5th G
copy 1

S0-BDL-781

Noxon Road Elementary School
Old Noxon Road
Poughkeepsie, N.Y.
12603

World Book's

Science
Desk Reference

Noxon Road Elementary School
Old Noxon Road
Poughkeepsie, N.Y.
12603

World Book, Inc.
a Scott Fetzer company

Chicago London Sydney Toronto

The material in this volume
is excerpted from
The World Book Encyclopedia

© 1990 World Book, Inc. All rights reserved. This volume
may not be reproduced in whole or in part in any form
without prior written permission from the publisher.

1991 Revised Printing

World Book, Inc.
525 W. Monroe St.
Chicago, Illinois 60661

ISBN 0-7166-3242-X

Library of Congress Catalog Number 91-65996

Printed in the United States of America

B/IA

Staff

Publisher

William H. Nault, Ed.D., Litt.D.

Editor in Chief
Robert O. Zeleny, B.A.

Executive Editor
A. Richard Harmet, M.S.J.

Editorial

Science Editors
William Graham, B.S.
Karin C. Rosenberg, M.A.

Contributing Editor
Jacqueline L. Rubenstein, B.A.

Art

Art Director
Alfred de Simone, M.A.

Assistant Art Director
Richard B. Zinn

Senior Artist
Isaiah W. Sheppard, Jr., B.F.A.

Contributing Artist
Linda Kinnaman, B.A.

Product Production

Manufacturing
Henry Koval, B.A., *Director*
Sandra Van den Broucke, B.S., *Manager*

Pre-press Services
J. J. Stack, A.B., *Director*
Janice Rossing, B.A., *Coordinator*
Randi Park

Consultant Committees

Biological Sciences

Lawrence C. Bliss, B.S., M.S., Ph.D.
Professor of Botany,
University of Washington

Anne Innis Dagg, B.A., M.A., Ph.D.
Academic Director, Independent
Studies,
University of Waterloo (Ont.)

John B. Hanson, B.A., Ph.D.
Professor of Agronomy and
Plant Biology Emeritus,
University of Illinois

C. Anderson Hedberg, M.D.
Associate Professor of Medicine,
Rush-Presbyterian-St. Luke's
Medical Center and
Rush Medical College

Charlotte P. Mangum, A.B.,
M.S., Ph.D.
Professor of Biology,
College of William and Mary

Irwin Rubenstein, B.S., Ph.D.
Head, Department of Plant Biology,
and Professor of Plant Biology,
University of Minnesota,
Twin Cities Campus

Physical Sciences

A. Louis Allred, B.S., Ph.D.
Professor of Chemistry,
Northwestern University

Francis T. Cole, A.B., Ph.D.
Physicist,
Fermi National Accelerator
Laboratory

Jay M. Pasachoff, A.B., A.M., Ph.D.
Field Memorial Professor and
Director, Hopkins Observatory
of Williams College

John G. Truxal, A.B., B.S., Sc.D.
Distinguished Teaching Professor,
Department of Technology
and Society,
State University of New York
at Stony Brook

About this book

Why does the moon have phases? What is the difference between a butterfly and a moth? How many bones does the human skeleton have? When did the dinosaurs live?

You will find the answers to these and countless other questions about the world of science in *World Book's Science Desk Reference.*

Looking up information in the *Science Desk Reference* is very much like looking up information in *World Book.* Like *World Book,* articles in the *Science Desk Reference* are arranged in alphabetical order. Let's say your question is "Why does the moon have phases?" The first step is to select the *key word*—the most important word in the question: "Moon." In most cases, the key word will be the

same as an article in this volume. So start looking through this book looking for articles that begin with "M."

You will note that there are *guide words* at the top of the pages that tell you what article is on that page. If you come upon the guide words **Mammal** or **Mars,** you know you haven't gone far enough. If you find **Muscle** or **Mushroom,** you know you must go back to find the **Moon** article in its proper alphabetical order. As you can see, finding an article in the *Science Desk Reference* is very much like finding a word in a dictionary.

The articles in the *Science Desk Reference* have been taken from *The World Book Encyclopedia* and adapted for your use. In many cases, there is more

Illustrations play a key role in communicating information in the *Science Desk Reference.* For example, a photograph shows the antennae of a male moth. A diagram conveys how heat decreases the orderly arrangement of water molecules. Artwork depicts the parts of the eye and reconstructs scenes of prehistoric dinosaurs.

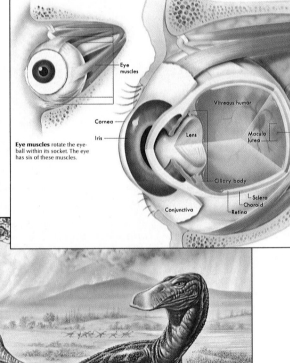

Eye muscles rotate the eyeball within its socket. The eye has six of these muscles.

Eye muscles

Vitreous humor

Cornea

Iris

Lens

Macula lutea

Ciliary body

Sclera
Choroid
Retina

Conjunctiva

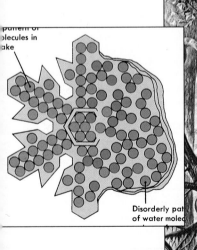

pattern of
molecules in
ake

Disorderly pat
of water molec

information on a subject in *World Book*. A box at the end of an article will tell you what additional information can be found in *World Book*. For example, after reading the **Moon** article, the box tells you there is more information in *World Book* on: What the moon is like, How the moon was formed, and The moon in history.

Within articles, you will sometimes find *cross-references*. The **Jet propulsion** article, for example, says "see **Rocket**" for information on how rockets used the principles of jet propulsion to fly in the airless expanse of outer space. Other cross-references direct you to related information in *World Book* itself. The **Environmental pollution** article says "For more information on soil and how it is damaged,

see the articles in *World Book* on **Soil** and **Erosion**."

Of course, this single volume cannot contain or even direct you to the wealth of information contained in *World Book*'s more than 5,400 science articles. If you cannot find the information you are seeking in the *Science Desk Reference,* please check the *World Book* in your classroom or library.

Above all, use and enjoy the *Science Desk Reference*. Whether looking up information for a school assignment or just browsing for your own interest, the *Science Desk Reference* provides a wonderful window to the world of science.

The editors

Special features facilitate the search for information in the *Science Desk Reference*. Tables of terms define certain words or phrases used in discussing scientific subjects. Facts in brief tables provide important information at a glance. Interesting facts presentations bring to life the unusual aspects of a topic.

Computer terms

Binary code is used by computers to represent information. It consists of the 0's and 1's of the binary numeration system.
Bit, an abbreviation of the term *binary digit,* may be either the digit 0 or 1.
Byte is a group of bits that act as a single unit of information, such as a letter or numeral.
Database is an organized collection of information stored on a magnetic disk or other direct-access storage device.
File storage device is any device used to save information until it is needed again.
Hardware refers to the physical parts of a computer system.
Input is any information that a user enters into a computer.
Mainframe is a large, powerful computer that many people can use at once. It can store large amounts of information.
Memory is the part of a computer that stores information.
Microprocessor is a miniature electronic device consisting of thousands of transistors and related circuitry on a silicon chip. The device is often called a "computer on a chip" because it can hold the processor and some memory.
Modem is a device that allows computer users to communicate with one another over telephone lines.
Network is a system consisting of two or more computers connected by high-speed communication lines
Operating system is a type of software th tion of a computer system.
Output is any result provided by a comput
Peripheral equipment consists of input d vices, and file storage devices.
Personal computer is a desktop or handh signed for general-purpose use.
Program is a set of instructions to be carri puter, written in a computer language.
Simulation is the representation or imitati system on a computer, usually with a math purpose is to predict and analyze what is li various conditions.
Software refers to the programs used by a form desired tasks.

Interesting facts about elephants

The skin of an elephant is gray and wrinkled. An adult elephant's skin measures up to $1\frac{1}{2}$ inches (3 centimeters) thick and weighs about 1 short ton (0.9 metric ton). However, it is surprisingly tender. Flies, mosquitoes, and other insects can bite into the skin.

An angry or frightened elephant can run at a speed of more than 25 miles (40 kilometers) an hour for a short distance. On a long journey, a herd of elephants travels at about 10 miles (16 kilometers) an hour.

es its trunk as a hand. The trunk can carry a ilogram) log or an object as small as a coin. Ele-he and smell with their trunks.

Mars at a glance

Mars, shown in blue in the diagram, is the next planet beyond the earth. The ancient symbol for Mars, *right,* is still used today.

Pluto
Neptune
Uranus
Saturn
Jupiter
Mars
Earth
Venus
Mercury
Sun

Contents

Air 8
Air pollution 11
Airplane 12
Airship 17
Amphibian 18
Animal 20
Ant 40
Ape 44
Aquarium 45
Astronomy 46
Atom 50
Bacteria 52
Bark 53
Bat 54
Bear 55
Beaver 57
Bee 60
Beetle 63
Bird 66
Brain 75
Butterfly 78
Camel 82
Cat 84
Cave 87
Cell 88
Circulation 91
Classification, Scientific 92
Climate 94
Cloud 96
Coal 98
Color 101
Comet 103
Computer 104
Condor 107
Crane 108
Crustacean 109
Deer 111
Desert 114
Digestive system 115

Dinosaur 116
Dog 120
Dolphin 123
Duck 126
Eagle 128
Ear 130
Earth 133
Earthquake 138
Eclipse 140
Ecology 141
Electric motor 142
Electric power 143
Electricity 146
Electronics 149
Element, Chemical 152
Elephant 156
Environmental pollution 160
Evolution 164
Eye 167
Fish 170
Flower 176
Fly 180
Forest 182
Fossil 186
Frog 188
Fruit 190
Gas 192
Giraffe 194
Glacier 195
Gorilla 197
Hawk 199
Heart 200
Heat 203
Hippopotamus 206
Horse 207
Human body 210
Insect 212
Invention 217
Jet propulsion 219

Jupiter 222
Kangaroo 223
Laser 224
Leaf 226
Light 230
Lightning 233
Lion 234
Lobster 236
Lung 237
Lymphatic system 238
Machine 239
Mammal 240
Mars 244
Mercury 245
Meteor 246
Metric system 247
Mineral 250
Molecule 253
Mollusk 254
Monkey 255
Moon 258
Moth 263
Mountain 265
Mouse 268
Muscle 270
Mushroom 271
Nervous system 273
Nuclear energy 275
Ocean 278
Octopus 283
Ostrich 284
Petroleum 285
Planet 288
Plant 292
Prehistoric animal 301
Rabbit 305
Radio 306
Rain 309
Rainbow 310

Rat 311
Reptile 312
Respiration 314
Rhinoceros 315
Rock 316
Rocket 318
Root 322
Saturn 323
Seal 325
Season 327
Seed 328
Shark 329
Skeleton 331
Skin 332
Snake 334
Solar energy 337
Solar system 339
Sound 341
Space travel 344
Spider 352
Squirrel 356
Star 358
Stem 362
Sun 363
Swan 369
Teeth 370
Television 374
Tiger 378
Tornado 379
Tree 380
Turtle 385
Venus 388
Volcano 390
Water 394
Water pollution 400
Weather 401
Weights and measures 404
Whale 409
Woodpecker 415

Artstreet

Dave Woodward, Atoz Images

The air around us is invisible. But we can feel the air when it pushes against us as gusts of wind, *left.* Wind is simply moving air. We can also tell that air has weight. This weight enables hot-air balloons to rise above the earth because they are lighter than the surrounding air, *right.*

Air

Air is the mixture of gases that surrounds the earth. It is often called the *atmosphere*. Air covers the land and sea and extends far above the earth's surface. We cannot see, smell, or taste air. Yet it is as real as land or water. When the wind blows, it is the air you feel against your face. Wind is simply moving air. You can also see the effect of wind in drifting clouds, pounding waves, and trembling leaves. Moving air can turn windmills and blow large sailboats across the ocean.

Without air, there could be no life on the earth. All living things—animals and plants—need air to stay alive. You are breathing air now. You must breathe air, or you will die. People have lived more than a month without food and more than a week without water. But a person can live only a few minutes without air.

Air does much more than make it possible for us to breathe. Air shields the earth from certain harmful rays from the sun and other objects in outer space. At the same time, it traps the heat that comes from the sun. In this way, air helps keep the earth warm enough to support life. Air protects us from meteors, most of which burn up in the atmosphere before they can strike the earth's surface. Clouds that form in the air bring us water in the form of rain and snow. All living things must have water to live, just as they must have air.

We also need air to hear. Sound must travel through the air or some other substance. Most of the sounds we hear travel through the air. Thus, the world would be silent if there were no air. Air has weight. This weight enables balloons filled with a light gas or heated air to rise high above the earth because they are lighter than the air around them. Air moving past the wings of airplanes, birds, and insects enables them to fly.

The earth has plentiful air. But the quality of the air depends largely on the amount of industrial wastes and other *pollutants* (impurities) that people add to the atmosphere. Air pollution is a serious problem in most of the world's big cities. Polluted air harms our health. It also injures plants and animals, damages building materials, and even affects the weather.

What is air?

Air consists of a mixture of gases that extends from the earth's surface to outer space. The earth's gravity holds the air in place around the earth. The gases of the air move about freely among one another. As sunlight passes through the earth's atmosphere, it strikes molecules of the gases. The molecules scatter the sunlight, which is a mixture of all colors, in every direction. The sky appears blue because much more blue light is scattered than any other color.

Many small particles of dust are suspended among the gases of the air. The air also carries tiny water droplets and ice crystals in the form of clouds. However, scientists do not consider the dust, water droplets, and ice crystals to be part of the air.

How air behaves

Weight and pressure. We do not usually notice the weight of air because air is much lighter than solids or liquids. However, we can prove that air has weight with a simple experiment. First, we remove the air from a bottle by means of a small vacuum pump. We then seal the bottle and weigh it. Next, we break the seal so that air rushes into the bottle. When we weigh the bottle again, it weighs more. The added weight is air.

The gases of the air

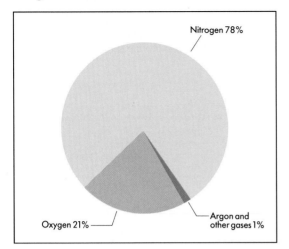

Air consists chiefly of nitrogen and oxygen. They make up about 99 per cent of *dry air*—air from which all water vapor has been removed. Argon and other gases account for about 1 per cent.

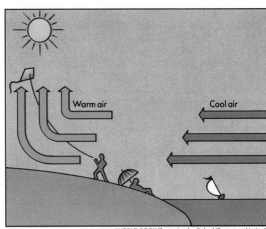

WORLD BOOK illustration by Oxford Illustrators Limited

Air movement. Wind results from differences in the temperature of the air. For example, on a sunny day, the air above an ocean shore is warmer than the air over the water. The warmer air over the shore expands, becomes lighter, and rises. The cooler air from the sea moves in, producing a sea breeze.

At sea level, each cubic foot (0.03 cubic meter) of air weighs only about 1 $\frac{1}{4}$ ounces (35 grams). But the weight of all the air around the world is more than 5,700,000,000,000,000 short tons (5,200,000,000,000,000 metric tons). The weight of the air pressing from the top of the atmosphere upon the layers of air below produces *air pressure*, also called *atmospheric pressure*. The air pressure at sea level averages 14.7 pounds per square inch (101.3 kilopascals). The air pressing down on your shoulders weighs about 1 short ton (0.9 metric ton). You do not feel this weight because you are supported by equal air pressure on all sides.

Air movement. Air moves across the surface of the earth in the form of wind. The sun causes the wind because it heats the earth's surface unevenly. Air above

warm areas of the earth expands and becomes lighter. It then rises, creating an area of low pressure near the surface. Wind is produced when cooler, heavier air flows toward the low-pressure area, replacing the rising air. Wind often develops along an ocean shore during the day because land heats up more quickly than water does. The air over the shore is thus warmer than the air over the water. As the warm air over the shore rises, the cooler air from the sea moves inland and replaces it, producing a sea breeze. At night, the air over the shore becomes cooler than the air over the water. Thus, the wind direction reverses, and a breeze blows out to sea.

Air resistance. Air resists the motion of objects traveling through it. This resistance occurs because moving objects rub against the atoms and molecules of the

Air pressure

The weight of the air pressing down all around us produces *air pressure*. The diagrams below show one common way we use air pressure as a force—to drink through a straw. Sucking on the straw creates a partial vacuum inside it. The greater air pressure outside then pushes the liquid in the glass up through the straw.

WORLD BOOK illustrations by Oxford Illustrators Limited

Air resistance

Air resists the motion of objects traveling through it. This resistance slows a parachute jumper's fall, *below*. The jumper meets minimum air resistance and falls rapidly until the parachute is opened. The greater resistance acting on the surface of the parachute enables the jumper to float safely to the ground.

WORLD BOOK illustrations by Oxford Illustrators Limited

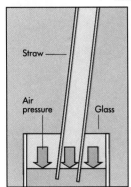

Equal air pressure

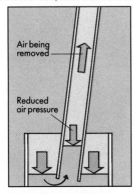

Unequal air pressure

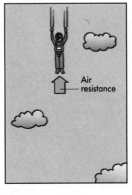

Minimum resistance

Maximum resistance

gases that make up the air. A piece of paper in the air floats slowly to the ground because of the air resistance acting on its surface. Air resistance slows down the speed of a parachute jumper's fall.

During the early days of aviation, airplanes flew slowly partly because such parts as the wing braces and landing wheels rubbed against the air. Aviation engineers found that they could reduce air resistance and thus increase the speed of a plane by streamlining its shape. They removed outside wing supports and installed landing wheels that could be pulled up into the plane. They found that even smoothing down rivet heads helped reduce air resistance.

Structure of the atmosphere

Scientists divide the earth's atmosphere into four lay-

ers according to differences in temperature. These layers, from the lowest to highest altitude, are (1) the troposphere, (2) the stratosphere, (3) the mesosphere, and (4) the thermosphere. The atmosphere becomes thinner with increasing height above the earth.

See **Air** in *World Book* for more information on the following topics:

- What is air?
- How air behaves
- Structure of the atmosphere
- Origin of the atmosphere
- The study of air

The layers of the atmosphere

Scientists divide the earth's atmosphere into four layers, according to differences in the temperature of the air. These layers are the *troposphere,* the *stratosphere,* the *mesosphere,* and the *thermosphere.* The outer atmosphere gradually fades into interplanetary space.

WORLD BOOK illustration by Oxford Illustrators Limited

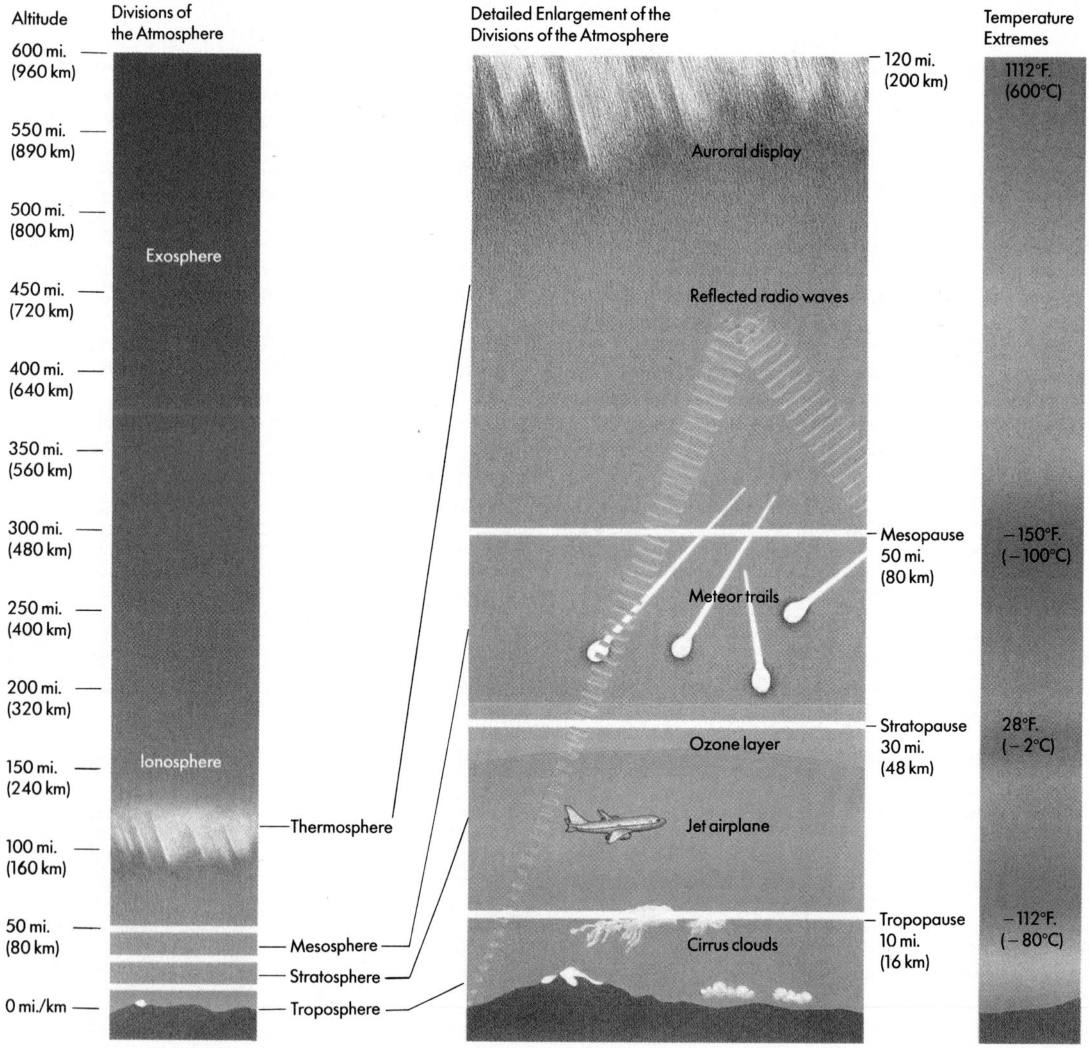

Altitude	Divisions of the Atmosphere	Detailed Enlargement of the Divisions of the Atmosphere	Temperature Extremes
600 mi. (960 km)		120 mi. (200 km)	1112°F. (600°C)
550 mi. (890 km)		Auroral display	
500 mi. (800 km)	Exosphere		
450 mi. (720 km)		Reflected radio waves	
400 mi. (640 km)			
350 mi. (560 km)			
300 mi. (480 km)		Mesopause 50 mi. (80 km)	−150°F. (−100°C)
250 mi. (400 km)		Meteor trails	
200 mi. (320 km)			
150 mi. (240 km)	Ionosphere	Ozone layer — Stratopause 30 mi. (48 km)	28°F. (−2°C)
100 mi. (160 km)	Thermosphere	Jet airplane	
50 mi. (80 km)	Mesosphere	Cirrus clouds — Tropopause 10 mi. (16 km)	−112°F. (−80°C)
0 mi./km	Stratosphere / Troposphere		

Air pollution occurs when wastes dirty the air. Artificially created wastes are the main sources of air pollution. They can be in the form of gases or *particulates* (tiny particles of liquid or solid matter). Such wastes result chiefly from the burning of fuel to power motor vehicles and to heat buildings. They also come from industrial processes and the burning of solid wastes. Natural *pollutants* (impurities) include dust, pollen, and soil particles.

The rapid growth of population and industry, and the increase in the number of automobiles and airplanes, has made air pollution an increasingly serious problem in many big cities since the 1950's. The air over these cities often becomes so filled with pollutants that it harms the health of people, and also harms plants, animals, fabrics, building materials, and the economy.

The damage caused by air pollution costs the people of the United States alone about $16 billion a year—or $75 per person. This money is spent for increased maintenance of buildings, cleaning and replacement of clothing, and health care.

Chief sources of air pollution

The major sources of air pollution vary from city to city. Automobiles produce nearly all the pollution in Los Angeles. Furnaces in apartment and office buildings cause most of the contamination in New York City. Chicago's air pollution comes equally from industry, motor vehicles, and heating plants.

Forms of transportation, such as airplanes, automobiles, ships, and trains, are a leading source of air pollution in the United States. Exhaust from engines contains various kinds of harmful pollutants. Such pollutants include carbon monoxide gas, *hydrocarbons* (compounds of hydrogen and carbon), and *nitrogen oxides* (compounds of nitrogen and oxygen). Nitrogen oxides in the air help produce a form of oxygen called *ozone.* Ozone reacts with hydrocarbons to form a type of air pollution known as *smog.*

Fuel combustion for heating homes, office buildings, and factories sharply increases the level of air pollution in urban areas. Furnaces that burn coal or fuel oil give off nitrogen oxides, particulates, and *sulfur oxides* (compounds of sulfur and oxygen). Electric power plants that use these fuels also release such pollutants into the atmosphere.

See **Air pollution** in *World Book* for more information on Effects of air pollution and Control of air pollution.

Major air pollutants and their sources   Most air pollution is caused by artificially created wastes in the form of gases and tiny particles of liquid and solid matter. The five principal sources of these pollutants are shown below at the left. The charts show the approximate percentage of each kind of pollutant that these sources contributed to air pollution in the United States.

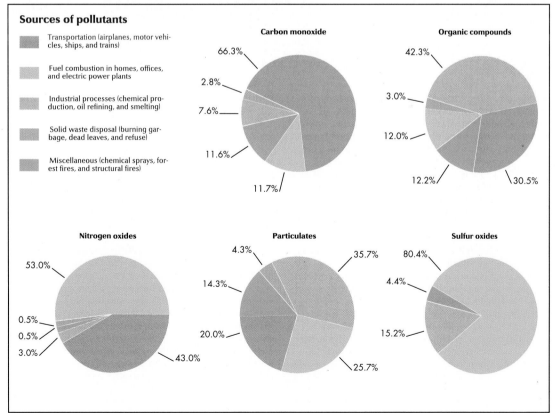

Sources of pollutants

- Transportation (airplanes, motor vehicles, ships, and trains)
- Fuel combustion in homes, offices, and electric power plants
- Industrial processes (chemical production, oil refining, and smelting)
- Solid waste disposal (burning garbage, dead leaves, and refuse)
- Miscellaneous (chemical sprays, forest fires, and structural fires)

Carbon monoxide
66.3%
2.8%
7.6%
11.6%
11.7%

Organic compounds
42.3%
3.0%
12.0%
12.2%
30.5%

Nitrogen oxides
53.0%
0.5%
0.5%
3.0%
43.0%

Particulates
4.3%
14.3%
20.0%
35.7%
25.7%

Sulfur oxides
80.4%
4.4%
15.2%

Figures are for 1987. Source: U.S. Environmental Protection Agency.

Boeing Commercial Airplane Company

A giant jet airliner is designed to fly large numbers of passengers long distances. The world's largest airplane, the Boeing 747-400, *above,* can carry over 400 passengers a third of the way around the world without refueling.

Airplane

Airplane is one of the newest and fastest means of transportation. Only spacecraft travel faster than airplanes. A modern jet transport plane can carry a heavy load of passengers and cargo across the United States in less than 5 hours. It can fly halfway around the world —from Chicago to Calcutta, India—in about 15 hours. Passengers can ride in comfort 30,000 to 45,000 feet (9,100 to 13,700 meters) above the ground. On many long flights, they can watch a movie or listen to music. The largest jets can hold nearly 500 passengers.

Rocket planes, the world's fastest airplanes, have been flown at speeds faster than 4,500 miles per hour (mph), or 7,240 kilometers per hour (kph). Rocket planes are used mainly for research.

Most airplanes are not so large or powerful as jets and rocket planes. About 80 per cent of all the planes in the United States have only one engine and can carry only a few passengers at a time. Many people use these light airplanes for short business or pleasure trips.

An airplane is a heavier-than-air machine. The largest transport planes weigh more than 350 short tons (320 metric tons) when fully loaded. A plane's engines, wings, and *control surfaces* enable it to fly. The engine or engines move the plane forward through the air. As the plane moves, the air that flows over the wings moves faster—and therefore has less pressure—than the air

under the wings. This difference in air pressure, called *lift,* keeps the plane in the air. The pilot keeps the plane balanced in flight by adjusting the control surfaces, which are movable sections of the wings and tail.

The activity of designing, building, and flying aircraft is called *aeronautics.* During the late 1700's, people used balloons to make their first flights into the air. Balloons can fly because they are lighter than air. After the first balloon flights, inventors tried to develop a heavier-than-air flying machine. Some inventors experimented with *gliders* (engineless planes). They studied birds' wings and discovered that they are curved. By giving their gliders curved wings instead of flat ones, they could make them fly hundreds of feet or meters. During the 1800's, inventors made the first gasoline engines, which could give a plane the power it needed for flight.

Finally, on Dec. 17, 1903, two American bicycle manufacturers—Orville and Wilbur Wright—made the first airplane flights in history, near Kitty Hawk, N.C. Orville made the first flight. He flew their wood, wire, and cloth airplane 120 feet (37 meters). After the Wright brothers' success, pilots and inventors worked continually to improve airplane design. Almost every year, planes flew faster and farther than they had flown the year before. By the early 1950's, airliners were making daily nonstop flights across the Atlantic Ocean.

J. R. Eyerman

A huge propeller-driven plane, an Aero Spacelines Super Guppy, dwarfs a light jet plane. The Super Guppy hauls rocket parts for the U.S. space program. The jet carries passengers.

U.S. Air Force

The fastest planes have jet or rocket engines. The Lockheed SR-71A, *above,* a U.S. Air Force plane, is one of the fastest jets. It can fly at a speed of more than 2,000 mph (3,200 kph).

© Chris Sorensen, The Stock Market

A powerful jet cargo plane can carry tons of goods nonstop for thousands of miles or kilometers. Privately operated parcel services use planes like the one above to deliver tons of mail. Jets have brought all parts of the world within easy reach of one another.

Important dates in airplane development

c. 1500 The Italian artist and inventor Leonardo da Vinci made drawings of flying machines with flapping wings.

1783 Two Frenchmen—Jean F. Pilâtre de Rozier and the Marquis d'Arlandes—made the first free lighter-than-air ascent. They made the ascent in a hot-air balloon.

1804 Sir George Cayley of Great Britain flew the first successful model glider.

1843 William S. Henson, a British inventor, patented plans for a steam-driven airplane that had many of the basic parts of a modern plane.

1848 John Stringfellow of Great Britain built a small model based on Henson's plane. It was launched but remained in the air only briefly.

1891-1896 Otto Lilienthal, a German, became the first person to successfully pilot gliders in flight.

1896 Samuel P. Langley of the United States flew a steam-powered model plane.

1903 Orville and Wilbur Wright of the United States made the first engine-powered, heavier-than-air flights, near Kitty Hawk, N.C. Their first flight went 120 feet (37 meters) and lasted only about 12 seconds.

1906 Trajan Vuia, a Romanian inventor, built the first full-sized monoplane, but it could not fly.

1909 Louis Blériot of France became the first person to fly across the English Channel.

1913 Igor I. Sikorsky, a Russian inventor, built and flew the first four-engine plane.

1915 The first flight of an all-metal, cantilever-wing plane, the Junkers J 1, took place in Germany.

1924 The first all-metal, trimotor transport, the Junkers G 23, was test-flown in Germany.

1927 The Lockheed Vega, a single-engine transport, flew for the first time. It became one of the most popular transport planes of the 1920's and early 1930's.

1936 Douglas DC-3 transport planes entered airline service in the United States. They became the most widely used airliners in history.

1939 The first successful flight of a jet-engine airplane took place in Germany.

1942 The Bell Aircraft Company built the first jet airplane in the United States. It was flown by Robert M. Stanley at Muroc Dry Lake, Calif.

1947 Charles Yeager, a U.S. Air Force captain, made the first supersonic flight, in a Bell X-1 rocket plane.

1952 De Havilland Comets, the world's first large commercial jetliners, began service.

1953 The first turboprop transport, the Vickers Viscount, began regular airline service.

1953 The North American F-100 Super Sabre jet fighter became the first operational supersonic fighter.

1958 The Boeing 707 began the first U.S. jet transport service between the United States and Europe.

1968 Russian pilots test-flew the world's first supersonic transport plane, the Tu-144.

1970 The first jumbo jet, the Boeing 747, entered airline service.

1976 The Concorde, a supersonic transport plane built by Britain and France, began passenger service.

The parts of an airplane

This drawing of a light plane, a Piper Cherokee, shows the parts of an airplane. The basic parts are the wing, *fuselage* (body), tail assembly, landing gear, and engine. Some other parts, such as the ribs and spars in the wings, are structural. Still other parts, including the ailerons, flaps, rudder, and stabilator, are movable surfaces used to control the plane. The drawing also shows the wing's root, tip, and leading and trailing edges.

WORLD BOOK illustration by Tom Morgan; courtesy of Piper Aircraft Corp.

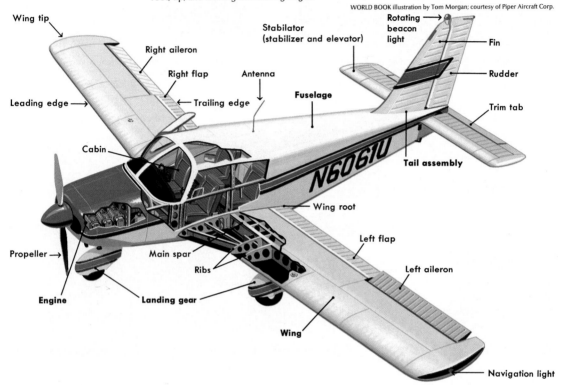

Wing tip

Right aileron

Right flap

Antenna

Leading edge →

← Trailing edge

Stabilator (stabilizer and elevator)

Rotating beacon light

Fin

Rudder

Fuselage

Trim tab

Cabin

N6061U

Tail assembly

Wing root

Left flap

Propeller →

Main spar

Ribs

Left aileron

Engine

Landing gear

Wing

Navigation light

How an airplane flies

Four basic forces govern the flight of an airplane: (1) *gravity,* (2) *lift,* (3) *drag,* and (4) *thrust.* Gravity is the natural force that pulls a plane toward the ground. Lift is the force that pushes a plane upward against the force of gravity. It is created by the movement of a plane's wing through the air. Drag is the natural force of air opposing an airplane's forward movement. Thrust is the force that opposes drag and moves a plane forward. Thrust is created by a plane's propeller or by its jet engines. When a plane's lift equals the force of gravity and its thrust equals the drag, the plane is in level, *cruising* flight. When any of the four forces changes, the plane begins to climb, turn, or change its direction or position.

This section discusses some of the ways in which the four basic forces affect the flight of an airplane.

Gravity and lift. Gravity tends to keep an airplane on the ground or to pull it to the earth when in flight. The force of gravity on the ground equals the weight of the plane on the ground. For a plane to become airborne and to stay in the air, its wing must create a lifting force greater than the downward force of gravity. Lift is created by a change of air pressure around an airplane's wing as the plane moves along the ground or through the air.

Early attempts to fly with wings failed because people did not yet understand that it is the curved shape of

WORLD BOOK diagram

Four forces act on an airplane in flight: (1) *gravity,* (2) *lift,* (3) *drag,* and (4) *thrust.* Gravity is the natural force that pulls a plane toward the ground. Lift opposes gravity and pushes the plane upward. Drag is the natural force of air opposing a plane's forward movement. Thrust opposes drag and moves the plane forward.

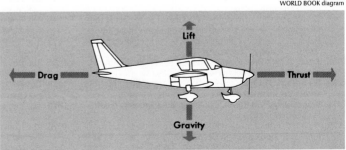

Lift

Drag

Thrust

Gravity

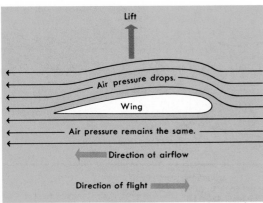

WORLD BOOK diagram

Lift is created by a drop in air pressure over an airplane's wing. An airplane wing has a curved upper surface. As a plane moves forward, the pressure of the air that rushes over this curved surface falls. A high-pressure area always moves toward a low-pressure area. The high-pressure area below the wing thus rises toward the low-pressure area above it and so lifts the plane into the air.

a bird's wings that creates lift. After this fact was discovered, people began to build airplane wings that were slightly curved and so created lift in much the same way a bird's wings do.

When a plane stands on the ground, the air pressure above and below its wing is the same. As the plane starts to move forward, air begins to flow over and under the wing. The air moving over the curved upper surface flows in a curve. As it does so, its speed increases and its pressure drops. The air moving under the flat bottom of the wing moves in a straight line. Its speed and pressure are not changed by the wing. A high-pressure area always moves toward a low-pressure area, and so the air under the wing tries to move upward to the air over the wing. But the wing is in the way. Instead of meeting the low-pressure area, the high-pressure area lifts the wing into the air. The faster the airplane moves, the greater the lift its wing produces. As an airplane increases its speed down the runway before take-off, its wing builds up more and more lift. The air pressure beneath the wing finally becomes greater than the weight of the plane, and so the force of the lift becomes greater than the force of gravity. The plane then takes off.

Drag and thrust. A wing can produce lift only if it is moving forward through the air. A plane needs engine thrust to create the required forward movement. As thrust increases, it moves a plane forward faster than before. However, as a plane's speed increases, drag increases also. To oppose drag, the plane needs still more thrust.

In a jet airplane, the rapid movement of gases through the jet engine produces thrust. Propellers produce thrust in turboprop planes and planes powered by reciprocating engines. Propeller blades are shaped much like airplane wings. As the propeller spins, the air pressure on the front surface of the blades is reduced. The higher pressure on the back of the blades moves toward the lower pressure on the front. As it does so, it pushes against the propeller blades and moves the

plane forward. The faster the jet engine works or the propeller spins, the greater the force of thrust.

To help increase thrust, engineers design airplane bodies to be as streamlined as possible. They give them a sleek, trim shape, and they design every part on the outside so that it will knife through the air smoothly.

Changing altitude. An airplane cruising in level flight has lift balanced against gravity and thrust balanced against drag. To make the airplane descend, the pilot must decrease the power of the engine. The propeller or jet engines slow down, reducing the plane's thrust. The reduction in thrust also reduces lift, and the airplane begins to move downward. At the same time, drag increases its effect, which further slows the airplane and adds to the rate at which the plane descends.

How thrust is produced

Propellers produce thrust in gasoline-powered and turboprop planes. Jet engines produce thrust in jet planes.

WORLD BOOK diagrams

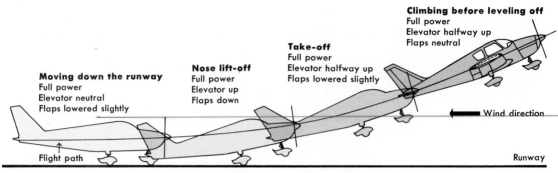

Climbing before leveling off
Full power
Elevator halfway up
Flaps neutral

Take-off
Full power
Elevator halfway up
Flaps lowered slightly

Nose lift-off
Full power
Elevator up
Flaps down

Moving down the runway
Full power
Elevator neutral
Flaps lowered slightly

Wind direction

Flight path

Runway

For take-off, a plane moves down the runway at high speed. The wind rushes around the wing, building up lift. To get more lift, the pilot raises the elevator, increasing the angle of attack. The pilot may also lower the flaps. When lift becomes greater than gravity, the plane takes off.

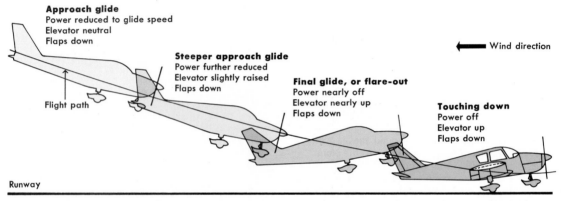

Approach glide
Power reduced to glide speed
Elevator neutral
Flaps down

Wind direction

Steeper approach glide
Power further reduced
Elevator slightly raised
Flaps down

Final glide, or flare-out
Power nearly off
Elevator nearly up
Flaps down

Touching down
Power off
Elevator up
Flaps down

Flight path

Runway

WORLD BOOK diagrams

For landing, a plane's speed must be reduced as much as possible, and so the pilot decreases the engine power. But reducing speed also reduces lift. The plane must recover enough lift to keep from crashing. To recover lift, the pilot increases the angle of attack and lowers the flaps.

In order to climb, the pilot increases the engine power. The propeller or jet engines work faster, creating more thrust. The increased thrust also increases lift, and the plane begins to climb. However, climbing increases drag, and so the plane needs still more lift. To get the added lift, the pilot increases the plane's *angle of attack*—that is, the angle at which the wing cuts through the air. The pilot uses the controls to make the nose point up slightly so that the wing is at an upward angle to the path of the plane's flight. The flow of air over the upper part of the wing increases in speed, and the air pressure over the wing becomes less than the pressure over the wing in cruising flight. The area of high pressure under the wing moves toward the area of lower pressure over the wing, producing lift. But increasing the angle of attack disturbs the flow of air over the wing, which increases drag. The pilot brings the four forces of flight into balance again by increasing engine power to gain more thrust.

Changing direction. A pilot turns a plane by increasing the lift on one wing or the other. To make a left turn, for example, the pilot operates controls that put the airplane into a *left bank*. That is, the left wing dips lower than the right one. Lift always occurs at a right angle to the surface of the wing. When the wing is not horizontal to the ground, lift takes place at an angle to the ground.

As the left wing dips, the lift on the right wing increases, which pulls the plane around the turn. The pilot uses the rudder to keep the airplane's nose steady. The rudder is not used to turn the plane. It is the lifting force of the wing, occurring at an angle to the horizon, that makes the airplane turn.

For more information on how an airplane flies and on how basic forces act on a plane in flight, see **Aerodynamics** in *World Book.*

See **Airplane** in *World Book* for more information on the following topics:

•History and development
•Airplanes of today
•The parts of an airplane
•Power for flight

•Flying an airplane
•Flight navigation
•Building an airplane

Airship is a lighter-than-air aircraft. An airship has a huge main body that contains a lighter-than-air gas. The gas raises the craft and keeps it aloft in the same way a gas balloon is lifted. However, airships, unlike balloons, have engines that move them through the air and nearly all have equipment for steering. Balloons are moved by the wind, and cannot be steered. They thus travel in the direction the wind blows. Airships also differ from helicopters and airplanes, which are heavier than air. Helicopters and airplanes use their engines and blades or wings to lift them and keep them aloft.

Airships were introduced in the 1800's as the first manned flying machines capable of prolonged flight and of being steered. This feature of these craft led to their being called *dirigibles,* which comes from the Latin word *dirigere,* meaning *to direct.* In World War I (1914-1918), airships were used as bombers, for protecting ships against submarine attack, and for other duties. Before and after the war, they were used to carry passengers. Airship passenger services reached their height in the 1930's, but a series of disastrous crashes and the increasing popularity and long-range capability of the airplane brought airship passenger services to an end.

How airships fly

Lift is the force that raises an airship off the ground and keeps it aloft. Airships generate lift because the gas they contain has a lower density than the air outside the craft. Airships hold enough of this lighter-than-air gas to overcome their own weight and rise from the ground.

Early airships contained hydrogen, the lightest of all gases. But hydrogen is highly flammable, and this property of the gas was an important factor in a number of airship disasters. As a result, helium eventually replaced hydrogen for use in airships.

Thrust is the force that moves an airship through the air. Most airships use engines and propellers to obtain thrust. On large rigid airships, the engines and propellers were in *gondolas* (cars) attached to the hull. Such craft had separate gondolas for the passengers and crew. On most nonrigid airships, engines are on a gondola that also holds the crew and passengers.

Control. Most airships have tail structures that include *fins, rudders,* and *elevators.* Fins are large, fixed surfaces. Typically, four fins are set equally distant from one another around the ship's *stern* (rear). The smaller, movable rudders and elevators are surfaces attached to the fins. A pilot moves the rudders to steer and the elevators to raise or lower the ship's nose.

For improved control, rigid airships contained *ballast.* Ballast was usually water. When released, the water helped the craft gain height by making it lighter. Rain or other weather conditions that made the craft heavier during flight often required the pilot to release ballast to lighten the craft to maintain its altitude.

Ballonets are air-filled bags or compartments inside nonrigid and semirigid pressure craft. One ballonet lies in the *bow* (front) of the envelope, and another lies in the stern. Ballonets help maintain the shape of the envelope. For example, if the gas pressure in the envelope decreases, air is pumped into the ballonets so that the envelope will not sag.

Kinds of airships   There are three main types of airships. A *nonrigid airship* has no framework supporting its gas-filled *envelope* (outer skin). In a *semirigid airship,* metal supports brace the craft's gas-filled bag. An extensive inner framework of wood or metal supports the gas bags of a *rigid airship.*

WORLD BOOK illustrations by Tony Gibbons, Linden Artists Ltd.

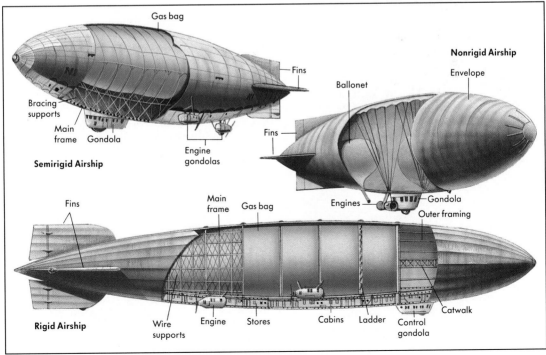

Gas bag

Fins

Nonrigid Airship

Envelope

Ballonet

Bracing supports

Main frame   Gondola

Fins

Engine gondolas

Semirigid Airship

Engines

Gondola

Outer framing

Fins

Main frame   Gas bag

Rigid Airship   Wire supports   Engine   Stores   Cabins   Ladder   Control gondola

Catwalk

Amphibian, *am FIHB ee uhn,* is an animal with scaleless skin that—with a few exceptions—lives part of its life in water and part on land. There are about 3,200 kinds of amphibians, and they make up one of the classes of *vertebrates* (animals with backbones). Amphibians include frogs, toads, salamanders, and caecilians.

Most amphibians hatch from eggs laid in water or moist ground, and begin life as water-dwelling *larvae* (young). Through a gradual process called *metamorphosis,* the larvae change into adults. The adults look very different from the larvae. Some adults continue to live in water, but most spend their lives on land. Almost all return to water to find mates and produce young.

Amphibians are generally smaller than such other vertebrates as fish, birds, and mammals. Most amphibians are no more than 6 inches (15 centimeters) long and weigh less than 2 ounces (60 grams). The smallest frog in the world can sit on a person's thumbnail. The largest amphibian is the Japanese giant salamander. Adults can be more than 5 feet (1½ meters) long.

Amphibians are cold-blooded—that is, their body temperature stays about the same as the temperature of their surroundings. Those that live in regions with harsh winters hibernate during the cold weather. Many of those that live in warm, dry climates *estivate*—that is, become inactive during summer.

Amphibians live on every continent except Antarctica. They generally live in moist habitats near ponds, lakes, or streams. Certain tropical tree frogs never leave the trees. They lay their eggs in rain water that collects at the base of leaves. Some amphibians live in dry regions. They survive for weeks or months in moist places un-

derground, waiting for rain to create puddles. After a rainfall, they gather at the puddles to mate and lay their eggs. The eggs hatch and the larvae develop quickly, before the puddles dry up.

Most amphibians eat insects. In some areas of the world, amphibians are quite numerous, and they play an important role in maintaining the balance of nature. Amphibians aid people by eating insects and insect larvae that destroy crops and carry disease. In some places, people use amphibians as food.

Kinds of amphibians

Zoologists divide amphibians into three groups: (1) frogs and toads; (2) salamanders; and (3) caecilians.

Frogs and toads have four legs and no tail. Their hind legs are very long and are used for jumping. Frogs generally have longer legs than toads. There are about 2,700 species of frogs and toads. Most of them live in tropical climates. But two species occur as far north as the Arctic Circle, and others are found as far south as Tierra del Fuego, at the tip of South America.

Salamanders have long tails and four—or in a few species, two—short, weak legs. There are about 370 species of salamanders. Most live in *temperate zones*—that is, in areas of the world having seasonal changes in temperature. Salamanders are also common in warm, humid areas of Central America and South America.

Caecilians have no legs and look like large earthworms. There are about 150 species of caecilians, which are found only in tropical regions. Most caecilians live in underground burrows, but some are aquatic.

The bodies of amphibians

Skin of amphibians has no external scales, hair, or feathers. Most amphibians have smooth skin, but some toads have thick, leathery skin. The outer layer of skin, called the *epidermis,* protects the animal's deeper tissues. Adult amphibians shed the outermost portion of the epidermis several times a year. The inner layer of skin, called the *dermis,* contains many nerves and blood vessels. It also has many glands, which open onto the skin surface. Many of them produce *mucus,* a thick, slimy substance that moistens and protects the skin. Other glands produce poisons that can hurt or kill an enemy.

Many frogs and salamanders have brightly colored skin. The color results from *pigments* (coloring matter) found in special cells that lie just below the epidermis. Movement of the pigments in the cells allows some species to change color rapidly. For example, some change color when the temperature goes up or down.

Breathing. Most land-dwelling adult amphibians breathe with lungs. Water-dwelling adults and larvae breathe by means of gills, as do fish. Some adults have both lungs and gills. In addition, all amphibians take in oxygen through the skin and through the lining of the mouth and throat. Some small salamanders have no lungs and breathe only through the skin and mouth.

Digestive system of amphibians includes the mouth, *esophagus* (tube to the stomach), stomach, and intestines. Food is mixed and partially *digested* (broken down) in the stomach, but most digestion takes place in the small intestine. The walls of the stomach and small intestine contain numerous glands that secrete digestive

Caecilian
Typhlonectes compressicauda
18 inches (45.7 centimeters)

Marbled Salamander
Ambystoma opacum
3½ to 4¼ inches (8.9 to 10.8 centimeters)

Plains Spadefoot Toad
Scaphiopus bombifrons
1½ to 2½ inches (3.8 to 6.3 centimeters)

WORLD BOOK illustration by Richard Lewington

Amphibians are divided into three main groups: (1) caecilians, (2) salamanders, and (3) frogs and toads. The drawings above show representatives from each of these three groups.

Interesting facts about amphibians

WORLD BOOK illustrations by James Teason

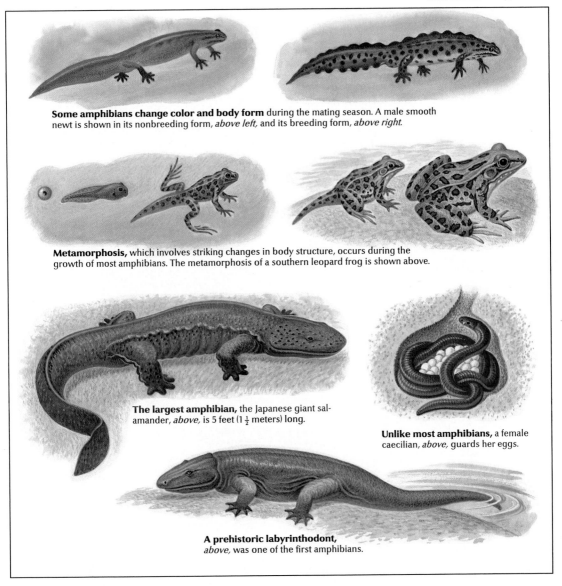

Some amphibians change color and body form during the mating season. A male smooth newt is shown in its nonbreeding form, *above left,* and its breeding form, *above right.*

Metamorphosis, which involves striking changes in body structure, occurs during the growth of most amphibians. The metamorphosis of a southern leopard frog is shown above.

The largest amphibian, the Japanese giant salamander, *above,* is 5 feet (1½ meters) long.

Unlike most amphibians, a female caecilian, *above,* guards her eggs.

A prehistoric labyrinthodont, *above,* was one of the first amphibians.

juices, which break food down into substances that can be absorbed and used by the animal's body. In addition, two large glands—the liver and pancreas—pour digestive juices into the small intestine. The digested food is absorbed from the small intestine, and the remaining wastes travel down the large intestine to the *cloaca,* a chamber that opens to the outside of the body. Waste products, eggs, and sperm (male sex cells) all pass out of the body through the cloaca.

Sense organs. Most frogs, toads, and salamanders have good eyesight, which helps them catch insects. Caecilians' eyes are either very small or completely absent. Caecilians have little use for eyes in their underground burrows. Water-dwelling amphibians also have a *lateral line system,* which is a set of sensitive organs

along the sides of the body. It allows an animal to sense movement in the surrounding water.

Frogs and toads can hear a wider range of sounds than salamanders and caecilians. Frogs and toads have well-developed voices. Their calls are important in mating. Caecilians and most salamanders have no voices.

Most amphibians smell and taste by means of the *Jacobson's organ,* a pair of tiny cavities in the roof of the mouth. The tissues that line these cavities respond to chemical changes in the mouth or nose.

See **Amphibian** in *World Book* for more information on Ways of life and The history of amphibians.

Arctic terns

Sea fan

The variety of animal life is almost endless. Animals range from complex, humanlike apes, such as gibbons, to tiny parasites, such as flukes. Some animals, such as arctic terns, travel great distances each year. Others, including the plantlike sea fan, spend most of their lives fixed to the bottom of the ocean.

WORLD BOOK illustration by John F. Eggert

Fluke

Gibbon

WORLD BOOK illustrations by Alex Ebel except where noted

Animal

Animal. Animals of many shapes and sizes live in all parts of the world. They walk or crawl on land, fly in the air, and swim in the water. Horses, canaries, toads, goldfish, butterflies, and worms are all animals. So are oysters, beetles, elephants, lobsters, sponges, seals, and snakes. Many animals are so small that they can be seen only with a microscope. The largest animal is the blue whale. It is longer than five elephants in a row.

No one knows exactly how many kinds of animals there are. So far, scientists have *classified* (grouped) more than a million kinds of animals. But each year, hundreds of new kinds are discovered.

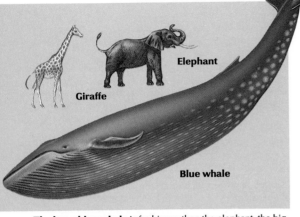

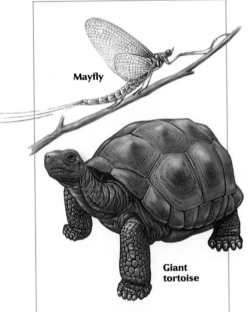

Kinds of animals. Scientists have classified more than a million kinds of animals. They have identified about a million kinds of insects alone. There are about 21,700 kinds of fishes, 8,600 kinds of birds, 6,000 kinds of reptiles, 3,200 kinds of amphibians, and 4,000 kinds of mammals.

The largest ears of all animals are those of the African elephant. They grow as large as 4 feet (1.2 meters) across. The largest eyes of all land animals are those of the horse and ostrich. They are about one and a half times the size of human eyes.

The hummingbird can fly straight up like a helicopter. It can hover in front of a flower to suck the nectar. The *bee hummingbird,* which grows to only 2 inches (5 centimeters) long, is the smallest of all birds.

The chameleon's tongue is as long as its body. This lizard swiftly shoots out its tongue to capture insects for food. Certain chameleons can quickly change color, and even develop spots and streaks that make them seem to be part of their background.

The most dangerous bird is the cassowary of Australia and New Guinea. It has powerful legs and knifelike claws. A kick from a cassowary can cripple or even kill a person.

A tree-climbing crab lives on many tropical islands. It is called the *coconut crab* because it cracks coconuts with its powerful claws and eats the sweet meat.

Coconut crab

The flying dragon is a lizard that lives in Asia and the East Indies. It can spread out folds of skin to form "wings" that it uses to glide through the air from tree to tree.

The platypus, a mammal, has a bill like a duck and lays eggs as birds do. But it nurses its young with milk as do other mammals. It lives only on mainland Australia and the island of Tasmania.

Platypus

The huge blue whale is far bigger than the elephant, the biggest land animal, or the giraffe, tallest of all the animals.

Lives of animals range from several hours to many years. An adult mayfly lives only a few hours or days. Some giant tortoises have lived over 100 years.

Many scientists divide living things into five main *kingdoms* (groups)—animals, plants, fungi, protists, and monerans. It is usually easy to tell animals from other types of organisms. For example, most animals move around, but most plants and fungi are held to the places where they grow by roots or rootlike structures. Most animals are made up of a number of different types of cells. Protists and monerans typically consist of only one cell.

Each kind of animal is different from all other kinds. Each has its own way of life. Each is especially suited to the place where it lives and to the food it eats. However, many animals are similar in certain ways. For example, some animals can be kept as pets. Some are raised for meat. Some animals are wild. Some animals live on land, and others live in water. Animals can also be grouped in many other ways, such as according to the number of legs they have. Arranging animals according to such similarities is a handy way of dividing the animal kingdom into a few large groups.

Where animals live

Animals live everywhere—in all climates on land, and at all levels of the oceans. Many kinds of animals often live in the same place. Usually they are the same kinds of animals that have lived in those surroundings for thousands of years. As a result, the animals have developed bodies and ways of life that suit them especially to that particular place. There they can move about easily, find food, and produce more of their own kind. An animal's surroundings are called its environment.

This section tells about the major animals, grouped according to their environments:

● *Animals of the mountains*

● *Animals of the grasslands*

● *Animals of the temperate forests*

● *Animals of the tropical forests*

● *Animals of the deserts*

● *Animals of the polar regions*

● *Animals of the oceans*

Animals of the mountains

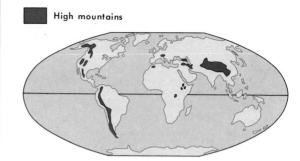

High mountains

Mountain ranges include all kinds of climates and animal environments. Few animals except insects and spiders live in the bitter cold of snow-covered mountain peaks. Below the snowfields, most mountains have rocky cliffs and crags. There live such sure-footed animals as goats and sheep. The rabbitlike pika and other small animals also live in the high, rocky areas. Many birds build their nests among the crags. The Nepalese swift of the Himalaya may be found at heights of over 20,000 feet (6,100 meters). Almost every mountain level has grass-covered plateaus and slopes, or forested valleys. Grazing animals such as vicuñas and yaks live in the grassy places. Many mountain animals move from one level to another to find food as the seasons change.

Yak   Asia

FPG

Bighorn sheep
North America

Rocky Mountain pika
North America

Peterson, Photo Researchers

Vicuña South America

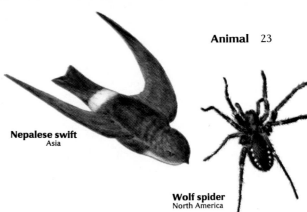

Nepalese swift
Asia

Wolf spider
North America

Okapia, Publix

Mountain gorilla Africa

Roy Pinney, Publix

Chinchilla South America

Russ Kinne, Photo Researchers

Giant panda Asia

Himalayan ibex
Asia

Marco Polo sheep
Asia

Rocky Mountain goat
North America

Snow leopard
Asia

WORLD BOOK illustrations by Margaret L. Estey

Animals of the grasslands

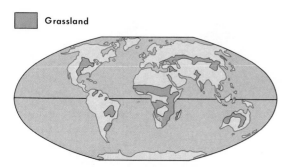

Grassland

Most of the largest animals and many of the swiftest animals live on vast stretches of open country called grasslands. Among the large grassland animals are the elephant, hippopotamus, and rhinoceros. Fast-running animals of the grasslands include the blackbuck, kudu, ostrich, pronghorn, and zebra. Africa has more kinds of grassland animals than any other continent. The lion hunts chiefly in Africa, and the giraffe is also an African grassland animal. Australia's most familiar grassland animal is the kangaroo. Many of the small grassland animals dig tunnels for homes. Among them is the prairie dog of North America.

GIRAFFE

ZEBRA

OSTRICH

AARDVARK

GNU

Africa

Pronghorn
North America

Kudu
Africa

Blackbuck
Asia

Indian rhinoceros   Asia

Ylla, Rapho Guillumette

African elephant

Secretary bird   Africa

Guggisberg, Photo Researchers

Hippopotamus   Africa

Conzett & Huber

African vulture

Peterson, Photo Researchers

Simon Trevor

African lion

Kangaroo
Australia

Prairie dog
North America

WORLD BOOK illustrations by René Martin

Animals of the temperate forests

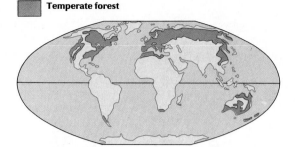

■ Temperate forest

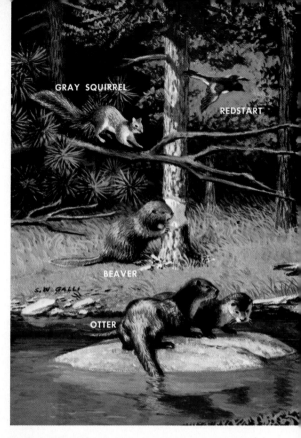

GRAY SQUIRREL

REDSTART

BEAVER

S. W. GALLI

OTTER

North America

Most animals that live in the temperate forests have small bodies. These animals can move easily through the underbrush. They include the chipmunk, opossum, porcupine, raccoon, skunk, and squirrel. A few kinds of large animals, such as bear, boar, deer, and moose, also live there. The shores of the ponds, lakes, and streams of temperate forests shelter many animals that live both on land and in water. These animals include the beaver, frog, muskrat, otter, salamander, and turtle. Many birds nest in temperate forests. They feed on the insects and worms that live in great numbers among the plants and in the rich soil. Most temperate forests are in Asia, Europe, and North America. Australia has some temperate forests where the echidna and the koala are found.

Russ Kinne, Photo Researchers

European brown bear

FPG

Moose   North America

Barred owl
North America

Wood frog
North America

Garter snake
North America

Red-backed salamander
North America

DOWNY WOODPECKER

WHITE-TAILED DEER

OVENBIRD

CHIPMUNK

RACCOON

WOODCHUCK

MUSKRAT

PORCUPINE

SKUNK

OPOSSUM

SNAPPING TURTLE

Okapia, Publix

Wild boar Europe

Geoffroy Kinns, Photo Researchers

Red deer Europe

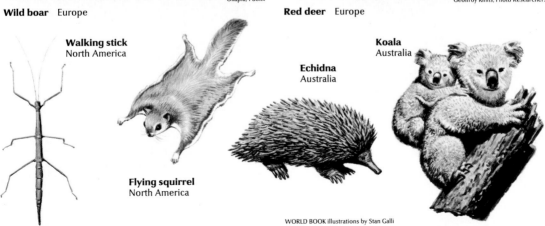

Walking stick
North America

Koala
Australia

Echidna
Australia

Flying squirrel
North America

WORLD BOOK illustrations by Stan Galli

Animals of the tropical forests

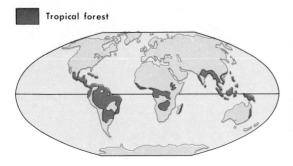

▮ Tropical forest

Animals of the tropical forests have an environment that stays hot all year around. Anteaters, jaguars, leopards, tapirs, and tigers live in these forests. Tropical forests include lightly wooded areas with moderate rainfall, and huge rain forests—densely wooded places with heavy rainfall. In the tropical rain forests, the tops of the trees and vines form a thick overhead covering called a *canopy*. Climbing animals, such as monkeys and sloths, live in the canopy. Gibbons, orangutans, and other apes are also found in tropical rain forests. In addition, brightly colored parrots and numerous other birds nest in the trees. Many birds of the tropical rain forests feed mostly on large colonies of ants and other insects. Snakes, such as the boa constrictor; and spiders, including the tarantula, grow to giant size in the tropical rain forests.

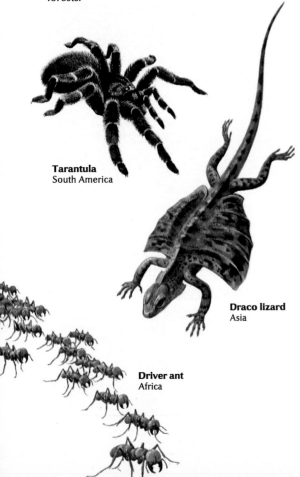

Tarantula
South America

Draco lizard
Asia

Driver ant
Africa

BLACK HOWLER MONKEY

COMMON MARMOSET

MACAW

SPIDER MONKEY

COATI

IGUANA

TWO-TOED SLOTH

PARASOL ANT

OCELOT

TREE FROG

TREE BOA CONSTRICTOR

South American Rain Forest

Axis deer
Asia

South American tapir

Malayan tapir
Asia

Chevrotain
Asia

Des Bartlett, Photo Researchers

Bongo Africa

Okapia, Publix

Gibbon   Asia

Orangutan
Asia

James Simon, Photo Researchers

Woolly monkey   South America

James Simon, Photo Researchers

Giant anteater   South America

Tiger Asia

Ylla, Rapho Guillumette

Leopard Africa, Asia

Jaguar
Central and South
America, Mexico

WORLD BOOK illustrations by Robert Kuhn

Animals of the deserts

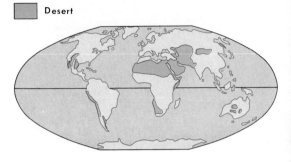

☐ Desert

Most animals of the deserts have small bodies. Their size helps them escape from the heat that scorches most deserts during the daytime. Some desert animals dig into the ground when the hot sun beats down. Others find shade under brush, rocks, or trees. After sunset, most deserts become quite cool, and the animals go in search of food. Some lizards, snakes, and tortoises like the high daytime temperatures. But even they must seek shade during the hottest times. Most desert animals can live without water for several days. The dromedary is famous for being able to travel many days without drinking. Small desert animals include mice, hares, rabbits, kangaroo rats, and spadefoot toads. Among the larger desert animals are the coyote, dingo, and mule deer.

Southwestern United States

David Fleay

Dingo   Australia

Cy LaTour

Scorpion   North America

FPG

Dromedary   Africa, Asia

PALLID BAT

COYOTE

BOBCAT

MULE DEER

ANTELOPE JACK RABBIT

CACTUS WREN

KIT FOX

GILA MONSTER

WORLD BOOK illustration by Rudolf Freund

Nathan Cohen

Shovel-nosed snake North America

Cy LaTour

Saiga Asia

Lewis W. Walker, Photo Researchers

Elf owl North America

David Fleay

Horned dragon Australia

Animals of the polar regions

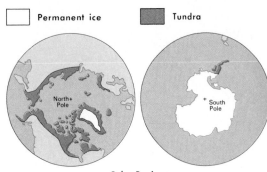

Permanent ice   Tundra

Polar Regions

Few land animals live in areas of the polar regions that have ice and snow all year around. But even the coldest arctic and antarctic waters have great numbers of fishes. In the far north, these fishes provide food for the polar bears that live on the arctic islands and ice floes. In the Antarctic, penguins and other birds feed on the fishes of the southern polar seas. Many animals live in the arctic *tundra* (swampy plains) of northern Asia, Canada, and Europe. They include grazing animals such as the caribou and musk ox. Other arctic animals are the hare, ermine, fox, grizzly bear, lemming, wolf, and wolverine. Arctic birds include the loon, rock ptarmigan, sandhill crane, snowy owl, and golden plover.

SNOWY OWL

MUSK OX

ARCTIC HARE

ROCK PTARMIGAN

ERMINE

Arctic winter

Polar bear   Arctic

Cy LaTour

Arctic bumble bee

Emperor penguin   Antarctica

Emil Schulthess, Black Star

Steve McCutcheon

Alaska brown bear

SANDHILL CRANE

ARCTIC LOON

GOLDEN PLOVER

CARIBOU

ARCTIC FOX

WORLD BOOK illustrations by Guy Tudor

Arctic summer

Walrus Arctic

Steve McCutcheon

Collared lemming
Arctic

Animals of the oceans

Animals live everywhere in the vast ocean waters, which cover 70 per cent of the earth's surface. Many small animals, including the shrimplike copepod, make up the animal part of plankton, a mass of organisms that drifts with the ocean currents and tides. Whales, the world's largest animals, also live in the oceans. Other large ocean animals include the sea cow, octopuses, sharks, and sting rays. Many kinds of brightly colored fishes often live close to the reefs in tropical ocean waters. Most fishes live near the continents, but some, such as the flying fish, are found in the open seas. Many animals with shells, such as marine clams, and spiny animals, such as sea urchins, live on the ocean floor.

Copepod   Worldwide

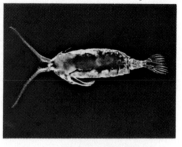

Douglas P. Wilson

Blood-red starfish
North Atlantic

Purple sea urchin
Pacific Coast
North America

Flatworm
Tropical seas

Fingered limpet
Pacific Coast
North America

Margiocco from Paul Popper
Sea pen   Warm seas

G. Tomsich, Photo Researchers
Fan worm   European Coast

Common octopus
Americas

Giant spider crab
Japan

Margiocco from Paul Popper
Disk jellyfish
Mediterranean

Verne Peckham, NAS
Dahlia anemone
Northern seas

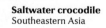

Saltwater crocodile
Southeastern Asia

Manatee
Tropical Atlantic

Killer whale
Pacific

Squirrelfish and coral Bahamas

Russ Kinne, Photo Researchers

Flying fish Warm seas

Deep-sea angler Atlantic and Pacific

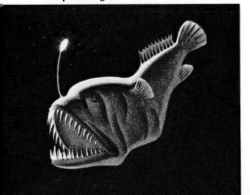

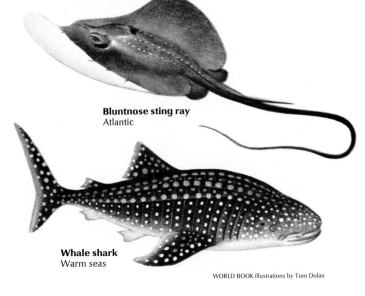

Bluntnose sting ray
Atlantic

Whale shark
Warm seas

WORLD BOOK illustrations by Tom Dolan

Animal camouflage

Protective coloration helps many animals hide from their enemies. Flatfish have body colors that change to match the ocean bottom. This makes them seem to disappear. Many birds, such as the pheasant, have colors that make them seem to be part of the surroundings in which they nest. The spotted fawn of the white-tailed deer is hard to see because its colors resemble those of its woodland home. The gray bark crypsis is typical of many moths whose coloring makes them seem to disappear when they rest on certain trees. An animal that uses protective coloration to fool an enemy usually remains motionless until danger passes.

Lilo Hess, Three Lions

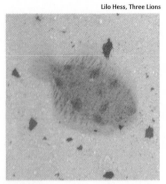

Flatfish

Lilo Hess, Three Lions

White-tailed deer fawn

David G. Allen

Pheasant

Alexander B. Klots

Gray bark crypsis

Protective resemblance helps many kinds of animals stay alive by deceiving their enemies. The bodies of these animals are shaped to make them look like a part of their surroundings, or like another animal. A treehopper on the stem of a rosebush looks so much like a thorn that birds often overlook the insect. The razor fish holds its body straight up and down when it swims. Its long, slender body looks like the thin leaves of a sea plant. The wings of a dead-leaf mantis resemble leaves. Some robber flies look so much like a bumble bee that enemies often avoid them. Other insects are protected because they look like twigs or flowers.

Pierre Labout, Jacana

Frank Roche, Animals Animals

Dead-leaf mantis

Breck Kent, Animals Animals

E. R. Degginger

Treehopper

Razor fish

Robber fly

Animal defenses and weapons

The armadillo's armor protects the animal from harm. The bony plates of the armor fit together so well that the armadillo can roll up tightly into a ball when an enemy comes near.

© Leonard Lee Rue III

Sharp quills help protect a porcupine from attack. When touched, the barbed quills come off the porcupine and hook into the attacker's flesh, where they can cause painful wounds.

E. R. Degginger

Speed is the impala's main defense. An impala can run as fast as 50 miles (80 kilometers) per hour in bounding leaps.

E. R. Degginger

Broad, curved tusks make the wild boar dangerous to its enemies. This ferocious animal fights savagely if attacked.

E. R. Degginger

A lobster's claws are powerful weapons. The animal uses its claws to seize crabs, fish, snails, and other prey. The strong, toothed claws then crush the prey and tear it into pieces.

Zig Leszczynski, Animals Animals

Rattlesnake fangs inject deadly poison. The needlelike fangs fold back against the roof of the mouth when not in use. They move forward when the snake opens its mouth to strike.

Alan Blank, Bruce Coleman Inc.

A saw-whet owl spreads its *talons* (claws) to capture a mouse. Owls also use their talons to defend their nests from intruders.

Ted Levin, Animals Animals

Large, heavy horns protect the Cape buffalo of southern Africa. This powerful animal can even kill an attacking lion.

A. J. Deane, Bruce Coleman Ltd.

Animals and their young

The young of many animals need no care from their parents. As soon as they are born, they can move about and find food. The young of other animals need help for some time after birth. Their parents feed and protect them until they can care for themselves.

Many kinds of newborn ocean animals get along by themselves. These ocean animals include mollusks, sea urchins, and starfish. Their parents pay no attention to them. Some fishes, such as salmon, may travel thousands of miles or kilometers to lay their eggs in certain streams. But then they leave the eggs, and the baby fishes that hatch must get along as best they can. Sea turtles climb onto the beach to lay their eggs in the sand. Then they crawl right back into the sea, letting the young turtles that hatch develop by themselves. Some frogs and toads leave their eggs in ponds and ignore the tadpoles that hatch. Most insects do no more than lay their eggs in places where the young will be able to find food.

On the other hand, the sea horse is famous for the way it helps its young. The male sea horse carries the female's eggs in a pouch on its underside. After the young hatch, the father lets them out one by one into seaweed where they can find food.

The stickleback, a spiny fish that lives in many waters of the Northern Hemisphere, also helps its young. The male stickleback builds a nest of roots and sticks for the eggs. It guards the young for several days after they hatch. Kangaroos and opossums keep their newborn babies in a pouch on the front of the mother's body. There the youngster is fed and protected by the mother.

Ants and bees take special care of their young. Certain members of each colony bring food to the young, and spend most of their time as nursemaids. Many birds and mammals not only take care of their young, but also train them in important ways. They keep their young warm, feed them, and teach them to fly or to hunt for their food.

See **Animal** in *World Book* for more information on the following topics:

- Kinds of animals
- The importance of animals
- Ways of life
- Animal bodies
- A classification of the animal kingdom

Turtles give their young no care at all. The mother sea turtle digs a hole on a beach and lays her eggs. Then she covers them with sand and returns to sea. The sun hatches the eggs.

Jane Burton, Photo Researchers

Monkeys take good care of their babies. These crab-eating macaques show great affection for their young and train them carefully. Most monkeys fight fiercely to protect their babies.

B. Amadeus Rubel, Shostal

Names of animals and their young

Animal	Male	Female	Young	Group	Approximate gestation period*
Albatross (royal)			fledgling	flock	81 days*
Antelope	buck	doe	kid	herd	9 months
Bear	boar	sow	cub	sloth	6-8 months
Beaver			kit	colony	3 months
			pup	family	
Bobcat	tom	lioness	kit		65 days
Cat	tom	queen	kitten	clowder	63 days
Cattle	bull	cow	calf	herd	9 months
				drove	
Chicken	cock	hen	chick	flock	21 days*
	rooster				
Deer	buck	doe	fawn	herd	7 months
	hart	hind			
	stag	roe			
Dog	dog	bitch	pup	kennel	58-63 days
Donkey	jackass	jennet	foal	pace	12 months
		jenny	colt		
Elephant	bull	cow	calf	herd	18-23 months
Fox	dog	vixen	cub	skulk	49-55 days
			pup		
Giraffe	bull	cow	calf	herd	14-15 months
Goat	billy	nanny	kid	herd	151 days
	buck	doe			
Goose	gander	goose	gosling	flock	30 days*
				gaggle	
Hog	boar	sow	shoat	herd	114 days
			farrow	drove	
			piglet		
Horse	stallion	dam	foal	herd	11 months
	stud	mare	colt (male)		
			filly (female)		
Kangaroo	buck	doe	joey	herd	30-40 days
	boomer	flier		troop	
				mob	
Lion	lion	lioness	cub	pride	108 days
Ostrich	cock	hen	chick	flock	42 days*
Rabbit	buck	doe	kit	warren	30-32 days
Rat	buck	doe			22 days
Seal	bull	cow	pup	herd	8-12 months
			whelp	trip	
Sheep	buck	dam	lamb	flock	5 months
	ram	ewe	lambkin	herd	
			teg		
Swan	cob	pen	cygnet	flock	35 days*
Turkey	cock	hen	poult	flock	28 days*
	gobbler				
	tom				
Whale	bull	cow	calf	herd	10-17 months
Zebra	stallion	mare	colt	herd	11-12 months

*Approximate incubation period.

David Fleay

A baby wallaby stays with its mother—in her pouch—until it can care for itself. Wallabies are small-sized kangaroos.

Fur seals start life in a group with many other pups and their mothers. Each mother seal nurses and tends only her own young.

Karl W. Kenyon, NAS

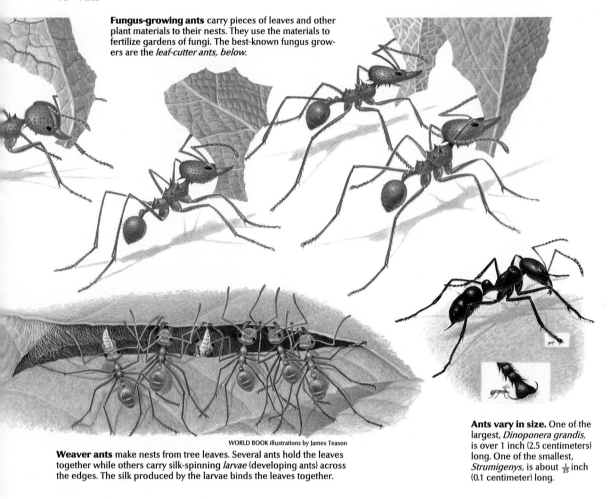

Fungus-growing ants carry pieces of leaves and other plant materials to their nests. They use the materials to fertilize gardens of fungi. The best-known fungus growers are the *leaf-cutter ants, below.*

WORLD BOOK illustrations by James Teason

Weaver ants make nests from tree leaves. Several ants hold the leaves together while others carry silk-spinning *larvae* (developing ants) across the edges. The silk produced by the larvae binds the leaves together.

Ants vary in size. One of the largest, *Dinoponera grandis,* is over 1 inch (2.5 centimeters) long. One of the smallest, *Strumigenys,* is about $\frac{1}{25}$ inch (0.1 centimeter) long.

Ant

Ant is an insect that lives in organized communities. Ants are therefore known as *social insects.* Other social insects include some kinds of bees, all termites, and certain wasps. However, ants are perhaps the most highly developed social insects.

A community of social insects is called a *colony.* An ant colony may have a dozen, hundreds, thousands, or millions of members. Each colony has one or several *queens.* A queen's chief job is to lay eggs. Most members of an ant colony are *workers.* All the workers, like the queens, are females. The workers build the nest, search for food, care for the young, and fight enemies. *Males* live in the nest only at certain times. Their only job is to mate with young queens. After mating, the males soon die.

Ants have many different ways of life. For example, *army ants* live by hunting other insects. Some kinds of army ants march across the land in enormous swarms, eating most of the insects they meet. Ants known as *slave makers* raid the nests of other ants and steal the young, which they raise as slaves. *Harvester ants* gather seeds and store them inside their nests. Certain kinds of *dairying ants* keep insects that give off a sweet liquid when the ants "milk" them.

Ants live everywhere on land, except for extremely cold areas. They are most numerous in regions that have a warm climate. Some ants live in underground tunnels, and some build earthen mounds. Others live inside trees or in hollow parts of certain other plants. Still other ants construct their nests from tree leaves. Some kinds of ants, such as army ants, do not have permanent nests.

There are about 10,000 kinds of ants. Most kinds have drab colors, such as black, brown, or rust. But some are yellow, green, blue, or purple.

The different kinds of ants vary in size, but most are small. The largest kinds are more than 1 inch (2.5 centimeters) long. The smallest kinds are about $\frac{1}{25}$ inch (0.1 centimeter) long.

In spite of their small size, ants are amazingly strong. Most ants can lift objects that are 10 times heavier than their bodies. Some can lift objects that are 50 times heavier than their bodies.

Scientists believe that ants gradually developed from

Some ants build earthen mounds over their underground nests. The mounds of harvester ants, *above,* are a common sight in the Southwestern United States.

Ants use their antennae to smell one another. In this way, ants recognize nestmates. The antennae are organs of touch, taste, and hearing as well as of smell.

Ant nestmates share food by *regurgitation.* Two ants stand mouth to mouth, and one spits up food for the other. Food is shared among all members of a colony.

Janitor ants make nests in tunnels in tree branches. The large workers, called *soldiers,* have a pluglike head. A soldier blocks the nest entrance with its head, *above,* to keep out enemies.

Balzekas Museum of Lithuanian Culture (WORLD BOOK photo)

Fossils of ants indicate that ants have lived on the earth for more than 100 million years. This fossil ant, which became preserved in amber, is about 30 million years old.

wasps more than 100 million years ago. Ants resemble wasps more than they do any other insects. In fact, one kind of wasp looks so much like an ant that it is commonly called a *velvet ant.* But an ant has a *node* (knotlike growth) on top of its waist. This node distinguishes ants from most antlike wasps.

The bodies of ants

Among most species of ants, the queens, workers, and males differ in size. In many cases, the queens are several times larger than the workers. The males are also larger than the workers, but they are smaller than the queens. In addition, the workers among a particular species may differ in size. The largest workers, which are called *soldiers,* may have a bigger head than the other workers have.

Like other insects, ants have a hard, shell-like covering called an *exoskeleton.* This covering protects the internal organs. An ant's muscles are attached to the inside walls of the exoskeleton.

An ant's body has three main parts. They are (1) the head, (2) the trunk, and (3) the metasoma. An ant's internal organs and sense organs are similar to those of many other insects.

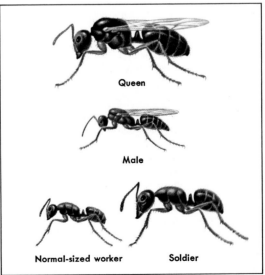

WORLD BOOK illustrations by James Teason

The classes of ants—queens, males, and workers—differ in size. In most cases, queens are the largest, followed by males and workers. Among carpenter ants, *above,* some workers are larger than males. These large workers are called *soldiers.*

The body of an ant

The external anatomy

An ant's body has three main parts: (1) the head, (2) the trunk, and (3) the metasoma. The main features of the head are the eyes, antennae, and mandibles. Three pairs of legs extend from the bottom of the trunk. The narrow front part of the metasoma is called the *waist,* and the large back part is called the *gaster.* Some ants have a sting at the tip of the gaster.

The internal anatomy

An ant's internal organs include a brain and nerve cord and a tube-shaped heart. The animal breathes through *spiracles* (tiny openings along the sides of the body). Its digestive system includes a food pouch that squeezes the liquid out of food. The liquid moves through a food passage to the *crop,* a storage pouch, and then to the stomach, where digestion occurs. Wastes pass through the rectum and out of the body.

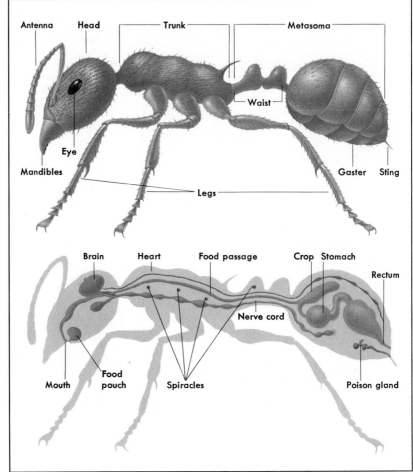

WORLD BOOK illustration by James Teason

Life in an ant colony

All ants are social insects. But except for the fact that they all live in groups, ants vary greatly in their ways of life. This section chiefly discusses the general features of life in an ant colony.

Castes. In almost all ant colonies, the members are divided into three *castes* (classes). The castes are the queen, workers, and males. In most cases, a young queen starts a new colony after mating with one or several males. After she has established a colony, the queen lays eggs for the rest of her life. The queen does not rule the colony. But the workers, all of whom are females, feed and lick her, as they do one another. Some colonies have only one queen, but others may have several. Besides caring for the queen, the workers enlarge, repair, and defend the nest; care for the young; and gather food. A worker may chiefly do one job throughout its life or change jobs from time to time. Males do not do any work in the colony. They live a short time, and their only function is to mate with young queens.

Among many species of ants, the workers differ in size and shape. The largest workers are the soldiers. They have a big head and large mandibles. In some species, the soldiers' chief job is to defend the colony from

enemies. In other species, the soldiers have no special job. Among *janitor ants,* the soldiers have a blunt, plug-shaped head. Janitor ants make their nests in tunnels in the branches of trees. A soldier keeps enemies out of the nest by blocking the entrance with its head.

Nests. Ants build many types of nests. Most species make their homes underground, carving tunnels and chambers in the soil. Some of these species build large mounds of soil, twigs, and pine needles over their underground nests.

The large black or brown *carpenter ants* make their nests in the trunks and branches of trees and even in the wooden beams of houses. These ants, unlike termites, do not eat wood. They chew tunnels in wood only to make nesting space.

Many kinds of ants make their homes in rotten logs, under the bark of trees, or in hollow parts of the leaves or thorns of certain plants. Some species chew up plant fibers and then use the material to build "cardboard" nests.

Tropical *weaver ants* construct nests from tree leaves. To make a nest, some of the workers hold the edges of leaves together, while other workers carry silk-spinning *larvae* back and forth across the edges. Larvae are ants in an early stage of development. The larvae produce a thick sheet of silken webbing that binds the edges of the leaves together.

Ant nests vary greatly in size. Some ants live in nests that may have only one chamber no bigger than your finger. Such a nest may have as few as 12 ants or as many as 300. Some tropical ants build huge underground nests that may extend 40 feet (12 meters) below the surface of the ground. More than 10 million ants may live in such a nest. Some North American and European ants build nests that consist of 12 or more mounds connected by underground tunnels. The nesting site may cover an area the size of a tennis court, and some mounds may be 3 feet (0.9 meter) high or higher. Millions of ants may live in the mounds and underground chambers.

Most ant nests have a number of chambers. One chamber houses the queen and her eggs. Several other chambers serve as "nurseries," to which the workers move the growing young. If one chamber becomes too cold or too wet for the young, the workers move them to a warmer or drier chamber. Many chambers serve as gathering or resting places for the workers. The nests of some ants have rooms in which food is stored or fungi are raised. As a colony grows, the workers enlarge the nest by making more rooms and passageways. Ants that live in regions with cold winters move to the deepest parts of their nests during the winter. They emerge from their nests again in spring.

Life span. Queen, worker, and male ants have different life spans. Queens live the longest, from about 10 to 20 years. Workers may live from less than 1 year to more than 5. Males live only a few weeks or months before they go on the mating flight, after which they soon die.

The importance of ants

Ants play an important role in the balance of nature. They eat large numbers of insects and so help keep them from becoming too plentiful. In the tropics, for example, ants eat more than half the termites hatched each year. Ants, in turn, are an important food source for birds, frogs, lizards, and many other animals.

Ants are both beneficial and harmful to farmers. Some species aid farmers by killing insects that damage crops. Ants that dig underground nests improve the soil by breaking it up, loosening it, and mixing it. Loose soil absorbs water more easily than does hard-packed soil. Ants can also be agricultural pests. Some dairying ants protect aphids and other insects that harm crops. *Fire ants* are serious pests in the Southern United States. They build large mounds that interfere with the cutting of hay. They also have a painful sting, to which some people are allergic.

Many kinds of ants are household pests. For example, *carpenter ants* damage houses by tunneling through wooden beams. *Pharaoh's ants* and *thief ants* invade houses, restaurants, hospitals, and other buildings and eat stored food. Poison sprays or baits can sometimes help rid ants from houses. But before using indoor sprays or baits, a person should check with the state or county agricultural extension office to make sure they are both effective and safe to use.

See **Ant** in *World Book* for more information on The bodies of ants, Life in an ant colony, and Kinds of ants.

Inside an ant nest

This drawing shows the nest of a colony of harvester ants. The nest consists of various rooms and connecting tunnels. The tunnels extend through the mound and deep underground. One chamber houses the queen and her eggs. Several rooms serve as "nurseries," where the workers care for the growing young. Some chambers are gathering or resting places for the workers. Harvester ants also have rooms for storing seeds, which they gather outside the nest. As a colony grows, the workers make more rooms and tunnels. The ants spend the winter in the deepest rooms of the nest.

WORLD BOOK illustration by James Teason

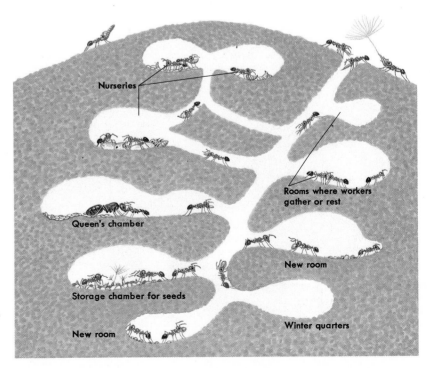

Nurseries

Rooms where workers gather or rest

Queen's chamber

New room

Storage chamber for seeds

New room

Winter quarters

Ape is a member of a group of animals that most closely resemble human beings. There are four major kinds of apes—chimpanzees, gibbons, gorillas, and orangutans. All these animals have hairy, tailless bodies; longer arms than legs; and long fingers and toes. They also have large brains and rank as the most intelligent animals next to human beings.

Most scientists believe that apes and human beings developed from a common ancestor. Apes resemble human beings in body structure more than any other animals do. They have similar bones, muscles, and organs. But human beings also differ from apes in many ways. For example, human beings walk on two legs and have longer legs and less body hair. They also have a larger brain than that of apes. For more information on the differences between human beings and apes, see **Human being** (Physical characteristics) in *World Book*.

Scientists divide the apes into two groups, based chiefly on size. Gibbons, the smallest apes, are called *lesser apes.* Chimpanzees, gorillas, and orangutans are called *great apes.* Gorillas are the largest, followed by orangutans and chimpanzees.

Differences between apes and monkeys. Many people confuse apes with monkeys, but the two groups of animals differ in many ways. Most monkeys have tails and seem less intelligent. The great apes are much larger and have longer fingers and toes. Apes are skillful tree climbers. On the ground, chimpanzees and gorillas walk in a semiupright posture, supporting the front part of their bodies on their knuckles. Orangutans walk infrequently on the ground, but when they do they support themselves on their fists. Gibbons spend almost all their time in trees but often walk on two legs on branches. By contrast, monkeys run and jump on all fours, both in trees and on the ground.

Way of life. Apes live in tropical Africa and Asia. All apes except gorillas eat mostly fruit. Gorillas eat mainly ground plants, such as wild celery and bamboo shoots.

Gibbons live in the tropical forests of Southeast Asia. They spend much time hanging from tree branches or swinging from branch to branch. Gibbons form family groups of a male and a female and their young.

Chimpanzees live in a wide range of habitats from western to eastern Africa. They are found in rain forests as well as dry grasslands. They live both in trees and on the ground. Scientists recognize two kinds of chimpanzees. One kind is known simply as the chimpanzee. The other, more slender, variety is called the pygmy chimpanzee. Chimpanzees live in groups that vary from 20 to 40 members. Often, the females leave their group and join another. Pygmy chimpanzees live in groups of males, females, and their young. These groups may contain 5 to 30 individuals.

Gorillas live in the lowland forests of western and central Africa and in the mountain forests of eastern Africa. Large males often sleep on the ground, but females and the young sleep in trees. Gorillas travel in groups of up to 20 individuals. Older males develop a patch of white or silvery hair on their backs and are called *silverbacks.* One of these males leads each group.

Orangutans live in the tropical forests of Borneo and Sumatra. They spend most of the time in trees, though large males are often seen on the ground. Orangutans usually travel alone, but a female and her offspring travel together.

The number of apes is decreasing because people hunt them for food and for pets and to sell to zoos and research centers. In addition, roads, farms, and the forest industry have destroyed much of the forests where apes once lived.

The four kinds of apes   There are four major kinds of apes: gorillas, chimpanzees, gibbons, and orangutans. These animals live in the tropical regions of Africa and Asia. Gorillas, chimpanzees, and orangutans are known as the *great apes.* Gibbons, the smallest apes, are called *lesser apes.*

WORLD BOOK illustrations by James Teason

Gibbon
Hylobates lar
Height: about 31 inches
(80 centimeters)

Gorilla
Gorilla gorilla
Height: about 69 inches (174 centimeters)

Chimpanzee
Pan troglodytes
Height: about 48 inches (123 centimeters)

Orangutan
Pongo pygmaeus
Height: 49 inches (124 centimeters)

Aquarium is a place where people keep fish and other water animals. Aquariums range in size from small glass tanks to large buildings that display water animals of all kinds and sizes. Large tanks called *oceanariums* are used to keep large *marine* (salt-water) animals, such as dolphins and porpoises.

Starting a home aquarium

Basic equipment for a home aquarium includes (1) a tank and tank cover, (2) a filter, (3) a heater, and (4) a thermometer.

A rectangular tank that holds 10 to 20 gallons (38 to 76 liters) makes a good aquarium for a beginning aquarist. One popular type of tank has a metal frame, glass sides and ends, and a slate or glass bottom. Most covers include an incandescent or fluorescent lamp that shines down into the tank. Such covers, called *light reflectors,* make it easy to see the fish. Lids that cover the entire top prevent fish from jumping out of the tank and reduce the amount of heat lost from the tank.

The aquarium filter removes dirt suspended in the water and keeps the water clean. Most filters are connected to an electrically operated air pump. The pump produces a stream of air that pushes water through the filter. *Trap-type* filters pass the water through such materials as activated charcoal and glass wool, which remove particles and some impurities. *Undergravel filters* suck wastes into the gravel at the bottom of the tank. Bacteria in the gravel use the wastes as food. Filters circulate water and help *disperse* (scatter) harmful gases.

The electric heater warms the water to the proper temperature to keep the fish healthy. For most fish, the water must be kept between 72° and 80° F. (22° and 27° C). Most heaters hang on the tank's edge and extend into the water. The thermometer should be located away from the heater where it can be easily read.

Setting up an aquarium. A new tank should be washed inside and out with lukewarm, salty water and then rinsed thoroughly. The tank should be placed in its permanent location on a level, strong surface near an electrical outlet. The aquarium should be located away from direct sunlight, drafts, and radiators. The gravel should be rinsed and put into the tank in a layer about 1 inch (2.5 centimeters) deep. Undergravel filters should be placed in the tank before the gravel is added.

The tank should be filled with tap water. It is best to fill the tank a little at a time, and to watch for leaks. Plants that root in the gravel should be placed into the tank when it is about two-thirds full. The filter and heater should be put in just before the tank is completely filled.

In most cases, the water will be suitable for fish two to three days after the tank is filled and the electrical equipment is started. The water will be cloudy at first due to unsettled particles of dirt. Bubbles of gas may also appear. The cloudiness and bubbles will disappear in a day or two. After that time, a new cloudiness might appear, caused by bacteria. This condition will also probably clear up in a few days.

A home aquarium for tropical fish

A home aquarium should have an air pump and a filter to keep the water clean. The lid prevents fish from jumping out of the tank. The heater, controlled by a thermostat, keeps the water at the desired temperature. Gravel and decorative plants give the aquarium a pleasing appearance.

WORLD BOOK illustration by James Teason

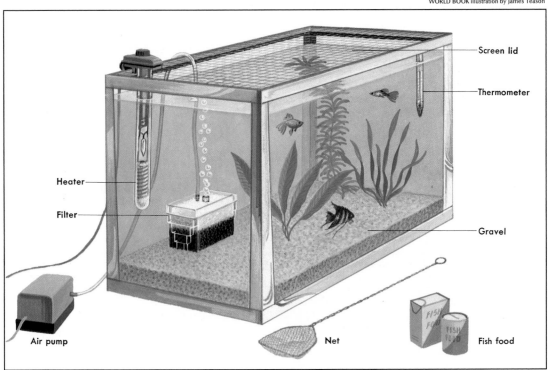

Screen lid

Thermometer

Heater

Filter

Gravel

Air pump

Net

Fish food

Jet Propulsion Laboratory

Uranus and a moon, *foreground*

Jay M. Pasachoff

Total solar eclipse

© California Institute of Technology (Palomar Observatory)

The Great Galaxy in Andromeda

Halley's comet in 1985

David F. Malin, Anglo-Australian Observatory

Objects studied by astronomers include comets, galaxies, *nebulae* (clouds of dust and gas), planets, and stars. Astronomers also observe eclipses and other events in the heavens.

Astronomy

Astronomy is the study of the stars, planets, and other objects that make up the universe. Astronomers observe the locations and motions of heavenly bodies. However, almost all astronomers are interested in more than just observing these objects. They also seek answers to such questions as "What are stars made of?" and "How do they create their light?" For this reason, most astronomers are also *astrophysicists*—that is, they study physical and chemical processes that occur in the universe.

Astronomy is one of the oldest sciences. It began in ancient times with the observation that the heavenly bodies go through regular cycles of motion. Throughout history, the study of these cycles has served such practical purposes as keeping time, marking the arrival of the seasons, and navigating accurately at sea.

As early as 200 B.C., the Babylonians charted the positions of the heavenly bodies to predict events on the earth. The making of such predictions is called *astrology* and is based on the belief that the positions of stars and planets influence what happens on the earth. The ancient Egyptians, Greeks, and Romans also practiced astrology, and many early astronomers believed in it. By the 1700's, however, most scientists had come to reject astrology. Scientists today consider it a *pseudoscience* (false science). They explain events on the earth and in space by the laws of physics and chemistry, which provide no basis for a belief in astrology. In addition, many scientists do not simply ignore astrology but actively oppose it as superstition that slows the advance of science.

Observing the sky

The daytime sky. The sun is an interesting object in the daytime sky. A variety of storms and other activities can be seen on the surface of the sun from day to day. However, the sun is too bright to observe safely without using special equipment. Sunlight also makes the sky too bright to observe other stars and planets during the day. The moon, however, is sometimes visible in daylight. As sunlight passes through the earth's atmosphere, it strikes molecules of the gases that make up the atmosphere. The molecules scatter the sunlight, which is a mixture of all colors, in every direction. The sky appears blue because blue light is scattered much more than any other color.

The nighttime sky. The moon is the brightest and most easily seen object in the sky at night. As a result, the most familiar astronomical observation is of the moon's *phases,* such as the full moon, half moon, and crescent. The phases occur because the amount of

© 1979 Royal Observatory Edinburgh (David F. Malin, Anglo-Australian Observatory)
The Horsehead nebula in the constellation Orion

the moon's sunlit area that can be seen from the earth changes as the moon orbits the earth. The moon completes one set of phases about once a month.

On some nights, the moon shines so brightly that few stars or planets can be seen. But on a dark, moonless night, many stars and planets become visible. The planets usually appear first. Not until the sky is truly dark do the stars come out. Planets and stars look much alike in the night sky. However, the planets shift position nightly in relation to the stars. In addition, planets shine steadily, and stars appear to twinkle. Twinkling occurs because moving layers of air in the earth's atmosphere bend starlight, making the images of the stars appear to vary in brightness and dance around slightly.

Five planets—Venus, Jupiter, Mars, Saturn, and Mercury—can be seen easily without a telescope. Venus is usually the brightest planet, and Jupiter the next brightest. Mars stands out because of its reddish tinge. Although Saturn can be seen with the naked eye, a small telescope is needed to view its beautiful rings. Mercury is often too close to the sun to be visible. But at times, Mercury appears low in the western sky just after sunset or low in the eastern sky just before sunrise.

About 6,000 stars shine bright enough to be seen without a telescope. Sirius is the brightest star. Other bright stars include Canopus, Arcturus, and Vega. In ancient times, astronomers divided the stars into classes of brightness called *magnitudes.* They classified the brightest stars as first magnitude, slightly fainter stars as second magnitude, and so on. The faintest stars visible to the naked eye were classified as sixth magnitude. Astronomers today use a modified version of this system.

Every few years, a bright *comet* may be observed with the unaided eye. A comet is a ball of ice and dust that follows a regular orbit around the sun. When nearing the sun, a comet may brighten enough to be seen from the earth. A few comets develop a long tail that extends across one-sixth or more of the sky. However, most comets can be seen only with a telescope, and even bright comets remain visible to the naked eye for only a few days or weeks.

Glowing meteors are far more common in the night sky than comets. A meteor is a chunk of rock or metal that is burning up as it enters the earth's atmosphere. It appears as a streak of light. Meteors are also known as *falling stars* or *shooting stars.* On any clear night, a person can see a few meteors an hour. Showers of meteors take place regularly at certain times of the year. These showers probably result from the passage of the earth through the orbit of a comet that has broken up.

Astronomy terms

Astronomical unit (AU) is the average distance between the earth and the sun—about 93 million miles (150 million kilometers). This unit is used to measure distances within the solar system.

Astrophysics is the study of the chemical composition of astronomical bodies and of the physical processes that occur in space.

Big bang refers to the explosion that nearly all astronomers believe started the universe.

Black hole is an object that is invisible because it has so much gravitational force that not even light can escape from it.

Celestial equator is an imaginary line through the sky directly over the earth's equator.

Celestial poles are points in the sky directly above the North Pole and the South Pole.

Cosmology is the study of the structure and history of the entire universe.

Declination tells how far north or south of the celestial equator a place is in the sky. Declination is measured in degrees.

Ecliptic refers to the apparent yearly path of the sun through the sky with respect to the stars.

Light-year is the distance light travels in one year—about 5.88 trillion miles (9.46 trillion kilometers). Astronomers use this unit to measure distances outside the solar system.

Magnitude is a measurement of the brightness of an astronomical object. *Apparent magnitude* is an object's brightness as seen from the earth. *Absolute magnitude* is a measure of how bright an object would be if it were 32.6 light-years from the earth.

Nebula means a cloud of gas and dust among the stars.

Neutron star is a small, extremely dense star composed of tightly packed neutrons.

Pulsar is a neutron star that sends forth regular bursts of radio waves.

Quasar is an object that looks much like a star but has a tremendous red shift. Quasars are the most distant objects yet detected in the universe. They give off enormous amounts of energy.

Red shift refers to a shift in the *spectrum* (color pattern) of radiation from an astronomical object toward the longer wavelengths. In the visible part of the *spectrum,* the longer wavelengths are red. The presence of a red shift indicates that an object is moving away from the earth.

Right ascension tells how far east a place in the sky is from the point where the sun crosses the celestial equator on about March 21. Right ascension is measured in *hours.* One hour equals an angle of 15 degrees.

The sky at different latitudes. People who observe the night sky at different latitudes have different views of it. A person at the North Pole can never see the stars in the southern half of the sky. Similarly, a person at the South Pole can never see the stars in the northern half. At the equator, a person can see all the stars in the sky during the course of the year.

People anywhere on the earth can see a band of light across the night sky called the *Milky Way*. The Milky Way is the collection of stars, gas, and dust that makes up the galaxy in which our sun is located. One nearby galaxy, in the constellation Andromeda, is faintly visible in the sky of the Northern Hemisphere. Observers in the Southern Hemisphere can see two other galaxies, called the *Magellanic Clouds*.

Why the stars seem to move. The positions of the stars in the sky change slightly over many years. How-

ever, the stars seem to sweep across the sky each night. Their seeming movement is due to the earth's rotation. As the earth rotates on its axis, we on the earth are always moving from west to east. But because we do not sense this motion, it appears to us that the stars revolve overhead from east to west. Only the North Star does not seem to move because it is almost directly above the North Pole. The North Star has served as a guide for navigators since ancient times.

The appearance of the sky also changes from night to night because of the earth's annual revolution around the sun. The sun always blocks part of the sky—that is, some stars cannot be seen because they are in the sky during the daytime. But as the earth moves around the sun, the portion of the sky that is visible at night changes gradually. The earth completes a revolution around the sun in about 365 days. The stars thus rise and

The stars and constellations of the Northern Hemisphere

This map shows the sky as it appears from the North Pole with Polaris, the North Star, directly overhead. To use the map, face south and turn the map so that the current month appears at the bottom. The stars in about the bottom two-thirds of the map will be visible at some time of the night from most areas of the U.S. and southern Canada.

WORLD BOOK illustration by W. J. M. Tirion

set $\frac{1}{365}$ of 24 hours, or about 4 minutes, earlier each night. As the year goes on, the stars in the night sky set earlier and earlier until they are lost in the twilight. Other stars rise earlier and earlier and so become part of the night sky.

Constellations are groups of stars within a particular region of the sky. When astronomers in ancient Egypt, Greece, and other lands began to study the sky, they divided it into regions that had fairly distinct groups of stars. They named these constellations after the figures the stars seemed to form and associated the figures with stories about heroes, heroines, and beasts. Most of the constellations to which we refer today are the groupings devised by the ancient Greeks.

Some star groups, such as the Big Dipper and Little Dipper, do not make up complete constellations. Such groups are called *asterisms*. The Big Dipper is part of

the constellation Ursa Major (Big Bear), and the Little Dipper is part of Ursa Minor (Little Bear).

The stars in a constellation do not necessarily have any relationship with one another. Some stars in a constellation may be relatively near the earth, and others relatively far away. For mapping purposes, however, astronomers divide the sky into 88 constellations. Each star is associated with only one constellation.

See **Astronomy** in *World Book* for more information on the following topics:

- An astronomer's view of the universe
- Astronomers at work
- History
- Careers

The stars and constellations of the Southern Hemisphere

This map shows the sky as it appears from the South Pole. There is no "South Star," but the constellation Octans would be almost directly overhead if you were at the South Pole. To use the map, an observer in the Southern Hemisphere would face north and turn the map so that the current month appears at the bottom.

WORLD BOOK illustration by W. J. M. Tirion

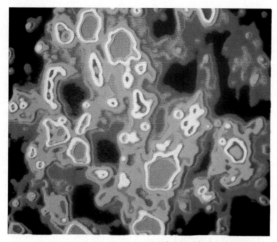

A. V. Crewe, M. Ohtsuki, and M. Utlaut,
Enrico Fermi Institute, University of Chicago

Individual atoms of the metals platinum and palladium magnified about 3 million times appear as yellow dots in this photo made with an electron microscope. The yellow areas with red or purple centers are clusters of atoms. Color was added electronically to improve the image. Atoms themselves have no color.

Atom is one of the basic units of matter. Everything around us is made up of atoms. An atom is incredibly tiny—more than a million times smaller than the thickness of a human hair. The smallest speck that can be seen under an ordinary microscope contains more than 10 billion atoms.

Atoms form the building blocks of the simplest substances, the *chemical elements.* Familiar elements include hydrogen, oxygen, iron, and lead. Each chemical element consists of one basic kind of atom. *Compounds* are more complicated substances composed of two or more kinds of atoms linked together in units called *molecules.* Water, for example, is a compound in which each molecule consists of two atoms of hydrogen linked to one atom of oxygen.

Atoms vary greatly in weight, but they are all about the same size. For example, an atom of plutonium, the heaviest element found in nature, weighs more than 200 times as much as an atom of hydrogen, the lightest known element. However, the diameter of a plutonium atom is only about 3 times that of a hydrogen atom.

The parts of an atom

Tiny as atoms are, they consist of even more minute particles. The three basic types are *protons, neutrons,* and *electrons.* Each atom has a definite number of these *subatomic* particles. The protons and neutrons are crowded into the *nucleus,* an exceedingly tiny region at the center of the atom. If a hydrogen atom were about 4 miles (6.4 kilometers) in diameter, its nucleus would be no bigger than a tennis ball. The rest of an atom outside the nucleus is mostly empty space. The electrons whirl through this space, completing billions of trips around the nucleus each millionth of a second. The fantastic speed of the electrons makes atoms behave as if they were solid, much as the fast-moving blades of a fan prevent a pencil from being pushed through them.

Atoms are often compared to the solar system, with the nucleus corresponding to the sun and the electrons corresponding to the planets that orbit the sun. This comparison is not completely accurate, however. Unlike the planets, the electrons do not follow regular, orderly paths. In addition, the protons and neutrons constantly move about at random inside the nucleus.

The nucleus makes up nearly all the *mass* of an atom. Mass is the quantity of matter in an atom. Each proton has a mass roughly equal to that of 1,836 electrons, and it would take 1,839 electrons to equal the mass of a neutron. Each proton carries one unit of positive electric charge. Each electron carries one unit of negative charge. Neutrons have no electric charge. Under most conditions, an atom has the same number

The parts of an atom

An atom consists of three basic types of particles called *protons, neutrons,* and *electrons.* Protons have a positive electric charge, and electrons have a negative charge. Neutrons are electrically neutral. The protons and neutrons are clustered in the *nucleus,* a tiny region near the center of the atom. The electrons whirl at fantastic speeds through the empty space outside the atom's nucleus.

WORLD BOOK illustration by Leonard E. Morgan

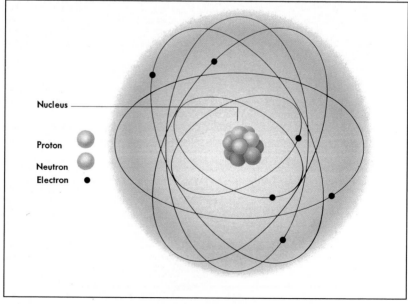

Nucleus

Proton

Neutron

Electron

of protons and electrons, and so the atom is electrically neutral.

Protons and neutrons are about 100,000 times smaller than atoms, but they are in turn made up of even smaller particles called *quarks*. Each proton and neutron consists of three quarks. In the laboratory, scientists can cause quarks to combine and form other kinds of subatomic particles besides protons and neutrons. All these other particles break down and change into ordinary particles in a small fraction of a second. Thus, none of them is found in ordinary atoms. However, scientists first learned that protons and neutrons consist of quarks through the study of other subatomic particles. In *World Book*, see **Particle physics** for information on these other particles.

The electrons, unlike the protons and neutrons, do not seem to have smaller parts. Electrons have very little mass. The mass of an electron in grams may be written with a decimal point followed by 27 zeros and a 9.

Opposite electric charges attract. The positively charged nucleus therefore exerts a force on the negatively charged electrons that keeps them within the atom. However, each electron has energy and so is able to resist the attraction of the nucleus. The more energy an electron has, the farther from the nucleus it will be. Thus, electrons are arranged in *shells* at various distances from the nucleus according to how much energy they have. Electrons with the least energy are in inner shells, and those with more energy are in outer shells.

See **Atom** in *World Book* for more information on the following topics:

- The parts of an atom
- The properties of atoms
- The forces within an atom
- How scientists study atoms
- Development of the atomic theory

Fermilab

Tracks made by atomic particles from a *particle accelerator,* a device that speeds up the particles, are recorded on film. Physicists study the tracks to learn about the characteristics of the particles that produced them.

WORLD BOOK illustration by Leonard E. Morgan

How atoms compare in weight and size

Atoms vary greatly in weight, but they are all about the same size. The smallest and lightest atom is the hydrogen atom. It consists of 1 proton and 1 electron. The largest and heaviest atom found in nature is the plutonium atom. It has 94 protons, 150 neutrons, and 94 electrons. An atom of plutonium weighs more than 200 times as much as an atom of hydrogen. However, a plutonium atom is only about 3 times as large in diameter as a hydrogen atom.

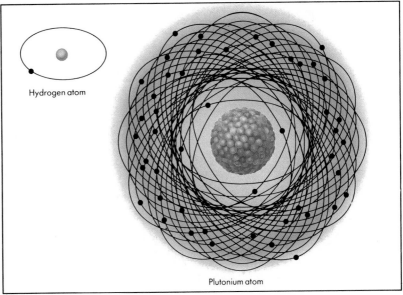

Hydrogen atom

Plutonium atom

Bacteria are simple organisms that consist of one cell. They are among the smallest living things. Most bacteria measure from 0.3 to 2.0 *microns* in diameter and can be seen only through a microscope. (One micron equals 0.001 millimeter or 0.000039 inch.) Some scientists classify bacteria as plants. Others believe bacteria are neither plants nor animals. These scientists classify bacteria as either *monerans* or *protists.*

Bacteria exist almost everywhere. There are thousands of kinds of bacteria, most of which are harmless to human beings. Large numbers of bacteria live in the human body but cause no harm. Some species cause diseases, but many others are helpful.

The importance of bacteria

Helpful bacteria. Certain kinds of bacteria live in the intestines of human beings and other animals. These bacteria help in digestion and in destroying harmful organisms. Intestinal bacteria also produce some vitamins needed by the body.

Bacteria that live in soil and water play a vital role in recycling carbon, nitrogen, sulfur, and other chemical elements used by living things. Many bacteria help *decompose* (break down) dead organisms and animal wastes into chemical elements. Without bacterial decomposition, the elements would remain in dead organisms and animal wastes, and all life would soon stop. Other bacteria help change chemical elements into

forms that can be used by plants and animals. For example, certain kinds of bacteria convert nitrogen in the air and soil into nitrogen compounds for use by plants.

Harmful bacteria. Some kinds of bacteria cause diseases in human beings. These diseases include cholera, gonorrhea, leprosy, pneumonia, syphilis, tuberculosis, typhoid fever, and whooping cough. Bacteria enter the body through natural openings, such as the nose or mouth, or through breaks in the skin. In addition, air, food, and water carry bacteria from one person to another. Harmful bacteria prevent the body from functioning properly by destroying healthy cells.

Certain bacteria produce *toxins* (poisons), which cause such diseases as diphtheria, scarlet fever, and tetanus, and a form of food poisoning called *botulism.* Some toxins are produced by living bacteria, but others are released only after a bacterium dies.

Bacteria that usually live harmlessly in the body may cause infections if a person's resistance is low. For example, if bacteria in the throat reproduce faster than the body can dispose of them, a person may get a sore throat.

See **Bacteria** in *World Book* for more information on the following topics:

- The importance of bacteria
- The structure of bacteria
- The life of bacteria
- History

A bacterial cell

A bacterial cell may have up to three protective layers. These layers surround the cytoplasm, which contains the cell's nuclear body. Hairlike flagella extend through the layers and help the bacterium to move.

WORLD BOOK diagram by Lou Bory

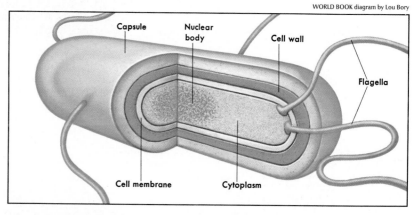

Capsule · Nuclear body · Cell wall · Flagella · Cell membrane · Cytoplasm

The four basic kinds of bacteria

Scientists classify bacteria according to shape. Cocci are round and are linked together. Bacilli look like rods, and vibrios resemble bent rods. Spirilla have a spiral shape. The type of spirilla shown below can cause disease, but other spirilla are harmless.

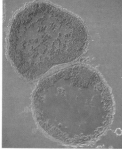

CNRI/SPL from Photo Researchers

Cocci

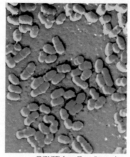

CNRI/SPL from Photo Researchers

Bacilli

SPL from Photo Researchers

Vibrios

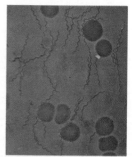

Eric Gravé, Photo Researchers

Spirilla

Bark is the outer covering of most kinds of trees and shrubs. It protects the stem, roots, and branches from injury, insects, disease, and loss of water. Tissues in bark also carry sugar from the leaves to other parts of the plant.

Bark is made up of circular layers of tissues that lie outside the woody core of trees and shrubs. These tissues are divided into two parts, *inner bark* and *outer bark.* Tissues in the inner bark transport and store food. The outer bark serves as a protective covering.

Most trees and shrubs begin to develop bark during their first year. New layers of inner and outer bark form every year, and the bark gradually grows thicker.

Inner bark is composed of layers of living, growing tissues. These layers, from innermost to outermost, are the (1) phloem, (2) phelloderm, and (3) cork cambium, or phellogen.

Phloem consists primarily of *sieve tubes,* which conduct sugar down from the leaves. Bands of fibers may support these tubes. The phloem also includes certain other kinds of cells, including companion cells and ray cells. The phloem in mature woody plants is produced by tissue called the *cambium,* which lies between the wood and the bark. Cell division in the cambium produces new layers of wood and inner bark, and causes the stem of the plant to grow wider. As new phloem accumulates, it pushes the older phloem out and crushes it into the outer bark.

The phelloderm is a layer of food storage cells. It is produced by the cork cambium, which acts similarly to the cambium in the production of new tissues. The growth of new phloem stretches the phelloderm and the cork cambium until they break apart and die. New layers of phelloderm and cork cambium then develop to replace the dead tissues.

Outer bark consists chiefly of *cork,* a tough, dead tissue produced by the cork cambium. Patches of dead phloem occur throughout the outer bark of mature trees and shrubs. This dead phloem has been pushed out by the growth of new phloem.

Cork cells have thick walls that contain a waxy, waterproof substance called *suberin.* Suberin protects the plant from losing water and prevents gases from passing in and out. Gases enter and leave the stem through *lenticels,* which are round or oval blisters in the surface of the bark. In young stems, the outer bark is also marked by scars at points where buds and leaves were once attached.

Young trees and shrubs have a thin, smooth layer of cork. As the stem of the plant grows wider, this layer splits, and new cork cells develop beneath it. This process continues throughout the life of the plant and causes the outer bark to become rough and scaly. The outer bark of a few kinds of trees remains smooth because it stretches easily. Trees with smooth bark include beeches and birches.

The cork cambium produces a new layer of cork annually. The thickness of the bark of most trees does not increase greatly because they lose some older bark each year. However, the outer bark of a large California redwood can measure more than 2 feet (61 centimeters) thick near its base. This thick outer bark protects the trees from the damage that can be caused by the heat of fire.

How people use bark. Early peoples used bark to make canoes, clothing, and shelters. The bark of many kinds of trees has become commercially valuable through the years and is used in manufacturing a wide variety of products.

Manufacturers use cork from the extremely thick outer bark of the cork oak tree in making bottle stoppers, flooring, insulation materials, and many other products. The bark of certain trees contains tannic acid, a substance used in tanning hides to make leather.

The structure of bark Bark consists of *inner bark* and *outer bark.* The tissues of inner bark transport and store food. Outer bark is dead tissue that serves as a protective covering. The diagram on the left shows bark as it appears on a tree. The diagram on the right is an enlarged view of the individual tissues.

WORLD BOOK diagrams by David Cunningham and Marion Pahl

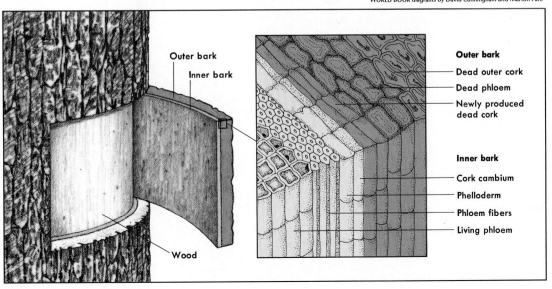

Bat is the only mammal that can fly. Bats have a furry body, and their wings are covered by smooth, flexible skin. Most species of bats live in attics, caves, or other sheltered places. Some species live in trees. Bats seem uncommon in many regions because they roost in dark places and come out only at night, when most people are asleep. Bats hang upside down when they are resting.

There are more than 900 species of bats. Bats live in all parts of the world except Antarctica and the Arctic. Most kinds make their home in the tropics, where they can find food the year around. About 40 species of bats live in Canada and the United States.

The body of a bat. Bats vary in appearance and size, depending on the species. Bats that live in the open may have bright colors and markings. Those that live in dark, sheltered areas have black, brown, gray, red, or yellow fur.

The largest bats, called flying foxes, have a wingspan of over 5 feet (1.5 meters) and a body about the size of a pigeon's. The Kitti's hog-nosed bat of Thailand, the smallest species, is about the size of a bumble bee and weighs only about $\frac{1}{14}$ ounce (2 grams). It is one of the smallest known mammals. Many common North American bats have a wingspan of about 12 inches (30 centimeters) and weigh from $\frac{1}{6}$ to $\frac{2}{3}$ ounce (5 to 19 grams).

The skeleton of a bat resembles that of other mammals. Like many other mammals, a bat has hands with fingers and feet with toes. A bat's breathing rate, heartbeat, and body temperature, unlike those of many other mammals, vary greatly, depending on its activities and the temperature of its surroundings. Among some species, the temperature of a resting bat becomes the same as that of its environment.

The life of a bat. Many species of bats live in colonies that may have thousands or even millions of members. Others live alone or in small groups. Most bats

The skeleton of a bat

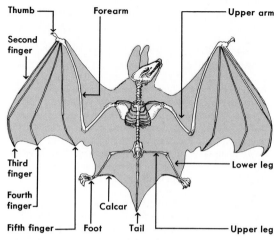

WORLD BOOK illustration by Marion Pahl

spend the day sleeping in their roost. They also may groom their fur and wings or tend their young during the day.

About an hour before dusk, bats start to move around or take short flights. At dusk, they begin to fly from their roost and head for their feeding grounds. Many species eat insects, and each species seeks its own kind of feeding area. Some bats feed in open areas. Other kinds feed in heavy jungles or above a pond.

See **Bat** in *World Book* for more information on The body of a bat, The life of a bat, and Some kinds of bats.

S. C. Bisserot, Bruce Coleman Ltd.

The sight of a flying bat frightens many people unnecessarily. Bats do little harm to people or to crops and livestock. These expert fliers even help people by catching and eating large numbers of destructive insects.

Bear is a large, powerful animal with thick, shaggy fur. Bears prey on other animals and are classified by zoologists as *carnivores*—that is, animals that eat chiefly meat. But most bear species also eat other foods, including fruit, nuts, leaves, insects, and fish.

The Alaskan brown bear is the largest carnivore that lives on land. It grows about 9 feet (2.7 meters) long and may weigh up to 1,700 pounds (770 kilograms). The sun bear, also called the Malayan bear, is the smallest bear. It is 3 to 4 feet (91 to 120 centimeters) long and weighs only 60 to 100 pounds (27 to 45 kilograms).

Most wild bears live north of the equator. They are found in Asia, Europe, and North America, and in the Arctic near the North Pole. Only one species, the spectacled bear, lives in South America. No wild bears live in Africa, Antarctica, or Australia.

The body of a bear

Most bears have heavy bodies with long, thick fur, loose skin, and large, hairy heads. Bears have small eyes and cannot see well. Their small, rounded ears stand straight up, but they hear only fairly well. They have an excellent sense of smell.

Bears have short, strong legs and large feet. Each foot has five toes, and each toe ends in a long, heavy claw. The claws can always be seen because, unlike those of a cat, they have no covering. A bear uses its claws to dig up roots, ants, termites, and other food, or to tear its prey.

Skeleton of a grizzly bear

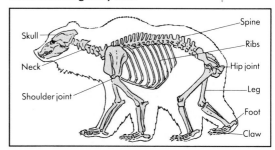

Grizzly bear tracks

WORLD BOOK illustration by Tom Dolan

A bear's walk differs from that of most other animals. Most animals walk and run on their toes. A bear, like a human being, puts the entire sole of its foot on the ground with each step and the heel of the foot strikes the ground first. The hind feet of a large bear may be 12 to 16 inches (30 to 41 centimeters) long. The large feet, the short legs, and heel-first way of stepping make bears look slow and clumsy. But bears are agile and can move

David Goodnow

A mother brown bear and her cubs fish for salmon.

Shapes and sizes of bears These drawings show the differences in size and body shape of bears. The sizes given are the average adult length. The scientific names of the bears appear in italics.

WORLD BOOK illustrations by John D. Dawson

Alaskan brown bear
Ursus arctos middendorffi
9 feet (2.7 meters)

Polar bear
Ursus maritimus
8¼ feet (2.67 meters)

American black bear
Euarctos americanus
5 feet (1.5 meters)

Asiatic black bear
Selenarctos thibetanus
5 feet (1.5 meters)

Sloth bear
Melursus ursinus
5 feet (1.5 meters)

Spectacled bear
Tremarctos ornatus
5 feet (1.5 meters)

Giant panda
Ailuropoda melanoleuca
5 feet (1.5 meters)

Sun bear
Helarctos malayanus
3 feet (0.9 meter)

fast. Polar bears can run at speeds of up to 35 miles (56 kilometers) an hour.

The life of a bear

Bears usually live alone and never gather in groups. During the mating season in the summer, a male and a female bear may live together for about a month. Then the male wanders away and the female prepares a place for her cubs to be born.

Winter sleep. Some bears spend much of the winter in a state similar to sleeping. Many scientists consider the bear's winter sleep to be an example of hibernation. Many other scientists, however, do not consider bears to be true hibernators. They point out that a bear's body temperature, unlike that of other hibernating mammals, does not drop greatly during winter sleep. In addition, a bear awakens easily and may become fairly active on mild winter days. These scientists use such terms as "winter lethargy" or "incomplete hibernation" to describe the bear's sleep period.

A bear prepares for its winter sleep by eating large amounts of food during late summer and storing fat within its body for energy. When food becomes scarce, the bear goes to its den. The den may be a cave or a

brush pile, or a burrow that the bear has dug under the roots of a large tree. Some kinds of bears may build shelters of twigs or dig shallow holes in hillsides. Female polar bears find ice caves or dig dens in the snow.

Brown bears and black bears, both of which live in regions that have harsh winters, almost always have a period of winter sleep. Species found in areas with milder winters may enter dens for only brief periods. Tropical species, such as sun bears and sloth bears, do not have a winter sleep period. Although polar bears live in the Arctic, they normally remain active during the winter. These bears spend the winter wandering the polar ice near open water and preying on seals and other marine mammals that come ashore.

Cubs. Most bear cubs are born during the mother's winter sleep period. A female bear usually has two cubs at a time, but the number may vary from one to four. The cubs weigh only ½ to 1 pound (0.23 to 0.5 kilogram) at birth. Their eyes are closed, and they have no fur. The eyes open about a month after birth, and by that time the body is covered with thick, soft fur. The cubs stay in the den with their mother for about two months. In spring, they come out, frisky and playful. They grow rapidly and may weigh 40 pounds (18 kilograms) by autumn. Cubs stay with the mother for one or two years. She teaches them to hunt for food.

Facts in brief

Names: *Male,* boar or he-bear; *female,* sow or she-bear; *young,* cub; *group,* pack or sloth.
Gestation period: 7 to 9 months, depending on the species.
Number of newborn: 1 to 4, usually 2.
Length of life: 15 to 30 years.
Where found: Arctic, Asia, Europe, North and South America.
Scientific classification: Bears belong to the class Mammalia, and the order Carnivora. They make up the bear family, Ursidae. Some scientists place the giant panda in the raccoon family, Procyonidae.

See **Bear** in *World Book* for more information on The life of a bear and Kinds of bears.

Simon, Photo Researchers

After cutting down a tree, a beaver moves it to a nearby pond.

Beaver is a furry animal with a wide, flat tail that looks like a paddle. Beavers are known for their skill at cutting down trees with their strong front teeth. They eat the bark and use the branches to build dams and *lodges* (homes) in the water. Beavers almost always seem to be busy working. For this reason, we often call a hard-working person an "eager beaver" or say that the person is "busy as a beaver."

Beavers live in rivers, streams, and freshwater lakes near woodlands. They are excellent swimmers and divers. A beaver can swim underwater for $\frac{1}{2}$ mile (0.8 kilometer), and can hold its breath for 15 minutes.

There are more beavers in the United States and Canada than anywhere else in the world. Beavers are also found in Asia and Europe. Hunters in the United States and Canada trap over 500,000 beavers a year. Beaver fur is soft and shiny, and it wears well. Clothing manufacturers use it to make fur coats. They also use it to trim the collars and cuffs of cloth coats. Beaver fur is also squeezed together with other kinds of fur to make a cloth called *felt*.

Beavers were probably the most hunted animals in North America from the late 1500's through the 1800's. The pioneers and Indians ate beaver meat, and traded the furs for things they needed. In the late 1600's, a person could trade 12 beaver skins for a rifle. One beaver skin would buy four pounds of shot, or a kettle, or a pound of tobacco. Trading companies shipped beaver

fur throughout the world to be made into coats or hats. Hunters killed so many beavers that hardly any were left in North America by the late 1800's. The U.S. and Canadian governments passed laws to protect the animals. Today, beavers, like many other wild animals, can be trapped only at certain times of the year.

The body of a beaver

North American beavers are 3 to 4 feet (91 to 120 centimeters) long, including the tail, and weigh from 40 to 95 pounds (18 to 43 kilograms). They are the largest *rodents* (gnawing animals) in the world except for the capybara of South America. Unlike most other kinds of mammals, beavers keep growing throughout their lives. Most beavers look larger than they really are because of their humped backs and thick fur. Thousands of years ago, some beavers of North America were about $7\frac{1}{2}$ feet

Facts in brief

Names: *Male,* none; *female,* none; *young,* kit or pup; *group,* family or colony.
Gestation period: About 3 months.
Number of newborn: 2 to 4.
Length of life: About 12 years.
Where found: Asia, Europe, North America.
Scientific classification: Beavers make up the beaver family, Castoridae. The North American beaver is *Castor Canadensis.* The European beaver is *C. Fiber.*

(2.3 meters) long, including the tail—almost as long as the grizzly bears. No one knows why these huge beavers disappeared.

Head. The beaver has a broad head, with large and powerful jaws. Its rounded ears and small nostrils can close tightly to keep water out. A beaver has three eyelids on each eye. Two outer eyelids, one upper and one lower, fit around the eye. A transparent inner eyelid slides down over the eye and lets the animal see under water. On land, it protects the eye from sharp twigs when the animal cuts trees. The beaver cannot see well, and depends on its keen hearing and smell to warn it of danger.

Teeth. A beaver has 20 teeth—4 strong, curved front teeth for gnawing, and 16 back teeth for chewing. The front teeth, called *incisors,* have a bright orange outer covering that is very hard. The back part of the incisors is made of a much softer substance. When a beaver gnaws, the back part of its incisors wears down much faster than the front part. As a result, these teeth have a sharp, chisel-like edge. The incisors never wear out because they keep growing throughout the animal's life. The back teeth have flat, rough edges and stop growing when the beaver is about 2 years old.

There are large gaps between the beaver's incisors and its back teeth. Flaps of skin, one on each side of the mouth, fold inward and meet behind the incisors. These skin flaps seal off the back of the mouth. They let the animal gnaw wood on land or in the water without getting splinters or water in its mouth. The flaps open when the beaver wants to eat or drink.

Feet. The beaver's legs are short, and its feet are black. Tough skin, with little hair, covers the feet. Each front paw ends in five toes that have long, thick claws. A beaver uses its claws to dig up the roots of bushes and trees for food. When swimming, the animal usually makes tight fists of its front paws and holds them against its chest. Sometimes, when a beaver swims through underwater brush or grass, it uses its front paws to push the plants aside.

The back feet are larger than the front ones, and may be 6 to 7 inches (15 to 18 centimeters) long. The toes are webbed and end in strong claws. Two claws on each foot are split. The beaver uses these split claws to comb its fur. The webbed feet serve as flippers, and help make the animal a powerful swimmer and diver.

Tail of a beaver is one of the animal's most interesting features. The stiff, flat tail looks like a paddle. It is about 12 inches (30 centimeters) long, 6 to 7 inches (15 to 18 centimeters) wide, and $\frac{3}{4}$ inch (19 millimeters) thick. A small part of the tail nearest the beaver's body has the same kind of fur as the body. The rest is covered with black, scaly skin and has only a few stiff hairs. The beaver uses its tail to steer when it swims. The tail is used as a prop when the animal stands on its hind legs to eat or to cut down trees. A beaver slaps its tail on the water to make a loud noise to warn other beavers of danger.

Fur. Beaver fur varies from shiny dark brown to yellowish brown. It looks black when wet. A beaver's coat consists of two kinds of fur: (1) short, soft underfur; and (2) long, heavy guard hairs. The guard hairs lie over the underfur and protect it. The underfur helps keep a beaver comfortable in the water. This fur traps air and holds it close to the animal's skin. The trapped air acts as a protective blanket that keeps the beaver warm, even in icy water.

The life of a beaver

Beavers usually live in family groups. As many as 12 beavers may make up a family, but generally there are 6

The body of a beaver

Hans Reinhard, Bruce Coleman Inc.
Front foot

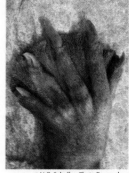

© V. B. Scheffer, Photo Researchers
Hind foot

© Leonard Lee Rue III, Photo Researchers
Front teeth

© V. B. Scheffer, Photo Researchers
Scales on tail

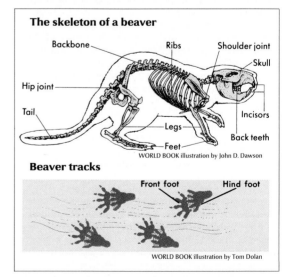

The skeleton of a beaver

Backbone
Ribs
Shoulder joint
Skull
Hip joint
Tail
Incisors
Legs
Back teeth
Feet

WORLD BOOK illustration by John D. Dawson

Beaver tracks

Front foot
Hind foot

WORLD BOOK illustration by Tom Dolan

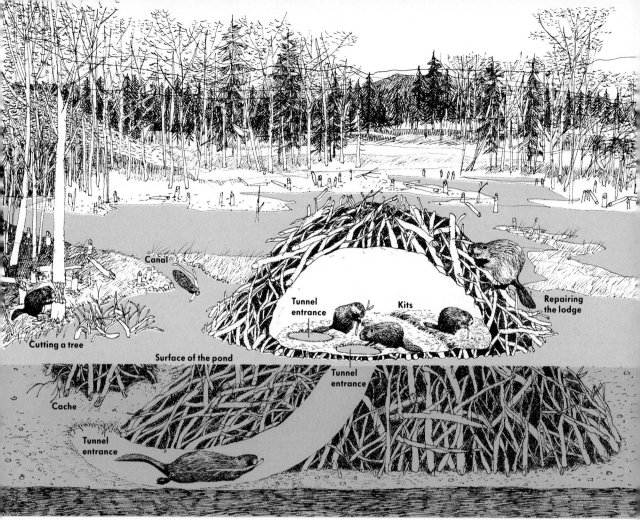

Canal

Cutting a tree

Tunnel entrance

Kits

Repairing the lodge

Surface of the pond

Tunnel entrance

Cache

Tunnel entrance

WORLD BOOK illustration by George Suyeoka

A beaver colony bustles with activity. Beavers cut down trees to build a dam and repair their lodge. They store food in a cache for winter, and take twigs into the lodge for the young.

or fewer. The group includes the adult male and female, the young born the year before, and the newborn.

Building dams and canals. The beaver's habits of building and of storing food seem to be *instinctive* (unlearned). A beaver cuts down trees even if it has no place to build a dam or a lodge, and even if it has more than enough food.

A whole beaver family, and sometimes beavers from other families, may join in building a dam. Beaver dams are made of logs, branches, and rocks plastered together with mud. Beavers use mud and stones for the base of a dam. Then they add brush and log poles. They strengthen the dam by placing the poles so that the tips lean in the same direction as the water flows. The beavers plaster the tops and sides of the poles with more mud, stones, and wet plants. They do most of this work with their front teeth and front paws. They bring mud from the river bottom by holding it against their chests with their front paws.

The beavers build their dam so that the top is above the water. Some dams are more than 1,000 feet (300 meters) long. Beavers may keep their dams in good condition for many years. Most beavers that live in lakes do

not build dams, but some build dams across the outlets of small lakes.

Building lodges. A beaver lodge looks somewhat like a tepee. A family of beavers builds its lodge with the same materials and in much the same way as it builds a dam. The lodge may stand on the riverbank or in the water like an island. The tops of most lodges are 3 to 6 feet (91 to 180 centimeters) above the water. Each lodge has several underwater entrances and tunnels, all of which lead to an inside chamber. The floor of the chamber is 4 to 6 inches (10 to 15 centimeters) above the water. Here, young beavers can stay warm and dry in winter, and the adults can dry off after bringing in food. Holes between the branches in the ceiling let in fresh air.

Beavers that live in large lakes or in swift rivers may dig dens in the banks. These beaver dens, like the lodges, have underwater entrances and tunnels.

See **Beaver** in *World Book* for more information on The life of a beaver.

Ron Larsen, Van Cleve Photography

A honey bee worker hovers over a flower, sucking up nectar with its tongue. These bees also gather pollen, which they carry in areas called *baskets* on their hind legs.

Bee

Bee is an insect that lives in almost every part of the world except near the North and South poles. Bees are one of the most useful of all insects. They produce honey, which people use as food; and beeswax, which is used in such products as adhesives, candles, and cosmetics. There are about 20,000 *species* (kinds) of bees. Only the kinds known as *honey bees* make honey and wax in large enough amounts to be used by people.

Flowers provide food for bees. The bees collect tiny grains of pollen and a sweet liquid called nectar from the blossoms they visit. They make honey from the nectar, and use both honey and pollen as food. During their food-gathering flights, bees spread pollen from one flower to another, thus *pollinating* (fertilizing) the plants they visit. This enables the plants to reproduce. Many

important food crops, including fruits and vegetables, depend on bees for fertilization.

Bees probably developed from wasplike ancestors that first got their food by eating other insects. These creatures gradually switched to flowers as their food source. In time, bees became completely dependent on flowers for food. The flowers, in turn, benefited from the bees. Scientists believe that over the years, bees helped create the wide variety of flowers in the world today by spreading pollen among various plants.

Like most insects, bees have three pairs of legs and four wings. They also have a special stomach, called a *honey stomach,* in which they carry nectar. All female bees have a sting, which they use for self-defense.

Bees can be grouped into two general categories. Most are *solitary bees.* That is, they live alone. Honey bees and bumble bees are examples of *social bees* that live and work together in large groups, or *colonies.*

Three kinds of bees make up a honey bee colony. The colony consists of thousands of workers, one queen, and a few hundred drones.

WORLD BOOK illustrations by James Teason

Worker   **Queen**   **Drone**

Hive life in spring and summer

Bees perform a variety of jobs in warm weather. Nurse bees, *left,* clean the empty cells and care for the grubs. The queen, *center,* lays eggs, one in a cell. Workers defend the hive by stinging an invading wasp to death, *bottom center.* Field workers, *right,* return to the hive loaded with nectar and pollen. Bees at the entrance to the hive fan in fresh air with their wings, *bottom right.*

WORLD BOOK illustration by James Teason

Hive life in fall

As cold weather sets in, the queen and workers cluster together on the honeycomb for warmth. They feed on honey that the colony stored up during the spring and summer. In this picture, the bees have already eaten the honey that had been stored in some of the cells, *bottom left.* Some workers, *right,* collect food out of full cells. Others, *bottom right,* push the drones out of the hive.

WORLD BOOK illustration by James Teason

The honey bee colony. A typical honey bee colony is made up of one *queen,* tens of thousands of *workers,* and a few hundred *drones.* The queen is the female honey bee that lays eggs. The workers are the unmated female offspring of the queen. The drones are the male offspring.

Honey bees live in hives. The hive is a storage space, such as a hollow tree or a box, which contains a *honeycomb.* The honeycomb is a mass of six-sided compartments called *cells.* Worker bees build the honeycomb of wax produced by their bodies. They also collect a sticky substance called *propolis,* or *bee glue,* from certain kinds of trees. They use it to repair cracks in the hive.

The honeycomb is used to raise young bees and to store food. The queen bee lays one egg in each cell in part of the honeycomb. In general, the cells containing the eggs and developing bees are in the center of the hive. This area is called the *brood nest.* The bees store pollen and honey in cells above and around the brood nest. The same cells may be used for different purposes. During spring and summer, many cells are used to raise young bees. In fall, brood production stops, and more cells are available for storing honey through the winter.

The contents of the hive are a prized source of food for many animals, including bees from other colonies. Several workers always guard the entrance to the hive. The bees in each hive have their own special odor. The guard bees can detect bees from other hives by their smell. The guard bees attack strangers, whether they are bees from outside the colony, bears, or human beings.

The body of the honey bee. The honey bee, like all insects, has a body that is divided into three sections: the head, the *thorax* (chest), and the abdomen. The insect's *honey stomach,* in which it carries nectar, is located in the abdomen. The bee's body is thickly covered with fine hairs. When a bee travels from flower to flower, grains of pollen stick to these hairs. Honey bees range in color from black to shades of light brown. Drones are slightly larger than workers, and queens are longer than both workers and drones.

> See **Bee** in *World Book* for more information on the following topics:
>
> • The body of the honey bee   • Kinds of bees
> • Life of the honey bee   • Beekeeping

Interesting facts about bees

Fossil bees found trapped in amber probably lived 80 million years ago.
The largest bee is *Chalicodoma pluto,* a mason bee about $1\frac{1}{2}$ inches (3.8 centimeters) long. The largest honey bee, called the giant honey bee, is about $\frac{3}{4}$ inch (19 millimeters) long.
Size of a bee colony. A strong, healthy colony may contain between 50,000 and 60,000 bees.
The smallest bee is *Trigona minima,* a stingless bee only $\frac{1}{12}$ inch (2 millimeters) long. The dwarf bee, the smallest honey bee, is under $\frac{1}{2}$ inch (13 millimeters).
Speed. Worker bees fly about 15 miles (24 kilometers) per hour.
Taste. Honey bees can identify a flavor as sweet, sour, salty, or bitter.
A worker honey bee collects enough nectar in its lifetime to make about $\frac{1}{10}$ pound (45 grams) of honey.

Five kinds of bees

WORLD BOOK illustrations by James Teason

Stingless bees often build their nests in hollow tree trunks. Colonies of these social bees may have from 50 to several thousand members. They live only in tropical and semitropical areas.

The carpenter bee bores a tunnel in wood for its nest. It divides the tunnel into several cells, separated by wood chips mixed with saliva. Each cell contains an egg and some food.

The leafcutting bee also nests in tunnels. It fills the tunnels with cells made of small pieces of leaf mixed with saliva.

The mining bee burrows into loose ground to make its nest. Mining bees are considered solitary insects, but many share the same main tunnel to the surface of the ground.

The mason bee sometimes builds its nest on a stone wall. The nest consists of several cells made of clay and saliva.

Thomas Eisner

A bombardier beetle, *above,* defends itself by squirting a hot, irritating jet of gas at its attacker. It produces this spray by mixing chemicals from two organs located at the end of its body.

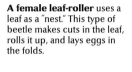

A female leaf-roller uses a leaf as a "nest." This type of beetle makes cuts in the leaf, rolls it up, and lays eggs in the folds.

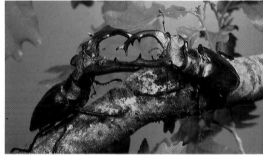

Hans Reinhard, Bruce Coleman Inc.

WORLD BOOK illustrations by John F. Eggert

A male eastern Hercules beetle, *above,* has a long horn. This beetle is also one of the largest beetles in North America. It grows to $2\frac{1}{2}$ inches (6 centimeters) long.

Male stag beetles have long jaws that they use to defend themselves. Stag beetles get their name from the jaws, which resemble the antlers of a *stag* (male deer).

Beetle is one of the most common of all insects. There are about 300,000 *species* (kinds) of beetles. They live everywhere on earth except in the oceans. Beetles are found in rain forests and in deserts. They live in freezing cold areas and in hot springs. They inhabit mountain lakes and can even survive in polluted sewers.

Beetles have typical insect body parts, including antennae, three pairs of legs, and a tough *exoskeleton* (external skeleton). However, unlike other insects, adult beetles have a pair of special front wings called *elytra.* These wings form leathery covers that protect the beetle's body. Because of their shell-like skeleton and hard wing covers, beetles have been called the "armored tanks" of the insect world.

Beetles vary greatly in shape, color, and size. Some, such as click beetles and fireflies, are long and slender. Others, including ladybugs, are round. Most beetles are brown, black, or dark red in color. But some have bright, shiny, rainbow colors. The smallest beetles, feather-winged beetles, measure less than $\frac{1}{50}$ inch (0.5 millimeter) long. One of the largest beetles is the Goliath beetle of Africa. It grows about 5 inches (13 centimeters) long and weighs over $1\frac{1}{2}$ ounces (42 grams).

Most species of beetles are *solitary insects*—that is, they live alone and have no family life. The young develop without help from their parents. A few species of

beetles are *social insects.* These beetles spend at least part of their life in family groups.

Beetles have many enemies, including birds, reptiles, and other insects. Most beetles protect themselves from enemies by hiding or by flying away. A few beetles produce bad-smelling chemicals that discourage attackers. Some beetles can bite.

Many beetles are pests because they feed on farm crops, trees, or stored food. But some beetles are helpful to people. For example, ladybugs and certain other beetles save crops by eating insect pests. Other beetles are important because they eat dead plants and animals and thus remove them from the environment.

The bodies of beetles

Like other insects, beetles have a body that is divided into three main parts. These parts are: (1) the head, (2) the thorax, and (3) the abdomen.

The head includes the beetle's mouthparts, eyes, and a pair of antennae. The eyes and antennae are the insect's chief sense organs.

Mouthparts. Beetles have chewing mouthparts. In beetles called *weevils,* the mouthparts are part of a long snout. A beetle's jaws are called *mandibles.* A number of beetles have large, pincerlike mandibles.

Eyes. Beetles have a *compound eye* on each side of

Some kinds of beetles

There are more than 300,000 species of beetles. They live in nearly every type of environment on earth except in the oceans. These drawings and photographs provide examples of the great variety of sizes, shapes, and colors of beetles.

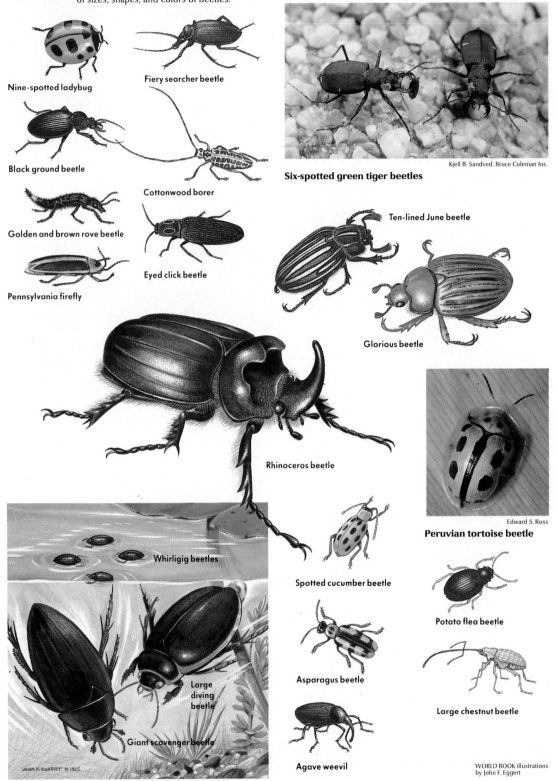

Nine-spotted ladybug

Fiery searcher beetle

Black ground beetle

Cottonwood borer

Golden and brown rove beetle

Eyed click beetle

Pennsylvania firefly

Six-spotted green tiger beetles

Kjell B. Sandved, Bruce Coleman Inc.

Ten-lined June beetle

Glorious beetle

Rhinoceros beetle

Peruvian tortoise beetle

Edward S. Ross

Whirligig beetles

Large diving beetle

Giant scavenger beetle

Spotted cucumber beetle

Potato flea beetle

Asparagus beetle

Large chestnut beetle

Agave weevil

WORLD BOOK illustrations
by John F. Eggert

JOHN F. EGGERT © 1995

The external anatomy of a beetle

WORLD BOOK illustrations by John F. Eggert

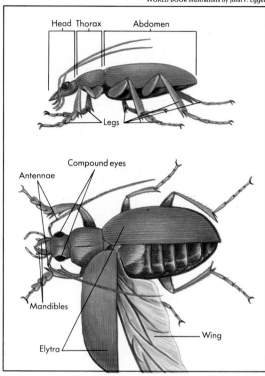

the head. Each eye consists of a bundle of tiny, light-sensitive lenses. Each lens contributes a small bit of the total image that a beetle sees. Most beetles see motion and colors quite well. A few species are blind.

Antennae vary greatly among beetles. Many beetles have antennae made up of threadlike or beadlike segments. In many of these beetles, the tip segments of the antennae are club-shaped. Some beetles have elbow-shaped or featherlike antennae. A beetle's antennae are covered with hairs and special organs that can detect specific odors. Some beetles have special sense organs near the base of the antennae that provide a simple type of hearing. These organs send messages to the brain when certain sounds vibrate the antennae.

The thorax forms the middle of the beetle's body. It consists of three segments, each with a pair of legs. The second and third segments each have a pair of wings.

Legs. Each leg of a beetle has five segments and claws at the end. Most beetles that are fast runners have long, slender legs. Other beetles have short, stout legs, often with flat pads on the bottom. These pads have hundreds of expanded hairs that act like suction cups and enable the beetle to walk upside down on slick surfaces. The legs of digging beetles have toothlike projections that are used to scrape away soil. Most swimming beetles have flattened hind legs. In some species, these legs are fringed with long hairs to form paddles.

Wings. A beetle's front wings, the elytra, are attached to the second thorax segment. The hind wings are attached to the third segment. In most species, the elytra cover the hind wings when the insect is not flying. To fly, a beetle pops open the elytra and holds them upward and outward so it can move its hind wings freely.

The abdomen contains the reproductive organs and the chief organs of digestion. It typically consists of 10 segments, though only 5 to 8 segments may be visible. The segments are usually soft on the upper surface where they are covered by the elytra. The undersurface is harder for protection. Each segment of the abdomen has a pair of tiny holes called *spiracles*. Oxygen enters the beetle's body through the spiracles.

> See **Beetle** in *World Book* for more information on The life cycle of beetles and Kinds of beetles.

The life cycle of a beetle

A beetle goes through four stages of development: (1) egg, (2) larva, (3) pupa, and (4) adult. The illustration below shows the development of a broad-nosed beetle. The egg, laid in the ground, hatches into a larva. As the larva grows, it sheds its outer skin several times before becoming a pupa. The adult organs develop in the pupa. When this process is complete, the adult emerges.

WORLD BOOK illustration by John F. Eggert

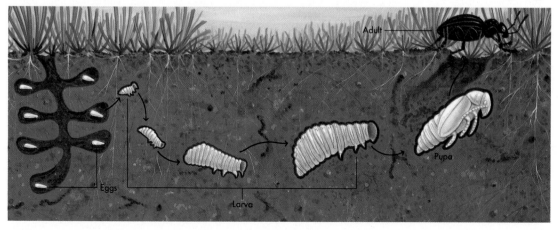

The California condor is almost extinct. Its natural habitat has been nearly destroyed, and the bird lays only one egg every two years.

A male Count Raggi's bird of paradise courts a mate by spreading his elegant feathers.

A dipper walks underwater in search of insects and small fish. Strong claws and sturdy legs enable it to grip a stream bed even in a fast current.

WORLD BOOK illustrations by Tom Dunnington

Bird

Bird is an animal with feathers. All birds have feathers, and they are the only animals that have them. But when people think of birds, they usually think first of their flying ability. All birds have wings. The fastest birds can reach speeds well over 100 miles (160 kilometers) per hour. No other animals can travel faster than birds. However, not all birds can fly. For example, ostriches and penguins are flightless. Instead of flying, ostriches walk or run. They use their wings only for balance. Penguins swim. They use their wings like flippers.

People have always been fascinated by birds. Their marvelous flying ability makes them seem to be the freest of all animals. Many birds have gorgeous colors or sing sweet songs. The charms of birds have inspired poets, painters, and composers. Certain birds also serve as symbols. People have long regarded the owl as a symbol of wisdom and the dove as a symbol of peace. The eagle has long represented political and military might. The bald eagle, which lives only in North America, is the national symbol of the United States. Birds also played a role in the development of the airplane. Inventors built successful planes only after they patterned the wings after the shape of a bird's wings.

There are about 8,600 kinds of birds. The smallest

bird is the bee hummingbird, which grows only about 2 inches (5 centimeters) long. The largest bird is the ostrich, which may grow up to 8 feet (2.4 meters) tall. Birds live in all parts of the world, from the polar regions to the tropics. They are found in forests, deserts, and cities; on grasslands, farmlands, mountaintops, and islands; and even in caves. Ducks, gulls, and certain other birds always live near water. Most such birds can swim. Some birds, especially those in the tropics, stay in the same general area throughout life. Even in the Arctic and the Antarctic, some hardy birds stay the year around. But many birds of cool or cold regions migrate each year to warm areas to avoid winter, when food is hard to find. In spring, they fly home again to nest.

All birds hatch from eggs. Among most kinds of birds, the female lays her eggs in a nest built by herself or her mate or by both of them. The majority of birds have one mate at a time, with whom they raise one or two sets of babies a year. Some birds keep the same mate for life. Others choose a new mate every year. Most baby birds remain in the nest for several weeks or months after hatching. Their parents feed and protect them until they can care for themselves. Most birds leave their parents when they are a few months old.

The ptarmigan hides from enemies by blending with its surroundings. In winter, the bird has white feathers, making it almost invisible against the snow, *above*. In summer, the ptarmigan's feathers are speckled and so match the vegetation on the
ground, where the bird makes its nest, *below*.

© David C. Fritts, Animals Animals

© Charles G. Summers Jr., DPI

Birds belong to the large group of animals called *vertebrates*. Vertebrates are animals with a backbone. The
group also includes fish, reptiles, and mammals. Birds
have two forelimbs and two hindlimbs, as do cats, dogs,
monkeys, and most other mammals. But in birds, the
forelimbs are wings rather than arms or front legs. Like
mammals, and unlike fish and reptiles, birds are *warm-
blooded*—that is, their body temperature always remains about the same, even if the temperature of their
surroundings changes. Unlike most other vertebrates,
birds lack teeth. Instead, they have a hard bill, or beak,
which they use in getting food and for self-defense.

Many birds are valuable to people. Such birds as
chickens and ducks provide meat and eggs for food.
Birds help farmers by eating insects that attack their
crops. Some types of birds eat farmers' grain and fruit.
But in general, birds do much more good then harm.

Since the 1600's, about 80 kinds of birds have died
out. People have killed off most of them by overhunting
or by destroying their environment to create farms and
cities. Today, most countries have laws to protect birds
and help prevent any more kinds from dying out.

Interesting facts about birds

The highest flyer is the bar-
headed goose. Some flocks of
bar-headed geese fly over the
world's highest mountain
range, the Himalaya in Asia, at
an altitude of more than
25,000 feet (7,625 meters).

**Bar-Headed
Goose**

The fastest diver is the peregrine falcon. The bird's
broad, powerful wings and
streamlined body enable it to
swoop down on its prey at a
speed of more than 200 miles
(320 kilometers) per hour.

Peregrine Falcon

The largest bird is the male
African ostrich. It may grow as
tall as 8 feet (2.4 meters) and
weigh as much as 300 pounds
(140 kilograms).

Ostrich

The smallest bird is the bee
hummingbird. When fully
grown, it measures about 2
inches (5 centimeters) and
weighs about $\frac{1}{10}$ ounce (3
grams). The nest of a bee
hummingbird is the size of
half a walnut shell.

**Bee
Hummingbird**

The greatest traveler. Arctic terns migrate farther than
any other bird. They travel
about 11,000 miles (17,700 kilometers) each way between
their breeding grounds in the
Arctic and winter home in the
Antarctic.

Arctic Tern

Emperor penguin

The deepest diver is the
emperor penguin. Emperor
penguins have been recorded
underwater at depths of almost 900 feet (270 meters).
They use their wings to propel themselves through the
water.

WORLD BOOK illustrations by Venner Artists,
Ltd., James Teason, and John F. Eggert

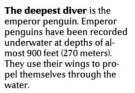

How birds feed   Birds find food in many places—in the air, on the ground, underwater, inside flowers and trees, and even in mud. Their diets include insects, fish, meat, seeds, fruit, and sap. In most cases, the structure of a bird's bill or feet—or of its bill and feet—is adapted to the bird's feeding habits.

© Shelly Grossman, Woodfin Camp, Inc.

A hawk captures a snake. Birds of prey use their sharp claws to seize animals and their razorlike bill to tear off flesh.

Ducrot, Jacana

The swift feeds only on flying insects. The bird's extremely wide mouth enables it to catch insects in the air.

© Jan L. Wassink, Tom Stack & Assoc.

A Bohemian waxwing eats a berry. Its short, broad bill is well adapted to picking berries and other small fruits.

Joseph VanWormer, Bruce Coleman Inc.

The red-legged partridge uses its small but powerful beak to crack open grain and other seeds.

Wayne Lankinen, Bruce Coleman Ltd.

The yellow-bellied sapsucker makes a hole in a tree with its long, pointed bill and then feeds on the sap.

M. D. England, Ardea London

A red-backed shrike has used its strong bill to spear a grasshopper onto the end of a sharp twig.

© Earl L. Kubis, Photographics

The anhinga uses its extremely sharp bill to spear fish. The bird's long, flexible neck and webbed feet help it in fishing.

Eric & David Hosking

The flamingo feeds on the tiny plants and animals in muddy waters. Its bill filters mud and water from food.

E. R. Degginger

A black skimmer scoops up fish by plowing the water with its bill. The lower part of the bill is shaped like a flat blade.

How a bird flies

During a flapping flight, a bird's wings make two kinds of movements. The inner part of each wing moves up and down. The outer part moves in a circle. The circular movement begins on the full upstroke (1) and continues counterclockwise through the start of the downstroke (2), the full downstroke (3), and the start of the upstroke (4). The wing tips push forward on the downstroke, which propels the bird through the air.

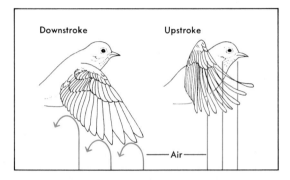

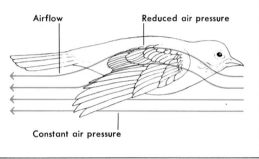

WORLD BOOK diagrams by Jean Helmer

The wing feathers overlap on the downstroke so no air can pass through. On the upstroke, the feathers twist open, allowing the air to pass through and making it easier to lift the wing.

A bird stays aloft because air flowing over the wings drops in pressure. Air pressure under the wings remains the same. High pressure moves toward low pressure, which keeps the bird up.

How wing shape affects flying skills

The shape of a bird's wings determines the type of flying that the bird does best. Gulls, *below left,* and other birds with long, pointed wings excel at soaring and gliding. Most fast fliers, such as swifts, *center,* have narrow, tapered wings. Pheasants, *right,* and most other fowllike birds have short, broad, rounded wings. These birds can take off quickly but can fly fast only a short distance.

WORLD BOOK illustrations by John D. Dawson

Gull

Chimney swift

Ring-necked pheasant

Building a nest. Many kinds of birds do not build a nest. Most falcons and nightjars, for example, simply lay their eggs on bare ground. Certain other birds nest in hollow trees, in holes in the ground, or in the abandoned nests of other birds. Such birds include many bluebirds, house sparrows, parrots, purple martins, wrens, and some owls. Starlings often chase other birds from their nests and then use the nests themselves. However, most birds build nests, some of which are elaborate structures. In most cases, the female does all or most of the work. If the males help, they chiefly provide building materials.

Most bird nests are bowl- or saucer-shaped structures made of such materials as twigs, grass, and leaves. Birds build such nests on the ground, in bushes and trees, on ledges, and in holes. The nests of the smallest hummingbirds measure only about 1 inch (2.5 centimeters) high. In North America, ospreys build the largest nests, which may be as high as 6 feet (1.8 meters). Many species of birds cement the building material together with sticky substances. Blue jays and American robins use mud. Hummingbirds and gnatcatchers use sticky threads from spider webs. Swifts use their own saliva, which is thick and gummy. The hardened saliva not only holds the nest together but also cements it to the nesting place, such as the wall of a cave or the inside of a chimney.

Some kinds of birds do not build bowl- or saucer-shaped nests. Most woodpeckers and kingfishers nest in holes that they make by using their bill as a digging tool. Woodpeckers dig the holes in dead trees. Kingfishers dig them in banks of sand or clay. Many birds make nests that are completely enclosed except for a small entrance. Weaverbirds of tropical Africa use their bill and feet to weave such nests of grasses and plant fibers. The nests hang from tree branches or reeds. Some kinds of swallows construct enclosed nests of mud cemented to the sides of cliffs, caves, hollow trees, or even houses and office buildings.

Kinds of bird nests

Birds build an enormous variety of nests, ranging from simple hollows in the ground to elaborate structures suspended from tree branches. Some of the many kinds of nests are pictured below.

WORLD BOOK illustrations by John D. Dawson

Grebes build their nests on lakes and ponds. They make the nests of weeds and sticks and anchor them to rushes.

Weaverbirds use their bill to weave elaborate, enclosed nests of grass. The nests hang from tree branches.

Barn swallows use pellets of mud to construct nests on the walls of cliffs, caves, and farm buildings.

Tailorbirds sew leaves together to form a nest. They use their bill as a needle, and natural fibers as thread.

Woodpeckers make holes in trees for their nests. The holes have little or no lining, except for wood chips.

Killdeers nest in a slight hollow on bare ground. They may line the hollow with gravel or twigs.

Birds' eggs The eggs of most birds have a similar shape, but they vary greatly in color and size. Most eggs that are laid in sheltered nests or holes in the ground are white. Most of those laid in uncovered nests have protective coloring. The eggs pictured below are shown in their actual size.

Field Museum of Natural History, Chicago (WORLD BOOK photo)

Rose-Breasted Grosbeak   Robin   Bluebird   Goldfinch   Cedar Waxwing

Cardinal   House Sparrow   Scarlet Tanager   House Wren   Starling

Purple Martin   Yellow Warbler   White-Breasted Nuthatch   Catbird   Brown Thrasher

Baltimore Oriole   Bobolink   Song Sparrow   Towhee   Red-Winged Blackbird

Yellow-Billed Cuckoo   Golden-Crowned Kinglet   Hermit Thrush   Scissor-Tailed Flycatcher   Meadow Lark

Painted Redstart   Mockingbird   Blue Jay   Chickadee   Whippoorwill

The external features of a bird

The drawing at the right shows the main external features of a typical bird, the domestic pigeon. Feathers are the most prominent feature. They cover all the body except the eyes, bill, legs, and feet. The feathers grow in groups, such as the *primaries, secondaries, scapulars, tertials,* and various sets of *coverts.*

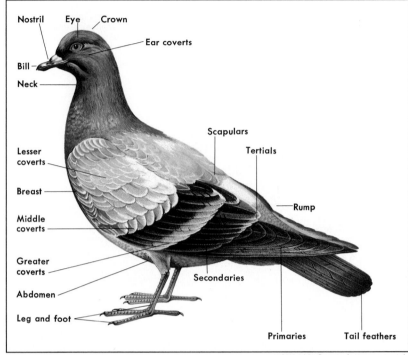

Nostril Eye Crown
Ear coverts
Bill
Neck
Scapulars
Tertials
Lesser coverts
Breast
Rump
Middle coverts
Greater coverts
Secondaries
Abdomen
Leg and foot
Primaries Tail feathers

WORLD BOOK illustration by Venner Artists, Ltd.

The bodies of birds

The bodies of birds are adapted for flying. The skeleton, feathers, and internal organs are all exceptionally lightweight. The body as a whole is streamlined. Birds' bodies differ mainly in size and in the adaptations for getting food, avoiding enemies, and attracting a mate.

External features

The most striking external feature of a bird is its feathers. Feathers cover all the main parts of a bird's body except the eyes, bill, legs, and feet. In some species, including some owls and grouses, even the legs and feet have feathers.

Feathers. Birds have about 940 to 25,000 feathers, depending on the species. Most feathers have a stiff central *shaft,* on each side of which is a flat *vane.* The vane consists of hundreds of slender parallel branches from the shaft. These branches are called *barbs.* The largest feathers are the long *flight feathers* of the wings and tail. The flight feathers near the tip of the wing are called *primaries.* Those closer to the body are known as *secondaries.* A layer of smaller feathers, called *coverts,* covers the base of the flight feathers.

In addition to vaned feathers, some birds have *down feathers* or *plumes* or both down feathers and plumes. Most down feathers have a short shaft and soft, fuzzy barbs that are not connected into vanes. Many water birds have a thick coat of down under the vaned feathers. Plumes are generally long feathers with flexible shafts and barbs. They may grow from different parts of the body and are used in courtship displays.

In many species of birds, the male's feathers are more brightly colored than the female's. In a few species, the females are more colorful. In other species, the male and female look alike.

Birds shed their feathers at least once a year and grow a new set. This process, called *molting,* generally occurs after the breeding season. Most birds that molt twice a year have a different appearance during different seasons. The majority of these birds, including grebes, loons, and scarlet tanagers, are brightly colored in spring and summer and dull in fall and winter. In some species, such as bobolinks and many ducks, only the males alternate between a colorful and dull appearance.

Bills. The bills of birds differ mainly according to how the birds feed. Finches, grosbeaks, and most other seed-eating birds have a hard, cone-shaped bill, which they use like a nutcracker. Many fruit eaters also have a cone-shaped bill. But these birds use the sharp point of the bill to pierce the skin of oranges and other thick-skinned fruits. Woodpeckers have a chisellike bill, which they use to bore into trees in search of insects.

Many ducks eat the plant matter that floats on bodies of water. These birds have an exceptionally broad bill with hundreds of tiny filters along the edges. The broadness of the bill enables the birds to take big mouthfuls of water. The filters along the edges of the bill trap the food particles and let the water drain away. Most fish-eating birds, such as herons and terns, have a long, pointed bill, which they use to spear fish. Pelicans and a few other fish eaters use their unusually large bill to scoop fish from the water. Some land birds, such as

Types of bills The bills of birds vary according to what they eat and their feeding methods. The drawings below illustrate the widely different bill adaptations among six kinds of birds. Birds also use their bills in nest building and self-defense as well as in feeding.

WORLD BOOK illustrations by John D. Dawson

Chisel bill
Woodpeckers hunt insects by drilling into trees with their chisellike bill.

Prober bill
Brown creepers use their bill to probe the bark of trees for insects.

Cracker bill
Grosbeaks have an unusually strong bill, which they use to crack seeds.

Trap bill
The nighthawk's bill opens wide, trapping insects in midair.

Scoop bill
Skimmers use the bottom half of their bill to scoop fish from the water.

Detector bill
A spoonbill sweeps its bill back and forth through the water to find prey.

Types of feet Most birds have four toes on each foot, and all birds have a claw at the tip of each toe. However, the arrangement and size of the toes and the size and shape of the claws vary according to the ways of life of different species. These drawings show six of the most common variations.

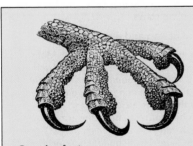

Grasping foot
Ospreys use their large, curved claws to snatch fish from the water.

Scratching foot
Pheasants and other birds that scratch the soil for food have rakelike toes.

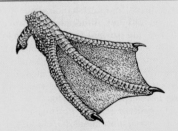

Swimming foot
Ducks and other web-toed swimming birds use their feet like paddles.

Perching foot
Robins have a long hind toe, which helps them grip a perch tightly.

Running foot
Killdeers and many other fast-running birds have three toes instead of four.

Climbing foot
A woodpecker's hind toes enable it to climb without falling backward.

The skeleton of a bird

A bird's skeleton is both light-weight and strong. It is light-weight because many of the bones are hollow. The skeleton is strong because many of the bones are *fused* (joined together).This drawing shows the skeleton of the domestic pigeon.

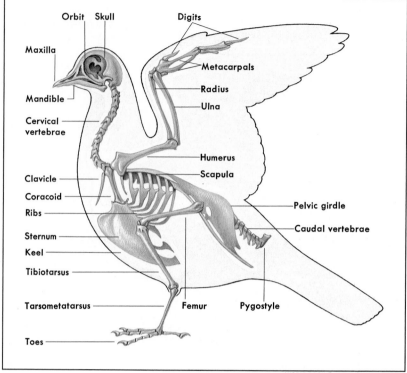

WORLD BOOK illustration by James Teason

hornbills and toucans, have a large, brightly colored bill. Most hornbills and toucans are fruit eaters, however. The huge size and bright colors of the bill are apparently unrelated to the method of feeding. They probably serve mainly for courtship display.

Legs and feet. Although all birds have two legs and two feet, the size and structure of the limbs differ greatly among various species. Birds that spend most of their time in the air have exceptionally short legs. The legs of most tree climbers are also shorter than the average. On the other hand, most wading birds and fast runners have especially long legs.

The great majority of birds have four toes on each foot. Among most species, including all songbirds, three toes point forward and one points backward. A perching bird steadies itself by curling the hind toes around a branch or other perch. Some birds that are good climbers, including parrots and woodpeckers, have two toes pointing forward and two pointing backward. The hind toes help provide an extra grip for the birds as they climb. Emus and most other flightless, fast-running birds have three toes on each foot. The ostrich is the only two-toed bird.

Many swimming birds have webs of skin connecting their toes. The webbing enables the birds to use their feet like paddles. In such birds as ducks and gulls, the webbing connects only the three front toes. Cormorants, pelicans, and related birds have all four toes connected by webs. Instead of webbing, coots, grebes, and phalaropes have broad, paddlelike toes. Gallinules and screamers are also good swimmers, but their feet differ little from those of four-toed land birds.

All birds have a claw at the tip of each toe, but the claws are not equally prominent in all species. Birds with large, sharp, curved claws include birds of prey and birds that cling to vertical surfaces, such as creepers, nuthatches, swifts, and woodpeckers. Most running birds have short, blunt claws.

Skeleton and muscles

A bird's skeleton is lightweight but strong. Many bones that are separate in mammals are *fused* (joined together) in birds. The fused bones give the skeleton exceptional strength. The skeleton is lightweight chiefly because many of the bones are hollow.

The wings of a bird correspond to the arms of a human being. Each wing has three main parts: (1) the outermost part, or *hand;* (2) the middle part, or *forearm;* and (3) the part nearest the body, or *upper arm.* The primary flight feathers are attached to the hand. The secondary flight feathers are attached to the forearm. The upper arm carries the muscles that move the wing.

In birds that fly, the largest muscles are those that move the wings. Most birds have strong leg muscles, but these muscles are especially well developed in fast runners. Small muscles at the base of each feather enable a bird to maneuver, fluff, or display its feathers.

See **Bird** in *World Book* for more information on the following topics:

•The importance of birds
•The distribution of birds
•Birds of North America
•Birds of other regions
•How birds live

•Family life of birds
•Bird migration
•The bodies of birds
•Bird study and protection
•The development of birds

Brain

Brain is the master control center of the body. The brain constantly receives information from the senses about conditions both inside the body and outside it. The brain rapidly analyzes this information and then sends out messages that control body functions and actions. The brain also stores information from past experience, which makes learning and remembering possible. In addition, the brain is the source of thoughts, moods, and emotions.

In such simple animals as worms and insects, the brain consists of small groups of nerve cells. All animals with a backbone have a complicated brain made up of many parts. Animals that have an exceptionally well developed brain include apes, dolphins, and whales. Human beings have the most highly developed brain of all. It consists of billions of interconnected cells and enables people to use language, solve difficult problems, and create works of art.

The human brain is a grayish-pink, jellylike ball with many ridges and grooves on its surface. A newborn baby's brain weighs less than 1 pound (0.5 kilogram). By the time a person is 6 years old, the brain has reached its full weight of about 3 pounds (1.4 kilograms). Most of the brain cells are present at birth, and so the increase in weight comes mainly from growth of the cells. During this six-year period, a person learns and acquires new behavior patterns at the fastest rate in life.

A network of blood vessels supplies the brain with the vast quantities of oxygen and food that it requires. The human brain makes up only about 2 per cent of the total body weight, but it uses about 20 per cent of the oxygen used by the entire body when at rest. The brain can go without oxygen for only three to five minutes before serious damage results.

The brain is located at the upper end of the spinal cord. This cable of nerve cells extends from the neck about two-thirds the way down the backbone. The spinal cord carries messages between the brain and other parts of the body. In addition, 12 pairs of nerves connect the brain directly with certain parts of the body.

The brain works somewhat like both a computer and a chemical factory. Brain cells produce electrical signals and send them from cell to cell along pathways called *circuits.* As in a computer, these electrical circuits receive, process, store, and retrieve information. Unlike a computer, however, the brain creates its electrical signals by chemical means. The proper functioning of the brain depends on many complicated chemical substances produced by brain cells.

Scientists in various fields work together to study the structure, function, and chemical composition of the brain. Together, their field of study is called *neuroscience* or *neurobiology.* This field is rapidly increasing our understanding of the brain. But much remains to be learned. Scientists do not yet know how much of the brain's activity can be explained by current laws of physics and chemistry.

The parts of the brain

The brain has three main divisions: (1) the cerebrum, (2) the cerebellum, and (3) the brain stem. Each part con-

sists chiefly of nerve cells, called *neurons,* and supporting cells, called *glia.*

The cerebrum makes up about 85 per cent of the weight of the human brain. A thin layer of nerve cell bodies called the *cerebral cortex* or *cortex* forms the outermost part of the cerebrum. Most of the cerebrum beneath the cortex consists of nerve cell fibers. Some of these fibers connect parts of the cortex. Others link the cortex with the cerebellum, brain stem, and spinal cord.

The cerebral cortex folds in upon itself and so forms a surface with many ridges and grooves. This folding greatly increases the surface area of the cortex within the limited space of the skull. Some areas of the cortex, called the *sensory cortex,* receive messages from the sense organs as well as messages of touch and temperature from throughout the body. Others areas, called the *motor cortex,* send out nerve impulses that control the movements of all the skeletal muscles. But the largest portion of the cortex is the *association cortex.* The association cortex analyzes, processes, and stores information and so makes possible all our higher mental abilities, such as thinking, speaking, and remembering.

A *fissure* (large groove) divides the cerebrum into halves called the *left cerebral hemisphere* and the *right cerebral hemisphere.* The hemispheres are connected by bundles of nerve fibers, the largest of which is the *corpus callosum.* Each hemisphere, in turn, is divided into four *lobes* (regions). They are (1) the frontal lobe, at the front; (2) the temporal lobe, at the lower side; (3) the parietal lobe, in the middle; and (4) the occipital lobe, at

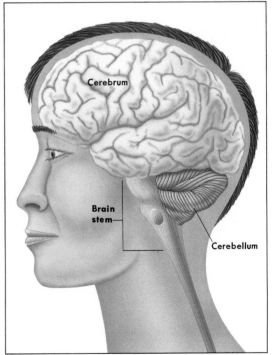

WORLD BOOK diagram by Colin Bidgood

The human brain weighs about 3 pounds (1.4 kilograms) and has three major divisions—the cerebrum, cerebellum, and brain stem. The parts of the brain are grayish-pink or white, not the colors used for clarity in the illustrations for this article.

the rear. Each lobe is named after the bone of the skull that lies above it. Fissures in the cerebral cortex form the boundaries between the lobes. The two major fissures are the *central fissure* and the *lateral fissure.*

The cerebellum is the part of the brain most responsible for balance, posture, and the coordination of movement. It is located below the back part of the cerebrum. The cerebellum consists of a large mass of closely packed *folia* (leaflike bundles of nerve cells). The cerebellum has a right hemisphere and a left hemisphere joined by a finger-shaped structure called the *vermis.* Nerve pathways connect the right half of the cerebellum with the left cerebral hemisphere and the right side of the body. Pathways from the left half connect with the right cerebral hemipshere and the left side of the body.

The brain stem is a stalklike structure that connects the cerebrum with the spinal cord. The bottom part of the brain stem is called the *medulla oblongata* or *medulla.* The medulla has nerve centers that control breathing, heartbeat, and many other vital body processes. The major sensory and motor pathways between the body and the cerebrum cross over as they pass through the medulla. Each cerebral hemisphere thus controls the opposite side of the body.

Just above the medulla is the *pons,* which connects the hemispheres of the cerebellum. The pons also contains nerve fibers that link the cerebellum and the cerebrum. Above the pons lies the *midbrain.* Nerve centers in the midbrain help control movements of the eyes and the size of the pupils.

At the upper end of the brain stem are the *thalamus* and the *hypothalamus.* There are actually two thalami, one on the left side of the brain stem and one on the right side. Each thalamus receives nerve impulses from various parts of the body and routes them to the appropriate areas of the cerebral cortex. The thalami also relay impulses from one part of the brain to another. The hypothalamus regulates body temperature, hunger, and other internal conditions. It also controls the activity of the nearby *pituitary gland,* the master gland of the body.

A network of nerve fibers called the *reticular formation* lies deep within the brain stem. The reticular formation helps regulate the brain's level of awareness. Sensory messages that pass through the brain stem stimulate the reticular formation, which in turn stimulates activity and alertness throughout the cerebral cortex.

The work of the brain

Most functions of the brain involve the coordinated activity of many brain areas. Scientists have developed numerous methods to study these functions. Experiments on animal brains have revealed a great deal about the workings of various areas of the brain. Studying the human brain is more difficult because of the risk of interfering with its vital functions. However, scientists have learned much about the normal activity of the human brain by studying people with brain damage caused by illness or injury.

Surgeons have mapped the functions of many areas of the cerebral cortex by electrically stimulating the brain during brain surgery. Brain operations do not require that the patients be unconscious because the brain feels no pain directly. Thus, the patients can tell

The cerebrum   The cerebrum consists of a left hemisphere and a right hemisphere. Each hemisphere is divided into four lobes by grooves in the *cortex,* a layer of nerve cell bodies that covers the cerebrum. This diagram shows the left cortex and indicates some major functions of each of its parts.

WORLD BOOK diagram by Colin Bidgood

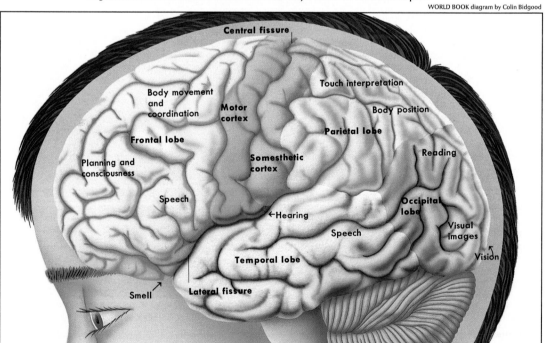

the surgeons what they experience when particular brain areas are stimulated.

Brain surgery has revealed that certain functions of the cerebrum occur chiefly in one hemisphere or the other. Surgeons treat some cases of epilepsy by cutting the corpus callosum, which connects the cerebral hemispheres. This operation produces a condition called the *split brain,* in which no communication occurs between the hemispheres. Studies of split-brain patients suggest that the left hemisphere largely controls our ability to use language, mathematics, and logic. The right hemisphere is the main center for musical ability, the recognition of faces and complicated visual patterns, and the expression of emotion.

See **Brain** in *World Book* for more information on the following topics:

- The parts of the brain
- How the brain is protected
- The work of the brain
- The chemistry of the brain
- Disorders of the brain
- The brain in animals

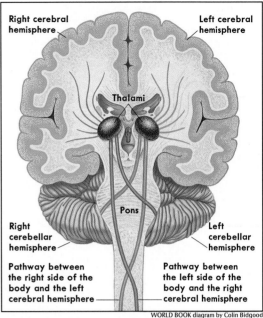

WORLD BOOK diagram by Colin Bidgood

Nerve pathways cross over as they pass through the brain stem. As a result, each cerebral hemisphere controls the opposite side of the body. Similarly, each side of the cerebrum is linked with the opposite side of the cerebellum.

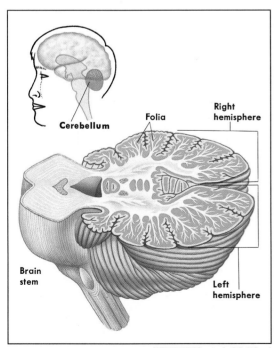

WORLD BOOK diagrams by Colin Bidgood

The cerebellum is the part of the brain most responsible for balance and coordination. The cross section of the cerebellum clearly shows the *folia,* which are leaflike bundles of nerve cells.

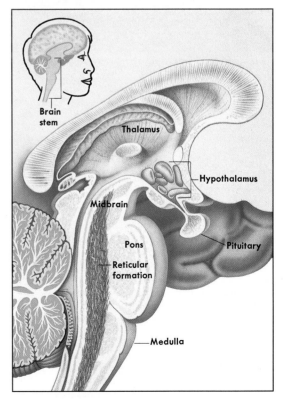

The brain stem is a stalklike structure that links the cerebrum with the spinal cord. The larger diagram shows a cross section of the brain stem and the nearby pituitary gland.

© Edward S. Ross

A copper butterfly stops at a flower and sucks up nectar with its long, tubelike *proboscis.* Most adult butterflies feed only on nectar. The proboscis coils up when not in use.

Butterfly

Butterfly is one of the most beautiful of all insects. People have always been charmed by the delicate, gorgeously colored wings of butterflies. The beauty and grace of these insects have inspired artists and poets. Butterflies have also played a part in religious beliefs. The ancient Greeks believed that the soul left the body after death in the form of a butterfly. Their symbol for the soul was a butterfly-winged girl named Psyche.

Butterflies live almost everywhere in the world. Tropical rain forests have the most kinds of butterflies. Other kinds of butterflies live in woodlands, fields, and prairies. Some butterflies live on cold mountaintops, and others live in hot deserts. Many butterflies travel great distances to spend the winter in a warm climate.

There are about 15,000 to 20,000 *species* (kinds) of butterflies. The largest butterfly, Queen Alexandra's birdwing of Papua New Guinea, has a wingspread of about 11 inches (28 centimeters). One of the smallest

butterflies is the western pygmy blue of North America. It has a wingspread of about $\frac{3}{8}$ inch (1 centimeter). Butterflies are every color imaginable. The colors may be bright, pale, or shimmering and arranged in fantastic patterns. The word *butterfly* comes from the Old English word *buterfleoge,* meaning *butter* and *flying creature. Buter* probably referred to the butter-yellow color of some European butterflies.

Butterflies and moths together make up an insect group called Lepidoptera. The name comes from two Greek words: *lepis,* which means *scale;* and *pteron,* which means *wing.* The name refers to the powdery scales that cover the two pairs of wings of both butterflies and moths. However, butterflies differ from moths in a number of important ways, including the following four. (1) Most butterflies fly during the day. The majority of moths, on the other hand, fly at dusk or at night. (2) Most butterflies have knobs at the ends of their anten-

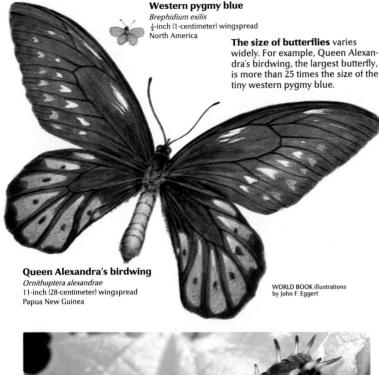

Western pygmy blue
Brephidium exilis
⅜-inch (1-centimeter) wingspread
North America

Queen Alexandra's birdwing
Ornithoptera alexandrae
11-inch (28-centimeter) wingspread
Papua New Guinea

WORLD BOOK illustrations
by John F. Eggert

The size of butterflies varies widely. For example, Queen Alexandra's birdwing, the largest butterfly, is more than 25 times the size of the tiny western pygmy blue.

How butterflies differ from moths

Butterflies and moths together make up the insect group Lepidoptera. But butterflies differ from moths in a number of ways. (1) Most butterflies fly during the daytime. Most moths fly at night. (2) The majority of butterflies have knobs at the ends of their antennae. The antennae of most moths are not knobbed. (3) Most butterflies have slender, hairless bodies. Most moths have plump, furry bodies. (4) Most butterflies rest with their wings upright over their bodies. Most moths rest with their wings stretched out flat.

Butterfly

Moth

WORLD BOOK illustrations by Patricia Wynne

© Edward S. Ross

A caterpillar feeds on plants until it reaches full size, *above.* It then forms a shell, inside which the wormlike caterpillar develops into a beautiful butterfly.

nae. The antennae of most moths are not knobbed. (3) Most butterflies have slender, hairless bodies. The majority of moths have plump, furry bodies. (4) Most butterflies rest with their wings held upright over their bodies. Most moths rest with their wings spread out flat.

A butterfly begins its life as a tiny egg, which hatches into a caterpillar. The caterpillar spends most of its time eating and growing. But its skin does not grow, and so the caterpillar sheds it and grows a larger one. It repeats this process several times. After the caterpillar reaches its full size, it forms a protective shell. Inside the shell, an amazing change occurs—the wormlike caterpillar becomes a beautiful butterfly. The shell then breaks open, and the adult butterfly comes out. The insect expands its wings and soon flies off to find a mate and produce another generation of butterflies.

Butterfly caterpillars have chewing mouthparts, which they use to eat leaves and other plant parts. Some kinds of caterpillars are pests because they damage crops. One of the worst pests is the caterpillar of the cabbage butterfly. It feeds on cabbage, cauliflower, and related plants.

Adult butterflies may have sucking mouthparts. The adults feed mainly on nectar and do no harm. In fact, they help pollinate flowers. Many flowers must have pollen from other blossoms of the same kind of flower to produce fruit and seeds. When a butterfly stops at a flower to drink nectar, grains of pollen cling to its body. Some of the pollen grains rub off on the next blossom the butterfly visits.

The bodies of butterflies. Butterflies have certain body features in common with other insects. For example, a butterfly has a hard, shell-like skin called an *exoskeleton* (outer skeleton). The exoskeleton supports the body and protects the internal organs. A butterfly's body, also like that of any other insect, has three main parts: (1) the head, (2) the thorax, and (3) the abdomen.

The life cycle of butterflies. The life of an adult butterfly centers on reproduction. The reproductive cycle begins with courtship, in which the butterfly seeks a mate. If the courtship proves successful, mating occurs.

Butterflies use both sight and smell in seeking mates. Either the male or the female may give signals, called *cues,* of a certain kind or in a particular order. If a butterfly presents the wrong cue, or a series of cues in the wrong sequence, it will be rejected.

In courtship involving visual cues, a butterfly reveals certain color patterns on its wings in a precise order. Many visual cues involve the reflection of ultraviolet light rays from a butterfly's wing scales. The cues are invisible to the human eye, but butterflies see them clearly. The visual cues help the insects distinguish between males and females and between members of different species.

Usually, a butterfly that presents an appropriate scent will be immediately accepted as a mate. The scent comes from chemicals, called *pheromones,* that are released from special wing scales. A pheromone may attract a butterfly a great distance away.

In most cases, the male butterfly dies soon after mating. The female goes off in search of a place to lay her eggs. She usually begins laying the eggs within a few hours after mating.

Every butterfly goes through four stages of development: (1) egg, (2) larva, (3) pupa, and (4) adult. This process of development through several forms is called *metamorphosis.*

How butterflies protect themselves. Butterflies have many enemies, including other insects and birds. To escape their enemies, butterflies have developed various means of self-defense.

Many butterflies and caterpillars escape harm because they blend with their surroundings. This form of defense is known as *protective coloration.* Butterflies may look like bark or other vegetation. Most caterpillars are green or brown. Green ones blend with the plants they eat. Brown ones look like dead leaves or twigs.

Many butterflies have chemical defenses. Among certain swallowtails, the caterpillar has an organ just behind the head that gives off an unpleasant odor when the caterpillar is disturbed. Some butterflies are protected as both larvae and adults because they taste bad to enemies. During the larval stage, many of these butterflies eat plants that have bitter or poisonous juices. The juices are stored in the tissues, making the insects distasteful to enemies. Most such butterflies have bright colors and so advertise that they taste unpleasant. This form of protection is called *warning coloration.* An animal that has eaten one of these butterflies will probably avoid eating another butterfly with that coloration.

Some nonprotected butterflies resemble, or *mimic,* distasteful species. Enemies cannot tell them apart and so leave both alone. The most familiar mimic in North America is the viceroy butterfly, which looks like the monarch butterfly. Enemies avoid the viceroy because the monarch tastes unpleasant. Some protected butterflies even resemble other protected ones. By mimicking each other, these insects gain extra protection.

See **Butterfly** in *World Book* for more information on the following topics:

- Kinds of butterflies
- The bodies of butterflies
- The life cycle of butterflies
- Hibernation and migration
- How to collect butterflies

The anatomy of a butterfly   A butterfly's body has three main parts: (1) the head, (2) the thorax, and (3) the abdomen. The drawings below show the chief external features and internal organs of a typical female butterfly.

WORLD BOOK illustrations by Patricia Wynne

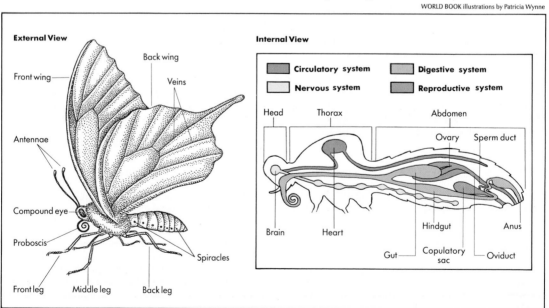

External View

- Back wing
- Front wing
- Veins
- Antennae
- Compound eye
- Proboscis
- Spiracles
- Front leg
- Middle leg
- Back leg

Internal View

- Circulatory system
- Nervous system
- Digestive system
- Reproductive system

Head   Thorax   Abdomen

- Ovary
- Sperm duct
- Brain
- Heart
- Hindgut
- Anus
- Gut
- Copulatory sac
- Oviduct

The life cycle of a butterfly

A butterfly goes through four stages of development: (1) egg; (2) larva, or caterpillar; (3) pupa; and (4) adult. This process of development is called *metamorphosis*.

© John Shaw, Bruce Coleman Inc.

The egg is typically green or yellow. The eggs of some species hatch in a few days, but others take months.

After emerging from the egg, a caterpillar immediately begins to eat. This photograph shows a newly hatched caterpillar eating its own eggshell.

The larval stage lasts two weeks or more. During this period, a caterpillar eats leaves and grows rapidly. After reaching full size, *above,* it is ready to become a pupa.

Hanging from a twig, a pupa starts to form a hard shell, *above.* Inside the shell, larval structures will re-form into those of an adult butterfly.

© David Overcash, Bruce Coleman Inc.

A newly formed monarch butterfly pulls free of its pupal shell, *above.* About an hour after leaving its shell, it may be ready to fly.

© John Shaw, Bruce Coleman Ltd.

Protective coloration helps many butterflies escape their enemies. The two butterflies above are hard to see because their color blends with their surroundings.

© Edward S. Ross

A swarm of monarch butterflies rests on a branch after migrating south for the winter. Monarchs may migrate from as far north as Canada to California, Florida, or Mexico.

George Holton, Photo Researchers

Herds of Bactrian camels graze in the Gobi Desert. These sturdy animals, whose ancestors roamed wild, can carry heavy packs for long distances over rocky mountain trails.

Camel is a large, strong desert animal. Camels can travel great distances across hot, dry deserts with little food or water. They walk easily on soft sand where trucks would get stuck, and carry people and heavy loads to places that have no roads. Camels also serve the people of the desert in many other ways.

The camel carries its own built-in food supply on its back in the form of a hump. The camel's hump is a large lump of fat that provides energy for the animal if food is hard to find.

There are two chief kinds of camels: (1) the Arabian camel, also called *dromedary,* which has one hump, and (2) the Bactrian camel, which has two humps. In the past, *hybrids* (crossbreeds) of the two species were used widely in Asia. These hybrid camels had one extra-long hump and were larger and stronger than either parent.

Camels have been domesticated by people for thousands of years. Arabian camels may once have lived wild in Arabia, but none are wild today. There are several million Arabian camels, and most of them live with the desert people of Africa and Asia. The first Bactrian camels probably lived in Mongolia and in Turkestan, which was called Bactria in ancient times. A few hundred wild Bactrian camels may still roam in some parts of Mongolia, and over a million domesticated ones live in Asia.

Scientists believe that members of the camel family lived in North America at least 40 million years ago. Before the Ice Age, camels had developed into a distinct species and had moved westward across Alaska to western Asia. In Asia, two groups separated and gradually became the two chief kinds of camels known today. Meanwhile, smaller members of the camel family had moved southward from North America to South America. Today, four members of the camel family live in South America: (1) alpacas, (2) guanacos, (3) llamas, and (4) vicunas.

The body of a camel

A camel stands from 6 to 7 feet (1.8 to 2.1 meters) tall at the shoulders, and weighs from 550 to 1,500 pounds (250 to 680 kilograms). Its ropelike tail may be almost 21 inches (53 centimeters) long. Camels seem larger than they are because of their thick, woolly fur, which may be all shades of brown, from nearly white to almost black. An Arabian camel's fur is short and helps protect its body from the heat. A Bactrian camel's fur is longer. It

Facts in brief

Names: *Male,* bull; *female,* cow; *young,* calf, foal; *group,* herd.
Gestation period: About 13 months.
Number of young: Usually 1.
Length of life: up to 40 years.
Where found: Africa and Asia.
Scientific classification: Camels belong to the camel family, Camelidae. They are in the genus *Camelus.* The Arabian camel is *C. dromedarius.* The Bactrian camel is *C. bactrianus.*

may grow about 10 inches (25 centimeters) long on the animal's head, neck, and humps.

All camels lose their fur in spring and grow a new coat. The fur comes off so fast that it hangs in large pieces, making the animal appear ragged. A camel looks sleek and slender for several weeks after losing its coat, but a thick coat of new fur grows by autumn.

Camels have calluslike bare spots on their chests and on their leg joints. These spots look as though the hair had been rubbed off, but they are natural and not signs of wear. Even young camels have them. Thick, leathery skin grows there and becomes tough when the animal is about five months old.

The head. A camel has large eyes on the sides of its head. Each eye is protected by long, curly eyelashes that keep out sand. In the daytime, when the sun is high, the eyes do not allow excessive light in. Glands supply the eyes with a great deal of water to keep them moist. Thick eyebrows shield the eyes from the desert sun.

The camel's small, rounded ears are located far back on its head. The ears are covered with hair, even on the inside. The hair helps keep out sand or dust that might blow into the animal's ears. A camel can hear well, but, like the donkey, it often pays no attention to commands.

The camel has a large mouth and 34 strong, sharp teeth. It can use the teeth as weapons. A camel owner may cover the animal's mouth with a muzzle to keep it from biting. A working camel cannot wear a bit and bridle, as a horse does, because its mouth must be free to chew *cud* (regurgitated food).

The hump of a camel is mostly a lump of fat. Bands of strong tissue hold pads of fat together, forming the hump above the backbone. The hump of a healthy, well-fed camel may weigh 80 pounds (36 kilograms) or more.

Most kinds of animals store fat in their bodies, but only camels keep most of their fat in a lump. If food is hard to find, the fat in the hump provides energy. If a camel is starving, its hump shrinks. The hump may even slip off the animal's back and hang down on its side. After the camel has had a few weeks' rest and food, its hump becomes firm and plump again. The hump is not a storage place for water, as many people believe.

The legs and feet. Camels have long, strong legs. Powerful muscles in the upper part of the legs allow the animals to carry heavy loads for long distances. A camel can carry as much as 1,000 pounds (450 kilograms), but the usual load weighs about 330 pounds (150 kilograms). While working, the animals typically travel about 25 miles (40 kilometers) a day, at a speed of 3 miles (5 kilometers) an hour. Camels usually walk, especially if it is hot, but when they must go faster they either gallop or *pace*. The pace is a medium-speed movement in which both legs on the same side lift and come down together. This leg action produces a swaying, rocking motion that makes some riders "seasick." Camels are sometimes called "ships of the desert."

The tough, leathery skin pads on a camel's legs act as cushions when the animal kneels to rest. The camel bends its front legs and drops to its knees. Then it folds its hind legs and sinks to the ground. To get up, the camel straightens its hind legs and then jerks up its front legs. A camel can lie down and get up again even with a heavy load on its back.

Camels have two toes on each foot. A hoof that looks like a toenail grows at the front of each toe. Cows, horses, and many other animals walk on their hoofs. But a camel walks on a broad pad that connects its two long toes. This cushionlike pad spreads when the camel steps on it. The pad supports the animal on loose sand in much the same way that a snowshoe helps a person walk on snow. The camel's cushioned feet make almost no sound when the animal walks or runs.

> See **Camel** in *World Book* for more information on People and camels and The life of a camel.

Ernst A. Weber, Photo Researchers

A dromedary can be bred and trained for riding and racing. It can run about 10 miles (16 kilometers) per hour, and can travel as far as 100 miles (160 kilometers) in a day.

The skeleton of a camel

WORLD BOOK illustration by John D. Dawson

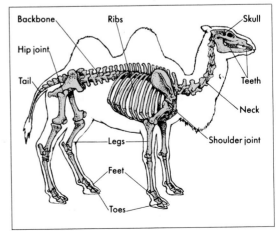

A kitten staring curiously at a vase

Hediye Kerman

Pete Pearson, Van Cleve Photography

A cat hunting in a field

© Hans Reinhard

A tabby clawing at a tree

A cat washing itself

© Hans Reinhard

Cat

Cat is a favorite pet of people around the world. Cats are intelligent and have an independent nature. These small animals can also be playful and entertaining. Many cats make affectionate, loyal pets, providing companionship for people of all ages. About 58 million cats are kept as pets in the United States. About 4 million pet cats live in Canada.

The word *cat* also refers to a family of meat-eating animals that includes tigers, lions, leopards, and panthers. This family also includes *domestic cats*—that is, those that people keep as pets. Domestic cats and their wild relatives share many characteristics. All these animals have long, powerful bodies and somewhat rounded heads. They have short, strong jaws and 30 sharp teeth. Members of the cat family are skillful hunters. They are able to catch other animals by approaching them swiftly and quietly on padded feet. Or they may wait motionless until an animal comes close and then spring upon it suddenly.

The body of a cat

Body size and structure. Adult cats average about 8 to 10 inches (20 to 25 centimeters) tall at the shoulder. Most cats weigh from 6 to 15 pounds (2.7 to 7 kilograms). But some cats weigh more than 20 pounds (9 kilograms).

Cats have the same basic skeleton and internal organs as human beings and other meat-eating mammals. The skeleton of a cat has about 250 bones. The exact number of bones varies, depending on the length of the cat's tail. The skeleton serves as a framework that supports and protects the tissues and organs of a cat's body. Most of the muscles attached to the skeleton are long, thin, and flexible. They enable a cat to move with great ease and speed. Cats can run about 30 miles (48 kilometers) per hour.

The arrangement of the bones and the joints that connect them permits a cat to perform a variety of movements. Unlike many animals, a cat walks by moving the front and rear legs on one side of its body at the same time, and then the legs on the other side. As a result, a cat seems to glide. Its hip joint enables a cat to leap easily. Other special joints allow a cat to turn its head to reach most parts of its body.

A cat has five toes on each forepaw, including a thumblike toe called a *dewclaw.* Each hindpaw has four toes. Some cats have extra toes. Each of a cat's toes ends in a sharp, hooklike claw. The claws usually are *retracted* (held back) under the skin by elastic ligaments, which are a type of connective tissue. However, when the claws are needed, certain muscles quickly pull the *tendons* (cordlike tissues) connected to the claws. This action extends the claws. A cat uses its claws in climbing, in catching prey, and in defending itself. Several spongy pads of thick skin cover the bottoms of a cat's feet. The pads cushion the paws and enable a cat to move quietly.

A cat's tail is an extension of its backbone. The flexible tail helps a cat keep its balance. When a cat falls, it whips the tail and twists its body to land on its feet.

Head. A cat's head is small and has short, powerful jaws. Kittens have about 26 needlelike temporary teeth, which they shed by about 6 months of age. Adult cats have 30 teeth, which are used for grasping, cutting, and shredding food. Unlike human beings, cats have no teeth for grinding food. But a cat's stomach and intestines can digest chunks of unchewed food. Tiny hooklike projections called *papillae* cover a cat's tongue, making it rough. The rough surface of the tongue helps

a cat lick meat from bones and groom its coat.

A cat has a small, wedge-shaped nose. The tip is covered by a tough layer of skin called *nose leather.* The nose leather may be various colors. It is usually moist and cool. A sick cat may have a warm, dry nose.

The colored part of a cat's eyes, called the *iris,* may be various shades of green, yellow, orange, copper, blue, or lavender. *Odd-eyed* cats have irises of different colors. For example, one eye may be green and the other blue. Muscles in the iris control the amount of light that enters a cat's eye through an opening called the *pupil.* In bright light, the iris protects the eye from glare by making the pupil contract and form a vertical slit. In dim light, the pupils widen and so permit more light to enter.

At the back of each eye, a cat has a special mirrorlike structure called the *tapetum lucidum.* It reflects light and so helps a cat see in dim light. It also produces *eyeshine,* the glow a person sees when light strikes the eyes of a cat at night. Each of a cat's eyes has a third eyelid at the inner corner. This structure, called the *nictitating membrane,* protects and lubricates the eyes.

A cat's ears are near the top of its skull. Each ear can move independently. A cat can aim the cup of its ears in the direction from which a sound is coming and so improve its hearing.

Senses. A cat's vision is not as keen as that of a human being. Cats probably see most colors as various shades of gray. However, they can detect the slightest motion, which is helpful in hunting. They see well in dim light but cannot see in total darkness.

Cats have a highly developed sense of smell. Newborn kittens, for example, are able to recognize their nest by scent alone. In addition to its nose, a cat has another sense organ in its mouth that detects scents.

Cats also have a keen sense of hearing. They hear a much broader range of sounds than people do. Deafness is rare among cats. However, it is an inherited defect among some white cats, particularly those with blue or odd-color eyes.

WORLD BOOK illustration by James Teason and John D. Dawson

The skeleton of a cat

The body of a cat includes about 250 bones. The exact number of bones varies, depending on how long a cat's tail is. The skeleton supports and protects the tissues and organs of the body.

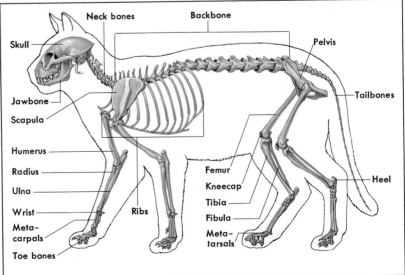

The paws of a cat

Spongy footpads, *right,* enable a cat to walk quietly. Each of a cat's toes ends in a sharp, hooked claw. When retracted, *below left,* the claws are held under the skin by ligaments. The claws extend when muscles tighten the tendons, *below right.*

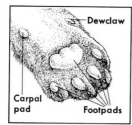

Dewclaw

Carpal pad

Footpads

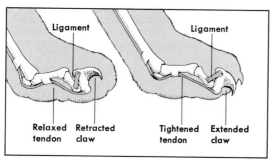

Ligament

Ligament

Relaxed tendon
Retracted claw

Tightened tendon
Extended claw

WORLD BOOK illustrations by John D. Dawson

The whiskers of a cat are special hairs that serve as highly sensitive touch organs. These hairs, called *vibrissae* or *tactile hairs,* grow on the chin, at the sides of the face, and above the eyes. The hairs are attached to nerves in the skin, which transmit signals to the brain when the whiskers brush against objects. The whiskers may help a cat protect its eyes, feel its way in the dark, and detect changes in wind direction.

The eyes of a cat

The illustrations below show some of the special features of a cat's eyes. Cats can see well in normal and dim light.

WORLD BOOK illustrations by Keith Freeman

Narrowing of the pupils in bright light allows less light into the eyes.

Widening of the pupils in dim light permits more light to enter the eyes.

A third eyelid, in the inner corner of each eye, protects and lubricates the eyes.

Irises of different colors are a feature of *odd-eyed* cats. The cats have normal vision.

The life of a cat

Most healthy cats live from 12 to 15 years. But many reach 18 or 19 years of age, and some have lived as long as 30 years.

Reproduction. A *queen* (female cat) can begin mating when it is between 5 and 9 months old, and a *tomcat* (male cat) can begin when it is between 7 and 10 months old. Tomcats can mate at any time. Queens mate only during a period of sexual excitement called *estrus* or *heat.* Estrus occurs several times a year and usually lasts from 3 to 15 days. If a queen is prevented from mating while she is in heat, she will probably come into heat again very soon. In most cases, this cycle recurs until she becomes pregnant.

The pregnancy period among cats lasts about nine weeks. When a queen is ready to give birth, she selects a quiet, safe spot as a nest. On the average, a queen bears from 3 to 5 kittens at a time. However, litters of more than 10 kittens have been reported. The mother can deliver the kittens herself with no human assistance, unless complications develop.

Most newborn kittens weigh about $3\frac{1}{2}$ ounces (99 grams). The mother licks the kittens and so dries them and stimulates their breathing and other body functions. Like other mammals, cats feed their young on milk produced by the mother's body. Newborn kittens cannot see or hear because their eyes and ears are sealed. They depend completely on their mother to nurse, clean, and protect them. The father cat plays no role in caring for the kittens.

Growth and development. Healthy kittens show a steady, daily weight gain. Their eyes open from 10 to 14 days after birth. Soon afterward, their ears open and the first teeth begin to appear. Kittens start to walk and explore their environment at about 3 weeks of age. But the mother watches over them and retrieves kittens that stray too far from the nest.

By about 4 weeks of age, kittens have their full set of temporary teeth. They then begin to eat solid foods and to lap water. The mother usually begins to *wean* (stop nursing) them at about this age.

When kittens are about 4 weeks old, owners should begin to handle them frequently and play with them gently. Kittens that receive such attention tend to become good pets. They learn faster and have fewer behavior problems than kittens that are ignored or overprotected. A kitten that has contact with a variety of people will be less fearful of strangers and new situations as an adult. Kittens can even learn not to fear dogs if they are allowed to play with a friendly dog.

By about 6 weeks of age, kittens have a fully developed brain and nervous system and can be safely separated from their mother. However, if possible, kittens should remain with their mother and their littermates until they are 9 or 10 weeks of age.

See **Cat** in *World Book* for more information on the following topics:

- The body of a cat
- Breeds of cats
- The life of a cat
- Caring for a cat
- Cat associations and shows
- History

A sectional view of a solution cave
A solution cave, such as the one shown below, is formed in limestone when water dissolves sections of the rock. Many of the cave's features develop from minerals deposited by the water.

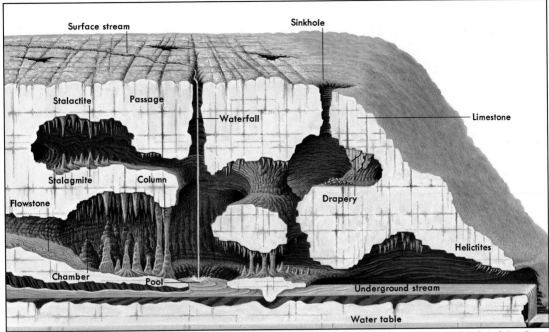

WORLD BOOK diagram by James Teason

Cave, also called *cavern,* is a naturally hollow area in the earth that is large enough for a person to enter. Some caves consist of a single chamber only a few yards or meters deep. Other caves are vast networks of passages and chambers. The longest cave ever explored is the Mammoth-Flint Ridge cave system in Kentucky, which extends more than 190 miles (306 kilometers).

The interior of a cave is a dark, damp place where sunlight never enters. However, artificial light supplied by explorers may reveal a strange underground landscape filled with beautiful, oddly shaped rock formations called *speleothems.* Many caves also have underground lakes, rivers, and waterfalls.

How caves are formed. Most caves are formed in limestone or in a related rock, such as marble or dolomite. Such caves, called *solution caves,* form as underground water slowly dissolves the rock. This process takes thousands of years. It begins when surface water trickles down through tiny cracks in the rock to the *water table,* the level at which the underground area is saturated with water. There the water dissolves some of the rock, forming passages and chambers. The water may form deep pits where the rock tilts sharply.

Limestone and similar rock are only slightly soluble in water. But the water that trickles down from the surface contains carbon dioxide, which has been absorbed from the air and soil above the rock. The carbon dioxide forms a mild acid in the water, and this acid helps dissolve the rock.

Eventually, the water table may drop below the level of the cave. Or, the cave may be raised above the water table by an earthquake or, more often, by a gradual uplifting of the ground. Most of the water then drains out, and air fills the cave. A surface stream may enter the

cave and flow through it. The stream continues the process of dissolving the rock and thus enlarges the cave. Connections from the cave to the surface may develop in several ways. For example, the rock above part of the cave may collapse, forming a vertical entrance called a *sinkhole.* A horizontal entrance may develop on a hillside or a valley slope, especially at a point where a spring or stream flows from the cave.

Other caves, called *lava caves,* form from molten lava. As lava flows down a slope, its outer surface cools and hardens, but the lava beneath remains molten. The molten lava continues to flow and eventually drains out, creating a cave. Lava caves are near the surface of the earth and have many openings in their thin roof. *Sea caves* form along rocky shores as the surf and wind wear away weak areas of the rock.

Speleothems. If the water table drops below the level of a cave, water may continue to seep in through cracks in the rock. The water contains dissolved minerals. As it enters the cave, some of the minerals crystallize and are deposited as speleothems. A speleothem may be white, brown, red, or multicolored, depending on the minerals that form it.

The best-known kinds of speleothems are *stalactites* and *stalagmites.* Stalactites are iciclelike formations that hang from the ceiling of a cave. Stalagmites are pillars that rise from the floor. A stalactite and a stalagmite may join and form a column. In *World Book,* see **Stalactite; Stalagmite.**

See **Cave** in *World Book* for more information on Speleothems, Life in caves, and Spelunking.

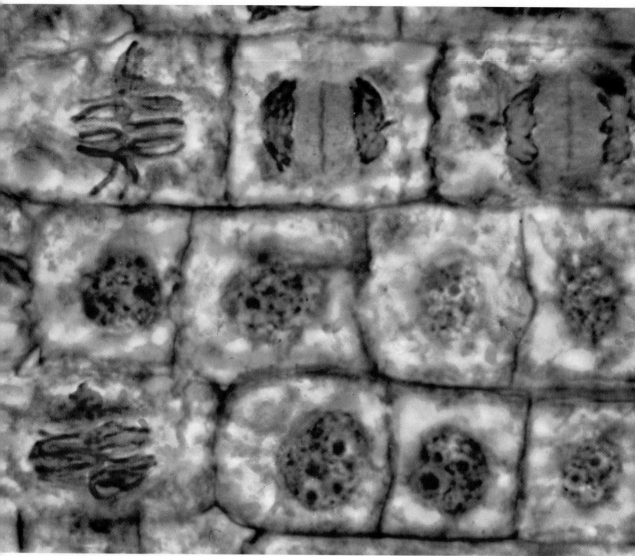

General Biological Supply

Cells, the building blocks of all living things, stand out clearly in this photograph of an onion root tip. The cells have been stained, and magnified about 1,200 times. The reddish stains show structures called *chromosomes* in cells that are dividing and becoming two cells.

Cell

Cell is the basic unit of all life. All living things—tigers, trees, mosquitoes, and people—are made up of cells. Some organisms consist of only one cell. Plants and animals are made up of many cells. For example, the body of a human being has more than 10 million million (10,000,000,000,000) cells.

Most cells are so small that they can be seen only under a microscope. It would take about 40,000 of your red blood cells to fill this letter *O*. It takes several million cells to make up the skin on the palm of your hand.

Some one-celled organisms lead independent lives. Others live in loosely organized groups. In plants and animals, the cells are specialists with particular jobs to do. As you read these words, for example, nerve cells in your eyes are carrying messages of what you are reading to your brain. Muscle cells attached to your eyeballs are moving your eyes across the page. Nerve cells, muscle cells, and other specialized cells group together to form *tissues,* such as nerve tissue or muscle tissue. Different kinds of tissues form *organs,* such as the eyes, heart, and lungs. All the specialized cells together form you—or a giraffe, a daisy, or a bluebird.

All cells have some things in common, whether they are specialized cells or one-celled organisms. A cell is

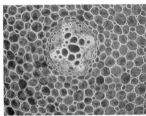

Buttercup root cells

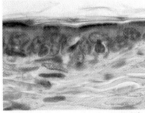

Rat skin cells

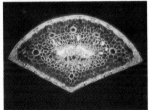

Pine needle cells

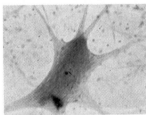

Ox nerve cell

alive—as alive as you are. It "breathes," takes in food, and gets rid of wastes. It also grows and *reproduces* (creates its own kind). And, in time, it dies.

A thin covering encloses each cell. Within the covering is a jellylike fluid called *cytoplasm*. This fluid contains many tiny structures. Each structure has a job to do, such as producing energy. Most cells have a structure called the *nucleus,* which is the cell's control point. The nucleus contains the cell's *genetic program,* a master plan that controls almost everything the cell does. The entire living substance that makes up the cell is often called *protoplasm.*

Just as all living things are made up of cells, every new cell is produced from an existing cell. Most cells reproduce by dividing, so that there are two cells where

there once was only one cell. When a cell divides, each of the two newly produced cells gets a copy of the genetic program.

The genetic program is "written" in a chemical substance called *DNA* (deoxyribonucleic acid). All DNA, whether it comes from an animal cell or a plant cell, looks much alike, and is made up of the same building blocks. But the genetic program carried in DNA makes every living thing different from all other living things. This program makes a dog different from a fish, a zebra different from a rose, and a willow different from a wasp. It makes you different from every other person on the earth.

Scientists are beginning to understand the genetic program and the chemical code in which it is written in DNA. After they have solved it, they may be able to control cancer and many other diseases that arise in the cell. Scientists also may be able to change the characteristics of plants and animals. They may even be able to create life in a test tube.

Inside a living cell

Cells differ greatly in size, in shape, and in the special jobs they do. But we can imagine a typical living cell that has the features found in almost all cells except those of bacteria. Such a typical cell can be thought of as a tiny chemical factory. It has a control center that tells it what to do and when. It has power plants for generating energy, and it has machinery for making its products or performing its services.

A thin covering called the *cell membrane* or *plasma membrane* encloses the cell and separates it from its surroundings. The cell has two main parts: (1) the nucleus and (2) the cytoplasm.

The nucleus is the control center that directs the activities of the cell. A *nuclear membrane* surrounds the nucleus and separates it from the cytoplasm. The nucleus contains two important types of structures, *chromosomes* and *nucleoli.*

Chromosomes are long, threadlike bodies that normally are visible only when the cell is dividing. Chromosomes consist chiefly of two substances—DNA and certain proteins. Lined up along the chromosomes' DNA are the *genes,* the basic units of heredity. Genes control the passing on of characteristics from parents to offspring. Each gene consists of part of a DNA molecule. The chemical structure of the DNA that makes up the genes determines that a dog will give birth to a dog instead of a fish. This chemical structure determines your height, the color of your eyes, the shape of your hands, the texture of your hair, and thousands of other characteristics.

DNA works its wonders chiefly by directing the production of complicated chemical substances called *proteins.* The cell's structures are built mostly of proteins. In addition, certain proteins called *enzymes* speed up chemical reactions in the cell. Without enzymes, these reactions would occur very slowly, and the cell could not function normally. Thus, the kinds of proteins a cell makes help determine the nature of the cell.

Nucleoli are round bodies that form in certain regions of specific chromosomes. Each nucleus may contain one or more nucleoli, though some cells have none at all. Nucleoli help in the formation of *ribosomes,* the

The structures of a cell   Cells differ in size, shape, and function. There is no "typical" cell. Yet almost all cells have many things in common. For this reason, it is helpful to imagine "typical" plant and animal cells like these.

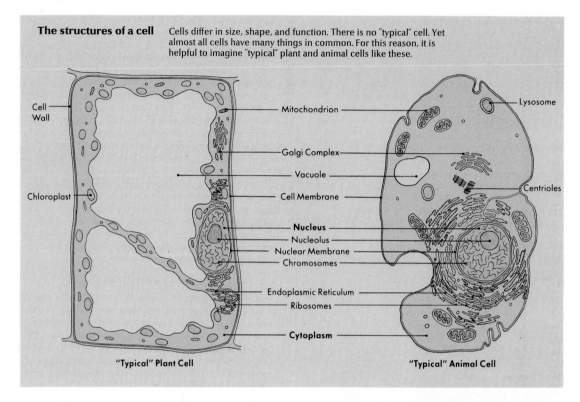

"Typical" Plant Cell

"Typical" Animal Cell

cell's centers of protein production. Nucleoli are made up of proteins and *RNA* (ribonucleic acid). RNA is chemically similar to DNA and plays important roles in making proteins.

The cytoplasm is all the cell except the nucleus. Proteins are made in the cytoplasm, and many of the cell's life activities take place there. Many tiny structures called *organelles* are located in the cytoplasm. Each has a particular job to do. These organelles are called *mitochondria, lysosomes,* the *endoplasmic reticulum, centrioles,* and the *Golgi complex.*

Mitochondria are the power producers of the cell. A cell may contain hundreds of mitochondria. These structures are sausage-shaped, and they produce almost all the energy the cell needs to live and to do its work.

Lysosomes are small, round bodies containing many different enzymes, which can break down many substances. For example, lysosomes help white blood cells break down harmful bacteria.

Endoplasmic reticulum is a complex network of membrane-enclosed spaces in the cytoplasm. The surfaces of some of the membranes are smooth. Others are bordered by ribosomes—tiny round bodies that contain large amounts of RNA. Ribosomes are the cell's protein manufacturing units. The proteins the cell needs to grow, repair itself, and perform hundreds of chemical operations are made on the ribosomes.

Centrioles look like two bundles of rods. They lie near the nucleus, and are important in cell reproduction.

The Golgi complex, also called *Golgi apparatus,* consist of a stack of flat structures. These structures store and eventually release various products from the cell.

Membranes enclose the entire cell, the nucleus, and all the organelles. The membranes hold the cell and each of its parts together. Most membranes consist of a double layer of a fatty substance called *phospholipid.* Proteins occur at various points and extend to different depths within the double layer of phospholipids. Only needed materials can enter the cell and its parts because of the structure and chemical composition of the membranes.

Plant cells have certain special structures. *Chloroplasts,* found in the cytoplasm, are organelles that contain a green substance called *chlorophyll.* In a process called *photosynthesis,* chlorophyll uses the energy of sunlight to produce energy-rich sugars. All life on the earth depends on these sugars. Plant cells also have a *cell wall* surrounding the cell membrane. The cell wall of most plants contains *cellulose,* a substance manufactured in the cytoplasm. Cellulose makes plant stems stiff. *Vacuoles* are common in plant cells. These large, fluid-filled cavities often take up a large part of the plant cell.

See **Cell** in *World Book* for more information on the following topics:

•Looking at a cell
•Inside a living cell
•Cell division
•Cell research

•The work of a cell
•The code of life
•The cell in disease

Circulatory system is a network that carries blood throughout the body. All animals except the simplest kinds have some type of circulatory system.

In some *invertebrates* (animals without a backbone), the circulatory system consists of a simple network of tubes and hollow spaces. Other invertebrates have pumplike structures that send blood through a system of blood vessels. In human beings and other *vertebrates* (animals with a backbone), the circulatory system consists primarily of a pumping organ—the heart—and a network of blood vessels.

The human circulatory system supplies the cells of the body with the food and oxygen they need to survive. At the same time, it carries carbon dioxide and other wastes away from the cells. The circulatory system also helps regulate the temperature of the body and carries substances that protect the body from disease. In addition, the system transports chemical substances called *hormones,* which help regulate the body's activities.

See **Circulatory system** in *World Book* for more information on the following topics:

- Parts of the circulatory system
- Functions of the circulatory system
- Disorders of the circulatory system
- The circulatory system in other animals

The human circulatory system

A person's circulatory system consists chiefly of a pump—the heart—and a network of blood vessels. These vessels—arteries, veins, and capillaries—carry blood throughout the body.

WORLD BOOK illustration by Colin Bidgood

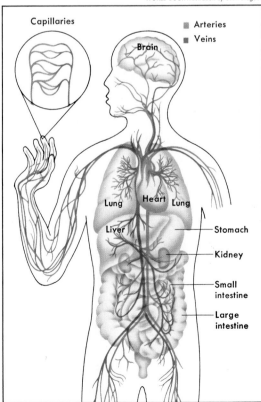

Capillaries

■ Arteries
■ Veins

Brain

Lung   Heart   Lung
Liver

Stomach

Kidney

Small intestine

Large intestine

Some functions of the circulatory system

WORLD BOOK illustrations by Colin Bidgood

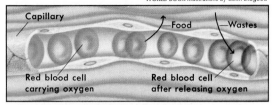

Capillary   Food   Wastes

Red blood cell carrying oxygen   Red blood cell after releasing oxygen

In maintaining body tissues. The circulatory system supplies tissues of the body with essential food and oxygen, and carries away carbon dioxide and other wastes. Substances leave and enter the bloodstream through thin capillary walls.

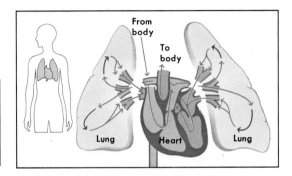

From body

To body

Lung   Heart   Lung

In respiration. Blood carrying carbon dioxide, *blue,* flows to the heart. The heart pumps it to the lungs, where it gives up carbon dioxide and picks up oxygen. The oxygen-rich blood, *red,* returns to the heart and is pumped to all parts of the body.

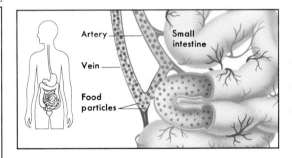

Artery   Small intestine

Vein

Food particles

In nutrition. The circulatory system carries digested food particles to the cells of the body. These particles enter the bloodstream through the walls of the small intestine.

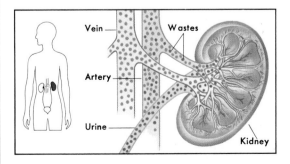

Vein   Wastes

Artery

Urine

Kidney

In removal of wastes. Waste products from body tissues are carried by the blood to the kidneys. The kidneys filter out these substances and expel them in the urine.

Classification, Scientific. Scientific classification is a method scientists have developed to arrange all of the world's organisms in related groups. It is the orderly arrangement of all living things. Scientific classification indicates certain relationships among all organisms. Detailed scientific classifications also show how ancient and extinct biological groups fit into this arrangement. The classification of organisms is a science called *taxonomy* or *systematics.*

Groups in classification. Seven chief groups make up a system in scientific classification. The groups are: (1) kingdom, (2) phylum or division, (3) class, (4) order, (5) family, (6) genus, and (7) species. The kingdom is the largest group. The species is the smallest. Every known organism and plant has a particular place in each group.

Kingdom is the largest unit of biological classification. Until the 1960's, most biologists formally recognized only two major kingdoms—Animalia, the animal kingdom, and Plantae, the plant kingdom. But as more information about the microscopic structure and biochemistry of organisms became known, scientists real-

ized that a two-kingdom classification system was not exact enough. Today, most biologists use a system that recognizes five kingdoms of organisms. These kingdoms are Animalia, Plantae, Fungi, Protista, and Monera.

The kingdom Animalia is the largest kingdom. It has more than 1 million named species. These species include the organisms that most people easily recognize as animals, such as human beings, deer, fish, insects, and snails. The kingdom Plantae consists of more than 350,000 species. It includes those organisms that most people easily recognize as plants, such as magnolias, sunflowers, grasses, pine trees, ferns, and mosses. The kingdom Fungi has more than 100,000 species. These species include fungi, such as mushrooms and bread molds, as well as the lichens. The kingdom Protista has more than 100,000 species. This kingdom includes green, golden, brown, and red algae; ciliates; sporozoans; sarcodines; and flagellates. The kingdom Monera, also called *Prokaryotae,* consists of bacteria, including blue-green algae or cyanobacteria. There are more than 10,000 known species in this kingdom.

How organisms are classified

The illustrated tables below are simplified examples of classification. They show how a red squirrel (*Tamiasciurus hudsonicus*) and a common buttercup (*Ranunculus acris*) can be separated from any other species of animal or plant. As you go down the tables, from kingdom to species, the animals and plants in each group have more and more features in common. The captions list these features. Individuals in a species have so many similar features that they look alike.

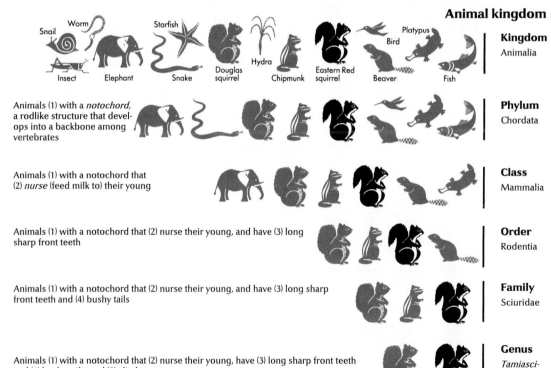

Animal kingdom

Kingdom
Animalia

Animals (1) with a *notochord,* a rodlike structure that develops into a backbone among vertebrates

Phylum
Chordata

Animals (1) with a notochord that (2) *nurse* (feed milk to) their young

Class
Mammalia

Animals (1) with a notochord that (2) nurse their young, and have (3) long sharp front teeth

Order
Rodentia

Animals (1) with a notochord that (2) nurse their young, and have (3) long sharp front teeth and (4) bushy tails

Family
Sciuridae

Animals (1) with a notochord that (2) nurse their young, have (3) long sharp front teeth and (4) bushy tails, and (5) climb trees

Genus
Tamiasciurus

Animals (1) with a notochord that (2) nurse their young, have (3) long sharp front teeth and (4) bushy tails, (5) climb trees, and (6) have brown fur on their backs and white fur on their underparts

Species
Tamiasciurus hudsonicus

Division, or *phylum,* is the second largest group. The kingdoms Protista, Fungi, and Plantae are classified into *divisions.* In the animal kingdom, the term *phylum* is used instead of division. Scientists disagree on which term should be used for the kingdom Monera.

The animal kingdom may be divided into 20 or more phyla. All animals with backbones belong to the phylum Chordata. The plant kingdom has 10 divisions. All plants that have flowers belong to the division Anthophyta.

Class members have more characteristics in common than do members of a division or phylum. For example, mammals, reptiles, and birds all belong to the phylum Chordata. But each belongs to a different class. Apes, bears, and mice are in the class Mammalia. Mammals have hair on their bodies and feed milk to their young. Reptiles, including lizards, snakes, and turtles, make up the class Reptilia. Scales cover the bodies of all reptiles, and none of them feed milk to their young. Birds make up the class Aves. Feathers grow on their bodies, and they do not feed milk to their young.

Order consists of groups that are more alike than those in a class. In the class Mammalia, all the animals produce milk for their young. Dogs, moles, raccoons, and shrews are all mammals. But dogs and raccoons eat flesh, and are grouped together in the order Carnivora, with other flesh-eating animals. Moles and shrews eat insects, and are classified in the order Insectivora, with other insect-eating animals.

Family is made up of groups that are even more alike than those in the order. Wolves and cats are both in the order Carnivora. But wolves are in the family Canidae. All members of this family have long snouts and bushy tails. Cats belong to the family Felidae. Members of this family have short snouts and short-haired tails.

Genus consists of very similar groups, but members of different groups usually cannot breed with one another. Both the coyote and the timber wolf are in the genus *Canis.* But coyotes and timber wolves generally do not breed with one another.

Species is the basic unit of scientific classification. Members of a species have many common characteristics, but they differ from all other forms of life in one or more ways. Members of a species can breed with one another, and the young grow up to look very much like the parents. No two species in a genus have the same scientific name. The coyote is *Canis latrans,* and the gray wolf is *Canis lupus.* Sometimes groups within a species differ enough from other groups in the species that they are called *subspecies* or *varieties.*

Plant kingdom

WORLD BOOK illustrations by John M. Bolt, Jr., and Trudy Rogers

Kingdom
Plantae

Cattail Fern Larkspur Sunflower Common buttercup Pine Grass Water crowfoot Magnolia Hornwort Maple Moss

Division
Anthophyta

Plants that have (1) flowers with reproductive organs called *ovaries* that protect *ovules* (structures that can develop into seeds)

Class
Dicotyledonae

Plants that (1) have flowers with ovaries and (2) develop from plant embryos with two *cotyledons* or *seed leaves*

Order
Ranales

Plants that have (1) flowers that have ovaries, (2) embryos with two cotyledons, and (3) *floral parts* (petals, sepals, stamens) that grow from beneath the ovary

Family
Ranunculaceae

Plants that have (1) flowers that have ovaries, (2) embryos with two cotyledons, (3) floral parts growing from beneath the ovary, and (4) many spirally arranged stamens

Genus
Ranunculus

Plants that have (1) flowers that have ovaries, (2) embryos with two cotyledons, (3) floral parts growing from beneath the ovary, (4) many spirally arranged stamens, and (5) all petals identical

Species
Ranunculus acris

Plants that have (1) flowers that have ovaries, (2) embryos with two cotyledons, (3) floral parts growing from beneath the ovary, (4) many spirally arranged stamens, (5) all petals identical, and (6) yellow flowers

What the world's climate is like

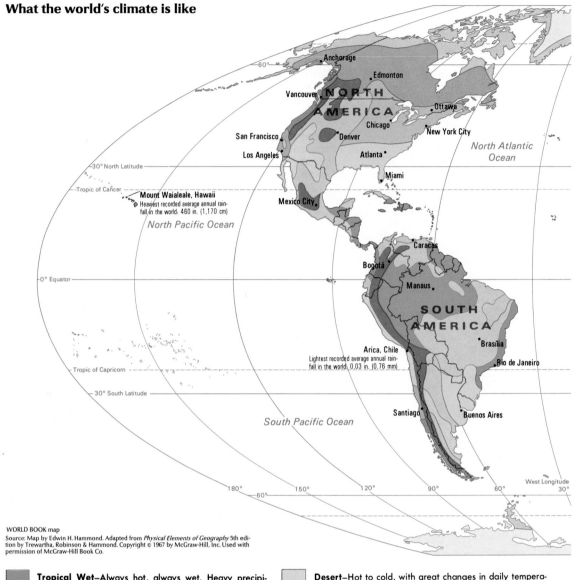

WORLD BOOK map
Source: Map by Edwin H. Hammond. Adapted from *Physical Elements of Geography* 5th edition by Trewartha, Robinson & Hammond. Copyright © 1967 by McGraw-Hill, Inc. Used with permission of McGraw-Hill Book Co.

Tropical Wet–Always hot, always wet. Heavy precipitation well distributed throughout the year.

Tropical Wet and Dry–Always hot, with alternate wet and dry seasons. Heavy precipitation in the wet season.

Highlands–These areas are affected by altitude and are generally cooler and wetter than the adjacent climates.

Desert–Hot to cold, with great changes in daily temperature except in coastal areas. Very little precipitation.

Steppe–Hot to cold, with great changes in daily temperature except in coastal areas. Little precipitation.

Subtropical Dry Summer–Hot, dry summers and mild, rainy winters. Moderate precipitation in winter.

Climate is the sum of all weather events in an area during a long period of time. *Climatologists* (scientists who study climate) often describe the climate in terms of an area's average monthly and yearly (1) temperatures and (2) amounts of *precipitation.* Precipitation consists of rain, snow, hail, and other forms of moisture that fall to earth. Climatologists also describe the year-to-year changes that produce major wet and dry spells.

Climate and weather are not the same. Weather is the condition of the atmosphere during a brief period. The weather may change from day to day. One day's weather may be stormy, wet, and cool. The next day's may be

sunny, dry, and somewhat warmer. To determine the climate of an area, scientists study the daily weather conditions over many years.

Every place on the earth, no matter how small, has its own climate. Places that lie far apart may have a similar climate. Yet there may be important differences between the climate of a hill and a nearby valley, or of a city and the surrounding countryside.

The scientific study of climate is called *climatology.* In describing the climate of a certain place, a climatologist considers a number of characteristics of the atmosphere. The most important of these characteristics are

Subtropical Moist—Warm to hot summers and cool winters. Moderate precipitation in all seasons.

Oceanic Moist—Moderately warm summer and mild, cool winter. Moderate precipitation in all seasons.

Continental Moist—Warm to cool summer and cold winter. Moderate precipitation in all seasons.

Subarctic—Short, cool summer and long, cold winter. Light to moderate precipitation, mostly in summer.

Polar—Always cold, with a brief chilly summer. Little precipitation in all seasons.

Icecap—Always cold, average monthly temperature never above freezing. Precipitation always in the form of snow.

temperature, precipitation, humidity, sunshine and cloudiness, wind, and air pressure.

Climatologists begin by describing the climate in terms of average temperature and precipitation amounts. They also consider the variations that occur between the different seasons of the year. For example, the average yearly temperature in both St. Louis and San Francisco is about 55° F. (13° C). Yet these two cities have different climates. St. Louis has fairly cold winters and hot summers, with precipitation the year around. San Francisco, on the other hand, has mild, rainy winters, and cool, almost rainless, summers.

Climatologists have developed various systems of climatic classification. However, many of these experts recognize 12 major kinds of climate: (1) tropical wet, (2) tropical wet and dry, (3) highlands, (4) desert, (5) steppe, (6) subtropical dry summer, (7) subtropical moist, (8) oceanic moist, (9) continental moist, (10) subarctic, (11) polar, and (12) icecap.

See **Climate** in *World Book* for more information on The importance of climate, Why climates differ, and The changing climate.

Cloud is a mass of small water droplets or tiny ice crystals that floats in the air. Fluffy white clouds floating across a blue sky, or the colors of clouds at sunset, are part of the beauty of nature. Clouds also play an important part in the earth's weather. The water that they bring as rain and snow is necessary to all forms of life. Clouds can also bring destruction or even death, in the form of hail or tornadoes.

Some clouds are great fleecy masses, and others look like giant feathers. Still others are dull gray or black sheets that darken the earth. Most clouds change shape continually. They do so because parts of the cloud evaporate when mixed with air that is drier than the cloud. Cloud shapes also change because of the action of winds and air movements.

Kinds of clouds

Scientists give names to clouds that describe their appearance. For example, the prefix *strato-* means *layerlike* or *sheetlike.* Clouds that appear as layers or sheets are called *stratus* clouds. The prefix *cumulo-* means *pile* or *heap,* and *cumulus* clouds are piled-up masses of white clouds. The prefix *cirro-* means *curl,* and *cirrus* clouds are curly white clouds. These terms and a few others are used to form the names of the most common clouds. The various types of clouds are grouped into different classes according to their height above the ground.

Low clouds. Two kinds of clouds, *stratus* and *stratocumulus,* are usually seen near the earth. The *bases* (lower edges) of most of these clouds are less than 6,000 feet (1,800 meters) above sea level. A stratus cloud looks like a smooth, even sheet. Drizzle often falls from it. A stratocumulus cloud is not as even in thickness as a stratus cloud. It has light and dark areas on the bottom, indicating, as its name suggests, that there are piles of clouds in the layer.

Middle clouds, called *altostratus, altocumulus,* and *nimbostratus,* usually lie from 6,000 to 20,000 feet (1,800 to 6,100 meters) above the earth. Nimbostratus clouds sometimes may be closer to the ground. An altostratus cloud forms a smooth white or gray sheet across the sky. If the cloud is not too thick the sun may be seen through it. An altocumulus cloud appears in many shapes. It may be seen as unconnected piles or as a layer of clouds piled together. A nimbostratus cloud is a smooth layer of gray. Frequently, the cloud itself cannot be seen because of the rain or snow that is falling from it.

High clouds, called *cirrus, cirrostratus,* and *cirrocumulus,* are formed entirely of ice crystals. Other clouds are mainly water droplets. Cirrus clouds are the delicate wispy clouds that appear high in the sky, sometimes higher than 35,000 feet (10,700 meters). A cirrostratus cloud is a thin sheet of cloud. It often causes a halo to appear around the sun or moon. This halo is a good way to recognize a cirrostratus cloud. Cirrocumulus clouds look like many small tufts of cotton hanging high in the sky. These clouds rarely form.

Clouds at more than one height. *Cumulus* and *cumulonimbus* clouds may rise to great heights while their bases are near the ground. Cumulus clouds are heaped-up piles of cloud. They may float lazily across the sky or change into the most spectacular of all clouds, the cumulonimbus. A cumulonimbus cloud may reach heights as great as 60,000 feet (18,000 meters) from its base. Its top, which contains ice crystals, spreads out in the shape of an anvil. This kind of cloud is often called a *thunderhead* because heavy rain, lightning, and thunder come from it. Sometimes hail or, on rare occasions, a deadly tornado comes from a cumulonimbus cloud.

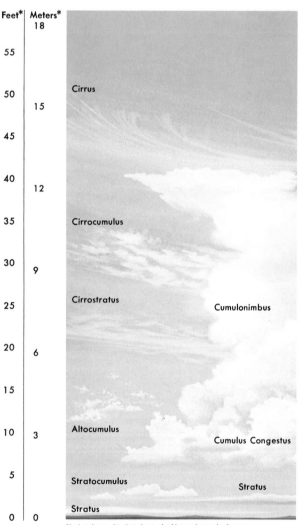

Feet*	Meters*
	18
55	
50	15
45	
40	12
35	
30	9
25	
20	6
15	
10	3
5	
0	0

Cirrus

Cirrocumulus

Cirrostratus

Cumulonimbus

Altocumulus

Cumulus Congestus

Stratocumulus

Stratus

Stratus

*Scale indicates altitude in thousands of feet or thousands of meters.
WORLD BOOK diagram by Herb Herrick

Different clouds are seen at various altitudes above the earth. This diagram shows examples of some common clouds and their approximate altitudes. Many clouds are found only within a certain range of altitudes. Other clouds, such as the cumulonimbus, extend from very low to very high altitudes.

See **Cloud** in *World Book* for more information on How clouds form and Clouds and the weather.

How clouds form

Clouds form when moist air rises and becomes cooler. The air usually rises by (1) convection, (2) lifting, or (3) frontal activity. Cool air cannot hold so much water vapor as warm air can, and the excess vapor changes into tiny drops of water or crystals of ice. These drops or crystals form clouds.

By convection. Solar radiation heats the ground and the air next to it, *right*. The warm air becomes lighter and *convection* (a flow of air) carries it upward. As the air rises, it becomes cooler. If the air is moist, some water vapor condenses and forms clouds, such as the cumulus clouds shown below.

Ray Atkeson

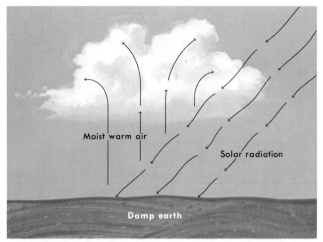

Moist warm air

Solar radiation

Damp earth

By lifting. Warm, moist air blowing over mountains or hills is lifted, *right*. When the air rises, it cools and cannot hold all its water vapor. This vapor *condenses* (changes to drops of liquid) and forms clouds over the high ground, *below*. Clouds formed in this way cover the tops of some mountains permanently.

WORLD BOOK photo by Val L. Mitchell

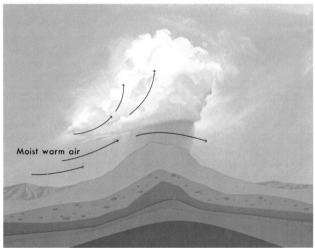

Moist warm air

WORLD BOOK diagram by Herb Herrick

By frontal activity. A weather front occurs when two masses of air at different temperatures come together. The diagram, *right,* shows cool air moving under warm air along a cold front. The warm air is cooled as it rises above the cool air. Many clouds form, *below,* along the front at all altitudes.

Robert H. Glaze, Artstreet

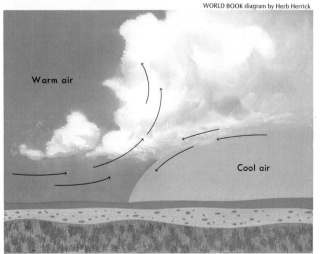

Warm air

Cool air

Fossil ferns and a lump of coal, *left,* were both formed from the remains of plants that died many millions of years ago. While the plants lived, they stored up energy from the sun. The plants that became fossils gave up their store of energy in the process. Only the outline of their appearance remains. But the energy of the coal-forming plants is preserved in the coal. When the coal is burned, it releases this energy in the form of heat.

WORLD BOOK photo

Coal

Coal is a black or brown rock that can be ignited and burned. As coal burns, it produces energy in the form of heat. The heat from coal can be used to heat buildings and to make or process various products. But the heat is used mainly to produce electricity. Coal-burning power plants supply about half the electricity used in the United States and nearly two-thirds of that used throughout the world. Coal is also used to make *coke,* an essential raw material in the manufacture of iron and steel. Other substances obtained in the coke-making process are used to manufacture such products as drugs, dyes, and fertilizers.

Coal was once the main source of energy in all industrial countries. Coal-burning steam engines provided most of the power in these countries from the early 1800's to the early 1900's. Since the early 1900's, petroleum and natural gas have become the leading sources of energy throughout much of the world. Unlike coal, petroleum can easily be made into gasoline and the other fuels needed to run modern transportation equipment. Natural gas is often used in place of coal to provide heat. But the world's supplies of petroleum and natural gas are being used up rapidly. If they continue to be used at the present rate, petroleum supplies may be exhausted by the early 2000's, and natural gas by the mid-2000's. The world's supply of coal can last about 220 years at the present rate of use.

Increased use of coal, especially for producing electricity, could help relieve the growing shortage of gas and oil. However, the use of coal involves certain problems. The burning of coal has been a major cause of air

pollution. Methods have been developed to reduce the pollution, but these methods are costly and not yet fully effective. They must be improved before the use of coal can be increased greatly. In addition, some coal lies deep underground and so is difficult to mine.

Coal developed from the remains of plants that died 400 million to 1 million years ago. For this reason, it is often referred to as a *fossil fuel.* The coal-forming plants probably grew in swamps. As the plants died, they gradually formed a thick layer of matter on the swamp floor.

Uses of coal in the United States

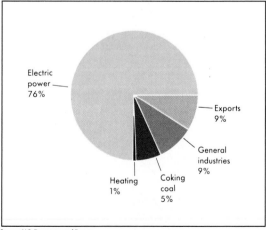

Electric power — 76%

Exports 9%

General industries 9%

Coking coal 5%

Heating 1%

Source: U.S. Department of Energy.

Kinds of underground mines

There are three main kinds of underground mines: (1) shaft mines, (2) slope mines, and (3) drift mines. In a shaft mine, the entrance and exit passages are vertical. In a slope mine, they are dug on a slant. In a drift mine, the passages are dug into the side of a coal bed exposed on a slope.

WORLD BOOK diagrams

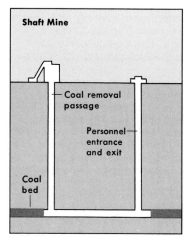

Shaft Mine

Coal removal passage

Personnel entrance and exit

Coal bed

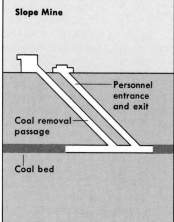

Slope Mine

Personnel entrance and exit

Coal removal passage

Coal bed

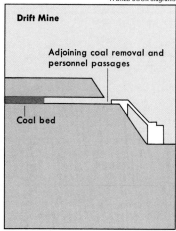

Drift Mine

Adjoining coal removal and personnel passages

Coal bed

Types of underground-mining equipment

WORLD BOOK illustrations by Robert Addison

Conventional-mining equipment. The conventional method of mining involves a series of steps, three of which require special machinery. First, a cutting machine, *left,* cuts a deep slit along the base of the coal *face* (coal exposed on the surface of a mine wall). Another machine, *center,* drills holes into the face. Miners load the holes with explosives and then set the explosives off. The undercutting along the bottom of the face causes the shattered coal to fall to the floor. A loading machine, *right,* gathers the coal onto a conveyor belt.

Continuous-mining equipment eliminates the series of steps in mining a face. A continuous-mining machine, *right,* gouges out the coal and loads it onto a shuttle car in one operation.

The development of coal

The formation of coal involved three main steps. (1) The remains of dead plants turned into a substance called *peat.* (2) The peat became buried. (3) The buried peat was subjected to great pressure. After thousands or millions of years under pressure, the peat turned into coal. Each of these steps is illustrated below.

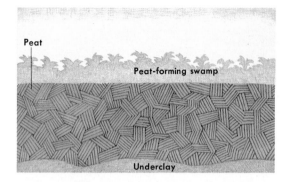

A thick layer of peat developed as plant matter accumulated and hardened on the floor of a swamp. The matter built up as plants that grew in the swamp died and sank to the bottom. Peat-forming swamps once covered much of the earth.

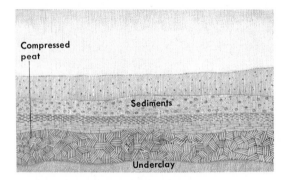

Deposits of loose mineral matter, called *sediments,* completely covered the peat bed. As these sediments continued to pile up over the bed, they compressed the peat.

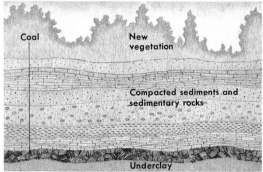

WORLD BOOK diagrams by Jean Helmer

Pressure on the peat increased as the sediments became more compact and heavier. Some sediments hardened into rock. The increasing pressure turned the peat into coal.

Over the years, this matter hardened into a substance called *peat.* In time, the peat deposits became buried under sand or other mineral matter. As the mineral matter accumulated, some of it turned into such rocks as sandstone and shale. The increasing weight of the rock layers and of the other overlying materials began to change the peat into coal. Coal, sandstone, and other rocks formed from deposited materials are called *sedimentary rocks.*

Coal mines can be divided into two main groups: (1) surface mines and (2) underground mines. In most cases, surface mining involves stripping away the soil and rock that lie over a coal deposit. This material is known as *overburden.* After the overburden has been removed, the coal can easily be dug up and hauled away. Underground mining involves digging tunnels into a coal deposit. Miners must go into the tunnels to remove the coal.

Surface mining is usually limited to coal deposits within 100 to 200 feet (30 to 61 meters) of the earth's surface. The more overburden that must be removed, the more difficult and costly surface mining becomes. Most coal deposits deeper than 200 feet are mined underground. Surface mines produce about 60 per cent of the coal mined in the United States. Underground mines produce the rest.

See **Coal** in *World Book* for more information on the following topics:

- How coal was formed
- Where coal is found
- The uses of coal
- How coal is mined
- Cleaning and shipping coal
- The coal industry
- History of the use of coal

Bucyrus-Erie Company

Strip mining depends on giant earthmoving machines like the one at the top of this picture. The earthmover strips away the soil and rock that lie over a coal deposit. A coal-digging machine, *center,* then scoops up the coal and loads it into a truck.

John Shaw, Tom Stack & Assoc.

H. Armstrong
Roberts

Dwight R. Kuhn,
Bruce Coleman Inc.

Zig Leszczynski,
Animals Animals

The great variety of colors in nature includes the dazzling colors of autumn leaves, *top,* and the appetizing colors of ripe fruits and vegetables, *above left.* A brightly colored flower, *above center,* attracts a honeybee to its pollen. The brilliant blue and yellow of a South American arrow poison frog, *above right,* serve as a vivid warning to the animal's enemies.

Color

Color fills our world with beauty. We delight in the colors of a magnificent sunset and in the bright red and golden-yellow leaves of autumn. We are charmed by gorgeous flowering plants and the brilliantly colored arch of a rainbow. We also use color in various ways to add pleasure and interest to our lives. For example, many people choose the colors of their clothes carefully and decorate their homes with colors that create beautiful, restful, or exciting effects. By their selection and arrangement of colors, artists try to make their paintings more realistic or expressive.

Color serves as a means of communication. In sports, different colored uniforms show which team the players are on. On streets and highways, a red traffic light tells drivers to stop, and a green light tells them to go. On a map printed in color, blue may stand for rivers and other bodies of water, green for forests and parks, and black for highways and other roads.

We use the names of colors in many common expressions to describe moods and feelings. For example, we say a sad person *feels blue* and a jealous one is *green with envy.* We say an angry person *sees red.* A coward may be called *yellow.*

Color plays an important part in nature. The brilliant colors of many kinds of blossoms attract insects. The insects may pollinate the flowers, causing the plants to develop seeds and fruits. Colorful fruits attract many kinds of fruit-eating animals, which pass the seeds of the fruits in their droppings. The seeds may then sprout wherever the droppings fall. In this way, fruit-bearing plants may be spread naturally to new areas.

The colors of some animals help them attract mates. For example, a peacock spreads his brightly colored feathers when courting a female. The colors of many other animals help them escape from enemies. For example, Arctic hares have brownish fur in summer. In winter, their fur turns white, making it difficult for enemies to see the hares in the snow.

Although we speak of seeing colors or objects, we do not actually see them. Instead, we see the light that objects reflect or give off. Our eyes absorb this light and change it into electrochemical signals. The signals travel through nerves to the brain, which interprets them as colored images. However, there is much that scientists still do not know about how our eyes and brain enable us to sense color.

The relation between color and light. To understand how we see color, we must first know something about the nature of light. Light is a form of energy that behaves in some ways like waves. Light waves have a range of *wavelengths*. A wavelength is the distance between any point on one wave and the corresponding point on the next wave. Different wavelengths of light appear to us as different colors. Light that contains all wavelengths in the same proportions as sunlight appears white. See **Light**.

When a beam of sunlight passes through a specially shaped glass object called a *prism,* the rays of different wavelengths are bent at different angles. The bending breaks up the sunlight into a beautiful band of colors. This band contains all the colors of the rainbow and is called the *visible spectrum.* At one end of the spectrum, the light appears as violet. It consists of the shortest wavelengths of light that we can see. Farther along the spectrum, the light has increasingly longer wavelengths. It appears as blue, green, yellow, orange, and red, each shading into its neighboring colors in the spectrum. The longest wavelengths of light that we can see appear deep red in color.

Light waves are a form of *electromagnetic waves,* which consist of patterns of electric and magnetic energy. The visible spectrum is only a small part of the *electromagnetic spectrum*—the entire range of electromagnetic waves. Beyond the violet end of the visible spectrum are ultraviolet rays, X rays, and gamma rays. Beyond the red end of the visible spectrum are infrared rays and radio waves. In *World Book,* see **Electromagnetic waves.**

Such objects as traffic lights and neon signs appear colored because the light that they give off contains a limited range of wavelengths. However, most objects appear colored because their chemical structure absorbs certain wavelengths of light and reflects others. When sunlight strikes a carrot, for example, molecules in the carrot absorb most of the light of short wavelengths. Most of the light of longer wavelengths is reflected. When these longer wavelengths of light reach our eyes, the carrot appears orange.

An object that reflects most of the light of all wavelengths in nearly equal amounts appears white. An object that absorbs most of the light of all wavelengths in nearly equal amounts appears black.

See **Color** in *World Book* for more information on the following topics:

- How we see color
- Color vision in animals
- Methods of color production
- Producing color harmony
- Characteristics of color
- How colors are classified
- History of color studies

The visible spectrum   A band of colors called the *visible spectrum* forms when white light passes through a *prism* (a specially shaped glass object). The prism bends the shortest light waves most. They appear violet. It bends the longest waves least. They appear red. All other colors lie in between. Ultraviolet and infrared fall outside the spectrum and are invisible to people. The length of light waves is measured in *nanometers.* One nanometer is a billionth of a meter, or about $\frac{1}{25,000,000}$ of an inch.

WORLD BOOK illustration by Leonard Morgan

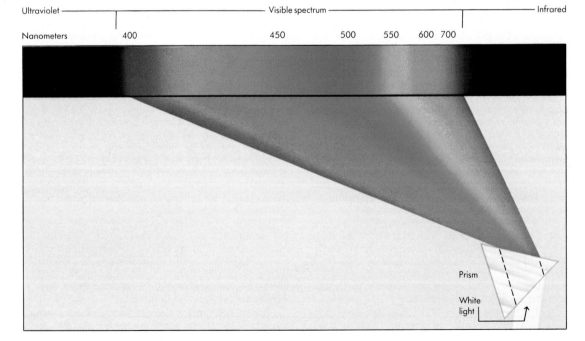

Ultraviolet ————————————————— Visible spectrum ————————————— Infrared

| Nanometers | 400 | 450 | 500 | 550 | 600 | 700 |

Prism

White light

Comet, *KAHM iht,* is an object that resembles a fuzzy star and travels along a definite path through the solar system. Some of the brightest comets develop a long, shining tail when they come near the sun. The tail of a comet may stream across space as far as 100 million miles (160 million kilometers). A comet has a distinct center called a *nucleus* that measures less than 10 miles (16 kilometers) in diameter. A hazy cloud called a *coma* surrounds the nucleus. Its diameter may be as large as 1 million miles (1.6 million kilometers). The coma and nucleus make up the comet's head.

Most comets cannot be seen without a telescope. Some are visible to the unaided eye, but only for several weeks or months when they pass closest to the sun. Halley's Comet is probably the best-known comet. It was named for the English astronomer Edmond Halley, who recognized that it could be seen an average of every 77 years as it orbited the sun. Astronomers determined that the comet would complete two orbits during the 1900's—in 1910 and in 1986.

A number of other extremely bright comets have been seen since 1910. For example, Comet Arend-Roland and Comet Mrkos appeared in 1957 and Comet Ikeya-Seki in 1965. In 1973, Comet Kohoutek became the first comet to be studied by men in space. Astronauts in the Skylab space station photographed it and so provided much new information about comets.

For centuries, many people believed the coming of a comet would bring a disaster, such as a war or an epidemic. Halley's Comet revived these fears in 1910, but the earth passed through the edge of the comet's tail with no harm. However, a collision between the earth and a comet's nucleus could be very destructive.

The composition of comets. Scientists once believed the nucleus of a comet consisted of tiny solid particles held together loosely by gravitation. Today, most astronomers think the nucleus resembles a dirty snowball that was formed in the cold, distant regions of the solar system. The nucleus probably consists of frozen gases and ice mixed with dust. The gases include ammonia, carbon dioxide, carbon monoxide, and methane. The gases and water make up from 70 to 80 per cent of the total mass. The remaining 20 to 30 per cent may re-

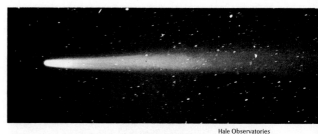

Hale Observatories

Halley's Comet appears an average of every 77 years as it orbits the sun. It was seen as early as 240 B.C.

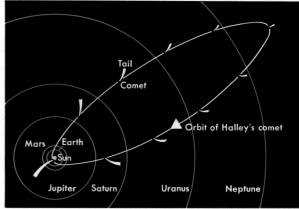

WORLD BOOK diagram by Mas Nakagawa

A comet travels through the solar system along an egg-shaped orbit called an *ellipse.* The orbit of Halley's Comet, shown in the diagram above, crosses the orbits of the earth and other planets. A comet's tail always points away from the sun.

semble meteoric particles. This portion consists of fine grains and larger chunks of metals and rocky material.

As a comet approaches the sun, the heat causes the outer layers of the icy nucleus to evaporate. The evaporation releases dust and gases, which form the coma around the nucleus. The pressure of the sun's light may push the smallest dust particles and gas molecules away from the coma, forming one or more tails. This pressure makes a comet's tail point away from the sun. When a comet approaches the sun, its tail brings up the rear. But when the comet moves away from the sun, its tail leads.

All of a comet's light comes from the sun. The brightness of a comet results partly from sunlight reflected by its nucleus and coma. In addition, when a comet is closest to the sun, gas molecules in the coma release energy absorbed from the sun's rays.

The paths of comets. Most comets travel around the sun in *elliptical* (oval-shaped) paths. The time it takes a comet to make a complete orbit is called its *period.* Some comets have short periods of less than seven years. Others travel in such huge orbits that they pass near the sun only once in thousands or even millions of years. No comet seems to have approached the sun from beyond the limits of the solar system. Therefore, all comets seen by astronomers are considered part of the solar system.

Famous comets

Name	First seen	Period of orbit (Years)
Halley's Comet	Before 240 B.C.	76-79*
Tycho Brahe's Comet	1577	Unknown
Biela's Comet	1772	6.6-6.8*
Encke's Comet	1786	3.3
Comet Flaugergues	1811	3,000
Comet Pons-Winnecke	1819	5.6-6.3*
Great Comet of 1843	1843	513
Donati's Comet	1858	2,000
Great Comet of 1882	1882	760
Comet Morehouse	1908	Unknown
Comet Schwassmann-Wachmann 1	1927	16.1-16.4*
Comet Humason	1961	2,900
Comet Ikeya-Seki	1965	880
Comet Tago-Sato-Kosaka	1969	420,000
Comet Bennett	1969	1,680
Comet Kohoutek	1973	75,000
Comet West	1976	500,000

*Period changes

© George Haling, Photo Researchers

Computers come in a wide range of sizes. A *mainframe* computer system may fill a large room, *above.* A *personal computer, left opposite page,* fits on a desk top. The tiniest computers consist of a *microprocessor,* a chip that fits through the eye of a needle, *right opposite page.*

Computer

Computer is a machine that performs calculations and processsses information with astonishing speed and precision. A computer can handle vast amounts of information and solve complicated problems. It can take thousands of individual pieces of data and turn them into more usable information—with blinding speed and almost unfailing accuracy. The most powerful computers can perform billions of calculations per second.

Computers handle many tasks in business, education, manufacturing, transportation, and other fields. They provide scientists and other researchers with a clearer understanding of nature. They give people who work with words an effective way to create documents. They enable designers and artists to see things that have never been seen before. Computers produce new information so quickly and accurately that they are changing people's views of the world. For these and other reasons, the computer is one of the most interesting and important machines ever invented.

The most common type of computer, by far, is the *digital computer. Digital* means *having to do with numbers.* Digital computers perform tasks by changing one set of numbers into another set. All data—numerals, pictures, sounds, symbols, and words—are translated into numbers inside the computer. Everything a digital computer can do is based on its ability to perform simple procedures on numbers—such as adding, subtracting, or comparing two numbers to see which is larger. Digital computers are so widespread that the word *com-*

puter alone almost always refers to a digital computer. The largest digital computers are parts of computer systems that fill a large room. The smallest digital computers—some so tiny they can pass through the eye of a needle—are found inside wrist watches, pocket calculators, and other devices.

All digital computers have two basic parts—a *memory* and a *processor.* The memory receives data and holds them until needed. The memory is made up of a huge collection of switches. The processor changes data into useful information by converting numbers into other numbers. It reads numbers from the memory, performs basic arithmetic calculations such as addition or subtraction, and puts the answer back into the memory. The processor performs this activity over and over until the desired result is achieved. Both the memory and the processor are *electronic*—that is, they work by sending electrical signals through wires.

The smallest digital computers consist only of the memory and the processor. But larger digital computers are part of systems that also contain *input equipment* and *output equipment.* The operator uses an input device, such as a keyboard, to enter instructions and data into the computer. After processing is complete, an output device translates the processed data into a form understandable to the user—words or pictures, for example. Typical output devices include printers and visual displays that resemble television screens.

People can think about problems and figure out how

© Henley & Savage from The Stock Market

Bell Laboratories

to solve them. But computers cannot think. A person must tell the computer in very simple terms exactly what to do with the data it receives. A list of instructions for a computer to follow is called a *program.*

People have used calculating devices since ancient times. The first electronic digital computer, built in 1946, filled a huge room. Since then, rapid improvements in computer technology have led to the development of smaller, more powerful, and less expensive computers.

Basic principles of computers

A computer receives individual pieces of data, changes the data into more useful information, and then tells the operator what the information is. For example, a person who wants to find the sum of four numbers enters them into the computer. In only a fraction of a second, signals that represent these numbers are changed into signals that represent the sum. The computer then displays the sum for the user.

How a computer operates. People use input devices to enter data into computers. One of the most common input devices is the *computer terminal,* which looks like a typewriter keyboard combined with a television screen. Data that are typed on the keyboard appear on the screen. At the same time, the data go to the memory. The memory also stores a program—the step-by-step series of instructions for the computer to follow. The processor manipulates the data according to the program.

The processed information is sent to an output device, which presents it to the computer user. In many cases, the computer terminal that served as the input device also acts as the output device, and its screen displays the results. Printers are another important kind of output device. *File storage devices* are used to save in-

Computer terms

Binary code is used by computers to represent information. It consists of the 0's and 1's of the binary numeration system.
Bit, an abbreviation of the term *bi*nary digi*t,* may be either the digit 0 or 1.
Byte is a group of bits that act as a single unit of information, such as a letter or numeral.
Database is an organized collection of information stored on a magnetic disk or other direct-access storage device.
File storage device is any device used to save information until it is needed again.
Hardware refers to the physical parts of a computer system.
Input is any information that a user enters into a computer.
Mainframe is a large, powerful computer that many people can use at once. It can store large amounts of information.
Memory is the part of a computer that stores information.
Microprocessor is a miniature electronic device consisting of thousands of transistors and related circuitry on a silicon chip. The device is often called a "computer on a chip" because it can hold the processor and some memory.
Modem is a device that allows computer users to communicate with one another over telephone lines.
Network is a system consisting of two or more computers connected by high-speed communication lines.
Operating system is a type of software that controls the operation of a computer system.
Output is any result provided by a computer.
Peripheral equipment consists of input devices, output devices, and file storage devices.
Personal computer is a desktop or handheld computer designed for general-purpose use.
Program is a set of instructions to be carried out by a computer, written in a computer language.
Simulation is the representation or imitation of a situation or system on a computer, usually with a mathematical model. The purpose is to predict and analyze what is likely to occur under various conditions.
Software refers to the programs used by a computer to perform desired tasks.

formation and programs to be used in the future.

All data handled by computers, including words, enter the processor in the form of digits. Computers commonly use the digits of the *binary numeration system* (in *World Book,* see **Numeration systems** [The binary system]). Unlike the familiar decimal system, which uses 10 digits, the binary system uses only two digits: 0 and 1. These digits are called *bits.* Different combinations of bits represent letters, symbols, and decimal numerals. Each such combination of bits is called a *byte.* For example, according to one standard code, the binary representation for the letter A is 100 0001, while the binary representation for the letter Z is 101 1010. Each symbol and decimal numeral also is represented by a specific combination of 0's and 1's.

Each of a computer's thousands of tiny electronic circuits operates much like an ordinary light switch. When a circuit is off, it corresponds to the binary digit 0. When a circuit is on, it corresponds to the digit 1. Binary digits, like decimal numbers, can be added, subtracted, multiplied, and divided. Thus, a computer can perform all the basic arithmetic operations.

Computer hardware and software. The physical equipment that makes up a computer system is called *hardware.* Hardware includes input and output devices, file storage devices, the memory, and the processor. The input and output devices and the file storage devices also are known as *peripheral equipment.*

Computer *software* consists of the programs that a computer uses to perform a task. People can either create or purchase software. Computers have vast and varied capabilities because of the many different kinds of available software.

See **Computer** in *World Book* for more information on the following topics:

- The importance of the computer
- Kinds of computers
- How a computer works
- Programming a computer
- The computer industry
- The development of the computer
- Problems of the computer age

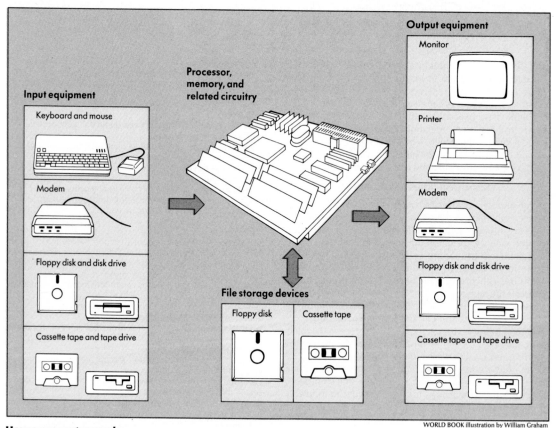

Input equipment

Keyboard and mouse

Modem

Floppy disk and disk drive

Cassette tape and tape drive

Processor, memory, and related circuitry

File storage devices

Floppy disk

Cassette tape

Output equipment

Monitor

Printer

Modem

Floppy disk and disk drive

Cassette tape and tape drive

WORLD BOOK illustration by William Graham

How a computer works

Computer systems come in a wide range of sizes and contain varying types of equipment. Nevertheless, all digital computers work essentially the same way. The diagram above illustrates the flow of information through a personal computer system. A human operator uses *input equipment* to provide data and instructions to the computer. The *processor* then performs calculations on the data, while the *memory* stores information during processing. The results then are sent to the *output equipment,* which presents them to the user. *File storage devices* enable information to be saved for future use.

California condor
Gymnogyps californianus
Found only in captivity
Body length 50 inches
(127 centimeters)

Andean condor
Vultur gryphus
Found in the Andes, from
Venezuela and Colombia to
the Strait of Magellan
Body length 52 inches
(132 centimeters)

WORLD BOOK illustrations by Albert E. Gilbert

Condor is either of two large vultures found in the Western Hemisphere. The *California condor,* which once lived wild in southern California, has nearly died out. Only about 25 California condors survive, all in captivity. The *Andean condor* of South America is more common, but it also is in danger of extinction. Andean condors live in the Andes Mountains from Colombia to the Strait of Magellan, and along the coast of Peru.

Appearance. California condors are the largest flying land birds in North America, with a wingspan of 8 to 9½ feet (2.4 to 2.9 meters). The slightly larger Andean condor has a wingspread of about 10 feet (3 meters). Black feathers cover most of an adult condor's body. California condors have white on the underside of the wings. The upper wing surface of Andean condors is white. A collar of feathers circles the base of the neck—black feathers on California condors and white feathers on Andean condors. The featherless neck and head are red-orange in California condors and dark blue in Andean condors. Male Andean condors have a fleshy crest on the head.

Habits. In the wild, condors spend much of the day resting on high perches. Condors do not build nests. Instead, their eggs are laid in caves, in holes, or among boulders. A female California condor lays just one egg every two years. A female Andean condor also reproduces only every second year, laying one or two eggs.

Condors are powerful, graceful fliers. They can soar and glide for long distances, flapping their wings an average of only once an hour. They may search the ground for food as they fly. Like other vultures, condors eat the remains of dead animals.

Outlook for the California condor. By the 1980's, only a small number of California condors survived. Many California condors had been shot. Others may have died from eating poisoned animal bodies set out to kill coyotes. Increasingly, the growth of urban areas posed a major threat to condor survival. The condor's way of life requires vast areas of open, hilly country, and urban growth destroys such habitat.

In 1982, biologists began a program to capture all wild California condors. They hope to breed condors in captivity and eventually return the birds to the wild. The last wild California condor was captured in 1987. Despite this effort, the future of the bird remains in doubt.

Scientific classification. Condors belong to the New World vulture family, Cathartidae. The California condor is classified as *Gymnogyps californianus.* The Andean condor is *Vultur gryphus.*

Crane is the name of a family of large birds with long legs and a long neck. Cranes live in marshy areas in many parts of the world. South America and Antarctica are the only continents that have no cranes. Cranes resemble herons, but they can easily be distinguished in flight. Cranes extend their head and neck straight ahead when they fly, but herons bend theirs into an S-shape.

Appearance. Cranes have long and slender legs, necks, and bills. The tallest cranes stand about 5 feet (1.5 meters) high, and the shortest are about $2\frac{1}{2}$ feet (0.8 meter) tall. A crane's wingspan can measure up to $7\frac{1}{2}$ feet (2.3 meters). The male and female look alike. They range in color from white to dark gray and brown. Most adult cranes have a patch of red skin on the head.

Habits. Most cranes that live in the Northern Hemisphere migrate south each fall from nesting grounds in the north. They return to their nesting ground each spring. Other cranes remain the year around in warm areas. A crane's powerful, buglelike voice carries for a great distance. The birds call to each other in flight, perhaps to keep the flock together during migration.

Cranes mate after they reach their nesting grounds. The male and female perform a dance before mating. The birds alternately circle around each other with opened wings, bow their heads, and leap into the air.

Cranes build nests in shallow water in a marsh, swamp, or other wet, open area. Both the male and the female help pile grasses, weeds, and other plants into a mound. A female crane usually lays only two eggs in a season. Both parents care for the eggs and young.

Cranes eat a variety of foods, including frogs, insects, snails, and grain and other plants. They are a pest in some areas because they take grain from farmers' fields.

WORLD BOOK illustrations by Walter Linsenmaier

Sarus crane
Grus antigone
Found in southern Asia
from India to the Philippines
Body length: 60 inches
(152 centimeters)

Demoiselle crane
Anthropoides virgo
Found in
south-central Eurasia
Body length: 38 inches
(97 centimeters)

Sandhill crane
Grus canadensis
Found in northern and
southeastern North America
and the northern Soviet Union
Body length: 44 inches
(112 centimeters)

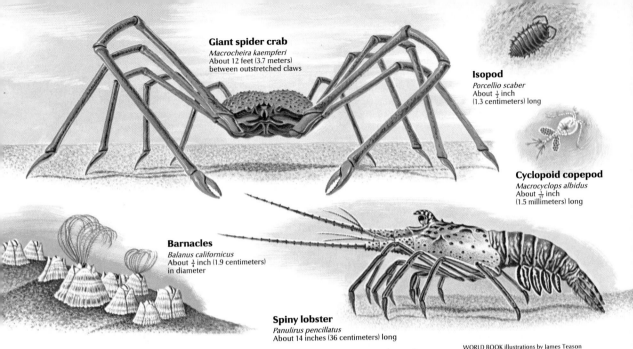

Giant spider crab
Macrocheira kaempferi
About 12 feet (3.7 meters)
between outstretched claws

Isopod
Porcellio scaber
About $\frac{1}{2}$ inch
(1.3 centimeters) long

Cyclopoid copepod
Macrocyclops albidus
About $\frac{1}{17}$ inch
(1.5 millimeters) long

Barnacles
Balanus californicus
About $\frac{3}{4}$ inch (1.9 centimeters)
in diameter

Spiny lobster
Panulirus pencillatus
About 14 inches (36 centimeters) long

WORLD BOOK illustrations by James Teason

Crustaceans include a wide variety of animals. The largest crustacean, the giant spider crab, measures up to 12 feet (3.7 meters) long between its outstretched claws.

Crustacean, *kruhs TAY shuhn,* is an invertebrate animal with many jointed legs. A crustacean has no bones. A shell called an *exoskeleton* covers its body. Crabs, crayfish, lobsters, and shrimp are crustaceans, as are barnacles, water fleas, and wood lice.

There are about 30,000 species of crustaceans. The largest crustacean, the giant spider crab of Japan, measures up to 12 feet (3.7 meters) long between its outstretched claws. The smallest species, such as copepods and water fleas, may be less than $\frac{1}{24}$ inch (1 millimeter) long. Most kinds of crustaceans live in salt water, but some inhabit fresh water. A few kinds, including certain crabs and wood lice, live on land.

Crustaceans play a major role in aquatic ecology. In most aquatic environments, diatoms and other microorganisms are the basic food producers. Many small crustaceans feed on these microorganisms. The small crustaceans, in turn, serve as food for fish and other larger aquatic animals. Crustaceans thus form a key link between food-producing microorganisms and the larger animals in the aquatic food chain.

People in many parts of the world eat crabs, lobsters, shrimp, and other crustaceans. On the other hand, some kinds of crustaceans cause problems for people. For example, certain marine wood lice burrow into, and eventually destroy, wooden wharves. Barnacles attach themselves to the hulls of ships and greatly reduce the vessels' speed. Certain crabs and other crustaceans damage rice crops by burrowing into the dikes that surround rice paddies, or by eating the young plants.

The body of a crustacean

Outer body. The body of most adult crustaceans has three main parts, each of which consists of many segments. These three parts are (1) the head, (2) the thorax, and (3) the abdomen.

Crustaceans have two pairs of antennae, which extend from the head. The head also includes the mouth, three pairs of jaws, and the eyes. The eyes may be even with the surface of the head or at the end of stalks.

Each segment of the thorax has a pair of legs. Most crustaceans have 6 to 14 pairs of legs. A few species have more, and some have less. Crustaceans use some of their legs mainly for swimming or walking. Other legs may be pincers used for catching food, for fighting, or for other activities.

The abdomen of most species of crustaceans lacks legs. But *malacostracans,* a major group that includes lobsters and shrimp, have small abdominal legs. These legs are used for swimming, for breathing, and, in the females of some species, for carrying eggs. Many malacostracans also have a flattened tail, which they snap rapidly to swim backward.

A crustacean's exoskeleton protects and supports the

The body of a shrimp

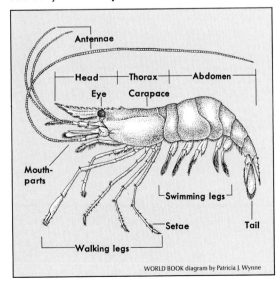

Antennae

Head — Thorax — Abdomen

Eye   Carapace

Mouth-
parts

Swimming legs

Setae   Tail

Walking legs

WORLD BOOK diagram by Patricia J. Wynne

internal organs. The exoskeleton may be soft or very hard. It is soft and thin at the joints to allow for bending. Some species have a shield of exoskeleton called a *carapace* that extends from the back of the head over the thorax.

Internal organs of crustaceans resemble those of insects. In most kinds of crustaceans, a heart pumps the blood throughout the body. Some small species of crustaceans have no heart, and their body movements promote circulation of the blood.

A crustacean's digestive system has three main parts. In malacostracans, food is ground up in the *foregut* and is further digested in the *midgut,* or stomach. The *hindgut,* or intestine, compacts and stores undigested materials until they are eliminated from the body.

Crustaceans have a small brain. It is connected to a nerve cord that extends along the underside of a crustacean's body. Clusters of nerve cell bodies along the cord have some control over various activities.

Most crustaceans, unlike land-dwelling insects, breathe through gills. However, most small species have no gills. They breathe through their skin.

Senses. Most adult crustaceans have a pair of *compound eyes.* These eyes have many separate lenses and can easily detect movement (in *World Book,* see **Compound eye**). Many species also have a *simple eye,* which senses light but does not form an image. Most young crustaceans, and the adults of copepods and a few other species, have only a simple eye.

Tiny hairlike *setae* cover various parts of the body. Certain of them are sensitive to touch, smell, and taste. These sensory setae are concentrated on the antennae, mouthparts, and pincers.

See **Crustacean** in *World Book* for more information on The life of a crustacean.

Interesting facts about crustaceans

WORLD BOOK illustrations by James Teason

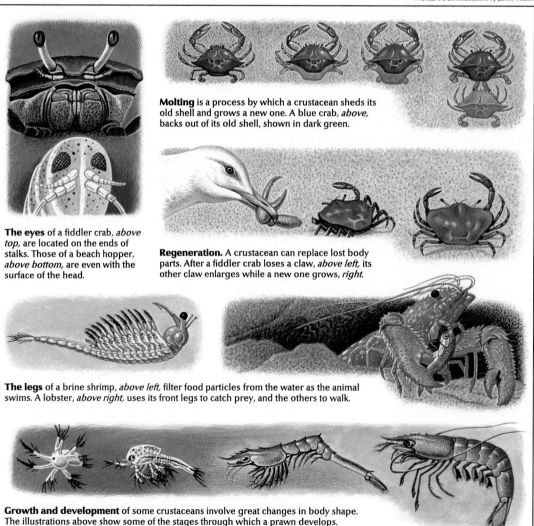

Molting is a process by which a crustacean sheds its old shell and grows a new one. A blue crab, *above,* backs out of its old shell, shown in dark green.

The eyes of a fiddler crab, *above top,* are located on the ends of stalks. Those of a beach hopper, *above bottom,* are even with the surface of the head.

Regeneration. A crustacean can replace lost body parts. After a fiddler crab loses a claw, *above left,* its other claw enlarges while a new one grows, *right.*

The legs of a brine shrimp, *above left,* filter food particles from the water as the animal swims. A lobster, *above right,* uses its front legs to catch prey, and the others to walk.

Growth and development of some crustaceans involve great changes in body shape. The illustrations above show some of the stages through which a prawn develops.

Stephen Collins, N.A.S.

New antlers of a white-tailed deer, *above,* and moose, *below,* have a furry cover called *velvet* which the animals soon rub off.

D. Lichtenberg, N.A.S.

Fritz Prenzel, Pix from Publix

A mother white-tailed deer guards her fawns while they search for food. Fawns may stay with their mothers for more than a year.

Deer are the only animals with bones called *antlers* on their heads. Antlers differ from horns, which are strong, hard layers of skin with a bony core. Deer are among the most common large land mammals and are well-known for their running ability.

There are more than 60 species of deer, including caribou, elk, marsh deer, moose, mule deer, musk deer, and reindeer. Some deer live in the hot, dry deserts. Others live in cold regions above the Arctic Circle. However, most species of deer live in prairies, swamps, or woodlands that have a mild climate.

Deer vary widely in size. They are among the largest wild animals in North America and Europe. The North American moose is the largest deer in the world. Some males grow $7\frac{1}{2}$ feet (2.3 meters) tall at the shoulders and weigh over 1,800 pounds (816 kilograms). The smallest deer is the pudu of western South America. It is about 1 foot (30 centimeters) tall at the shoulders and weighs about 20 pounds (9 kilograms).

Among most species of deer, only the males have antlers. In caribou and reindeer, however, both males and females have antlers.

Most male deer are called *bucks.* But male caribou, elk, and moose are called *bulls,* and male red deer are *stags* or *harts.* Most female deer are called *does.* But female caribou, elk, and moose are *cows,* and female red deer are *hinds.* Most young deer are called *fawns,* but young caribou, elk, and moose are *calves.*

Since early times, people have used deer meat for food and deer skins for clothing. After white settlers came to North America, they killed so many deer that the animal was wiped out in large regions of the continent. In some areas, deer populations recovered after the animals were reintroduced from other regions and protected by hunting laws. However, hunting laws fail to protect many of the animals that prey on deer, such as coyotes and cougars. These predators are now scarce or absent in some areas where deer live, and some deer populations have grown too large. As a result, today many deer are killed simply to reduce their numbers.

The body of a deer

Deer are *mammals*—that is, animals whose young feed on milk produced by the mother. Like other mam-

The skeleton of a deer

WORLD BOOK illustration by John D. Dawson

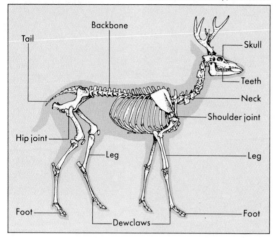

mals, deer are *warm-blooded,* which means their body temperature remains fairly constant regardless of the surrounding temperature. Deer have a covering of hair on the body that helps keep them warm in cold weather. Caribou of the Far North have a thick coat of hair. Most other deer have shorter, shiny hair that lies flat so that the animals' coat looks smooth. Deer in tropical regions have a much thinner coat.

Legs and hoofs. All deer have long, thin legs and are good runners. They move their legs rapidly and take long strides. A deer's foot is really two center toes. Each of the two toes is protected by a hard covering called a *hoof.* A deer runs on tiptoe with a springing or bouncing motion. Two other toes, called *dewclaws,* grow higher on the leg and have no use when the animal runs. The dewclaws often leave dots at the back of a deer's track in snow.

Deer use their speed to avoid predators. A frightened white-tailed deer can run as fast as 40 miles (64 kilometers) per hour and can leap 15 to 20 feet (4.6 to 6.1 meters) forward. Even the moose, with its large, powerful body, can run about 20 miles (32 kilometers) per hour.

Head. Deer have narrower heads and somewhat smaller noses and mouths than do cattle. The deer's lips move easily, and the animal uses them to grasp food. Most kinds of deer have only bottom teeth in the front of the mouth. A thick pad of rough skin takes the place of upper front teeth. The lower teeth press against this pad of skin when the deer tears off leaves and twigs to eat. The upper and lower back teeth have many sharp-pointed tips. The deer uses these teeth to chew its food.

A deer has large eyes at the sides of its head. However, the animal depends on its ears and its nose to catch the first warnings of danger. A deer has keen hearing and smell. Its large ears are always erect, and they can be moved to catch sounds from any direction. A deer can identify the direction from which a sound is coming. A deer usually faces into the wind when it eats or rests. The wind carries sounds and smells of approaching predators.

Antlers are outgrowths of bone that are part of a deer's skull. Their hard, bony structure and sharp points

make them extremely dangerous weapons. Male deer use antlers chiefly to fight for mates or for leadership of a herd. Deer that live in mild or cold climates shed their antlers each winter and begin to grow a new set in late spring. Deer that live in warm or hot climates may lose their antlers and grow new ones at other times of the year.

New antlers are soft and tender and grow rapidly. A thin layer of skin grows over the antlers and stimulates their development. This skin layer is called *velvet* because it is covered by short, fine hairs that give it a soft appearance. As the antlers reach full size, the velvet dries and the deer scrapes it off on the ground or against trees or bushes.

All antlers have branches that end in *tines* (points or prongs). But the shape of the antlers varies among species of deer. Moose and caribou are easy to distinguish from other deer by the antlers alone. Moose antlers have areas that are broad and flat. In caribou, a branch of one antler extends forward above the nose of the animal.

The size and shape of a deer's antlers depend on the animal's size, age, and health. A deer first grows antlers when it is 1 or 2 years old. In most deer, these first antlers are short and somewhat straight. Each year, the antlers grow longer and larger, and form branches.

The life of a deer

Deer have no permanent homes, dens, or nesting sites. They spend their lives roaming an area called a *home range* in search of food. Deer also claim and de-

The tracks of a deer

WORLD BOOK illustration by Tom Dolan

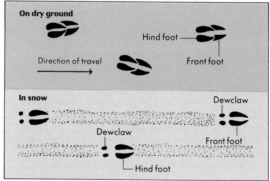

How a deer's antlers grow

Deer lose their antlers each winter and begin to grow new ones in late spring. The new antlers are soft and tender. Thin skin with short, fine hairs called *velvet* covers the growing antlers. Full-grown antlers are hard and strong, and have no velvet.

WORLD BOOK illustration by Tom Dolan

Deer of North America

These drawings show the differences in size, body shape, and antlers of the five major kinds of North American deer. The sizes given are the average shoulder height of the adult deer. Deer, especially the moose and elk, are among the largest wild animals of North America.

WORLD BOOK illustrations by John D. Dawson

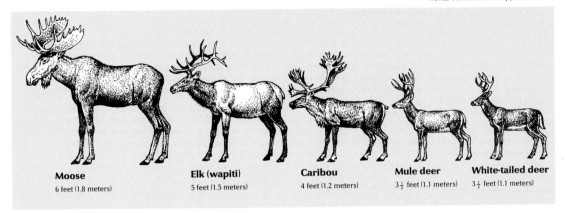

Moose	Elk (wapiti)	Caribou	Mule deer	White-tailed deer
6 feet (1.8 meters)	5 feet (1.5 meters)	4 feet (1.2 meters)	3½ feet (1.1 meters)	3½ feet (1.1 meters)

fend areas within the home range to attract mates. Deer may live in groups or alone, depending on their age, sex, and species. Moose spend most of their time alone. But caribou may form herds with up to 100,000 animals.

Many deer move to more favorable locations when the seasons change. Deer that live in the mountains move to lower lands for the winter. These deer usually stay near the edges of forests. There, trees and grasses supply food, and bushes serve as a place to sleep, to hide from predators, or to give birth.

Some deer migrate long distances each year. Caribou may travel 1,000 miles (1,600 kilometers) between feeding grounds. They spend the summer in the flat, marshy land of the Arctic Circle. In late summer, they gather in large herds and travel to warmer areas for the winter. In early spring, the caribou return north.

Young. A female deer carries her young inside her body for about six to nine months, depending on the species. She chooses a hidden spot away from other deer to give birth. The young deer remain hidden until they can walk well enough to follow their mother.

Fawns of white-tailed deer weigh from 3½ to 6 pounds (1.6 to 2.7 kilograms) at birth. They stay hidden for four to five weeks. Newborn moose calves weigh about 25 to 35 pounds (11 to 16 kilograms). They can follow their mother when they are about 10 days old. Caribou calves, most of which are born during the herd's spring migration, weigh about 10 pounds (4.5 kilograms) at birth. They can walk with the herd several hours later.

Most kinds of deer have one young at a time. Occasionally, twins are born. Chinese water deer, which live along the Yangtze River, give birth to the most young—four to seven fawns at a time.

Food. Deer eat a wide variety of plants and plant parts. In spring, when food is relatively plentiful, deer eat mostly grasses, flowers, buds, and young leaves. In summer, when grasses and leaves dry up, deer eat twigs, stems, and mature leaves. In winter, deer often gather in small herds and tramp the snow on their feeding grounds to reach twigs and small tree branches. When food becomes extremely scarce, deer will feed on bark and other hard parts of trees.

Deer do not chew their food well before swallowing it. A deer's stomach has four chambers. One chamber serves as a storage place, which enables deer to eat large amounts of food quickly. Thus, deer do not need to spend long periods at their feeding grounds, where predators might see them. Later, when a deer has found a safe place, the stored food is returned to the mouth in a ball-like glob. The deer then chews this food, called *cud.* After the chewed food has been swallowed, it goes to other parts of the stomach. Animals that digest their food in this way are called *ruminants* (in *World Book,* see **Ruminant**).

Habits. Deer use their keen senses, their knowledge of their home range, and their speed to avoid enemies. A healthy deer can outrun most predators, including bears, cougars, wolves, and human beings. But a deer's primary means of escaping danger is to avoid detection. Unless startled, most deer will stand motionless and let a predator pass by. White-tailed deer and mule deer feed only at dawn and dusk at the edges of forests, where they blend in best with their surroundings.

Wild deer live 10 to 20 years. In captivity, some deer live longer. However, the roe deer of Europe lives 10 to 12 years in the wild but only 3 to 7 years in a zoo.

See **Deer** in *World Book* for more information on Kinds of deer.

Where deer live

The yellow areas of the map show the parts of the world in which deer live. Deer live on every continent except Antarctica.

Desert is generally thought of as a hot, barren region that receives little rainfall. Rainfall is scarce in all desert regions, but deserts are not barren wastelands. Deserts have a wide variety of land formations and soil substances, and most of them have at least one permanent stream. Deserts cannot support the abundant plant and animal life found in humid climates. But many kinds of plants and animals thrive in deserts.

Scientists do not agree on a single definition for deserts. Some classify a desert as any region that receives an average of less than 10 inches (25 centimeters) of rain annually. Other scientists use the type of soil or vegetation to determine whether a region is a desert. Still others consider all these factors. They define a desert as a region that can support little vegetation because of both insufficient rainfall and dry soil.

Most deserts are in warm climates, but some regions near the North and South poles are also considered deserts. These areas are so cold that moisture freezes there and cannot stimulate plant growth. This article discusses deserts in warm climates.

Deserts cover about a seventh of the earth's land area. The largest desert in the world is the Sahara in northern Africa. The Sahara spreads over about $3\frac{1}{2}$ million square miles (9 million square kilometers). Other large deserts include the Australian Desert; the Arabian Desert on the Arabian Peninsula; and the Gobi in China and Mongolia. Deserts also cover about 500,000 square miles (1.3 million square kilometers) in North America.

Deserts do not support large numbers of people. People who do live in a desert region must adjust to the hot, dry climate. In North American deserts, for example, many Indians and Mexicans live in adobe or mud houses that provide insulation from the heat. Many desert dwellers in Africa and Asia are herders who move from place to place in search of water and grazing land. They live in tents and wrap themselves in long cloth robes for protection against the scorching sun and blowing sand. Air-conditioning and irrigation projects have made life more comfortable for other desert dwellers.

WORLD BOOK illustration by Jean Helmer

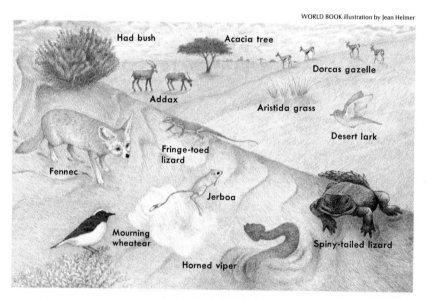

Many kinds of plants and animals live in desert regions. The illustration at the left shows some plant and animal life of the Sahara. These organisms have developed various ways to survive the extremely hot, dry climate of the desert.

Deserts cover about a seventh of the earth's land surface. Most deserts lie near the Tropic of Cancer and the Tropic of Capricorn. These regions are high-pressure zones in which cool air descends. The descending air becomes warm and absorbs moisture instead of releasing it as precipitation. Other deserts are in (1) regions separated from the ocean by mountains and (2) coastal areas.

Desert

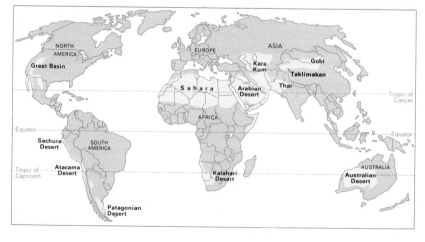

WORLD BOOK map

Digestive system is the group of organs that break down food into smaller particles, or molecules, for use in the human body. This breakdown makes it possible for the smaller digested particles to pass through the intestinal wall into the bloodstream. The particles are then distributed to nourish all parts of the body.

The fats, proteins, and carbohydrates (starches and sugars) in foods are made up of very complex molecules and must be digested, or broken down. When digestion is completed, starches and complex sugars are broken down into simple sugars, fats are digested to fatty acids and glycerol, and proteins are digested to amino acids and peptides. Simple sugars, fatty acids and glycerol, and amino acids and peptides are the digested foods that can be absorbed into the bloodstream. Such foods as vitamins, minerals, and water do not need digestion.

From mouth to stomach. Digestion begins in the mouth. Chewing is very important to good digestion for two reasons. When chewed food is ground into fine particles, the digestive juices can react more easily. As the food is chewed, it is moistened and mixed with saliva, which contains the enzyme *ptyalin.* Ptyalin changes some of the starches in the food to sugar.

After the food is swallowed, it passes through the esophagus into the stomach. In the stomach it is thoroughly mixed with a digestive juice by a vigorous, to-and-fro churning motion. This motion is caused by contractions of strong muscles in the stomach walls.

The digestive juice in the stomach is called *gastric juice.* It contains hydrochloric acid and the enzyme *pepsin.* This juice begins the digestion of protein foods such as meat, eggs, and milk. Starches, sugars, and fats are not digested by the gastric juice. After a meal, some food remains in the stomach for two to five hours. But liquids and small particles begin to empty almost immediately. Food that has been churned, partly digested, and changed to a thick liquid is called *chyme.* Chyme passes from the stomach into the small intestine.

In the small intestine, the digestive process is completed on the partly digested food by pancreatic juice, intestinal juice, and bile. The pancreatic juice is produced by the pancreas and pours into the small intestine through a tube, or duct. The pancreatic juice contains the enzymes *trypsin, amylase,* and *lipase.* Trypsin breaks down the partly digested proteins, amylase changes starch into simple sugars, and lipase splits fats into fatty acids and glycerol. The intestinal juice is produced by the walls of the small intestine. It has milder digestive effects than the pancreatic juice, but carries out similar digestion. Bile is produced in the liver, stored in the gall bladder, and flows into the small intestine through the bile duct. Bile does not contain enzymes, but it does contain chemicals that help break down and absorb fats.

When the food is completely digested, it is absorbed by tiny blood and lymph vessels in the walls of the small intestine. It is then carried into the circulation for nourishment of the body. Food particles are small enough to pass through the walls of the intestine and blood vessels only when they are completely digested.

Almost no digestion occurs in the large intestine. The large intestine stores waste food products and absorbs small amounts of water and minerals.

Digestion

Digestion is the process that breaks food down into simple substances the body can use. The digestive system includes all the organs and tissues involved in this process.

Parts of the digestive system

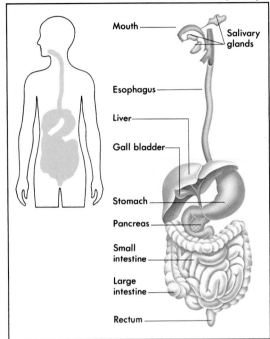

WORLD BOOK illustrations by Colin Bidgood

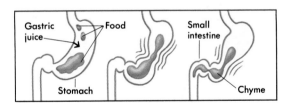

The stomach churns food and adds gastric juice, which breaks down proteins. Food exits the stomach as *chyme,* a thick liquid.

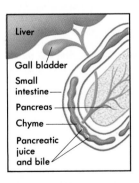

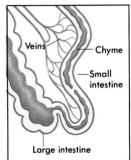

Bile and pancreatic juice act on the chyme in the upper small intestine. Pancreatic juice digests proteins, fats, and sugars and starches. Bile helps break down fats.

Digested foods are absorbed into the bloodstream from the small intestine. The indigestible remains pass into the large intestine and are eliminated from the body.

Dinosaurs of the Jurassic Period (205 million to 138 million years ago) included the longest known dinosaur, the 90-foot (27-meter) diplodocus, *above right*. Other dinosaurs included the plated stegosaurus, *upper left*, the allosaurus, *center*, and the camptosaurus, *lower right.*

Dinosaur

Dinosaur is the name of a kind of reptile that lived millions of years ago. The word *dinosaur* comes from two Greek words meaning *terrible lizard*. Dinosaurs were not lizards. But the size of some dinosaurs was terrifying. The biggest ones were the largest animals ever to live on land. They weighed more than 10 times as much as a full-grown elephant. Only a few kinds of whales grow to be larger than these dinosaurs.

The first dinosaurs appeared on the earth around 220 million years ago. For about 150 million years, they ruled the land. They lived in most parts of the world and in a variety of surroundings, from swamps to open plains. Then about 63 million years ago, dinosaurs died out rather suddenly.

Dinosaurs varied greatly in size, appearance, and habits. But the most famous kinds include such giants as the apatosaurus, diplodocus, and tyrannosaurus rex. Apatosaurs, also called brontosaurs, grew about 80 feet (24 meters) long. The diplodocus grew even longer—to about 90 feet (27 meters). Both the apatosaurus and the diplodocus were plant-eaters. They had a tiny head and

an extremely long neck and tail. Tyrannosaurs were fierce meat-eaters. They stood almost 10 feet (3 meters) tall at the hips and had an enormous head and long, pointed teeth. But not all dinosaurs were giants. The smallest kind was about the size of a chicken.

In some ways, dinosaurs were like most present-day reptiles. For example, some had teeth, bones, and skin like those of crocodiles and other reptiles living today. Many probably were also about as intelligent as crocodiles. But dinosaurs differed from present-day reptiles in other ways. For example, no modern reptiles grow as large as large dinosaurs. Another important difference is in posture. The legs of lizards, turtles, and most other reptiles are pushed out to the sides of the body, giving the animals a sprawling posture. But a dinosaur's legs were under the body like the legs of a horse. This leg structure lifted the dinosaur's body off the ground and enabled some kinds to walk on their hind legs.

Dinosaurs lived during a time in the earth's history called the *Mesozoic Era.* This era lasted from about 240 million to 63 million years ago. The Mesozoic Era is also called the *Age of Reptiles* because reptiles ruled the land, sea, and sky during that time. The most important reptiles belonged to a group of animals called *archo-*

WORLD BOOK illustrations by Alex Ebel

Dinosaurs of the Cretaceous Period (138 million to 63 million years ago) included the tyranno-saurus rex, *upper left,* and the horned triceratops. Two anatosaurs stand in the foreground. Flow-ering plants appeared during this period, and opossums, snakes, and lizards were common.

saurs (ruling reptiles). In addition to dinosaurs, this group included *thecodonts,* the ancestors of the dino-saurs; crocodiles; and flying reptiles. By the close of the Mesozoic Era, all archosaurs except crocodiles had died out, and the Age of Reptiles ended.

Scientists do not know why dinosaurs disappeared. They once thought that dinosaurs had left no *descend-ants* (offspring). But scientists now believe that certain small meat-eating dinosaurs were the ancestors of birds.

Scientists learn about dinosaurs by studying dinosaur *fossils*—that is, the preserved bones, teeth, eggs, and tracks of dinosaurs. They also study living reptiles and other animals that resemble dinosaurs in some ways.

The world of the dinosaurs

When dinosaurs lived, the earth was much different from the way it is today. For example, the Alps, the Him-alaya, and many other surface features had not yet been formed. The first flowering plants did not appear until late in the Mesozoic Era. The mammals of the Mesozoic Era were extremely small, and many of the plants and animals that were common then are now rare or extinct.

The land and climate. Scientists believe that the continents once formed a single land mass surrounded by an enormous sea. During the Mesozoic Era, this land mass began to break up into continents. The continents slowly drifted apart toward their present locations. But for many centuries, dinosaurs could wander freely over the land connections between continents.

As the continents moved apart, their surface features and climate changed. For a time, shallow seas covered much of North America, Europe, and southern Asia. Thick forests bordered drier plains, and swamps and deltas lined the seacoasts. Later in the Mesozoic Era, the Rocky Mountains began to form, and the seas drained from North America.

Throughout much of the Mesozoic Era, dinosaurs probably lived in an almost tropical climate. Areas near the seas may have had mild, moist weather all year. In-land regions probably had an annual dry season. To-ward the end of the Mesozoic Era, the climate grew cooler and drier.

See **Dinosaur** in *World Book* for more informa-tion on the following topics:

- The world of the dinosaurs
- Kinds of dinosaurs
- How dinosaurs lived
- Why dinosaurs died out
- Learning about dinosaurs

When dinosaurs lived

Dinosaurs lived during the Mesozoic Era, which lasted from about 240 million to 63 million years ago. The era is divided into three periods—the Triassic, the Jurassic, and the Cretaceous. Some kinds of dinosaurs lived throughout the era. Others lived during only one or two periods.

Corals and mollusks were common. Fish appeared. Land was bare.	Algae were plentiful.	Spore-bearing plants appeared on land.	Forests developed, and insects and amphibians appeared.	Mosses developed. Reptiles appeared.

Paleozoic Era (570 million to 240 million years ago)

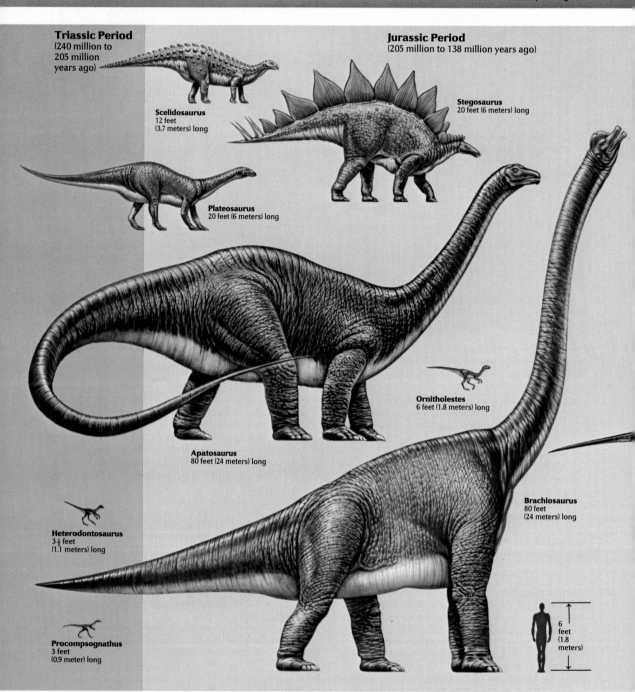

Triassic Period (240 million to 205 million years ago)

Jurassic Period (205 million to 138 million years ago)

Scelidosaurus 12 feet (3.7 meters) long

Stegosaurus 20 feet (6 meters) long

Plateosaurus 20 feet (6 meters) long

Apatosaurus 80 feet (24 meters) long

Ornitholestes 6 feet (1.8 meters) long

Brachiosaurus 80 feet (24 meters) long

Heterodontosaurus 3½ feet (1.1 meters) long

Procompsognathus 3 feet (0.9 meter) long

6 feet (1.8 meters)

WORLD BOOK illustrations by Alex Ebel

| Seed plants developed. | Dinosaurs and mammals appeared. | Birds appeared. | Flowering plants developed. | Dinosaurs died out. | Fruits, grains, and grasses developed. | Early human beings appeared. |

Mesozoic Era (240 million to 63 million years ago) **Cenozoic Era** (63 million years ago to the present)

Cretaceous Period
(138 million to 63 million years ago)

Camptosaurus
15 feet (4.8 meters) long

Ankylosaurus 15 feet (4.8 meters) long

Corythosaurus
30 feet (9 meters) long

Iguanodon
30 feet (9 meters) long

Compsognathus
2 ½ feet (0.8 meter) long

Torosaurus
30 feet
(9 meters) long

Deinonychus 9 feet (2.7 meters) long

Allosaurus
30 feet (9 meters) long

Tyrannosaurus rex
40 feet (12 meters) long

Ornithomimus
14 feet (4.3 meters) long

Dog

Dog is a popular pet throughout the world. At least 12,000 years ago, dogs became the first animals to be tamed. Today, these affectionate and obedient animals can be found almost anywhere there are people to love and serve. About 49 million dogs live as pets in the United States, and about 3 million live in Canada.

Many people recognize only such favorite breeds of dogs as the collie, German shepherd, and poodle. But through careful breeding, human beings have produced hundreds of breeds. Each breed has its own particular abilities and physical features. Some breeds have highly unusual characteristics. For example, the chow chow has a black tongue. The Mexican hairless has no hair except for a small patch on top of its head. The coat of the shar-pei is harsh in texture. A shar-pei puppy's skin is so loose that it appears too large for the dog's body. The basenji, which originated in Africa, is the only dog that cannot bark.

Dogs vary greatly in size. The smallest breed is the Chihuahua. On the average, Chihuahuas weigh only about 4 pounds (1.8 kilograms) and stand about 5 inches (13 centimeters) high at the shoulders. The tallest breed is the Irish wolfhound, which may grow 34 inches (86 centimeters) in height. The St. Bernard is the heaviest dog. It weighs as much as 200 pounds (90 kilograms).

Dogs belong to a small family of meat-eating animals that also includes wolves, coyotes, foxes, and jackals. Dogs resemble these animals in body structure and behavior. The dingo of Australia and certain animals that live in other parts of the world are commonly called *wild dogs.*

The body of a dog

The size, shape, and other characteristics of a dog's body vary widely from breed to breed. But in spite of their differences, all dogs share certain basic physical features.

Coat. Most dogs have two coats—an outer coat of long *guard hairs* and an undercoat of shorter, fluffy hair. The guard hairs protect the dog against rain and snow, and the undercoat keeps the dog warm. Most dogs shed the undercoat in late spring and grow it back in autumn. Dogs also have a number of long, stiff whiskers about the mouth. The whiskers serve as highly sensitive touch organs.

The texture, length, and color of the coat differ greatly among the various breeds. The hair may be curly, as on the poodle, or straight, as on the German shepherd. The collie's coat feels rough, and the Kerry blue terrier's coat is soft. Such breeds as the Afghan hound and the Pekingese have a long, silky coat. The boxer and the whippet have an extremely short coat. The color of the coat may vary even within a breed. For example, a Labrador

Some breeds of dogs have extremely unusual characteristics. A shar-pei puppy, *left,* has a wrinkled coat that looks too large for its body. A black tongue is the distinguishing feature of the chow chow, *center.* The puli, *right,* has a coat that becomes tangled into long, ropelike cords.

WORLD BOOK photo by Brent Jones   WORLD BOOK photo   WORLD BOOK photo by Dave G. Wacker

Dogs provide companionship for people of all ages. These children's affectionate friend is a *mongrel* (mixed-breed dog). In general, mongrels have a good disposition and make excellent pets.

WORLD BOOK photo

Specially trained dogs perform many tasks. This German shepherd uses its keen sense of smell to detect drugs being smuggled into the United States.

WORLD BOOK photo

retriever's coat may be black, yellow, or chocolate-brown.

Body structure is determined mainly by a dog's skeleton. Female dogs have 310 bones. Male dogs have one additional bone, located in the penis. Although all breeds have the same number of bones, the size and shape of the bones differ greatly from breed to breed. For example, the basset hound has very short, thick leg bones. In contrast, the greyhound has unusually long leg bones.

Dogs have four toes on each foot plus an extra thumblike toe called a *dewclaw* on each front foot. Some dogs also have a dewclaw on each hind foot. Dewclaws do not reach the ground. They serve no purpose and can easily be caught on objects and torn. For this reason, a veterinarian should remove the hind dewclaws when a puppy is a few days old. Each of a dog's toes has a blunt toenail, or claw. But unlike cats, dogs cannot pull their claws back. The bottoms of a dog's paws have cushiony pads covered with tough skin.

Some dogs, such as borzois and collies, have an unusually long, narrow skull. The skull shape gives the dogs a long, slender face. Some other breeds, including bulldogs and Pekingeses, have a very short, broad skull, which makes the face look pushed in. Most dogs have a skull shape between these two extremes.

Puppies have 32 temporary teeth, which they begin to lose when they are about 5 months old. Adult dogs have 42 teeth. A dog uses its 12 small front teeth, called *incisors,* to pick up food. The dog tears meat with its 4 large, pointed *canine teeth,* or *fangs.* It uses the 26 other teeth, called the *premolars* and *molars,* to grind and crush food.

Many breeds of dogs have pointed ears that stand straight up. Other breeds have *pendulous* ears, which hang down. Many people have the ears of certain pendulous-eared breeds *cropped* (cut) to make them stand up. Such breeds include Doberman pinschers and miniature schnauzers. Cropping is done at an age when puppies are highly sensitive to pain. Some countries have outlawed cropping as a cruel practice. On terriers and some other breeds, the tail is also *docked* (cut short). Docking is done a few days after birth and so is much less painful than ear cropping.

Dog terms

Bitch is an adult female dog.
Canine is another word for *dog* or *doglike.* The term comes from *canis,* the Latin word for *dog.*
Crossbred means a dog whose parents belong to different breeds.
Dog is an adult male dog. However, the term is generally used for all dogs, regardless of age or sex.
Litter refers to a group of puppies born at one time.
Mongrel is a dog of such mixed ancestry that no one breed can be recognized.
Pedigree is a record of a purebred dog's ancestors.
Puppy is a dog less than 1 year old.
Purebred means a dog whose parents belong to the same breed.
Studbook is a book in which breeders register the pedigrees of dogs.
Whelp is an unweaned puppy—that is, one that still feeds on its mother's milk. The term also means to give birth to puppies.

Body functions of a dog differ only slightly from those of a human being. For example, a dog's heart beats 70 to 120 times per minute. The human heart, on the average, beats 70 to 80 times per minute. A dog's normal body temperature is 101.5° F. (38.6° C), only a little higher than a person's normal temperature of 98.6° F. (37° C). But unlike human beings, dogs do not cool the body by sweating. Instead, a dog sticks out its tongue and pants. As the dog pants, evaporation of water from the mouth cools its body. Dogs do have sweat glands, but they play only a small role in reducing the body temperature.

Senses. A dog's most highly developed sense is its sense of smell. Dogs recognize objects chiefly by smell, much as people recognize them by sight. Dogs can detect some odors that are millions of times too faint for people to detect. By sniffing a group of objects, a dog can pick out the ones that a particular person touched. Fluid from a gland inside the nose keeps the tip of a dog's nose moist. The moisture helps a dog detect odors. A dog also licks its nose to help keep it moist. In addition, a dog's whiskers may sense the wind direction and so help the dog determine the direction from which an odor is coming.

Dogs also have a much better sense of hearing than people have. Dogs can hear high-pitched sounds far

The sizes of dogs   The Chihuahua is the smallest breed of dog. The St. Bernard is the heaviest breed, and the Irish wolfhound is the tallest. Other breeds of dogs range in size between these extremes. The measurements given for each dog pictured below are the average weight and shoulder height for the breed.

WORLD BOOK illustration by Jean Helmer

Chihuahua
1-6 lb. (0.5-3 kg)
5 in. (13 cm)

Cocker spaniel
22-28 lb. (10-13 kg)
14-15 in. (36-38 cm)

Collie
50-75 lb. (23-34 kg)
22-26 in. (56-66 cm)

St. Bernard
165-200 lb. (75-90 kg)
25½-30 in. (65-76 cm)

Irish wolfhound
126-145 lb. (57-66 kg)
32-34 in. (81-86 cm)

The body of a dog

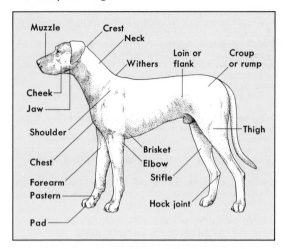

Muzzle
Crest
Neck
Withers
Loin or flank
Croup or rump
Cheek
Jaw
Shoulder
Brisket
Thigh
Chest
Elbow
Forearm
Stifle
Pastern
Hock joint
Pad

The skeleton of a dog

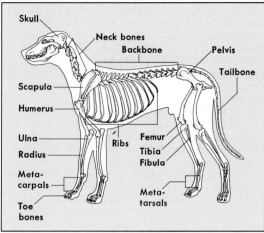

Skull
Neck bones
Backbone
Pelvis
Tailbone
Scapula
Humerus
Ulna
Radius
Ribs
Femur
Tibia
Fibula
Meta-carpals
Meta-tarsals
Toe bones

WORLD BOOK illustrations by Jean Helmer

above the limit of human hearing. They can also hear sounds at much greater distances than people can. In addition, dogs have a highly developed ability to recognize different complicated sounds. For example, many dogs can recognize the sound of their owner's automobile and so tell it apart from other cars.

Dogs cannot see as well as people. Dogs detect movement well, which helps make them good hunters. But they see patterns and forms much more poorly than people do. Dogs are also color blind. They can tell colors apart only by recognizing various shades of gray.

The senses of taste and touch are well developed in all breeds of dogs. However, some dogs are much more sensitive to touch and pain than others. Toy breeds are the most sensitive, and breeds used for hunting or attacking game are the least sensitive. Dogs will groom each other and enjoy being stroked and petted by people. But dogs that have been mistreated may show "touch-shyness" and avoid any human contact.

WORLD BOOK photo

A mother nurses her puppies until they are about 6 weeks old. Most litters consist of 1 to 12 pups, but litters of 15 or more have been reported. These dogs are Chesapeake Bay retrievers.

The life of a dog

Life history. A female dog carries her young for nine weeks before they are born. In most cases, a dog gives birth to a litter of 1 to 12 puppies, though litters of 15 or more have been reported. Dogs are mammals, and so they feed their young on milk produced by the mother's body. A mother dog nurses her pups until they are about 6 weeks old.

Puppies are born with their eyes closed and their ears sealed. Their eyes and ears open about 13 to 15 days after birth. Until that time, they depend entirely on their senses of touch and smell to detect things in their environment. These senses are well developed at or shortly after birth. During the third week of life, puppies begin to walk and to respond to sights and sounds.

Between 4 and 10 weeks of age, a puppy forms emotional attachments to its mother and its littermates. If the puppy is to become a good pet, it must have contact with people during this period. Such contact is the key to developing a close relationship with the dog that will last throughout its life. For this reason, the ideal time to adopt a puppy is when it is about 6 to 8 weeks old.

Dogs become fully grown at 8 months to 2 years of age, depending on the size of the breed. Large dogs develop more slowly than smaller breeds. It is difficult to compare the age of a dog to that of a human being. However, a 6-month-old puppy generally compares in development to a 10-year-old child, and a 2-year-old dog compares to a 24-year-old person. After a dog's second year, each year equals about four or five years of a person's life. On the average, dogs live about 12 to 15 years. Most of the larger breeds have shorter life spans, however.

See **Dog** in *World Book* for more information on the following topics:

- Kinds of dogs
- The life of a dog
- Choosing a dog
- Caring for a dog
- Training a dog
- History

Dolphin, *DAHL fuhn,* is a small, toothed whale. Like all whales, dolphins are mammals, not fish. Mammals, unlike fish, feed their young with milk that is produced in the mother's body. Also unlike fish, dolphins have lungs and are *warm-blooded*—that is, their body temperature always stays about the same, regardless of the temperature of their surroundings. Many scientists believe that dolphins rank among the most intelligent animals, along with chimpanzees and dogs.

Dolphins and other whales make up a group of mammals called *cetaceans.* This article deals with *marine dolphins.* Most species of marine dolphins live only in salt water. These animals inhabit nearly all the oceans. Many species remain near land for most of their lives, but some marine dolphins live in the open sea. A different family of cetaceans, called *river dolphins,* live in fresh or slightly salty water. The word *dolphin* also refers to a large game fish. In *World Book,* see **River dolphin; Dolphin** (fish).

Marine dolphins are closely related to porpoises, another group of sea mammals. Most zoologists classify marine dolphins and porpoises into one family consisting of about 40 species. The chief differences between dolphins and porpoises occur in the snout and teeth. "True" dolphins have a beaklike snout and cone-shaped teeth. "True" porpoises have a rounded snout and flat or spade-shaped teeth. But these characteristics are not present in all species. Some scientists distinguish between dolphins and porpoises. Other experts use the term *dolphin* or the term *porpoise* for all members of the family. In this article, the word *dolphin* refers to all members of the family of marine dolphins and porpoises.

Types of dolphins

The various species of dolphins range from 4 to 30 feet (1.4 to 9 meters) long and weigh from 100 pounds (45 kilograms) to 5 short tons (4.5 metric tons). The most familiar types include *bottle-nosed dolphins, common dolphins,* and *common porpoises.*

Bottle-nosed dolphins are the best-known species. Their short beaks give these dolphins an expression that looks like a smile. Most of the performing dolphins in amusement parks, aquariums, and zoos are bottle-nosed dolphins. Members of this species measure up to 15 feet (4.6 meters) long and can weigh as much as 440 pounds (200 kilograms). They are gray, but their backs are darker than their undersides. Bottle-nosed dolphins show apparent great friendliness toward people and often swim alongside ships. They also adapt well to life in captivity.

Bottle-nosed dolphins live in warm or tropical waters. Most of them stay within 100 miles (160 kilometers) of land. Many live in bays and protected inlets, where the water is relatively shallow. Bottle-nosed dolphins frequently appear off the coast of Florida. They range as far north as Japan and Norway and as far south as Argentina, New Zealand, and South Africa.

Common dolphins have several distinct features. For example, a dark band around their eyes extends to the end of their long, narrow beak. Common dolphins also have black backs, white undersides, and prominent gray and yellowish-brown stripes on their sides. These dolphins grow from 6 to 8 feet (1.8 to 2.4 meters) long and

Jim Annan

A trained dolphin, *above,* leaps high out of the water to snatch an object from a trainer's hand. A dolphin can jump through a hoop and use its mouth to catch and throw a ball.

weigh up to 165 pounds (75 kilograms).

Common dolphins live in warm or tropical waters. They often swim in large schools and are frequently seen in the open ocean. Common dolphins sometimes follow ships for many miles. As they do so, these playful dolphins may leap out of the water.

Common porpoises are one of the smallest species of dolphins. They seldom grow longer than 6 feet (1.8 meters), and they weigh from 100 to 120 pounds (45 to 54 kilograms). These dolphins, which are sometimes called *harbor porpoises,* usually travel alone or in small groups. They avoid people and lack the playfulness of some other species.

Common porpoises have black backs and white undersides. Many live in the cool waters of the North Atlantic Ocean and in other oceans, but they are rarely seen in the tropics. Members of this species sometimes swim up rivers in search of food. They have been seen in several major European rivers, including the Thames in England and the Seine in France.

Other species include the largest dolphins, which are called *killer whales.* They measure as long as 30 feet (9 meters) and may weigh 4 or 5 short tons (3.6 or 4.5 metric tons). Members of another species, known as *pilot whales,* or *blackfish,* grow 15 to 20 feet (4.6 to 6 meters) long. Pilot whales differ from other large dolphins because of their almost entirely black bodies and their bulging foreheads. Among the most numerous species of dolphins are *spinner dolphins,* which sometimes spin on their sides when they leap out of the water.

Many kinds of dolphins have distinguishing colors or

other markings. For example, *Risso's dolphins* are brown and gray, and most of them have many irregular white streaks. *White-sided dolphins* have gray, white, and yellow stripes on their sides. Their colorful markings make them popular attractions at many aquariums and zoos. *Spotted dolphins* are named for their white spots. *Striped dolphins* have black stripes on their undersides. *Dall's porpoises* are identified by their black bodies and white sides and are slightly larger than common porpoises.

The bodies of dolphins

All dolphins have torpedo-shaped bodies, which enable the animals to move through the water quickly and easily. They have a pair of paddle-shaped forelimbs called *flippers,* but no hindlimbs. Most species of dolphins also have a *dorsal fin* on their back. This fin, along with the flippers, helps balance the animal when it swims. Powerful tail fins, called *flukes,* propel dolphins through the water.

Some kinds of dolphins

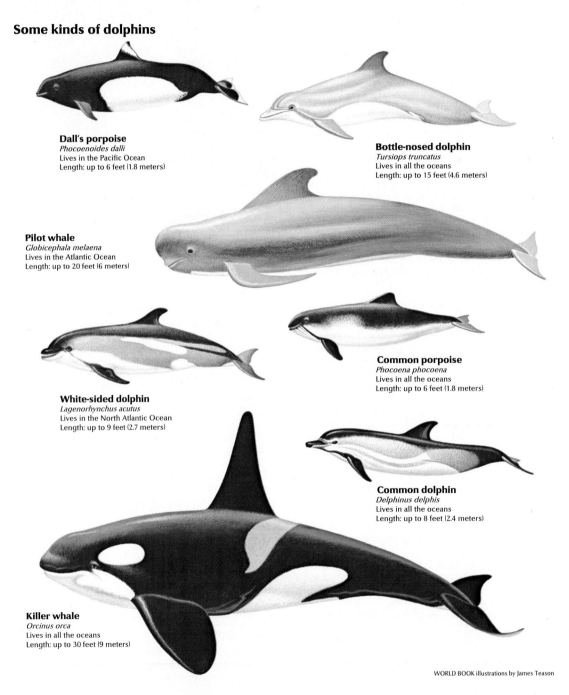

Dall's porpoise
Phocoenoides dalli
Lives in the Pacific Ocean
Length: up to 6 feet (1.8 meters)

Bottle-nosed dolphin
Tursiops truncatus
Lives in all the oceans
Length: up to 15 feet (4.6 meters)

Pilot whale
Globicephala melaena
Lives in the Atlantic Ocean
Length: up to 20 feet (6 meters)

Common porpoise
Phocoena phocoena
Lives in all the oceans
Length: up to 6 feet (1.8 meters)

White-sided dolphin
Lagenorhynchus acutus
Lives in the North Atlantic Ocean
Length: up to 9 feet (2.7 meters)

Common dolphin
Delphinus delphis
Lives in all the oceans
Length: up to 8 feet (2.4 meters)

Killer whale
Orcinus orca
Lives in all the oceans
Length: up to 30 feet (9 meters)

WORLD BOOK illustrations by James Teason

The skin of dolphins is smooth and rubbery. A layer of fat, called *blubber,* lies beneath the skin. The blubber keeps dolphins warm and acts as a storage place for food. It is lighter than water, and so it probably also helps dolphins stay afloat.

Like all other mammals, dolphins have lungs. The animals must surface regularly to breathe air and usually do so once or twice a minute. A dolphin breathes through a *blowhole,* a nostril on top of its head. The animal seals its blowhole by means of powerful muscles most of the time while underwater.

Dolphins have a highly developed sense of hearing. They can hear a wide range of low- and high-pitched sounds, including many that are beyond human hearing. Dolphins also have good vision, and the entire surface of their bodies has a keen sense of touch. All these senses function well both above and below the surface of the water. Dolphins have no sense of smell and little, if any, sense of taste.

Dolphins have a natural sonar system called *echolocation,* which helps them locate underwater objects in their path. A dolphin locates such objects by making a series of clicking and whistling sounds. These sounds leave the animal's body through the *melon,* an organ on top of the head. The melon consists of special fatty tissue that directs the sounds forward. Echoes are produced when the sounds reflect from an object in front of the dolphin. By listening to the echoes, the animal determines the location of the object.

Most kinds of dolphins have a large number of teeth. Some species have more than 200. Dolphins use their teeth only to grasp their prey, which are chiefly fish and octopuslike animals called *squids.* Dolphins swallow their food whole and usually eat the prey headfirst.

The life of dolphins

Most dolphins mate in spring and early summer. During courtship, the males, called *bulls,* and the females, called *cows,* bump heads and also take part in other rituals. The pregnancy period for most species of dolphins lasts from 10 to 12 months. The females almost always give birth to one baby, called a *calf,* at a time. One or more female dolphins may help the mother during birth. The calf is born tailfirst and immediately swims to the surface, sometimes with its mother's help, for its first breath of air. A newborn dolphin is about a third as long as its mother.

Wometco Miami Seaquarium

Baby dolphins are born in the water. The mother and other female dolphins push the infant to the surface for its first breath of air. The mother nurses its baby with milk for about a year. Dolphins breathe through a *blowhole* on top of the head.

Female dolphins, like all female mammals, have special glands that produce milk. The calf drinks the milk from its mother's nipples. The females nurse and protect their young for more than a year. Male dolphins take no part in caring for the young.

Most species of dolphins live at least 25 years. Some pilot whales reach 50 years of age. Sharks are the chief natural enemies of dolphins.

Some dolphins die after swimming into extremely shallow water and stranding themselves on the shore. The animals cannot live long out of water because their bodies become overheated. Scientists do not know why dolphins beach themselves. Some believe the beachings result from a malfunction in the echolocation system.

See **Dolphin** in *World Book* for more information on The life of dolphins and Dolphins and people.

Tom Stack

Many sharp teeth line the dolphin's jaws. A fatty organ called the *melon* causes a bulge on top of the animal's head.

The body of a common dolphin

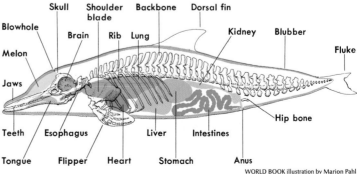

Skull · Shoulder blade · Backbone · Dorsal fin · Blowhole · Brain · Rib · Lung · Kidney · Blubber · Melon · Fluke · Jaws · Hip bone · Teeth · Esophagus · Liver · Intestines · Tongue · Flipper · Heart · Stomach · Anus

WORLD BOOK illustration by Marion Pahl

Dr. Paul A. Johnsgard

A wood duck and her ducklings stay close together so she can protect them from enemies. Most ducklings can swim on the day they are born, but they cannot fly for several weeks.

Duck is a bird with waterproof feathers and webbed feet. Ducks are related to geese and swans. But ducks have shorter necks and wings and flatter bills, and they quack or whistle rather than honk. Male ducks are called *drakes,* and females are called *ducks.*

Ducks live throughout the world in wetlands, including marshes and areas near rivers, ponds, lakes, and oceans. They live in arctic, temperate, and tropical regions for some or all of the year. Many kinds of ducks migrate long distances annually between their breeding grounds, where they rest and raise their young, and their wintering areas, where the water does not freeze. Some ducks migrate thousands of miles.

The features of a duck

Ducks spend a lot of time in water, where their webbed feet serve as paddles for swimming and diving. They are graceful on water, but waddle clumsily when walking on land because their legs are set on the sides and toward the rear of the body. Most common wild ducks weigh from 2 to 4 pounds (0.9 to 1.8 kilograms), but some of the smaller species weigh less than 1 pound (0.45 kilogram).

The various kinds of ducks get their food in different ways, depending on their body features. Some ducks extend their long necks down through shallow water to pick food off the bottom. Others dive for food in deep water. Ducks that sift food have wide bills with edges that strain seeds, insects, and snails from the water. Some ducks have short bills that they use to pry barnacles from rocks or to grab clams. Others have long, narrow bills with sawlike edges for catching and holding fish.

Ducks protect themselves from cold water by waterproofing their feathers. They use their bills to rub the

feathers with a waxy oil from a gland at the base of the tail. Under the oiled feathers is a layer of soft, fluffy feathers called *down.* Down helps insulate a duck's body because it traps air under the outside feathers.

Most drakes have bright-colored feathers. Their colors include green, blue, red, and chestnut. But drakes of some species are mostly black and white. Most females are brown and can hide by blending with the surroundings when incubating eggs or taking care of ducklings.

The life of a duck

Ducks seek mates during winter. The bright colors of the drakes attract females. A female usually leads her drake to the breeding grounds during the spring migration, often returning to the same wetland where she was hatched. The ability of ducks and other birds to return to the same places each year is called *homing behavior.* Once on the breeding grounds, each male defends a small territory from which he drives away other males or other pairs of his own species. The female builds a nest in a clump of grass or reeds, or in a hole in a tree.

Ducklings. The female duck lays from 5 to 12 eggs. After she starts to sit on the eggs to warm and protect them, the drake leaves to join other males. The ducklings hatch from three weeks to a month later.

Female redhead ducks of North America sometimes lay eggs in the nests of other species. They often de-

Two types of duck bills

Diving ducks have long, narrow bills, *top,* with toothlike edges to hold fish. Dabbling ducks have short, broad bills for prying.

WORLD BOOK diagram by Margaret Estey

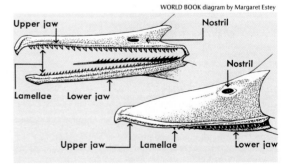

Facts in brief

Names: *Male,* drake; *female,* duck; *young,* duckling; *group,* flock.
Incubation period: 23 to 30 days, depending on species.
Number of eggs: 5 to 12, depending on species.
Length of life: 2 to 12 years (shoveler and mallard reported to 20 years).
Where found: All parts of the world except Antarctica.

pend on the other ducks to hatch the eggs and care for the young. Most ducklings look alike, and the new mother accepts them.

Ducklings can run, swim, and find food for themselves within 36 hours of hatching. A group of ducklings is called a *brood.* A mother duck keeps her brood together so she can protect it from predators. Animals that prey on ducklings include turtles, raccoons, hawks, and large fish. Sometimes the ducklings in one brood mix with another. As a result, some females end up with broods of 15 to 25 ducklings, while others have only 2 or 3. Ducklings grow quickly and have most of their feathers in about a month. They learn to fly in five to eight weeks.

Food. Ducks that do not dive for food are called *dabbling ducks.* They eat mostly wetland plants, including the seeds of aquatic weeds, grasses, sedges, and rushes. They also eat insects and other small animals that they find on or under the water. *Pochard ducks* dive to the bottom for roots, seeds, snails, insects, and small clams. In fresh water, pochards and dabbling ducks may eat many kinds of insects, including beetles, bugs, and dragonflies. In salt water, they feed on snails, barnacles, shrimp, and mussels, as well as on plants. *Wood ducks* eat acorns, small fruits, insects, and seeds.

Mergansers, a kind of sea duck, eat mostly fish, which they catch in either salt water or fresh water. *Eiders* and other sea ducks pull crabs, barnacles, and shrimp off rocks and weeds. They dig snails, cockles, mussels, and clams from the bottom, and also catch fish.

See **Duck** in *World Book* for more information on The life of a duck, Kinds of ducks, and Protection of ducks.

Types of ducks   Scientists classify ducks into eight separate groups called *tribes.* Members of six of the tribes are illustrated below. They are the dabbling duck, pochard, perching duck, sea duck, shelduck, and stiff-tailed duck. The other two tribes are called the steamer duck and the torrent duck.

Shelduck illustration by John F. Eggert; other illustrations by Athos Menaboni

Dabbling ducks (*Anatini*)

Mallard
Anas platyrhynchos
Found in Northern Hemisphere
(28 inches, or 71 centimeters)

Pochards (*Aythyini*)

Greater scaup
Aythya marila
Found in Northern Hemisphere
(20 inches, or 51 centimeters)

Perching ducks (*Cairinini*)

Mandarin duck
Aix galericulata
Found in eastern Asia and Japan
(20 inches, or 51 centimeters)

Sea ducks (*Mergini*)

Red-breasted merganser
Mergus serrator
Found in polar region, Northern Hemisphere
(23 inches, or 58 centimeters)

Shelducks (*Tadornini*)

Common shelduck
Tadorna tadorna
Found in Europe and Asia
(24 inches, or 61 centimeters)

Stiff-tailed ducks (*Oxyurini*)

Ruddy duck
Oxyura jamaicensis
Found in North and South America and West Indies
(17 inches, or 43 centimeters)

WORLD BOOK illustration by Stanley W. Galli

A bald eagle, its powerful wings spread wide, returns to its *aerie* (nest) with food for its hungry young. The bald eagle's white head feathers give it the appearance of baldness.

Eagle is the name of some of the largest and most powerful birds in the world. Among birds of prey, only condors and some species of vultures are larger than eagles. Eagles look fierce and proud, and they sometimes soar gracefully high in the air. They are often pictured as courageous hunters and have long been symbols of freedom and power. The *golden eagle* best fits this description and is sometimes called "king of birds." But eagles are not always as bold and fierce as they look. Most will eat whatever flesh is easiest to get, including *carrion* (dead animals).

The body of an eagle

Eagles vary in size, depending on the species and the individual. Females are generally larger than males. Wingspreads of different species and individuals range from about 4 to 8 feet (1.2 to 2.4 meters). Most eagles weigh about 7 to 12 pounds (3.2 to 5.4 kilograms), but some weigh as much as 20 pounds (9.1 kilograms).

If the wind and other flying conditions are favorable, some species of eagles may be able to carry prey weighing nearly as much as themselves. Normally, however, eagles can only carry smaller prey.

The head of an eagle is large and covered with feathers. An eagle has large eyes that are located on the sides of its head. However, it can see straight ahead. Most birds have keener sight than humans and other animals, but eagles and hawks are said to have the keenest sight of all. Eagles can probably sight their prey while soaring

high in the air. But they usually watch from perches or fly close to the ground while they are hunting. Eagles have large, strong, hooked beaks, which they use to tear up their prey. The golden eagle's beak measures about 2 inches (5 centimeters) long and 1 inch (2.5 centimeters) from top to bottom. The bald eagle's beak is even larger.

Feet and legs. Eagles have strong legs and feet. Most eagles have scaly, bright yellow skin on their feet. Eagles seize and kill prey with their long, curved talons. They also use their talons to carry prey to a feeding place. When eagles fight, they dive at each other and try to strike with their talons. The legs of golden eagles and several other species are covered with feathers. The lower part of the bald eagle's legs is bare.

Feathers and wings. Eagles have such long, broad wings and tails that they look clumsy when they are on the ground. But the wings easily support their heavy

Facts in brief

Names: Adult, eagle; young, eaglet or eyass.
Incubation period: 35-42 days or more, depending on species.
Length of life: 20-50 years.
Where found: Throughout the world, except in Antarctica and where people have killed them off or destroyed their habitat.
Scientific classification: Eagles belong to the class Aves, the order Falconiformes, and the family Accipitridae. Within the family, the larger species are generally called *eagles* and the smaller species *hawks* or *buzzards,* but there is no rigid distinction.

bodies when they fly. Eagles can glide great distances without flapping their wings. The long feathers in their wings are strong and stiff, and they are shaped so the air flows smoothly over the surface of the wing. When the eagle soars, the feathers spread out like fingers and bend up at the tips.

The life of an eagle

Wild eagles that survive to adulthood are thought to live from 20 to 30 years. In captivity, eagles may live 50 years or more. Most young eagles first breed when they are about 5 years old. Mated eagles are thought to stay together. If one member of a pair dies, the other may find another mate. In winter, bald eagles may gather in areas with plentiful food. But during the breeding season, each pair claims a territory around its nest and keeps other eagles away. The golden eagle may defend a territory of about 20 to 60 square miles (50 to 160 square kilometers). The bald eagle holds a smaller territory.

Nests of eagles are called *aeries* or *eyries* (both pronounced *AIR eez* or *IHR eez*). Bald eagles usually build their aeries in the tops of tall trees that are near water. Some nest on cliffs. Golden eagles usually nest on high cliffs in the mountains. Some eagles in Asia nest on the ground. Eagles tend to use the same aerie every year. However, some eagles have two or more aeries. They use one aerie one year and another the next year.

Eagles build aeries mainly with sticks. They often decorate the aerie with fresh leaves while they are using it. They usually add new material each year they use an aerie, so many old aeries are very big. A new aerie may be 6 feet (1.8 meters) across and 18 inches (46 centimeters) deep. But an old aerie may be up to 10 feet (3 meters) across and 15 feet (4.5 meters) deep.

Eggs are about 3 inches (7.6 centimeters) long and 2 inches (5 centimeters) across. Females lay one, two, or—rarely—three eggs each year. The eggs of golden eagles

The harpy eagle lives in Central and South American rain forests and feeds on monkeys, sloths, and other animals.

WORLD BOOK illustration
by Stanley W. Galli

Steller's sea eagle is one of the largest and most powerful eagles. It breeds on the coast of Siberia and in Korea.

WORLD BOOK
illustration by
Stanley W. Galli

are white or spotted with reddish-brown or gray. Those of bald eagles are white and become stained with yellow in the nest. Northern eagles lay eggs in March. Bald eagles in Florida lay eggs during the fall and winter.

The eggs hatch in five to six weeks or more, depending on the species. During that time, the female *incubates* the eggs—that is, she sits on them to keep them warm. The male incubates them occasionally, and brings food to the female while she sits. After the eggs hatch, both parents guard the nest and take food to the young.

Young eagles are called *eaglets* or *eyasses*. Eaglets are hatched with their eyes open. They are covered with a grayish-white *down* (fuzz). Their regular feathers begin to grow when they are 2 to 3 weeks old. Eaglets are not able to tear up their own food until they are 6 or 8 weeks old. They leave the nest when they are 11 to 12 weeks old, but they cannot fly very well at first. They stay near the aerie for several weeks. The parents feed them for a few more months until they can hunt well enough to get their own food.

Some species of eagles hatch two eggs. But it is unusual for both eaglets to survive. One usually hatches two or three days before the other. The older eaglet is larger and takes more than its share of food. It also attacks the smaller eaglet repeatedly and may kill it.

Food. Eagles hunt only during the day. They spend the night in their aeries or on a safe perch. Often, two eagles hunt together. Some eagles eat only certain types of prey. But most hunt a wide variety of prey and occasionally eat carrion or steal prey from other animals.

See **Eagle** in *World Book* for more information on The life of an eagle and Kinds of eagles.

Ear

Ear is the sense organ that makes it possible for us to hear. Hearing is one of our most important senses. It enables us to communicate with one another through speech. The development of speech itself depends mostly on hearing. Children learn to talk by listening to and imitating the speech of other people. Hearing can also alert us to danger. We hear the warning honk of an automobile horn or the whistle of an approaching train. Even while asleep, we may hear a fire alarm or the barking of a watchdog. In addition, hearing provides pleasure. For example, it enables us to enjoy music, the singing of birds, and the sound of the surf.

Hearing is a complicated process. Everything that moves makes a sound. Sound consists of vibrations that travel in waves. Sound waves enter the ear and are changed into nerve signals that are sent to the brain. The brain interprets the signals as sounds.

Besides enabling us to hear, our ears help us keep our balance. The ears have certain organs that respond to movements of the head. These organs inform the brain about any changes in the position of the head. The brain then sends messages to various muscles that keep our head and body steady as we stand, sit, walk, or move in any way.

The sense of hearing

Sound consists of vibrations that travel in waves through the air, the ground, or some other substance or surface. Sounds vary in *frequency* and *intensity.* Fre-

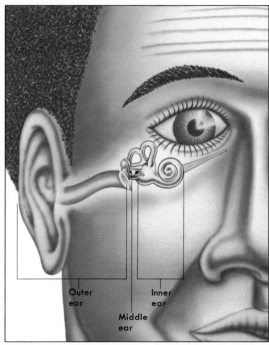

WORLD BOOK illustration by Colin Bidgood

The human ear extends deep into the skull. Its main parts are (1) the outer ear, (2) the middle ear, and (3) the inner ear.

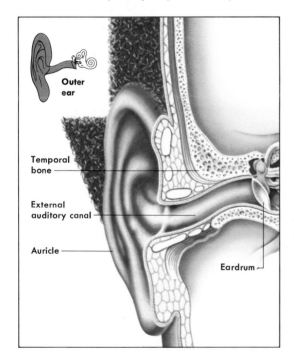

The outer ear consists of the *auricle,* the fleshy part of the ear on the side of the head, and the *external auditory canal,* a passageway that leads to the *eardrum.* The inner two-thirds of the auditory canal is surrounded by the *temporal bone.*

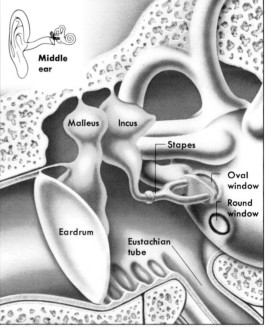

WORLD BOOK illustrations by Colin Bidgood

The middle ear has three bones—the *malleus, incus,* and *stapes.* They link the eardrum to the *oval window,* a membrane of the inner ear. The *Eustachian tube* leads from the middle ear to the back of the throat.

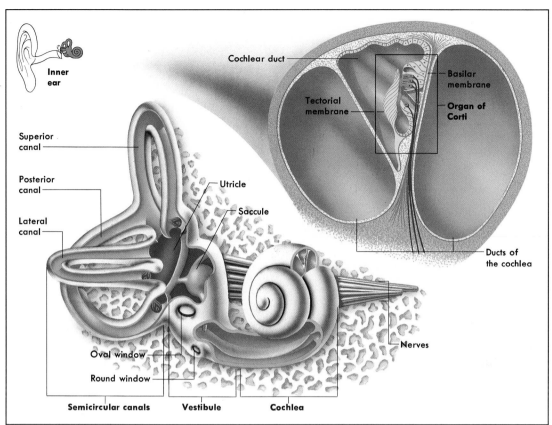

Inner ear

Cochlear duct

Tectorial membrane

Basilar membrane

Organ of Corti

Superior canal

Posterior canal

Lateral canal

Utricle

Saccule

Ducts of the cochlea

Nerves

Oval window

Round window

Semicircular canals   Vestibule   Cochlea

WORLD BOOK illustrations by Colin Bidgood

The inner ear consists of the *vestibule, semicircular canals,* and *cochlea.* The vestibule includes the *utricle* and *saccule,* which with the semicircular canals form the ear's organs of balance. The cochlea has three fluid-filled ducts, shown enlarged at the right above. One wall of the central *cochlear duct* is formed by the *basilar membrane,* which has many hair cells. The hair cells make up the *organ of Corti,* the actual organ of hearing. The *tectorial membrane* lies above the hair cells.

quency is the number of vibrations produced per second and is measured in *hertz.* One vibration per second equals 1 hertz. A high-frequency sound has a high pitch, and a low-frequency sound has a low pitch. The full range of normal human hearing extends from 20 to 20,000 hertz. As a person grows older, however, the ability to hear high-frequency sounds decreases. Intensity is the amount of energy in a sound wave. It is measured in *decibels.* A person can barely hear a sound of zero decibels. Sounds above 140 decibels can be painful to the ears. In some cases, they may seriously damage the ears.

How sounds travel to the inner ear. Sound waves enter the external auditory canal of the outer ear and strike the eardrum, causing it to vibrate. The vibrations from the eardrum then flow across the three auditory ossicles of the middle ear—from the malleus, which is attached to the eardrum, to the incus and then to the stapes. The footplate of the stapes vibrates within the oval window, which lies between the middle and inner ears. These movements of the footplate create waves in the fluid that fills the ducts of the cochlea of the inner ear.

Besides transmitting sound waves to the oval window, the auditory ossicles of the middle ear *amplify* (strengthen) the waves. Sound waves do not travel as easily through the cochlear fluid of the inner ear as they do through the air. They diminish by about 30 decibels as they pass through the cochlear fluid. But amplification of the sound waves by the auditory ossicles makes up for the loss in intensity.

Sound waves can also be conducted to the inner ear through the bones of the skull. This process is called *bone conduction.* Some of the sound produced by your voice travels to your inner ears in this way.

How sounds reach the brain. The movements of the footplate of the stapes in the oval window produce waves in the cochlear fluid. The cochlear fluid pushes against the basilar membrane, causing it to move. The hair cells of the organ of Corti on the basilar membrane slide against the overhanging tectorial membrane. The hairs bend and so create impulses in the cochlear nerve fibers attached to the hairs. The cochlear nerve transmits the impulses to the *temporal lobe,* the hearing center of the brain. The brain interprets the impulses as sounds.

Sounds of high-, middle-, and low-frequency affect hair cells at different locations along the basilar membrane. High-frequency sounds move hair cells near the

How sounds travel to the inner ear

Sound waves enter the ear through the external auditory canal. They strike the eardrum, causing it to vibrate. The vibrations flow across the malleus, incus, and stapes. The footplate of the stapes vibrates within the oval window, creating waves in the fluid that fills the ducts of the cochlea.

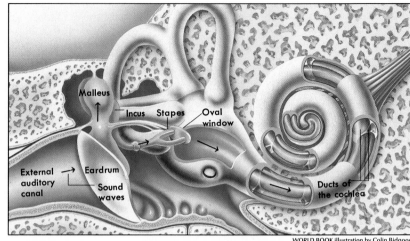

WORLD BOOK illustration by Colin Bidgood

base of the spiraling cochlea. Middle-frequency sounds move hair cells near the middle of the spiral, and low-frequency sounds affect those near the top. In addition, the nerve fibers of the basilar membrane send impulses of the same frequency as that of a particular sound.

The intensity of a sound determines how many hair cells are affected and how many impulses the cochlear nerve sends to the brain. For example, loud sounds move a large number of hair cells, and the cochlear nerve transmits many impulses.

A person's ability to tell the direction from which a sound comes depends on *binaural hearing*—that is,

hearing with both ears. For example, a sound coming from the right side of a person reaches the right ear a fraction of a second sooner than it reaches the left ear. The sound is also slightly louder in the right ear. The brain recognizes this tiny difference in time and loudness to determine the direction of the sound.

See **Ear** in *World Book* for more information on the following topics:

- Parts of the ear
- The sense of balance
- Disorders of the ear
- The ears of animals

Interesting features of the ears of various animals

WORLD BOOK illustrations by Patricia J. Wynne

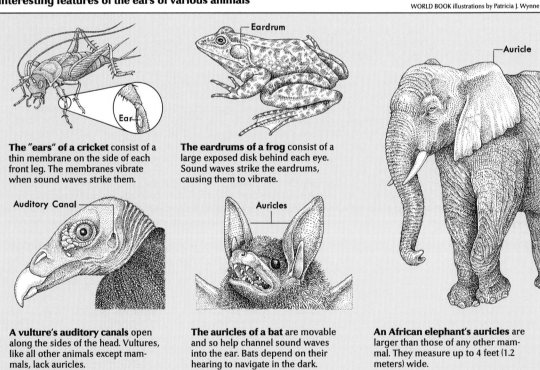

The "ears" of a cricket consist of a thin membrane on the side of each front leg. The membranes vibrate when sound waves strike them.

The eardrums of a frog consist of a large exposed disk behind each eye. Sound waves strike the eardrums, causing them to vibrate.

A vulture's auditory canals open along the sides of the head. Vultures, like all other animals except mammals, lack auricles.

The auricles of a bat are movable and so help channel sound waves into the ear. Bats depend on their hearing to navigate in the dark.

An African elephant's auricles are larger than those of any other mammal. They measure up to 4 feet (1.2 meters) wide.

NASA

A photograph of the earth, taken from a satellite 22,300 miles (35,900 kilometers) out in space, shows clouds over North America, *upper left,* South America, *center,* and Africa, *upper right.* Water covers about 70 per cent of the earth. Land covers only about 30 per cent.

Earth

Earth means many things to the people who live on it. To a farmer, earth is rich soil. To a road builder, earth means mountains of hard rock. For a sailor, earth is water as far as the eye can see. A pilot's view of earth may include part of an ocean, a mountain, and patches of farmland. An astronaut speeding through space sees the earth's round shape and the outline of lands and oceans. Each of these different views helps describe the earth but none really tells what the earth is.

The earth is a huge *sphere* (ball) covered with water, rock, and soil, and surrounded by air. It is one of nine *planets* that travel through space around the sun. The sun is a star—one of billions of stars that make up a *galaxy* called the Milky Way. The Milky Way and billions of other galaxies make up the *universe.*

The planet earth is only a tiny part of the universe, but it is the home of human beings and many other living things. Animals and plants live almost everywhere on the earth's surface. They can live on the earth because it is just the right distance from the sun. Living things need the sun's warmth and light for life. If the earth were too close to the sun, it would be too hot for living things. If the earth were too far from the sun, it would be too cold for anything to live. Most living things—both plants and animals—also must have water to live. The earth has plenty. Water covers most of the earth's surface.

All life on the earth is found on and above a skinlike *crust* made of rock. The crust lies under the land and water that we know as the earth's surface. Beneath the crust, the earth is a hot, lifeless ball of rock and metal that no human being has ever seen or sampled.

The earth is always moving. It spins like a top and also travels around the sun at the same time. We use these two motions of the earth to measure the length of days and years. One day is the time it takes the earth to spin around once. One year is the time it takes the earth to travel once around the sun. The earth, like some of the other planets, has a ball-shaped moon traveling around it. The other planets that have moons all have two or more, except Pluto, which only has one.

The study of the earth is called *geology,* and scientists who study the earth are *geologists.*

The earth in the universe

The earth as a planet. The earth ranks fifth in size among the planets. It has a diameter of about 8,000 miles (13,000 kilometers). The diameter of Jupiter, the largest planet, is about 11 times that of the earth. The diameter of Pluto, the smallest planet, is less than one-fifth the diameter of the earth.

The earth is about 93 million miles (150 million kilometers) from the sun. Only two planets—Mercury and Venus—are closer to the sun. Scientists believe these planets have surface temperatures of 600° to 800° F. (316° to 427° C). The average temperature of the earth's surface is 57° F. (14° C). All the other planets except Mars are

The earth at a glance

Age: At least $4\frac{1}{2}$ billion years.

Mass: 6,600,000,000,000,000,000,000,000 (6.6 sextillion) short tons (6.0 sextillion metric tons).

Motion: *Rotation* (spinning motion around an imaginary line connecting the North and South poles)—once every 23 hours, 56 minutes, 4.09 seconds. *Revolution* (motion around the sun)—once every 365 days, 6 hours, 9 minutes, 9.54 seconds.

Size: *Polar diameter* (distance through the earth from North Pole to South Pole)—7,899.83 miles (12,713.54 kilometers). *Equatorial diameter* (distance through the earth at the equator)—7,926.41 miles (12,756.32 kilometers). *Polar circumference* (distance around the earth through the poles)—24,859.82 miles (40,008.00 kilometers). *Equatorial circumference* (distance around the earth along the equator)—24,901.55 miles (40,075.16 kilometers).

Area: *Total surface area*—196,800,000 square miles (509,700,000 square kilometers). *Land area*—approximately 57,300,000 square miles (148,400,000 square kilometers), 29 per cent of total surface area. *Water area*—approximately 139,500,000 square miles (361,300,000 square kilometers), 71 per cent of total surface area.

Surface features: *Highest land*—Mount Everest, 29,028 feet (8,848 meters) above sea level. *Lowest land*—shore of Dead Sea, about 1,310 feet (399 meters) below sea level.

Ocean depths: *Deepest part of ocean*—area of the Mariana Trench in Pacific Ocean southwest of Guam, 36,198 feet (11,033 meters) below surface. *Average ocean depth*—12,200 feet (3,730 meters).

Temperature: *Highest,* 136° F. (58° C) at Al Aziziyah, Libya. *Lowest,* −128.6° F. (−89.6° C) at Vostok Station in Antarctica. *Average surface temperature,* 57° F. (14° C).

Atmosphere: *Height*—more than 99 per cent of the atmosphere is less than 50 miles (80 kilometers) above the earth's surface,

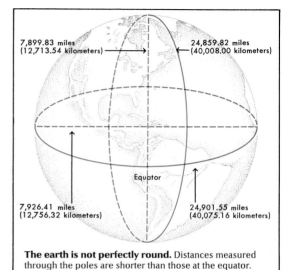

7,899.83 miles (12,713.54 kilometers)

24,859.82 miles (40,008.00 kilometers)

Equator

7,926.41 miles (12,756.32 kilometers)

24,901.55 miles (40,075.16 kilometers)

The earth is not perfectly round. Distances measured through the poles are shorter than those at the equator.

but particles of the atmosphere are 1,000 miles (1,600 kilometers) above the surface. *Chemical makeup of atmosphere*—about 78 per cent nitrogen, 21 per cent oxygen, 1 per cent argon with small amounts of other gases.

Chemical makeup of the earth's crust (in per cent of the crust's weight): oxygen 46.6, silicon 27.7, aluminum 8.1, iron 5.0, calcium 3.6, sodium 2.8, potassium 2.6, magnesium 2.0, and other elements totaling 1.6.

very cold, with temperatures ranging from −236° to −369° F. (−149° to −223° C). The temperature on Mars, however, may reach as high as −81° F. (−27° C) at noon near the equator. It drops as low as −191° F. (−124° C) on the side away from the sun.

Only the atmosphere of the earth contains enough oxygen to support animal life. The atmosphere of Mars consists chiefly of carbon dioxide, with only a trace of oxygen. The atmosphere of Venus is also made up primarily of carbon dioxide. Mercury has very little atmosphere. Jupiter, Saturn, Uranus, and Neptune all have atmospheres that include hydrogen, helium, and methane, a gas that makes up most of the natural gas found on the earth. Pluto appears to have frozen methane gas on its surface. It also appears to have an atmosphere composed chiefly of methane.

How the earth moves. The earth has three motions. It (1) spins like a top, (2) travels around the sun, and (3) moves through the Milky Way with the rest of the solar system.

The earth spins around its *axis,* an imaginary line that connects the North and South poles. The spinning motion makes the sun appear to move from east to west, and causes day and night on earth. The "day" side of the earth faces the sun, and the "night" side faces away from the sun. As the earth spins eastward, some parts of the earth move from the night side to the day side. People in these regions see the sun "come up" in the east. Other parts of the earth move from the day side to the night side. People there see the sun "set" in the west.

It takes 23 hours, 56 minutes, and 4.09 seconds for the earth to spin around once. This length of time is called a *sidereal day.*

The earth travels 595 million miles (958 million kilometers) around the sun in 365 days, 6 hours, 9 minutes, and 9.54 seconds. This length of time is called a *sidereal year.* During this period, the earth travels at an average speed of 66,600 miles (107,200 kilometers) an hour. As the earth moves around the sun, the night sky changes slowly. Some groups of stars are visible in the night sky, and other groups disappear into the sunlit day sky.

The path of the earth around the sun is called the earth's *orbit.* The orbit lies on an imaginary flat surface that cuts through the sun. This surface is the earth's *orbital plane.* The earth's axis does not stick straight up from the orbital plane. It tilts about $23\frac{1}{2}$° from the straight-up position. This tilt and the earth's motion around the sun cause the change of seasons. For example, the northern half of the earth tilts toward the sun in summer. In winter, the northern half of the earth tilts away from the sun.

The whole Milky Way spins around like a giant wheel. The solar system is about three-fifths of the way from the center to the edge of the Galaxy. It revolves around the center of the Galaxy at a speed of about 155 miles (250 kilometers) per second.

Outside and inside the earth

The earth's shape and size. The earth may be thought of as a ball with the North Pole at the top and the South Pole at the bottom. Halfway between the poles is an imaginary circle around the earth called the *equa-*

Three motions of the earth

WORLD BOOK diagram by Cynthia Fujii

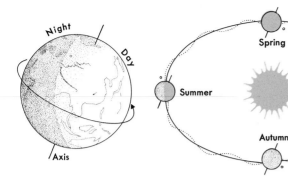

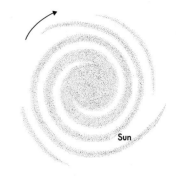

The earth spins around its axis once every 24 hours. This motion creates day and night.

The earth travels around the sun once every 365 days. This motion creates years. The moon's gravitation makes the earth follow a wobbly path, *dotted line.*

The earth moves with the sun as the sun circles the Milky Way once about every 250 million years.

tor. The earth is not perfectly round. It is slightly flattened at the poles. The diameter of the earth measured from pole to pole is shorter than the diameter at the equator. At the poles, the diameter is 7,899.83 miles (12,713.54 kilometers). This distance is 26.58 miles (42.78 kilometers) shorter than the diameter at the equator—7,926.41 miles (12,756.32 kilometers).

Similarly, the distance around the earth is shorter at the poles than at the equator. At the poles, the earth

Inside the earth

Beneath the earth's crust are the mantle, the outer core, and the inner core. Scientists learn about the inside of the earth by studying how waves from earthquakes travel through the earth.

WORLD BOOK illustration by Raymond Perlman

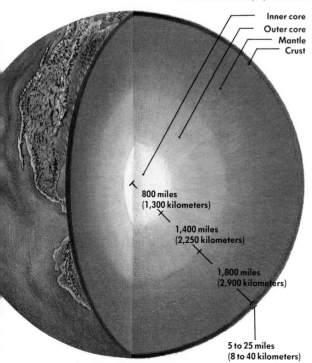

Inner core
Outer core
Mantle
Crust

800 miles
(1,300 kilometers)

1,400 miles
(2,250 kilometers)

1,800 miles
(2,900 kilometers)

5 to 25 miles
(8 to 40 kilometers)

measures 24,859.82 miles (40,008.00 kilometers) around. At the equator, it measures 24,901.55 miles (40,075.16 kilometers) around. It takes almost two days for a jet airplane to fly around the earth. An astronaut in space circles the earth in about 90 minutes.

The equator does not mark the earth's "fattest" part. The distance around the earth is greatest along a circle slightly south of the equator. The earth's shape is somewhat like that of a pear, which has its fattest part just below its "middle." But this bulge is so small that the earth still looks like a perfectly round ball.

Inside the earth. Beneath the crust, the earth is a sphere of hot rock and metal. By studying the records of earthquake waves, scientists have learned that the inside of the earth is divided into three parts: the *mantle,* the *outer core,* and the *inner core.*

The mantle is a thick layer of solid rock below the crust. It goes down about 1,800 miles (2,900 kilometers). The rock in the mantle is made of silicon, oxygen, aluminum, iron, and magnesium. The upper part of the mantle has a temperature of about 1600° F. (870° C). This temperature gradually increases down through the mantle to about 8000 °F. (4400 °C) where the mantle meets the next lower section, the outer core.

The outer core begins about 1,800 miles (2,900 kilometers) below the earth's surface. Scientists believe the outer core is about 1,400 miles (2,250 kilometers) thick and is made of melted iron and nickel. Its temperature ranges from about 4000° F. (2200° C) in the uppermost parts to about 9000° F. (5000° C) in the deepest parts.

The ball-shaped inner core lies within the outer core and makes up the center of the earth. The boundary between the outer and inner cores is about 3,200 miles (5,150 kilometers) below the earth's surface. The center of the inner core is about 800 miles (1,300 kilometers) below this boundary, or about 4,000 miles (6,400 kilometers) below the earth's surface. Scientists believe the inner core consists of solid iron and nickel. The temperature there may be as high as 9000° F. (5000° C).

See **Earth** in *World Book* for more information on the following topics:

- The earth in the universe
- Outside and inside the earth
- How the earth changes
- How the earth began
- History of the earth

Outline of the earth's history

This geological time scale outlines the development of the earth and of life on the earth. The earth's earliest history appears at the bottom of the chart, and its most recent history is at the top.

	Period or epoch and its length	Beginning (years ago)	Development of life on the earth	
Cenozoic Era — Quaternary Period	Holocene Epoch 10 thousand years	10 thousand	Human beings hunted and tamed animals; developed agriculture; learned to use metals, coal, oil, gas, and other resources; and put the power of wind and rivers to work.	Cultivated plants
Quaternary Period	Pleistocene Epoch 2 million years	2 million	Modern human beings developed. Mammoths, woolly rhinos, and other animals flourished but died out near the end of the epoch.	Human beings
Tertiary Period	Pliocene Epoch 3 million years	5 million	Sea life became much like today's. Birds and many mammals became like modern kinds and spread around the world. Humanlike creatures appeared.	Horses
Tertiary Period	Miocene Epoch 19 million years	24 million	Apes appeared in Asia and Africa. Other animals included bats, monkeys, and whales, and primitive bears and raccoons. Flowering plants and trees resembled modern kinds.	Apes
Tertiary Period	Oligocene Epoch 14 million years	38 million	Primitive apes appeared. Camels, cats, dogs, elephants, horses, rhinos, and rodents developed. Huge rhinoceroslike animals disappeared near the end of the epoch.	Early horses
Tertiary Period	Eocene Epoch 17 million years	55 million	Birds, amphibians, small reptiles, and fish were plentiful. Primitive bats, camels, cats, horses, monkeys, rhinoceroses, and whales appeared.	Grasses
Tertiary Period	Paleocene Epoch 8 million years	63 million	Flowering plants became plentiful. Invertebrates, fish, amphibians, reptiles, and mammals were common.	Small mammals
Mesozoic Era	Cretaceous Period 75 million years	138 million	Flowering plants appeared. Invertebrates, fish, and amphibians were plentiful. Dinosaurs with horns and armor became common. Dinosaurs died out at the end of the period.	Flowering plants
Mesozoic Era	Jurassic Period 67 million years	205 million	Cone-bearing trees were plentiful. Sea life included shelled squid. Dinosaurs reached their largest size. The first birds appeared. Mammals were small and primitive.	Birds
Mesozoic Era	Triassic Period 35 million years	240 million	Cone-bearing trees were plentiful. Many fish resembled modern kinds. Insects were plentiful. The first turtles, crocodiles, and dinosaurs appeared, as did the first mammals.	Dinosaurs
Paleozoic Era	Permian Period 50 million years	290 million	The first seed plants—cone-bearing trees—appeared. Fish, amphibians, and reptiles were plentiful.	Seed plants
Paleozoic Era — Carboniferous Period	Pennsylvanian Period 40 million years	330 million	Scale trees, ferns, and giant scouring rushes were abundant. Fish and amphibians were plentiful. The first reptiles appeared. Giant insects lived in forests where coal later formed.	Reptiles
Carboniferous Period	Mississippian Period 30 million years	360 million	Trilobites had nearly died out. Crustaceans, fish, and amphibians were plentiful. Many coral reefs were formed.	Amphibians
Paleozoic Era	Devonian Period 50 million years	410 million	The first forests grew in swamps. Many kinds of fish, including sharks, armored fish, and lungfish, swam in the sea and in fresh waters. The first amphibians and insects appeared.	Fish
Paleozoic Era	Silurian Period 25 million years	435 million	Spore-bearing land plants appeared. Trilobites and mollusks were common. Coral reefs formed.	Corals
Paleozoic Era	Ordovician Period 65 million years	500 million	Trilobites, corals, and mollusks were common. Tiny animals called graptolites lived in branching *colonies* (groups).	Graptolites
Paleozoic Era	Cambrian Period 70 million years (?)	570 million (?)	Fossils were plentiful for the first time. Shelled animals called trilobites, and some mollusks, were common in the sea. Jawless fish appeared.	Trilobites
Precambrian Time Almost 4 billion years (?)		$4\frac{1}{2}$ billion (?)	Coral, jellyfish, and worms lived in the sea about 1,100 million years ago. Bacteria lived as long ago as $3\frac{1}{2}$ billion years. Before that, no living things are known.	Bacteria

60 million years ago
Paleocene Epoch

Earth scientists believe that the positions of the earth's land masses are continually shifting. The map at the right shows the locations of the continents about 60 million years ago. At that time, the individual continents were approaching their present positions, which are shown in black outline.

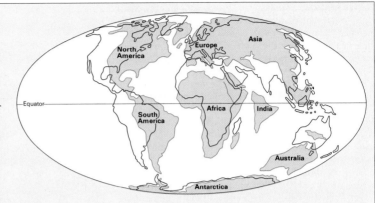

120 million years ago
Cretaceous Period

Scientists theorize that the continents were formed by the breakup of two great land masses: (1) Laurasia to the north, and (2) Gondwanaland to the south. In the map at the right, these two land masses are shown as they may have appeared about 120 million years ago. Laurasia eventually broke up to form Eurasia and North America. Gondwanaland separated into Africa, Antarctica, Australia, India, and South America.

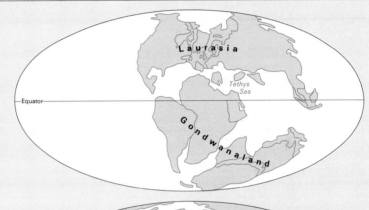

180 million years ago
Jurassic Period

Scientists believe that Laurasia and Gondwanaland were formed by the breakup of a single giant land mass called Pangaea, *right*. This huge land mass probably was surrounded by a single ocean called Panthalassa. Scientists theorize that Pangaea started breaking apart to form Laurasia and Gondwanaland about 200 million years ago.

360 million years ago
Mississippian Period

Little is known about the position of the earth's land before 200 million years ago. But some scientists theorize that a number of land masses came together to form Pangaea. The map at the right shows possible positions of such land masses about 360 million years ago.

WORLD BOOK maps. Based on University of Chicago Paleographic Atlas Project.

Earthquake is a sudden shaking or shock in the earth. There may be as many as a million earthquakes in a single year. Most of them take place beneath the surface of the sea. Few of these cause any damage. But those that occur near large cities cause much damage and loss of life, especially if the cities rest on soft ground. The energy released by a large earthquake may equal that of about 200 million short tons (180 million metric tons) of TNT. Its energy may be 10,000 times as great as that of the first atomic bomb. The strength of an earthquake is often measured on a scale of numbers called the *Richter scale.* The largest earthquakes are commonly measured using figures called *strain-energy magnitudes.*

Large earthquakes cause violent motions of the earth's surface. Coastal earthquakes may cause huge sea waves that sweep up on land and add to the general destruction. Such waves often occur in the Pacific Ocean, where coastal earthquakes are most common. Geologists use a Japanese word, *tsunami,* for these destructive waves.

Why earthquakes occur. According to the *plate tectonics* theory, the earth's surface consists of seven large rigid plates and about as many smaller ones that are in slow, continuous motion. This motion squeezes and stretches rocks at the plates' edges. If the force becomes too great, the rocks *rupture* (break) and shift, causing an earthquake. Most of these ruptures, or *faults,* lie beneath the surface. But some, such as the San Andreas Fault in California, are visible.

Much of the energy released in an earthquake travels away from the fault in waves called *seismic waves.* Near the *focus* (place where the rupture begins), vibrations of the seismic waves can be destructive. As the waves travel away from the focus, their vibrations weaken. Seismographic stations around the world record seismic waves from a great earthquake.

Seismic waves consist of compressional waves, shear waves, and surface waves. *Compressional waves* are really sound waves, and travel at a speed of 5 miles (8 kilometers) a second. They pass through the earth in about 20 minutes. The rocks vibrate in the direction traveled by the wave from inside the earth. This causes the

Bob Schalkwijk, Black Star

Earthquakes can destroy buildings, roads, and other structures. Such damage may result from changes in the level of the ground that sometimes occur during an earthquake.

rocks to change volume. *Shear waves* travel about half as fast as compressional waves. The rocks vibrate at right angles to the direction traveled by the wave from inside the earth. This causes the rocks to change shape. *Surface waves* travel slightly slower than shear waves. They are confined to the earth's surface in much the same way that ocean waves are limited to the surface of the sea. By measuring the speed of seismic waves, scientists can obtain some idea of the kinds of rocks that are found below the surface of the earth.

Location of earthquakes. Seismologists use the time intervals between different seismic waves to compute the distance of the focus from a seismographic station. To locate the focus more precisely, they draw circles on a map to show the distance of the earthquake from several stations. The earthquake is located where the circles intersect. The focus of most earthquakes occurs less than 25 miles (40 kilometers) beneath the surface of the earth. But some may occur at depths as great

Strongest earthquakes since 1900*

Year	Location	Magnitude†	Year	Location	Magnitude†
1905	Northern India	8.0	1958	Southeastern Alaska	8.1
	Western Mongolia	8.4		Kuril Islands	8.4
1906	San Francisco	8.1	1960	Southern Chile	9.7
1920	Gansu, China	8.4	1963	Kuril Islands	8.3
1923	Kamchatka, Soviet Union	8.5	1964	Southern Alaska	9.2
1933	Pacific Ocean floor, near Japan	8.3	1965	Aleutian Islands	8.5
1934	Nepal	8.3	1966	Western Peru	8.0
1938	Banda Sea floor, near Indonesia	8.6	1968	Pacific Ocean floor, near Japan	8.1
1939	Eastern Turkey	8.0	1969	Kuril Islands	8.0
1944	Southern Honshu, Japan	8.0	1970	Western Peru	7.9
1946	Aleutian Islands	8.3	1972	Southeastern Alaska	7.9
	Pacific Ocean floor, near Japan	8.0	1976	Mindanao, Philippines	7.9
1949	Queen Charlotte Islands, British Columbia	8.2	1977	Lesser Sunda Islands, Indonesia	8.8
1950	Assam, India	8.8	1983	New Ireland, Papua New Guinea	7.9
1952	Pacific Ocean floor, Japan	8.7	1985	Mexico City	8.1
	Kamchatka, Soviet Union	8.9	1986	Aleutian Islands	8.3
1957	Aleutian Islands	9.1		Kermadec Islands, South Pacific	8.4
	Southwestern Mongolia	8.1	1989	Pacific Ocean floor, near New Zealand	8.5

*In *World Book,* see **Disaster** (table) for a list of the earthquakes that have caused the most deaths.
†Magnitudes given are strain-energy magnitudes, which measure strong earthquakes more accurately than Richter magnitudes.
Sources: G. Purcaru and H. Berckhemer in *Tectonophysics* 49 (1978), © Elsevier Scientific Publishing Company, Amsterdam; U.S. National Geophysical Data Center.

Causes and effects of earthquakes

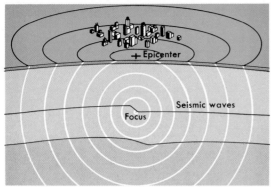

WORLD BOOK diagram by Mas Nakagawa

An earthquake occurs when forces inside the earth cause a sudden rock movement. The site of the movement is the quake's *focus.* Seismic waves created by the quake are strongest at the *epicenter,* the point on the surface above the focus.

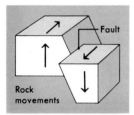
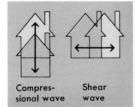

WORLD BOOK diagrams

An earthquake focus is centered in rocks that have broken and slid past one another. Geologists call such places *faults.*

Seismic waves include *compressional waves,* which shake buildings vertically, and *shear waves,* which move them horizontally.

tinents and sea floor are stable regions that have few quakes. Most earthquakes take place within two belts. The *circum-Pacific* belt lies along plate boundaries around the Pacific Ocean. The *Alpide* belt follows plate boundaries across southern Europe and Asia.

Prediction of earthquakes is not yet possible, but scientists are optimistic that they will find a method. Scientists know the regions where earthquakes are likely to occur. They may use the history of previous earthquakes to estimate how often a certain region may expect earthquakes. For example, California may expect a catastrophic earthquake once every 50 to 100 years. In such regions, engineers have developed buildings to withstand the severest earthquakes.

Seismologists are closely monitoring selected areas where large earthquakes are expected. They hope to record small earthquakes or distortions in the ground which might signal that a large earthquake is about to occur. However, progress toward successful earthquake prediction is slow.

Damage by earthquakes. Most earthquakes pass unnoticed. Light earthquakes may be mistaken for the rumbling of a truck. But large, destructive earthquakes do occur from time to time. Most of the destruction takes place shortly after the first tremor is felt.

Most deaths and damage from an earthquake result from the collapse of buildings or other structures. The earthquake may loosen the bricks in a chimney or cause a wall or roof to cave in. Falling material may kill or injure someone or damage other property. Earthquakes may also topple bridges, break water pipes, cut electric lines, and rupture gas mains. Fire is one of the greatest dangers in an earthquake.

as 400 miles (640 kilometers) beneath the surface of the earth.

Most earthquakes occur along the boundaries where plates separate, collide, or slide past each other. These places are the earth's most geologically active regions. Volcanoes, new mountain ranges, and deep ocean trenches—in addition to earthquakes—occur along the edges of the plates. In contrast, the flat parts of the con-

Where earthquakes occur

Almost all the world's major earthquakes occur in two great belts—the circum-Pacific belt and the Alpide belt. Each dot on the map represents five earthquakes during a nine-year period. The circum-Pacific belt, sometimes called the *Ring of Fire,* accounts for more than three-fourths of the world's earthquakes. Most of the other quakes occur in the Alpide belt, which cuts across Europe and Asia from Burma to southern Europe and North Africa. Other active earthquake areas include the mid-oceanic ridges that form undersea mountain chains.

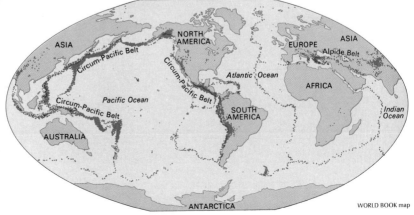

WORLD BOOK map

Eclipse is the darkening of a heavenly body. It occurs when the shadow of one object in space falls on another object or when one object moves in front of another to block its light. A *solar eclipse* takes place when the sun appears to become dark as the moon passes between the sun and the earth. A *lunar eclipse* occurs when the moon darkens as it passes through the earth's shadow.

When eclipses occur. The earth and the moon always cast shadows into space, and the moon orbits the earth about once every month. But an eclipse—either solar or lunar—does not occur every month. The moon's orbit is tilted about 5° to the earth's orbit around the sun. For this reason, the moon's shadow generally misses the earth, and so a solar eclipse does not occur. Likewise, the moon most often escapes being eclipsed by passing above or below the shadow of the earth. Thus, a solar or a lunar eclipse can occur only when the earth, sun, and moon are in nearly a straight line.

Astronomers can predict eclipses with great accuracy. At least two solar eclipses and as many as three lunar eclipses may be seen each year from various places on the earth.

Solar eclipses occur when the moon's shadow sweeps across the face of the earth. The shadow usually moves from west to east across the earth at a speed of about 2,000 miles (3,200 kilometers) per hour. People in the path of the shadow may see one of three kinds of eclipses. A *total eclipse* occurs if the moon completely blots out the sun. If the moon is at its farthest point from the earth when a total eclipse occurs, the eclipse may be only an *annular eclipse.* In such an eclipse, the moon darkens only the middle of the sun, leaving a bright ring around the edges. A *partial eclipse* occurs if the moon covers only part of the sun.

A total solar eclipse can be seen only in certain parts of the world. These areas lie in the *path of totality,* the path along which the moon's shadow passes across the earth. The path of totality is never wider than about 170 miles (274 kilometers).

A solar eclipse should never be viewed directly. Radiation from the sun—even from just the corona—can damage the eyes. Even the use of darkened film, smoked glass, or sunglasses does not eliminate the danger of watching a solar eclipse. Solar eclipses should be viewed indirectly with a *pinhole projector* or a similar device.

Dennis Milon

A total eclipse of the moon is seen from the night side of the earth. During most lunar eclipses, the moon does not become completely dark but appears reddish in color.

Lunar eclipses take place when the moon passes through the shadow of the earth. A *total eclipse* occurs if the entire moon passes through the earth's shadow. A *partial eclipse* occurs if only part of the moon passes through the shadow. A total lunar eclipse may last up to 1 hour 40 minutes. A lunar eclipse may be seen by most of the people on the night side of the earth. There is no danger in viewing a lunar eclipse.

The moon does not become completely dark during most lunar eclipses. In many cases, it becomes reddish. The earth's atmosphere bends part of the sun's light around the earth and toward the moon. This light is red because the atmosphere scatters the other colors present in sunlight in greater amounts than it does red.

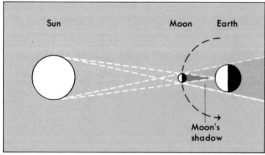

WORLD BOOK diagram

A solar eclipse occurs when the moon passes between the sun and the earth. The sun is blocked out by the moon and cannot be seen from areas on the earth that lie in the moon's shadow.

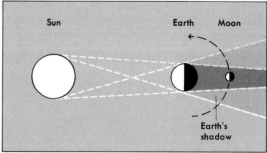

WORLD BOOK diagram

A lunar eclipse takes place when the earth is directly between the sun and the moon. The moon gradually becomes darker as it moves into the shadow of the earth.

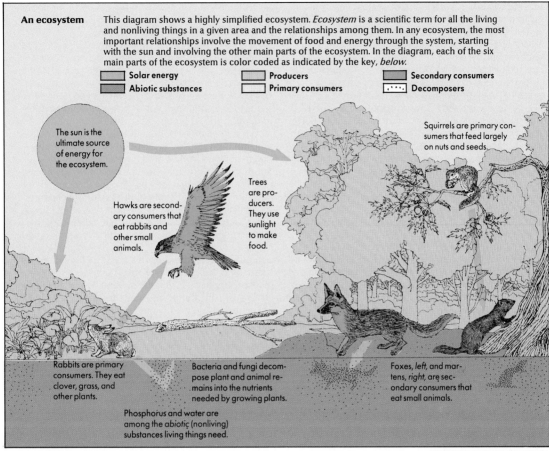

An ecosystem This diagram shows a highly simplified ecosystem. *Ecosystem* is a scientific term for all the living and nonliving things in a given area and the relationships among them. In any ecosystem, the most important relationships involve the movement of food and energy through the system, starting with the sun and involving the other main parts of the ecosystem. In the diagram, each of the six main parts of the ecosystem is color coded as indicated by the key, *below.*

- Solar energy
- Abiotic substances
- Producers
- Primary consumers
- Secondary consumers
- Decomposers

The sun is the ultimate source of energy for the ecosystem.

Squirrels are primary consumers that feed largely on nuts and seeds.

Hawks are secondary consumers that eat rabbits and other small animals.

Trees are producers. They use sunlight to make food.

Rabbits are primary consumers. They eat clover, grass, and other plants.

Bacteria and fungi decompose plant and animal remains into the nutrients needed by growing plants.

Foxes, *left*, and martens, *right*, are secondary consumers that eat small animals.

Phosphorus and water are among the *abiotic* (nonliving) substances living things need.

WORLD BOOK diagram by George Suyeoka

Ecology

Ecology, *EE KAHL uh jee,* is the branch of science that deals with the relationships living things have to each other and to their environment. Scientists who study these relationships are called *ecologists.*

The world includes a tremendous variety of living things, from complex plants and animals to simpler organisms, such as fungi, amebas, and bacteria. But whether large or small, simple or complex, no organism lives alone. Each depends in some way upon other living and nonliving things in its surroundings. For example, a moose must have certain plants for food. If the plants in its environment were destroyed, the moose would have to move to another area or starve to death. In turn, plants depend upon such animals as moose for the *nutrients* (nourishing substances) they need to live. Animal wastes and the decay of dead animals and plants provide many of the nutrients plants need.

The study of ecology increases our understanding of the world and its life. This is important because our survival and well-being depend on ecological relationships throughout the world. Even changes in distant parts of the world and its atmosphere affect us and our environment.

Although ecology is considered a branch of biology, ecologists use knowledge from many disciplines, including chemistry, physics, mathematics, and computer science. They also rely on such fields as climatology, geology, meteorology, and oceanography to learn about air, land, and water environments and their interactions. This multidisciplinary approach helps ecologists understand how the physical environment affects living things. It also aids them in assessing the impact of environmental problems, such as acid rain or the greenhouse effect.

Ecologists study the organization of the natural world on three main levels: (1) populations, (2) communities, and (3) ecosystems. They analyze the structures, activities, and changes that take place within and among these levels. Ecologists normally work out of doors, studying the operations of the natural world. They often conduct field work in isolated areas, such as islands, where the relationships among the plants and animals may be simpler and easier to understand. Many ecological studies focus on solving practical problems. For example, ecologists search for ways to curb the harmful effects of air and water pollution on living things.

See **Ecology** in *World Book* for more information on the following topics:

- Populations
- Communities
- Ecosystems
- Applied ecology

Electric motor is a machine that changes electric energy into mechanical power to do work. Electric motors are used to operate a variety of machines and machinery. Washing machines, air conditioners, and vacuum cleaners include electric motors, as do hairdriers, sewing machines, and power drills and saws. Various kinds of motors power machine tools, robots, and other equipment to keep factories running smoothly.

There are two general types of electric motors, based on the type of electricity they use. They are (1) alternating current (AC) motors and (2) direct current (DC) motors. Alternating current usually reverses the direction of its flow 60 times per second. Alternating current is available from electrical outlets in homes, and so AC motors are commonly used in household appliances. Direct current flows in only one direction. Its chief source is a battery. DC motors are commonly used to run machinery in factories. They are also used as starters for gasoline engines.

Electric motors depend on electromagnets to produce the force that is necessary for driving a machine or machinery. The machine or machinery driven by an electric motor is known as its *load.* A drive shaft connects the motor to the load.

Basic principles. The operation of an electric motor is based on three main principles: (1) An electric current produces a magnetic field; (2) the direction of a current in an electromagnet determines the location of the magnet's poles; and (3) magnetic poles attract or repel each other.

When an electric current passes through a wire, it produces a magnetic field around the wire. If the wire is wound in a coil around a metal rod, the magnetic field around the wire becomes strengthened and the rod becomes magnetized. This arrangement of rod and wire coil is a simple electromagnet, with its two ends serving as north and south poles. In *World Book,* see **Electromagnet.**

The *right-hand rule* is one way of showing the relationship between the direction of the current and the magnetic poles. Hold a coil of wire in your right hand. Supposing the coil is an electromagnet, wrap your fingers around it so that they point in the direction of the current. Your thumb then points toward the electromagnet's north pole. This method works only when a current flows from a positive terminal to a negative one.

Like poles, such as two north poles, repel each other. Unlike poles attract each other. If a bar magnet is suspended between the ends of a horseshoe magnet, it will rotate until its north pole is opposite the horseshoe magnet's south pole. The bar magnet's south pole will be opposite the horseshoe magnet's north pole.

> See **Electric motor** in *World Book* for more information on Parts of an electric motor, Kinds of electric motors, and History.

How an electric motor works   An electric motor basically consists of a stationary magnet and a moving conductor. Lines of force between the poles of the magnet form a permanent magnetic field. When an electric current passes through the conductor, the conductor becomes an electromagnet and produces another magnetic field. The two magnetic fields strengthen each other and push against the conductor.

WORLD BOOK diagrams by William Graham

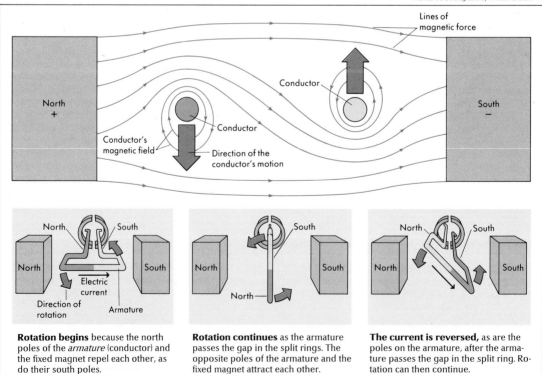

Rotation begins because the north poles of the *armature* (conductor) and the fixed magnet repel each other, as do their south poles.

Rotation continues as the armature passes the gap in the split rings. The opposite poles of the armature and the fixed magnet attract each other.

The current is reversed, as are the poles on the armature, after the armature passes the gap in the split ring. Rotation can then continue.

Artstreet

Distribution substation

WORLD BOOK photo

WORLD BOOK photo

Artstreet

Coal-burning electric power plant

Typical uses of electric power

An electric power system begins with power plants, which produce large amounts of electricity. Wires carry high-voltage electric current from the power plants to substations, where the voltage is reduced. The electricity is then distributed to homes, offices, businesses, and factories.

Electric power

Electric power is the use of electric energy to do work. It lights, heats, and cools many homes. Electricity also provides power for television sets, refrigerators, vacuum cleaners, and many other home appliances. Electric power runs machinery in factories. Escalators, elevators, and computers and other business machines in stores and offices use electric power. Electricity drives many trains and subway systems. On farms, electric machinery performs such tasks as pumping water, milking cows, and drying hay.

Huge electric generators in power plants produce almost all the world's electricity. The majority of these plants burn coal, oil, or natural gas to run the generators. Most other plants drive the generators by means of nuclear energy or the force of falling water. Wires carry the electricity from power plants to the cities or other areas where it is needed. The electricity is then distributed to individual consumers.

Electric power is measured in units called *watts.* For example, it takes 100 watts of electric power to operate a 100-watt light bulb. Ten 100-watt bulbs require 1,000 watts, or 1 *kilowatt.* The amount of energy used is expressed in *kilowatt-hours.* A kilowatt-hour equals the amount of work done by 1 kilowatt in one hour. If you burn ten 100-watt bulbs for one hour or one 100-watt bulb for 10 hours, you use 1 kilowatt-hour of electric power.

The world's electric power plants can produce more than $2\frac{1}{4}$ billion kilowatts of electricity at any given time. The United States leads all other countries in generating capacity. American power plants can generate as much as 672 million kilowatts. Canadian plants can produce about 96 million kilowatts.

Sources of electric power

Large electric power plants supply nearly all the electricity that people use. The power plants first create mechanical energy by harnessing the pressure of steam or flowing water to turn the shaft of a device called a *turbine.* The turning shaft drives an electric generator, which converts the mechanical energy into electricity.

An electric generator has a stationary part called a *stator* and a rotating part called a *rotor.* In the huge electric generators used in power plants, the stator consists of hundreds of windings of wire. The rotor is a large electromagnet that receives electricity from a small separate generator called an *exciter.* An external source of mechanical energy turns the rotor. The magnetic field created by the rotor turns as the rotor turns. As the magnetic field rotates, it produces a voltage in the wire windings of the stator that causes a flow of electric current.

The major types of electric power plants are (1) fossil-fueled steam electric power plants, (2) hydroelectric power plants, and (3) nuclear power plants. Various other kinds of power plants produce smaller amounts of electricity.

Fossil-fueled steam electric power plants generate about 64 per cent of the world's electric power and about 70 per cent of the electric power produced in the United States. Such plants burn coal, oil, or natural gas. These substances are called *fossil fuels* because they developed from *fossils* (the remains of prehistoric plants and animals). The fuel is burned in a *combustion chamber* to produce heat. The heat, in turn, is used to convert water to steam in a boiler. The steam then flows through a set of tubes in a device called a *superheater.* Hot combustion gases surround the steam-filled tubes in the superheater, increasing the temperature and pressure of the steam in the tubes.

The superheated, high-pressure steam is used to drive a huge steam turbine. A steam turbine has a series of wheels, each with many fanlike blades, mounted on a shaft. As the steam rushes through the turbine, it pushes against the blades, causing both the wheels and the turbine shaft to spin. The spinning shaft turns the rotor of the electric generator, thereby producing electricity.

Hydroelectric power plants generate about 20 per cent of the world's electric power and about 15 per cent of the electricity produced in the United States. Such

plants convert the energy of falling water into electric energy. A hydroelectric plant uses water that is stored in a reservoir behind a dam. The water flows through a tunnel or pipe to a *water turbine,* or *hydraulic turbine.* As the water rushes through the turbine, it spins the turbine shaft, which drives the electric generator.

Nuclear power plants generate about 16 per cent of the world's electric power and about 15 per cent of the electricity generated in the United States. Nuclear plants produce electricity in much the same way that fossil-fueled plants do. But instead of a fuel-burning combustion chamber, a nuclear power plant has a device called a *nuclear reactor.* A nuclear reactor produces enormous amounts of heat by *fissioning* (splitting) the nuclei of atoms of a heavy element. Most nuclear plants use the element uranium as the fuel in their reactors.

Heat from the nuclear fission is used to convert water into steam. The steam drives the steam turbine that runs the electric generator. After the steam has left the turbine, it is condensed and recycled through the plant. Many nuclear power plants use cooling towers to cool the water from the condenser pipes.

Transmitting and distributing electric power

The electricity generated by power plants is transmitted to cities or other areas. It is then distributed to

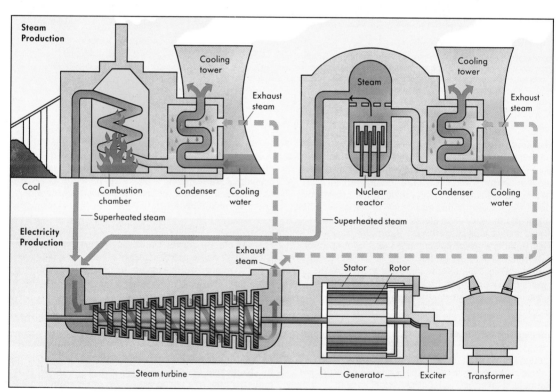

WORLD BOOK illustration by Oxford Illustrators Limited

Steam electric power plants create steam by heating water in a nuclear reactor or in a combustion chamber, where coal, oil, or gas is burned. The steam turns a turbine that runs a generator. The generator has a rotating electromagnet called a *rotor* and a stationary part called a *stator.* A separate generator called an *exciter* powers the rotor, creating a magnetic field that produces an electric charge in the stator. The charge is transmitted as electricity. A transformer boosts the voltage. Exhaust steam passes cool water pipes in a condenser and turns back to water for reheating. The water that has absorbed the steam's heat in the condenser is piped to a cooling tower.

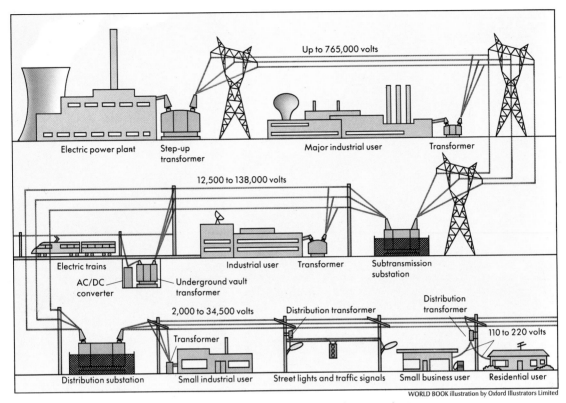

Up to 765,000 volts

Electric power plant   Step-up transformer   Major industrial user   Transformer

12,500 to 138,000 volts

Electric trains   AC/DC converter   Underground vault transformer   Industrial user   Transformer   Subtransmission substation

Distribution transformer   Distribution transformer

2,000 to 34,500 volts   Distribution transformer   110 to 220 volts

Transformer

Distribution substation   Small industrial user   Street lights and traffic signals   Small business user   Residential user

WORLD BOOK illustration by Oxford Illustrators Limited

An electric power delivery system has power lines to carry current and transformers to change its voltage. Step-up transformers boost voltages so that current can be transmitted long distances. Substations and transformers reduce voltages to levels needed by consumers. Some industrial users and transportation systems that require high voltages have their own transformers.

houses, factories, farms, offices, and other individual consumers.

Transmission. Most electricity travels from power plants along overhead wires called *transmission lines.* Laying underground or underwater cables generally costs more than stringing overhead wires. Cables are thus used far less frequently than overhead wires.

As electric current moves along transmission lines, the lines resist the current flow. The resistance causes the current to lose energy. Power plants limit energy losses by transmitting electricity at high voltages. As voltage is increased, the amount of current needed to transmit a particular amount of electric power decreases. Because less current flows through the line, there is less energy lost due to resistance.

Electric current may be either *direct current* (DC) or *alternating current* (AC). Direct current flows in only one direction. Alternating current reverses direction many times each second. It is easier to boost the voltage of alternating current than that of direct current. Alternating current is therefore easier to transmit. For this reason, electric power plants generate alternating current.

The typical power plant generator can produce about 1 million kilowatts of electric power at up to 22,000 volts. Devices called *step-up transformers* then boost this voltage as high as 765,000 volts for transmission.

Distribution. Some large industries require high-voltage current and receive it directly from transmission lines. But high-voltages are unsafe in homes, offices, and most factories. The voltage must therefore be decreased before electricity is distributed to them.

High-voltage electricity is carried by the transmission lines to *subtransmission substations* near the area where the power will be used. These substations have devices called *step-down transformers* that reduce the voltage to 12,500 to 138,000 volts. The voltage is then further reduced at *distribution substations* to 2,000 to 34,500 volts. *Distribution lines* may carry this medium-voltage current directly to commercial, industrial, or institutional users. Distribution lines also carry electric power to *distribution transformers* on poles, on the ground, or in underground vaults. Distribution transformers reduce the voltage to the levels needed by most users. Wires from the transformers run to homes, stores, offices, and other users. Nearly all such consumers in the United States and Canada receive electric power at about 110 or 220 volts.

See **Electric power** in *World Book* for more information on the following topics:

- Sources of electric power
- Transmitting and distributing electric power
- The electric power industry
- History

Lightning

© Frank Lane, Bruce Coleman Inc.

WORLD BOOK photo

Incandescent bulb

Electricity is an important form of energy. Lightning is a natural flash of light caused by electric energy. An incandescent bulb provides light generated by electricity from a power plant.

Electricity

Electricity is one of the most important forms of energy. We cannot see, hear, or smell electricity, but we know about it by what it does. Electricity produces light and heat, and it provides power for household appliances and industrial machinery. Electric power also enables us to have telephones, computers, motion pictures, television, and radio.

Most of the electricity that we use daily consists of a flow of tiny particles called *electrons*. Electrons are the smallest units of electricity. They are much too tiny to be seen, even with a microscope. Everything around us, including our bodies, contains electrons. Therefore, everything can be thought of as partly electrical. Some of the effects of electricity may be seen in nature. For example, lightning is a huge flash of light caused by electricity. Certain eels and other fishes give electric shocks.

Almost all the world's electricity is produced at power plants by large machines called *generators*. Most of these plants burn coal or oil to make steam, which provides the energy to run the generators. Thick wires carry electricity from the plants to homes, schools, stores, farms, factories, and other places where people need it.

Electricity is a handy source of energy, but it must be used with great care. Faulty wiring or an overloaded socket can cause a fire. An electric current—even one of low-voltage—can kill you if you touch a bare wire with wet hands or while standing on a wet floor.

Sources of electricity

The sources of electricity produce electric energy from some type of nonelectric energy. The main sources are (1) generators, (2) batteries, and (3) solar cells.

Generators convert mechanical energy into electricity. They produce most of our electricity. If a loop of wire rotates between the poles of a magnet, electric current is *induced* (produced) in the wire. Most modern generators work by means of magnets whirled past stationary coils of wire. However, the principle is the same. The amount of electric energy produced by a generator is approximately equal to the amount of mechanical energy that is used in moving the magnet or wire. One generator can provide enough power for a city of 500,000 people.

Batteries change chemical energy into electricity. A battery consists of one or more units called *electric cells*. Each cell has two *electrodes*, which are structures made of different chemically active materials. One of the electrodes is positively charged, and the other is negatively charged. An electric cell also contains a liquid or paste called an *electrolyte*. The electrolyte is a chemical substance that conducts electric current in the cell. When the electrodes of a battery are connected to an electric circuit, the battery produces current, which flows through the circuit.

**The flow of
electric current
in metals**

Electric current in metals consists of a flow of free electrons. For example, if a copper wire is connected to the poles of a battery, free electrons in the wire flow from the negative to the positive
pole, producing electric current. The current is in the opposite direction as the electron flow.

WORLD BOOK diagram

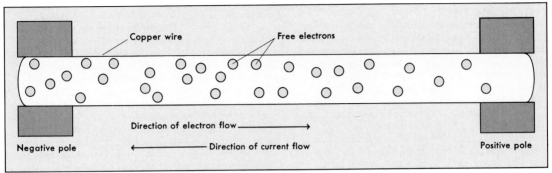

Copper wire

Free electrons

Direction of electron flow ⟶

◀— Direction of current flow

Negative pole

Positive pole

Solar cells convert sunlight into electricity. They provide nearly all the electric power for artificial satellites
and space vehicles. Most solar cells are made of a silicon crystal.

Principles of electricity

Conduction of electric current. A substance that
conducts electricity must contain charged particles that
are free to move. These particles may be electrons or
ions, or both. Certain metals, such as aluminum, copper,
and silver, are good conductors of electricity because
they have at least one free electron per atom. Free electrons are not bound tightly to their atoms and so can
move easily from one atom to another. Electric current
in a metal wire consists of a flow of free electrons. Some
metals, such as lead and tin, became *superconductors*
of electricity at temperatures near *absolute zero,* which
is −273.15° C.

The electrons of some materials, such as glass, plastic, and rubber, are bound so tightly to their atoms that
few electrons can move freely. These materials, called
insulators, conduct hardly any electricity. Other substances, including germanium and silicon, conduct electricity better than insulators do but not as well as conductors. Such substances are known as *semiconductors.*
Pure semiconductor materials would be insulators because they would have no free electrons. But certain impurities in semiconductors produce free electrons or
holes, both of which can form an electric current.

In liquid conductors, electric current consists of both
positively and negatively charged ions. For example,
table salt consists of positive sodium ions and negative
chloride ions. When salt is dissolved in water, these
ions separate and are free to move. If an electromotive
force is passed through the solution, the chloride ions
will move in one direction, and the sodium ions will
travel in the opposite direction. The flow of the ions
forms an electric current. Gases also conduct electricity.
The atoms of a gas constantly collide, producing both
free electrons and positive ions that can form a current.

Direction of current flow. In an electric current that
consists of both positive and negative particles, the positive particles flow in one direction, and the negative
ones flow in the opposite direction. The current travels
in the same direction as the flow of positive particles. In
a metal wire, only negatively charged electrons flow.

Electric current in a wire travels in the opposite direction as the flow of electrons.

Some scientists refer to the flow of electrons in a wire
as an *electronic current.* Such current travels in the
same direction as the flow of electrons but in the opposite direction as the electric current in the wire.

Effects of electricity

The flow of electric current through a conductor produces several useful effects. They include (1) heat, (2)
light, (3) magnetism, and (4) chemical effects.

Heat. When electricity flows through a conductor,
the resistance of the conductor converts some of the
electric energy into heat energy. Certain electric devices, such as ranges, heaters, toasters, and waffle irons,
generate heat by passing current through special *heat-*

Terms used in electricity

Alternating current is an electric current that reverses the di-
rection of its flow many times a second.
Conductor is a substance that transmits electricity.
Direct current is an electric current that flows in only one di-
rection.
Electric circuit is the path or paths followed by an electric cur-
rent.
Electric current is a flow of electrons or ions.
Electric field is the space around a charged particle in which
its charge has an effect.
Electric induction is the process by which an electrically
charged object charges another object without touching it.
Electromotive force, also called *voltage,* is the pressure that
pushes an electric current through a circuit.
Electron is a particle of an atom that carries one unit of nega-
tive charge.
Fuse is a device that prevents too much current from flowing
through a circuit.
Insulator is a substance that conducts hardly any electricity.
Ion is an atom that has either gained or lost electrons and is
electrically charged.
Proton is a particle of an atom that carries one unit of positive
charge.
Resistance is the opposition to the flow of an electric current in
a circuit.
Rheostat is a device that increases or decreases the resistance
in an electric circuit.
Semiconductor is a substance that conducts electricity better
than an insulator but not as well as a conductor.
Static electricity is electrons or ions that are not moving.
Transformer is a device that increases or decreases the volt-
age of alternating current.

ing units. These units are made of materials that have a fairly high resistance to current. In an electric range, for example, electricity travels through coils of special wire in the heating unit. The resistance of the coils causes them to become red hot.

Light. The atoms of all substances contain energy. Ordinarily, an atom has a certain *energy level.* If an atom absorbs additional energy, it moves to a higher energy level. Such an atom is called an *excited atom.* After absorbing the additional energy, the atom soon drops back to a lower energy level. When the atom drops back, it gives off its excess energy in the form of light.

The flow of current in a conductor generates heat energy that can cause the conductor to give off light. An *incandescent light bulb* works on this principle. Current flows through the filament of the bulb. As the filament gets hotter, some of its atoms are excited by being heated. When the atoms drop back to lower energy levels, the filament glows and gives off light.

Magnetism. The region around a magnet, where the force of magnetism can be felt, is called a *magnetic field.* A conductor carrying electricity is always surrounded by a magnetic field. For example, current flowing through a wire sets up a magnetic field around the wire. You can observe a field by running a vertical wire through a thin sheet of cardboard on which iron filings have been sprinkled. Connect the two ends of the wire to a battery so that current flows through the wire. Then tap the cardboard. The iron filings will form a series of circles around the wire. These circles outline the magnetic field surrounding the wire.

If a wire carrying current is wound into a coil, the magnetic field surrounding the wire is strengthened. Such a coil is called a *solenoid.* If a soft iron rod is placed inside the solenoid, the current in the solenoid magnetizes the iron, and an even stronger magnetic field results. Most electromagnets consist of a solenoid wound around an iron core. Such devices as doorbells and telephones operate by means of an electromagnet.

Chemical effects. When electric current flows through a conducting solution, it causes a chemical reaction. This process is known as *electrolysis.* For example, if the solution consists of water with dilute sulfuric acid added, electrolysis breaks up the water into hydrogen gas and oxygen gas. In the electrolysis of water, a battery is connected to carbon or platinum electrodes, which are placed in the solution. When current flows, hydrogen collects at the negative electrode, and oxygen collects at the positive electrode. Manufacturers use electrolysis in such processes as plating silverware, producing chemicals and metals, and purifying copper.

> See **Electricity** in *World Book* for more information on the following topics:
>
> •Uses of electricity   •Electric circuits
> •Kinds of electricity   •History
> •Sources of electricity

Effects of electricity

The flow of electric current through a conductor produces several useful effects. For example, electricity generates heat in a conductor. Ranges, toasters, and other electric devices work on this principle. Other effects of electricity include light, magnetism, and chemical effects.

WORLD BOOK diagrams by Zorica Dabich

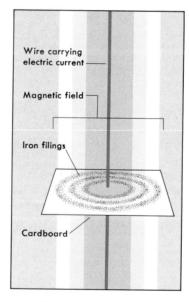

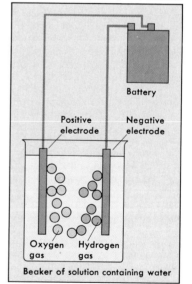

Light. When electricity flows through the filament of an incandescent bulb, the filament gets hot. The heat energizes some atoms of the filament. These *excited atoms* soon give off their additional energy in the form of light.

Magnetism. Electric current in a wire creates a magnetic field around the wire. If the wire is run through a sheet of cardboard on which iron filings have been sprinkled, the filings will form a series of circles outlining the field.

Chemical effects. If electricity is passed through a conducting solution, it causes a chemical reaction to take place. If the solution contains water, the electric current breaks up the water into hydrogen gas and oxygen gas.

Hewlett-Packard
Laser-operated measuring device

Singer Company
Automated checkout system

Jim Howard, Tom Stack & Assoc.
Stereo equipment

NASA
Spacecraft navigation system

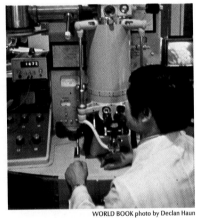
WORLD BOOK photo by Declan Haun
Electron microscope

Hewlett-Packard
Pocket-sized calculator

The amazing world of electronics gives us radio, TV, and other modern wonders, as shown in the photographs above. In less than 100 years, electronics has revolutionized such fields as communications, medicine, business and factory operations, and entertainment.

Electronics

Electronics is a branch of science and engineering closely related to the science of electricity. But electronics does jobs that electricity alone cannot do. Electronics makes possible such modern wonders as television, radio, stereo systems, radar, X rays, tape recorders, and high-speed computers.

The science of electronics began less than 100 years ago. But it has quickly changed people's lives in many ways. Television, radio, videocassette recorders (VCR's), and compact disc players have revolutionized communications and entertainment. Computers and robots speed up business and industrial operations. X-ray machines and other electronic equipment help physicians save lives. Air, sea, and space travel depend on navigation by radar, radio, and computers. Modern weapons systems use a wide variety of electronic equipment for target identification, range finding, and missile guidance.

Electronics depends on certain highly specialized *electron devices.* A television set, computer, or other piece of electronic equipment may contain from hun-

dreds to millions of these devices. The best-known and most important electron device is the *transistor.*

Transistors still operate millions of stereos, radios, and television sets. But engineers can now put more than a hundred thousand transistors on a single chip of silicon that is smaller than a fingernail. Such a chip forms an *integrated circuit.* Chips of this type can be wired together on circuit boards to produce electronic equipment that is smaller and less expensive—but far more powerful—than ever before.

Basic principles. To understand how electron devices work, a person must know something about the nature of atoms. Every atom has one or more *electrons*—particles that carry a negative electric charge. In substances called *conductors,* which include metals, each atom has one or more *free electrons* that can flow from atom to atom. This flow forms an electric current. The pressure that drives the electrons is called *voltage.*

Electronics and the science of electricity both deal with electric current. But each focuses on a different use of current. Electricity deals with current mainly as a form of energy that can operate lights, motors, and other equipment. Electronics treats electric current chiefly as a means of carrying information. Currents that carry information are called *signals.*

A steady, unchanging electric current can carry energy. But the current must vary in some way to serve as a signal. Some electron devices change a current's behavior to produce or modify signals. Others interpret the signals. The signals may represent sounds, pictures, numbers, letters, or computer instructions. Signals also can be used to count objects, measure time or temperature, or detect chemicals or radioactive materials.

The signals in electronic circuits may be classified as either *digital* or *analog.* A digital signal is like an ordinary electric switch—it is either on or off. An analog signal can have any value within a certain range.

Computers are the main users of digital signals. Different combinations of on and off switches can represent different numbers, letters, or other symbols that make up data stored by a computer. Other combinations tell the computer to carry out certain operations. As en-

gineers have learned to pack more and more transistors into each integrated circuit, the operation of computers has become increasingly faster. This is because the signals that travel between transistors do not have to travel as far when the transistors are closer together. Modern computers perform calculations billions of times faster than human beings can and thousands of times faster than the first electronic computers.

Analog signals are widely used to represent sounds and pictures because light levels and the frequencies of sound waves can have any value within a given range. Analog signals can be converted into digital signals, and digital signals into analog. For example, compact disc players convert digital sound signals on discs to analog signals for playback through loudspeakers.

The fast and reliable control of both digital and analog signals by electronic equipment is made possible by the unique properties of such *semiconductor* materials as silicon and germanium. Semiconductors are neither good conductors nor good *insulators* (nonconductors). But if they are altered in certain ways, they can both conduct and control electric currents.

WORLD BOOK illustrations by David Cunningham

Three basic electronic functions

Amplification strengthens a weak signal. Radio, TV, and other electronic signals consist of an electric current that pulses, or vibrates, much as alternating current (AC) does. But the pulses are usually too weak to operate such equipment as a radio or TV set. The equipment uses an *amplifier,* represented by the man at the right, to strengthen the pulses.

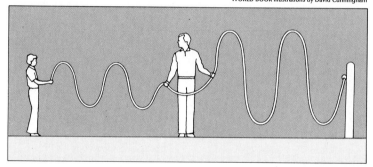

Switching allows a signal to be directed to one or more of several destinations. A type of switching called *rectification* changes alternating current (AC) to direct current (DC)—that is, it allows the current to flow in just one direction instead of back and forth continually. *Rectifiers* perform this job. In the drawing at the right, AC is represented by the wavy rope, and DC by the straightened rope. The man represents a rectifier.

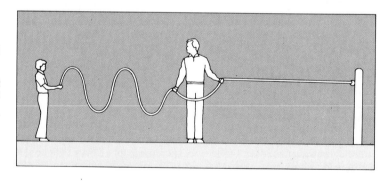

Oscillation changes direct current to a signal of a desired *frequency* (number of vibrations per second). An *oscillator,* represented by the man at the right, does this job. Oscillators have many uses, including the production of signals for radio and TV broadcasting and timing signals for various electronic equipment.

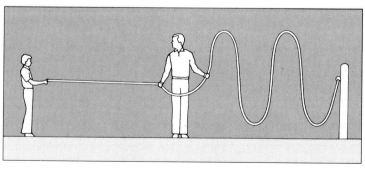

Terms used in electronics

Alternating current is an electric current that continually reverses its direction of flow.

Amplification is the strengthening of a weak signal to produce a strong one.

Direct current is an electric current that always flows in one direction only.

Electric current is a flow of electric charges. Most electric current consists of a flow of electrons.

Electron is a particle of an atom that carries a negative electric charge.

Electron device is any apparatus that controls an electric signal to change its basic character in some way. Electron tubes and solid-state devices are the main kinds of electron devices.

Electron tube is an electron device that controls a signal flowing in either a vacuum or a gas.

Frequency is the number of times a second that an electric signal vibrates—that is, changes its direction of flow.

Integrated circuit is a common solid-state device. Most integrated circuits consist of a tiny semiconductor chip. The chip can do the work of thousands of individual electron devices.

Oscillation is the changing of direct current to a signal of a desired frequency.

Rectification is the changing of alternating current to direct current.

Semiconductor device, especially the type called a *transistor,* is a common solid-state device. It is made largely of such materials as germanium or silicon, which are neither good conductors of electricity nor good *insulators* (nonconductors).

Signal is the pulse in an electric current that may represent sound, picture, or other information.

Solid-state device is an electron device that controls a signal flowing in certain solid materials, especially semiconductor materials.

Switching is the directing of an electric current to one or more of several destinations.

Electronics is based on the amplifying ability of transistors. Older equipment—as well as some new equipment—uses vacuum tubes to provide amplification. In addition to electronic amplifiers, almost all electronic equipment uses some nonelectronic devices to help process information. For example, broadcasting and receiving equipment for radio and television requires such nonelectronic devices as microphones and speakers. Microphones in a broadcasting studio change sound waves into weak electric signals. Speakers in television or radio receivers change the signals back into sound waves. But the electric signals must go through a number of changes from the time they leave the microphone until the speakers change them back into sound. Electron devices in the broadcasting and receiving equipment make most of these changes.

Electron devices perform three main functions: (1) amplification, (2) switching, and (3) oscillation. Electron devices perform these functions as part of *circuits.* A circuit consists of a series of connected electron devices and other parts. By combining the three functions in various ways, engineers design electronic equipment that performs many other special functions, such as the high-speed operations of computers.

See **Electronics** in *World Book* for more information on the following topics:

- Background to electronics
- Basic electronic functions
- Devices and circuits
- The development of electronics
- The electronics industry

Devices used in microelectronics

Microelectronics, a field of electronics, uses tiny electron devices called *integrated circuits* to run compact equipment. In an electronic watch, for example, such a circuit replaces springs and wheels. The time is shown in digits formed when an electric current passes through patterns of liquid crystals.

RCA; Pulsar (WORLD BOOK photo); Seiko Time Corporation (WORLD BOOK photo by Ryan Roessler); Seiko Time Corporation

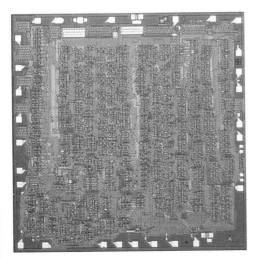

An integrated circuit used in an electronic watch is shown greatly magnified, *above,* and actual size, *above right.* This circuit contains 1,238 transistors and other devices that can be seen only under a microscope.

Inside the watch, *above right,* the integrated circuit is attached behind a tiny square of plastic, which can be seen in the middle of the photograph. A quartz crystal serves as the watch's timekeeping device. The integrated circuit, which is powered by a battery, keeps the crystal vibrating and translates the vibrations into electric impulses. These impulses contain such information as the time and the date. They activate liquid crystals, which become visible on the watch face as dark digits and characters, *right.*

Periodic table of the elements

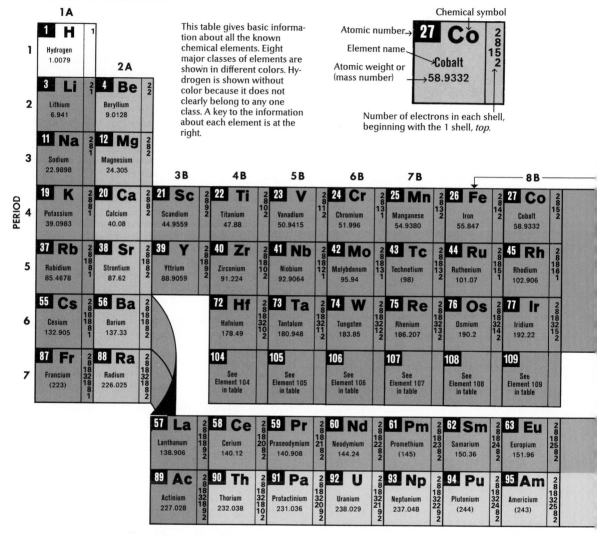

This table gives basic information about all the known chemical elements. Eight major classes of elements are shown in different colors. Hydrogen is shown without color because it does not clearly belong to any one class. A key to the information about each element is at the right.

Chemical symbol
Atomic number → 27 Co
Element name →Cobalt
Atomic weight or (mass number) → 58.9332

Number of electrons in each shell, beginning with the 1 shell, *top.*

Element, Chemical, is any one of the known kinds of basic chemical substances. All chemical substances are elements or *compounds* (combinations of elements). For example, hydrogen and oxygen are elements, and water is a compound of hydrogen and oxygen.

The International Union of Pure and Applied Chemistry recognizes 103 elements. Since 1964, several groups of scientists claim to have created six new elements. But none of the claims has yet been accepted officially.

A chemical element can be defined in either of two ways. It is (1) a substance that cannot be broken down chemically into simpler substances, or (2) a substance that contains only one kind of *atom.* Atoms are tiny bits of matter, so small that billions of them are needed to make even a small speck of any substance.

The idea that all things are elements or combinations of elements can be found in the writings of the ancient Greeks and other early peoples. Although this idea may seem simple, it is very difficult to decide whether a substance is an element or a compound. Many mistakes

were made in the discovery of the elements. For example, 7 of the 33 elements listed by the French chemist Antoine Lavoisier in the 1700's were not true elements.

Twelve chemical elements were known in ancient times, but it was not known that they were elements. Another 76 elements were discovered between 1557 and 1925. Since 1937, 21 other elements have been discovered. Eighteen of the known elements do not occur naturally on or in the earth. They have been artificially created. They were made when high-speed atomic particles hit and changed the makeup of other atoms.

Oxygen is the most plentiful element in the earth's crust. It accounts for nearly half the crust's weight. Other elements make up only a small fraction of the crust.

Nearly all elements on or in the earth are found combined with other elements. Pure elements are obtained by breaking down compounds that contain the desired elements. Artificially created elements are not plentiful. Only small amounts of most of them have been made. All artificially created elements and some of the ele-

8A

Alkali metals	Actinide series								**2** He	2
									Helium 4.00260	

Alkaline earth metals	Other metals		**3A**	**4A**	**5A**	**6A**	**7A**			

| Transition metals | Nonmetals | | **5** B | 2 3 | **6** C | 2 4 | **7** N | 2 5 | **8** O | 2 6 | **9** F | 2 7 | **10** Ne | 2 8 |
| | | | Boron 10.81 | | Carbon 12.011 | | Nitrogen 14.0067 | | Oxygen 15.9994 | | Fluorine 18.9984 | | Neon 20.179 | |

| Lanthanide series | Noble gases | | **13** Al | 2 8 3 | **14** Si | 2 8 4 | **15** P | 2 8 5 | **16** S | 2 8 6 | **17** Cl | 2 8 7 | **18** Ar | 2 8 8 |
| | | | Aluminum 26.9815 | | Silicon 28.0855 | | Phosphorus 30.9738 | | Sulfur 32.06 | | Chlorine 35.453 | | Argon 39.948 | |

1B   **2B**

28 Ni	2 8 16 2	**29** Cu	2 8 18 1	**30** Zn	2 8 18 2	**31** Ga	2 8 18 3	**32** Ge	2 8 18 4	**33** As	2 8 18 5	**34** Se	2 8 18 6	**35** Br	2 8 18 7	**36** Kr	2 8 18 8
Nickel 58.69		Copper 63.546		Zinc 65.39		Gallium 69.72		Germanium 72.59		Arsenic 74.9216		Selenium 78.96		Bromine 79.904		Krypton 83.80	

| **46** Pd | 2 8 18 18 0 | **47** Ag | 2 8 18 18 1 | **48** Cd | 2 8 18 18 2 | **49** In | 2 8 18 18 3 | **50** Sn | 2 8 18 18 4 | **51** Sb | 2 8 18 18 5 | **52** Te | 2 8 18 18 6 | **53** I | 2 8 18 18 7 | **54** Xe | 2 8 18 18 8 |
| Palladium 106.42 | | Silver 107.868 | | Cadmium 112.41 | | Indium 114.82 | | Tin 118.71 | | Antimony 121.75 | | Tellurium 127.60 | | Iodine 126.905 | | Xenon 131.29 | |

| **78** Pt | 2 8 18 32 17 1 | **79** Au | 2 8 18 32 18 1 | **80** Hg | 2 8 18 32 18 2 | **81** Tl | 2 8 18 32 18 3 | **82** Pb | 2 8 18 32 18 4 | **83** Bi | 2 8 18 32 18 5 | **84** Po | 2 8 18 32 18 6 | **85** At | 2 8 18 32 18 7 | **86** Rn | 2 8 18 32 18 8 |
| Platinum 195.08 | | Gold 196.967 | | Mercury 200.59 | | Thallium 204.383 | | Lead 207.2 | | Bismuth 208.980 | | Polonium (209) | | Astatine (210) | | Radon (222) | |

64 Gd	2 8 18 25 9 2	**65** Tb	2 8 18 27 8 2	**66** Dy	2 8 18 28 8 2	**67** Ho	2 8 18 29 8 2	**68** Er	2 8 18 30 8 2	**69** Tm	2 8 18 31 8 2	**70** Yb	2 8 18 32 8 2	**71** Lu	2 8 18 32 9 2
Gadolinium 157.25		Terbium 158.925		Dysprosium 162.50		Holmium 164.930		Erbium 167.26		Thulium 168.934		Ytterbium 173.04		Lutetium 174.967	

| **96** Cm | 2 8 18 32 25 9 2 | **97** Bk | 2 8 18 32 26 9 2 | **98** Cf | 2 8 18 32 28 8 2 | **99** Es | 2 8 18 32 29 8 2 | **100** Fm | 2 8 18 32 30 8 2 | **101** Md | 2 8 18 32 31 8 2 | **102** No | 2 8 18 32 32 8 2 | **103** Lr | 2 8 18 32 32 9 2 |
| Curium (247) | | Berkelium (247) | | Californium (251) | | Einsteinium (252) | | Fermium (257) | | Mendelevium (258) | | Nobelium (259) | | Lawrencium (260) | |

ments found on or in the earth are radioactive.

Names and symbols of elements. The names of some elements came from Greek or Latin words. The word *bromine* comes from the Greek word for *stench* (bad smell). Many artificially created elements are named in honor of a place or individual. Scientists at the University of California at Berkeley discovered berkelium and named it in honor of that city. Einsteinium was named in honor of the physicist Albert Einstein.

Each element—except elements 104 through 109—has a symbol consisting of one or two letters. Chemists use the symbol as an abbreviation for the element. In some cases, the symbol is the first letter of the element's name. For example, C is the symbol for carbon. If the names of two or more elements begin with the same letter, two letters of a name are used. Calcium has the symbol Ca, and zinc has the symbol Zn. Some symbols came from an old word for the element. The symbol for lead, Pb, comes from the Latin word for lead, *plumbum.*

Chemists use the symbols of elements to write formulas for compounds. The formulas tell which elements and how many atoms of each are in a compound. The symbols also provide an international language for chemists. The symbols for all the elements are in the *Periodic table* and the alphabetic *Table of the elements* with this article.

How to use the periodic table. The easiest way to locate elements on the table is by their atomic numbers. The *Table of the elements* gives the atomic number of each element. Chemists place the elements into classes that have some similar properties. These classes are shown in color on the periodic table.

See **Element, Chemical,** in *World Book* for more information on The periodic table, How to use the periodic table, and Development of the periodic table.

Table of the elements and their discoverers

Name	Symbol	Atomic weight*	Atomic number	Density (g/cm³) at 20° C	Discoverer	Country of discovery	Date of discovery
Actinium	Ac	227.028	89	10.07†	André Debierne	France	1899
Aluminum	Al	26.9815	13	2.70	Hans Christian Oersted	Denmark	1825
Americium	Am	[243]	95	13.67	G. T. Seaborg; R. A. James; L. O. Morgan; A. Ghiorso	United States	1945
Antimony	Sb	121.75	51	6.691			Known to ancients
Argon	Ar	39.948	18	0.00166	Sir William Ramsay; Baron Rayleigh	Scotland; Eng.	1894
Arsenic	As	74.9216	33	5.73			Known to ancients
Astatine	At	[210]	85	0.0175†	D. R. Corson; K. R. MacKenzie; E. Segrè	United States	1940
Barium	Ba	137.33	56	3.5	Sir Humphry Davy	England	1808
Berkelium	Bk	[247]	97	14.0**	G. T. Seaborg; S. G. Thompson; A. Ghiorso	United States	1949
Beryllium	Be	9.0128	4	1.848	Friedrich Wöhler; A. A. Bussy	Germany; Fr.	1828
Bismuth	Bi	208.980	83	9.747			Known to ancients
Boron	B	10.81	5	2.34	H. Davy; J. L. Gay-Lussac; L. J. Thenard	England; Fr.	1808
Bromine	Br	79.904	35	3.12	Antoine J. Balard; Carl J. Löwig	France; Germany	1826
Cadmium	Cd	112.41	48	8.65	Friedrich Stromeyer	Germany	1817
Calcium	Ca	40.08	20	1.55	Sir Humphry Davy	England	1808
Californium	Cf	[251]	98	————	G. T. Seaborg; S. G. Thompson; A. Ghiorso; K. Street, Jr.	United States	1950
Carbon	C	12.011	6	2.25			Known to ancients
Cerium	Ce	140.12	58	6.768	W. von Hisinger; J. Berzelius; M. Klaproth	Sweden; Germany	1803
Cesium	Cs	132.905	55	1.873	Gustav Kirchhoff, Robert Bunsen	Germany	1860
Chlorine	Cl	35.453	17	0.00295	Carl Wilhelm Scheele	Sweden	1774
Chromium	Cr	51.996	24	7.19	Louis Vauquelin	France	1797
Cobalt	Co	58.9332	27	8.9	Georg Brandt	Sweden	1737
Copper	Cu	63.546	29	8.96			Known to ancients
Curium	Cm	[247]	96	13.51†	G. T. Seaborg; R. A. James; A. Ghiorso	United States	1944
Dysprosium	Dy	162.50	66	8.550	Paul Émile Lecoq de Boisbaudran	France	1886
Einsteinium	Es	[252]	99	————	Argonne; Los Alamos; U. of Calif.	United States	1952
Element 104	——	————	104	————	Claimed by G. Flerov and others	Soviet Union	1964
					Claimed by A. Ghiorso and others	United States	1969
Element 105	—	————	105	————	Claimed by G. Flerov and others	Soviet Union	1968
					Claimed by A. Ghiorso and others	United States	1970
Element 106	—	————	106	————	Claimed by G. Flerov and others	Soviet Union	1974
					Claimed by A. Ghiorso and others	United States	1974
Element 107	—	————	107	————	Claimed by G. Flerov; Y. Oganessian and others	Soviet Union	1976
					Claimed by P. Armbruster and others	Germany	1981
Element 108	—	————	108	————	Claimed by P. Armbruster and others	Germany	1984
Element 109	—	————	109	————	Claimed by P. Armbruster and others	Germany	1982
Erbium	Er	167.26	68	9.15	Carl Mosander	Sweden	1843
Europium	Eu	151.96	63	5.245	Eugène Demarçay	France	1901
Fermium	Fm	[257]	100	————	Argonne; Los Alamos; U. of Calif.	United States	1953
Fluorine	F	18.9984	9	0.00158	Henri Moissan	France	1886
Francium	Fr	[223]	87	————	Marguerite Perey	France	1939
Gadolinium	Gd	157.25	64	7.86	Jean de Marignac	Switzerland	1880
Gallium	Ga	69.72	31	5.907	Paul Émile Lecoq de Boisbaudran	France	1875
Germanium	Ge	72.59	32	5.323	Clemens Winkler	Germany	1886
Gold	Au	196.967	79	19.32			Known to ancients
Hafnium	Hf	178.49	72	13.31	Dirk Coster; Georg von Hevesy	Denmark	1923
Helium	He	4.00260	2	0.0001664	Sir William Ramsay; Nils Langlet; P. T. Cleve	Scotland; Sweden	1895
Holmium	Ho	164.930	67	8.79	J. L. Soret	Switzerland	1878
Hydrogen	H	1.0079	1	0.00008375	Henry Cavendish	England	1766
Indium	In	114.82	49	7.31	Ferdinand Reich; H. Richter	Germany	1863
Iodine	I	126.905	53	4.93	Bernard Courtois	France	1811
Iridium	Ir	192.22	77	22.65	Smithson Tennant	England	1804
Iron	Fe	55.847	26	7.874			Known to ancients
Krypton	Kr	83.80	36	0.003488	Sir William Ramsay; M. W. Travers	Great Britain	1898
Lanthanum	La	138.906	57	6.189	Carl Mosander	Sweden	1839
Lawrencium	Lr	[260]	103	————	A. Ghiorso; T. Sikkeland; A. E. Larsh; R. M. Latimer	United States	1961
Lead	Pb	207.2	82	11.35			Known to ancients

*A number in brackets indicates the mass number of the most stable isotope.
†The density is calculated and not based on an actual measurement.
**Estimated.

Table of the elements and their discoverers

Name	Symbol	Atomic weight*	Atomic number	Density (g/cm³) at 20° C	Discoverer	Country of discovery	Date of discovery
Lithium	Li	6.941	3	0.534	Johann Arfvedson	Sweden	1817
Lutetium	Lu	174.967	71	9.849	Georges Urbain	France	1907
Magnesium	Mg	24.305	12	1.738	Sir Humphry Davy	England	1808
Manganese	Mn	54.9380	25	7.3	Johan Gahn	Sweden	1774
Mendelevium	Md	[258]	101	————	G. T. Seaborg; A. Ghiorso; B. Harvey; G. R. Choppin; S. G. Thompson	United States	1955
Mercury	Hg	200.59	80	13.546			Known to ancients
Molybdenum	Mo	95.94	42	10.22	Carl Wilhelm Scheele	Sweden	1778
Neodymium	Nd	144.24	60	7.0	C. F. Auer von Welsbach	Austria	1885
Neon	Ne	20.179	10	0.0008387	Sir William Ramsay; M. W. Travers	England	1898
Neptunium	Np	237.048	93	20.25	E. M. McMillan; P. H. Abelson	United States	1940
Nickel	Ni	58.69	28	8.902	Axel Cronstedt	Sweden	1751
Niobium	Nb	92.9064	41	8.57	Charles Hatchett	England	1801
Nitrogen	N	14.0067	7	0.001165	Daniel Rutherford	Scotland	1772
Nobelium	No	[259]	102	————	A. Ghiorso; G. T. Seaborg; T. Sikkeland; J. R. Walton	United States	1958
Osmium	Os	190.2	76	22.48	Smithson Tennant	England	1804
Oxygen	O	15.9994	8	0.001332	Joseph Priestley; Carl Wilhelm Scheele	England; Sweden	1774
Palladium	Pd	106.42	46	12.02	William Wollaston	England	1803
Phosphorus	P	30.9738	15	1.83	Hennig Brand	Germany	1669
Platinum	Pt	195.08	78	21.45	Julius Scaliger	Italy	1557
Plutonium	Pu	[244]	94	19.86	G. T. Seaborg; J. W. Kennedy; E. M. McMillan; A. C. Wahl	United States	1940
Polonium	Po	[209]	84	9.24	Pierre and Marie Curie	France	1898
Potassium	K	39.0983	19	0.862	Sir Humphry Davy	England	1807
Praseodymium	Pr	140.908	59	6.769	C. F. Auer von Welsbach	Austria	1885
Promethium	Pm	[145]	61	7.22	J. A. Marinsky; Lawrence E. Glendenin; Charles D. Coryell	United States	1945
Protactinium	Pa	231.036	91	15.37†	Otto Hahn; Lise Meitner; Frederick Soddy; John Cranston	Germany; England	1917
Radium	Ra	226.025	88	5.0	Pierre and Marie Curie	France	1898
Radon	Rn	[222]	86	0.00923	Friedrich Ernst Dorn	Germany	1900
Rhenium	Re	186.207	75	21.02	Walter Noddack; Ida Tacke; Otto Berg	Germany	1925
Rhodium	Rh	102.906	45	12.41	William Wollaston	England	1803
Rubidium	Rb	85.4678	37	1.532	R. Bunsen; G. Kirchhoff	Germany	1861
Ruthenium	Ru	101.07	44	12.41	Karl Klaus	Russia	1844
Samarium	Sm	150.36	62	7.49	Paul Émile Lecoq de Boisbaudran	France	1879
Scandium	Sc	44.9559	21	2.989	Lars Nilson	Sweden	1879
Selenium	Se	78.96	34	4.79	Jöns Berzelius	Sweden	1817
Silicon	Si	28.0855	14	2.33	Jöns Berzelius	Sweden	1823
Silver	Ag	107.868	47	10.50			Known to ancients
Sodium	Na	22.9898	11	0.971	Sir Humphry Davy	England	1807
Strontium	Sr	87.62	38	2.60	A. Crawford	Scotland	1790
Sulfur	S	32.06	16	2.07			Known to ancients
Tantalum	Ta	180.948	73	16.6	Anders Ekeberg	Sweden	1802
Technetium	Tc	[98]	43	11.50†	Carlo Perrier; Émilio Segrè	Italy	1937
Tellurium	Te	127.60	52	6.24	Franz Müller von Reichenstein	Romania	1782
Terbium	Tb	158.925	65	8.25	Carl Mosander	Sweden	1843
Thallium	Tl	204.383	81	11.85	Sir William Crookes	England	1861
Thorium	Th	232.038	90	11.66	Jöns Berzelius	Sweden	1828
Thulium	Tm	168.934	69	9.31	Per Theodor Cleve	Sweden	1879
Tin	Sn	118.71	50	7.2984			Known to ancients
Titanium	Ti	47.88	22	4.507	William Gregor	England	1791
Tungsten	W	183.85	74	19.3	Fausto and Juan José de Elhuyar	Spain	1783
Uranium	U	238.029	92	19.07	Martin Klaproth	Germany	1789
Vanadium	V	50.9415	23	6.1	Nils Sefström	Sweden	1830
Xenon	Xe	131.29	54	0.005495	Sir William Ramsay; M. W. Travers	England	1898
Ytterbium	Yb	173.04	70	6.959	Jean de Marignac	Switzerland	1878
Yttrium	Y	88.9059	39	4.472	Johann Gadolin	Finland	1794
Zinc	Zn	65.39	30	7.133	Andreas Marggraf	Germany	1746
Zirconium	Zr	91.224	40	6.506	Martin Klaproth	Germany	1789

*A number in brackets indicates the mass number of the most stable isotope.
†The density is calculated and not based on an actual measurement.

Cynthia Moss

Most elephants live in herds that consist of a number of adults and their young. The majority of herds are led by an old female called a *matriarch.* This picture shows a herd of African elephants grazing in a grassy clearing in Kenya. The matriarch stands in the center foreground.

Elephant is the largest animal that lives on land. Among all animals, only some kinds of whales are larger. The elephant is also the second tallest member of the animal kingdom. Only the giraffe is taller. Elephants are the only animals that have a nose in the form of a long trunk, which they use as a hand. They have larger ears than any other animal, and their tusks are the largest teeth.

There are two chief kinds of elephants, *African elephants* and *Asiatic elephants,* also known as *Indian elephants.* African elephants live only in Africa south of the Sahara. Asiatic elephants live in parts of India and Southeast Asia.

Elephants are extremely strong and highly intelligent. People have tamed and trained them for thousands of years. The logging industry in some Asian countries uses elephants to carry heavy loads. People throughout the world enjoy watching elephants in circuses and zoos. Trained circus elephants stand on their heads, lie down and roll over, dance, and perform other tricks.

One of the earliest recorded uses of elephants took place in war. In 331 B.C., a Macedonian army led by Alexander the Great defeated Persian soldiers who rode elephants in battle. In 218 B.C., the famous general Hannibal of Carthage used elephants when he crossed the Alps from France and invaded Italy.

During the 1800's, an African elephant named Jumbo was featured by the London Zoo for more than 24 years. Visitors came from all parts of the world to see Jumbo, the largest animal in captivity at that time. He stood 11 feet (3.4 meters) tall and weighed more than $7\frac{1}{4}$ short tons (6.6 metric tons). In 1882, the American showman P. T. Barnum purchased Jumbo and made the elephant a star attraction of his circus. The word *jumbo* became a common adjective for anything extremely large.

Through the years, people have killed large numbers of elephants. They also have settled on much of the land where the animals lived. As a result, the survival of wild elephants became seriously endangered during the late 1900's. Hunters kill elephants chiefly for their tusks, which are made of ivory. The ivory is used for jewelry and other items. Many African and Asian nations have passed laws to protect elephants from hunters. Some countries, including the United States and Canada, forbid the importing of ivory and ivory products. However, hunters continue to kill thousands of elephants illegally year after year.

The body of an elephant

The height of an adult elephant about equals the animal's length. An elephant has a short, muscular neck and an enormous head with huge, triangular ears. The trunk extends from the upper jaw, and a tusk grows from each side of the jaw at the base of the trunk. Massive legs support the body. An elephant's tail is small in relation to the rest of the animal. It measures about $3\frac{1}{3}$ feet (1 meter) long.

Skin and hair. Elephants have gray, wrinkled skin that hangs in loose folds. The skin of an adult measures up to $1\frac{1}{2}$ inches (3 centimeters) thick. It weighs about 1 short ton (0.9 metric ton). However, an elephant's skin is surprisingly tender. Some insects, including flies and mosquitoes, can bite into the skin.

Elephants are called *pachyderms,* a term that comes from a Greek word meaning *thick-skinned.* But elephants, unlike some other mammals, do not have a layer of fat under their skin to protect them from the cold. They get stomach cramps if the temperature drops below about 35° F. (2° C).

An elephant has no sweat glands, and so it must cool

off in other ways. It may get rid of excess body heat by flapping its enormous ears or by spraying water on itself. Elephants also stay cool by rolling in mud. The mud dries on their skin and thus shields it from the sun.

At birth, elephants are covered with brown hair. This hair becomes black through the years, and much of it wears off. Adult elephants have so little hair that they appear almost hairless. Patches of black bristles may grow around the ears, eyes, and mouth, and the end of the tail has a bunch of long bristles.

Trunk. An elephant's trunk is a combined nose and upper lip. It consists of a strong, flexible, boneless mass of flesh. The trunk of an adult elephant measures about 5 feet (1.5 meters) long.

An elephant breathes and smells with its trunk and uses it when eating and drinking. The animal sniffs the air and the ground almost constantly with its trunk. It carries food and water to its mouth with its trunk. It also gives itself a shower by shooting a stream of water through its trunk. The trunk of an adult can hold about $1\frac{1}{2}$ gallons (6 liters) of water.

An elephant grasps objects with its trunk much as a person does with a hand. The trunk can carry a log that weighs as much as 600 pounds (272 kilograms). The tip of the trunk can pick up an object as small as a coin. An elephant also uses its trunk to stroke its mate and its young. When fighting, the animal may use its trunk to grasp an enemy. But sometimes the trunk is protected by curling it under the chin.

Tusks and teeth. An elephant's tusks are actually long, curved upper teeth called *incisors.* They are made of ivory. About two-thirds of each tusk extends from the upper jaw. The rest is in the skull. Elephants use their tusks to dig for food and to fight. The tusks can lift and carry a load weighing as much as 1 short ton (0.9 metric ton). Most Asiatic females and some Asiatic males have no tusks.

Baby elephants grow *milk tusks,* which measure no longer than 2 inches (5 centimeters). These tusks fall out before the elephant is 2 years old. Permanent tusks replace them and continue to grow throughout the animal's life.

Elephants also have four *molars* (back teeth). The molars of an adult may measure 1 foot (30 centimeters) long and weigh about $8\frac{1}{2}$ pounds (4 kilograms). These teeth have jagged edges that help grind food. One molar lies on each side of both jaws, and additional molars form in the back of the mouth. The molars in front gradually wear down and drop out, and the ones in back push forward and replace them. An elephant grows six sets of molars during its lifetime. Each set consists of four teeth. The last set of molars appears when the animal is about 40 years old.

Legs and feet. The legs of an elephant are pillarlike structures. The feet are nearly round. Each foot has a thick pad of tissue that acts as a cushion. The foot expands under the elephant's weight and contracts when the animal lifts the leg. Elephants may sink deep into mud, but they can pull their legs out easily because the feet become smaller when lifted.

Senses. The trunk provides a keen sense of smell, and elephants depend on this sense more than on any other. They frequently wave their trunks high in the air to catch the scent of food or enemies. An elephant can

Interesting facts about elephants

The skin of an elephant is gray and wrinkled. An adult elephant's skin measures up to $1\frac{1}{2}$ inches (3 centimeters) thick and weighs about 1 short ton (0.9 metric ton). However, it is surprisingly tender. Flies, mosquitoes, and other insects can bite into the skin.

An angry or frightened elephant can run at a speed of more than 25 miles (40 kilometers) an hour for a short distance. On a long journey, a herd of elephants travels at about 10 miles (16 kilometers) an hour.

An elephant uses its trunk as a hand. The trunk can carry a 600-pound (272-kilogram) log or an object as small as a coin. Elephants also breathe and smell with their trunks.

Elephants love water and frequently bathe in lakes and rivers. They are excellent swimmers. An elephant gives itself a shower by shooting a stream of water from its trunk.

WORLD BOOK illustrations
by James Teason

Neal Ulevich

Trained elephants, such as the Asiatic elephant shown above, are used in the logging industry in several Asian countries. An elephant can carry heavy loads with its trunk or on its back.

How African and Asiatic elephants differ
The two chief kinds of elephants, African elephants and Asiatic elephants, differ in size, disposition, and body features. For example, African elephants are larger and fiercer and have bigger tusks. These drawings show various physical differences between the two species.

WORLD BOOK illustrations by John D. Dawson

African Elephant

Back dips
Ears cover shoulder
Forehead forms smooth curve
Loose fold of skin
Three toes
Four or five toes
Two knobs of flesh on tip of trunk

Asiatic Elephant

Two humps on forehead
Ears do not cover shoulder
Arched back
One knob of flesh on tip of trunk
Five toes
Four toes

smell a human being more than a mile (1.6 kilometers) away.

Elephants also have good hearing. Their huge ears pick up sounds of other animals from as far as 2 miles (3.2 kilometers) away. When an elephant is curious about a sound, its ears stand straight out.

The elephant's sense of touch is in the sensitive tip of its trunk. An elephant can recognize the shape of an object and whether the object is rough or smooth and hot or cold.

Elephants have poor sight and are color blind. Their eyes are small in relation to the enormous head. An elephant cannot turn its head completely, and so it can see only in the front and to the sides. The animal must turn around to see anything behind it.

Intelligence. Elephants have one of the largest brains and rank high in intelligence among animals. An elephant can learn to perform a variety of tasks and tricks if commands and signals are repeated over and over again.

Most elephants chosen for any type of training are 15 to 20 years old. Younger elephants can be trained more easily, but they cannot do heavy work. The training process starts after an elephant has been in captivity for a

WORLD BOOK illustration by James Teason and John D. Dawson

Internal anatomy of a female African elephant

This view of a female African elephant shows the animal's skeleton and some of its internal organs. An elephant's organs resemble those of other mammals but are much larger. For example, an elephant's heart is about 5 times as large as a human heart and more than 50 times as heavy.

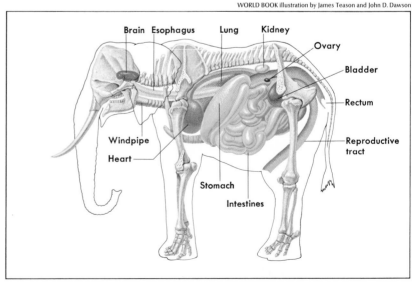

Brain
Esophagus
Lung
Kidney
Ovary
Bladder
Rectum
Reproductive tract
Windpipe
Heart
Stomach
Intestines

number of weeks. A trainer mounts the animal and gradually teaches it to obey signals. The trainer gives signals by gently kicking the elephant behind its ears. These signals include commands to kneel, stand up, turn around, and walk forward and backward. A well-trained elephant can also learn about 30 verbal commands.

Elephants have an excellent memory and rarely forget what they learn. They can remember both pleasant and unpleasant experiences years later.

The life of an elephant

Elephant herds. Most elephants live in herds. The size of an elephant herd probably depends mainly on the amount of food and water available. A herd of African elephants may have up to 1,000 members, but Asiatic elephants live in groups of only 5 to 60 animals. A herd of elephants consists of a number of families, each of which is made up of several adults and their young. Most herds of elephants are led by an old *cow* (female elephant) called a *matriarch.*

Some elephants leave the herd and live alone. Many of them are dangerous *bulls* (male elephants) called *rogues,* which may have been driven from the herd by other bulls because of their vicious behavior. Rogues usually attack immediately when they come upon another animal or a human being. The savageness of these elephants probably results from constant pain caused by decayed teeth, a wound, or a disease.

Elephants have no permanent homes. They roam wherever they can find enough food and water. A herd may wander over an area of about 390 square miles (1,000 square kilometers). Elephants in Kenya roam areas as large as 1,900 square miles (5,000 square kilometers). Sometimes, two or more herds gather and move to a new location. They may travel hundreds of miles together. Elephants often leave an area that has ample food and water. Zoologists believe they do so to avoid insect pests.

Wild elephants usually eat for about 16 hours every day. They bathe in lakes and rivers and like to roll in muddy water. After a mud bath, an elephant may cover

Peter Davey, Bruce Coleman Inc.

A baby elephant stays with its mother until it reaches adulthood at the age of 10 to 14 years. The youngster drinks the mother's milk for two to six years and then starts to graze.

itself with dirt. The dirt coating helps protect the animal's skin from the sun and insects. Elephants often play by tussling among themselves with their tusks and trunks.

Elephants communicate with one another in various ways. For example, they touch with their trunks as a greeting. A mother elephant calls to her young by slapping her ears against her head. Elephants also communicate by means of rumbling, grunting, and squealing noises.

See **Elephant** in *World Book* for more information on the following topics:

•The importance of ele-
  phants
•Kinds of elephants

•The life of an elephant
•Protecting elephants

C. Haagner, Bruce Coleman Inc.

Elephants cool off by bathing. They especially like to roll in muddy water. The mud dries on the animal's skin and helps protect it from the sun. An elephant needs water and mud for cooling because its skin has no sweat glands.

Ralph Crane, *Life,* © Time, Inc.   Hugh Rogers, Monkmeyer   David Muench, Van Cleve Photography

Environmental pollution damages our surroundings. Gases and smoke in the air, chemicals and other substances in water, and solid wastes on land are all common forms of pollution.

Environmental pollution

Environmental pollution is a term that refers to all the ways by which people pollute their surroundings. People dirty the air with gases and smoke, poison the water with chemicals and other substances, and damage the soil with too many fertilizers and pesticides. People also pollute their surroundings in various other ways. For example, they ruin natural beauty by scattering junk and litter on the land and in the water. They operate machines and motor vehicles that fill the air with disturbing noise. Nearly everyone causes environmental pollution in some way.

Environmental pollution is one of the most serious problems facing humanity today. Air, water, and soil—all harmed by pollution—are necessary to the survival of all living things. Badly polluted air can cause illness, and even death. Polluted water kills fish and other marine life. Pollution of soil reduces the amount of land available for growing food. Environmental pollution also brings ugliness to our naturally beautiful world.

Everyone wants to reduce pollution. But the pollution problem is as complicated as it is serious. It is complicated because much pollution is caused by things that benefit people. For example, exhaust from automobiles causes a large percentage of all air pollution. But the automobile provides transportation for millions of people. Factories discharge much of the material that pollutes air and water, but factories provide jobs for people and produce goods that people want. Too much fertilizer or pesticide can ruin soil, but fertilizers and pesticides are important aids to the growing of crops.

Thus, to end or greatly reduce pollution immediately,

people would have to stop using many things that benefit them. Most people do not want to do that, of course. But pollution can be gradually reduced in several ways. Scientists and engineers can work to find ways to lessen the amount of pollution that such things as automobiles and factories cause. Governments can pass and enforce laws that require businesses and individuals to stop, or cut down on, certain polluting activities. And—perhaps most importantly—individuals and groups of people can work to persuade their representatives in government, and also persuade businesses, to take action toward reducing pollution.

People have always polluted their surroundings. But throughout much of history, pollution was not a major problem. Most people lived in uncrowded rural areas, and the *pollutants* (waste products) they produced were widely scattered. People had no pollution-causing machines or motor vehicles. The development of crowded industrial cities in the 1700's and 1800's made pollution a major problem. People and factories in these cities put huge amounts of pollutants into small areas. During the 1900's, urban areas continued to develop and automobiles and other new inventions made pollution steadily worse. By the mid-1900's, pollution had affected the water in every major lake and river and the air over every major city in the United States and other industrial countries. Since the late 1960's, millions of people have become alarmed by the dangers of pollution. Large numbers of people are now working to reduce pollution.

Kinds of pollution

There are several kinds of environmental pollution. They include air pollution, water pollution, soil pollution, and pollution caused by solid wastes, noise, and radiation.

All parts of the environment are closely related to one another. (The study of the relationships among living things, and between living things and other parts of the environment, is called *ecology* [see **Ecology**].) Because of the close relationships, a kind of pollution that chiefly harms one part of the environment may also affect others. For example, air pollution harms the air. But rain washes pollutants out of the air and deposits them on the land and in bodies of water. Wind, on the other hand, blows pollutants off the land and puts them into the air.

Air pollution turns clear, odorless air into hazy, smelly air that harms health, kills plants, and damages property. People cause air pollution by pouring hundreds of millions of tons of gases and *particulates* into the atmosphere each year. Particulates are tiny particles of solid or liquid matter. One of the most common forms of air pollution is smog.

Most air pollution results from *combustion* (burning) processes. The burning of gasoline to power motor vehicles and the burning of coal to heat buildings and help manufacture products are examples of such processes. Each time a fuel is burned in a combustion process, some type of pollutant is released into the air. The pollutants range from small amounts of colorless poison gas to clouds of thick black smoke.

Weather conditions can help reduce the amount of pollutants in the air. Wind scatters pollutants, and rain and snow wash them into the ground. But in many areas, pollutants are put into the air faster than weather conditions can dispose of them. In crowded cities, for example, thousands of automobiles, factories, and furnaces may add tons of pollutants to a small area of the atmosphere each day.

At times, weather conditions cause pollutants to build up over an area instead of clearing them away. One such condition—called *thermal inversion*—occurs when a layer of warm air settles over a layer of cooler air that lies near the ground. The warm air holds down the cool air and prevents pollutants from rising and scattering. A serious pollution problem results when a thermal inversion occurs over a city that is pouring tons of pollutants into the air.

One serious result of air pollution is its harmful effect on human health. Both gases and particulates burn people's eyes and irritate their lungs. Particulates can settle in the lungs and worsen such respiratory diseases as asthma and bronchitis. Some experts believe that particulates may even help cause such diseases as cancer, emphysema, and pneumonia. In cities throughout the world, long periods of heavy air pollution have caused illness and death rates to increase dramatically.

Air pollution also harms plants. Poisonous gases in the air can restrict the growth of, and eventually kill, nearly all kinds of plants. Forests in Tennessee, citrus groves near Los Angeles, and vegetable gardens in New Jersey have all been seriously damaged by air pollution.

Most materials get dirty and wear out more quickly in polluted air than in clean air. Polluted air even harms such hard and strong materials as concrete and steel. In some cities, statues and other art objects that stood outdoors for centuries have been moved indoors because air pollution threatened to destroy them.

Air pollutants may also affect the weather. Both gases and particulates can cause changes in the average temperatures of an area. Particulates scatter the sun's rays and reduce the amount of sunlight that reaches the ground. Such interference with sunlight may cause average temperatures in an area to drop. Some gases, including carbon dioxide, allow sunlight to reach the ground, but prevent the sunlight's heat from rising out of the atmosphere and flowing back into space. This development, called a *greenhouse effect,* may cause average temperatures to rise.

For more details on air pollution, see **Air pollution.** In *World Book,* see **Smog.**

Water pollution reduces the amount of pure, fresh water that is available for such necessities as drinking and cleaning, and for such activities as swimming and fishing. The pollutants that affect water come mainly from industries, farms, and sewerage systems. Industries dump huge amounts of waste products into bodies of water each year. These wastes include chemicals, wastes from animal and plant matter, and hundreds of other substances. Wastes from farms include animal wastes, fertilizers, and pesticides. Most of these materials drain off farm fields and into nearby bodies of water. Sewerage systems carry wastes from homes, offices, and industries into water. Nearly all cities have waste treatment plants that remove some of the most harmful wastes from sewage. But even most of the treated sewage contains material that harms water.

Natural cycles work to absorb small amounts of wastes in bodies of water. During a cycle, wastes are turned into useful, or at least harmless, substances. Bacteria called *aerobic bacteria* use oxygen to decay natural wastes such as dead fish and break them down into chemicals, including nitrates, phosphates, and carbon dioxide. These chemicals, called *nutrients,* are used as food by *algae* (simple organisms) and green plants in the water. The algae serve as food for microscopic animals called *zooplankton.* Small fish, such as minnows, eat the zooplankton. The small fish, in turn, are eaten by larger fish, which eventually die and are broken down by bacteria. The cycle then begins again.

The same natural cycles work on wastes poured into water by people. Bacteria break down chemicals and other wastes and turn them into nutrients, or else into substances that will not harm fish or sea plants. But if too much waste matter is poured into the water, the whole cycle will begin to break down, and the water becomes dirtier and dirtier. The bacteria that work to decay the wastes use up too much oxygen during the decaying process. As a result, less oxygen is available for the animals and plants in the water. Animals and plants then die, adding even more wastes to the water. Finally, the water's entire oxygen supply is used up and, without oxygen, *anaerobic bacteria,* rather than aerobic bacteria, decay wastes. The anaerobic decaying process causes wastes to give off smelly gases.

Nutrients in water cause a similar process—called *nutrient enrichment,* or *eutrophication*—to take place. Nutrients that people add to water, such as nitrates from agricultural fertilizers and phosphates from detergents in sewage, greatly increase the growth of algae in water. As larger amounts of algae grow, larger amounts also die. The dead algae become wastes, and, as they decay, they use up the water's oxygen supply.

The addition of heated water to a body of water also upsets cycles. Heated water can kill animals and plants that are accustomed to living at lower temperatures. It also reduces the amount of oxygen that water can hold. The addition of heated water is called *thermal pollution.* Most heated water comes from industries and power plants that use water for cooling.

Another major pollutant is oil, which enters oceans primarily from oil tankers. Such oil spills ruin beaches and kill birds and marine life.

For more details on water pollution, see **Water pollution.**

Soil pollution damages the thin layer of fertile soil that covers much of the earth's land and is essential for growing food. Natural processes took thousands of years to form the soil that supports crops. But, through careless treatment, people can destroy soil in a few years.

In nature, cycles similar to those that keep water clean work to keep soil fertile. Plant and animal wastes, including dead organisms, accumulate in the soil. Bacteria and fungi decay these wastes, breaking them down into nitrates, phosphates, and other nutrients. The nutrients feed growing plants, and when the plants die the cycle begins again.

People use fertilizers and pesticides to grow more and better crops. Fertilizers add extra nutrients to the soil and increase the amount of a crop that can be grown on an area of land. But the use of large amounts of fertilizer may decrease the ability of bacteria to decay wastes and produce nutrients naturally.

Pesticides destroy weeds and insects that harm crops. But pesticides may also harm bacteria and other helpful organisms in the soil.

Much damage to soil results from *erosion.* Erosion is the wearing away of soil. It can result from the removal of trees, grass, and other plants that hold soil in place. Wind can then blow the bare soil away and rain can wash it away. Careless farming methods are a major cause of erosion. The clearing of land for construction projects, such as roads and real estate developments, also causes erosion.

Water pollution   Most of the pollutants that people put into water come from treated and untreated sewage, from agricultural drainage, and from industrial wastes. The pollutants reduce valuable supplies of pure, fresh water by upsetting the natural cycles that work to keep water clean. By upsetting the cycles, the pollutants harm the animals and plants that live in the water.

WORLD BOOK diagram by George Suyeoka

Untreated sewage contains large amounts of wastes from animal and plant matter. The wastes decay in water, and some of the water's oxygen is used up in the decaying process. If too much oxygen is used, organisms in the water cannot survive.

Treated sewage contains nitrates and phosphates. These substances cause large amounts of *algae* (simple organisms) to grow. The algae multiply quickly, and also die quickly. After they die, they decay and use up oxygen.

For more information on soil and how it is damaged, see the articles in *World Book* on **Soil** and **Erosion**.

Solid wastes are probably the most visible forms of pollution. People throw away billions of tons of solid material each year. Much of this waste ends up littering roadsides, floating in lakes and streams, and collecting in ugly dumps. Examples of solid wastes include junked automobiles, tires, refrigerators, and stoves; cans and other packaging materials; and scraps of metal and paper. Such solid pollutants are most common in the heavily populated areas in and near cities. Slag and other wastes from mining processes pollute much land away from cities.

Solid wastes present a serious problem because most of the methods used to dispose of them result in some type of damage to the environment. When the wastes are put into open dumps, they ruin the attractiveness of the surrounding areas. Dumps also provide homes for disease-carrying animals, such as cockroaches and rats. Some solid wastes can be destroyed by burning them. But burning produces smoke that causes air pollution. When wastes are dumped in water, they contribute to various forms of water pollution.

In the mid-1980's, more than 2 billion short tons (1.8 billion metric tons) of solid wastes were produced in the United States each year. This amounted to an average of about 45 pounds (20 kilograms) of solid wastes for each person in the country each day. Most solid wastes are disposed of in open dumps. But in many areas, especially near large cities, the land available for dumping is

running out. In the meantime, the production of solid wastes is increasing rapidly. In addition, more and more wastes that are difficult to dispose of are being produced. Tin and steel cans that rust and can be absorbed by the soil are being replaced by aluminum cans that stay in their original state for many years. Paper and cardboard packaging that decays and burns easily is being replaced by plastics that will not decay and that give off harmful gases when burned.

Other kinds of pollution. Some things that pollute the environment cannot be classified as air, water, or soil pollutants, or as solid wastes. They travel through and affect various parts of the environment. These pollutants include noise, radiation, acid rain, pesticides, and such metals as mercury and lead.

See **Environmental pollution** in *World Book* for more information on the following topics:

- Kinds of pollution
- Causes of pollution
- Controlling pollution
- History

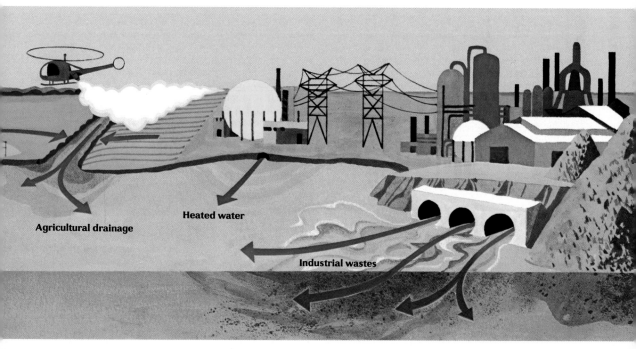

Agricultural drainage includes animal wastes, which decay; fertilizers, which increase the growth of algae; and pesticides, which kill animals and plants.

Heated water kills animals and plants that are accustomed to living in cooler water. Most heated water comes from industries that use water for cooling.

Industrial wastes include chemicals, wastes from animal and plant matter, and hundreds of other substances. They ruin water by upsetting natural cycles.

Evolution

Evolution is a process of gradual change. The word *evolution* may refer to various types of change. For example, scientists generally describe the formation of the universe as having occurred through evolution. Many astronomers believe the stars and planets evolved from clouds of hot gases. Anthropologists study the evolution of human culture from tribal societies to complex, industrialized societies.

However, the process of evolution most commonly refers to the formation and development of life on the earth. The idea that living things evolved from nonliving matter and changed through the ages is called the *theory of organic evolution,* or simply the *theory of evolution.* According to this theory, the first single-celled organisms appeared about $3\frac{1}{2}$ billion years ago, soon after the earth's crust had formed and cooled. As time passed, more complex organisms gradually developed specialized characteristics that helped them adapt to their environment. This evolutionary process eventually produced all the species that inhabit the earth today.

The theory of evolution helps explain two fundamental facts of nature—the tremendous variety of living organisms and their basic similarities. Scientists estimate that more than 2 million species of living things inhabit the earth. Yet all these organisms share certain characteristics, such as cell structure and genetic code (in *World Book,* see **Cell** [The genetic code]). According to the theory of evolution, variations among species have resulted chiefly from evolutionary adaptations to different environments. On the other hand, living things remain basically alike because they have evolved from common ancestors.

The process of organic evolution goes on and on. Most biologists believe that it is occurring as fast today as at any time in the past. During the last few million years—a relatively brief period in the earth's history—hundreds of species have become extinct and hundreds of others have developed.

Although the theory of evolution is supported by a vast amount of scientific evidence, it is not universally accepted. Some people reject the theory because they claim there are too many gaps in the evolutionary record. Others believe the theory conflicts with the Biblical account of the creation of life. A number of people object to the idea that human beings are related to lower forms of life.

Main ideas of evolutionary theory

Most scientists believe that evolution is governed largely by two processes—*natural selection* and *heredity.* Natural selection determines the general trend of evolutionary changes. Heredity provides the mechanism for passing on these changes from one generation to the next. The interaction of these two processes may produce a series of gradual changes that eventually result in the development of new species.

Natural selection is a process by which organisms best suited to their environment become the ones most likely to survive and leave descendants. This process is sometimes called *survival of the fittest.* It enables species to evolve in response to changes in their environ-ment. For example, as such factors as climate and the food supply change, characteristics suitable to the new conditions tend to replace less useful traits.

The operation of natural selection was first documented by the British naturalist Charles Darwin in the mid-1800's. According to Darwin, natural selection depends chiefly on three factors: (1) hereditary variability, (2) the tendency toward overpopulation, and (3) the struggle for existence.

Hereditary variability is the way in which the members of a species vary in such inherited traits as color, size, and the ability to withstand cold. Some of these variations may determine how successfully individuals adapt to their environment. An animal whose color matches its surroundings may be able to capture prey or escape its enemies more readily than one with highly visible coloring.

The tendency toward overpopulation results from the fact that living things are capable of producing more offspring than are necessary to replace themselves. For example, among animals and plants that reproduce sexually, two parents can produce far more than two offspring.

All living things are engaged in a constant struggle for existence, chiefly because of the tendency toward overpopulation. Increasing numbers of organisms must compete for a limited supply of food, water, space, and other necessities of life. The individual plants and animals whose variations are best adapted to the environment have an advantage in this struggle. They will be the most likely ones to survive, reproduce, and pass their favorable characteristics on to their offspring. After many generations, these traits will be widespread among the members of the species.

Natural selection can be illustrated by a cactus called the prickly pear, which normally grows close to the ground and has soft spines. On the Galapagos Islands, in the Pacific Ocean, prickly pears are the chief food of giant tortoises. A tortoise is more likely to eat an ordinary prickly pear than a tall one with tough spines. As a result, tall, tough-spined prickly pears have survived and reproduced in greater numbers through the years. Today, they are the most common form of prickly pears on the majority of the islands. But on the islands with no tortoises, almost all the prickly pears are short and have soft spines.

Heredity is the passing on of characteristics from parents to offspring. It controls the development of individual organisms and determines how well they adapt to their environment.

How characteristics are inherited. Hereditary characteristics are carried by tiny particles called *chromosomes.* Chromosomes are in the nuclei of cells and carry large numbers of *genes,* which are segments of a substance called *deoxyribonucleic acid* (DNA). DNA contains the coded information that determines the various characteristics of the organism.

Among animals and higher plants, each body cell has an identical double set of chromosomes. Offspring inherit one set of chromosomes from each parent. The chromosomes are transmitted during sexual reproduction. Egg cells and sperm cells are formed in a special way and have only one set of chromosomes. A sperm fertilizes an egg during the reproductive process, and

**The evolutionary
tree of life**

This diagram shows how living things evolved into some of their present forms. Scientists believe the first living things—bacteria and other one-celled organisms—appeared about 3½ billion years ago. Mammals and flowering plants are among the youngest branches on the evolutionary tree.

WORLD BOOK illustrations by Patricia J. Wynne

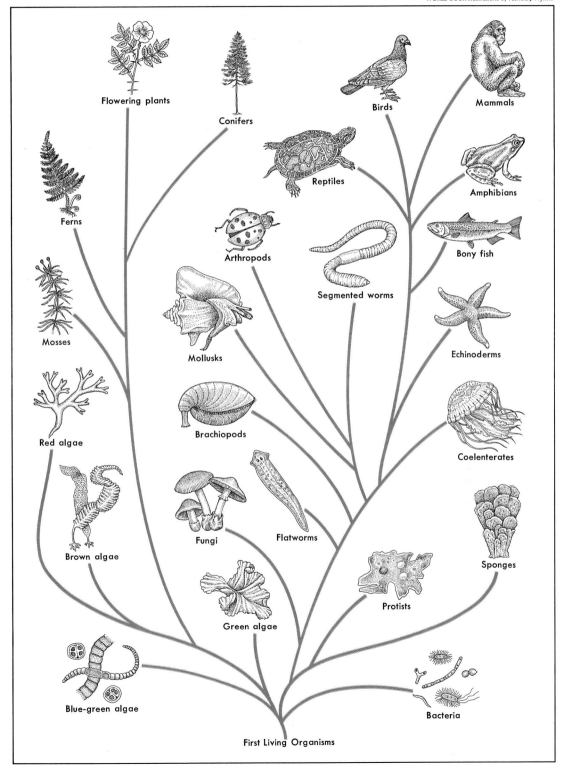

Flowering plants

Conifers

Birds

Mammals

Reptiles

Amphibians

Ferns

Arthropods

Bony fish

Segmented worms

Mosses

Mollusks

Echinoderms

Red algae

Brachiopods

Coelenterates

Brown algae

Fungi

Flatworms

Sponges

Green algae

Protists

Blue-green algae

Bacteria

First Living Organisms

the fertilized egg then contains two sets of chromosomes.

As the fertilized egg cell begins to grow, each chromosome in the nucleus of the cell duplicates itself. The chromosome and its duplicate lie next to each other in pairs. When the cell divides into two cells, one of each pair of chromosomes goes each of the new cells. Thus, the two new cells contain chromosomes that are identical with those in the original cell. This process of growth through cell division continues until it has produced all the cells that make up an organism.

How hereditary characteristics change. If chromosomes had always duplicated themselves exactly since life began, all organisms would now be identical. However, such duplication did not occur because chromosomes or genes may undergo certain changes. There are two principal types of changes—*mutation* and *recombination.*

A mutation is a change in the structure of a gene. Mutations may be caused by environmental factors, such as chemicals and radiation, which affect the DNA in genes. After a gene has changed, it duplicates itself in its changed form. These *mutant genes* may alter some inherited characteristics.

Mutations occur regularly but infrequently, and most of them produce unfavorable traits. *Albinism* is a fairly common mutation. Albino animals have mutant genes that do not allow the production of normal skin pigment. In most cases, such mutant genes are eliminated by natural selection because most of the organisms that have them die before producing any offspring. However, some mutations help organisms adapt better to their environment. A plant in a dry area might have a mutant gene that causes it to grow larger and stronger roots. The plant would have a better chance of survival than others of its species because its roots could absorb more water. This type of beneficial mutation provides the raw material for evolutionary change.

Recombination involves changes in the arrangement of genes. During the formation of egg or sperm cells, genes from one of a pair of chromosomes may change places with genes from the other chromosome. As a result, the offspring may inherit different combinations of traits from their parents. Unlike mutation, recombination does not introduce new hereditary characteristics. However, recombination enables natural selection to act upon different combinations of such traits.

Development of new species. Evolution through natural selection causes a species to change so that it can adapt to changes in its environment. However, natural selection does not entirely explain how several species develop from one common ancestor species. This type of species development is called *speciation.*

A species is a group of plants or animals whose members are more closely related to one another than to members of any other group. Among organisms that reproduce sexually, members of a species can interbreed and produce fertile offspring. Most biologists believe speciation occurs after a species has been separated into two or more isolated populations. Each of these isolated populations develops different traits through natural selection. If the isolation lasts long enough, the populations may become so dissimilar that members of one group cannot successfully breed with those of another. Speciation will then have occurred.

The isolation that marks the beginning of speciation may be *geographic, ecological,* or *genetic.* In geographic isolation, groups of organisms are separated by such physical barriers as deserts, mountains, or bodies of water. Members of each group may develop different adaptations to their particular environment and eventually evolve into separate species.

Ecological isolation involves populations that live in the same area but occupy different habitats. Some members of a species may have a way of life that requires specialized adaptations. For example, birds that eat nuts and seeds need a stronger beak than those that feed on nectar from flowers. After many generations, the organisms that develop such adaptations may form distinct species.

Genetic isolation results from mutations that affect sexual traits. Organisms with such mutations may be able to breed with one another but not with other members of the species. Genetic isolation may follow long periods of geographic or ecological isolation, or it may occur within one or a few generations in a stable population. Rapid genetic isolation is especially common among plants, in which major changes in the number and organization of chromosomes can produce a new species within a single generation.

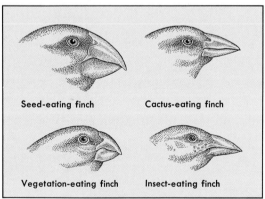

Seed-eating finch   Cactus-eating finch

Vegetation-eating finch   Insect-eating finch

WORLD BOOK illustrations by Patricia J. Wynne; adapted from *Darwin's Finches* by David Lack, used with permission of Cambridge University Press

Specialized adaptations in finches on the Galapagos Islands resulted from competition for limited food. Different groups of finches developed beaks adapted to various kinds of food. After many generations, these groups evolved into separate species.

See **Evolution** in *World Book* for more information on the following topics:

•Evidence of evolution   •Acceptance of evolution
•History of the theory of   •Evolution and religion
  evolution

Eye

Eye is the organ of sight. It is our most important organ for finding out about the world around us. We use our eyes in almost everything we do—reading, working, watching movies and television, playing games, and countless other activities. Sight is our most precious sense, and many people fear blindness more than any other disability.

The human eyeball measures only about 1 inch (25 millimeters) in diameter. Yet the eye can see objects as far away as a star and as tiny as a grain of sand. The eye can quickly adjust its focus between a distant point and a near one. It can be accurately directed toward an object even while the head is moving.

The eye does not actually see objects. Instead, it sees the light they reflect or give off. The eye can see in bright light and in dim light, but it cannot see in no light at all. Light rays enter the eye through transparent tissues. The eye changes the rays into electrical signals. The signals are then sent to the brain, which interprets them as visual images.

How we see

Focusing. Light rays that enter the eye must come to a point on the retina for a clear visual image to form. However, the light rays that objects reflect or give off do not naturally move toward one another. Instead, they either spread out or travel almost parallel. The focusing parts of the eye—the cornea and the lens—bend the rays toward one another. The cornea provides most of the *refracting* (bending) power of the eye. After light rays pass through the cornea, they travel through the aqueous humor and the pupil to the lens. The lens bends the rays even closer together before they go through the vitreous humor and strike the retina. Light rays from objects at which the eyes are aimed come together at the *fovea centralis,* a tiny pit in the center of the macula. It is the area of sharpest vision. Light rays from objects to the sides strike other areas of the retina.

The refracting power of the lens changes constantly as the eye shifts focus between nearby objects and distant ones. Light rays from nearby objects spread out, and those from distant objects travel nearly parallel. Therefore, the lens must provide greater bending

Parts of the eye   The visible parts of the eyeball are the white *sclera* and the colored *iris.* A membrane called the *conjunctiva* covers the sclera. The clear *cornea* lies in front of the iris. The *lens* is connected to the *ciliary body.* Inside the eyeball is a clear substance called *vitreous humor.* The *retina,* which underlies the *choroid,* changes light rays into electrical signals. The *optic nerve* carries the signals to the brain. The *fovea centralis,* a pit in the *macula lutea,* is the area of sharpest vision.

WORLD BOOK illustrations by Charles Wellek

Eye muscles rotate the eyeball within its socket. The eye has six of these muscles.

power for the light rays from nearby objects to come together. This additional power is produced by a process called *accommodation.* In this process, one of the muscles of the ciliary body contracts, thereby relaxing the fibers that connect the ciliary body to the lens. As a result, the lens becomes rounder and thicker and thus more powerful. When the eye looks at distant objects, the muscle of the ciliary body relaxes. This action tightens the fibers that are connected to the lens, and the lens becomes flatter. For this reason, the eye cannot form a sharp image of a nearby object and a distant one at the same time.

Depth perception is the ability to judge distance and to tell the thickness of objects. The lens system of

the eye, like the lens of a camera, reverses images. Thus, the images that form on the retina are much like those produced on film in a camera. The images are upside down and reversed left to right. They are also flat, as in a photograph. However, the brain interprets the images as they really are. The ability of the brain to interpret retinal images right-side up, unreversed, and in depth comes from experience that begins at a person's birth.

The optic nerves from the two eyes meet at the base of the brain at a point called the *optic chiasm.* At the optic chiasm, half the nerve fibers from each eye cross over and join the fibers from the other eye. Each side of the brain receives visual messages from both eyes. The nerve fibers from the right half of each eye enter the

How the eye focuses

Distance vision

Distant objects reflect or give off light rays that are nearly parallel as they enter the eye. The cornea and the lens bend the rays toward one another, which makes them come together on the retina and form a clear visual image.

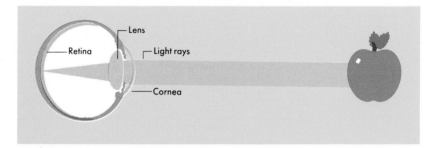

Near vision

Nearby objects reflect or give off light rays that are spreading out as they enter the eye. Greater bending power is thus needed to bring these rays together. The lens provides this power by becoming rounder and thicker in a process called *accommodation.*

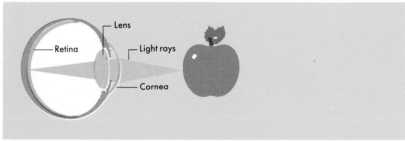

WORLD BOOK diagrams by Linda Kinnaman

How we see in depth

WORLD BOOK diagram

Depth perception is the ability to judge distance and to tell the thickness of objects. Because the eyes are set slightly apart, each one sees objects from a slightly different angle. As a result, each eye sends a slightly different message to the brain. Some of the nerve fibers from each eye cross over at the *optic chiasm.* Each side of the brain thus receives visual messages from both eyes. The brain puts the images together and so provides depth perception.

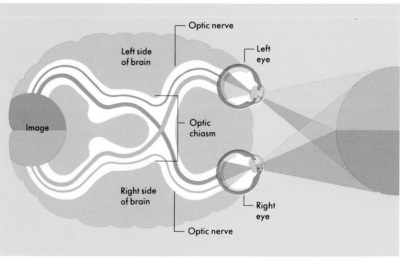

right side of the brain. These fibers carry visual messages from objects that are to a person's left. The nerve fibers from the left half of each eye enter the left side of the brain. These fibers carry visual messages from objects that are to a person's right. Thus, if one side of the brain becomes damaged, the opposite side of a person's field of vision may be reduced. Such damage may occur as a result of a stroke or tumor.

The eyes are about $2\frac{1}{2}$ inches (6.4 centimeters) apart from center to center. For this reason, each eye sees things from a slightly different angle and sends slightly different messages to the brain. The difference can be demonstrated by focusing on a nearby object first with one eye closed and then with the other eye closed. The image seen with each eye is slightly different. The brain puts the images together and thus provides depth perception, also called *stereoscopic vision* or *three-dimensional vision*. The image formed by the brain has thickness and shape, and the brain can judge the distance of the object.

Normal depth perception requires that the eyes work together in a process called *binocular vision* or *fusion*. In this process, the eye muscles move the eyes so that light rays from an object fall at a corresponding point on each retina. When viewing objects close up, the eyes turn slightly inward. When viewing distant objects, the eyes are almost parallel. If images do not fall at a corresponding point on each retina, they will be blurred or be seen as double or the brain will ignore one of them.

In most people, visual messages are stronger in one eye and on one side of the brain than the other. Most people are "right-eyed" or "left-eyed," just as they are right-handed or left-handed. For example, they favor one eye or the other when aiming a camera or a rifle.

Adaptation to light and dark is partly controlled by the pupil. In strong light, the pupil may become as small as a pinhead and so prevent the eye from being damaged or dazzled by too much light. In the dark, it can get almost as large as the entire iris, thus letting in as much light as possible. However, the most important part of adaptation to light and dark occurs in the retina.

Light rays are absorbed by pigments in the retina's rods and cones. The pigments consist of protein and vitamin A. Vitamin A helps give the pigments their color. The color enables the pigments to absorb light. Light changes the chemical structure of the vitamin A and bleaches out the color in the pigments. This process generates an electrical signal that the optic nerve transmits to the brain. After the pigments have been bleached, the vitamin A moves into a part of the retina known as the *retinal pigmented epithelium* (RPE). The vitamin regains its original chemical structure in the RPE and then returns to the rods and cones. There, it joins with protein molecules and forms new pigments.

See **Eye** in *World Book* for more information on the following topics:

- Parts of the eye
- How we see
- Defects of the eye
- Diseases of the eye
- Care of the eye
- Eyes of animals

Some animal eyes   Most animals have organs of some kind that sense light. In some animals, these organs can only tell light from dark. The eyes of certain other animals can see objects clearly even in dim light.

WORLD BOOK illustrations by John Dawson

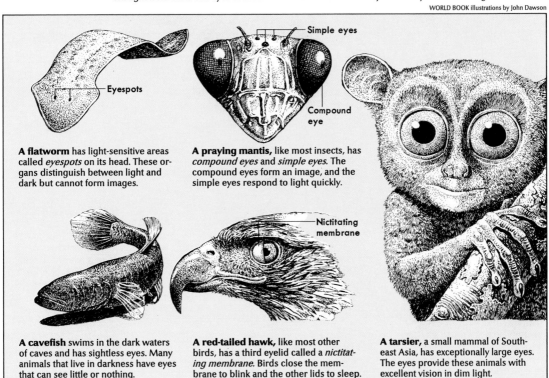

A flatworm has light-sensitive areas called *eyespots* on its head. These organs distinguish between light and dark but cannot form images.

A praying mantis, like most insects, has *compound eyes* and *simple eyes*. The compound eyes form an image, and the simple eyes respond to light quickly.

A cavefish swims in the dark waters of caves and has sightless eyes. Many animals that live in darkness have eyes that can see little or nothing.

A red-tailed hawk, like most other birds, has a third eyelid called a *nictitating membrane*. Birds close the membrane to blink and the other lids to sleep.

A tarsier, a small mammal of Southeast Asia, has exceptionally large eyes. The eyes provide these animals with excellent vision in dim light.

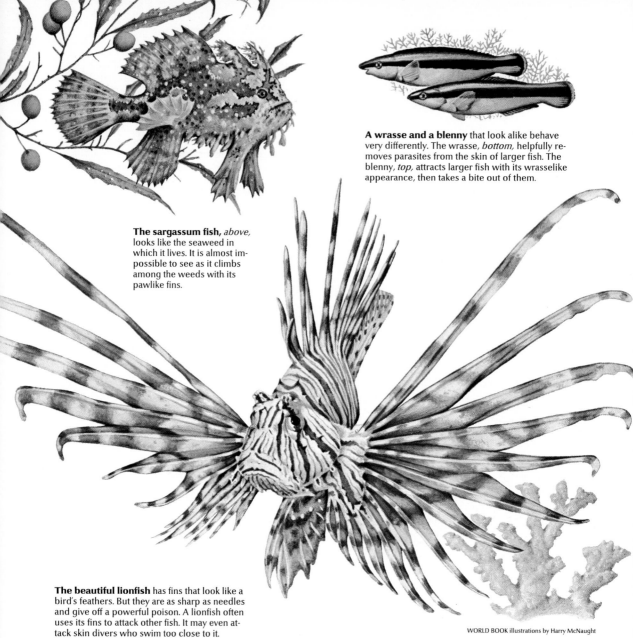

The sargassum fish, *above,*
looks like the seaweed in
which it lives. It is almost impossible to see as it climbs
among the weeds with its
pawlike fins.

A wrasse and a blenny that look alike behave
very differently. The wrasse, *bottom,* helpfully removes parasites from the skin of larger fish. The
blenny, *top,* attracts larger fish with its wrasselike
appearance, then takes a bite out of them.

The beautiful lionfish has fins that look like a
bird's feathers. But they are as sharp as needles
and give off a powerful poison. A lionfish often
uses its fins to attack other fish. It may even attack skin divers who swim too close to it.

WORLD BOOK illustrations by Harry McNaught

Fish

Fish are *vertebrates* (backboned animals) that live in
water. There are more kinds of fish than all other kinds
of water and land vertebrates put together. The various
kinds of fish differ so greatly in shape, color, and size
that it is hard to believe they all belong to the same
group of animals. For example, some fish look like
lumpy rocks, and others like wriggly worms. Some fish
are nearly as flat as pancakes, and others can blow
themselves up like balloons. Fish have all the colors of
the rainbow. Many have colors as bright as the most
brightly colored birds. Their rich reds, yellows, blues,
and purples form hundreds of beautiful patterns, from
stripes and lacelike designs to polka dots.

The smallest fish is the pygmy goby of the Philippines, which grows less than $\frac{1}{2}$ inch (13 millimeters)
long. The largest fish is the whale shark, which may
grow more than 40 feet (12 meters) long and weigh over
15 short tons (14 metric tons). It feeds on small sea animals and plants and is completely harmless to most
other fish and to human beings. The most dangerous
fish weigh only a few pounds or kilograms. They include
the deadly stonefish, whose poisonous spines can kill a
human being in a matter of minutes.

Fish live almost anywhere there is water. They are
found in the near-freezing waters of the Arctic and in
the steaming waters of tropical jungles. They live in
roaring mountain streams and in quiet underground rivers. Some fish make long journeys across the ocean.
Others spend most of their life buried in sand on the
bottom of the ocean. Most fish never leave water. Yet

The porcupinefish is covered with protective spines. For added protection, the fish fills itself with water to change from its normal appearance, *bottom,* to that of a prickly balloon, *top.*

Roy Pinney, Globe

An archerfish catches an insect resting above the surface by spitting drops of water at it. The drops strike with enough force to knock the insect into the water, where the fish can eat it.

some fish are able to survive for months in dried-up riverbeds.

Fish have enormous importance to human beings. They provide food for millions of people. Fishing enthusiasts catch them for sport, and people keep them as pets. In addition, fish are important in the *balance of nature.* They eat plants and animals and, in turn, become food for plants and animals. Fish thus help keep in balance the total number of plants and animals on the earth.

All fish have two main features in common. (1) They have a backbone, and so they are vertebrates. (2) They breathe mainly by means of gills. Nearly all fish are also *cold-blooded* animals—that is, they cannot regulate their body temperature, which changes with the temperature of their surroundings. In addition, almost all fish have fins, which they use for swimming. All other water animals differ from fish in at least one of these ways. Dolphins, porpoises, and whales look like fish and have a backbone and fins, but they are *mammals* (animals that feed their young with the mother's milk). Mammals breathe with lungs rather than gills. They are also *warm-blooded*—their body temperature remains about the

Interesting facts about fish

The smallest fish is the pygmy goby of the Philippines. It measures less than $\frac{1}{2}$ inch (13 millimeters) when fully grown.

The largest fish is the whale shark. It may weigh more than 15 short tons (14 metric tons) —over twice as much as an African elephant. This fish is harmless to people. It eats small sea plants and animals.

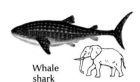

Whale shark

A four-eyed fish, the anableps, has eyes divided in two. When the fish swims just below the surface, the top half of each eye sees above the surface and the bottom half sees underwater.

Anableps

The black swallower can swallow fish twice its own size. Its jaws have "hinges" that enable them to open wide, and its stomach can stretch to several times its normal size. A fish swallowed whole is gradually digested.

Black swallower

The flying hatchet fish is one of the few fish that can really fly. A hatchet fish can take off from the water's surface and fly as far as 10 feet (3 meters). The fish uses its side fins as wings.

Flying hatchet fish

The walking catfish lives for days out of water and even "walks" on land from one lake to another. The fish has special air-breathing organs and uses its side fins and tail to help it crawl on the ground.

Walking catfish

The largest group of fish are bristlemouths, a kind of tiny salt-water fish. Scientists believe that bristlemouths number in the billions of billions.

same when the air or water temperature changes. Some water animals are called *fish,* but they do not have a backbone and so are not fish. These animals include jellyfish and starfish. Clams, crabs, lobsters, oysters, scallops, and shrimps are called *shellfish.* But they also lack a backbone.

The first fish appeared on the earth about 500 million years ago. They were the first animals to have a backbone. Most scientists believe that these early fish became the ancestors of all other vertebrates.

In some ways, a fish's body resembles that of other vertebrates. For example, fish, like other vertebrates, have an internal skeleton, an outer skin, and such internal organs as a heart, intestines, and a brain. But in a number of ways, a fish's body differs from that of other vertebrates. For example, fish have fins instead of legs, and gills instead of lungs.

The chief kinds of fish

WORLD BOOK illustration by Marion Pahl

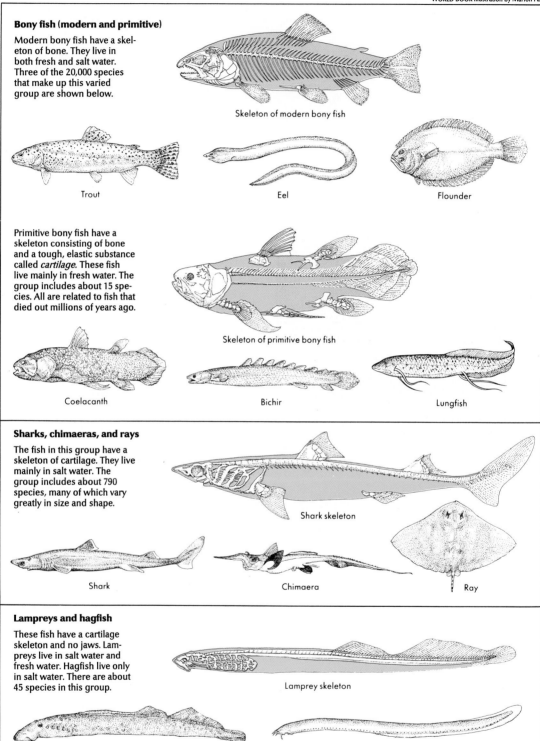

Bony fish (modern and primitive)

Modern bony fish have a skeleton of bone. They live in both fresh and salt water. Three of the 20,000 species that make up this varied group are shown below.

Skeleton of modern bony fish

Trout

Eel

Flounder

Primitive bony fish have a skeleton consisting of bone and a tough, elastic substance called *cartilage*. These fish live mainly in fresh water. The group includes about 15 species. All are related to fish that died out millions of years ago.

Skeleton of primitive bony fish

Coelacanth

Bichir

Lungfish

Sharks, chimaeras, and rays

The fish in this group have a skeleton of cartilage. They live mainly in salt water. The group includes about 790 species, many of which vary greatly in size and shape.

Shark skeleton

Shark

Chimaera

Ray

Lampreys and hagfish

These fish have a cartilage skeleton and no jaws. Lampreys live in salt water and fresh water. Hagfish live only in salt water. There are about 45 species in this group.

Lamprey skeleton

Lamprey

Hagfish

External anatomy of a fish

This drawing of a yellow perch shows the external features most fish have in common. Many kinds of fish do not have all the fins shown here, or they lack such features as gill covers or scales. For example, lampreys and hagfish have no scales and no pelvic or pectoral fins.

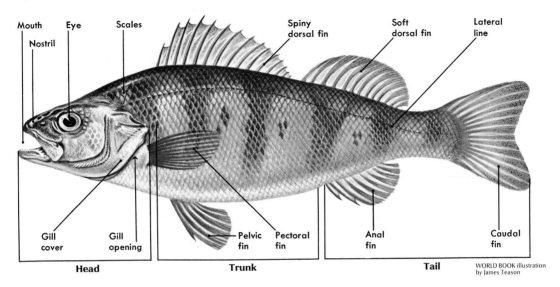

Mouth — Eye — Scales — Spiny dorsal fin — Soft dorsal fin — Lateral line — Nostril — Gill cover — Gill opening — Pelvic fin — Pectoral fin — Anal fin — Caudal fin — Head — Trunk — Tail

WORLD BOOK illustration by James Teason

Systems of the body

The internal organs of fish, like those of other vertebrates, are grouped into various systems according to the function they serve. The major systems include the respiratory, digestive, circulatory, nervous, and reproductive systems. Some of these systems resemble those of other vertebrates, but others differ in many ways.

Respiratory system. Unlike land animals, almost all fish get their oxygen from water. Water contains a certain amount of dissolved oxygen. To get oxygen, fish gulp water through the mouth and pump it over the gills. Most fish have four pairs of gills enclosed in a *gill chamber* on each side of the head. Each gill consists of two rows of fleshy *filaments* attached to a *gill arch.* Water passes into the gill chambers through *gill slits.* A flap of bone called a *gill cover* protects the gills of bony fish. Sharks and rays do not have gill covers. Their gill slits form visible openings on the outside of the body.

In a bony fish, the breathing process begins when the gill covers close and the mouth opens. At the same time, the walls of the mouth expand outward, drawing water into the mouth. The walls of the mouth then move inward, the mouth closes, and the gill covers open. This action forces the water from the mouth into the gill chambers. In each chamber, the water passes over the gill filaments. They absorb oxygen from the water and replace it with carbon dioxide formed during the breathing process. The water then passes out through the gill openings, and the process is repeated.

Digestive system, or *digestive tract,* changes food into materials that nourish the body cells. It eliminates materials that are not used. In fish, this system leads from the mouth to the *anus,* an opening in front of the anal fin. Most fish have a jawed mouth with a tongue and teeth. A fish cannot move its tongue. Most fish have their teeth rooted in the jaws. They use their teeth to

seize prey or to tear off pieces of their victim's flesh. Some of them also have teeth on the roof of the mouth or on the tongue. Most fish also have teeth in the *pharynx,* a short tube behind the mouth. They use these teeth to crush or grind food.

In all fish, food passes through the pharynx on the way to the *esophagus,* another tubelike organ. A fish's esophagus expands easily, which allows the fish to swallow its food whole. From the esophagus, food passes into the *stomach,* where it is partly digested. Some fish have their esophagus or stomach enlarged into a *gizzard.* The gizzard grinds food into small pieces before it passes into the intestines. The digestive process is completed in the intestines. The digested food enters the blood stream. Waste products and undigested food pass out through the anus.

Circulatory system distributes blood to all parts of the body. It includes the heart and blood vessels. A fish's heart consists of two main chambers—the *atrium* and the *ventricle.* The blood flows through *veins* to the atrium. It then passes to the ventricle. Muscles in the ventricle pump the blood through *arteries* to the gills, where the blood receives oxygen and gives off carbon dioxide. Arteries then carry the blood throughout the body. The blood carries food from the intestines and oxygen from the gills to the body cells. It also carries away waste products from the cells. A fish's kidneys remove the waste products from the blood, which returns to the heart through the veins.

Nervous system of fish, like that of other vertebrates, consists of a *spinal cord, brain,* and *nerves.* However, a fish's nervous system is not so complex as that of mammals and other higher vertebrates. The spinal cord, which consists of soft nerve tissue, runs from the brain through the backbone. The brain is an enlargement of the spinal cord and is enclosed in the skull. The nerves extend from the brain and spinal cord to every part of

Internal organs of a fish

This view of a yellow perch shows the chief internal organs found in most fish. These organs are parts of the systems that perform such body processes as breathing and digestion.

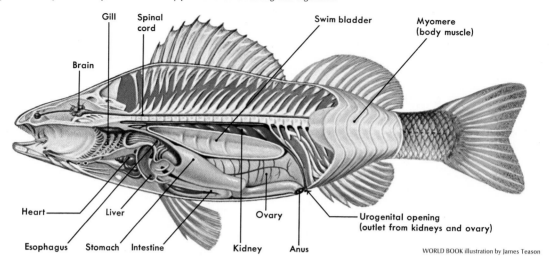

Gill | Spinal cord | Swim bladder | Myomere (body muscle)
Brain
Heart | Liver | Ovary | Urogenital opening (outlet from kidneys and ovary)
Esophagus | Stomach | Intestine | Kidney | Anus

WORLD BOOK illustration by James Teason

the body. Some nerves, called *sensory* nerves, carry messages from the sense organs to the spinal cord and brain. Other nerves, called *motor* nerves, carry messages from the brain and spinal cord to the muscles. A fish can consciously control its skeletal muscles. But it has no conscious control over the smooth muscles and heart muscles. These muscles work automatically.

Reproductive system. As in all vertebrates, the reproductive organs of fish are *testes* in males and *ovaries* in females. The testes produce male sex cells, or *sperm.* The sperm is contained in a fluid called *milt.* The ovaries produce female sex cells, or *eggs.* Fish eggs are also called *roe* or *spawn.* Most fish release their sex cells into the water through an opening near the anus. The males of some species have special structures for transferring sperm directly into the females. Male sharks, for example, have such a structure, called a *clasper,* on each

pelvic fin. The claspers are used to insert sperm into the female's body.

Special organs

Most bony fish have a swim bladder below the backbone. This baglike organ is also called an air bladder. In most fish, the swim bladder provides *buoyancy,* which enables the fish to remain at a particular depth in the water. In lungfish and a few other fish, the swim bladder serves as an air-breathing lung. Still other fish, including many catfish, use their swim bladders to produce sounds as well as to provide buoyancy. Some species communicate by means of such sounds.

A fish would sink to the bottom if it did not have a way of keeping buoyant. Most fish gain buoyancy by inflating their swim bladder with gases produced by their blood. But water pressure increases with depth. As a

The lateral line system

The lateral line system makes a fish sensitive to vibrations in the water. It consists of a series of tubelike *canals* in a fish's skin. Vibrations enter the canals through *pores* (openings in the skin) and travel to sensory organs in the canals. Nerves connect these organs to the brain.

WORLD BOOK illustrations by Marion Pahl and Zorica Dabich

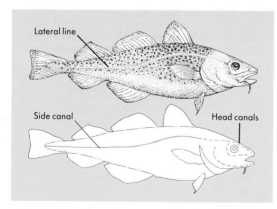

Lateral line
Side canal | Head canals

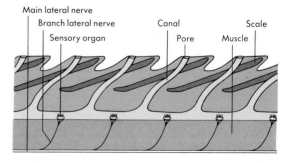

Main lateral nerve
Branch lateral nerve | Canal | Scale
Sensory organ | Pore | Muscle

The skeleton of a fish

The skeletons of most fish consist mainly of (1) a skull, (2) a backbone, (3) ribs, (4) fin rays, and (5) supports for fin rays or fins. The skeleton of a yellow perch is shown below.

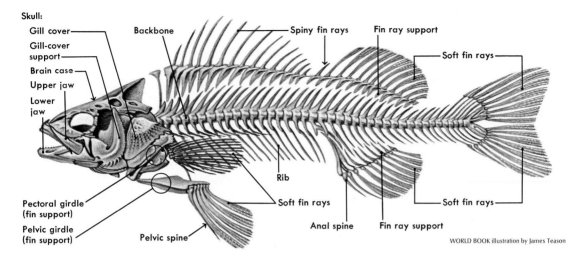

Skull:
Gill cover
Gill-cover support
Brain case
Upper jaw
Lower jaw

Backbone

Spiny fin rays

Fin ray support

Soft fin rays

Soft fin rays

Pectoral girdle (fin support)
Pelvic girdle (fin support)
Pelvic spine

Rib

Soft fin rays

Anal spine   Fin ray support

Soft fin rays

WORLD BOOK illustration by James Teason

fish swims deeper, the increased water pressure makes its swim bladder smaller and so reduces the fish's buoyancy. The amount of gas in the bladder must be increased so that the bladder remains large enough to maintain buoyancy. A fish's nervous system automatically regulates the amount of gas in the bladder so that it is kept properly filled. Sharks and rays do not have a swim bladder. To keep buoyant, these fish must swim constantly. When they rest, they stop swimming and so sink toward the bottom. Many bottom-dwelling bony fish also lack a swim bladder.

Many fish have organs that produce light or electricity. But these organs are simply adaptations of structures found in all or most fish. For example, many deep-sea fish have light-producing organs developed from parts of their skin or digestive tract. Some species use these organs to attract prey or possibly to communicate with others of their species. Various other fish have electricity-producing organs developed from muscles in their eyes, gills, or trunk. Some species use these organs to stun or kill enemies or prey.

See **Fish** in *World Book* for more information on the following topics:

- The importance of fish
- Kinds of fish
- Where fish live
- The bodies of fish
- The senses of fish

- How fish live
- How fish reproduce
- The development of fish
- A classification of fish

How a fish's gills work

Like all animals, fish need oxygen to change food into body energy. These drawings show how a fish's gills enable it to get oxygen from the water and to get rid of carbon dioxide, a body waste.

WORLD BOOK illustration by Margaret Ann Moran

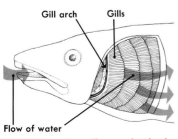

Gill arch   Gills

Flow of water

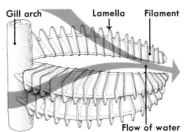

Gill arch   Lamella   Filament

Flow of water

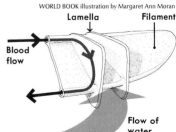

Lamella   Filament

Blood flow

Flow of water

Most fish have four gills on each side of the head. Water enters the mouth and flows out through the gills. Each gill is made up of fleshy, threadlike *filaments*.

Water from the mouth passes over the filaments, which are closely spaced along a *gill arch* in two rows. Three of the many filaments of a gill are shown above.

Each filament has many tiny extensions called *lamellae*. Blood flowing through a lamella takes oxygen from the water and releases carbon dioxide into the water.

David Muench

Desert wild flowers thrive in the hot, dry climate of the Southwestern United States. A variety of flowering plants, such as cactuses, can survive for many months without rain. The seeds of these plants lie buried during dry periods and then sprout after the rains return.

Flower

Flower is a blossom or an entire plant that is known for its blossoms. Most plants have flowers. In some cases, however, the flowers are so small and plain that few people think of them as flowers. Most people think of flowers as being brightly colored and showy. Plants that have such blossoms include buttercups, dandelions, orchids, roses, tulips, violets, and hundreds of other garden flowers and wild flowers. Some trees, such as catalpas and horse chestnuts, have beautiful blossoms. However, the trees themselves are never referred to as flowers. All of the plants classified as either garden flowers or wild flowers are smaller than trees. Also, most of these flowering plants have soft stems rather than woody stems.

People prize flowers for their attractive shapes, gorgeous colors, and delightful fragrance. Because of their beauty, flowers are a favorite form of decoration. People also use flowers to express their deepest feelings. For more than 50,000 years, people have placed flowers on the graves of loved ones as a sign of remembrance and respect. Flowers are used at weddings to symbolize love, faithfulness, and long life. Certain flowers also have a religious meaning. Among Christians, for example, the white Easter lily stands for purity. Buddhists and Hindus regard the lotus, which is a type of water lily, as a sacred flower.

Originally, all flowers were wild flowers. Prehistoric people found wild flowers growing nearly everywhere, from the cold wastes of the Arctic to the steaming jungles of the tropics. In time, people learned to grow plants from seeds. They could then raise the prettiest and sweetest-smelling wild flowers in gardens. By 3000

Interesting facts about flowers

Robert W. Mitchell,
Tom Stack & Associates

Werner Stoy,
Camera Hawaii

Yucca flowers of the American Southwest are pollinated by female yucca moths, which lay their eggs in the flowers' seed-producing organs. The eggs hatch into caterpillars, which feed on the seeds.

The night-blooming cereus is a climbing cactus with large, fragrant, white flowers that open only at night. The plant grows in Hawaii, the West Indies, and other areas that have a tropical climate.

Red-hot pokers have long, slender stems topped by spikes of small, brilliantly colored flowers. They belong to the lily family and may reach a height of 5 feet (1.5 meters). Most red-hot pokers grow wild in South Africa.

M. Fogden, Bruce Coleman Inc.

Stone plants of South Africa have leaves that look like the stones among which the plants grow. Each plant has two fleshy leaves. A white or yellow flower grows in a slit between the tops of the leaves.

Edward S. Ross

The fly orchid of southern Ecuador has the shape and coloring of a female tachinid fly. This resemblance attracts male tachinid flies. The males pollinate fly orchids as they travel between blossoms.

© James H. Carmichael, Jr.

Gloriosa lilies have long, graceful *stamens* (male reproductive parts) that grow outside the petals. The stems may measure up to 6 feet (1.8 meters) tall. The flowers grow in Asia and Africa.

Diana & Rick Sullivan,
Bruce Coleman Ltd.

D. Ruble from Edward S. Ross

The rafflesia is the world's largest flower. It measures up to 3 feet (91 centimeters) across. Rafflesias grow in Indonesia. They have no stems or leaves and are parasites on other plants.

William H. Allen, Jr.

Dick Keen, Acadia Multi-Image

Poinsettias have petallike leaves called *bracts, left,* that surround the plants' tiny flowers, *right.* Most poinsettias have red bracts. The plants are native to Mexico and Central America.

B.C., the Egyptians and other peoples of the Middle East had begun to cultivate a variety of garden flowers, including jasmines, poppies, and water lilies. Gardeners have since developed many other kinds, and cultivated flowers are now raised in every country. Thousands of species of flowering plants still grow in the wild throughout the world. But many of these species are becoming rare as more and more wilderness areas are leveled to make room for farms and cities.

Although people admire flowers for their beauty, the function of the blossoms is to make seeds. Every blossom has male or female parts—or both male and female parts. The male and female parts together produce the seeds. The seeds develop in a female part called an *ovary,* which is a hollow structure at the base of a flower. Before the seeds can develop, however, they

must be fertilized by sex cells in the pollen produced by the male parts of a flower. Among most kinds of flowering plants, the pollen is carried from the male parts of one flower to the female parts of another flower. The wind pollinates some kinds of flowers, especially those that have small, plain blossoms. Insects or birds pollinate most plants with showy or sweet-smelling flowers. In some kinds of flowering plants, the plants pollinate themselves.

Plants that have flowers are classed scientifically as *angiosperms.* The word *angiosperm* comes from two Greek words meaning *covered* and *seed.* All angiosperms bear their seeds in the protective covering. Before the seeds are fertilized, they are protected in the ovary. After the seeds are fertilized, the ovary grows into a structure called a *fruit.* The fruit encloses and protects

Parts of a flower A typical flower has four main parts. They are (1) the calyx, (2) the corolla, (3) the stamens, and (4) the pistils. The calyx forms the outermost part and consists of leaflike *sepals.* The corolla consists of the petals. The stamens and pistils make up a flower's reproductive parts.

WORLD BOOK illustration by James Teason

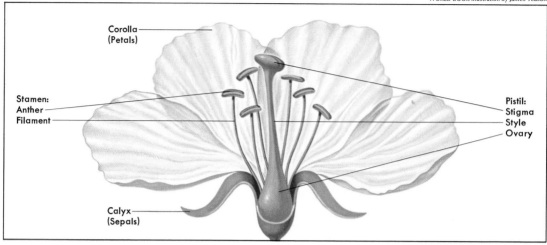

Corolla
(Petals)

Stamen:
Anther
Filament

Pistil:
Stigma
Style
Ovary

Calyx
(Sepals)

the ripening seeds. The rest of the blossom then dies.

Scientists estimate that there are more than 350,000 species of plants throughout the world. About 250,000 species are flowering plants, or angiosperms. All garden flowers and wild flowers belong to this large group, as do nearly all other familiar plants. One major exception is cone-bearing plants. Like angiosperms, cone-bearing plants reproduce by means of seeds. The seeds are produced by the cones. The cones develop from structures that resemble the plain flowers of some angiosperms. But these structures lack an ovary and therefore are not considered to be flowers in the strict sense of the word.

The parts of a flower

The typical flower develops at the tip of a flower stalk. The tip is somewhat enlarged, forming a cup-shaped structure called a *receptacle.* A bud grows from the receptacle and develops into a flower.

Most flowers have four main parts: (1) the calyx, (2) the corolla, (3) the stamens, and (4) the pistils. The calyx is the outermost part of a flower. It consists of a set of leaflike or petallike structures called *sepals.* The corolla consists of a flower's petals. The stamens and pistils make up the reproductive parts of flowers. The stamens are the male parts, and the pistils are the female parts. Every flower has either stamens or pistils—or both stamens and pistils. Flowers that have all four main parts are called *complete flowers.* Flowers that lack one or more of the parts are called *incomplete flowers.* In addition to the main parts, many flowers have glands that produce nectar. These glands, which are called *nectaries,* lie near the base of the flower.

In most flowers, each main part consists of three, four, or five elements or of multiples of three, four, or five elements. In a trillium, for example, three sepals form the calyx, and three petals form the corolla. The flower has six stamens, and the pistil is composed of three equal parts. The elements may be separate from one another, like the petals of a poppy or a rose. Or the elements may be *fused* (joined together). In flowers with fused petals, for example, the corolla is shaped like a tube, bell, trumpet, pouch, or saucer. Flowers that have such corollas include morning-glories, daffodils, and petunias. In such species as evening primroses and verbenas, the petals are fused at the base and free at the tip. The corolla thus has a tubelike or bell-like base and a fringed edge.

In buttercups, morning-glories, and most other flowers, all the main parts are arranged around the center of the flower in a circular fashion. If the flower is divided in half in any direction, the halves will be alike. Such flowers are *radially symmetrical.* Orchids, snapdragons, sweet peas, and certain other flowers can be divided into identical halves only if the blossoms are cut through lengthwise. Such kinds of flowers are *bilaterally symmetrical.*

The calyx. The sepals, which make up the calyx, are the first parts to form among the majority of flowers. They protect the developing inner parts of the flower. In most cases, the sepals remain attached to the flower after it opens.

In many flowers, such as buttercups and magnolias, the sepals are greenish, leaflike structures that are on the underpart of the flower. Other flowers have sepals that look like petals. Among many members of the iris, lily, and orchid families, the sepals and the petals look so much alike that they cannot be told apart. Botanists call these petallike structures *tepals.* Certain kinds of flowers have colorful sepals in place of petals. These flowers include anemones, hepaticas, larkspurs, and marsh marigolds.

The corolla, which consists of a flower's petals, is the showy, brightly colored part of most flowers. The colors of the petals—and of colored sepals—attract insects or birds that help spread a flower's pollen. The colors come from certain chemicals in a plant's tissues. These chemicals are present in all parts of the plant, not only the petals or sepals. But they are masked in the other parts by large amounts of green or brown pigments. Many flowers also have spots, stripes, or other markings on their petals that attract insects or birds. In most cases, the odors of flowers come from oily substances in the petals. Strong odors, like bright colors, attract animals.

The stamens are the male, pollen-producing parts of a flower. They are not particularly noticeable in most flowers. In some cases, however, the stamens make up a flower's most attractive part. Male acacia flowers, for example, consist mainly of a large feathery tuft of colorful stamens.

In most flowers, each stamen has two parts—a *filament* and an *anther.* The filament is a threadlike or ribbonlike stalk with an enlarged tip. The enlarged tip forms the anther. The anther consists of four tiny baglike structures that produce pollen. After the pollen is ripe, these structures split open, which releases the pollen grains.

The stamens are separate from one another in many flowers. But in such species as hollyhocks and sweet peas, some or all of the filaments are fused and form a tube around the pistil. In some flowers, the stamens are fused with one or more other flower parts. For example, the stamens of gentians are fused to the petals, and the stamens of most orchids are fused to the pistils.

The pistils are the female, seed-bearing parts of a flower. Some flowers, including all members of a pea family, have only one pistil. But most flowers have two or more. In many species, the pistils are fused into one *compound pistil.* A compound pistil is often referred to simply as a pistil. The individual pistils that make up a compound pistil are called *carpels.*

Among most flowers, each pistil or carpel has three parts—a *stigma,* a *style,* and an *ovary.* The stigma is a

sticky area at the top. The style consists of a slender tube that leads from the stigma to the ovary. The ovary is a hollow structure at the base. It contains one or more structures called *ovules.*

Variations in flower structure. Many kinds of flowers grow in clusters called *inflorescences.* In some species, such as bridal wreaths and snapdragons, the individual flowers in each cluster are easy to identify as flowers. In numerous other species, however, the inflorescence looks like one flower and the individual flowers that make up the inflorescence look like petals. These species include the many members of the *composite family,* such as asters, chrysanthemums, daisies, dandelions, and sunflowers.

Among the members of the composite family, the flowers grow from a *head* at the tip of the flower stalk. Each head has several or many flowers, depending on the species. A dandelion head, for example, may have 100 or more tiny yellow flowers. Each flower, or *floret,* looks like a petal but consists of a calyx, a corolla, stamens, and a pistil. One petal makes up the corolla. The dandelion florets grow so close together that only their corollas can be seen.

Many plants that have inflorescences also have leaflike structures called *bracts* just beneath each flower cluster. In most cases, bracts are small, green, and barely noticeable. But in a few species, they are so large and showy that most people mistake them for part of the flower. The showy "petals" of bougainvilleas, dogwoods, and poinsettias are bracts. The flowers are small, plain-looking inflorescences at the center of the bracts.

See **Flower** in *World Book* for more information on the following topics:

- The uses of flowers
- Garden flowers
- Wild flowers
- The role of flowers in reproduction
- Flower hobbies
- How flowers are named and classified

Variations in flower structure

Flowers vary in the shape, number, and color of their main parts. In addition, some species lack one or more of these parts. The examples below illustrate four variations in flower form.

WORLD BOOK illustrations by James Teason

 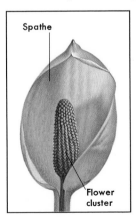  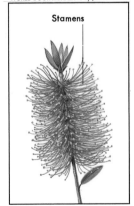

A composite flower is many small flowers. The daisy has tiny *disk flowers* in the center and individual *ray flowers* that look like petals.

A leaflike spathe surrounds the tiny flowers of the skunk cabbage. The flowers grow in a cluster on a stalk. Some spathes have bright colors.

Large white bracts encircle the flowers of the dogwood. Many people mistakenly think that the attractive bracts are part of the flower.

Long red stamens make up the showiest part of bottlebrush blossoms. The stamens form a spike that resembles a brush used to wash bottles.

Fran Hall, N.A.S.

A horse fly's eyes act as prisms, breaking light into bands of color.

Jane Burton

Grace A. Thompson, N.A.S.

A house fly searches for food on a crust of bread. The stiff hairs on the fly's body and legs may carry many disease germs that brush off on anything the insect touches.

The greenbottle fly is named for the color of its shiny coat.

Fly is an insect with one pair of well-developed wings. The common house fly is one of the best known kinds of flies. Other kinds include black flies, blow flies, bot flies, crane flies, deer flies, fruit flies, gnats, horse flies, leaf miners, midges, mosquitoes, robber flies, sand flies, tsetse flies, and warble flies.

A number of other insects are often called flies, but they have four wings and are not true flies. These insects include butterflies, caddisflies, damselflies, dragonflies, mayflies, and scorpionflies.

Some flies are among the most dangerous pests known. They carry germs inside their bodies, on the tip of their mouthparts, or in the hair on their bodies. When a fly "bites," or when it touches any object, it may leave some of these germs behind. Flies carry germs that cause such serious diseases as malaria, sleeping sickness, filariasis, and dysentery. These insects also cause diseases in animals and plants.

Scientists have developed many ways to control flies. Some swamps are drained. Others are covered with oil or sprayed with insecticides. These treatments kill newly hatched mosquitoes and other flies that grow in water. Proper disposal of garbage, decaying plants, and animal wastes is important for control of other kinds of flies.

Some kinds of flies are helpful. They carry pollen from one plant to another, much as bees do. Others eat insect pests. Scientists use fruit flies in the study of *heredity.* These flies have provided valuable information

on how characteristics are passed on from one generation to the next.

Flies live throughout the world. Among the smallest are the midges called *no-see-ums,* which are found in forests and coastal marshes. They are about $\frac{1}{20}$ inch (1.3 millimeters) long. One of the largest flies, the *mydas fly,* is found in South America. It is 3 inches (7.6 centimeters) long and also measures 3 inches from the tip of one wing to the tip of the other.

Flies are among the fastest of all flying insects. The buzzing of a fly is the sound of its wings beating. A house fly's wings beat about 200 times a second, and some midges move their wings 1,000 times a second. House flies fly at an average speed of $4\frac{1}{2}$ miles (7.2 kilometers) per hour. They can fly even faster for short distances to escape their enemies, which include people and many birds.

There are about 100,000 kinds of flies. They make up

Facts in brief

Names: *Male,* none; *female,* none; *young,* maggots or wrigglers; *group,* swarm.
Number of newborn: 1 to 250 at a time, depending on species. As many as 1,000 a year for each female.
Length of life: Average 21 days in summer for house flies.
Where found: Throughout the world.
Scientific classification: Flies belong to the class Insecta, and make up the order Diptera.

an *order* (chief group) of insects. The scientific name of the order is *Diptera,* which comes from Greek words that mean *two wings*.

The body of a fly

A fly's body has three main parts: (1) the head, (2) the thorax, and (3) the abdomen. The body wall consists of three layers and is covered with fine hair. Many kinds of flies have dull black, brown, gray, or yellowish bodies. A few kinds, including soldier flies and hover flies, may have bright orange, white, or yellow markings. Some kinds, such as bluebottle flies and greenbottle flies, are shiny blue or green. They seem to sparkle with brassy, coppery, or golden lights.

Head. A fly has two large eyes that cover most of its head. The males of some species have eyes so large that they squeeze against each other. The eyes of most female flies are farther apart.

Like most other kinds of insects, a fly has *compound* eyes made up of thousands of six-sided lenses. A house fly has about 4,000 lenses in each eye. No two lenses point in exactly the same direction, and each lens works independently. Everything a fly sees seems to be broken up into small bits. The insect does not have sharp vision, but it can quickly see any movement.

A fly has two antennae that warn it of danger and help it find food. The antennae grow near the center of the head between the eyes. The size and shape of the antennae vary widely among different species of flies, and even between males and females of the same species. A house fly's antennae are short and thick; a female mosquito's are long and covered with soft hair; and a male mosquito's are long and feathery. The antennae can feel changes in the movement of the air, which may warn of an approaching enemy. Flies also smell with their antennae. The odor of the chemicals in rotting meat and garbage attracts house flies. The odors of certain chemicals bring vinegar flies to wine cellars.

The mouth of a fly looks somewhat like a funnel. The broadest part is nearest the head, and tubelike part called the *proboscis* extends downward. A fly uses its proboscis as a straw to sip liquids, which are its only food.

Flies do not bite or chew because they cannot open their jaws. Mosquitoes, sand flies, stable flies, and other kinds of "biting" flies have sharp mouthparts hidden in the proboscis. They stab these sharp points into a victim's skin and inject saliva to keep the blood from clotting. Then the flies sip the blood. Blow flies, fruit flies, and house flies do not have piercing mouthparts. Instead, they have two soft, oval-shaped parts called *labella* at the tip of the proboscis. The flies use these parts somewhat like sponges to lap up liquids, which they then suck into the proboscis. They sip liquids, or turn solid foods such as sugar or starch into liquids by dropping saliva on them.

Thorax. A fly's muscles are attached to the inside wall of the thorax. These strong muscles move the insect's legs and wings. A fly has six legs. It uses all its legs when it walks, but often stands on only four legs. The legs of most kinds of flies end in claws, which help them cling to such flat surfaces as walls or ceilings. House flies and certain other flies also have hairy pads called *pulvilli* on their feet. A sticky substance on the feet helps the in-

sects walk on the smooth, slippery surfaces of windows and mirrors.

A fly's wings are so thin that the veins show through. The veins not only carry blood to the wings, but also help stiffen and support the wings. Instead of hind wings, a fly has a pair of thick, rodlike parts with knobs at the tips. These parts are known as *halteres*. The halteres give the fly its sense of balance. The halteres vibrate at the same rate as the wings beat when the insect is flying.

A fly is airborne as soon as it beats its wings. It does not have to run or jump to take off. In the air, the halteres keep the insect in balance and guide it so it can dart quickly and easily in any direction. A fly does not glide in the air or to a landing as do butterflies, moths, and most other flying insects. A fly beats its wings until its feet touch something to land on. If you pick up a fly, but leave the legs and wings free, the wings begin to beat immediately.

Abdomen. A fly breathes through air holes called *spiracles* along the sides of its body. The abdomen has eight pairs of spiracles, and the thorax has two pairs. Air flows through the holes into tubes that carry it to all parts of the fly's body.

See **Fly** in *World Book* for more information on The life of a fly.

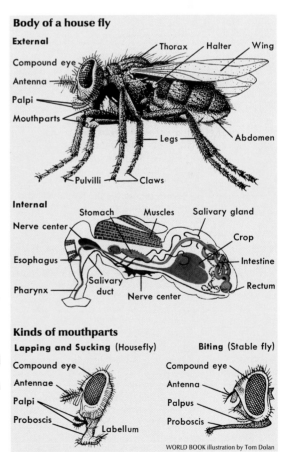

Body of a house fly

External — Thorax, Halter, Wing, Compound eye, Antenna, Palpi, Mouthparts, Legs, Abdomen, Pulvilli, Claws

Internal — Stomach, Muscles, Salivary gland, Nerve center, Crop, Esophagus, Intestine, Salivary duct, Rectum, Pharynx, Nerve center

Kinds of mouthparts

Lapping and Sucking (Housefly) — Compound eye, Antennae, Palpi, Proboscis, Labellum

Biting (Stable fly) — Compound eye, Antenna, Palpus, Proboscis

WORLD BOOK illustration by Tom Dolan

Jerry Frank, DPI

Tropical rain forest

Robert Frerck, Dimensions

Tropical seasonal forest

Jacques Jangoux

Savanna

Different kinds of forests grow in different parts of the world. Many scientists divide the world's forests into the six main *formations* (types) shown in the photographs above and on the next page. The forests that make up each formation have similar plant and animal life.

Forest

Forest is a large area of land covered with trees. But a forest is much more than just trees. It also includes smaller plants, such as mosses, shrubs, and wild flowers. In addition, many kinds of birds, insects, and other animals make their home in the forest. Millions upon millions of living things that can only be seen under a microscope also live in the forest.

Climate, soil, and water determine the kinds of plants and animals that can live in a forest. The living things and their environment together make up the forest *ecosystem.* An ecosystem consists of all the living and nonliving things in a particular area and the relationships among them.

The forest ecosystem is highly complicated. The trees and other green plants use sunlight to make their own food from the air and from water and minerals in the soil. The plants themselves serve as food for certain animals. These animals, in turn, are eaten by other animals. After plants and animals die, their remains are broken down by bacteria and other organisms, such as protozoans and fungi. This process returns minerals to the soil, where they can again be used by green plants to make food.

Although individual members of the ecosystem die, the forest itself lives on. If the forest is wisely managed, it provides us with a continuous source of wood and many other products.

Before people began to clear the forests for farms and cities, great stretches of forestland covered about 60 per cent of the earth's land area. Today, forests occupy about 30 per cent of the land. The forests differ greatly from one part of the world to another. For example, the steamy, vine-choked rain forests of central Africa are far different from the cool, towering spruce and fir forests of northern Canada.

The importance of forests

Forests have always had great importance to human beings. Prehistoric people got their food mainly by hunting and by gathering wild plants. Many of these people lived in the forest and were a natural part of it. With the development of civilization, people settled in towns and cities. But they still returned to the forest to get timber and to hunt. Today, people depend on forests more than ever, especially for their economic, environmental, and enjoyment value. The science of forestry is concerned with increasing and preserving these values by careful management of forestland.

The structure of forests

Every forest has various *strata* (layers) of plants. The five basic forest strata, from highest to lowest, are (1) the canopy, (2) the understory, (3) the shrub layer, (4) the herb layer, and (5) the forest floor.

The canopy consists mainly of the *crowns* (branches and leaves) of the tallest trees. The most common trees

Jen and Des Bartlett, Bruce Coleman Inc.

Temperate deciduous forest

Ray Atkeson, DPI

Temperate evergreen forest

Jacques Jangoux

Boreal forest

in the canopy are called the *dominant* trees of the forest. Certain plants, especially climbing vines and epiphytes, may grow in the canopy. *Epiphytes* are plants that grow on other plants for support but absorb from the air the water and other materials they need to make food.

The canopy receives full sunlight. As a result, it produces more food than does any other layer. In some forests, the canopy is so dense it almost forms a roof over the forest. Fruit-eating birds, and insects and mammals that eat leaves or fruit, live in the canopy.

The understory is made up of trees shorter than those of the canopy. Some of these trees are smaller species that grow well in the shade of the canopy. Others are young trees that may in time join the canopy layer. Because the understory grows in shade, it is not as productive as the canopy. However, the understory provides food and shelter for many forest animals.

The shrub layer consists mainly of shrubs. Shrubs, like trees, have woody stems. But unlike trees, they have more than one stem, and none of the stems grows as tall as a tree. Forests with a dense canopy and understory may have only a spotty shrub layer. The trees in such forests filter out so much light that few shrubs can grow beneath them. Most forests with a more open canopy and understory have heavy shrub growth. Many birds and insects live in the shrub layer.

The herb layer consists of ferns, grasses, wild flowers, and other soft-stemmed plants. Tree seedlings also make up part of this layer. Like the shrub layer, the herb layer grows thickest in forests with a more open canopy and understory. Yet even in forests with dense tree layers, enough sunlight reaches the ground to support some herb growth. The herb layer is the home of forest animals that live on the ground. They include such small animals as insects, mice, snakes, turtles, and ground-nesting birds and such large animals as bears and deer.

The forest floor is covered with mats of moss and with the wastes from the upper layers. Leaves, twigs, and animal droppings—as well as dead animals and plants—build up on the forest floor. Among these wastes, an incredible number of small organisms can be found. They include earthworms, fungi, insects, and spiders, plus countless bacteria and other microscopic life. All these organisms break down the waste materials into the basic chemical elements necessary for new plant growth.

Kinds of forests

Many systems are used to classify the world's forests. Some systems classify a forest according to the characteristics of its dominant trees. A *needleleaf forest,* for example, consists of a forest in which the dominant trees have long, narrow, needlelike leaves. Such forests are also called *coniferous* (cone-bearing) because the trees bear cones. The seeds grow in these cones. A *broadleaf forest* is made up mainly of trees with broad, flat leaves. Forests in which the dominant trees shed all their leaves during certain seasons of the year, and then grow new ones, are classed as *deciduous forests.* In an *evergreen forest,* the dominant trees shed old leaves and grow new ones continuously and so remain green throughout the year.

In some other systems, forests are classified according to the usable qualities of the trees. A forest of broadleaf trees may be classed as a *hardwood forest* because most broadleaf trees have hard wood, which makes fine furniture. A forest of needleleaf trees may be classed as a *softwood forest* because most needleleaf trees have softer wood than broadleaf trees have.

Many scientists classify forests according to various *ecological systems.* Under such systems, forests with similar climate, soil, and amounts of moisture are grouped into *formations.* Climate, soil, and moisture determine the kinds of trees found in a forest formation. One common ecological system groups the world's forests into six major formations. They are (1) tropical rain forests, (2) tropical seasonal forests, (3) temperate deciduous forests, (4) temperate evergreen forests, (5) boreal forests, and (6) savannas.

Tropical rain forests grow near the equator, where the climate is warm and wet the year around. The largest of these forests grow in the Amazon River Basin of South America, the Congo River Basin of Africa, and throughout much of Southeast Asia.

Of the six forest formations, tropical rain forests have the greatest variety of trees. As many as 100 species—none of which is dominant—may grow in 1 square mile (2.6 square kilometers) of land. Nearly all the trees of tropical rain forests are broadleaf evergreens, though some palm trees and tree ferns can also be found. In most of the forests, the trees form three canopies. The upper canopy reaches about 150 feet (46 meters) high. A few exceptionally tall trees, called *emergents,* tower above the upper canopy. The understory trees form the two lower canopies.

The shrub and herb layers are thin because little sunlight penetrates the dense canopies. However, many climbing plants and epiphytes crowd the branches of the canopies, where the sunlight is fullest.

Most of the animals of the tropical rain forests also live in the canopies, where they can find plentiful food. These animals include such flying or climbing creatures as bats, birds, insects, lizards, mice, monkeys, opossums, sloths, and snakes.

Tropical seasonal forests grow in certain regions of the tropics and subtropics. These regions have a definite wet and dry season each year or a somewhat cooler climate than that of the tropical rain forest. Such conditions occur in Central America, central South America, southern Africa, India, eastern China, and northern Australia and on many islands in the Pacific Ocean.

Tropical seasonal forests have a great variety of tree species, though not nearly as many as the rain forests. They also have fewer climbing plants and epiphytes. Unlike the trees of the rain forest, many tropical seasonal species are deciduous. The deciduous trees are found especially in regions with distinct wet and dry seasons. The trees shed their leaves in the dry season.

Tropical seasonal forests have a canopy about 100 feet (30 meters) high. One understory grows beneath the canopy. Bamboos and palms form a dense shrub layer, and a thick herb layer blankets the ground. The animal life resembles that of the rain forest.

Temperate deciduous forests grow in eastern North America, western Europe, and eastern Asia. These regions have a *temperate* climate, with warm summers and cold winters.

The canopy of temperate deciduous forests is about 100 feet (30 meters) high. Two or more kinds of trees dominate the canopy. Most of the trees in these forests

The structure of the forest

Every forest has various *strata* (layers) of plants. The five basic strata, from highest to lowest, are (1) the canopy, (2) the understory, (3) the shrub layer, (4) the herb layer, and (5) the forest floor. This illustration shows the strata as they might appear in a temperate deciduous forest.

WORLD BOOK illustration by Jean Helmer

Canopy

Understory

Shrub Layer

Herb Layer

Forest Floor

are broadleaf and deciduous. They shed their leaves in fall. The understory, shrub, and herb layers may be dense. The herb layer has two growing periods each year. Plants of the first growth appear in early spring, before the trees have developed new leaves. These plants die by summer and are replaced by plants that grow in the shade of the leafy canopy.

Large animals of the temperate deciduous forests include bears, deer, and, rarely, wolves. These forests are also the home of hundreds of smaller mammals and birds. Many of the birds migrate south in fall, and some of the mammals hibernate during the winter.

Some temperate areas support mixed deciduous and evergreen forests. In the Great Lakes region of North America, for example, the cold winters promote the growth of heavily mixed forests of deciduous and evergreen trees. Forests of evergreen pine and deciduous oak and hickory grow on the dry coastal plains of the Southeastern United States.

Temperate evergreen forests. In some temperate regions, the environment favors the growth of evergreen forests. Such forests grow along coastal areas that have mild winters with heavy rainfall. These areas include the northwest coast of North America, the south coast of Chile, the west coast of New Zealand, and the southeast coast of Australia. Temperate evergreen forests also cover the lower mountain slopes in Asia, Europe, and western North America. In these regions, the cool climate favors the growth of evergreen trees.

The strata and the plant and animal life vary greatly from one temperate evergreen forest to another. For example, the mountainous evergreen forests of Asia, Europe, and North America are made up of conifers. The coastal forests of Australia and New Zealand, on the other hand, consist of broadleaf evergreen trees.

Boreal forests are found in regions that have an extremely cold winter and a short growing season. The word *boreal* means *northern.* Vast boreal forests stretch across northern Europe, Asia, and North America. Similar forests also cover the higher mountain slopes on these continents.

Boreal forests, which are also called *taiga,* have the simplest structure of all forest formations. They have only one uneven layer of trees, which reaches up to about 75 feet (23 meters) high. In most of the boreal forests, the dominant trees are needleleaf evergreens—either spruce and fir or spruce and pine. The shrub layer is spotty. However, mosses and lichens form a thick layer on the forest floor and also grow on the tree trunks and branches. There are few herbs.

Many small mammals, such as beavers, mice, porcupines, and snowshoe hares, live in the boreal forests. Larger mammals in these forests include bears, caribou, foxes, moose, and wolves. Birds of the boreal forests include ducks, loons, owls, warblers, and woodpeckers.

Savannas are areas of widely spaced trees. In some savannas, the trees grow in clumps. In others, individual trees grow throughout the area, forming an uneven, widely open canopy. In either case, most of the ground is covered by shrubs and herbs, especially grasses. As a result, some biologists classify savannas as grasslands. Savannas are found in regions where low rainfall, poor soil, frequent fires, or other environmental features limit tree growth.

The largest savannas are tropical savannas. They grow throughout much of Central America, Brazil, Africa, India, Southeast Asia, and Australia. Animals of the tropical savannas include giraffes, lions, tigers, and zebras.

Temperate savannas, also called *woodlands,* grow in the United States, Canada, Mexico, and Cuba. They have such animals as bears, deer, elk, and pumas.

See **Forest** in *World Book* for more information on the following topics:

- The importance of forests
- Forests of the United States and Canada
- The life of the forest
- Forest succession
- The history of forests

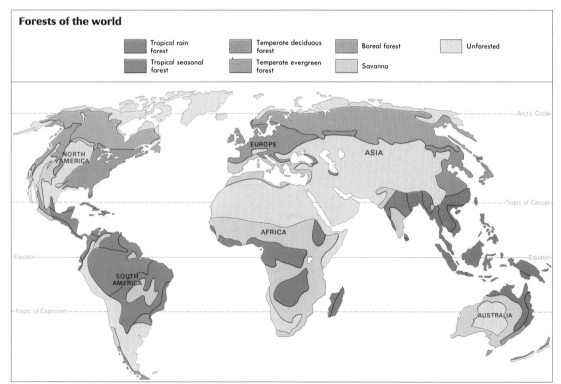

Forests of the world

WORLD BOOK map: adapted from *Physical Elements of Geography* by Trewartha, Robinson, and Hammond. Copyright © 1967 by McGraw-Hill, Inc. Used with permission of McGraw-Hill Book Company.

© Catherine Ursillo, Photo Researchers

Fossils, such as these dinosaur skeletons, help museum visitors visualize ancient species. Scientists study fossils to learn about the development and ways of life of prehistoric organisms.

Fossil

Fossil is the mark or remains of a plant or animal that lived thousands or millions of years ago. Some fossils are leaves, shells, or skeletons that were preserved after a plant or animal died. Others are tracks or trails left by moving animals.

Most fossils are found in *sedimentary rocks*. These fossils formed from plant or animal remains that were quickly buried in *sediments*—the mud or sand that collects at the bottom of rivers, lakes, swamps, and oceans. After thousands of years, the weight of upper layers of sediment pressing down on the lower layers turned them into rock. A few fossils are whole plants or animals that have been preserved in ice, tar, or hardened sap.

The oldest fossils are microscopic traces of bacteria that scientists believe lived about $3\frac{1}{2}$ billion years ago. The oldest animal fossils are remains of *invertebrates* (animals without a backbone) estimated to be about 700 million years old. The oldest fossils of *vertebrates* (animals with a backbone) are fossil fish about 500 million years old.

Fossils are more common and easier to find than many people realize. For example, fossils are plentiful in nearly every state in the United States. Even so, scientists believe that only a small portion of the countless plants and animals that have lived on earth have been pre-

served as fossils. Many species are thought to have lived and died without leaving any trace whatsoever in the fossil record.

Although the fossil record is incomplete, many important groups of animals and plants have left fossil remains. These fossils help scientists discover what forms of life existed at various periods in the past and how these prehistoric species lived. Fossils also indicate how life on earth has gradually changed over time. This article explains how fossils provide information on ancient life. For a description of animals of the past, see **Prehistoric animal.**

How fossils reveal the past

In the distant past, when most fossils formed, the world was different from today. Plants and animals that have long since vanished inhabited the waters and land. A region now covered with high mountains may have been the floor of an ancient sea. Where a lush tropical forest thrived millions of years ago, there may now be a cool, dry plain. Even the continents have drifted far from the positions they occupied hundreds of millions of years ago. No human beings were present to record these changes. But *paleontologists* (scientists who study prehistoric life) have been able to piece together much of the story of the earth's past by examining its fossil record.

How fossils form

The great majority of plants and animals die and decay without leaving any trace in the fossil record. Bacteria and other microorganisms break down such soft tissues as leaves or flesh. As a result, these tissues rarely leave fossil records. Even most hard parts, such as bones, teeth, shells, or wood, are eventually worn away by moving water or dissolved by chemicals. But when plant or animal remains have been buried in sediment, they may become fossilized. These remains are occasionally preserved without much change. Most, however, are altered after burial. Many of the remains disappear completely, but still leave a fossil record in the sediment.

Fossils may be preserved in several ways. The main processes of fossilization are (1) the formation of impressions, molds, and casts; (2) carbonization; and (3) the action of minerals.

Formation of impressions, molds, and casts. Some fossils consist of the preserved form or outline of animal or plant remains. Impressions, also called *prints* or *imprints,* are shallow fossil depressions in rock. They form when thin plant or animal parts are buried in sediment and then decay. After the sediment has turned to stone, only the outline of the plant or animal is preserved. Many impressions consist of small grooves left by the bones of fish or the thick-walled veins found inside leaves. Sometimes even delicate soft parts, such as feathers or leaves, are preserved as impressions.

Molds form after hard parts have been buried in mud, clay, or other material that turns to stone. Later, water dissolves the buried hard part, leaving a mold—a hollow space in the shape of the original hard part—inside the rock. A cast forms when water containing dissolved minerals and other fine particles later drains through a mold. The water deposits these substances, which eventually fill the mold, forming a copy of the original hard part. Many seashells are preserved as molds or casts.

Carbonization results when decaying tissues leave behind traces of carbon. Living tissues are made up of compounds of carbon and other chemical elements. As decaying tissues are broken down into their chemical parts, most of the chemicals disappear. In carbonization, a thin, black film of carbon remains in the shape of the organism. Plants, fish, and soft-bodied creatures have been preserved in precise detail by carbonization.

The action of minerals. Many plants and animals became fossilized after water that contained minerals soaked into the pores of the original hard parts. This action is called *petrifaction.* In many such fossils, some or all of the original material remains, but it has been strengthened and preserved by the minerals. This process is called *permineralization.* The huge tree trunks in the Petrified Forest of Arizona were preserved by permineralization.

In other cases, the minerals in the water totally replaced the original plant or animal part. This process, called *replacement,* involves two events that happen at the same time: The water dissolves the compounds that make up the original material, while the minerals are de-

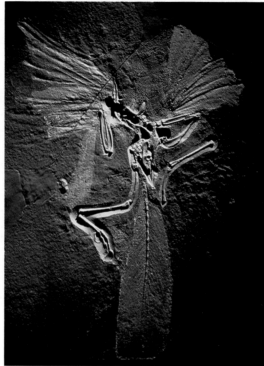
American Museum of Natural History

An impression of an archaeopteryx began to form when the bird was buried in soft silt. The silt turned to limestone, preserving the delicate outlines of the bird's wing and tail feathers.

American Museum of Natural History

A mold preserved the three-dimensional form of a trilobite after its body decayed.

Runk/Schoenberger from Grant Heilman

A carbonized fossil of a fern consists of traces of carbon in the shape of the leaf.

posited in their place. Replacement by minerals can duplicate even microscopic details of the original hard part.

See **Fossil** in *World Book* for more information on How fossils reveal the past and Studying fossils.

E. R. Degginger

Harold Hungerford

Frogs vary greatly in color and size. The spotted, brownish-green leopard frog, *above,* measures from 2 to 3½ inches (5 to 9 centimeters) long. The colorful arrow poison frog, *top right,* grows from 1 to 2 inches (2.5 to 5 centimeters) long. The green tree frog, *bottom right,* is less than 2 inches long.

Alvin E. Staffan

Frog

Frog is a small, tailless animal with bulging eyes. Almost all frogs also have long back legs. The strong hind legs enable a frog to leap distances far greater than the length of its body. Frogs live on every continent except Antarctica. But tropical regions have the greatest number of species. Frogs are classified as *amphibians.* Most amphibians, including most frogs, spend part of their life as a water animal and part as a land animal.

The body of a frog

The giant, or Goliath, frog of west-central Africa ranks as the largest frog. It measures nearly a foot (30 centimeters) long. The smallest species grow only ½ inch (1.3 centimeters) long. Frogs also differ in color. Most kinds are green or brown, but some have colorful markings.

Although different species may vary in size or color, almost all frogs have the same basic body structure. They have large hind legs, short front legs, and a flat head and body with no neck. Adult frogs have no tail, though one North American species has a short, taillike structure. Most frogs have a sticky tongue attached to the front part of the mouth. They can rapidly flip out the tongue to capture prey.

Like higher animals, frogs have such internal organs as a heart, liver, lungs, and kidneys. However, some of the internal organs differ from those of higher animals. For example, a frog's heart has three chambers instead of four. And although adult frogs breathe by means of lungs, they also breathe through their skin.

Legs. A few burrowing species have short hind legs and cannot hop. But all other frogs have long, powerful hind legs, which they use for jumping. Many frogs can leap 20 times their body length on a level surface. Frogs also use their large hind legs for swimming. Most water-

dwelling species have webbed toes on their hind feet. The smaller front legs, or arms, prop a frog up when it sits. The front legs also help break the animal's fall when it jumps. Frogs that live in trees have tiny, sticky pads on the ends of their fingers and toes. The pads help the animal cling to the tree trunk as it climbs.

Skin. Most frogs have thin, moist skin. Many species have poison glands in their skin. The poison oozes onto the skin and helps protect the frog. If an enemy grabs a frog, the poison irritates the enemy's mouth and causes the animal to release the frog. Frogs have no hair, though the males of one African species, the so-called hairy frog, look hairy during the mating season. At that time, tiny, blood-rich growths called *papillae,* which resemble hair, grow from the sides of the frog's body. These structures provide males with extra oxygen during a period when they are very active.

In water, a frog uses its strong hind legs for swimming. Many water-dwelling species, such as the North American bullfrog, *above,* have webbed toes on their hind feet as well.

Treat Davidson, NAS

Skeleton of a grass frog

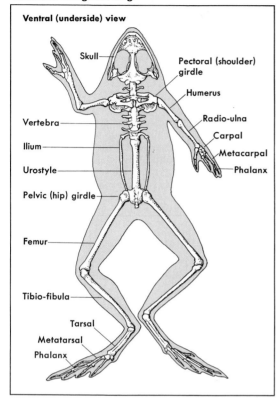

Ventral (underside) view

Skull
Pectoral (shoulder) girdle
Humerus
Radio-ulna
Vertebra
Carpal
Ilium
Metacarpal
Urostyle
Phalanx
Pelvic (hip) girdle
Femur
Tibio-fibula
Tarsal
Metatarsal
Phalanx

Some species of frogs change their skin color with changes in the humidity, light, and temperature. Frogs shed the outer layer of their skin many times a year. Using their forelegs, they pull the old skin off over their head. They then usually eat the old skin.

Senses. Frogs have fairly good eyesight, which helps them in capturing food and avoiding enemies. A frog's eyes bulge out, enabling the animal to see in almost all directions. Frogs can close their eyes by pulling the eyeballs deeper into their sockets. This action closes the upper and lower eyelids. Most species also have a thin, partly clear inner eyelid attached to the bottom lid. This inner eyelid, called the *nictitating membrane,* can be moved upward when a frog's eyes are open. It protects the eyes without completely cutting off vision.

Most frogs have a disk of skin behind each eye. Each disk is called a *tympanum,* or eardrum. Sound waves cause the eardrums to vibrate. The vibrations travel to the inner ear, which is connected by nerves to the hearing centers of the brain.

Most frogs have a delicate sense of touch. It is particularly well developed in species that live in water. The tongue and mouth have many taste buds, and frogs often spit out bad-tasting food. The sense of smell varies among species. Frogs that hunt mostly at night or that live underground have the best sense of smell.

Voice. Male frogs of most species have a voice, which they use mainly to call females during the mating season. In some species, the females also have a voice. But the female's voice is not nearly so loud as the male's.

A frog produces sound by means of its *vocal cords.* The vocal cords consist of thin bands of tissue in the *larynx* (voice box), which lies between the mouth and lungs. When a frog forces air from its lungs, the vocal cords vibrate and give off sound.

Among many species, the males have a *vocal sac,* which swells to great size while a call is being made. Species that have a vocal sac produce a much louder call than do similar species that have no sac. Some species have a vocal sac on each side of the head. Others have a single sac in the throat region.

See **Frog** in *World Book* for more information on The life of a frog, Kinds of frogs, and Frogs and human beings.

The life of a frog A frog's life has three stages: (1) egg, (2) tadpole, and (3) adult frog. Most female frogs lay a clump of several hundred eggs in water. A male frog clings to the female's back and fertilizes the eggs as she lays them. Tiny fishlike tadpoles hatch from the eggs. As the tadpoles grow, they develop legs and a froglike body. In time, they become adult frogs and can live out of water.

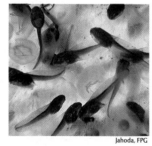

Jahoda, FPG

Newly hatched tadpoles

E. S. Ross

Older tadpole, with legs

Giuseppe Mazza

Frog near completion of metamorphosis

Jane Burton, Bruce Coleman Inc.

Frog eggs and egg laying

Fruit is the part of a flowering plant that contains the plant's seeds. Fruits include acorns, cucumbers, tomatoes, and wheat grains. But the word *fruit* commonly refers to the juicy, sweet or tart kinds that people enjoy eating. The word comes from the Latin word *frui,* meaning *enjoy.* Popular fruits include apples, bananas, grapes, oranges, peaches, pears, and strawberries.

Many fruits are nutritious as well as appetizing. For example, oranges and strawberries contain large amounts of Vitamin C. Most fruits have a high sugar content, and so they provide quick energy. Fruits alone cannot provide a balanced diet, however, because the majority of them supply little protein.

The world's fruit growers raise millions of tons of fruit annually. Fruit growing is a branch of *horticulture,* a field of agriculture that also includes the raising of nuts, vegetables, flowers, and landscape crops. Most nuts are actually fruits, as are such vegetables as cucumbers, green peppers, and tomatoes. To prevent confusion, horticultural scientists define a fruit as an edible seed-bearing structure that (1) consists of fleshy tissue and (2) is produced by a *perennial.* A perennial is a plant that lives for over two years without being replanted. The horticultural definition of a fruit excludes nuts and vegetables. Nuts are firm, not fleshy. Most vegetables are *annuals*—that is, the plants live for only one season.

In some cases, the horticultural definition of a fruit conflicts with the definition used by botanists and with common usage. For example, watermelons and musk-melons are fruits, and most people regard them as such. But they grow on vines that must be replanted annually, and so horticulturists regard melons as vegetables. Rhubarb is sometimes considered a fruit. But people eat the leafstalk of the plant, not the seed-bearing structure. Thus, horticulturists classify rhubarb as a vegetable.

How botanists classify fruits. Fruit, the seed-bearing structure of a flowering plant, develops from the *ovaries* of the flowers. An ovary is a hollow structure near the base of a flower. It may hold one seed or more than one, depending on the species of the plant.

The wall of an ovary of mature fruit, in which the seed is fully developed, has three layers. The outer layer is called the *exocarp,* the middle layer is known as the *mesocarp,* and the inner layer is the *endocarp.* The three layers together are called the *pericarp.*

Botanists classify fruits into two main groups, simple fruits and compound fruits. A simple fruit develops from a single ovary, and a compound fruit develops from two or more ovaries.

See **Fruit** in *World Book* for more information on the following topics:

- How horticulturists classify fruits
- Growing fruit
- Marketing fruit
- Developing new varieties of fruit
- How botanists classify fruits

How horticulturists classify fruits

Any seed-bearing structure produced by a flowering plant is a fruit. But the word *fruit* has a more limited meaning in common usage and in horticulture, the branch of agriculture that includes fruit growing. Thus, the word usually refers to the edible sweet or tart fruits that are popular foods and widely grown farm crops. Horticulturists classify these fruits into three groups, based on temperature requirements for growth: (1) temperate fruits, (2) subtropical fruits, and (3) tropical fruits. Some examples of each of these types are shown below.

WORLD BOOK illustrations by James Teason

Temperate fruits must have an annual cold season. They are raised mainly in the Temperate Zones, the regions between the tropics and the polar areas.

Subtropical fruits need warm or mild temperatures throughout the year but can survive occasional light frosts. They are grown chiefly in subtropical regions.

Tropical fruits cannot stand frost. They are raised mainly in the tropics. Large quantities of some species, especially bananas and pineapples, are exported.

Simple fruits   Simple fruits are classified into two main groups, depending on whether their tissue is fleshy or dry. Fleshy simple fruits include most of the seed-bearing structures that are commonly called fruits. They are divided into three main types: (1) berries, (2) drupes, and (3) pomes. The drawings below show some examples of each of these types and of several dry simple fruits.

WORLD BOOK illustrations by James Teason

Berries consist entirely of fleshy tissue, and most species have many seeds. The seeds are embedded in the flesh. This group includes only a few of the fruits that are commonly known as berries.

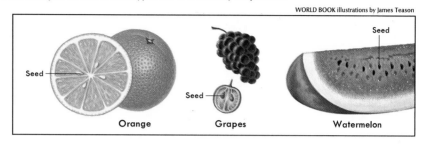

Orange   Grapes   Watermelon

Drupes are fleshy fruits that have a hard inner stone or pit and a single seed. The pit encloses the seed.

Peach   Cherries   Plum

Pomes have a fleshy outer layer, a paperlike core, and more than one seed. The seeds are enclosed in the core.

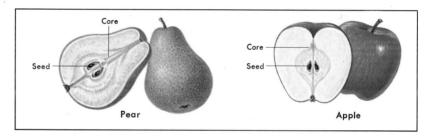

Pear   Apple

Dry simple fruits are produced by many kinds of trees, shrubs, garden plants, and weeds. The seed-bearing structures of nearly all members of the grass family, including corn and wheat, belong to this group.

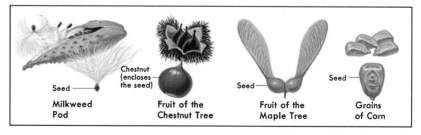

Milkweed Pod   Fruit of the Chestnut Tree   Fruit of the Maple Tree   Grains of Corn

Compound fruits   A compound fruit consists of a cluster of seed-bearing structures, each of which is a complete fruit. Compound fruits are divided into two groups, (1) aggregate fruits and (2) multiple fruits.

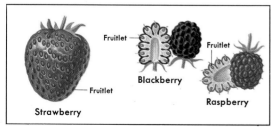

Strawberry   Blackberry   Raspberry

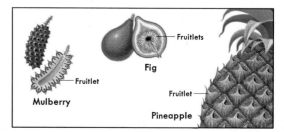

Mulberry   Fig   Pineapple

Aggregate fruits include most of the fruits that are commonly called berries. Each fruitlet of a blackberry or raspberry is a small drupe. Each "seed" of a strawberry is a dry fruitlet.

Multiple fruits include mulberries, figs, and pineapples. Mulberry fruitlets are small drupes. Each "seed" in a fig and each segment of a pineapple is a fruitlet.

Trans-Canada Pipe Lines Ltd.

Industrial use of natural gas accounts for about a third of the gas burned in the United States and Canada. This gas-burning furnace is used to harden gears in an automobile factory.

Gas

Gas (fuel) is one of our most important resources. We burn it to provide heat and to produce energy to run machinery. The chemical industry uses the chemicals in gas to make detergents, drugs, plastics, and many other products.

People sometimes confuse gas with gasoline, which is often called simply *gas.* But gasoline is a liquid. On the other hand, gas fuel—like air and steam—is a *gaseous* form of matter. That is, it does not occupy a fixed amount of space as liquids and solids do.

Gas has many uses as a fuel. Millions of people use it to heat their homes, cook meals, burn garbage, heat water, dry laundry, and cool the air. Hotels, restaurants, hospitals, schools, and many other businesses and institutions burn gas for cooking, heating buildings and water, air conditioning, and generating steam. Gas produces little air pollution when it is burned.

Industry has many uses for gas in addition to using it as a raw material in making products. These uses range from burning off the quills of chickens to hardening the nose cones of spacecraft.

There are two kinds of gas—*natural gas* and *manufactured gas.* Almost all the gas used in the United States and Canada is natural gas. Most scientists believe that natural gas has been forming beneath the earth's surface for hundreds of millions of years. The natural forces that created gas also created petroleum. As a result, natural gas is often found with or near oil deposits. The same methods are used to explore and drill into the earth for both fuels.

Manufactured gas is produced chiefly from coal or petroleum, using heat and chemical processes. Manufactured gas costs more than natural gas and is used in regions where large quantities of the natural fuel are not available.

The Soviet Union, the United States, Canada, and the Netherlands—in that order—are the leading producers of natural gas. Until the 1960's, large quantities of natural gas were not available in most European countries, and manufactured gas was used widely. During the 1960's, the development of newly discovered gas fields led to the rapid expansion of Europe's natural gas industry. Expansion was especially rapid in the Soviet Union and the Netherlands. The world's largest known gas field was discovered in the Soviet Union in 1966. Great Britain also began to produce much natural gas from deposits that were found under the North Sea in the mid-1960's.

The gas industry consists of three main activities: (1) producing gas, either by drilling natural gas wells or by manufacturing gas; (2) transmitting gas, usually by pipeline, to large market areas; and (3) distributing gas to the user. Each part of the gas industry requires its own special skills and equipment. Some gas companies conduct all three of these activities, but most companies handle only one.

The natural gas industry began in the United States. The industry started to expand rapidly in the late 1920's with the development of improved pipe for transmitting gas great distances economically. By the 1930's, gas produced in Texas was being carried by pipeline to the Midwest. Today, long-distance gas pipelines serve many parts of the world.

In the 1970's and 1980's, the gas industry launched a number of programs to meet an increasing demand for gas. For example, the industry began seeking ways of producing gas from coal.

How natural gas was formed. Most scientists believe that natural gas was formed millions of years ago, when water covered much more of the earth's surface than it does today. Down through the ages, tremendous quantities of tiny marine organisms called *plankton* died and settled to the ocean floors. There, fine sand and mud drifted down over the plankton. Layer upon layer of these deposits piled up. The great weight of the deposits, plus bacteria, heat, and other natural forces, changed the chemical compounds in the plankton into natural gas and oil. The gas and oil flowed into the holes in limestone, sandstone, and other kinds of porous rocks. Layers of solid rocks formed over the porous rocks and sealed the gas and oil beneath them. Later, movements in the earth's crust caused the ancient seas to draw back, and dry land appeared over many gas and oil deposits.

The composition of natural gas. Pure natural gas is made up of chemical compounds of the elements hydrogen and carbon. These compounds are called *hydrocarbons.* Some hydrocarbons are naturally gaseous, some are liquid, and some are solid. The form depends on the number and arrangement of the hydrogen and carbon atoms in the hydrocarbon molecule.

Natural gas is composed chiefly of methane, the lightest hydrocarbon. In a methane molecule, one atom of carbon is bound together with four atoms of hydrogen. Its chemical formula is CH_4. Other gaseous hydrocarbons usually found in natural gas include ethane (C_2H_6), propane (C_3H_8), and butane (C_4H_{10}). Natural gas that is impure may contain such gases as carbon dioxide, helium, and nitrogen.

When natural gas burns, the hydrocarbon molecules break up into atoms of carbon and hydrogen. The atoms combine with the oxygen in the air and form new substances. The carbon and oxygen form carbon dioxide (CO_2), an odorless, colorless gas. The hydrogen and oxygen produce water vapor (H_2O). As the molecules break up and recombine, heat is released.

© Ted Czocowski, Image Finders

Drilling a well is the only sure way to find out if an area has gas. Tall derricks hold the well-drilling equipment.

See **Gas** in *World Book* for more information on the following topics:

- Uses of gas
- From well to user
- The chemical story of gas
- History of the gas industry

How natural gas was formed   Ages ago, the remains of tiny marine organisms sank to the sea floors and were buried by sediments, *left.* The decaying matter became gas and oil trapped in porous rock under nonporous rock, *center.* Later, the earth's crust shifted, and dry land appeared over many deposits, *right.*

WORLD BOOK diagram by George Suyeoka

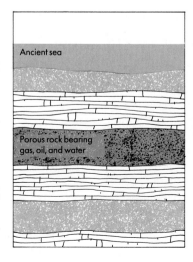

Ancient sea

Settling of dead organisms

Ocean floor

Nonporous rock

Porous rock

Nonporous rock

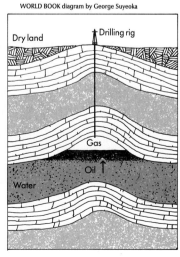

Ancient sea

Porous rock bearing gas, oil, and water

Dry land   Drilling rig

Gas

Oil

Water

Giraffe is the tallest of all animals. Male giraffes may grow more than 18 feet (5.5 meters) tall—5 feet (1.5 meters) taller than the African elephant, the second tallest animal. Most adult male giraffes stand about 17 feet (5.2 meters) tall, and most females grow to about 14 feet (4.3 meters) in height. The giraffe gets its great height from its legs, which are 6 feet (1.8 meters) long, and a neck that may be even longer. But even though giraffes tower over other animals, most adult males weigh only about 2,600 pounds (1,200 kilograms). A male African elephant may weigh more than five times as much.

Giraffes live in Africa south of the Sahara in open woodlands. They feed on the leaves, twigs, and fruit of trees and bushes. A giraffe, like a cow, chews a *cud,* which is food that has entered the stomach but is returned to the mouth for a second chewing. Giraffes can go without drinking water for many weeks.

The body of a giraffe. A giraffe's coat has patchlike markings of *tawny* (light brownish-yellow) to chestnut-brown. The lines that separate the patches are lighter tawny or white. This color pattern helps protect giraffes by making them hard to see when they stand among trees. Each giraffe has its own distinct coat pattern.

Two bony "horns" grow from a giraffe's skull. These horns, which are covered by skin and hair, resemble a deer's antlers before the antlers develop branches. They are not true horns because they do not have a horny covering. Some giraffes also have one or more short hornlike bumps on the forehead. The horns of the female are smaller than those of the male.

A giraffe can close its nostrils completely to keep out sand and dust. It uses its long upper lip and its tongue, which is about 21 inches (53 centimeters) long, to gather food from tree branches. Giraffes have good vision and hearing. A giraffe seldom uses its voice, though it can utter a variety of soft sounds.

Despite the length of its neck, a giraffe has only seven neck bones—the same number that human beings and most other mammals have. A short mane grows along the back of the neck from the head to the shoulders. The sloping back measures about 5 feet (1.5 meters) from the base of the neck to the base of the tail. The tail, which is about 3 feet (91 centimeters) long, ends in a tuft of long, black hairs. A giraffe's hoofs are split into two parts. Each part consists of the hardened tip of one toe. A giraffe's closest relative—and the only other member of the giraffe family—is the okapi.

The life of a giraffe. A female giraffe carries her young inside her body for about 15 months before giving birth. Giraffes bear one baby at a time, except for rare cases of twins. At birth, a *calf* (baby giraffe) may stand as tall as 6 feet (1.8 meters) and weigh as much as 150 pounds (68 kilograms). It can stand up within an hour. The *cow* (female giraffe) nurses its young with milk for 9 or 10 months, though the baby eats small amounts of green plants from the age of 2 weeks. A female can bear her first baby when she is 5 years old. In the wild, giraffes may live as long as 28 years.

Giraffes walk by moving both legs on one side of the body forward almost together and then both legs on the other side. When giraffes gallop, both hind feet swing forward and land outside and in front of the front feet. Giraffes can gallop up to 35 miles (56 kilometers) per hour.

See **Giraffe** in *World Book* for more information on The life of a giraffe and Giraffes and people.

The skeleton of a giraffe

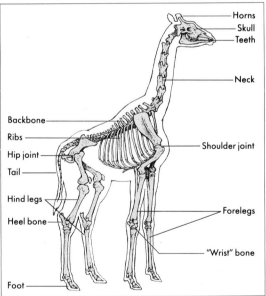

WORLD BOOK illustration by John D. Dawson

Giraffe tracks

A. Myers, De Wys, Inc.

Giraffes live in small groups on African grasslands. They feed on leaves, twigs, and fruit from trees that grow in scattered groves. Every giraffe has its own distinct coat pattern.

Glacier is a huge mass of ice that flows slowly over land. Glaciers form in the cold polar regions and in high mountains. The low temperatures in these places enable large amounts of snow to build up and turn into ice. Most glaciers range in thickness from about 300 to 10,000 feet (91 to 3,000 meters).

Kinds of glaciers. There are two main kinds of glaciers, *continental glaciers* and *valley glaciers.* They differ in shape, size, and location.

Continental glaciers are broad, extremely thick ice sheets that cover vast areas of land near the earth's polar regions. The continental glaciers on Greenland and Antarctica, for example, bury mountains and plateaus and conceal the entire landscape except for the highest peaks. Glaciers of this type build up at the center and slope outward toward the sea in all directions.

Valley glaciers are long, narrow bodies of ice that fill high mountain valleys. Many of them move down sloping valleys from bowl-shaped hollows located among the peaks. In mountains near the equator, such as the northern Andes of South America, valley glaciers occur at elevations of about 15,000 feet (4,570 meters) or higher. Valley glaciers occur at lower elevations in the European Alps, the Southern Alps of New Zealand, and other mountain ranges nearer the poles.

How glaciers form. Glaciers begin to form when more snow falls during the winter than melts and evaporates in summer. The excess snow gradually builds up in layers. Its increasing weight causes the snow crystals under the surface to become compact, grainlike pellets. At depths of 50 feet (15 meters) or more, the pellets are further compressed into dense crystals of ice. These crystals combine to form glacial ice. The ice eventually becomes so thick that it begins to move under the pressure of its own great weight.

Glaciers are affected by seasonal variations in snowfall and temperature. Most glaciers increase slightly in size during the winter because snow falls over much of their surface. The cold temperatures promote the build-up of snow, and limit the melting of the glaciers' lower parts as the ice masses move downslope. In areas away from the poles, the size of glaciers decreases in summer because the rising temperatures cause the lower parts to melt. In the always frigid polar regions, glaciers shrink for other reasons. When they reach the sea, for example, huge chunks of ice break away from them. These chunks fall into the water and become icebergs.

Glaciers may also increase or decrease in size as a result of changes in climate that occur over long periods. For example, the ice sheet that covers much of Greenland is growing smaller because of a gradual rise in temperature in the area since the early 1900's.

The movement of glaciers. A glacier flows downslope because of the pull of gravity. The ice crystals deep within the glacier glide over one another as a result of the pressure of the surface layers. These small movements of the individual crystals cause the entire ice mass to move. The melting and refreezing of the ice crystals along the base of a glacier also help it slide downslope. Heat from friction and from the earth's interior melts some of the crystals of the glacier's bottom layer. The water from the dissolved crystals flows down into nearby open spaces in the layer and refreezes, forming new ice crystals.

Bob and Ira Spring

A valley glacier flows down this mountain valley in Alaska. Dark strips of rock debris called *moraines* run through the ice. Melting ice forms a lake, *foreground,* at the end of the glacier.

John R. T. Molholm

A continental glacier covers most of Antarctica. The Ross Ice Shelf, *above,* forms part of the huge ice sheet. Its edge rises above the Ross Sea along the western edge of the continent.

**A sectional view of
a valley glacier**

A valley glacier moves downslope from a *cirque,* a bowl-shaped hollow near a mountain peak. As the glacier travels over uneven terrain, its surface splits and forms cracks called *crevasses.* The glacier picks up rocks and other materials and piles them up in narrow ridges called *moraines.*

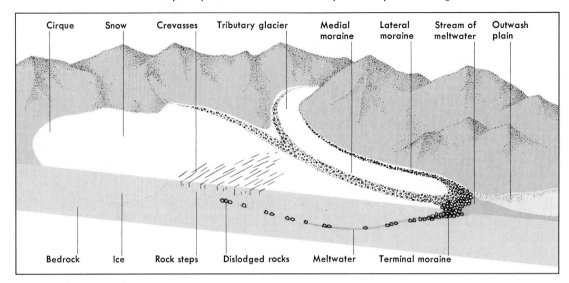

The surface of a glacier is stiff and rigid. It often fractures and forms deep cracks called *crevasses* as the glacier flows over uneven or steep terrain. Crevasses also develop because the upper layers of a glacier move more rapidly than its lower layers.

Most glaciers flow extremely slowly and move less than a foot (30 centimeters) per day. But sometimes a glacier may travel much faster for several years. For example, some glaciers at times flow more than 50 feet (15 meters) per day. The various parts of a glacier move at different speeds. The center and upper areas of a valley glacier flow the fastest. The sides and bottom move more slowly because they rub against the walls and floor of the valley. Scientists measure a glacier's speed by driving stakes into the ice at various points and recording the changes in their position.

How glaciers shape the land. As glaciers pass over an area, they help shape its features. They create a variety of land forms by means of erosion and by transporting and depositing rock debris. Glaciers greatly altered the surface of large parts of Europe and North America during the Pleistocene Ice Age, which ended about 10,000 years ago.

Glacial erosion occurs when an advancing ice mass scoops up rock fragments and drags them along its base. In doing so, the glacier grinds the *bedrock* (layer of solid rock beneath the loose rock fragments), producing a polished but often scratched surface. When a glacier decreases in size, it leaves behind broad humps of hard bedrock called *roches moutonnées.* One side of this kind of land form is smoothly rounded while the other side is rough and irregular.

A glacier in a mountain valley may produce a rounded hollow, called a *cirque,* near the peak of the mountain. A cirque forms when the upper part of a glacier removes blocks of rock from the surrounding cliffs. A glacier also can gouge out a U-shaped depression in a river valley. Such a depression that forms below sea

Land forms created by a glacier

As a glacier melts, it leaves behind humps of hard bedrock, and rounded hills and narrow ridges of rock debris. Hollows in the loose rocks trap water from the melting glacier, forming lakes.

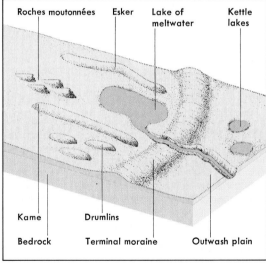

WORLD BOOK diagrams by Cynthia Fujii

level and is flooded by the ocean is called a *fiord.*

Glacial deposits consist of clay and sand, and rocks of various sizes. Glaciers pile up these materials, forming uneven ridges called *moraines.* The ridges along the sides of a valley glacier are known as *lateral moraines.* When two valley glaciers come together, the lateral moraines between them merge to form a *medial moraine* along the center of the combined ice mass. The hilly ridge at the lower end of a valley glacier is called a *terminal moraine.* Such a moraine also develops around the edge of a continental glacier.

Gorilla is the largest of the *anthropoid* (humanlike) apes. This powerful animal has huge shoulders, a broad chest, and long arms and short legs. A large male gorilla living in the wild may weigh 450 pounds (204 kilograms). Standing up on its legs, it may be 6 feet (1.8 meters) tall. Females usually weigh about 200 pounds (91 kilograms), and are shorter than males.

A gorilla looks fierce. It has a shiny black face and large canine teeth. A thick ridge of bone juts out above its eyes. Black or brownish hair covers all of a gorilla's body, except its face, chest, and the palms of its hands and soles of its feet. The adult male gorilla has a hairy crest on its head, and a grayish back. When a gorilla is excited or wants to frighten away intruders, it stands up on its legs and slaps its cupped hands against its chest one at a time. This produces a sound.

Actually, a gorilla is not as fierce as it looks. It will not hurt a human being unless it is threatened or attacked. Gorillas are shy, friendly animals that seem to need companionship and attention. The first gorillas kept in zoos did not live long, and some people believe they died from loneliness. Gorillas lack the outgoing personality of their relatives, the chimpanzees, and they are less eager to perform stunts and tricks.

The gorilla usually walks on all fours, with its feet flat on the ground and the upper part of its body supported on the knuckles of its hands. It often stands up on its legs, but walks only a few steps in this position. A gorilla usually travels on the ground, but sometimes it climbs into a tree to sit, eat, or sleep.

Gorillas are quiet animals, even though they can make about 20 different sounds. The most startling gorilla call is the roar given by an angry male. Babies whimper when distressed, and scream when frightened. Adults grumble softly when contented. Gorillas have no real enemies except human beings. People hunt gorillas for food, capture them for zoos, and cut down their forests. As a result, the gorilla has become rare in many parts of its African home, and its survival is threatened.

Dian Fossey, Bruce Coleman Inc.

Gorillas travel in groups looking for bamboo, bark, buds, fruit, and leaves to eat. The group is continually on the move and never spends more than one night in the same place.

Facts in brief

Gestation period: From 8 to 9 months.
Number of newborn: 1.
Length of life: Up to 50 years in captivity; in the wild, unknown.
Where found: East-central and west Africa.
Scientific classification: Gorillas belong to the anthropoid ape family, Pongidae. They are genus *Gorilla,* species *G. gorilla.*

San Diego Zoo

The gorilla is the largest kind of ape. Powerful male gorillas, such as the one at the left, may weigh as much as 450 pounds (204 kilograms). Gorillas can walk a few steps using only their legs. But they generally use their knuckles to support the upper part of their body.

The gorilla's home is in the rain forests of Africa near the equator. The *western lowland gorilla* lives in the forests of western Africa, from Nigeria south to the Congo River. The *eastern lowland gorilla* lives in the lowlands of eastern Zaire. The *mountain gorilla* inhabits upland regions in Rwanda, the Virunga Mountains of Zaire, and mountain forests in Uganda. It lives at altitudes of up to 13,000 feet (3,960 meters), where freezing temperatures occur every night of the year.

Gorillas lead a peaceful life. They travel through forests in groups of from 2 to 30. A group may be made up of one or more males, two or more females, and several young gorillas. An adult male always leads the group. He makes all the decisions, such as when to get up in the morning, where to go, and when to rest. This male also protects the group against danger. The extra males in the group sometimes leave their companions and wander alone through the forest. A new group forms when one or more females joins a lone male.

Each group wanders around in its own home range, which covers from 2 to 15 square miles (5 to 39 square kilometers). Gorillas never spend more than one night in the same place. Several groups may live in the same

The skeleton of a gorilla

WORLD BOOK illustration by John D. Dawson

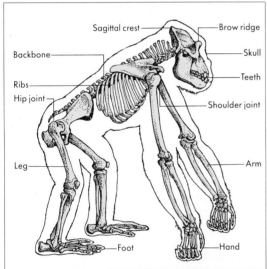

Sagittal crest — Brow ridge
Backbone — Skull
Ribs — Teeth
Hip joint — Shoulder joint
Leg — Arm
Foot — Hand

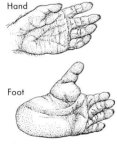

Hand

Foot

Ben McCall, FPG

A gorilla's foot has a "thumb" and resembles the animal's hand. Such feet help the gorilla climb trees.

A gorilla's head has a ridge of bone called a *sagittal crest* on top of the skull. A *brow ridge* is above the eyes.

Where gorillas live

The yellow areas on the map below show the regions of the world inhabited by gorillas. Most gorillas live in central Africa.

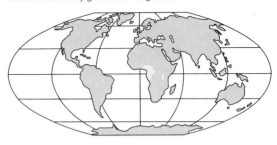

section of a forest, but they usually avoid each other.

The gorilla's day usually begins about an hour after sunrise. During the early morning, the apes feed on a wide variety of leaves, buds, barks, and fruits. Only gorillas living in captivity eat meat.

From the middle of the morning to the middle of the afternoon is nap time. The adults rest while the younger apes wrestle with each other, play games similar to *Follow the Leader* or *King of the Mountain,* and swing on vines. After the rest period, all the gorillas eat again.

Every evening just before dark, the gorillas build a simple nest where they sleep at night. They break or bend branches to make a crude platform, either on the ground or in trees. Adult gorillas build their own nests, but baby gorillas snuggle in with their mothers.

Life cycle. The gorilla's pregnancy lasts for from 8 to 9 months. The newborn gorilla is helpless. It weighs from 3 to 5 pounds (1.4 to 2.3 kilograms) at birth, and remains with its mother for about $3\frac{1}{2}$ years. At first, the mother carries her baby by holding it gently to her chest. After about three months, the baby is strong enough to hold on by itself. Then the baby may ride on its mother's back, holding on to her long hair. The baby is able to crawl by the age of 3 months, and walk by 5 months. But it usually rides "piggyback" until it is almost 3 years old. Then it travels by itself.

Female gorillas usually mate when they are about 8 years old, and males reach full adulthood at about 12 years old. No one knows how long wild gorillas live. Some gorillas in captivity have lived up to 50 years. Most wild gorillas probably do not live such a long time. They suffer from many diseases, especially those caused by parasites in the blood and intestines. They also may suffer from respiratory disorders and colds.

Gorillas in captivity. The gorilla was not discovered until 1847. In 1911, the first gorilla was exhibited in a United States zoo. In 1956, Colo, the first gorilla born in captivity, was born in a zoo in Columbus, Ohio.

Gorillas rank among the most intelligent animals. For many years, people have wondered whether gorillas could learn to use language. In 1972, researchers at Stanford University began to teach sign language to a female gorilla named Koko. Koko developed a vocabulary of several hundred signs and used them to communicate with her teachers.

Hawk refers to a type of bird of prey. Hawks belong to a large family of birds that includes ospreys, kites, harriers, Old World vultures, and eagles. Hawks live on every continent except Antarctica.

There are two types of hawks, *accipiters* and *buteos.* Accipiters include such species as the *goshawk* and *Cooper's hawk.* These hawks watch and wait for prey from a perch, such as a tree branch. They have relatively short wings and long tails. Buteos generally have longer wings than accipiters and fan-shaped tails, and they frequently soar in search of prey. They include such species as the *red-tailed hawk* and *Swainson's hawk.*

Hawks hunt a wide variety of animals, including small mammals, reptiles, fish, insects, and other birds. Hawks that prey chiefly on birds have long, thin toes with sharp, curving *talons* (claws). These "bird hawks" include most accipiters. Hawks that eat mammals and reptiles have stouter legs, shorter toes, and thicker talons than do bird hawks. Most buteos belong to this group.

Buteo hawks use their excellent eyesight to spot prey from high up in the air. When a hawk sees its prey, it swoops down and may grasp the animal with its talons. After making a kill, the hawk tears off pieces of the animal with its sharp beak. Some hawks eat bones, feathers, and fur as well as flesh. Because hawks cannot digest everything they eat, they throw up masses of undigested food called *pellets.*

In all species of hawks, the female is larger than the male. Hawks measure from 10 to 27 inches (25 to 69 centimeters) in length and weigh from 3 ounces to 5 pounds (90 grams to 2 kilograms).

See **Hawk** in *World Book* for more information on Breeding, Migration, and North American hawks.

Northern harrier
Circus cyaneus
Found in temperate Northern Hemisphere
Body length 24 inches (61 centimeters)

WORLD BOOK diagram by Marion Pahl

Goshawk
Accipiter gentilis
Found in temperate Northern Hemisphere
Body length 26 inches (66 centimeters)

A hawk's vision is sharper than a human being's. Its eyes have more light-sensitive cells, and most kinds of hawks have more than one *fovea* (an area of the retina). At a great distance, a person sees a rabbit as a blur, but a hawk sees it clearly.

Human eye

Fovea

Retina

Hawk eye

Foveae

WORLD BOOK illustrations by Albert Gilbert

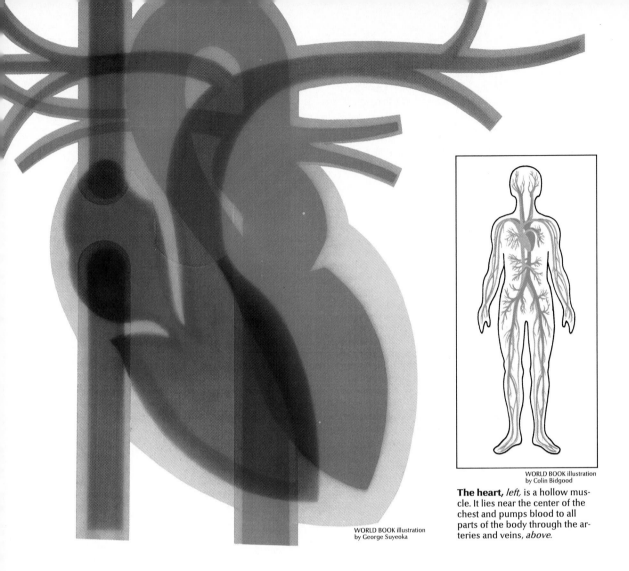

WORLD BOOK illustration
by Colin Bidgood

The heart, *left,* is a hollow muscle. It lies near the center of the chest and pumps blood to all parts of the body through the arteries and veins, *above.*

WORLD BOOK illustration
by George Suyeoka

Heart

Heart is a busy machine that pumps blood to all parts of the body. Blood carries oxygen to the brain and all other parts of your body. As long as your heart pumps blood, your body gets the oxygen it needs. If your heart stops, the oxygen is cut off and you will die unless a special device is used to circulate your blood.

The heart is a large hollow muscle. Tubes called *veins* bring blood to the heart. Other tubes called *arteries* carry blood away from the heart. Regulators called *valves* control the flow of blood through the heart itself.

Your heart is about the size of your fist, and the heart and fist grow at about the same rate. An adult's heart is about 5 inches (13 centimeters) long, $3\frac{1}{2}$ inches (9 centimeters) wide, and $2\frac{1}{2}$ inches (6.4 centimeters) thick. A man's heart weighs about 11 ounces (312 grams), and the heart of a woman weighs approximately 9 ounces (260 grams).

The heart lies in a slanting position near the middle of the chest toward the front. It is wider at the top than at the bottom. The wider end points toward the person's right shoulder. The narrower end points downward, to-

Your heart . . .

. . . is a busy pump linked by 100,000 miles (160,000 kilometers) of pipelines to all parts of your body.

. . . weighs less than 1 pound (0.5 kilogram).

. . . is as big as your fist.

. . . beats about 70 times a minute, and more than 100,000 times in a single day.

. . . pumps 5 quarts (4.7 liters) of blood through its chambers every 60 seconds.

. . . does enough work in one hour to lift a weight of $1\frac{1}{2}$ short tons (1.4 metric tons) more than 1 foot (30 centimeters) off the ground.

ward the front of the chest and to the left. The lower end is the part you can feel beating.

This article is about the human heart, but many kinds of animals have hearts. Earthworms, houseflies, snails, and some other *invertebrate animals* (animals without backbones) have hearts. Their hearts are not as well developed as human hearts. Often, they are just a thick-walled tube. All *vertebrate animals* (animals with backbones) have hearts. These animals include frogs, toads, lizards, snakes, and all birds and mammals.

Parts of the heart

The heart lies between the lungs at the center of the chest. The lower part of the heart points toward the left side of the body. Because the beating, or pumping, takes place in the lower part, many persons incorrectly think the heart is entirely on the left side of the body. This illustration shows the heart about two-thirds normal size.

The outer covering of the heart is a strong, thin membrane called the *pericardium.* The superior vena cava, aorta, and other large blood vessels lead in and out of the heart. Smaller blood vessels nourish the heart itself.

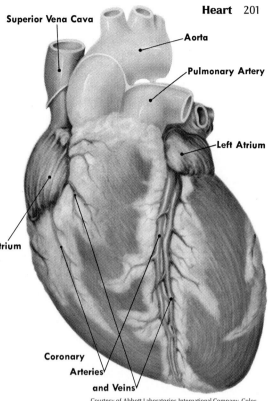

Superior Vena Cava

Aorta

Pulmonary Artery

Left Atrium

Right Atrium

Coronary Arteries and Veins

Courtesy of Abbott Laboratories International Company. Color reconstructions by Virginia Samter and Arnold R. Chalfant.

How the heart works

Each side of the heart performs a different pumping job. The right side takes blood from the body and pumps it to the lungs. The left side collects blood from the lungs and pumps it to the body. Blood entering the right side of the heart contains *carbon dioxide,* a waste product of the body. All blood entering the right side of the heart goes to the lungs before it reaches the left side of the heart. In the lungs, the carbon dioxide is removed, and oxygen is added to the blood. Blood that flows to the body from the left side of the heart contains fresh oxygen. The oxygen is used in the body cells to produce energy. See **Circulatory system.**

Right side. Blood from the body flows into the right atrium through two large veins. One of these veins, the *superior vena cava,* carries blood from the head and arms. The other vein, the *inferior vena cava,* carries blood from the trunk and legs.

Blood from the body fills the right atrium. The atrium then contracts, squeezing blood through the tricuspid valve into the ventricle. The tricuspid valve is made of three little triangular flaps of thin, strong fibrous tissue. These flaps permit the blood to flow into the ventricle, but they prevent it from flowing back into the atrium. The flaps are like doors that open only in one direction.

At first, the ventricle is relaxed, but it contracts when it is filled with blood. The resulting pressure closes the tricuspid valve and opens the semilunar valve between the ventricle and the *pulmonary artery.* Blood gushes through the semilunar valve into the pulmonary artery, which leads to the lungs. The valve is called *semilunar* because it is made up of three flaps that are shaped like half-moons. Blood squeezed from the ventricle pushes the flaps against the walls of the pulmonary artery.

Left side. From the lungs, the blood flows back to the heart through the four *pulmonary veins.* It flows out of the pulmonary veins into the left atrium. The left atrium, like its neighbor on the right, then contracts, squeezing blood through the mitral valve into the left ventricle. The mitral valve is similar to the tricuspid valve, except that it has only two flaps. The left ventricle contracts, forcing blood through another semilunar valve into the aorta. The aorta, with its numerous branches, carries blood throughout the body.

Phases. The two sides of the heart relax and fill, and then contract and empty themselves at the same time. The atria contract only a split second before the ventricles do. The relaxing and filling phase is called the *diastole.* The contracting and pumping phase is called the *systole.* The action felt as a heartbeat is the systole.

Blood pressure. The blood in the circulatory system is always under pressure, as is the water in the pipes of a water system. Blood pressure depends upon the amount of blood in the system, the strength and rate of the heart's contraction, and the elasticity of the arteries. The heart regulates blood pressure by producing a hormone called *atrial natriuretic factor.* This hormone helps the kidneys get rid of salt. Excess salt in the body may contribute to *hypertension* (high blood pressure). Doctors measure two phases of blood pressure—the *systolic pressure* and the *diastolic pressure.* The systolic pressure is the blood pressure when the heart is contracted. The diastolic pressure is the pressure when the heart relaxes between beats. Doctors use a device called a *sphygmomanometer* to measure a patient's blood pressure.

Beat of the heart. The walls of the heart are made of a special kind of muscle. The heart muscle contracts and relaxes regularly and automatically. A beat is one complete contraction and relaxation of the heart muscle.

A special system of muscles in the heart causes it to beat with a regular rhythm. One part of this system, the *sinoatrial (sinoauricular)* or *S-A node,* has the job of starting each heartbeat, setting the pace, and causing contraction of the heart muscle. It has been called the "pacemaker" of the heart. The impulse from this node spreads through the atria and reaches a second node,

How your heart works

These drawings show how blood flows through the heart. Blood in the right chambers, shown in blue, flows to the lungs. Blood in the left chambers, shown in red, goes to the rest of the body.

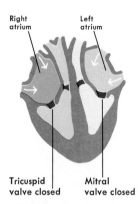

Right atrium | Left atrium

Tricuspid valve closed | Mitral valve closed

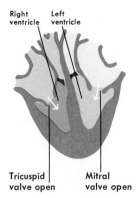

Right ventricle | Left ventricle

Tricuspid valve open | Mitral valve open

Semilunar valves open

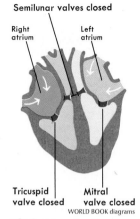

Pulmonary artery | Aorta

Tricuspid valve closed | Mitral valve closed

Semilunar valves closed

Right atrium | Left atrium

Tricuspid valve closed | Mitral valve closed

WORLD BOOK diagrams

The heart relaxes between beats during the *diastolic* phase. Blood flows into the heart from the veins, filling both atria. The tricuspid and mitral valves are closed.

The atria contract, forcing blood through the mitral and tricuspid valves and into the ventricles. This action is called *atrial systole.* The ventricles are still in diastole.

The ventricles contract in *ventricular systole.* Blood forces the mitral and tricuspid valves shut and opens the semilunar valves. It enters the aorta and pulmonary artery.

The heart again relaxes. The semilunar valves close, and the atria expand and fill with blood. These steps mark the beginning of diastole, and the cycle is repeated.

the *atrioventricular,* or *A-V node.* A part of this specialized system, called the *atrioventricular bundle* or the *bundle of His,* conducts the beating impulse from the atria and the A-V node to the rest of the heart. This system causes the heart to contract as a single unit.

Sometimes the heart may stop beating because of an accident, a heart attack, or surgical shock. Such an occurrence is called a *cardiac arrest.* If the heart stops during an operation, a doctor may open the patient's chest and massage the heart until it starts to beat again. In other emergency situations, doctors or other specially trained persons may give the victim *external heart massage.* They apply pressure to the chest in a certain way to restart the heartbeat.

Rate of beating. Without oxygen, the body cells stop working. Sometimes the body needs much oxygen. At other times, it requires little. An adult's heart normally beats about 70 times a minute, but the rate changes automatically to provide as much or as little oxygen as the body needs.

The body needs a lot of fuel for such strenuous exercises as swimming or ice skating. For this reason, the heart beats rapidly when a person swims or skates. It is

rushing more oxygen to the body by speeding the flow of blood. If the person stops exercising, the heart gradually slows down. It is regulating the flow of blood to the body's slower tempo.

There are many other examples of how the heart changes its rate of beating to meet a particular need. The heart beats faster when a person is angry, afraid, or excited. It is rushing more oxygen to the muscles to prepare the person for quick action, such as fighting or running away. During pregnancy, a woman's heart takes care not only of her own needs, but also the needs of the unborn baby. The woman's heart increases its output by half to three-fourths.

Heart diseases

Diseases of the heart and blood vessels are called *cardiovascular diseases.* The word *cardiovascular* comes from the word *cardiac,* meaning heart, and *vascular,* meaning blood vessel. Cardiovascular diseases cause about half of all deaths in the United States. The field of medicine that deals with the diagnosis and treatment of heart disease is called *cardiology.* Doctors who specialize in such medicine are called *cardiologists.*

The three most important kinds of heart disease are (1) *arteriosclerosis,* or hardening of the arteries; (2) *hypertension,* or high blood pressure; and (3) *rheumatic fever,* which often leads to *rheumatic heart disease* later in life. Certain infections, such as diphtheria, and syphilis in its late stages, can produce heart disease. Some children are born with imperfectly formed hearts. They suffer from *congenital heart disease.*

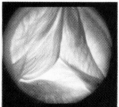

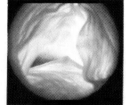

From the film *Red River of Life,* Moody Bible Institute of Science

The aortic valve controls the flow of blood from the left ventricle to the aorta, the main artery in the body. These photographs show how the flaps of the aortic valve open to let out blood as the left ventricle contracts. The structure of the valve prevents blood from flowing back into the ventricle.

See **Heart** in *World Book* for more information on the following topics:

- Its parts and development
- Heart diseases
- Heart attacks
- Treatment of heart problems

Fritz Henle, Photo Researchers

People use heat in many ways to do work and to make life more comfortable. In this foundry furnace, for example, heat is used to soften steel so that it can be shaped into the desired form. The steel becomes so hot it gives off light.

Heat

Heat is one of the most important forms of energy. When we think of heat, we usually think of how heat makes us feel. On a hot day, for example, it may make us feel uncomfortable. But heat is far more important in our lives than simply how it may make us feel.

We must have a carefully controlled amount of heat to live. Our bodies use the food we eat to produce the heat that keeps our temperature at about 98.6° F. (37° C). If our temperature rises too far above normal—or falls too far below—we can die. In cold weather, we wear heavy clothes to hold in our body heat. During warm weather, we wear light clothes to let the unneeded heat escape.

No one knows how high temperatures may climb, but the temperature inside the hottest stars is many millions of degrees. The lowest possible temperature, called *absolute zero,* is −459.67° F. (−273.15° C).

In our homes, we use heat in many ways. Heat warms our homes and cooks our food. It also provides hot water, dries the laundry, and makes electric light bulbs give off light.

In industry, the uses for heat are almost endless. Heat is used to separate metals from their ores and to refine crude oil. It is used to melt, shape, cut, coat, and harden metals and to join metals together. Heat is also used to make or process foods, glass, paper, textiles, and many other products.

Heat also runs our machinery. The heat from burning fuels in engines provides the power to move airplanes, automobiles, rockets, and ships. Heat causes the wheels of giant turbines to spin, driving generators that produce electricity. Electricity provides light and furnishes power to run all kinds of equipment—from electric pencil sharpeners to electric trains.

Sources of heat

Anything that gives off heat is a source of heat. The heat that we use or that affects life and events on the earth comes from six main sources. They are (1) the sun, (2) the earth, (3) chemical reactions, (4) nuclear energy, (5) friction, and (6) electricity.

We control some of these sources, and others we do not. We use the sources we control, such as electricity and nuclear energy, to heat buildings and do other work. But the sources we do not control also benefit us. For example, the sun provides the heat and light that make life possible. All sources of heat, even those that we normally control, can do great damage if they get out of control. For example, fires, which are chemical reactions, destroy much property every year.

The sun is our most important source of heat. If the sun should ever cool, the earth would become cold and lifeless. Only a tiny fraction of the heat produced in the sun strikes the earth. Yet it is enough to keep us—and all other organisms on the earth—alive.

The sun's heat is absorbed by the seas, the ground, plants, and the atmosphere. Large amounts of heat can be collected by using such devices as large *solar furnaces.* These furnaces have mirrors that reflect the sun's light from a wide area onto one spot. Some solar furnaces can generate enough heat to melt steel. Smaller ones can gather enough heat to cook food. See **Solar energy; Sun.**

The earth itself contains much heat deep inside. When a volcano erupts, some of this heat escapes to the surface. The lava from a volcano is rock melted by the heat deep within the earth. Some of the earth's heat also escapes in *geysers.* These springs shoot forth boiling water that has been heated by hot rocks within the earth. People have begun to use the earth's heat to generate electricity, heat houses, and do other work. See **Earth; Volcano.**

Chemical reactions can produce heat in a number of ways. A chemical reaction in which a substance combines with oxygen is called *oxidation.* Rapid oxidation produces heat fast enough to cause a flame. When coal, wood, natural gas, or any other fuel burns, substances in the fuel combine with oxygen in the air to form other compounds. This chemical reaction, which is known as *combustion,* produces heat—and fire.

People use fire in many ways. Fire in a gas stove produces heat to cook food. Coal, oil, or gas fires in furnaces and boilers heat buildings. Fire heats metals red-hot so that they can be shaped into a variety of forms. Special cutting torches can produce flames hot enough to cut through metal.

Another example of combustion is the burning of gasoline in the cylinders of an automobile engine. This process produces heat that causes the gases in the cylinders to expand and move parts that make the engine work.

The rusting of iron is also an example of oxidation. Unlike fire, however, rusting occurs so slowly that little heat and no flames are produced.

The mixing of certain kinds of chemicals also produces heat. For example, if sulfuric acid and water are combined, the mixture becomes boiling hot.

In all living things, food is changed into heat—as well as energy and living tissue—by the process of *metabolism.* Metabolism is a complicated series of chemical reactions carried out by living cells.

Nuclear energy can produce great quantities of heat. Nuclear weapons release so much heat so quickly that they destroy everything around them. Their heat cannot be put to useful work. But in a device called a *reactor,* heat can be produced from nuclear energy slowly enough to generate electricity and to do other jobs. See **Nuclear energy.**

Friction. When one object rubs against another, heat is produced. Friction is usually an unwanted source of heat because it may damage objects. In a machine, for example, the heat created as the moving parts rub against one another may cause those parts to wear down. For this reason, oil is used between moving machinery parts. The oil reduces friction and so decreases the generation of heat.

Electricity. The flow of electricity through metals, alloys, and other *conductors* (substances that carry electric current) generates heat. People make use of this heat in the operation of many appliances, including electric furnaces, ovens, ranges, dryers, heaters, toasters, and irons. See **Electricity.**

Sources of heat

WORLD BOOK illustrations

The sun produces heat from nuclear reactions deep inside it. All life on the earth depends on this heat.

Friction—the rubbing of one object against another—produces heat. Scouts learn to start a fire with friction.

Chemical reactions produce heat by causing a chemical change in substances. Fire is a chemical reaction.

The earth contains much heat deep inside. Some of this heat escapes to the surface when a volcano erupts.

Heat is a form of energy. Heat and energy cannot be seen, but the work they do can. For example, the burning of fuel in the engines of a jet airplane creates hot gases. These gases expand and provide the power that moves the plane.

Temperature and heat. All things are made up of atoms or molecules, which are always moving. The motion gives every object *internal energy*. The *level* of an object's internal energy depends on how rapidly its atoms or molecules move. If they move slowly, the object has a low level of internal energy. If they move violently, it has a high level. Hot objects have higher internal energy levels than do cold objects. The words *hot* and *cold* refer to an object's temperature.

Temperature is an indication of an object's internal energy level. A thermometer is used to measure temperature. Thermometers have a numbered scale so that temperature can be expressed in degrees. The two most common scales are the *Fahrenheit* and the *Celsius,* or *centigrade,* scales.

The temperature of an object determines whether that object will take on more internal energy or lose some when it comes into contact with another object. If a hot rock and a cold rock touch each other, some of the internal energy in the hot rock will pass into the cold rock as heat. If a thermometer were placed on the hot rock, it would show the rock's temperature falling steadily. A thermometer on the cold rock would show a steadily rising temperature. Eventually, the thermometers on the two rocks would show the same temperature. Then, no further flow of heat would occur.

Just as water flows only downhill, so heat flows only down a "temperature hill," passing from an object at a higher temperature to an object at a lower one. The greater the difference in temperature between two objects, the faster the heat will flow between them.

It is important to recognize that temperature and heat are not the same thing. Temperature is simply an indication of the level of internal energy that an object has.

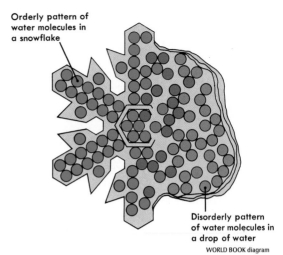

Orderly pattern of water molecules in a snowflake

Disorderly pattern of water molecules in a drop of water

WORLD BOOK diagram

Heat decreases the orderly arrangement of the atoms or molecules in an object. For example, the molecules of water in a snowflake are frozen in an orderly pattern. But as heat flows into the flake, its molecules move more rapidly. They become so disorderly that the snowflake begins to melt.

Heat, on the other hand, is the passage of energy from one object to another.

The three units most commonly used to measure heat are British thermal units (Btu's), calories, and joules. One *Btu* is the quantity of heat needed to raise the temperature of 1 pound of water 1° F. One *calorie* is the quantity of heat needed to raise the temperature of 1 gram of water 1° C. The calorie used to measure food energy is 1,000 times as large as this calorie. The Btu is generally used in engineering, and the calorie in the sciences. The *joule* can be used for measuring all forms of energy, including heat.

Disorder. Temperature and internal energy tell only part of the story about heat. To tell the whole story, we need to see what happens to the atoms or molecules of an object when heat flows into it.

As heat enters an object, that object's atoms or molecules move around more. The more heat that flows in, the more the object's atoms or molecules move around and the more disorderly they become. For example, the water molecules in a snowflake have an orderly pattern. But if a snowflake is taken into a warm room, it will melt and become a drop of water. Heat changes the orderly pattern of the snowflake into disorder. Scientists use the term *entropy* to describe the amount of disorder in an object.

Heat flowing into an object increases the internal energy and disorder in that object. Usually, the added heat also raises the temperature of the object. On the other hand, heat flowing out of an object decreases the internal energy and disorder in that object. Usually, the heat loss also lowers the temperature of the object.

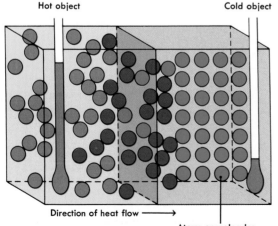

Hot object   Cold object

Direction of heat flow ———▶

Atoms or molecules

WORLD BOOK diagram

Heat energy flows from a hot to a cold object when they are in contact. The rapidly moving atoms or molecules in the hot object strike the less energetic atoms or molecules in the cold object and speed them up. In this way, internal energy in the form of heat passes from a hot object to a cold object.

See **Heat** in *World Book* for more information on the following topics:

- How heat travels
- What heat does
- Putting heat to work
- Learning about heat

A river hippopotamus has a stout, barrel-shaped body; short legs; and a huge head. It weighs as much as 5,800 pounds (2,630 kilograms) and ranks as one of the largest land animals. In spite of its clumsy appearance, the river hippopotamus is an excellent swimmer and can run as fast as a human being.

Mark Boulton, National Audubon Society

Hippopotamus, *HIHP uh PAHT uh muhs,* is the third largest animal that lives on land. Only the elephant and rhinoceros are larger. A large, wild river hippopotamus may weigh as much as 5,800 pounds (2,630 kilograms).

Hippopotamuses live in central, southern, and western Africa. They live close to water and spend much time in it. The word *hippopotamus* comes from two Greek words meaning *river horse.* However, the hippopotamus is more closely related to the hog than to the horse. There are two kinds of hippopotamuses: the *river hippopotamus,* also called the *common hippopotamus,* and the *pygmy hippopotamus.* The pygmy hippopotamus is much smaller than the river hippopotamus. It is also rarer.

The body of a river hippopotamus. The river hippopotamus has a large, barrel-shaped body; short legs; and a huge head. It generally weighs from 2,500 to 3,000 pounds (1,130 to 1,400 kilograms) and stands about 5 feet (1.5 meters) tall. It ranges from 12 to 15 feet (4 to 5 meters) long, not including the tail, which measures about 22 inches (56 centimeters) long. Each foot has four webbed toes.

The eyes of the river hippopotamus stick out from its head. The position of the ears, eyes, and nostrils enables the animal to hear, see, and breathe with most of its head underwater. The hippopotamus can also close its nostrils and ears when it swims or dives. Hippopotamuses have a good sense of smell, but their vision is only fair.

River hippopotamuses have thick, brownish-gray skin. They have no hair except for a few bristles on the head and tail. Special glands in the skin give off a clear, oily fluid that is either pink or red. This fluid keeps the animal's skin from getting too dry. The reddish color of the fluid led to the mistaken belief that hippopotamuses sweat blood.

A hippopotamus has long, curved front teeth. Its tusklike *canines* (side teeth) are even longer. All the teeth grow throughout the animal's life. But they seldom become too long, because the teeth of the upper and lower jaws grind together and wear each other away. The canines of a hippopotamus may grow more than 2 feet (61 centimeters) long, but only about half the tooth sticks out above the gum line.

See **Hippopotamus** in *World Book* for more information on The life of a river hippopotamus, The pygmy hippopotamus, and Hippopotamuses and people.

The skeleton of a river hippopotamus

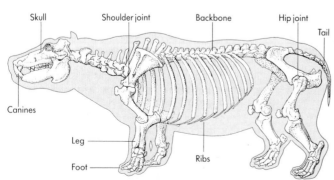

Skull Shoulder joint Backbone Hip joint Tail

Canines

Leg Ribs Foot

WORLD BOOK illustration by Marion Pahl

Tom Myers

A hippopotamus' tusklike canines can be seen when the animal opens its mouth. Hippopotamuses use their canines for fighting.

Walter Chandoha

The beauty of horses contributes to their great popularity. The powerful bodies and flowing manes and tails of the Arabian horses shown above give the animals a noble appearance.

Horse

Horse has been one of the most useful animals for thousands of years. Horses once provided the fastest and surest way to travel on land. Hunters on horseback chased animals and killed them for food or for sport. Soldiers charged into battle on sturdy war horses. The pioneers used horses when they settled the American West in the days of stagecoaches, covered wagons, and the pony express.

The horse is well-suited for working and running. For example, its wide nostrils help it breathe easily. Horses have a good sense of smell, sharp ears, and keen eyes.

They have strong teeth, but they eat only grain and plants, never meat. Long, muscular legs give horses the strength to pull heavy loads or to run at fast speeds. Horses also use their legs as their chief weapons. The kick of a horse can seriously injure a human being or an animal.

People have improved the natural qualities of the horse by breeding various kinds of horses. For example, horse raisers can breed a fast horse with a strong horse to produce an animal that has both speed and power.

Kinds of horses

There are more than 150 breeds and types of horses and ponies. The breeds vary greatly in size, strength, speed, and other characteristics. The smallest breed is the Falabella, which grows only 30 inches (76 centimeters) high. Falabellas were originally bred in Argentina and are kept as pets. The largest breed of horse is the shire, which was originally developed in England. Shires may measure over 68 inches (173 centimeters) high. They may weigh over 2,000 pounds (910 kilograms).

Shires and other large breeds, such as the Belgian, Clydesdale, and Percheron, are the strongest horses. They can pull loads that weigh more than a short ton (0.9 metric ton). The two fastest breeds are the quarter horse and the thoroughbred, which are often bred and trained for racing. The quarter horse can run $\frac{1}{4}$ mile (0.4 kilometer) in about 20 seconds. But the thoroughbred can run longer distances faster. It can cover a mile (1.6 kilometers) in about $1\frac{1}{2}$ minutes.

Horse terms

Bronco, or **Bronc,** is an untamed Western horse.
Colt, technically, is a male horse less than 4 years old. However, the word *colt* is often used for any young horse.
Crossbred means bred from a sire of one breed and a dam of another.
Dam is the mother of a foal.
Filly is a female horse less than 4 years old.
Foal is either a newborn male or a newborn female horse.
Frog is the elastic, horny, middle part of the sole of a horse's foot.
Gait is any forward movement of the horse, such as walking or galloping.
Gelding is a male horse that cannot be used for breeding because it has had some of its reproductive organs removed.
Grade is a horse or pony of mixed breed.
Hand is a unit used to measure the height of a horse, from the ground to the highest point of the withers. A hand equals 4 inches (10 centimeters).
Mare is a female horse more than 4 years old.
Mustang is the wild horse of the Western plains, descended from Spanish horses.
Pony is any small horse, but the word *pony* usually refers to a horse less than 58 inches (147 centimeters) tall when full-grown.
Purebred means bred from horses that are of the same breed.
Sire is the father of a foal.
Stallion is a male horse that can be used for breeding.
Yearling is a horse that is more than 1 and less than 2 years old. A race horse is considered a yearling from the first January 1 after its birth until the following January 1.
Withers is the ridge between a horse's shoulder bones.

The body of a horse

Coat and skin. The horse's body is covered by a coat of hair. A healthy, glowing coat gives a splendid appearance. A thick winter coat grows every autumn and is shed every spring. Horses never shed the hair of the mane or the tail. If the mane and tail become too thick, the horse's owner may pull out some hair to make the horse look better. Pulling the hair does not hurt because the animal has no nerves at the roots of its hair. A horse uses its tail to brush off insects. A horse also has special muscles for twitching the skin to get rid of insects.

Sweat glands on the surface of the horse's body help the animal stay cool. The heavy coats of horses used for fast work, such as racing or polo, should be clipped in winter. The horses can then cool off more easily when they sweat. When the animals are resting, they should be covered with a blanket to keep them warm.

Legs and hoofs. A horse's legs are suited for fast running. Large muscles in the upper part of the legs provide great speed with a minimum of effort. The long, thin lower legs give the horse a long stride. The front legs carry most of the horse's weight. They absorb the jolts when the animal runs or jumps. The rear legs provide power for running or jumping.

Thousands of years of evolution have given the horse feet ideally suited for running. Each foot is really a strong toe. Only the tip of the toe, protected by the strong, curved hoof, touches the ground. The remains of what were once two other toes grow as bony strips on the *cannon* bone of the horse's legs. The *frog* (an elastic mass on the sole of the foot) acts like a rubber heel. It helps absorb the jolt when the hoof strikes the ground. The horse's real heel bone is the *hock,* located about halfway up the leg. The hock never touches the ground.

Teeth. Most male horses have 40 teeth, and most females have 36. The *molars* (back teeth) grind food as the horse chews. These teeth have no nerves and never stop growing. Sometimes they grow unevenly and must be filed down so the horse can chew properly.

An expert on horses can tell a horse's age by counting the number of teeth and checking their condition. Most foals are born toothless but soon get two upper and two lower front teeth. When 4 months old, the horse has four upper and four lower teeth. At the age of 1 year, it has six pairs of upper and lower *incisors* (cutting teeth). At 5 years, a horse has 12 pairs of incisors and is said to have a full mouth. Adult horses have six pairs of molars. Males grow four extra teeth at the age of 5. By the time a horse is 8 years old, the rough grinding surfaces of the bottom incisors have been worn down.

Senses. Horses have larger eyes than any other land animals except ostriches. A horse's eyes are oval; and are set on the sides of the head. The eyes can be moved independently, each in a half circle. Thus, a horse can look forward with one eye and backward with the other. Because of the position of its eyes, a horse has a blind spot a short distance in front of it. It must turn its head to see a nearby object that lies directly ahead. The shape of a horse's eyes makes objects far to the side or back appear to move faster than they actually do. For this reason, a horse may *shy* (move suddenly) at the slightest movement of an object to the side or back.

Horses have keen hearing. They have short, pointed ears that they can move around to pick up sounds from almost any direction. Certain positions of the ears may indicate a horse's attitude. For example, when a horse points its ears forward, it is curious about an object in front of it. When a horse twitches its ears or lays them back against the head, it is angry and may kick.

Horses have a well-developed sense of smell. Their nostrils are very large and can pick up scents from long

The sizes of horses

Horses range in height from less than 3 feet (0.9 meter) to more than 5 feet (1.5 meters) at the withers. These illustrations show how various breeds compare in height to an average-sized man.

WORLD BOOK illustration

5 ft. 10 in. (178 cm)

Man Shetland Pony Arabian Quarter Horse American Saddle Horse Thoroughbred Shire

The skeleton of a horse

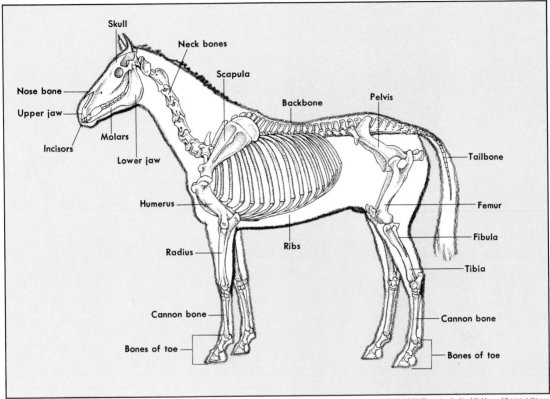

Skull
Neck bones
Scapula
Backbone
Pelvis
Nose bone
Upper jaw
Incisors
Molars
Lower jaw
Humerus
Radius
Ribs
Cannon bone
Bones of toe
Tailbone
Femur
Fibula
Tibia
Cannon bone
Bones of toe

WORLD BOOK illustration by Noel Sickles and Patricia J. Wynne

The foot of a horse

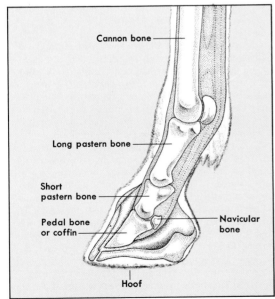

Cannon bone
Long pastern bone
Short pastern bone
Pedal bone or coffin
Navicular bone
Hoof

WORLD BOOK illustration by Noel Sickles and Patricia J. Wynne

A horse's foot has a single toe, which is formed by the pastern bones and the pedal bone. A horse walks on the tips of its toes, each of which is covered by a strong, hard hoof.

distances. A strong wind and heavy rain interfere with the sense of smell and cause horses to become nervous.

The sense of touch varies among different breeds of horses. The thin skin of most breeds of light horses is sensitive to insects and rough objects. Most breeds of heavy horses are less sensitive to such irritations.

Intelligence. Horses can learn to follow signals, but they must be taught through constant repetition. They also must be encouraged to overcome their fear of unfamiliar objects and situations. Horses have excellent memories and can recall experiences for years.

Life history. A mare carries her foal for about 11 months before giving birth. This period may vary from 10 to 14 months. Foals can stand shortly after birth, and within a few hours they are able to run about. The legs of newborn horses seem much too long for their bodies. As the horse matures, the legs grow more slowly than the rest of the body.

A year-old colt is about half grown. Most horses reach full height and weight by the age of 5. Most horse raisers breed mares at the age of 3 or 4, and stallions at the age of 2. Most mares have five or six foals during their life, but some have as many as 19.

See **Horse** in *World Book* for more information on the following topics:

- Kinds of horses
- The body of a horse
- Riding equipment
- How to ride
- Care of a horse
- Horse shows and sports
- Raising horses
- Horses in history

Tony Duffy, Focus on Sports

The human body can perform amazing acts of strength and grace. A highly trained athlete can push the body to the limits of its powers.

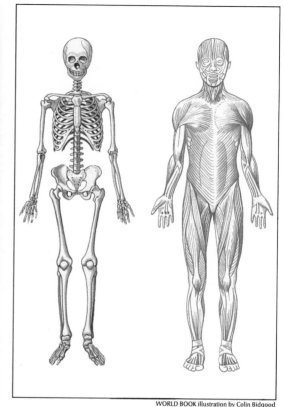

WORLD BOOK illustration by Colin Bidgood

The skeletal system includes more than 200 bones and makes up about 18 per cent of the body's weight. It provides the body with a sturdy framework. Bone is strong, yet light and flexible.

The muscular system consists of more than 600 muscles and makes up about 40 per cent of the body's weight. Muscles can *contract* (shorten). By contracting, the muscles enable the body to move.

Human body

Human body. People sometimes call the human body a machine—the most wonderful one ever built. Of course, the human body is not a machine. But it can be compared to one in many ways. Like a machine, the body is made up of many parts. Each part of the body, like each part of a machine, does special jobs. But all the parts work together and so make the body run smoothly. Also like a machine, the body needs energy to work. In such a machine as an automobile, for example, energy comes from gasoline. In the body, it comes from food and oxygen.

Although the human body can be compared to a machine, it is far more amazing than any machine. It can do things that no machine can do. For example, the body can grow. The body starts out as one cell. In time, this tiny cell develops into a body consisting of trillions of cells. The human body can also replace certain worn-out parts. Each day, about 2 billion of the body's cells wear out and are replaced. Thus, the body is always rebuilding itself. Every 15 to 30 days, for instance, the human body replaces the outermost layer of skin.

The human body can defend itself against hundreds of diseases. The body can also repair itself after most small injuries. Many body parts, such as the heart and kidneys, work continuously. The heart of a 70-year-old person, for example, has pumped at least 46 million gallons (174 million liters) of blood during that person's life. The person's kidneys have removed wastes from more than 1 million gallons (3.8 million liters) of blood.

By using its senses, the body can detect changes in its surroundings, such as changes in temperature, light, or sounds. It can adjust to these changes immediately. The body's senses are truly incredible. For instance, people can learn to identify thousands of odors, yet smell is one of the least developed senses in human beings. The human body can also detect changes that occur within itself, such as changes in body temperature. The various parts of the body continuously adjust their activities to keep the "inside" environment normal. Such adjustments rely on a system of nerves that carries messages from one part of the body to another. The messages travel at speeds of up to 100 yards (90 meters) per second.

The most remarkable part of the human body is the brain. The human brain is so highly developed that it makes people different from all other living things. Their

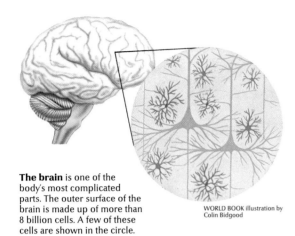

The brain is one of the body's most complicated parts. The outer surface of the brain is made up of more than 8 billion cells. A few of these cells are shown in the circle.

WORLD BOOK illustration by Colin Bidgood

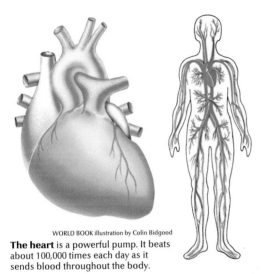

WORLD BOOK illustration by Colin Bidgood

The heart is a powerful pump. It beats about 100,000 times each day as it sends blood throughout the body.

magnificent brain makes people able to think. They can compose silly rhymes or beautiful poetry. They can imagine a dream world or study the mysteries of the atom. No animal—no matter how smart—and no computer—no matter how powerful—can think like a human.

What the body is made of

The human body has many parts. This section describes the organization of the body, from its smallest parts through its largest ones.

Chemical elements and molecules. Like all things—living and nonliving—the human body consists of atoms of chemical elements. The most common chemical elements in the body are carbon, hydrogen, nitrogen, and oxygen. The body also contains smaller amounts of many other elements, including calcium, iron, phosphorus, potassium, and sodium.

Atoms of chemical elements combine and form microscopic structures called *molecules.* The most common molecule in the human body is water. A molecule of water consists of two atoms of hydrogen and one atom of oxygen. Water makes up about 65 per cent of the body. Most of the chemical reactions that occur in the body require water.

Except for water, all of the chief molecules in the body contain the element carbon. The most important carbon-containing molecules are large, complicated structures called *macromolecules.* There are four main kinds of macromolecules in the body: *carbohydrates, lipids, proteins,* and *nucleic acids.* Carbohydrates provide energy that powers all the body's activities. Lipids have several jobs. Some lipids, particularly the fats, store extra fuel. Other lipids serve as one of the building materials for the cells that make up the body. Proteins also have various duties. Many proteins serve as building blocks for cells. Other proteins, called *enzymes,* speed up the chemical reactions within the body. Nucleic acids carry instructions that tell each cell how to perform its particular jobs.

Cells and tissues. The cell is the basic unit of all living things. The cells of the human body consist chiefly of molecules of water, proteins, and nucleic acids. The molecules that make up the cells are not alive, but the cells themselves are living things. Each of the body's cells is able to take in food, get rid of wastes, and grow. Most of the cells can also reproduce. A thin covering consisting of lipid molecules encloses each cell. This lipid envelope permits only certain substances to enter or leave the cell.

The body has many basic kinds of cells, such as blood cells, muscle cells, and nerve cells. Each kind of cell has special features and jobs. Cells of the same type form tissues. The body has four chief kinds of tissues. (1) *Connective tissue* helps support and join together various parts of the body. Most connective tissue is strong and elastic. (2) *Epithelial tissue* covers the body surface and so forms the skin. It also lines such body openings as the mouth and throat. Epithelial tissue prevents harmful substances from entering the body. (3) *Muscle tissue* consists of threadlike fibers that can *contract* (shorten). Muscle tissue makes it possible for the body to move. (4) *Nervous tissue* carries signals. It permits various parts of the body to communicate with one another.

Organs and organ systems. An organ consists of two or more kinds of tissues joined into one structure that has a certain task. The heart, for example, is an organ whose job is to pump blood throughout the body. Connective tissue, muscle tissue, and nervous tissue make up the heart.

Groups of organs form organ systems. Each organ system carries out a major activity in the body. For example, the digestive system consists of various organs that enable the body to use food. Similarly, the nervous system is made up of organs that carry messages from one part of the body to another.

See **Human body** in *World Book* for more information on the following topics:

- Anatomy of the human body (with Trans-Vision® showing major systems of the body)
- The skin
- The skeletal system
- The muscular system
- The digestive system

- The respiratory system
- The circulatory system
- The urinary system
- The reproductive system
- The endocrine system
- The nervous system

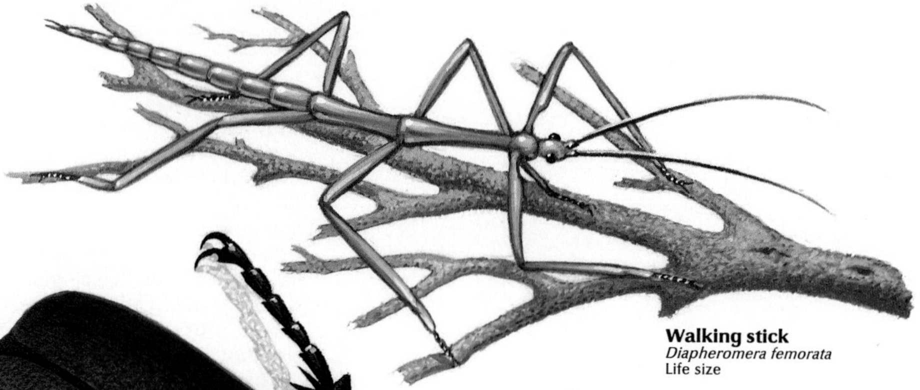

Walking stick
Diapheromera femorata
Life size

The variety of insect shapes is almost endless. The walking stick looks so much like a twig that the insect's enemies may not notice it.

Fairy fly
Alaptus magnanimus
Greatly enlarged

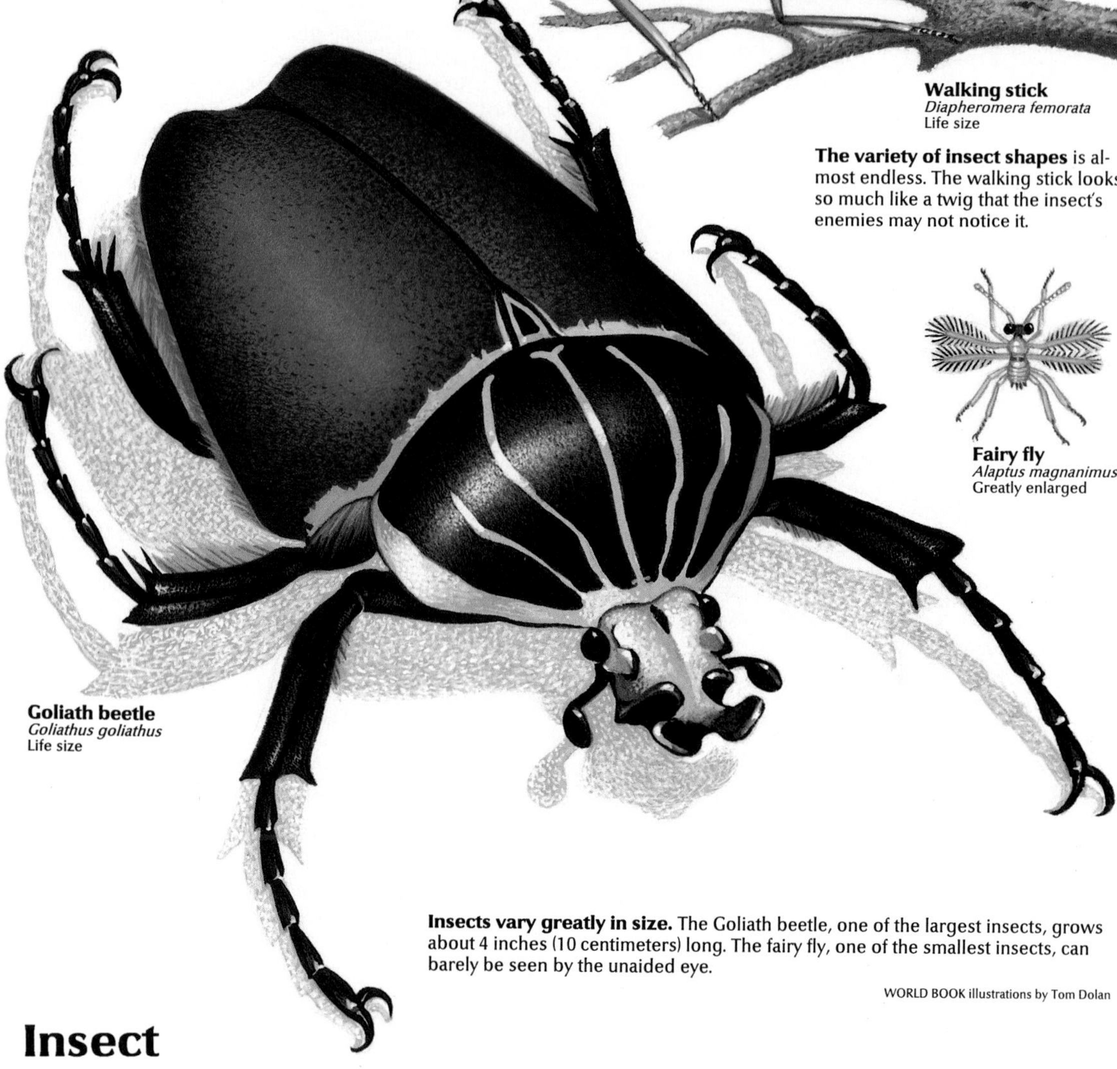

Goliath beetle
Goliathus goliathus
Life size

Insects vary greatly in size. The Goliath beetle, one of the largest insects, grows about 4 inches (10 centimeters) long. The fairy fly, one of the smallest insects, can barely be seen by the unaided eye.

WORLD BOOK illustrations by Tom Dolan

Insect

Insect is a small, six-legged animal. Bees, ants, wasps, butterflies, cockroaches, ladybugs, fireflies, termites, and moths are insects. So are houseflies, dragonflies, mosquitoes, silverfish, grasshoppers, lice, crickets, walking sticks, and fleas. The list could go on and on. If the scientific names of all the kinds of insects were printed in this book, it would take more than 6,000 pages to list them.

Scientists have described and named about a million kinds of animals. Of these, more than 800,000 are insects. Scientists discover from 7,000 to 10,000 new kinds of insects every year. They believe there may be from 1 million to 10 million kinds of insects still undiscovered.

Insects live almost everywhere on earth—from steamy tropical jungles to cold polar regions. They live high on snow-capped mountains, and in deserts below sea level. They can be found in caves deep in the earth, or flying high in the sky. Only in the oceans are few insects found.

We are constantly at war with some insects. They annoy us, bite us, and infect us with deadly diseases. They attack our crops, our pets, and our domestic animals. They invade our homes, eat our food, and damage our property. But insects also have great value to us. They pollinate many of our crops, provide us with honey and other products, and serve as food for fish, birds, and many other animals. In fact, life as we know it could not exist if all the insects were to disappear.

Insects are among the most fascinating animals on

WORLD BOOK photo courtesy Field Museum of Natural History

Fossil insects indicate that insects have lived on the earth at least 400 million years. This fossil dragonfly, shown half actual size, is about 150 million years old.

Moth
Chrysiridia madagascarensis
Life size

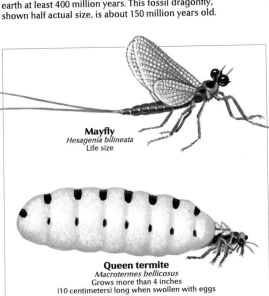

Mayfly
Hexagenia bilineata
Life size

Queen termite
Macrotermes bellicosus
Grows more than 4 inches
(10 centimeters) long when swollen with eggs

The life span of insects ranges from a few days or hours for adult mayflies to 50 years or more for some queen termites. Most insects live less than a year.

The gorgeous colors of some insects make them among the most beautiful of all animals. An outstanding example is the moth *Chrysiridia madagascarensis, above,* found on the island of Madagascar, off the southeastern coast of Africa. Many insects glow in the dark. These railroad worms, *below,* were photographed in their own light. The insects, shown about life size, are the larvae of a South American beetle.

Life magazine © Time Inc.

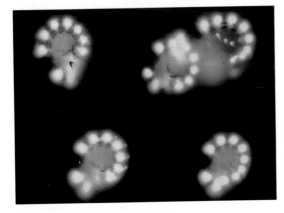

earth. They smell chiefly with their antennae, and some taste with their feet. Many insects hear by means of hairs on their bodies. Others have "ears" on their legs or on the sides of their bodies. Insects have no voices, but some make noises that can be heard 1 mile (1.6 kilometers) away. Insects have no lungs, but breathe through holes in their sides. Some insects have no eyes, and others have five eyes or more. Many insects have enormous strength. An ant can lift a weight 50 times as heavy as its body. If a 175-pound (79-kilogram) man could do as well, he could lift more than 4 short tons (3.6 metric tons)—with his teeth. A flea can broad-jump about 13 inches (33 centimeters). If a human being could do as well, he or she could jump 700 feet (210 meters).

Many insects do the same things we do. They build bridges and apartment houses. Some raise crops, and others keep "cattle" that they "milk." There are also insect carpenters, papermakers, guards, soldiers, nurses, slaves, hunters, trappers, thieves, and undertakers. Some insects even go to war against one another.

Many people think that such animals as spiders, centipedes, mites, and ticks are insects. But these animals differ from insects. For example, spiders have eight legs, and insects have six. A spider's body is divided into two main parts, but an insect's body has three. Most insects have wings and antennae, but spiders do not.

The bodies of insects

All insects have three pairs of legs, a body divided into three main parts—head, thorax, and abdomen—and a tough shell-like outer covering. Most insects also have wings and a pair of antennae.

Skeleton

The skeleton of an insect is on the outside of its body, and is called an *exoskeleton*. It is made up of several substances, the best known of which is *chitin*. The exoskeleton is lighter and stronger than bone, and serves as a suit of armor that protects the internal organs. The insect's muscles are attached to the inside wall of the exoskeleton.

The exoskeleton does not grow with an insect, as do the bones of a child. In time, the exoskeleton becomes too tight and must be shed. This process is called *molting*. The insect forms a new suit of armor underneath before it crawls out of the old suit. The new exoskeleton is soft, and so the insect gulps air to stretch it before the suit hardens. This process provides growing room until the next molt. Most insects continue to molt until they become adults.

The exoskeleton of an adult insect consists of about 20 ringlike parts. Some of these segments have become so completely *fused* (joined together) that they cannot be seen. Other segments are connected by flexible areas that serve as joints. The segments are grouped into the three main parts that make up the insect's body.

Head

An insect's head consists of five or six segments, but they are too tightly fused to be seen. The head includes the mouthparts, eyes, and antennae.

Mouthparts are a set of structures used for feeding. These structures surround the insect's actual mouth,

which is merely an opening in the head. The parts differ among insects, according to how the animal feeds. There are two main types of mouthparts. One type is adapted for chewing, and the other for sucking. Each order of insects has its own variation of one of these types, or a combination of both.

Chewing insects include grasshoppers, crickets, beetles, termites, and cockroaches. These insects have two powerful grinding jaws called *mandibles*. The jaws, which in most species are lined with teeth, work sideways, not up and down as ours do. An insect uses its jaws not only for chewing, but also for cutting or tearing off food. A second pair of less powerful jaws, called *maxillae*, is behind the mandibles. They also move sideways, and are used for handling food and pushing it down the throat. Chewing insects have two lips. The upper lip, called the *labrum*, is simply a flap that hangs down over the mouthparts and covers the mouth from the front. The lower lip, called the *labium*, covers the mouth from behind.

Sucking insects have mouthparts that developed from the basic chewing structures. The mouthparts of some sucking insects have changed so much to suit the animals' feeding habits that they are hard to recognize. The labium of bedbugs, chinch bugs, and other bugs has become a long, grooved beak. Four slender, sharp needles called *stylets* lie in the groove. The stylets developed from the mandibles and the maxillae. They are used for piercing plants or animals and then sucking up the juices or blood. The labrum serves as a flap that covers the groove in the beak.

In butterflies and moths, the mandibles have almost disappeared. Parts of the maxillae have become greatly lengthened and joined together to form a long, slender drinking tube. This tube, the *proboscis,* coils up when

WORLD BOOK illustration by James Teason

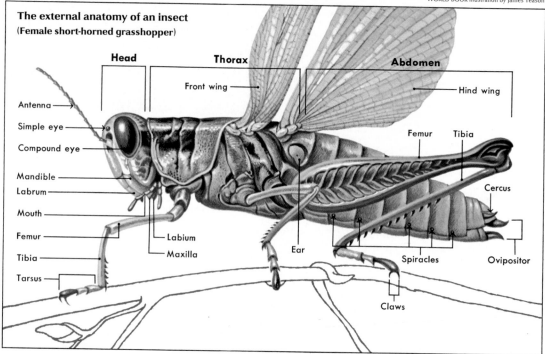

The external anatomy of an insect
(Female short-horned grasshopper)

Head   Thorax   Abdomen

Front wing

Hind wing

Antenna

Simple eye

Compound eye

Mandible

Labrum

Mouth

Femur

Tibia

Tarsus

Labium

Maxilla

Ear

Femur   Tibia

Cercus

Spiracles

Ovipositor

Claws

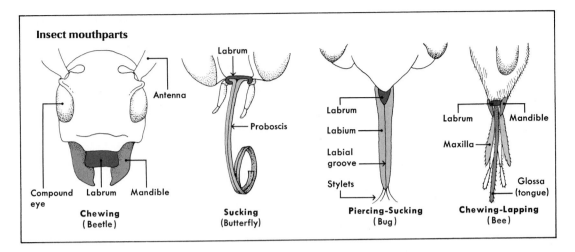

Insect mouthparts

Chewing
(Beetle)

Antenna

Compound eye   Labrum   Mandible

Sucking
(Butterfly)

Labrum

Proboscis

Piercing-Sucking
(Bug)

Labrum

Labium

Labial groove

Stylets

Chewing-Lapping
(Bee)

Labrum   Mandible

Maxilla

Glossa
(tongue)

the insect is not using it to suck liquids, such as nectar from flowers. In horseflies, the mandibles have become curved swords that can slash an animal's skin. The maxillae have developed into sharp-pointed rods that can be driven up and down into the victim's skin like a pneumatic drill. To feed, a horsefly plunges its sucking tube, formed from the labrum, into the bleeding wound made by the cutting tools.

Eyes and antennae. Most adult insects have two enormous *compound eyes.* These eyes are made up of separate lenses—as many as thousands of them. All the lenses combine to form a complete picture of what an insect sees.

Almost all insects have two antennae between their eyes. They use their antennae chiefly to smell and to feel. Some insects also use their antennae to taste and to hear. Most insects become distressed if their antennae are damaged or removed, and some insects become helpless.

Thorax

The thorax is the middle section of an insect's body. It consists of three tightly fused segments. The muscles that operate the legs and wings are attached to the inside wall of the thorax.

Legs. One pair of legs is connected to each segment of the thorax. Each leg has five main segments, with movable joints between the segments. When we walk, we balance ourselves on one leg as we step forward with the other. When insects walk, they usually move the middle leg on one side at the same time they move the front and hind legs on the other. In this way, the insects are always firmly supported—like a three-legged stool.

Many kinds of insects have legs adapted for special tasks. Giant water bugs, back swimmers, diving beetles, and a number of other insects that swim have long, flat hind legs that work like oars. Mole crickets and many types of dung beetles have strong, flat front legs that serve as shovels for digging. Locusts, fleas, and grasshoppers have long, muscular hind legs adapted for jumping. Honeybees have pollen-collecting brushes on their front legs and pollen-carrying baskets on their hind legs. Many kinds of butterflies have small, hairy front legs with special organs for finding food. Flies and bees have hooks and sticky pads on their feet. These in-

WORLD BOOK illustrations by Marion Pahl

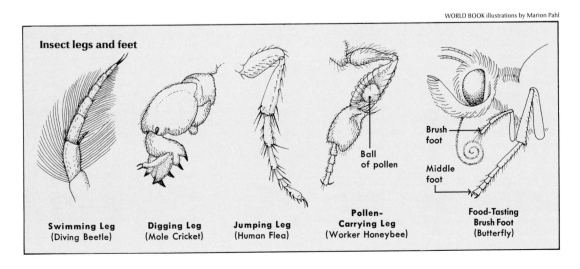

Insect legs and feet

Swimming Leg
(Diving Beetle)

Digging Leg
(Mole Cricket)

Jumping Leg
(Human Flea)

Ball of pollen

Pollen-
Carrying Leg
(Worker Honeybee)

Brush foot

Middle foot

Food-Tasting
Brush Foot
(Butterfly)

sects can walk on slippery surfaces, up and down walls, and upside down on ceilings.

Wings. Insects are the only animals besides birds and bats that have wings. Most adult insects have them. Houseflies, mosquitoes, tsetse flies, and all other true flies have two wings, which are attached to the middle segment of the thorax. Butterflies, dragonflies, moths, wasps, bees, and other winged insects have four wings. One pair is attached to the middle segment of the thorax, and the other pair to the hind segment.

Insects get their flying power from two sets of muscles. One set extends from top to bottom of the thorax. When these muscles contract, the thorax flattens, causing the wings to move up. The other set of muscles extends lengthwise. When they contract, the thorax arches upward, causing the wings to move down. As the two sets of muscles flatten and arch the thorax, they cause the wings to beat. Other muscles are attached directly to the bases of the wings, and control the direction of flight. They make it possible for many insects to fly in one place like a helicopter, or even to fly backward.

Among insects that have four wings, the two wings on each side often work together as if they were one wing. In some groups of insects, the two wings on each side overlap. In other groups, they lock together by means of hooks or hairs. Dragonflies beat their two pairs of wings alternately, with the front pair rising as the rear pair falls. Beetles do not use their front wings for flight. These wings form horny covers that protect the hind wings when the beetles are at rest. Flies have a pair of club-shaped balancing organs called *halteres,* which have replaced their hind wings. A fly usually will not try to fly if its halteres have been removed.

The fastest-flying insects are probably dragonflies. Some scientists estimate that these insects can fly as fast as 60 miles (97 kilometers) per hour. Butterflies and locusts can fly continuously for well over 100 miles (160 kilometers) on the food energy stored in their bodies. Tiny fruit flies can fly more than five hours without refueling. On the other hand, honeybees carry only enough fuel for a 15-minute flight. Large-winged butterflies beat their wings 4 to 20 times per second; houseflies, about 200 times per second; and some midges, about 1,000 times per second.

Abdomen

An insect's abdomen contains organs for digesting food, reproducing, and getting rid of waste products. The abdomen consists of 10 or 11 segments connected by flexible membranes. These membranes make it possible for the ringlike segments to slide into one another, like a telescope, when the abdomen is empty. The segments spread far apart when the abdomen is full. The abdomen of a queen termite may be so swollen with eggs that it is more than 1,000 times as large as the rest of her body. In some ant colonies, certain ants serve as food storage tanks. Their abdomens bulge with liquid sugar, with which they can feed other ants. The storage ants give up the liquid sugar through their mouths.

Many insects have a pair of feelers, called *cerci,* on the last segment of the abdomen. Mayflies, stone flies, and some roaches have especially long cerci. The cerci of earwigs and some other insects form a pair of tongs, which are used for self-defense or for capturing prey.

Walter Dawn

The "ears" of a cricket are on its legs. Each front leg has a drumlike membrane that vibrates when sound waves strike it.

Grant Heilman

The antennae of a male luna moth are covered with organs of smell that can pick up a female's scent over great distances.

The outer reproductive organs are attached to the eighth and ninth segments of the abdomen. In many males, these organs are part of a set of structures that hold the female during mating. The organs of many females are part of an egg-laying tool called the *ovipositor.* Females use the ovipositor to insert their eggs into such things as soil, wood, leaves, fruits, seeds, or the eggs or bodies of other animals. Some females have an ovipositor as long as or longer than the rest of the body. The ovipositor of bees, ants, and wasps has been adapted into a poisonous sting that can be withdrawn into the abdomen when not in use. Near the end of the abdomen is an opening called the *anus,* through which wastes and extra water pass from the insect's body.

See **Insect** in *World Book* for more information on the following topics:

- The world of insects
- The importance of insects
- The bodies of insects
- The senses of insects
- The life cycle of insects
- The ways of life of insects
- The orders of insects

Invention

Invention is the creation of a new device, process, or product. Our inventions have given us enormous control over our environment and enabled us to live better, easier, and happier lives. If we could not invent, we would be completely at the mercy of the climate and the land. Inventions have enabled human beings to survive the hazards of the environment and develop a civilized society.

Down through history, inventions have changed the way people live. Little by little, they have helped determine where people live and the kind of work they do. Inventions have also helped determine what people eat and wear and how they play and relax. Many thousands of years ago, people lived by hunting animals and gathering wild plants. To find food, people had to move from place to place. About 9000 B.C., people discovered they could grow their own food and raise livestock. The development of agriculture meant that people no longer had to wander about in search of food but could settle in farm villages. Then came the Industrial Revolution in the 1700's, with such inventions as spinning and weaving machines and the steam engine. These inventions produced another great change in the way people lived, as people flocked to the cities to work in factories. The modern way of life we know today exists largely because of inventions.

An invention differs from a discovery, but they are closely related. A discovery occurs when something that exists in nature is observed or recognized for the first time. An invention is the creation of something that never existed before. For example, people discovered fire. But they invented the match to start a fire. An invention is thus a combination of knowledge and skill applied to various discoveries and observations.

Before the 1900's, individual inventors working alone produced most inventions. Many of these inventors were craftworkers or mechanics who had little education. Today, most inventions are produced by teams of engineers and scientists who work together in laboratories in a common effort to invent.

See **Invention** in *World Book* for more information on the following topics:

- Why people invent
- How people invent
- The history of inventions
- Inventions of the future

Important inventions in history

People have invented since earliest times. But many of the most important inventions have been developed in the last 600 years. These inventions have revolutionized every element of civilization, including agriculture, communications, industry, science, transportation, and war. The drawings on this and the following page illustrate some major inventions.

WORLD BOOK illustrations by Mas Nakagawa

Flint Tools
About 1,750,000 B.C.

Plow
5000-3000 B.C.

Wheel
About 3000 B.C.

Archimedean Screw
200's B.C.

Paper
About A.D. 105

Magnetic Compass
1100's

Cannon
About 1350

Printing from Movable Type
About 1440

Compound Microscope
About 1590

Thermometer
1593

Telescope
1608

Steam Engine
1690-1769

Spinning Jenny
About 1764

Balloon
1783

Steamboat
1787-1807

Cotton Gin
1793

Food Canning
1795-1809

Steam Locomotive
1804

Stethoscope
1816

Photography
1826

Reaper
1831

Gas Refrigeration
1834

Telegraph
1837

Safety Match
1844

Pneumatic Tire
1845

Sewing Machine
1846

WORLD BOOK illustrations by Mas Nakagawa

Safety Pin
1849

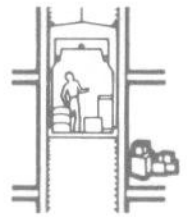

Safety Elevator
1853

Hypodermic Syringe
1853

Internal- Combustion
Engine
1860

Dynamite
1867

Typewriter
1867

Barbed Wire
1873

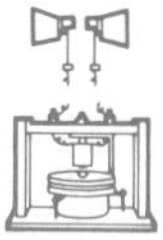

Telephone
1876

Phonograph
1877

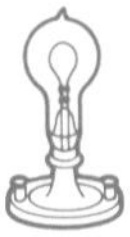

Incandescent Light
1879

Skyscraper
1885

Gasoline Automobile
1885

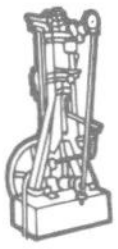

Diesel Engine
1892

Zipper
1893

Radio
1895

X-Ray Machine
1895

Safety Razor
1901

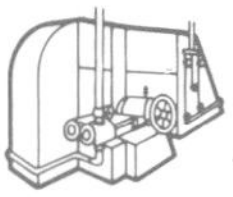

Air Conditioning
1902

Airplane
1903

Helicopter
1907

Television
1920's

Frozen Foods
1920's

Liquid-Fuel Rocket
1926

Analog Computer
1930

Fluorescent Light
About 1935

Radar
About 1935

Xerography
1938

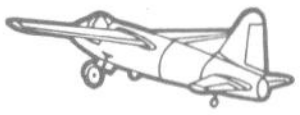

Jet Engine Aircraft
1939

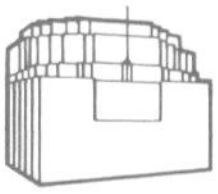

Nuclear Reactor
1942

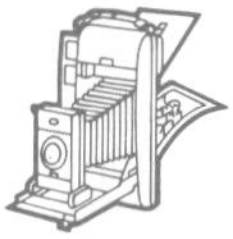

Polaroid Land Camera
1947

Transistor
1947

Polio Vaccine
1952-1955

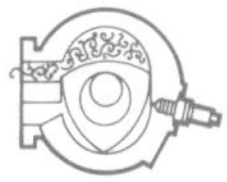

Wankel Engine
1956

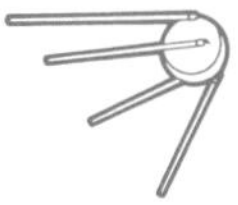

Artificial Satellite
1957

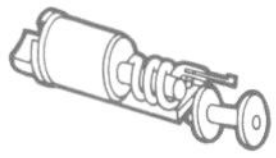

Laser
1960

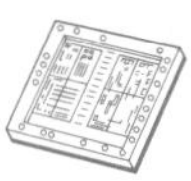

Microprocessor
1971

Jet propulsion is the production of motion in one direction by releasing a high-pressure stream of gas in the opposite direction. Rockets, guided missiles, and many airplanes are powered by jet propulsion.

Jet-propelled airplanes can reach much higher speeds than propeller-driven airplanes. Some jet aircraft fly faster than sound travels through the air. Jet propulsion also makes flight possible at extremely high altitudes—and even in outer space.

Jet engines cause less vibration than do piston engines, which are used in some airplanes to turn propellers. This smoothness of operation results in a safer and more comfortable ride. Jet engines are generally smaller and lighter in weight than piston engines that produce the same amount of *thrust* (forward-driving force). However, jet engines burn more fuel than piston engines do in order to create an equal amount of thrust.

How jet propulsion works. The principle of jet propulsion can be demonstrated with a simple garden hose connected to a water supply. When the nozzle at the end of the hose is closed, the water pushes in all directions against the inside surface of the nozzle. It also pushes back against the water in the hose that is trying to squeeze into the nozzle. When the nozzle is open, some of the water squirts out through the opening. This action upsets the balance of pressure inside the nozzle. It releases the pressure pushing forward just inside the nozzle opening. But the water that is still in the nozzle continues pressing backward and to the sides. If you let go of the nozzle, the unbalanced, backward-pushing pressure will propel it backward. The nozzle will move in the direction opposite that of the jet of water escaping from the nozzle.

The principle of jet propulsion was first described in 1687 by the English scientist Sir Isaac Newton in his third law of motion. This law states that for every action there is an equal and opposite reaction. In the above example, squirting water out of the end of the nozzle is the action. The equal and opposite reaction is the backward movement of the nozzle. Jet propulsion drives an aircraft engine in much the same way. Air pressure builds up inside the engine. The pressure pushing in one direction

Photri

A huge jet engine produces the power needed to fly airplanes with heavy loads of passengers and freight.

is released in a powerful stream of jet exhaust. The action of this exhaust escaping from the rear of the engine causes an equal and opposite reaction that pushes the engine forward.

Jet engines and rockets both use the principle of jet propulsion. However, they use different sources of oxygen to burn fuel. Jet engines use the oxygen in the air. For this reason, airplanes with jet engines cannot fly outside the earth's atmosphere. Rockets carry their own supply of oxygen to use in burning their fuel. As a result, rockets can fly in the airless expanse of outer space (see **Rocket**). Four major types of jet engines are described on the following pages.

See **Jet propulsion** in *World Book* for more information on How jet propulsion works, Types of jet engines, and Development of jet propulsion.

How a jet engine works

Air enters the jet engine, is compressed, mixed with fuel, and burned. The combustion gases push in all directions but can escape only at the rear of the engine. The action of these gases accelerating as they leave the engine creates a reaction that pushes the engine in the opposite direction.

WORLD BOOK diagram by William Graham

Air

Air

Air-stream compression

Fuel and air combustion

Gas-stream acceleration

Reaction—engine moves forward

Action—gases escape to the rear

Kinds of jet engines   The diagrams below show the principal parts of four major types of jet engines and how these engines produce power. The diagrams at the left show front views of the engines. The photographs on the opposite page show examples of aircraft that use these types of engines.

WORLD BOOK diagrams by James Magine

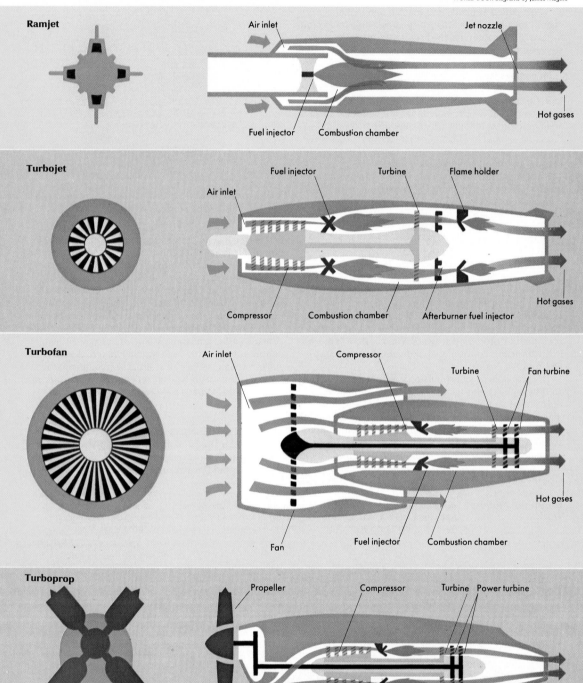

Ramjet

Air inlet

Jet nozzle

Hot gases

Fuel injector   Combustion chamber

Turbojet

Fuel injector   Turbine   Flame holder

Air inlet

Hot gases

Compressor   Combustion chamber   Afterburner fuel injector

Turbofan

Air inlet   Compressor

Turbine   Fan turbine

Hot gases

Fan   Fuel injector   Combustion chamber

Turboprop

Propeller   Compressor   Turbine   Power turbine

Hot gases

Air inlet   Fuel injector   Combustion chamber

A ramjet engine must be brought up to supersonic speed by a rocket or another jet engine before it can operate. Air rushes into the engine through the air inlets. The air slows down as it approaches the combustion chamber. It is compressed by more air entering the inlet behind it. In the combustion chamber, the compressed air is mixed with fuel supplied by the fuel injector and burned. The pressure produced by the burning fuel and air sends hot exhaust gases out the jet nozzle and drives the engine forward. Ramjets operate best at high, steady speeds. For this reason, they have been used chiefly to propel guided missiles, such as the one shown at the right.

LTV Missiles & Electronics Group

Turbojet engines have a compressor with fanlike blades that squeeze the incoming air. The compressor blades also force the compressed air into a set of combustion chambers. There, the compressed air is mixed with fuel and ignited, forming burning gases. The gases expand rapidly and rush through the blades of a turbine, making it spin. The turbine is connected by a shaft to the compressor and keeps the compressor turning. An afterburner gives a turbojet extra thrust by supplying the hot exhaust gases with extra fuel. This fuel is burned, increasing the speed of the jet exhaust. Metal grids called *flame holders* prevent the fast-moving gases from blowing out the flames. Turbojet engines power the F-5E Tiger II fighter aircraft pictured at the right.

Northrop Corporation

Turbofan engines resemble turbojet engines but have a huge propellerlike fan at the air inlet. Most of the air drawn through the fan passes around the rest of the engine, creating thrust. The rest of the air enters the enclosed engine, which operates like a turbojet to produce thrust. It consists of a compressor, combustion chambers, and two kinds of turbines. One turbine drives the compressor and the other, called a *fan turbine,* turns the fan. By using two methods to produce thrust, a turbofan can create more thrust at low speeds than a turbojet can. The turbofan also runs more quietly and uses less fuel. The turbofan is the most common type of jet engine. Turbofans power many commercial airliners, such as the DC-10 shown at the right.

United Airlines

Beech Aircraft Corporation

Turboprop engines consist of a propeller and a turbojet engine. The turbojet engine is used chiefly to turn the propeller, which supplies most of the turboprop's driving power. The propeller rotates when burning gases from the combustion chambers turn the power turbine. This turbine is connected to a shaft that drives the propeller by a system of gears. When the hot gases escape from the engine, they provide a small amount of additional thrust. Turboprop engines are most efficient at relatively low flight speeds. They are smaller and lighter in weight than piston engines that produce the same amount of power. Turboprops are widely used in small business aircraft, such as the Beechcraft Super King Air pictured at the right.

Jupiter is the largest planet in the solar system. The diameter of Jupiter at its equator is about 88,700 miles (142,700 kilometers), more than 11 times the diameter of the earth. It would take 1,000 earths to fill up the volume of the giant planet. Ancient astronomers named Jupiter after the king of the Roman gods.

Jupiter is the fifth closest planet to the sun. Its mean distance from the sun is about 483 $\frac{1}{2}$ million miles (778 million kilometers), compared with about 93 million miles (150 million kilometers) for the earth. At its closest approach to the earth, Jupiter is about 391 million miles (629 million kilometers) away.

Orbit. Jupiter travels around the sun in an *elliptical* (oval-shaped) orbit. Its distance from the sun varies from about 507 million miles (816 million kilometers) at its farthest point, to 460 million miles (740 million kilometers) at its closest point. Jupiter takes about 4,333 earth-days, or almost 12 earth-years, to orbit the sun, compared with 365 days, or one year, for the earth.

Rotation. As it orbits the sun, Jupiter spins on its *axis,* an imaginary line drawn through its center. Jupiter's axis is almost *perpendicular* (at an angle of 90°) to the planet's path around the sun. The axis tilts at an angle of 3° from the perpendicular position.

Jupiter spins faster than any other planet. It rotates once in 9 hours and 55 minutes, compared to 24 hours for the earth. Jupiter's rapid rotation causes it to bulge at its equator and flatten at its poles. The planet's diameter is 5,700 miles (9,170 kilometers) larger at the equator than between the poles.

Surface. Jupiter's surface cannot be seen from the earth because of the layers of dense clouds that surround the planet. These high-level clouds probably consist of frozen crystals of ammonia and methane. Most astronomers believe that Jupiter is a *fluid planet.* It consists primarily of gas, but it is composed of some liquid as well. The planet may have a small solid core con-

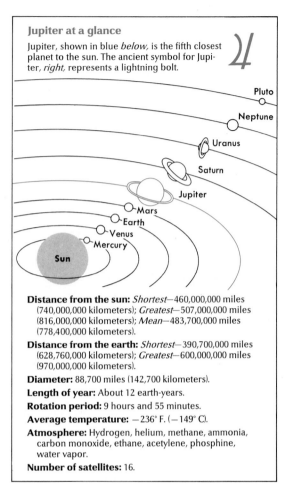

Jupiter at a glance

Jupiter, shown in blue *below,* is the fifth closest planet to the sun. The ancient symbol for Jupiter, *right,* represents a lightning bolt.

Pluto
Neptune
Uranus
Saturn
Jupiter
Mars
Earth
Venus
Mercury
Sun

Distance from the sun: *Shortest*—460,000,000 miles (740,000,000 kilometers); *Greatest*—507,000,000 miles (816,000,000 kilometers); *Mean*—483,700,000 miles (778,400,000 kilometers).

Distance from the earth: *Shortest*—390,700,000 miles (628,760,000 kilometers); *Greatest*—600,000,000 miles (970,000,000 kilometers).

Diameter: 88,700 miles (142,700 kilometers).

Length of year: About 12 earth-years.

Rotation period: 9 hours and 55 minutes.

Average temperature: −236° F. (−149° C).

Atmosphere: Hydrogen, helium, methane, ammonia, carbon monoxide, ethane, acetylene, phosphine, water vapor.

Number of satellites: 16.

Jet Propulsion Laboratory

The layers of dense clouds around Jupiter appear in a photograph of the planet taken by the *Voyager 1* space probe. The large, oval-shaped mark on the clouds is the Great Red Spot. The spot is believed to be an intense atmospheric disturbance.

sisting of rocky material.

When Jupiter is viewed through a telescope, a series of *belts* and *zones* can be seen on its clouds. The belts are dark lines that circle the planet parallel to its equator. The zones are light-colored areas between the belts. The widths and positions of the belts change slowly through the years. The belts and zones may be caused by various gases in the clouds.

A large, oval mark called the Great Red Spot can also be seen on Jupiter's clouds. The spot measures about 25,000 miles (40,200 kilometers) long—more than three times the diameter of the earth—and about 20,000 miles (32,000 kilometers) wide. The spot slowly changes its position from year to year. Most astronomers believe the spot is an intense atmospheric disturbance that resembles a hurricane. The spot seems to consist of violently swirling masses of gas.

See **Jupiter** in *World Book* for more information on the following topics:

•Surface and atmosphere
•Temperature
•Mass and density
•Radio radiation
•Satellites and ring
•Flights to Jupiter

Kangaroo is a furry animal that hops on its hind legs. Kangaroos are the largest members of a group of mammals called *marsupials*. Among most marsupials, including kangaroos, the females have a pouch on the stomach. They give birth to tiny offspring, which complete their development in this pouch.

This article deals mainly with the five larger species of kangaroos, sometimes called *great kangaroos*. They are the (1) eastern gray kangaroo, (2) western gray kangaroo, (3) red kangaroo, (4) wallaroo, and (5) antilopine wallaroo. These species live in the wild only in Australia.

The kangaroo family also includes about 40 species of smaller marsupials. Some of them live in New Guinea and on nearby islands, but most are found only in Australia. Many do not look like the larger kangaroos. However, the larger kangaroos and most of the smaller species have much larger hind legs than forelegs and a long, muscular tail. Nearly all the species eat plants.

The body of a kangaroo. Gray kangaroos and red kangaroos grow slightly larger than wallaroos and antilopine wallaroos. Most adult gray and red kangaroos stand about 6 feet (1.8 meters) tall and weigh about 100 pounds (45 kilograms). But some male red kangaroos grow 7 feet (2.1 meters) tall and weigh more than 150 pounds (68 kilograms). Female kangaroos are much smaller than the males.

Kangaroos have a small, deerlike head and a pointed snout. They have large, upright ears that they can turn from front to back. The body of a kangaroo is covered with short fur that varies in color among different species. Among most species, the fur is brown or gray. But animals of the same species may have different colors of fur. For example, male red kangaroos may be red or gray, and females may be bluish-gray.

Kangaroos have large, powerful hind legs and small front legs. The tail of the larger species grows more than 3 feet (91 centimeters) long. A kangaroo uses its tail for balance when hopping and for support when standing upright or walking on all four legs. When a kangaroo hops, it uses only its hind legs, which it moves together. Large kangaroos can hop as fast as 40 miles (64 kilometers) per hour for short distances. They can leap over obstacles as high as 6 feet (1.8 meters).

See **Kangaroo** in *World Book* for more information on The life of a kangaroo, Smaller members of the kangaroo family, and Kangaroos and people.

W. R. Taylor, Ardea Photographics

A kangaroo can hop on its powerful hind legs at speeds up to 40 miles (64 kilometers) per hour. The animal uses its long muscular tail for balance when hopping.

Warren Garst, Tom Stack & Associates

A *joey* (young kangaroo) spends the first several months of its life inside its mother's pouch. Shortly after the joey leaves the pouch, most female kangaroos give birth to a new baby.

The skeleton of a kangaroo

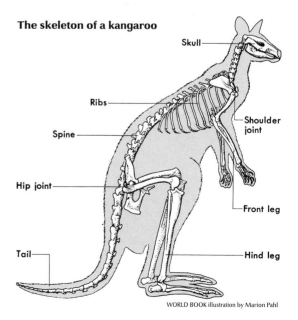

Skull

Ribs

Spine

Shoulder joint

Hip joint

Front leg

Tail

Hind leg

WORLD BOOK illustration by Marion Pahl

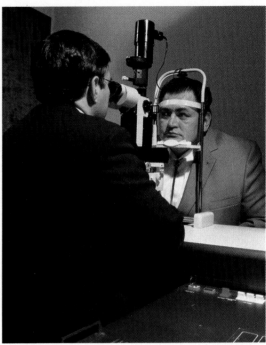

Korad

© Bob Hahn, Taurus

Lasers produce thin beams of light of varying intensity. The beam of a solid laser, *left,* is used to cut through a sheet of hard metal in a fraction of a second. In eye surgery, *right,* the physician uses a precisely focused beam from a gas laser to repair damaged tissue.

Laser, *LAY zuhr,* is a device that *amplifies* (strengthens) light. A laser produces a thin, intense beam of light that can burn a hole in a diamond or carry the signals of many different television pictures at the same time. The word *laser* stands for *l*ight *a*mplification by *s*timulated *e*mission of *r*adiation.

The light from a laser differs from the light produced by other sources, such as electric bulbs, fluorescent lamps, and the sun. The light from these other sources travels in all directions. Laser light is highly *directional*—that is, it travels in only one direction. Laser light travels in a narrow beam, and the sides of the beam stay almost parallel. For example, a beam $\frac{1}{2}$ inch (13 millimeters) wide may spread to only about 3 inches (7.6 centimeters) after traveling a mile (1.6 kilometers).

Laser light also differs from other light in terms of *frequency,* the number of vibrations of a light wave per second. Laser light consists of one or, at most, a few frequencies. The light that comes from other sources consists of many frequencies. Because laser light has so few frequencies, a laser beam has a narrow frequency range on the *electromagnetic spectrum*—an arrangement of frequencies from lowest to highest. The frequencies of a laser beam may be in only the visible region of the electromagnetic spectrum. Or they may be in only the infrared or ultraviolet regions, which are invisible.

How a laser works. Light is a form of energy that is released from individual atoms or molecules in a substance. To understand how a laser works, one must know something about the nature of atoms and how they interact with light and other forms of energy.

Every atom is a storehouse of energy. The amount of energy in an atom depends on the motion of the electrons that orbit the atom's nucleus. When an atom absorbs energy, its energy level increases, and the atom is said to be *excited.* The atoms of a substance become excited when they absorb heat, light, or other forms of energy that pass through the substance. An excited atom can return to its normal energy level by releasing its excess energy in the form of light. This release of energy is called *spontaneous emission.*

In spontaneous emission, excited atoms release light irregularly. As a result, the light has different frequencies and travels in different directions. Light released in this way is called *incoherent light.* Such light is pro-

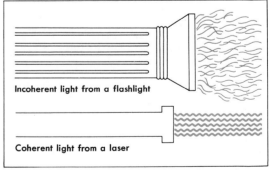

Incoherent light from a flashlight

Coherent light from a laser

WORLD BOOK diagram by Art Grebetz

Lasers produce coherent light. Waves of coherent light, unlike waves of incoherent light, move "in step" with one another. As a result, they spread only slightly—even over great distances.

duced by the sun and by ordinary electric bulbs.

Excited atoms also may release light systematically. This kind of release, called *stimulated emission,* is the main process that takes place in a laser. It occurs when the energy released from one atom interacts with an atom that is still excited. The interaction triggers the excited atom into releasing its own extra energy as light. Most of the light produced by stimulated emission has the same frequency as the triggering light. It also travels in the same direction, and so combines with and amplifies the triggering light. Such light is called *coherent light.*

The basic parts of a laser include a power source and a light-amplifying substance. The power source provides the energy that causes atoms in the light-amplifying substance to become excited. The total energy produced by a laser is always less than the energy produced by its power source. But the laser produces a much more intense light. The frequencies of the laser light depend on the light-amplifying substance used.

See **Laser** in *World Book* for more information on How lasers are used, Kinds of lasers, and History.

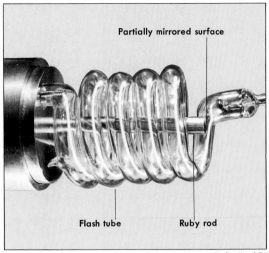

Hughes Aircraft Co.

A ruby crystal laser, *above,* produces powerful bursts of light. The flash tube generates laser light inside the ruby. The light shoots out through the partially mirrored surface.

How a ruby laser works

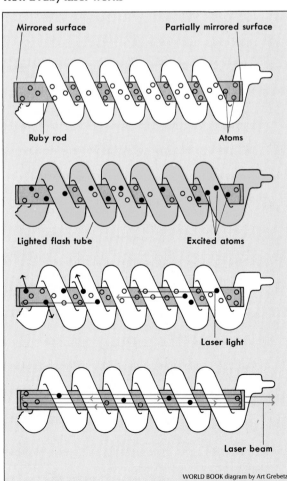

The diagrams at the left represent the light-amplifying material in a ruby laser. Each atom in the ruby has a certain amount of energy, depending on the motion of its electrons. This orbiting motion is shown in the diagrams at the right.

A flash tube sends intense light through the ruby. The light excites some of the ruby's atoms. These atoms are shown by the solid circles. An atom becomes excited when absorbed light energy changes the orbit of one of its electrons.

Excited atoms radiate light as their electrons drop back to low-energy orbits. Some of this light passes out the sides of the ruby. But part travels along the axis of the ruby as laser light.

The laser light is reflected back and forth by mirrors and stimulates other excited atoms into releasing their energy. This amplifies the laser light many times. Part of the amplified light passes through the partial mirror as an intense laser beam.

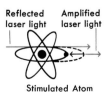

WORLD BOOK diagram by Art Grebetz

Edward S. Ross   Tony Castelvecchi, Foto Place   Leonard Lee Rue III, Bruce Coleman Inc.

Leaves, the chief food-making parts of plants, vary greatly in appearance. Most plants have broad, flat leaves, such as those of a maple tree, *left.* But oats, *center,* and other grasses have long, narrow leaves. Pines, *right,* and most other cone-bearing plants have needle leaves.

Leaf

Leaf is the main food-making part of almost all plants. Garden flowers, grasses, shrubs, and trees depend on their leaves to make food for the rest of the plant. So do many other plants, including ferns, vegetables, vines, and weeds.

Leaves work like tiny food factories. They capture energy from sunlight and use it to make food out of water from the soil and *carbon dioxide,* a gas in the air. This food provides plants with energy to grow, to produce flowers and seeds, and to carry on all their other activities.

Plants store the food made by leaves in their fruits, roots, seeds, and stems and even in the leaves themselves. Without this food, plants could not live. In addition, all the food that people and animals eat comes either from plants or from animals that eat plants.

Leaves vary tremendously in appearance. Some are round, and others oval. Still others are shaped like arrowheads, feathers, hands, hearts, or any number of other objects. However, most leaves can be divided into three groups according to their basic shape. (1) *Broad leaves* are the type of leaf that most plants have. These leaves are fairly wide and flat. Plants that have such leaves include maple and oak trees, pea plants, and rosebushes. (2) *Narrow leaves* are long and slender. Narrow leaves grow on grasses. Grasses include not only lawn grasses but also barley, corn, oats, wheat, and other cereal grasses. Lilies, onions, and certain other plants also have narrow leaves. (3) *Needle leaves* grow on firs, pines, spruces, and most other cone-bearing trees and shrubs. Needle leaves resemble short, thick sewing needles. A few other kinds of cone-bearing plants, including certain cedars and junipers, have scalelike leaves.

Most leaves grow from 1 to 12 inches (2.5 to 30 centimeters) in length. Some plants, however, have huge leaves. The largest leaves grow on the African raffia palm. The leaves of this tree measure up to 65 feet (20 meters) long. The giant water lily of South America has round, floating leaves that grow up to 6 feet (1.8 meters) across. In contrast, some plants have extremely small leaves. The true leaves of asparagus plants, for example, are so tiny that they are hard to see without a magnifying glass. In these plants, the stems, rather than the leaves, produce food.

The number of leaves on plants ranges from several to thousands. Most soft-stemmed plants have few leaves. For instance, a barley or wheat plant produces only 8 to 10 leaves each season. But trees may have an enormous number of leaves. A fully grown elm or pine tree may produce thousands of leaves.

Some simple plants that manufacture their own food do not have leaves. For example, algae, liverworts, and mosses are simple food-making plants that lack true leaves. In some of these simple plants, however, the green food-making tissues look like tiny leaves.

The importance of leaves

The chief job of leaves is to make food for plants. This food-making activity, called *photosynthesis,* occurs in fully grown leaves. But young leaves also are important. They wrap tightly around the tips of growing stems. They thus keep the delicate tips moist and help protect them from insects, cold, and other dangers.

Leaves are also vital to animals. Animals cannot make their own food. They depend on plants for their basic supply of food. Many animals eat leaves. For example, antelope, sheep, and other grazing animals eat grass leaves. People also eat leaves, such as those of cabbage, lettuce, and spinach plants. But even when people and animals eat the fruits, roots, seeds, and stems of plants, they are obtaining food made by leaves. In the same way, eggs, meat, milk, and all other animal foods can be traced back to food made by photosynthesis.

Leaves help make the air breathable. They release oxygen during photosynthesis. People and animals must have oxygen to live. Without the activities of leaves, the earth's supply of breathable oxygen would probably soon be used up.

People obtain many products from leaves in addition to food. For instance, we use the leaves of the tea plant to make tea. Peppermint and spearmint leaves contain oils used to flavor candy and chewing gum. Such leaves as bay, sage, and thyme are used in cooking to flavor foods. Some drugs come from leaves. For example, the drug digitalis, which is used to treat certain heart diseases, comes from the leaves of the purple foxglove, a common garden flower. Leaves of abacá and sisalana plants provide fiber used in making rope. The leaves of the tobacco plant are used to make cigarettes, cigars, and other tobacco products.

How a leaf makes food

A green leaf is a marvelous food-making factory. Using only the energy of the sun, it takes simple materials and turns them into energy-rich food. This section describes how a leaf obtains the raw materials needed to make food. It then provides a simple explanation of how the leaf produces food through photosynthesis. Finally, this section discusses *transpiration*, a process of water loss that plays a key role in the operation of the leaf food factory.

Obtaining the raw materials. A leaf needs three things to make food. They are (1) carbon dioxide, (2) water, and (3) light. The carbon dioxide and water serve as the raw materials of photosynthesis. The light, which is normally sunlight, provides the energy that powers photosynthesis.

Carbon dioxide enters a leaf from the air. The *epidermis* (outer surface) of the leaf has many tiny pores. These openings, called *stomata,* enable carbon dioxide to enter the leaf. Each pore is surrounded by two curved, bean-shaped *guard cells* that can swell and relax. When they swell, the pore is opened wide, and carbon dioxide enters the leaf. When the guard cells relax, the pore closes. In most plants, the stomata open during the day and close at night.

A leaf has many stomata. For example, a cottonwood leaf may have 1 million stomata, and a sunflower leaf nearly 2 million. However, the pores are so small that they make up less than 1 per cent of the leaf's surface. In most plants that grow in full sun, the majority of the stomata are in the shaded lower epidermis of the leaves. In many other plants, the stomata are about equally divided between the upper and lower epidermis.

Water. A leaf obtains water that has been absorbed by the plant's roots. This water travels up the stem and enters the leaf through the petiole. The leaf's veins carry the water throughout the blade. The smallest veins carry the water to nearly every cell in the blade.

Normally, the inside of the blade is very humid. The epidermis is covered by a waxy coating called the *cuticle.* The cuticle helps keep the leaf from drying out. Nevertheless, a leaf does lose much water. Most of this water escapes as vapor through the stomata by the process of transpiration.

Light. Leaves cannot make food without light. But most leaves work best when the sunlight is at a certain level of brightness. If the light is too dim, the leaf will not make enough food. But if the light is too bright, it can damage the food-making cells.

The leaves of many plants that grow in bright sunlight have an extremely thick cuticle, which helps filter out strong light and guards against excess water loss. The leaves may also have many hairs growing out of the epidermis. The hairs further reduce the intensity of bright light. The leaves of some plants have so many epidermal hairs that they feel fuzzy.

WORLD BOOK illustrations by James Teason

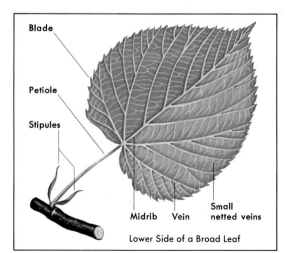

The parts of a leaf. Most leaves have two main parts: (1) a flat *blade* and (2) a stemlike *petiole.* The leaves of many plants also have a third main part, two small flaps called the *stipules.*

Blade
Petiole
Stipules
Midrib   Vein   Small netted veins
Lower Side of a Broad Leaf

Pinnately Veined
(Lower Side of Blue Beech)

Palmately Veined
(Lower Side of Sweet Gum)

Parallel Veined
(Upper and Lower Sides of Rye)

Center Veined
(Cross Section of White Pine)

Vein patterns differ among leaves. Most broad leaves have a *pinnate* (featherlike) or *palmate* (palmlike) vein pattern. Grasses have parallel veins. Needle leaves have one or two center veins.

Photosynthesis

Green leaves make food through *photosynthesis*. This process begins when sunlight strikes *chloroplasts,* small bodies that contain a green substance called *chlorophyll.* The chlorophyll absorbs energy from the sunlight. This energy splits water molecules into hydrogen and oxygen. The hydrogen combines with carbon dioxide, forming a simple sugar. Oxygen is released as a by-product.

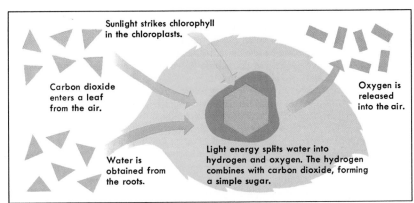

Sunlight strikes chlorophyll in the chloroplasts.

Carbon dioxide enters a leaf from the air.

Oxygen is released into the air.

Water is obtained from the roots.

Light energy splits water into hydrogen and oxygen. The hydrogen combines with carbon dioxide, forming a simple sugar.

WORLD BOOK diagram by Larry Miller, Graphic Direction, Inc.

Some plants, including the herbs, ferns, and shrubs of the forest floor, thrive in shade. The leaves of most of these plants have a thin cuticle and few epidermal hairs. These features allow as much of the dim light as possible to enter the leaves.

Photosynthesis occurs inside the leaf blade in two kinds of food-making cells—*palisade cells* and *spongy cells.* The tall, slender palisade cells are the chief food producers. They form one to three layers beneath the upper epidermis. The broad, irregularly shaped spongy cells lie between the palisade cells and the lower epidermis. Floating within both kinds of cells are numerous small green bodies known as *chloroplasts.* Each chloroplast contains many molecules of the green pigment chlorophyll.

Water enters the food-making cells from the tiny veins of the blade. Partly surrounding each palisade and spongy cell is an air space filled with carbon dioxide and other gases. The cells absorb carbon dioxide from this air space. When light strikes the chloroplasts, photosynthesis begins. The chlorophyll absorbs energy from the light. This energy splits the water molecules

into molecules of hydrogen and oxygen. The hydrogen then combines with carbon dioxide, which results in a simple sugar. This process is extremely complicated and involves many steps. The oxygen that is left over from the splitting of the water molecules enters the air through the stomata.

The sugar produced by photosynthesis is carried through the petiole to the stem and all other parts of the plant. In the plant cells, the sugar may be burned and thus release energy for growth or other activities. Or the sugar may be chemically altered and form fats and starches. In addition, the sugar may be combined with various minerals, and so produce proteins, vitamins, and other vital substances. The minerals enter the plant dissolved in the water absorbed by the roots.

Transpiration occurs as the sun warms the water inside the blade. The warming changes much of the water into water vapor. This gas can then escape through the stomata. Transpiration helps cool the inside of the leaf because the escaping vapor has absorbed heat.

Transpiration also helps keep water flowing up from the roots. Water forms a continuous column as it flows

Inside a green leaf

This cross section shows the many structures of a leaf blade. Palisade and spongy cells serve as food producers. In the veins, xylem tissue distributes water, and phloem tissue carries away food. *Stomata* (pores) on the underside of the blade enable gases to enter and leave the leaf.

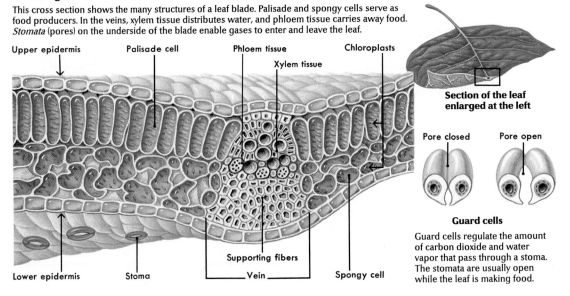

Upper epidermis   Palisade cell   Phloem tissue   Chloroplasts

Xylem tissue

Section of the leaf enlarged at the left

Pore closed   Pore open

Guard cells

Guard cells regulate the amount of carbon dioxide and water vapor that pass through a stoma. The stomata are usually open while the leaf is making food.

Lower epidermis   Stoma   Supporting fibers   Vein   Spongy cell

Specialized leaves   Some leaves perform special tasks in addition to or instead of food making. Such specialized leaves include protective leaves, storage leaves, tendrils, bracts, and insect-capturing leaves. Some specialized leaves, such as the spines of a cactus plant, do not even look like leaves. Botanists identify these structures as leaves because of their growth patterns.

Ray Hunold

Protective leaves include spines like those on the hedgehog cactus above. They keep animals from eating the plant.

WORLD BOOK photo

Food storage leaves include the bulb scales of a tulip, *above*. These fat leaves store food underground in winter.

Dick Keen

Water storage leaves are common on plants that grow in dry regions. Such plants include the stonecrop, *above*.

Edward S. Ross

Tendrils hold climbing plants in place. The tendrils of the garden pea plant above are wrapped around wires.

Robert H. Glaze, Artstreet

Bright red bracts surround the flowers of the poinsettia above. These leaves help attract pollinating insects to the flowers.

L. West, Bruce Coleman Inc.

Insect-capturing leaves attract, trap, and digest insects. Butterwort leaves, *above,* trap their prey in a sticky film.

through the roots, up the stem, and into the leaves. The molecules of water in this column stick to one another. Scientists believe that as molecules at the top of the column are lost through transpiration, the entire column of water is pulled upward. This pulling force is strong enough to draw water to the tops of the tallest trees. In addition, transpiration ensures a steady supply of dissolved minerals from the soil.

A plant may lose much water through transpiration. A corn plant, for example, may lose about 4 quarts (3.8 liters) of water on a hot day. If the roots cannot replace this water, the leaves wilt and photosynthesis stops.

Specialized leaves

Some leaves have special functions along with or instead of food making. Such specialized leaves include protective leaves, storage leaves, tendrils, bracts, and insect-capturing leaves.

See **Leaf** in *World Book* for more information on the following topics:

- The life story of a leaf
- The parts of a leaf
- Specialized leaves
- How to collect leaves

Light

© Ron Thomas, FPG

Light from the sun makes life on earth possible. Plants need sunlight to grow, and animals eat plants or plant-eating animals.

Light is so common that we often take it for granted. Yet the world would quickly change if suddenly there were no light. We could no longer see, because light that comes to our eyes makes seeing possible. Without light, we would have no food to eat or air to breathe. Green plants use the light from the sun to grow and to make food. All the food we eat comes from plants or animals that eat plants. As plants grow, they give off oxygen. This oxygen is a necessary part of the air we breathe.

Light gives us fuels. The energy in the sunlight that shone on the earth millions of years ago was stored by plants. After these plants died, they were changed into coal, natural gas, and oil. Today, we use the energy in these fuels to produce electricity and to operate machines.

Light from the sun also heats the earth. Without the sun's light, the earth would soon become so cold that nothing could live on it. Even if we burned all our fuels, we could not keep the earth warm enough for life to exist. For more information on light and energy from the sun, see the articles on **Solar energy** and **Sun.**

People have found ways of making and controlling light in order to see when there is no sunlight. At first, they produced light with campfires and torches. Later, they developed candles, oil lamps, gaslights, and electric lights.

People make and use light for many other purposes than to see by. For example, the pictures on a television screen consist of spots of light. Using scientific instruments, people can study light itself and learn much about the universe. For example, the light from distant stars can tell scientists what the stars are made of. It can also tell them if the stars are moving toward or away from the earth and how fast they are moving.

What is light? This question has been a puzzle for centuries. People once thought light was something that traveled from a person's eyes to an object and then back again. If anything blocked the rays from the eyes, the object could not be seen. Since the 1600's, scientists have made many discoveries about light. They have learned that light is a form of energy that can travel freely through space. The energy of light is called *radiant energy.* There are many kinds of radiant energy, including infrared rays, radio waves, ultraviolet rays, and X rays. We can see only a tiny part of all the different kinds of radiant energy. This part is called *visible light* or simply *light.*

Sources of light

Light makes it possible for us to see. Many of the things we see, such as the sun, a flashlight, and room lights, are *sources* of light. We see all other things because light from a source bounces off them and travels to us. Light sources can be classified as *natural* or *artificial.* Natural light comes from sources that we do not control. Such sources include the sun and the stars. Artificial light comes from sources that we control. These sources include candles and flashlights.

How light is produced. All light comes from atoms. It is produced by atoms that have gained energy either by absorbing light from another source or by being struck by other particles. An atom with such extra energy is said to be *excited*. Ordinarily, an atom stays excited only briefly. It de-excites by giving up its extra energy. It can either run into another atom to lose the energy, or it can *emit* (give off) light. The light then carries away the extra energy. The amount of energy needed to excite atoms and the amount of energy the atoms emit as light varies for different kinds of atoms.

Light is usually described as a wave, shaped much like a water wave that moves across a lake. But light can also be described as a small particle, called a *photon*. Each photon moves in a straight line, much as a pool ball does. In both descriptions, the light has energy. The amount of energy that is carried by the wave or photon largely determines the color of the light. For example, suppose you see a red apple on a blue chair. Each photon from the apple has less energy than a photon from the chair.

One way to excite atoms so that they emit light is by heating them. A poker may be heated until it is white-hot. Because of the heating, the atoms at the poker's surface collide violently with each other. When they collide, they excite one another. Each atom quickly emits its extra energy as light but is almost immediately re-excited by another collision. These collisions produce such a variety of states among the atoms that the photons released have a wide range of energies. The combination of all the resulting colors is white light. As the poker cools, fewer atoms are excited to high energies, and so the atoms emit fewer photons with the higher energies of blue light. Since red light is still being emitted, the cooling poker looks red.

Other sources of light. Many substances gain energy and emit light without being heated very much. They do this through a process called *luminescence*. Some luminescent materials glow in the dark long after they have received extra energy. They are said to be *phosphorescent*. Their atoms stay excited for some time before they de-excite and emit light.

Fireflies and a few other types of organisms emit light by a process called *bioluminescence*. In this process, chemicals within the organisms combine to produce a different chemical that has excited atoms. When the atoms de-excite, they emit photons.

The sun shines because nuclear reactions between hydrogen atoms within its core produce a tremendous amount of energy. Photons and other kinds of particles carry the energy to the sun's surface. At the surface, these particles excite atoms that then de-excite by emitting light. The earth receives part of that light. All stars emit light by this process.

An *aurora* such as the northern lights is an emission of light by molecules of air. When high-speed particles arrive at the earth from large eruptions on the sun, they crash into the air molecules. These collisions excite the molecules with extra energy. The molecules then release the energy by giving off light. When the collisions occur at night, the light emitted may be bright enough to be seen.

A *laser* is a device that produces a powerful, narrow beam of light in which all the photons have the same energy and travel in the same direction. Lasers serve as tools in scientific research, surgery, and telephone communications. They also have many industrial and military uses.

See **Light** in *World Book* for more information on the following topics:

- The nature of light
- How light behaves
- Measuring light
- Our understanding of light

Natural and artificial sources of light

Natural light sources, such as auroras and fireflies, are not controlled by people. People control artificial light sources, such as candles and lasers. All light comes from atoms.

© Ivan Polunin, Bruce Coleman Inc.
Firefly

© Hanson Planetarium from FPG
Aurora

© FPG
Candle

© Hank Morgan/SS from Photo Researchers
Laser

The behavior of light

In studying *optics* (the science of the behavior of light), physicists have discovered certain principles that describe how light behaves. The most important of these principles include (1) reflection, (2) refraction, (3) diffraction, and (4) interference.

Reflection

A beam of light will be reflected by a smooth surface. The beam coming toward the surface is called the *incident beam*. After the beam has been reflected, it is called the *reflected beam*. The angle the incident beam makes with an imaginary line *normal* (at right angles) to the surface equals the angle made by the reflected beam.

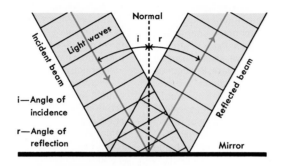

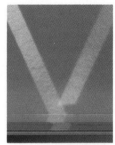

© E. R. Degginger

Refraction

Refraction causes a beam to bend as it passes from one substance into another. The beam bends toward the normal if it slows down when entering a substance, as shown in the diagram. The *angle of refraction* then is less than the *angle of incidence*. If light travels faster in the substance, the beam bends away from the normal.

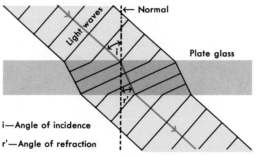

© E. R. Degginger

Diffraction

Light and other waves usually travel in a straight line. But when waves pass through a slit about the same size as their own wavelength, they *diffract* (spread out) into curving waves. The photograph shows water waves because light waves spread out so slightly that their diffraction is difficult to see.

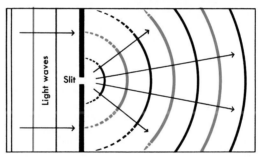

© E. R. Degginger

Interference

Light waves can interfere with each other in two ways. (1) Where the *crest* (peak) of one wave meets the crest of another—or where the *trough* (low point) of one wave meets the trough of another—the two waves combine and form a bright spot of light. This process is called *constructive interference*. (2) Where a crest meets a trough, the two waves cancel, leaving a dark spot. This process is called *destructive interference*. The photograph shows the interference pattern of water waves produced by two sources.

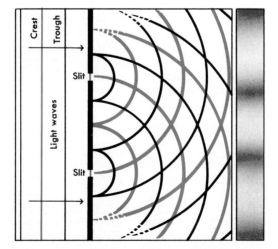

© E. R. Degginger

Lightning is a giant electrical spark in the sky. Most of the lightning people see takes place between a cloud and the ground. But lightning also occurs within a cloud, between a cloud and the air, and between two clouds. When lightning occurs in the atmosphere, its electrical energy scatters in the air. This energy may damage airplanes traveling through it, but it does not cause harm on the ground. But lightning that strikes the earth may kill people or cause fire.

Lightning that strikes the earth consists of one or more electrical discharges called *strokes.* The bright light that we see in a flash of lightning is called a *return stroke.* Return strokes travel at about the speed of light, which is 186,282 miles (299,792 kilometers) per second. They discharge about 100 million volts of electricity and heat the air in their paths to over 60,000° F. (33,000° C). Air heated by return strokes expands quickly, producing a wave of pressure called thunder. In *World Book,* see **Thunder.**

Flashes of lightning vary in length. A flash between a cloud and the ground may be up to 9 miles (14 kilometers) long. A lightning flash that travels through clouds side by side may be more than 90 miles (140 kilometers) long.

Serious study of lightning began in the 1700's. In 1752, Benjamin Franklin showed that lightning is electricity. He tied a metal key to the end of a kite string and flew the kite in a thunderstorm. Cloud electricity raised the voltage of the kite string. The high voltage caused a spark to jump from the key to grounded objects, proving that the cloud was electrified. Franklin's experiment was dangerous, and some people who have flown kites in storms have been electrocuted by lightning.

Forms of lightning

Lightning occurs in a variety of forms. A single flash of lightning often varies in appearance, depending on the position of an observer in relation to it.

The major forms of lightning include *forked lightning, streak lightning, ribbon lightning,* and *bead,* or *chain, lightning.* Forked lightning refers to a flash in which multiple branches of a stroke are visible. Streak lightning is a flash that seems to illuminate a single jagged line. Ribbon lightning appears as parallel streaks of light. It is formed when wind separates the strokes of a flash. Bead, or chain, lightning is a flash that breaks up into a dotted line as it fades.

Some electrical flashes in the sky—such as *heat lightning* and *sheet lightning*—are not really separate forms of lightning, though they appear different in some ways. Heat lightning, often seen on summer nights, seems to occur without thunder. Actually, it is lightning that occurs too far away from an observer for its accompanying thunder to be heard. The people underneath what looks from a distance like heat lightning are experiencing a normal thunderstorm. Sheet lightning appears as an illumination of a portion of the sky. But it is lightning whose distinct flashes either are too far away to be seen or are hidden from view by clouds.

A form of lightning called *ball lightning* differs greatly from ordinary lightning. Ball lightning appears as a glowing, fiery ball that floats for several seconds before disappearing. It has reportedly been seen during thunderstorms, usually after ordinary lightning has occurred. It is described as a red, yellow, or orange ball that may be as large as a grapefruit. It has been reported floating along the ground and inside houses, barns, and airplanes. No one knows how or why ball lightning occurs, or what it consists of.

A glowing light called *St. Elmo's fire* may resemble ball lightning in some ways. St. Elmo's fire is caused by electrical discharges from a sharp object during a thunderstorm. It sometimes appears around airplanes, the masts of sailing ships, towers, and treetops.

How lightning occurs

Lightning is caused by the movement of positive and negative electrical charges toward one another. During a storm, a thundercloud's particles collide and become electrically charged. The positively charged particles rise to the top of the cloud and the negatively charged particles fall to the cloud's base. When negative charges from the cloud's base move downward and meet with rising positive charges from the earth, *cloud-to-ground lightning* occurs. Lightning between charges within a cloud is called *intracloud lightning.* That which occurs between charges of different clouds is known as *cloud-to-cloud lightning.*

Before a storm

Particles collide

Charged particles separate

Cloud-to-ground lightning

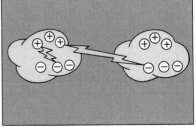

Intracloud and cloud-to-cloud lightning

WORLD BOOK diagrams by Arthur Grebetz

Norman Myers

A pride of lions moves across an open, grassy plain in Africa.

Lion is a big, powerful cat. It is probably the most famous member of the cat family. People are frightened by the lion's thundering roar and impressed by its strength and royal appearance. The lion is called the "king of beasts," and is a well-known symbol of both beauty and power.

Lions can live in cool climates and in the intense heat of semidesert areas. They do not like to live in thick forests. Most of them live in woodlands, grassy plains, and areas with thorny scrub trees. Lions live where they find a supply of food—deer, antelope, zebra, and other hoofed animals—and where they have a place to drink.

In ancient times, lions lived in Europe, the Middle East, India, and much of Africa. But human beings have killed thousands of lions as people settled in new areas. As a result, there are no more lions left in the Middle East and northern Africa. Only about 200 lions still live in Asia—all in the Gir Forest in India. Lions still live in the eastern part of central Africa and in southern Africa. But most of these lions live in national parks and areas called *reserves,* where the animals are protected from hunters.

Hundreds of lions also live in captivity in zoos throughout the world. And trained lions are popular performers in circuses.

The body of a lion

The lion and tiger are the largest members of the cat family. Lions are built for strength, not speed. A male

lion usually weighs from 350 to 400 pounds (159 to 180 kilograms), but some weigh up to 500 pounds (230 kilograms). Most males are about 9 feet (3 meters) long from the nose to the end of the tail. They are about $3\frac{1}{2}$ feet (107 centimeters) tall at the shoulder. *Lionesses* (females) are smaller than males. They weigh only 250 to 300 pounds (113 to 140 kilograms) and are about 1 foot (30 centimeters) shorter.

Male lions are the only cats with *manes.* This collar of long, thick hair covers the head, except the face, and the neck down to the shoulders and chest. The mane makes the male look even bigger and stronger than he is. It also protects him during fights. The long, thick hair softens the blows of his foes. Young males have a little hair around their heads when they are about a year old. The mane is not fully grown until the animal is about 5 years old. Manes may be blond, brown, or black. Most are a

Facts in brief

Names: *Male,* lion; *female,* lioness; *young,* cub; *group,* pride.
Gestation period: About $3\frac{1}{2}$ months.
Number in litter: 1 to 6, usually 2 or 3.
Length of life: 20 to 25 years, in captivity; in the wild, 15 to 20 years.
Where found: Africa south of the Sahara; the Gir Forest of India.
Scientific classification: Lions belong to the class Mammalia, and the order Carnivora. They are in the cat family, Felidae; genus *Panthera,* species *P. Leo.*

mixture of these colors. They darken as the lion grows.

The lion's coat is ideal for hiding. It is a brownish yellow, the same color as dead grass. Only the back of the ears and the tuft of hair at the end of the tail are black. *Cubs* (young lions) have spots on their coats.

The shoulders and forelegs of the lion are tremendously muscular. They give the lion the strength to clutch its prey and pull it to the ground. Each big, heavy paw is armed with curved claws that hook and hold the prey. When not in use, each claw withdraws into a sheath in the paw so the claws stay sharp.

The lion has 30 teeth. The four large *canine* (pointed) teeth are used to hold the prey, kill it, and to tear the meat. Four cheek teeth called the *carnassial* teeth are for cutting through tough skin and the *tendons* that join

The skeleton of a lion

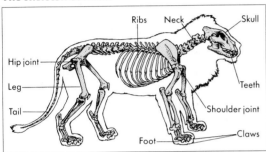

Lion tracks

WORLD BOOK illustration by John D. Dawson

Norman Myers, Photo Researchers

A lion's long, sharp teeth and huge paws are fearsome weapons. The lion can disable or kill some prey with one swipe, then use its pointed teeth to tear the prey apart.

muscles to bone. There are no teeth suitable for chewing. The lion swallows food in chunks.

The life of a lion

The lion is the most companionable of all cats. A *pride* (group) may include from 10 to 20 lions, or as many as 35. Each pride has from one to five adult males, several lionesses, and cubs. The members of the pride may not always be together. Some of the lions may hunt in one place, a few in another. But when they are reunited, they greet each other by rubbing cheeks.

Life within the pride is peaceful. Lions usually spend about 20 hours a day sleeping or resting. Cubs chase each other and wrestle. A lioness sometimes twitches her tail while one of her cubs tries to catch the tuft of hair at the end of the tail. Hungry cubs nurse on any lioness that has milk, not just their own mothers.

Lions usually walk about 5 miles (8 kilometers) in a day. If they have had a big meal, they may rest for 24 hours. But if they are hungry, they may travel as far as 15 miles (24 kilometers) in search of food.

Habits. Each pride stays in a specific *territory* (area). The territory has food and water for the lions. Where prey is plentiful, the territory may cover about 15 square miles (39 square kilometers). Where prey is scarce, it may be 100 square miles (260 square kilometers).

Lions do not allow strange animals to hunt in their territory. They warn intruders to stay away by roaring or by squirting a mixture of scent and urine on bushes. The strangers then know that the territory is occupied. If they ignore the warnings, they may be killed.

Pride members stay together like a family for years, but changes occur from time to time. All male cubs are chased from the territory by their fathers when they are between 2 and 3 years old. These young males then wander until they are fully grown. Then they may challenge some pride males. If they win, they can take over the territory and the lionesses it contains. Lions in captivity die of old age at about 20 to 25 years.

Cubs. A lioness becomes an adult and mates with the pride males when she is from 3 to 4 years old. About $3\frac{1}{2}$ months later, her cubs are born in a thicket. The cubs are blind and helpless at birth, and weigh about 3 pounds (1.4 kilograms) each. Lions do not have permanent dens. From time to time, the mother moves her cubs from one hiding place to another. She carries them in her mouth, one at a time. Hyenas, leopards, and even other lions may kill cubs while the mother is away hunting. Lions also have mated with tigers in captivity. Their offspring may be called a *tiglon,* a *tigon,* or a *liger.*

At first, the cubs live on milk. When they are about $1\frac{1}{2}$ months old, the mother leads them to an animal she has killed for their first meal of meat. The lioness usually does not have another litter until her cubs are 18 to 24 months old, old enough to hunt for themselves. Occasionally, a mother abandons her cubs. When food is scarce, the mother eats and lets the cubs starve. About half the cubs survive.

See **Lion** in *World Book* for more information on How a lion hunts and Lions and people.

Lobster is a hard-shelled animal that lives on the bottom of the ocean near the shore. A stiff shell covers the lobster's entire body like a suit of armor. The animal has two large claws that reach out in front and are almost as long as its body. The lobster's tail spreads out behind like a fan. Most kinds of lobsters have dark green or dark blue shells with spots on them. The shells of the animals turn bright red when the lobsters are cooked.

Lobsters have no backbone. They belong to a group of animals called *crustaceans.* The word *crustacean* comes from a Latin word meaning *hard shell.* Other crustaceans include crabs, crayfish, and shrimp.

The body of a lobster. The *common lobster* of the continent of North America, which is usually called the *American lobster,* measures 12 to 24 inches (30 to 61 centimeters) long and weighs 1 to 20 pounds (0.5 to 9 kilograms). Most European lobsters are smaller than American lobsters.

The lobster's body has 19 parts. The head has five parts, the *thorax* (center part) has eight, and the abdomen has six. Each part is covered by a section of the shell. The shell is thin and soft where the parts join, so the lobster can bend its body and move about. The lobster breathes through gills located beneath the shell on both sides of its thorax.

A lobster has two pairs of antennae on its head. The animal's eyes are on the ends of a pair of slender, jointed organs called *stalks.* Lobsters have *compound* eyes that consist of hundreds of lenses joined together. The lobster keeps its antennae and eye stalks moving constantly to search for food and to watch for enemies. The lobster's antennae, legs, and shell are covered with millions of tiny hairlike sensors that can detect chemicals. The sensors help the animal locate food.

A lobster has five pairs of jointed legs. Four pairs are thin, and the lobster uses them for walking. The fifth pair, which extend in front of the head, are thick and end in large claws. One of the claws is heavy and has thick teeth to crush prey. The other claw is smaller and has sharp teeth to tear food apart. All lobsters do not have the heavy claw on the same side. Some are "right-handed," and others are "left-handed." The front claws of a *spiny lobster* are long and slender. This lobster, named for the sharp spines on its shell, lives in coastal waters throughout much of the world.

The life of a lobster. Lobsters live on the bottom of

George H. Harrison, Bruce Coleman Inc.

An American lobster, *above,* has thick legs and huge front claws. It uses its claws to kill and handle prey. Lobsters eat crabs, snails, small fish, and other lobsters.

the ocean near shore, and hide in holes or under rocks at depths of 6 to 120 feet (1.8 to 37 meters). A lobster sits in its burrow all day, waving its feelers outside the entrance. It holds its claws ready and pounces on any prey that comes near. Lobsters eat crabs, snails, small fish, and other lobsters. At night, the lobster walks along the ocean bottom looking for food. If an enemy such as a large fish or an octopus comes near, the lobster scoots back into its burrow with powerful flips of its tail.

The body of a lobster

WORLD BOOK illustrations by Patricia Wynne

Heart   Stomach   Eye   Brain   Claw

Intestine

Blood vessel

Nerve cord   Liver   Mouth   Antenna

See **Lobster** in *World Book* for more information on The life of a lobster and Lobster fishing.

Facts in brief

Names: *Male,* cock; *female,* hen or chicken; *young,* none; *group,* none.
Gestation period: 11 to 12 months.
Number of newborn: 5,000 to 100,000 or more.
Length of life: About 15 years.
Where found: Atlantic Ocean, Pacific Ocean.
Scientific classification: Lobsters belong to the class Crustacea. Common lobsters make up the genus *Homarus.* Spiny lobsters make up the genus *Panulirus.*

Lung is the chief breathing organ of mammals, birds, reptiles, and most adult amphibians. The main job of the lungs is to exchange gases. As blood flows through the lungs, it picks up oxygen from the air and releases carbon dioxide. The body needs oxygen to burn food for energy, and it produces carbon dioxide as a waste product. This article discusses the human lungs, but the lungs of other animals function in a similar way.

Parts of the lungs. Human beings have two lungs—a left lung and a right lung—which fill up most of the chest cavity. A lung has a spongy texture and may be thought of as an elastic bag filled with millions of tiny air chambers, or sacs. If the walls of the air sacs could be spread out flat, they would cover about half a tennis court. The somewhat bullet-shaped lungs are suspended within the ribcage. They extend from just above the first rib down to the *diaphragm*, a muscular sheet that separates the chest cavity from the abdomen. A thin, tough membrane called the *visceral pleura* covers the outer surface of the lungs. The heart, large blood vessels, and *esophagus* (the tube connecting the mouth and stomach) lie between the two lungs.

The lungs are designed to receive air, which enters the body through the mouth or nose. The air passes through the *pharynx* (back of the nose and mouth) and the *larynx* (voice box) and enters the *airways*—a system of tubes that leads into the lungs. The largest of these tubes is the *trachea* (windpipe), which divides into two smaller tubes called *bronchi*. Each bronchus enters one lung, about a third of the way from the top to the bottom of the lung. Within the lung, the bronchus divides into smaller and smaller tubes, much as a tree limb divides into branches and twigs. The final "twigs" are tiny tubes called *bronchioles*. The smallest bronchioles, called *terminal bronchioles*, lead to the *respiratory units* of the lung. The respiratory units are made up of many *alveolar sacs*. Each sac contains about 20 tiny air spaces called *alveoli*. The walls of each alveolus contain networks of extremely small blood vessels called *pulmonary capillaries*. It is here that gas exchange takes place.

Three to five terminal bronchioles and the alveoli that they supply with air form a *lobule*. Many lobules unite to form the major subdivisions of the lung, called *lobes*. The left lung has two lobes, and the right lung has three. Each lobe has its own branches of bronchi and blood vessels, so a diseased lobe may be removed without sacrificing the usefulness of the other lobes.

Blood reaches the lung through two routes. Almost all of the blood comes through the *pulmonary circulation*. This blood has already circulated through the body tissues, where it has given up its oxygen and picked up carbon dioxide. A small amount of blood reaches the lungs through the *bronchial circulation*. This blood is rich in the oxygen and nutrients that the airway tissues—like all other body tissues—need.

See **Lung** in *World Book* for more information on Gas exchange in the lungs, Other jobs of the lungs, and Diseases of the lungs.

Parts of a human lung

The right lung consists of three lobes, and the left lung, two. Air enters a lung through a *bronchus*, which splits into *bronchioles*. Each bronchiole leads to a *respiratory unit* with *alveolar sacs*.

WORLD BOOK illustrations by Charles Wellek

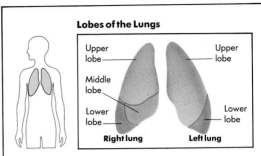

Lobes of the Lungs

Upper lobe

Upper lobe

Middle lobe

Lower lobe

Lower lobe

Right lung **Left lung**

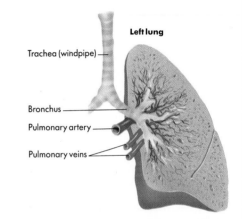

Left lung

Trachea (windpipe)

Bronchus

Pulmonary artery

Pulmonary veins

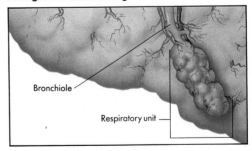

Enlarged Section of a Lung

Bronchiole

Respiratory unit

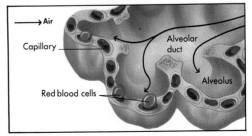

Cross Section of an Alveolar Sac

Air

Capillary

Alveolar duct

Alveolus

Red blood cells

An alveolar sac consists of an alveolar duct and about 20 alveoli. Blood picks up oxygen and releases carbon dioxide as it passes through the alveolar walls.

Lymphatic system, *lihm FAT ihk,* is a network of small vessels that resemble blood vessels. The lymphatic system returns fluid from body tissues to the blood stream. This process is necessary because fluid pressure in the body continuously causes water, proteins, and other materials to seep out of tiny blood vessels called *capillaries.* The fluid that has leaked out, called *interstitial fluid,* bathes and nourishes body tissues.

If there were no way for excess interstitial fluid to return to the blood, the tissues would become swollen. Most of the extra fluid seeps into capillaries that have low fluid pressure. The rest returns by way of the lymphatic system and is called *lymph.* Some scientists consider the lymphatic system to be part of the circulatory system because lymph comes from the blood and returns to the blood.

The lymphatic system also is one of the body's defenses against infection. Harmful particles and bacteria that have entered the body are filtered out by small masses of tissue that lie along the lymphatic vessels. These bean-shaped masses are called *lymph nodes.*

Work of the lymphatic system

Return of interstitial fluid. Interstitial fluid is produced continuously by seepage from the capillaries. For this reason, some of the fluid must constantly be returned from body tissues to the bloodstream. If the lymphatic vessels are blocked, fluid gathers in nearby tissues and causes swelling called *edema.*

The flow of lymph, after it reaches the larger lymphatic vessels, always takes place in the same direction —toward the thoracic duct. Much of the flow, including that within the thoracic duct, is upward. Yet lymph has no pump—as the blood has the heart—to keep it moving forward. The flow is caused by pressure from muscular movement, breathing, and the pulse beat in nearby blood vessels. Valves in the larger lymphatic vessels prevent the lymph from flowing backward. These valves resemble those in the veins.

Fighting infection. Lymphocytes and macrophages both play vital roles in fighting infection—lymphocytes by producing antibodies and macrophages by swallowing up foreign particles. During an infection, the lymph nodes that drain an infected area may swell and become painful. The swelling indicates that the lymphocytes and macrophages in the lymph nodes are fighting the infection and working to stop it from spreading. Such swellings are often called "swollen glands," though lymph nodes—not glands—are swollen.

Lymphocytes also flow into the bloodstream and circulate throughout the body combating infection. Many lymphocytes find their way to areas just under the skin. There they produce antibodies against bacteria and various substances that cause allergies.

Absorption of fats. Lymphatic vessels in the wall of the intestine have an important part in the absorption of fats by the body. These vessels are called *lacteals.* In the intestine, digested fats combine with certain proteins. The resulting particles enter the lacteals and give the lymph there a milky-white color.

See **Lymphatic system** in *World Book* for more information on Parts of the lymphatic system and Work of the lymphatic system.

The lymphatic system

The lymphatic system consists of a network of vessels throughout the body. Clusters of lymph nodes occur in the groin, neck, and armpits and near certain internal organs and blood vessels.

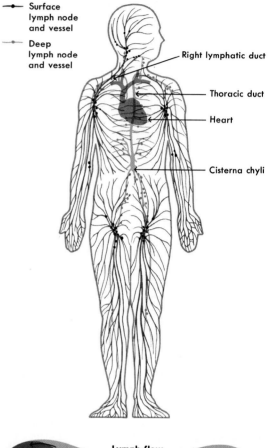

Surface lymph node and vessel

Deep lymph node and vessel

Right lymphatic duct

Thoracic duct

Heart

Cisterna chyli

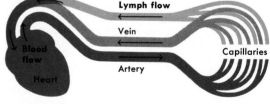

Lymph flow

Vein

Blood flow

Capillaries

Artery

Heart

Fluid seeps out of the capillaries and collects in the lymphatic vessels. The collected fluid, called lymph, flows in the lymphatic vessels and drains into blood veins near the heart.

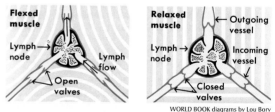

Flexed muscle

Lymph node

Lymph flow

Open valves

Relaxed muscle

Outgoing vessel

Lymph node

Incoming vessel

Closed valves

WORLD BOOK diagrams by Lou Bory

Flexing and relaxing of muscles near the lymphatic vessels produces a squeezing action that pushes lymph along its course. Valves in the vessels prevent lymph from flowing back.

Machine is a device that does work. Machines are designed to make life easier for us. Some machines perform tasks that would be impossible to do without them.

Principles of machines

A machine produces force and controls the direction and the motion of force. But it cannot create energy. A machine can never do more work than the energy put into it. It only transforms one kind of energy, such as electrical energy, and passes it along as mechanical energy. Some machines, such as diesel engines or steam turbines, change energy directly into mechanical motion. For example, the energy of steam rushing through the wheels of a turbine produces rotary motion. The mechanical energy of the turbine can be used to drive a generator that produces electricity. Other machines simply transmit mechanical work from one part of a device to another part. They include the six simple machines that are described on this page.

A machine's ability to do work is measured by two factors. They are (1) efficiency and (2) mechanical advantage.

Efficiency. The efficiency of a machine is the ratio between the energy it supplies and the energy put into it. No machine can operate with 100 per cent efficiency because the friction of its parts always uses up some of the energy that is being supplied to the machine. Although friction can be decreased by oiling any sliding or rotating parts, all machines produce some friction. For this reason, a perpetual-motion machine is impossible. In *World Book*, see **Perpetual motion machine**.

A simple lever is a good example of a machine that has a high efficiency. The work it puts out is almost equal to the energy it receives, because the energy used up by friction is quite small. On the other hand, an automobile engine has an efficiency of only about 25 per cent, because much of the energy supplied by the fuel is lost in the form of heat that escapes into the surrounding air.

Mechanical advantage. In machines that transmit only mechanical energy, the ratio of the force exerted by the machine to the force applied to the machine is known as *mechanical advantage*. Mechanical advantage can be demonstrated with a crowbar, which is a type of lever. When one end of the crowbar is directly under the weight, a part of the crowbar must rest on a *fulcrum* (support). The closer the fulcrum is to the load, the less the effort required to raise the load by pushing down on the handle of the crowbar, and the greater the mechanical advantage of the crowbar. For example, if the load is 200 kilograms, and the distance from the load to the fulcrum is one fourth of the distance from the handle to the fulcrum, it will take 50 kilograms of effort to raise the load. Therefore, the mechanical advantage will be four to one. But the distance the load will be moved will be only one-fourth of the distance through which the effort is applied.

See **Machine** in *World Book* for more information on Six simple machines and Designing machines.

Six simple machines

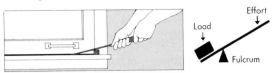

The lever is one of the earliest and simplest machines. Its advantage lies in the short distance between the fulcrum (pivotal point) and load, and in the long distance between the fulcrum and the point where effort is applied.

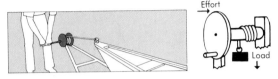

The wheel and axle has a rope attached to the axle to lift the load. The crank handle is the point where effort is applied. The effort is smaller than the load because it is at a greater distance from the axle which is the fulcrum.

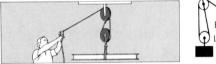

The pulley consists of a wheel with a grooved rim over which a rope is passed. It is used to change the direction of the effort applied to the rope. A block and tackle uses two or more pulleys to reduce the amount of effort needed to lift a load.

The inclined plane makes it easier to slide or skid a load upward than to lift it directly. The longer the slope, the smaller the effort required. The amount of work, however, is no less than if the load were lifted directly upward.

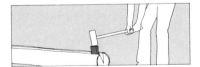

The wedge, when struck with a mallet or sledge, exerts a large force on its sides. A gently tapering, or thin, wedge is more effective than a thick one. The mechanical advantage of the wedge is of great importance.

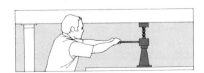

The screw is a spiral inclined plane. The jackscrew is a combination of the lever and the screw. It can lift a heavy load with relatively small effort. Therefore, it has a very high mechanical advantage for practical purposes.

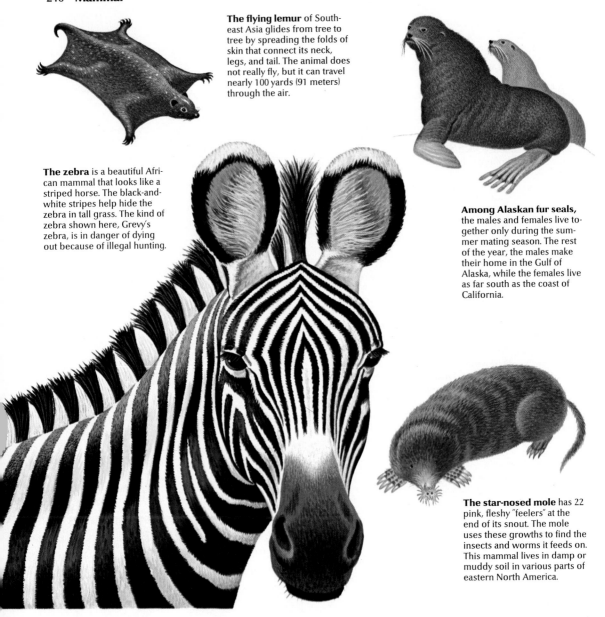

The flying lemur of Southeast Asia glides from tree to tree by spreading the folds of skin that connect its neck, legs, and tail. The animal does not really fly, but it can travel nearly 100 yards (91 meters) through the air.

The zebra is a beautiful African mammal that looks like a striped horse. The black-and-white stripes help hide the zebra in tall grass. The kind of zebra shown here, Grevy's zebra, is in danger of dying out because of illegal hunting.

Among Alaskan fur seals, the males and females live together only during the summer mating season. The rest of the year, the males make their home in the Gulf of Alaska, while the females live as far south as the coast of California.

The star-nosed mole has 22 pink, fleshy "feelers" at the end of its snout. The mole uses these growths to find the insects and worms it feeds on. This mammal lives in damp or muddy soil in various parts of eastern North America.

Mammal

Mammal is a *vertebrate* (backboned animal) that feeds its young on the mother's milk. There are about 4,000 kinds of mammals, and many of them are among the most familiar of all animals. Cats and dogs are mammals. So are such farm animals as cattle, goats, hogs, and horses. Mammals also include such fascinating animals as anteaters, apes, giraffes, hippopotamuses, and kangaroos. And people, too, are mammals.

Mammals live almost everywhere. Such mammals as monkeys and elephants dwell in tropical regions. Arctic foxes, polar bears, and many other mammals make their home near the North Pole. Such mammals as camels

and kangaroo rats live in deserts. Certain others, including seals and whales, dwell in the oceans. One group of mammals, the bats, can fly.

The largest animal that has ever lived, the blue whale, is a mammal. It measures up to 100 feet (30 meters) long and can weigh more than 220 short tons (200 metric tons). The smallest mammal is the Kitti's hog-nosed bat of Thailand. It is about the size of a bumblebee and weighs only about $\frac{1}{14}$ ounce (2 grams).

Some mammals live a long time. Elephants, for example, live for about 60 years, and some human beings reach the age of 100 years or more. On the other hand,

The sloth spends most of its life in the treetops. This South American mammal moves very slowly along the underside of branches, hanging upside down by its long claws.

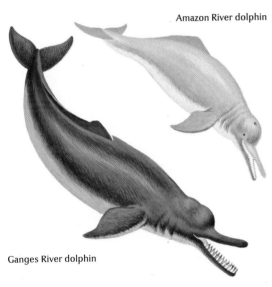

Amazon River dolphin

Ganges River dolphin

Dolphins are mammals that live in water. Most kinds of dolphins live in the ocean. However, the Amazon River dolphin and the Ganges River dolphin dwell in fresh water.

Interesting facts about mammals

The largest mammal—and the largest animal that has ever lived—is the blue whale. It measures up to 100 feet (30 meters) long when fully grown.

WORLD BOOK illustration by John Dawson

Kitti's hog-nosed bat

The Kitti's hog-nosed bat of Thailand is one of the smallest mammals. It is about the size of a bumblebee and weighs no more than a penny.

Potto

The potto, a small African tree dweller, has one of the strongest grips of all mammals. A potto can grasp a branch so tightly with its hands and feet that the animal may remain clinging to the branch even after it has died.

African rhinoceros

The rhinoceros has horns that look like closely packed hairs. Actually, they consist of many fibers of *keratin,* the horny substance that makes up the nails of people. African rhinos have two horns. Indian rhinos have one.

Marmosets

A young marmoset rides on its father's back. Most male mammals have little to do with raising their offspring. But among these South American monkeys, the father and mother share the job of carrying and protecting their babies.

Hyrax

The hyrax is a small mammal that looks much like a guinea pig. But scientists believe that its nearest relatives are actually elephants. Hyraxes, which are also known as conies, live in Africa and the Middle East.

WORLD BOOK illustrations by James Teason unless otherwise credited

many mice and shrews live for less than a year.

Mammals differ from all or most other animals in five major ways. (1) Mammals nurse their babies—that is, they feed them on the mother's milk. No other animals do this. (2) Most mammals give their young more protection and training than do other animals. (3) Only mammals have hair. All mammals have hair at some time in their life, though in certain whales it is present only before birth. (4) Mammals are *warm-blooded*—that is, their body temperature remains about the same all the time, even though the temperature of their surroundings may change. Birds are also warm-blooded, but nearly all other animals are not. (5) Mammals have a larger, more well-developed brain than do other animals. Some mammals, such as chimpanzees, dolphins, and especially human beings, are highly intelligent.

The senses and intelligence of mammals

Senses. Mammals rely on various senses to inform them of happenings in their environment. The major senses of mammals are (1) smell, (2) taste, (3) hearing, (4) sight, and (5) touch. However, the senses are not equally developed in each species of mammal. In fact, some species do not have all the senses.

Smell is the most important sense among the majority of mammals. Most species have large nasal cavities lined with nerves that are sensitive to odors. These animals rely heavily on smell to find food and to detect the presence of enemies. In many species, the members communicate with one another through the odors produced by various skin glands and body wastes. For example, a dog urinates on trees and other objects to tell other dogs it has been there. A few species of mammals, especially human beings, apes, and monkeys, have a poorly developed sense of smell. Dolphins and whales seem to lack the sense entirely.

Taste helps mammals identify foods and so decide what foods to eat. This sense is located mainly in *taste buds* on the tongue. However, much of the sense of taste is strongly affected by the odor of food.

Hearing is well developed in most mammals. The majority of species have an outer ear, which collects sound waves and channels them into the middle and inner ear. Only mammals have an outer ear. See the article **Ear** for a description of the human ear, which is typical of the ears of most mammals.

Some mammals use their sense of hearing to find food and avoid obstacles in the dark. Bats, for example, produce short, high-pitched sounds that bounce off surrounding objects. Bats can use these sounds and their echoes to detect insects and even thin wires. Dolphins and whales also use this system, called *echolocation,* to find food and avoid objects underwater. However, most of the sounds they make are pitched much lower than are the sounds made by bats. Other echolocating mammals include sea lions, seals, and shrews.

Sight is the most important sense among the *higher primates* (apes, monkeys, and people). The structure and function of the eye is similar in all mammals (see **Eye**). However, the eyes of the higher primates have more *cones* than do those of most other mammals. These structures give apes, monkeys, and people sharp daytime vision and the ability to tell colors apart. A few other mammals that are active during the day have some color vision, but most mammals are color blind. Many species of mammals that are active at night have large eyes with a reflector at the rear. This reflector, called the *tapetum lucidum,* helps the animal see in the dark. It produces the *eyeshine* a person sees when light strikes the eyes of a cat or a deer at night.

Touch. Most mammals have a good sense of touch. *Tactile nerves*—that is, nerves that respond to touch— are found all over a mammal's body. But some areas have an especially large number of these nerves and are very sensitive to touch. The whiskers of such mammals as cats, dogs, and mice have many tactile nerves at their

Some major characteristics of mammals

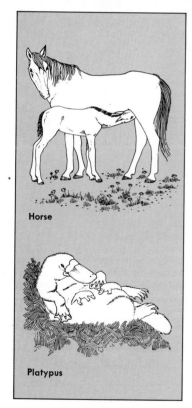

Horse

Platypus

Alpaca

Porcupine

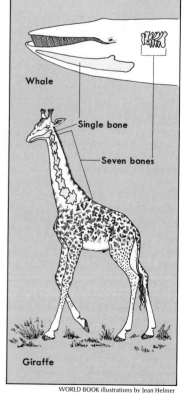

Whale

Single bone

Seven bones

Giraffe

WORLD BOOK illustrations by Jean Helmer

Mammals nurse their young. A colt, like most baby mammals, sucks milk from his mother's nipples. Baby platypuses lap milk from their mother's abdomen.

Mammals have hair. In the alpaca and most other mammals, a thick coat of hair provides warmth. The porcupine's quills are special hairs used for self-defense.

Mammals have similar skeletons. Only one bone forms each side of the lower jaw in mammals. Almost all mammals have seven bones in the neck.

base. These whiskers help the animals feel their way in the dark. Moles and pocket gophers have a highly sensitive tail, which aids them when backing up in dark, narrow tunnels. Primates' fingers have many tactile nerves.

Intelligence is related to the ability to learn. Through learning, an animal stores information in its memory and then later uses this information to act in appropriate ways. Mammals, with their highly developed cerebral cortex, can learn more than other kinds of animals.

Intelligence is hard to measure, even in human beings. But chimpanzees, dogs, and dolphins can learn much when trained by people. These species are among the most intelligent mammals. The amount of the sur-face area of the brain, especially of the cerebral cortex, generally indicates an animal's learning ability. In the more intelligent mammals, the cerebral cortex is fairly large and has many folds, which further increase its surface area.

See **Mammal** in *World Book* for more information on the following topics:

- The importance of mammals
- The bodies of mammals
- What mammals eat
- How mammals move
- How mammals reproduce
- Ways of life
- The evolution of mammals

How mammals reproduce

All mammals reproduce sexually. A new individual begins to form after a *sperm* (male sex cell) unites with an *egg* (female sex cell). This union is called *fertilization*. Mammals can be divided into three groups according to the way in which the fertilized egg develops into a new individual. These groups are (1) placentals, (2) marsupials, and (3) monotremes.

Norman Myers, Bruce Coleman Inc.

Placentals give birth to fairly well-developed offspring, such as the newborn zebra shown above. A young placental mammal develops inside its mother, receiving nourishment from her through an organ called the *placenta*. Placentals make up the vast majority of mammals.

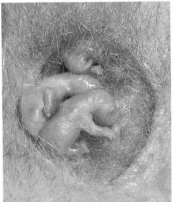

Leonard Lee Rue III, Bruce Coleman Inc.

Marsupials give birth to poorly developed young, such as these baby opossums. The young complete their development attached to the mother's nipples.

Warren Garst, Tom Stack & Assoc.

WORLD BOOK diagram by Jean Helmer

Monotremes, such as the platypus, *left,* lay eggs rather than bear their young alive. The female platypus digs a long tunnel in the bank of a stream, *right.* There she lays one to three eggs that have a leathery shell. The only other monotremes are the echidnas, or spiny anteaters. Platypuses and echidnas live in Australia and on nearby islands.

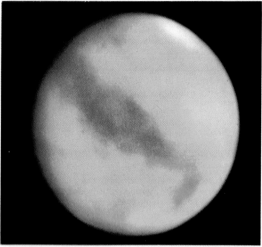

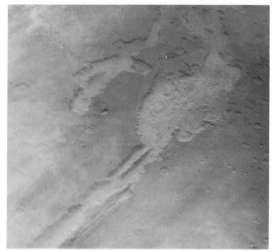

Hale Observatories

NASA

Mars' surface features, including light areas, dark areas, and polar cap, are visible in this photograph taken from the earth, *left.* The earth's atmosphere makes the picture blurry. A series of canyons called the Valles Marineris (Mariner Valleys) make up the diagonal landform in the photo at the right, taken by the *Viking 1.* This landform is more than 2,500 miles (4,000 kilometers) long.

Mars is the only planet whose surface can be seen in detail from the earth. It is reddish in color, and was named Mars after the bloody red god of war of the ancient Romans.

Mars is the fourth closest planet to the sun, and the next planet beyond the earth. Its mean distance from the sun is about 141,600,000 miles (227,900,000 kilometers), compared with about 93,000,000 miles (150,000,000 kilometers) for the earth. At its closest approach to the earth, Mars is 34,600,000 miles (55,700,000 kilometers) away. Venus is the only planet that comes closer.

Orbit. Mars travels around the sun in an *elliptical* (oval-shaped) orbit. Its distance from the sun varies from about 154,800,000 miles (249,200,000 kilometers) at its farthest point, to about 128,400,000 miles (206,600,000 kilometers) at its closest point. Mars takes about 687 earth-days to go around the sun, compared with about 365 days, or 1 year, for the earth.

Surface. The surface conditions on Mars are more like the earth's than are those of any other planet. But the present plants and animals of the earth could not live on Mars. The surface temperature on Mars is much lower than that on earth, rarely rising above the freezing point of water. The planet seems to have had large amounts of surface water millions of years ago, but almost none exists today. However, scientists think that water may be frozen in the planet's large polar caps or beneath its surface. The atmosphere of Mars contains only a trace of oxygen. In spite of the scarcity of liquid water and oxygen, many scientists believe some form of life may exist on Mars. But none has been found yet.

See **Mars** in *World Book* for more information on the following topics:

- Rotation
- Surface
- Atmosphere
- Temperature

- Density and mass
- Satellites
- Flights to Mars

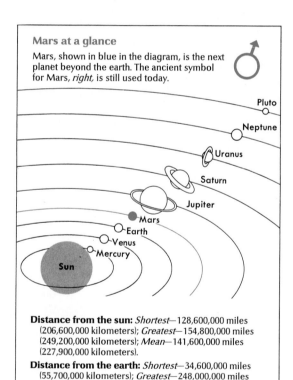

Mars at a glance

Mars, shown in blue in the diagram, is the next planet beyond the earth. The ancient symbol for Mars, *right,* is still used today.

Pluto
Neptune
Uranus
Saturn
Jupiter
Mars
Earth
Venus
Mercury
Sun

Distance from the sun: *Shortest*—128,600,000 miles (206,600,000 kilometers); *Greatest*—154,800,000 miles (249,200,000 kilometers); *Mean*—141,600,000 miles (227,900,000 kilometers).

Distance from the earth: *Shortest*—34,600,000 miles (55,700,000 kilometers); *Greatest*—248,000,000 miles (399,000,000 kilometers).

Diameter: 4,223 miles (6,796 kilometers).

Length of year: About 1 earth-year and $10\frac{1}{2}$ months.

Rotation period: 24 hours and 37 minutes.

Temperature: $-225.4°$ to 63° F. ($-143°$ to 17° C).

Atmosphere: Carbon dioxide, nitrogen, argon, oxygen, carbon monoxide, neon, krypton, xenon, and water vapor.

Number of satellites: 2.

Mercury is the planet nearest the sun. It has a diameter of 3,031 miles (4,878 kilometers), about two-fifths the earth's diameter. Mercury's mean distance from the sun is about 36 million miles (57.9 million kilometers), compared to 67,250,000 miles (108,230,000 kilometers) for Venus, the second closest planet.

Because of Mercury's size and nearness to the brightly shining sun, the planet is often hard to see from the earth without a telescope. At certain times of the year, Mercury can be seen low in the western sky just after sunset. At other times, it can be seen low in the eastern sky just before sunrise.

Orbit. Mercury travels around the sun in an *elliptical* (oval-shaped) orbit. The planet is about 28,600,000 miles (46 million kilometers) from the sun at its closest point, and about 43.4 million miles (69.8 million kilometers) from the sun at its farthest point. Mercury is about 57 million miles (91.7 million kilometers) from the earth at its closest approach.

Surface and atmosphere. Mercury's surface appears to be much like that of the moon. It reflects about 6 per cent of the sunlight it receives, about the same as the moon's surface reflects. Like the moon, Mercury is covered by a thin layer of minerals called *silicates* in the form of tiny particles. It also has broad, flat plains; steep cliffs; and many deep craters similar to those on the moon. Many astronomers believe the craters were formed by meteors or small comets crashing into the planet. Mercury does not have enough atmosphere to slow down approaching meteors and burn them up by friction.

Mercury is dry, extremely hot, and almost airless. The sun's rays are about seven times as strong on Mercury as they are on the earth. The sun also appears about $2\frac{1}{2}$ times as large in Mercury's sky as in the earth's. Mercury does not have enough gases in its atmosphere to reduce the amount of heat and light it receives from the sun. The temperature on the planet may reach 801° F. (427° C) during the day. But at night the temperature may drop as low as −279° F. (−173° C). Because of the lack of atmosphere, Mercury's sky is black, and stars probably can be seen during the day.

See **Mercury** in *World Book* for more information on the following topics:

- Orbit
- Rotation
- Phases
- Surface and atmosphere
- Density and mass
- Flights to Mercury

NASA

The planet Mercury was photographed in detail for the first time on March 29, 1974, by the U.S. probe *Mariner X*. The probe was about 130,000 miles (210,000 kilometers) from Mercury.

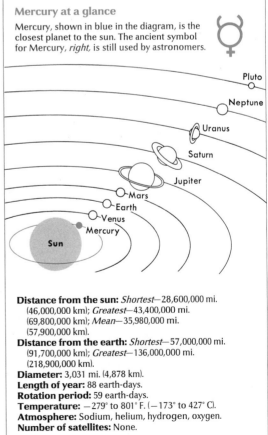

Mercury at a glance

Mercury, shown in blue in the diagram, is the closest planet to the sun. The ancient symbol for Mercury, *right*, is still used by astronomers.

Distance from the sun: *Shortest*—28,600,000 mi. (46,000,000 km); *Greatest*—43,400,000 mi. (69,800,000 km); *Mean*—35,980,000 mi. (57,900,000 km).
Distance from the earth: *Shortest*—57,000,000 mi. (91,700,000 km); *Greatest*—136,000,000 mi. (218,900,000 km).
Diameter: 3,031 mi. (4,878 km).
Length of year: 88 earth-days.
Rotation period: 59 earth-days.
Temperature: −279° to 801° F. (−173° to 427° C).
Atmosphere: Sodium, helium, hydrogen, oxygen.
Number of satellites: None.

Meteor is a bright streak of light seen briefly in the sky. Meteors are often called *shooting stars* or *falling stars* because they look like stars falling from the sky. Meteors result when chunks of metallic or stony matter called *meteoroids* enter the earth's atmosphere from space. Air friction makes the meteoroid so hot it glows and creates a trail of hot glowing gases. Meteoroids that reach the earth before burning up are called *meteorites.*

Scientists estimate that as many as 200 million visible meteors occur in the earth's atmosphere every day. These and invisible meteorites are estimated to add more than 1,000 short tons (910 metric tons) daily to the earth's weight. We first see most of these meteors when they are about 65 miles (105 kilometers) above the earth. Air friction heats them and the air around them to about 4000° F. (2200° C), and they burn out at altitudes of 30 to 50 miles (48 to 80 kilometers).

All known meteoroids belong to the solar system of which the earth is a part. They travel in a variety of orbits and velocities about the sun. The faster ones move at about 26 miles (42 kilometers) a second. The earth travels at about 18 miles (29 kilometers) a second. When meteoroids meet the earth's atmosphere head-on, the combined velocity may reach about 44 miles (71 kilometers) a second. Those traveling in the same direction as the earth hit the atmosphere at much slower speeds. Meteors rarely blaze for more than a few seconds. But occasionally one leaves a shining trail that lasts as long as several minutes. Most of the meteors we see were originally no larger than a pinhead or a grain of sand.

Meteorites sometimes explode into fragments with a noise that can be heard far away when they strike the earth or its atmosphere. In 1908, the famous Tunguska meteorite crashed into the earth in Siberia. People as far as 466 miles (750 kilometers) away saw it in full daylight, and felt its blast at a distance of 50 miles (80 kilometers). The meteorite had a weight estimated at a few hundred tons. It scorched a 20-mile (32-kilometer) area and flattened forests. In 1947, a meteorite exploded into fragments over the Sikhote-Alin Mountains in eastern Siberia. It left more than 200 craters in the earth.

There are two kinds of meteorites, stony and iron. *Stony meteorites* are made up of many stony minerals mixed with particles of iron. Some resemble minerals

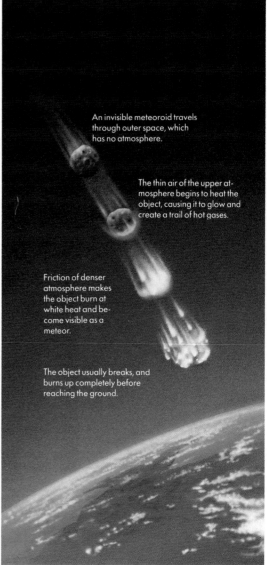

An invisible meteoroid travels through outer space, which has no atmosphere.

The thin air of the upper atmosphere begins to heat the object, causing it to glow and create a trail of hot gases.

Friction of denser atmosphere makes the object burn at white heat and become visible as a meteor.

The object usually breaks, and burns up completely before reaching the ground.

WORLD BOOK illustration by Rob Wood

A meteor appears in the sky whenever an object called a *meteoroid* hurtles into the earth's atmosphere from space.

from volcanoes. *Iron meteorites* consist chiefly of iron combined with nickel. They may have small amounts of cobalt, copper, phosphorus, carbon, and sulfur.

Meteor Crater Enterprises

The Meteor Crater of Arizona lies between the towns of Flagstaff and Winslow. Scientists believe that a meteorite struck the earth about 50,000 years ago and dug a hole about 4,150 feet (1,265 meters) across and 570 feet (174 meters) deep.

See **Meteor** in *World Book* for more information on Meteor showers and Meteorites.

WORLD BOOK photo

Students learn about the metric system by making various measurements with metric units.

Metric system

Metric system is a group of units used to make any kind of measurement, such as length, temperature, time, or weight. No other system of measurement ever used equals the metric system in simpleness. Scientists everywhere make measurements in metric units, and so do all other people in most countries.

The United States uses the *customary,* or *English,* system for most measurements. This system was developed in England from older units, beginning about the 1200's. In 1975, the U.S. Congress passed the Metric Conversion Act, which called for a voluntary changeover to the metric system. In the early 1970's, the Canadian government began to convert the nation to the metric system. All other major countries except these two were already using the metric system.

A group of French scientists created the metric system in the 1790's. The system has been revised several times. The official name of the present version is *Système International d'Unités* (International System of Units), usually known simply as *SI.* The term *metric* comes from the base unit of length in the system, the *meter,* for which the international spelling is *metre.*

Using the metric system

The scientists who created the metric system designed it to fit their needs. They made the system logical and exact. However, a nonscientist needs to know only a few metric units to make everyday measurements.

The metric system is simple to use for two reasons. First, it follows the decimal number system—that is, metric units increase or decrease in size by 10's. For example, a meter has 10 parts called *decimeters.* A decimeter

has 10 parts called *centimeters.* Units in the customary system have no single number relationship between them. For example, feet and yards are related by 3's, but feet and inches are related by 12's.

Also, the metric system has only 7 base units that make up all its measurements. The customary system has more than 20 base units for just its common measurements. Customary units used for special purposes add many more base units to that system.

The decimal arrangement. The metric system is a decimal system just as are the U.S. and Canadian money systems. In a decimal system, a unit is 10 times larger than the next smaller unit. For example, a meter equals 10 decimeters just as a dollar equals 10 dimes.

Most metric units have a prefix that tells the relationship of that unit to the base unit. These prefixes are the same no matter which base unit is used. This uniform system also simplifies metric measurement.

Greek prefixes are used to show multiples of a base unit. They make a base unit larger. For example, *hecto* means 100 times and *kilo* means 1,000 times. Latin prefixes are used to show the submultiples of the base unit. They make a base unit smaller. For example, *centi* means $\frac{1}{100}$ and *milli* means $\frac{1}{1,000}$.

See "The metric system at a glance" on the following pages.

See **Metric system** in *World Book* for more information on Using the metric system, Common measurements, and History.

The metric system at a glance

Length and distance

Length and distance measurements in the metric system are based on the meter. All units for length and distance are decimal fractions or multiples of the meter. Commonly used units include the millimeter, centimeter, meter, and kilometer.

One millimeter
About the thickness of a paper match

One centimeter
About the radius of a United States nickel

One meter
About the length of four volumes of *World Book* placed top-to-bottom

One kilometer
About the length of five city blocks

Surface or area

Surface or area measurements in the metric system are also based on the meter. But area is measured in square units. Common area units include the square centimeter, square meter, hectare (10,000 square meters), and square kilometer.

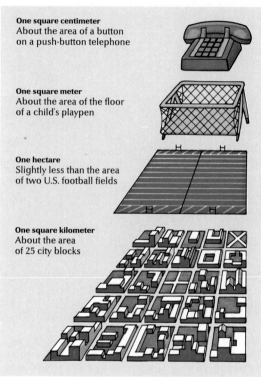

One square centimeter
About the area of a button on a push-button telephone

One square meter
About the area of the floor of a child's playpen

One hectare
Slightly less than the area of two U.S. football fields

One square kilometer
About the area of 25 city blocks

WORLD BOOK illustrations by George Suyeoka

Volume and capacity

Volume and capacity measurements in the metric system are based on the meter, but these measurements are made in cubic units. Common volume and capacity units include the cubic centimeter, liter (1,000 cubic centimeters), and cubic meter.

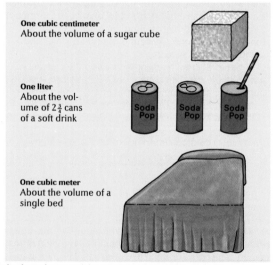

One cubic centimeter
About the volume of a sugar cube

One liter
About the volume of $2\frac{3}{4}$ cans of a soft drink

One cubic meter
About the volume of a single bed

The illustrations on these pages help show the size of the most common metric units. The metric conversion table will aid in the conversion of measurements into or out of the metric system.

Weight and mass

Weight measurement in the metric system is based on mass, the amount of matter an object contains. The metric unit for mass—and thus weight—is the gram. Commonly used weight units include the gram, kilogram, and metric ton (1,000 kilograms).

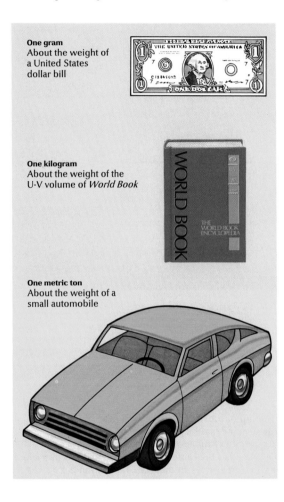

One gram
About the weight of a United States dollar bill

One kilogram
About the weight of the U-V volume of *World Book*

One metric ton
About the weight of a small automobile

Metric conversion table

When you know:	Multiply by:	To find:*
Length and distance		
inches (in.)	25	millimeters
feet (ft.)	30	centimeters
yards (yd.)	0.9	meters
miles (mi.)	1.6	kilometers
millimeters (mm)	0.04	inches
centimeters (cm)	0.4	inches
meters (m)	1.1	yards
kilometers (km)	0.6	miles
Surface or area		
square inches (sq. in.)	6.5	square centimeters
square feet (sq. ft.)	0.09	square meters
square yards (sq. yd.)	0.8	square meters
square miles (sq. mi.)	2.6	square kilometers
acres	0.4	hectares
square centimeters (cm²)	0.16	square inches
square meters (m²)	1.2	square yards
square kilometers (km²)	0.4	square miles
hectares (ha)	2.5	acres
Volume and capacity (Liquid)		
fluid ounces (fl. oz.)	30	milliliters
pints (pt.), U.S.	0.47	liters
pints (pt.), imperial	0.568	liters
quarts (qt.), U.S.	0.95	liters
quarts (qt.), imperial	1.137	liters
gallons (gal.), U.S.	3.8	liters
gallons (gal.), imperial	4.546	liters
milliliters (ml)	0.034	fluid ounces
liters (l)	2.1	pints, U.S.
liters (l)	1.76	pints, imperial
liters (l)	1.06	quarts, U.S.
liters (l)	0.88	quarts, imperial
liters (l)	0.26	gallons, U.S.
liters (l)	0.22	gallons, imperial
Weight and mass		
ounces (oz.)	28	grams
pounds (lb.)	0.45	kilograms
short tons	0.9	metric tons
grams (g)	0.035	ounces
kilograms (kg)	2.2	pounds
metric tons (t)	1.1	short tons
Temperature		
degrees Fahrenheit (° F.)	$\frac{5}{9}$ (after subtracting 32)	degrees Celsius
degrees Celsius (° C)	$\frac{9}{5}$ (then add 32)	degrees Fahrenheit

*Answers are approximations.

Temperature

Everyday temperature measurements in the metric system are made on the Celsius scale. This scale was once called the centigrade scale. Water freezes at 0° C and boils at 100° C.

Water at 0°C (ice) Water at 100°C (steam)

Metric prefixes

These prefixes can be added to most metric units to increase or decrease their size. For example, a kilometer equals 1,000 meters. Centi, kilo, and milli are the most commonly used prefixes.

Prefix	Symbol	Increase or decrease in unit	
exa (*EHK suh*)	E	1,000,000,000,000,000,000	(One quintillion)
peta (*PEH tuh*)	P	1,000,000,000,000,000	(One quadrillion)
tera (*TEHR uh*)	T	1,000,000,000,000	(One trillion)
giga (*JIHG uh*)	G	1,000,000,000	(One billion)
mega (*MEHG uh*)	M	1,000,000	(One million)
kilo (*KIHL uh*)	k	1,000	(One thousand)
hecto (*HEHK tuh*)	h	100	(One hundred)
deka (*DEHK uh*)	da	10	(Ten)
deci (*DEHS uh*)	d	0.1	(One-tenth)
centi (*SEHN tuh*)	c	0.01	(One-hundredth)
milli (*MIHL uh*)	m	0.001	(One-thousandth)
micro (*MY kroh*)	μ	0.000001	(One-millionth)
nano (*NAY nuh*)	n	0.000000001	(One-billionth)
pico (*PY koh*)	p	0.000000000001	(One-trillionth)
femto (*FEHM toh*)	f	0.000000000000001	(One-quadrillionth)
atto (*AT toh*)	a	0.000000000000000001	(One-quintillionth)

Hornblende

Feldspar

Quartz

Mica

Rocks are made of minerals. A chunk of granite, *left,* contains bits of hornblende, feldspar, quartz, and mica. Alone, these minerals appear as shown, *right.*

Mineral

Mineral is the most common solid material found on the earth. The earth's land and oceans all rest on a layer of rock made of minerals. All rocks found on the earth's surface also contain minerals. Even soil contains tiny pieces of minerals broken from rocks. Minerals are also found on our moon and on Mercury, Venus, and Mars.

Minerals include such common substances as rock salt and pencil "lead," and such rare ones as gold, silver, and gems. There are about 3,000 kinds of minerals, but only about 100 of them are common. Most of the others are harder to find than gold.

People use minerals to make many products. For example, graphite is used for pencil leads, and crayons and talcum powder are made from talc. Other products made from minerals include cement for building, fertilizers for farming, and chemicals for manufacturing.

Many people use the term *mineral* for any substance taken from the earth. Such substances include coal, petroleum, natural gas, and sand—none of which is a mineral. Certain substances in food and water, such as calcium, iron, and phosphorus, also are called minerals. But mineralogists, the scientists who study minerals, do not consider any of them minerals.

Mineralogists use the term *mineral* to mean a substance that has all of the four following features. (1) A mineral is found in nature. A natural diamond is a mineral, but a synthetic diamond is not. (2) A mineral is made up of substances that were never alive. Coal, petroleum, and natural gas are not minerals because they were formed from the remains of animals and plants. (3) A mineral has the same chemical makeup wherever it is found. Sand is not a mineral because samples from different places usually have different chemical makeups. (4) The atoms of a mineral are arranged in a regular pattern, and form solid units called *crystals.* The calcium and phosphorus found in milk are not minerals because they are dissolved in a liquid and are not crystals.

Minerals vary greatly in appearance and feel. On the following two pages, the terms *hardness* and *cleave* are used in describing the minerals shown. Mineralogists use a scale of from 1 to 10 to indicate hardness. The higher the number, the harder the mineral. A mineral cleaves if it splits into pieces that have flat surfaces. It does not cleave if it breaks into pieces with irregular surfaces.

See **Mineral** in *World Book* for more information on Identifying minerals, Inside minerals, and History of mineralogy.

Common minerals with nonmetallic luster

Azurite $Cu_3(CO_3)_2(OH)_2$. Blue. Hardness $3\frac{1}{2}$-4. Cleaves irregularly.

Cinnabar HgS. Dark red, earthy to metallic luster. Hardness 2-$2\frac{1}{2}$ Earthy form does not cleave.

Fluorite CaF_2. Green, blue, or purple cubes. Hardness 4. Cleaves in four directions.

Gypsum $Ca(SO_4)\cdot 2H_2O$. Colorless, white, gray, or yellow to brown. Hardness 2. Cleaves into plates.

Malachite $Cu_2(CO_3)(OH)_2$. Bright green. Hardness $3\frac{1}{2}$-4. Cleaves irregularly.

Muscovite $KAl_2(AlSi_3O_{10})(OH)_2$. Colorless. Hardness $2\frac{1}{2}$-3. Cleaves into tablets, sheets.

Potassium feldspar $K(AlSi_3O_8)$. White to pink. Leaves white streak. Hardness 6. Cleaves in two directions almost at right angles.

Quartz. SiO_2. Clear or tinted glassy crystals. Hardness 7. Does not cleave.

Rhodochrosite $Mn(CO_3)$. Pink. Hardness $3\frac{1}{2}$-4. Polyhedral cleavage.

Sulfur S. Yellow. Melts and burns with a match. Hardness $1\frac{1}{2}$-$2\frac{1}{2}$. Cleaves irregularly.

Talc $Mg_3(Si_4O_{10})(OH)_2$. Pale green. Feels greasy. Hardness 1-$1\frac{1}{2}$ Cleaves into tablets and sheets.

Wulfenite $Pb(MoO_4)$. Orange-yellow square tablets. Hardness 3. Cleaves into tablets.

Common minerals with metallic luster

Bornite Cu_5FeS_4. Copper-red with purple-blue tarnish. Hardness 3. Cleaves.

Chalcopyrite $CuFeS_2$. Brassy yellow. Leaves a green-black streak. Hardness $3\frac{1}{2}$-4. Does not cleave.

Copper Cu. Copper-red with brown tarnish. Hardness $2\frac{1}{2}$-3. Does not cleave.

Galena PbS. Bright metallic lead-gray cubes. Hardness $2\frac{1}{2}$. Cleaves to form cubes.

Gold Au. Yellow nuggets, grains, and flakes. Does not tarnish. Hardness $2\frac{1}{2}$-3. Does not cleave.

Graphite C. Steel-gray. Feels greasy. Hardness 1-2. Cleaves into tablets and sheets.

Magnetite Fe_3O_4. Black. Attracted by magnet and may act as magnet. Hardness $5\frac{1}{2}$-$6\frac{1}{2}$. Does not cleave.

Pyrite FeS_2. Pale brassy yellow. Leaves green- to brown-black streak. Hardness 6-$6\frac{1}{2}$. Does not cleave.

Pyrrhotite FeS. Bronze-yellow. Weakly attracted to magnet. Hardness $3\frac{1}{2}$-$4\frac{1}{2}$. Does not cleave.

Rutile TiO_2. Red to black with gem-like luster. Hardness 6-$6\frac{1}{2}$. Cleaves.

Silver Ag. Silver-white (above, as flecks in barite), tarnishing to black. Hardness $2\frac{1}{2}$-3. Does not cleave.

Stibnite Sb_2S_3. Gray columns with black tarnish. Hardness 2. Cleaves in one direction.

Molecule is one of the basic units of matter. It is the smallest particle into which a substance can be divided and still have the chemical properties of the original substance. If the substance were divided further, only atoms of chemical elements would remain. For example, a drop of water contains billions of water molecules. If the drop could be divided until only a single water molecule remained, that final drop would still have all the chemical properties of water. But if the water molecule were divided, only atoms of the elements hydrogen and oxygen would remain.

Molecules are made up of atoms held together in certain arrangements. Every atom consists of a positively charged nucleus surrounded by negatively charged electrons. In a molecule, there are an equal number of positive and negative charges.

Scientists use chemical formulas to show the composition of molecules. For example, a water molecule consists of two hydrogen atoms and one oxygen atom, and it has the formula H_2O. The size of a molecule depends on the size and number of its atoms. Molecules are made up of from two atoms to thousands of atoms. A molecule that consists of only two atoms, such as nitric oxide (NO), is called a *diatomic* molecule. A molecule that is made up of three atoms, such as water, is called a *triatomic* molecule.

Almost all gases, most common liquids, and many solids consist of molecules. But some substances are made up of different units called *ions* (atoms or groups of atoms with either a positive or a negative charge). These substances are called *ionic substances.*

Salts are examples of ionic substances. For example, sodium chloride, common table salt, consists of positive sodium ions and negative chloride ions. Electric forces among the ions hold the salt crystals together in a regu-

lar framework. Metals are also different from molecular substances. In addition to positive ions, metals consist of a large number of electrons that move about freely throughout the metal.

Molecules and matter. Molecules are held together in a group by forces called *Van der Waals forces.* These forces are usually weaker than those that hold the molecule itself together. The force between molecules depends on how far apart they are. When two molecules are widely separated, they attract each other. When they come very close together, they repel each other.

In a solid, the molecules are so arranged that the forces that attract and repel are balanced. The molecules vibrate about these positions of balance, but they do not move to different parts of the solid. As the temperature of a solid is raised, the molecules vibrate more strongly. When the Van der Waals forces can no longer hold the molecules in place, the solid melts and becomes a liquid.

In a liquid, the molecules move about easily, but they still have some force on one another. These forces are strong enough to form a filmlike surface on a liquid and prevent it from flying apart. Certain organic compounds called *liquid crystals* have properties of both liquids and solids. Within a particular temperature range, such a compound flows like a liquid, but has a more ordered molecular arrangement. Its molecules line up side by side and form tiny groups or clusters that slide past one another in certain directions.

In a gas, the molecules move about so fast that the attractive forces have little effect on them. When two molecules in a gas collide with each other, the repelling force sends them apart again. Therefore, gas molecules fill a container completely, because they move freely through all the space available.

Diagrams of some common molecules   Scientists study chemical compounds to learn how many atoms of each element are in the molecules and how these atoms are joined to each other. With this information, diagrams of molecules can be drawn with balls representing the individual atoms.

WORLD BOOK diagram

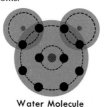

A molecule of water forms when two atoms of hydrogen and one of oxygen, *above,* join together in sharing their electrons, *below.* The electrons fill the vacancies in all the atoms.

Water Molecule

A carbon dioxide molecule has two oxygen atoms and a carbon atom.

An ammonia molecule has three hydrogen atoms and a nitrogen atom.

A butane molecule is a chain of carbon atoms with hydrogen atoms.

Giant snail

Mark Boulton, Bruce Coleman Ltd.

Flame scallop

Alex Kerstitch

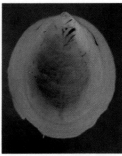

Robert Robertson

Monoplacophoran

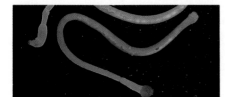

Robert Robertson

Aplacophoran

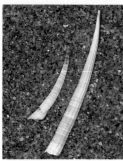

Jeff Foott, Bruce Colman Ltd.

Lined chiton

Jane Burton, Bruce Colman Ltd.

Octopus

Frieder Sauer, Bruce Coleman Ltd.

Tooth shell

Mollusk, *MAHL uhsk,* is a soft-bodied animal that has no bones. Snails, slugs, clams, mussels, oysters, squids, and octopuses are mollusks. Most mollusks have a hard shell that protects their soft bodies. Some, such as cuttlefish and squids, have no outside shell. A special shell grows inside their bodies. This shell is called a *cuttlebone* in cuttlefish and a *pen* in squids. A few kinds of mollusks, including octopuses and certain slugs, have no shell at all. For more information on mollusk shells and how they are formed, see **Shell** in *World Book.*

All mollusks have a skinlike organ called a *mantle* that makes the shell. The edges of the mantle release liquid shell materials and add them to the shell as the mollusk grows. In mollusks with no outside shell, the mantle forms a tough cover around the body organs.

Mollusks live in most parts of the world. Some kinds of mollusks live in the deepest parts of oceans. Others are found on the wooded slopes of high mountains. Still others live in hot, dry deserts. Wherever mollusks live, they must keep their bodies moist to stay alive. Most land mollusks live in damp places such as under leaves or in soil.

The importance of mollusks. Mollusks are used mainly for food. People in many parts of the world eat mollusks every day. Most Americans do not eat them nearly so often. The most popular kinds used as food in the United States are clams, oysters, and scallops.

Mollusk shells are made into many useful products, including pearl buttons, jewelry, and various souvenir items. Perhaps the best known mollusk products are the pearls made by pearl oysters.

Some mollusks are harmful to people. Certain small, freshwater snails of the tropics carry worms that cause an often fatal disease called *schistosomiasis.* Shipworm clams drill into rope and wooden boats and wharves, and cause millions of dollars worth of damage a year.

Kinds of mollusks. Mollusks make up the largest group of water animals. There are about 100,000 known kinds of living mollusks, and scientists find about 1,000 new species every year. The fossils of about 100,000 other species of mollusks have also been found.

The mollusks make up a *phylum* (major division) of the animal kingdom. The scientific name of the phylum is *Mollusca,* a Latin word meaning *soft-bodied.*

See **Mollusk** in *World Book* for more information on Kinds of mollusks.

Francisco Erize, Bruce Coleman Ltd.; E. R. Degginger

Monkeys live in many kinds of environments. Spider monkeys, *left,* dwell in forests of Central and South America. They swing and run swiftly among the tree branches. Baboons, *right,* roam African *savannas* (grasslands with scattered trees). They feed on the ground and sleep in caves or trees.

Monkey is one of many kinds of small, lively mammals that rank among the most intelligent animals. Scientists classify monkeys—together with human beings, apes, lemurs, and lorises—in the order Primates, the highest order of mammals. The intelligence of monkeys enables them to adapt to a broad range of environments. Their liveliness makes them favorites in zoos. Because of the similarities between monkeys and humans, scientists have used monkeys in research on human behavior and disease. For example, a blood substance called the *Rh factor* was discovered during experiments with the rhesus monkey (in *World Book,* see **Rh factor**).

There are about 200 species of monkeys. Most of them live in tropical regions in Central and South America, Africa, and Asia. Most species live in forests and some spend their entire life in the trees. Some African and Asian species live in *savannas* (grasslands with scattered trees) and spend most of their life on the ground. But even these monkeys sleep in trees—or on steep cliffs—for protection at night. All monkeys live together in various kinds of groups.

Monkeys vary greatly in size. The smallest species, the pygmy marmoset, measures only about 6 inches (15 centimeters) long, not including the tail. The mandrill, one of the largest species of monkeys, may grow as long as 32 inches (81 centimeters), not including the tail.

Scientists classify monkeys into two major groups, New World monkeys and Old World monkeys. New World monkeys live in Central and South America, and Old World monkeys are found in Africa and Asia. The two groups differ in several ways. For example, New World monkeys have nostrils spaced widely apart. The nostrils of Old World monkeys are close together. Most kinds of New World monkeys have 36 teeth. Old World monkeys have 32 teeth, as do humans. Some species of New World monkeys can grasp objects with their tail,

but no Old World monkey is able to do so.

New World monkeys have a remarkable variety of sizes, shapes, and colors. Scientists divide them into two main groups: (1) marmosets and tamarins; and (2) all other New World species, including capuchins, dourou-coulis, howlers, spider monkeys, squirrel monkeys, woolly monkeys, and woolly spider monkeys. All New World monkeys are *arboreal*—that is, they live in trees.

Old World monkeys include baboons, colobus monkeys, guenons, langurs, and macaques. Some Old World monkeys, including colobus monkeys and langurs, are *leaf-eating monkeys* and live mainly in trees. Many other Old World monkeys live on the ground. Among the monkeys that live on the ground, the males may be twice as large as the females.

Many people believe that apes—chimpanzees, gibbons, gorillas, and orangutans—are monkeys. But monkeys and apes differ in several ways. For example, apes are more intelligent than monkeys. Most monkeys have a tail, but none of the apes do. Monkeys are smaller than most apes. Apes are expert climbers. Monkeys generally run, jump, and leap among tree branches.

Human activities have greatly reduced the number of monkeys throughout the world. Some people hunt monkeys for food. Others catch them for pets. The clearing of land for agricultural, housing, and industrial developments has reduced the amount of living space available to monkeys. As a result, a number of species of New World and Old World monkeys are threatened with extinction.

The body of a monkey

All monkeys, including those that live on the ground, are the descendants of monkeys that live in trees. As a result, all monkeys have a body primarily suited for living in and moving through trees. For example, monkeys

The skeleton of a guenon monkey

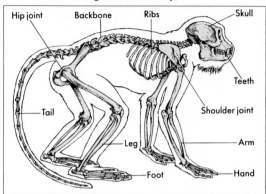

WORLD BOOK illustration by John D. Dawson

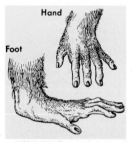

WORLD BOOK illustration by Marion Pahl

A monkey's hands and feet both can grasp objects. The big toe of a monkey looks and moves like a thumb.

Shelly Grossman, Woodfin Camp, Inc.

A monkey's tail provides balance for running and jumping. A spider monkey, *above,* can swing by its tail.

have long arms and legs that help them climb, leap, and run. They also can use their hands and feet to grasp objects—including tree branches. Most species have a long tail that helps them keep their balance. Some New World monkeys can use their tail like a hand to grasp branches and food while moving through the trees.

Head. Monkeys, unlike many other mammals, depend more on their eyes than their nose to gather information about their surroundings. They have large eyes that face forward. They can see in depth and distinguish colors. Their eyes help them judge distances and tell the size, shape, and ripeness of food.

Some monkeys, including baboons, mandrills, and sakis, have large, heavy jaws and eat grass and leaves. Smaller monkeys, such as marmosets and squirrel monkeys, have smaller, lighter jaws. They eat mostly fruit and insects. Many kinds of Old World monkeys have cheek pouches much like those of hamsters and squirrels. The pouches enable the monkeys to store food temporarily. No New World monkey has these cheek pouches.

Arms and legs. Monkeys usually walk and run on all fours, either on tree branches or on the ground. Most species have legs that are slightly longer than their arms. Many kinds of monkeys can stand and even run on their legs, but only for a short period of time. Monkeys usually stand or run on their legs when carrying food, peering over high grass, or threatening enemies or members of the group.

Hands and feet. Old World monkeys have *opposable* thumbs—that is, the thumb can be placed opposite any of the other fingers. This enables a monkey to grasp small food items. Most kinds of New World monkeys have thumbs that are only partly opposable. Their thumbs also do not move so freely as those of Old World monkeys. Two kinds of New World monkeys— spider monkeys and woolly spider monkeys—have only tiny thumbs or no thumbs at all. Among Old World monkeys, colobus monkeys have no thumbs.

The feet of most monkeys are larger and more powerful than their hands. All monkeys have five toes on each foot. The big toes look and function much like thumbs, giving the monkey an extra pair of grasping "hands." Marmosets and tamarins have claws on their fingers and toes, except for their big toes, which have a nail. All other kinds of monkeys have flat or flattish nails on all their fingers and toes.

Tail. Most monkeys that live on the ground have a shorter tail than do most that live in trees. Arboreal monkeys may have a tail longer than their body. They use their tail for balancing on tree branches. They also use it as an *air brake*—that is, to slow themselves down when they leap from branch to branch. Some New World monkeys, including howlers, spider monkeys, and woolly monkeys, can grasp objects with their tail. The tail of such monkeys has bare skin at the end. The tail of other monkeys is completely covered with hair.

See **Monkey** in *World Book* for more information on The life of a monkey.

R. C. Hermes, NAS   Lanceau, Agence de Presse Jacana

New World and Old World monkeys can be identified by their noses. The nostrils of New World monkeys, such as the woolly monkey, *left,* are widely spaced. Those of Old World monkeys, such as the mangabey, *right,* are close together.

Where monkeys live

The yellow areas of this map show the parts of the world in which monkeys live. Most species of monkeys live in the tropics.

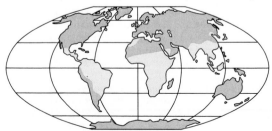

Douc langur
Pygathrix nemaeus nemaeus
Found in Laos and Vietnam
and on the island of Hainan
Body length: 22 to 32 inches
(56 to 81 centimeters)*

De Brazza's guenon
Cercopithecus neglectus
Found in central and eastern
African forests
Body length: 16 to 24 inches
(41 to 61 centimeters)*

Red uakari
Cacajao rubicundus
Found in eastern Peru and
northwestern Brazil
Body length: 14 to 19 inches
(36 to 48 centimeters)*

Woolly monkey
Lagothrix lagothricha
Found in the upper Amazon River
basin of South America
Body length: 15 to 23 inches
(38 to 58 centimeters)*

Douroucouli
Aotus trivirgatus
Found in forests of most of
South America and Panama
Body length: 10 to 19 inches
(25 to 48 centimeters)*

Patas monkey
Erythrocebus patas
Found in African grasslands
from Tanzania northward
Body length: 23 to 29 inches
(58 to 74 centimeters)*

Red colobus
Colobus badius
Found in tropical rain forests
of Africa
Body length: 18 to 24 inches
(46 to 61 centimeters)*

Proboscis monkey
Nasalis larvatus
Found in Borneo
Body length: 21 to 30 inches
(53 to 76 centimeters)*

*not including the tail

WORLD BOOK illustrations by Helmut Diller

NASA

The moon was photographed by the Apollo 11 astronauts during their return trip to the earth. They had made the first landing on the moon. The astronauts landed on the Sea of Tranquility, a large, dark-colored lava plain. The highland areas of the moon are lighter in color.

Moon

Moon is the earth's nearest neighbor in space. In 1969, this huge natural satellite of the earth became the first object in space to be visited by human beings.

The moon is the brightest object in the night sky, but it gives off no light of its own. When the moon "shines," it is *reflecting* (casting back) light from the sun. On some nights, the moon looks like a gleaming silver globe. On others, it appears as a thin slice of light. But the moon does not change its size or shape. Its appearance seems to change as different parts of it are lighted by the sun.

The moon travels around the earth once about every $27\frac{1}{3}$ days. The average distance between the centers of the earth and the moon is 238,857 miles (384,403 kilometers). A rocket journey from the earth to the moon and back takes about six days.

Because the moon is relatively close to the earth, it seems much larger than the stars and about the same size as the sun. The moon measures about 2,160 miles (3,476 kilometers) across. This distance is about a fourth the diameter of the earth and 400 times smaller than that of the sun. If the moon were seen next to the earth, it would look like a tennis ball next to a basketball.

The earth is not the only planet with a moon. For example, Jupiter has 16 known satellites. The earth's moon is the sixth largest of the more than 40 natural satellites of the planets. For more information on natural satellites, see the separate planet articles in *World Book.*

The moon has no life of any kind. Compared with the earth, it has changed little over billions of years. The moon has no air, wind, or water. On the moon, the sky is black—even during the day—and the stars are always visible. At night, the rocky surface becomes colder than any place on the earth. In the day, the temperature of the rocks is slightly higher than that of boiling water.

Through the centuries, people have gazed at the moon, worshiped it, and studied it. The long-time dream of traveling to the moon became history on July 20, 1969, when astronaut Neil A. Armstrong of the United States set foot on it.

Space flights and moon landings have provided many facts about the moon. Moon exploration has also helped solve many mysteries about the earth, the sun, and the planets. For more information on moon exploration, see the article on **Space travel.**

NASA

NASA

The far side of the moon has a rugged surface. The large crater in the center of the photograph is International Astronomical Union Crater No. 308. It is about 50 miles (80 kilometers) wide. The lunar footprint at the right was made by Edwin E. Aldrin, Jr., an Apollo 11 astronaut.

The moon at a glance

Age: About 4,600,000,000 (4.6 billion) years.
Distance from the earth: *Shortest*—221,456 miles (356,399 kilometers); *Greatest*—252,711 miles (406,699 kilometers); *Mean*—238,857 miles (384,403 kilometers).
Diameter: About 2,160 miles (3,476 kilometers).
Circumference: About 6,790 miles (10,927 kilometers).
Surface area: About 14,670,000 square miles (38,000,000 square kilometers).
Rotation period: 27 days, 7 hours, 43 minutes.
Revolution period around the earth: 27 days, 7 hours, 43 minutes.
Average speed around the earth: 2,300 miles (3,700 kilometers) per hour.
Length of day and night: About 15 earth-days each.
Temperature at equator: *Sun at zenith over maria,* 260° F. (127° C); *Lunar night on maria,* −280° F. (−173° C).
Surface gravity: About $\frac{1}{6}$ that of the earth.
Escape velocity: $1\frac{1}{2}$ miles (2.4 kilometers) per second.
Mass: $\frac{1}{81}$ that of the earth.
Volume: $\frac{1}{50}$ that of the earth.
Atmosphere: Little or none.

WORLD BOOK diagram

The diameter of the moon is about 2,160 miles (3,476 kilometers), or about a fourth of the earth's diameter. If the moon were placed on top of the United States, it would extend almost from San Francisco to Cleveland.

The orbit of the moon. The moon travels around the earth in an *elliptical* (oval shaped) path called an *orbit.* One such trip around the earth is called a *revolution.* The moon moves at an average speed of about 2,300 miles (3,700 kilometers) per hour along its 1.4-million-mile (2.3-million-kilometer) orbit.

The moon also travels with the earth as the earth circles the sun every 365¼ days, an earth year. The moon actually moves from west to east in the sky. But it seems to move from east to west as it rises and sets because the earth spins much faster than the moon revolves around the earth.

Because the moon's orbit is oval, the moon is not always the same distance from the earth. The point where the moon comes closest to the earth is 221,456 miles (356,399 kilometers) away. This point is called the moon's *perigee.* The moon's farthest point from the earth is 252,711 miles (406,699 kilometers) away. This point is the moon's *apogee.*

The gravitational pull of the earth keeps the moon in its orbit. If the earth or its gravitational force were to suddenly disappear, the moon would no longer orbit the earth. But the moon would still move in orbit around the sun.

Scientists measure the moon's revolution around the earth in *synodic months* and *sidereal months.* A synodic month—which equals about 29½ days—is the period from one new moon to the next new moon. It is the time that the moon takes to revolve around the earth in relation to the sun. If the moon started on its orbit from a spot exactly between the earth and the sun, it would return to almost the same place in about 29½ days. A synodic month equals a full day on the moon. This *lunar day* is divided into about two weeks of light and about two weeks of darkness.

A sidereal month—about 27⅓ days—is the time the moon takes to make one trip around the earth in relation to the stars. If the moon's revolution were to begin on a line with a certain star, it would return to the same position about 27⅓ days later.

A synodic month is longer than a sidereal month because the earth travels around the sun while the moon travels around the earth. By the time the moon has made one revolution around the earth, the earth has revolved $\frac{1}{13}$ of the way around the sun. Therefore, the moon has to travel slightly farther to be in the same position in relation to the sun.

Rotation. The moon rotates completely on its *axis* (an imaginary line through its north and south poles) only once during each trip around the earth. The moon rotates from west to east, the same direction that it travels around the earth. At its equator, the moon rotates at a speed of about 10 miles (16 kilometers) per hour. When you look up at the moon, you always see the same side.

How the moon gets its light

The moon gives off no light of its own. It shines by reflecting sunlight. Like the earth, half of the moon is always lighted by the sun's direct rays, and the other half is always in shadow. At times during the month, only a small slice of the moon's side that faces the earth is in full sunshine. The moon appears as a thin, bright *crescent. Earthshine* (sunlight reflected by the earth), dimly lights the moon's "dark" side when it faces the earth. Because the moon is made up chiefly of dark gray rocks and dust, it reflects only 10 per cent of the light it receives.

WORLD BOOK diagram

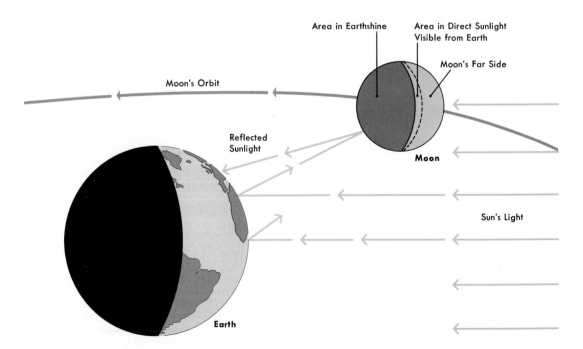

Area in Earthshine
Area in Direct Sunlight Visible from Earth
Moon's Far Side
Moon's Orbit
Reflected Sunlight
Moon
Sun's Light
Earth

The moon is held in this position by gravitational forces. We know that the moon is rotating because we can see only one side of it. If the moon did not rotate, we would be able to see its entire surface.

Sometimes we can see a short distance around the *limb* (edge) of the moon. The moon seems to swing from side to side and nod up and down during each revolution. These apparent motions are called *librations*. They are caused by slight changes in the moon's speed of revolution and by a five-degree tilt of the moon's orbit to the orbit of the earth. At different times, the librations enable us to see a total of 59 per cent of the moon's surface from the earth. The other 41 per cent of the moon's surface can never be seen from the earth. The moon's far side was a complete mystery until Oct. 7, 1959, when a Soviet rocket orbited the moon and sent back a few pictures of one far side area to the earth. On Dec. 24, 1968, the Apollo 8 astronauts became the first people to see the far side.

The phases of the moon. During a synodic month, we can see the moon "change" from a slim crescent to a full circle and back again. These apparent changes in the moon's shape and size are actually different conditions of lighting called *phases*. They are caused by changes in the amount of sunlight reflected by the moon toward the earth. The moon seems to change shape because we see different parts of its sunlit surface as it orbits the earth. Like the earth, half the moon is always lighted by the sun's rays except during eclipses. Sometimes the far side of the moon is in full sunlight even though it is out of view.

When the moon is between the sun and the earth, its sunlit side—the far side—is turned away from the earth. Astronomers call this darkened phase of the moon a *new moon*. In the new moon phase, the side of the moon that faces the earth is dimly lighted by *earthshine* (sunlight that is reflected from the earth to the moon).

A day after a new moon, a thin slice of light appears along the moon's eastern edge. The line between the sunlit part of the moon's face and its dark part is called the *terminator*. Each day, more of the moon's sunlit side is seen as the terminator moves from east to west. After about seven days, we can see half of a full moon. This half-circle shape is half of the moon's side that is exposed to sunlight and is the part that can be seen from the earth. This phase is called the *first quarter.*

About seven days after the first quarter, the moon has moved to a point where the earth is between it and the sun. We can now see the entire sunlit side of the moon. This phase is called *full moon*. A full moon seems bright on a clear night. But a whole sky of full moons would be only about a fifth as bright as the sun.

Why the moon has phases

The moon seems to change shape from day to day as it goes through *phases*. The moon changes from *new moon* to *full moon* and back again every 29 ½ days. The phases are caused by the moon's orbit around the earth as the earth and moon travel around the sun. Half of the moon is always in sunlight, but varying amounts of the lighted side are visible from the earth. As the moon and earth move along their orbits, more of the sunlit part is seen until it shines as a full moon. Then less and less of the sunlit part is seen until the dark new moon returns.

WORLD BOOK diagram

● Earth   ● Moon

Moon's Orbit Around the Earth

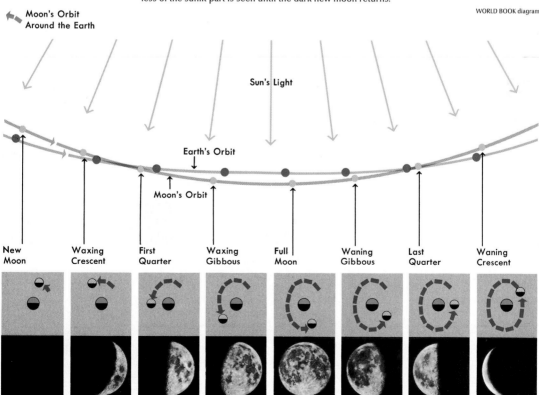

Sun's Light

Earth's Orbit

Moon's Orbit

New Moon | Waxing Crescent | First Quarter | Waxing Gibbous | Full Moon | Waning Gibbous | Last Quarter | Waning Crescent

About seven days after full moon, we again see half of a full moon. This phase is called the *last,* or *third,* quarter. After another week, the moon returns to a point between the earth and the sun for the new moon phase.

As the moon changes from new moon to full moon, it is said to be *waxing.* During the period from full moon back to new moon, it is said to be *waning.* When the moon appears smaller than half of a full moon, it is called *crescent.* When it looks larger than half of a full moon, yet is not a full moon, it is called *gibbous.*

The moon rises and sets at different times. In the new moon phase, it rises above the horizon with the sun in the east and travels close to the sun across the sky. With each passing day, the moon rises an average of about 50 minutes later and drops about 12 degrees farther behind in relation to the sun.

By the end of a week—at the first quarter phase—the moon rises at about noon and sets at about midnight. In another week—at full moon—it rises as the sun sets and sets as the sun rises. At last quarter, it rises at about midnight and sets at about noon. A week later—back at new moon—the moon and the sun rise together in the east.

Eclipses. The light of the sun causes both the earth and the moon to throw shadows into space. When a full moon passes through the earth's shadow, we see an *eclipse* of the moon. During a lunar eclipse, the moon is a dark reddish color. It is faintly lighted by red rays from the sun that have been *refracted* (bent) by the earth's atmosphere.

During another kind of eclipse, the new moon passes directly between the earth and the sun. When part or all of the sun is hidden by the moon, we see a *solar eclipse* (an eclipse of the sun). Solar eclipses occur where the shadow of the moon passes across the earth. The apparent size of the sun and the moon just happens by accident to be nearly equal. See **Eclipse.**

The moon and tides. Since ancient times, man has watched the rising and falling of the water level along the seashore. Just as the earth's gravity pulls on the moon, the moon's gravity pulls on the earth and its large bodies of water. The moon's gravity pulls up the water directly below the moon. On the other side of the earth, the moon pulls the solid body of the earth away from the water. As a result, two bulges called *high tides* are formed on the oceans and seas. As the earth turns, these tidal bulges travel from east to west. Every place along the seashore has two high tides and two low tides daily.

> See **Moon** in *World Book* for more information on What the moon is like, How the moon was formed, and The moon in history.

Why we see only one side of the moon

When we look at the moon, we always see the same side. This is because the moon turns once on its axis in the same time that it circles the earth. Astronomers call the moon's motion *synchronous* rotation. The force of gravity always keeps the same side of the moon toward the earth. This diagram shows why one side of the moon can never be seen from the earth. As the moon turns, a moon landmark such as a crater, shown as a red dot, stays in about the same position during the month. Sometimes the landmark is hidden in the dark part of the moon facing the earth. But because it does not move to the side of the moon opposite the earth, we know that we are seeing only one side of the moon. If the moon did not turn in its journey around the earth, the landmark would gradually seem to move across the visible surface of the moon. It would disappear around the moon's western edge and return to view on the moon's eastern edge about 14 days later.

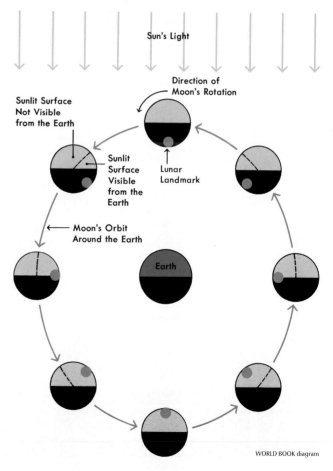

Sun's Light

Direction of Moon's Rotation

Sunlit Surface Not Visible from the Earth

Sunlit Surface Visible from the Earth

Lunar Landmark

← Moon's Orbit Around the Earth

Earth

WORLD BOOK diagram

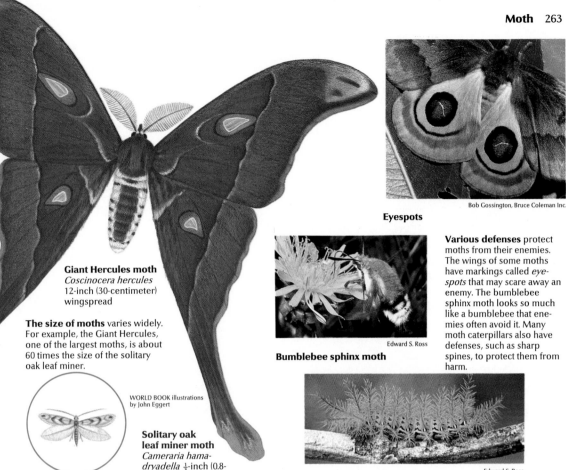

Eyespots

Bob Gossington, Bruce Coleman Inc.

Giant Hercules moth
Coscinocera hercules
12-inch (30-centimeter)
wingspread

The size of moths varies widely.
For example, the Giant Hercules,
one of the largest moths, is about
60 times the size of the solitary
oak leaf miner.

WORLD BOOK illustrations
by John Eggert

**Solitary oak
leaf miner moth**
*Cameraria hama-
dryadella* $\frac{1}{3}$-inch (0.8-
centimeter) wingspread

Various defenses protect
moths from their enemies.
The wings of some moths
have markings called *eyespots* that may scare away an
enemy. The bumblebee
sphinx moth looks so much
like a bumblebee that enemies often avoid it. Many
moth caterpillars also have
defenses, such as sharp
spines, to protect them from
harm.

Bumblebee sphinx moth

Edward S. Ross

Caterpillar with spines

Edward S. Ross

Moth is any of a wide variety of insects closely related
to butterflies. All butterflies and almost all moths have
two pairs of wings—a pair of large front wings and a
pair of smaller hind wings. Moths and butterflies together form the insect group *Lepidoptera.* The name
Lepidoptera comes from two Greek words: *lepis,* meaning *scale;* and *pteron,* meaning *wing.* The name refers to
the fine, powdery scales that cover the wings of butterflies and moths.

Moths live throughout the world, except in the
oceans. They inhabit steamy jungles near the equator,
and they have even been found on icecaps in the Arctic.
Moths vary greatly in size. The largest moths are the
Giant Hercules of Australia and the Giant Owl Moth of
South America. They have a wingspread of about 12
inches (30 centimeters). The smallest moths have wingspreads of about $\frac{1}{8}$ inch (3 millimeters). These moths belong to a group called *leaf miners.*

Like butterflies, moths change in form as they develop into adults. Only the adult form of a moth has
wings. Female adult moths lay many tiny eggs that hatch
into wormlike caterpillars. A caterpillar eats almost constantly, and it grows rapidly. After it is fully grown, the
caterpillar forms a shell-like covering around itself.
Within this shell, the insect goes through its final
changes. Eventually, the insect breaks out of the shell as
a fully developed adult moth.

Moths differ from butterflies in a number of important ways. For example, most moths fly at dusk or at
night. The majority of butterflies fly during the day.
Among most moths, the hind wing is attached to the
front wing by a hook or set of hooks, called a *frenulum.*
Butterflies lack a frenulum. In addition, most butterflies
have antennae that widen at the ends and resemble
clubs. The antennae of most moths are not club-shaped.

Some moths are regarded as pests because their caterpillars feed on and damage trees, food plants, or
clothing. However, many others are valuable to people
and nature. People use caterpillars of certain moths to
produce silk. Many adult moths help pollinate flowers.

The bodies of moths

A moth's body, like that of any insect, has three main
parts. They are: (1) the head, (2) the thorax, and (3) the abdomen.

The head bears the moth's eyes, antennae, and
mouthparts. These structures are the insect's most important sense organs.

Eyes. Moths have two large *compound eyes* on each
side of the head. These eyes consist of many separate
lenses, each of which supplies a complete image of part
of the moth's surroundings. Compound eyes are specially designed to help an insect spot movements, such
as the approach of an enemy.

The anatomy of a moth

A moth's body has three main parts: (1) head, (2) thorax, and (3) abdomen. The head bears the major sense organs, the thorax supports the wings and legs, and the abdomen contains various internal organs. The drawings below show external and internal features of a typical female moth.

WORLD BOOK illustrations by Zorica Dabich

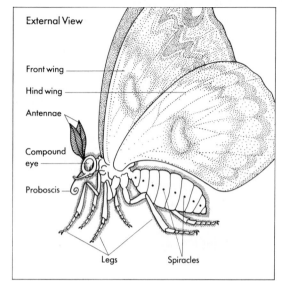

External View

Front wing

Hind wing

Antennae

Compound eye

Proboscis

Legs

Spiracles

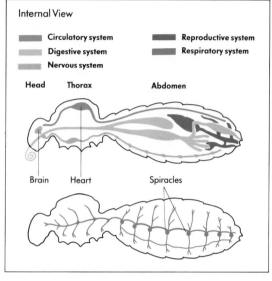

Internal View

- ▬ Circulatory system
- ░ Digestive system
- ▓ Nervous system
- ▬ Reproductive system
- ▬ Respiratory system

Head   Thorax   Abdomen

Brain   Heart   Spiracles

The life cycle of a moth

A moth goes through four stages of development: (1) egg, (2) larva, (3) pupa, and (4) adult. A female moth lays many tiny eggs, which hatch into larvae, or caterpillars. A caterpillar spends its life eating and growing. When fully grown, it forms a shell and becomes a pupa. The insect goes through its final changes within the shell. It emerges from the shell as an adult. These photos show stages in the development of a *Cecropia* moth.

Lyna M. Stone, Bruce Coleman Inc.
Female laying eggs

E. R. Degginger, Bruce Coleman Inc.
Larva

© Michael Lustbader, Photo Researchers
Pupal shell and adult

Antennae. Two antennae stick out from between a moth's eyes. Moths use their antennae chiefly to smell. The antennae are extremely sensitive to chemicals in the air. Female moths release chemicals called *pheromones* into the air to attract males for mating. The antennae of a male moth can "smell" a female as far as 5 miles (8 kilometers) away.

Mouthparts. Adult moths feed mostly on liquids, such as flower nectar and the juice of fruits. They suck up their food through a long, hollow tongue called a *proboscis*. The proboscis coils under the head when not in use.

The thorax forms the middle section of a moth's body. Attached to the thorax are the legs and wings of the insect.

Legs. Adult moths have three pairs of legs. Each leg consists of five segments. Joints connect the segments. Taste organs grow at the tips of the legs.

Wings. Two membranes form each of a moth's wings. A network of hollow tubes called *veins* supports the wings. Tiny scales cover the membranes and give the wings their colors and patterns. The females of some species lack wings and cannot fly.

The abdomen contains the organs of reproduction and the major organs of digestion. Tiny holes called *spiracles* on the sides of the abdomen lead into the insect's respiratory system. Oxygen enters the moth's body through the spiracles.

See **Moth** in *World Book* for more information on the following topics:

- •The life cycle of moths
- •Migration
- •Defenses against enemies
- •The importance of moths
- •Kinds of moths

© R. J. Rose, Miller Services

Majestic mountain peaks tower above their surroundings. These mountains, part of the rugged Rocky Mountain system, rise along the Athabaska River in Alberta, Canada.

Mountain

Mountain is a landform that stands much higher than its surroundings. Mountains generally are larger than hills, but what people call *hills* in one place may be higher than what people call *mountains* elsewhere. For example, the Black Hills of South Dakota and Wyoming stand higher above their surroundings than do the Ouachita Mountains of Arkansas and Oklahoma.

Mountains generally have steep slopes and sharp or slightly rounded peaks or ridges. Many geologists consider an elevated area a mountain only if it includes two or more zones of climate and plant life at different altitudes. In general, the climate becomes cooler and wetter with increasing elevation. In most parts of the world, a mountain must rise about 2,000 feet (600 meters) above its surroundings to include two climate zones.

A mountain may be a single peak, such as a lone volcano, or it may be part of a mountain range. A group of mountain ranges forms a mountain system. The Pacific Mountain System, for example, is made up of the Cascade Range and several other mountain ranges along the west coast of North America.

Mountains occur in the ocean as well as on land. Many islands are mountains on the ocean floor whose peaks rise above the surface of the water. The world's longest mountain system—the Mid-Atlantic Ridge—is almost totally underwater. It stretches more than 10,000 miles (16,000 kilometers) from the North Atlantic Ocean nearly to Antarctica. Some of the ridge's highest peaks form such islands as Iceland and the Azores.

The height of a mountain is usually expressed as the distance that its peak rises above sea level. Mount Everest, long considered the highest mountain in the world, rises 29,028 feet (8,848 meters) above sea level, according to a 1954 survey. Later surveys have suggested new

heights for Mount Everest, as well as for K2, which is also called Mount Godwin Austen or Dapsang. The surveys suggest that K2 may be a few feet higher than Mount Everest. But scientists will not conclude that K2 is higher until both mountains have been remeasured.

Mauna Kea, a volcano on the island of Hawaii, is the world's highest island peak. It stands 13,796 feet (4,205 meters) above sea level. Measured from its base on the floor of the Pacific Ocean, however, Mauna Kea is an astounding 33,476 feet (10,203 meters)—more than 6 miles (10 kilometers)—tall.

Mountain ranges are important because they determine the climate and water flow of surrounding regions. Mountains are also important for the plants and animals they support, and as a source of minerals. Mountain ranges influence human activities, shaping patterns of transportation, communication, and settlement.

See "Mountains of the world" on the following pages.

See **Mountain** in *World Book* for more information on the following topics:

- The importance of mountains
- How mountains are formed
- Major mountain systems
- Studying mountains

Mountains of the world

Some famous mountains

Name	In feet	In meters	Location	Interesting facts
	Height above sea level			
Aconcagua	22,831	6,959	Andes in Argentina	Highest peak in the Western Hemisphere
Annapurna	26,504	8,078	Himalaya in Nepal	Highest mountain climbed until 1953
Ararat	17,011	5,185	Eastern Plateau in Turkey	Noah's Ark supposed to have rested on Ararat
Chimborazo	20,561	6,267	Andes in Ecuador	For many years thought to be the highest mountain in the Western Hemisphere
Cotopaxi	19,347	5,897	Andes in Ecuador	One of the world's highest active volcanoes
Ixtacihuatl	17,343	5,286	Plateau of Mexico	Aztec name for *white woman*
Jungfrau	13,642	4,158	Alps in Switzerland	Electric railroad partway up the mountain
K2, or Mount Godwin Austen, or Dapsang	28,250 *	8,611 *	Karakoram, or Mustagh, in Kashmir	Second highest mountain in the world
Kilimanjaro	19,340	5,895	Isolated peak in Tanzania	Highest mountain in Africa
Lassen Peak	10,457	3,187	Cascade in California	One of the few active U.S. volcanoes
Matterhorn	14,692	4,478	Alps on Switzerland-Italy border	Favorite for daring mountain climbers
Mauna Kea	13,796	4,205	Island of Hawaii	Highest island peak in the world
Mauna Loa	13,677	4,169	Island of Hawaii	World's largest volcano
Mont Blanc	15,771	4,807	Alps on France-Italy-Switzerland border	Highest mountain in the Alps
Mount Cook	12,349	3,764	Southern Alps in New Zealand	Highest peak in New Zealand
Mount Elbrus	18,481	5,633	Caucasus in Soviet Union	Highest mountain in Europe
Mount Etna	11,122	3,390	Island of Sicily	Volcano known to have erupted over 260 times
Mount Everest	29,028	8,848	Himalaya on Nepal-Tibet border	Highest mountain in the world; first scaled in 1953
Mount Fuji	12,388	3,776	Island of Honshu in Japan	Considered sacred by many Japanese
Mount Hood	11,239	3,426	Cascade in Oregon	Inactive volcano with many glaciers
Mount Kanchenjunga, or Kinchinjunga	28,208	8,598	Himalaya on Nepal-India border	Third highest mountain in the world
Mount Kenya	17,058	5,199	Central Kenya	Base straddles the equator
Mount Kosciusko	7,310	2,228	Australian Alps	Highest peak in Australia
Mount Logan	19,524	5,951	St. Elias in Canada	Highest peak in Canada
Mount Makalu	27,824	8,481	Himalaya on Nepal-Tibet border	Fourth highest mountain in the world
Mount McKinley	20,320	6,194	Alaska Range in Alaska	Highest peak in North America
Mount Rainier	14,410	4,392	Cascade in Washington	Highest peak in Washington
Mount St. Helens	8,364	2,549	Cascade in Washington	One of the few active U.S. volcanoes
Mount Shasta	14,162	4,317	Cascade in California	Famous for its twin peaks
Mount Whitney	14,495	4,418	Sierra Nevada in California	Highest mountain in California
Olympus	9,570	2,917	Greece	Considered home of the gods by early Greeks
Orizaba, or Citlaltépetl	18,701	5,700	Plateau of Mexico	Highest peak in Mexico
Pikes Peak	14,110	4,301	Front Range in Colorado	Most famous of the Rocky Mountains
Popocatepetl	17,887	5,452	Plateau of Mexico	Aztec name for *smoking mountain*
Vesuvius	4,190	1,277	Italy	Only active volcano on the mainland of Europe

Each mountain listed has a separate article in *World Book*.   *Traditional measurement.

Sources: Rand McNally & Company; U.S. Geological Survey.

Major mountains of the Western Hemisphere

WORLD BOOK illustration by Robert Addison

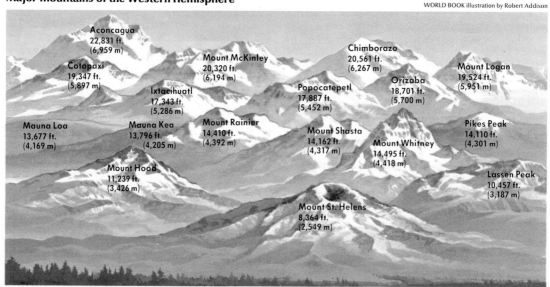

Aconcagua 22,831 ft. (6,959 m)

Cotopaxi 19,347 ft. (5,897 m)

Mount McKinley 20,320 ft. (6,194 m)

Chimborazo 20,561 ft. (6,267 m)

Mount Logan 19,524 ft. (5,951 m)

Ixtacihuatl 17,343 ft. (5,286 m)

Popocatepetl 17,887 ft. (5,452 m)

Orizaba 18,701 ft. (5,700 m)

Mauna Loa 13,677 ft. (4,169 m)

Mauna Kea 13,796 ft. (4,205 m)

Mount Rainier 14,410 ft. (4,392 m)

Mount Shasta 14,162 ft. (4,317 m)

Mount Whitney 14,495 ft. (4,418 m)

Pikes Peak 14,110 ft. (4,301 m)

Mount Hood 11,239 ft. (3,426 m)

Lassen Peak 10,457 ft. (3,187 m)

Mount St. Helens 8,364 ft. (2,549 m)

**Location of
the mountains**

This map locates the mountains listed in the table *Some famous mountains* and illustrated in the diagrams *Major mountains of the Eastern Hemisphere* and *Major mountains of the Western Hemisphere.* The diagrams also show how the mountains compare in height.

WORLD BOOK map

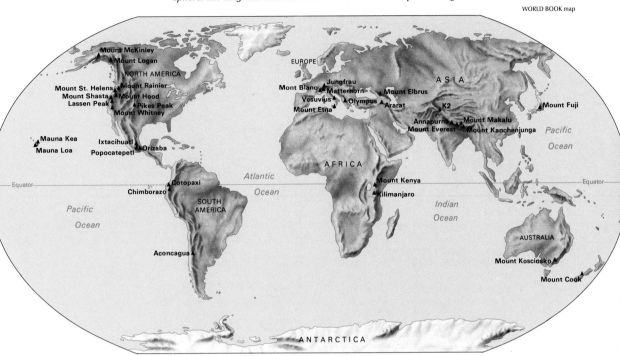

Major mountains of the Eastern Hemisphere

WORLD BOOK illustration by Robert Addison

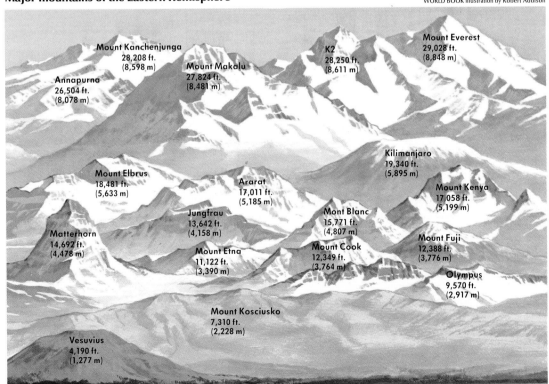

Cy La Tour

A house mouse eats stolen grain.

Mouse is a small animal with soft fur, a pointed snout, round black eyes, rounded ears, and a thin tail. The word *mouse* is not the name of any one kind of animal or family of animals. Many kinds of *rodents* (gnawing animals) are called mice. They include small rats, hamsters, gerbils, jerboas, lemmings, voles, harvest mice, deer mice, and grasshopper mice. All these animals have chisel-like front teeth that are useful for gnawing. A rodent's front teeth grow throughout the animal's life.

There are hundreds of kinds of mice, and they live in most parts of the world. They can be found in the mountains, in fields and woodlands, in swamps, near streams, and in deserts.

Probably the best known kind of mouse is the house mouse. It lives wherever people live, and often builds its nest in homes, garages, or barns. Some kinds of white house mice are raised as pets. Other kinds of house mice are used by scientists to learn about sickness, to test new drugs, and to study behavior.

House mice

House mice probably could be found in the homes of people who lived during ancient times. Those mice probably stole the people's food, just as mice do today.

Body of a house mouse is $2\frac{1}{2}$ to $3\frac{1}{2}$ inches (6.4 to 8.9 centimeters) long without the tail. The tail is the same length or a little shorter. Most house mice weigh $\frac{1}{2}$ to 1 ounce (14 to 28 grams). Their size and weight, and the

length of their tails, differ greatly among the many varieties and even among individual animals of the same variety.

The fur of most house mice is soft, but it may be stiff and wiry. It is grayish brown on the animal's back and sides, and yellowish white underneath. House mice raised as pets or for use in laboratories may have pure white fur, black or brown spots, or other combinations of colors. The house mouse's tail is covered by scaly skin.

A house mouse has a small head and a long, narrow snout. Several long, thin whiskers grow from the sides of the snout. These whiskers, like those of a cat, help the

Facts in brief

Common name	Scientific name	Gestation period	Number of young	Where found
*House mouse	*Mus musculus*	18-21 days	4-7	Worldwide
American harvest mouse	*Reithrodontomys fulvescens*	21-24 days	1-7	North and South America
Grasshopper mouse	*Onychomys leucogaster*	29-38 days	3-4	North America
Deer mouse	*Peromyscus maniculatus*	21-27 days	1-9	North and South America

*The house mouse belongs to the family of Old World rats and mice, Muridae. The American harvest, grasshopper, and deer mice belong to the family of New World rats and mice, Cricetidae.

mouse feel its way in the dark. The animal has rounded ears, and its eyes look somewhat like round black beads. A mouse can hear well, but it has poor sight. Probably because house mice cannot see well, they may enter a lighted room even if people are there.

Like all other rodents, mice have strong, sharp front teeth that grow throughout the animal's life. With these chisel-like teeth, mice can gnaw holes in wood, tear apart packages to get at food inside, and damage books, clothing, and furniture.

Food. A house mouse eats almost anything that human beings eat. It feeds on any meat or plant materials that it can find. Mice also eat such household items as glue, leather, paste, and soap. House mice that live out of doors eat insects, and the leaves, roots, seeds, and stems of plants. Mice always seem to be looking for something to eat, but they need little food. They damage much more food than they eat.

Homes. House mice live wherever they can find food and shelter. Any dark place that is warm and quiet makes an excellent home for mice. A mouse may build its nest in a warm corner of a barn, on a beam under the roof of a garage, or in a box stored in an attic or basement. The animal may tear strips of clothing or upholstery to get materials for its nest. It may line the nest with feathers or cotton stolen from pillows. House mice that live in fields or woodlands dig holes in the ground and build nests of grass inside. They may line the nests with feathers or pieces of fur.

Young. A female house mouse may give birth every 20 to 30 days. She carries her young in her body for 18 to 21 days before they are born. She has four to seven young at a time. Newborn mice have pink skin and no fur, and their eyes are closed. They are completely helpless. Soft fur covers their bodies by the time they are 10 days old. When they are 14 days old, their eyes open. Young mice stay near the nest for about three weeks after birth. Then they leave to build their own nests and start raising families. Most female house mice begin to have young when they are about 45 days old.

See **Mouse** in *World Book* for more information on House mice and Some other kinds of mice.

The skeleton of a mouse

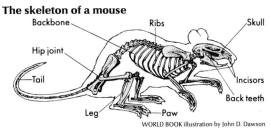

WORLD BOOK illustration by John D. Dawson

Mouse tracks

Hind foot   Front foot

WORLD BOOK illustration by Tom Dolan

J. M. Conrader

White-footed mouse and her young

Jane Burton, Photo Researchers

Harvest mouse

Grasshopper mouse

Cordell Andersen, NAS

Muscle is the tough, elastic tissue that makes body parts move. All animals except the simplest kinds have some type of muscle.

People use muscles to make various movements, such as walking, jumping, or throwing. Muscles also help in performing activities necessary for growth and for maintaining a strong, healthy body. For example, people use muscles in the jaw to chew food. Other muscles help move food through the stomach and intestines, and aid in digestion. Muscles in the heart and blood vessels force the blood to circulate. Muscles in the chest make breathing possible.

Muscles are found throughout the body. As a person grows, the muscles also get bigger. Muscle makes up nearly half the body weight of an adult.

Kinds of muscles. The human body has more than 600 major muscles. About 240 of them have specific names. There are two main types of muscles: (1) skeletal muscles and (2) smooth muscles. A third kind of muscle, called *cardiac muscle,* has characteristics of both skeletal and smooth muscles. It is found only in the heart.

See **Muscle** in *World Book* for more information on the following topics:

- Kinds of muscles
- How muscles work
- Disorders of the muscles
- Muscles in other animals

Skeletal muscles

The human body has more than 600 major muscles. About 240 of these muscles have specific names. The illustrations below show some of the most important external skeletal muscles. These muscles are identified by their Latin names, which are the names used by medical personnel.

WORLD BOOK illustrations by Charles Wellek

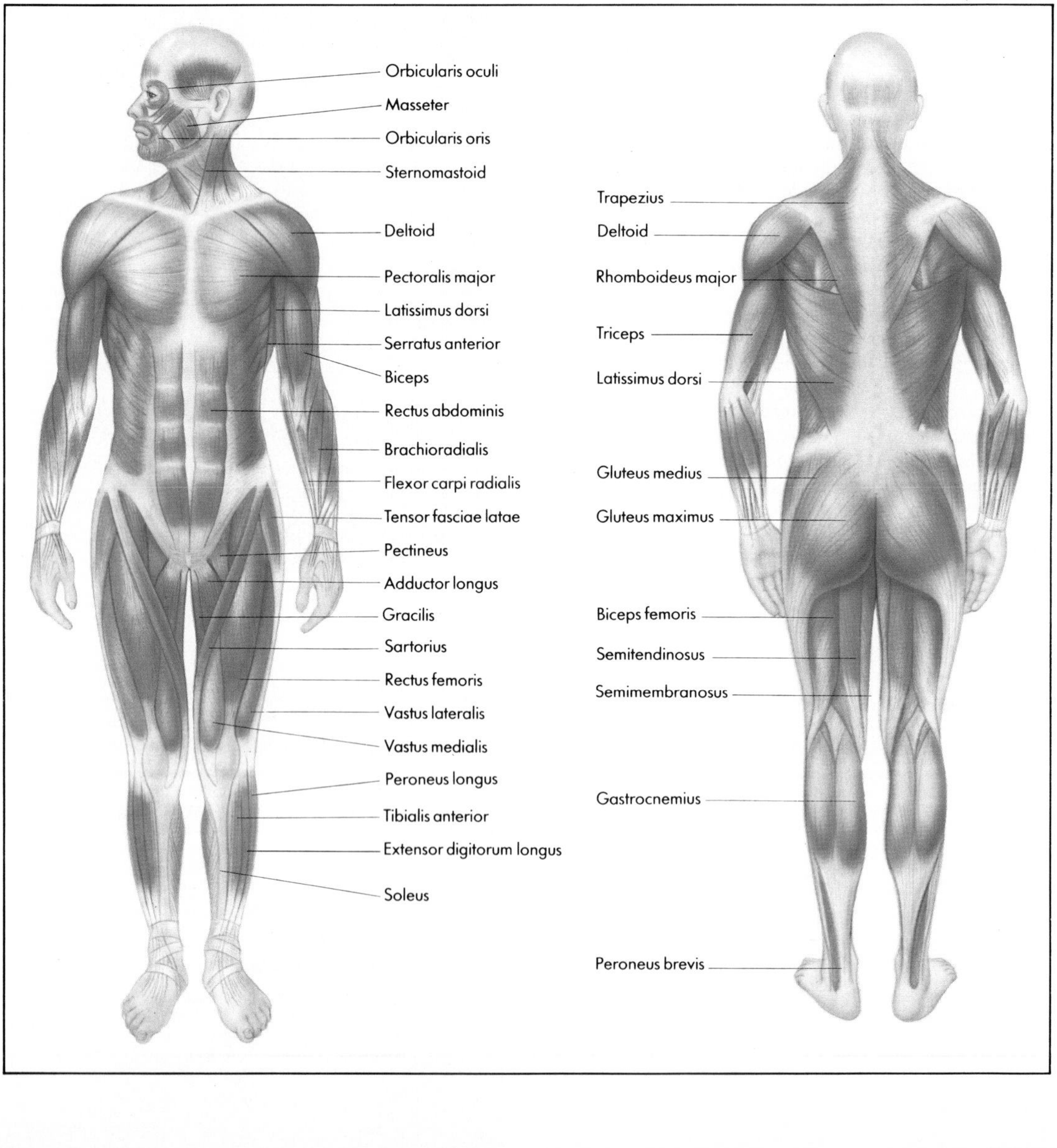

Orbicularis oculi
Masseter
Orbicularis oris
Sternomastoid
Deltoid
Pectoralis major
Latissimus dorsi
Serratus anterior
Biceps
Rectus abdominis
Brachioradialis
Flexor carpi radialis
Tensor fasciae latae
Pectineus
Adductor longus
Gracilis
Sartorius
Rectus femoris
Vastus lateralis
Vastus medialis
Peroneus longus
Tibialis anterior
Extensor digitorum longus
Soleus

Trapezius
Deltoid
Rhomboideus major
Triceps
Latissimus dorsi
Gluteus medius
Gluteus maximus
Biceps femoris
Semitendinosus
Semimembranosus
Gastrocnemius
Peroneus brevis

Mushroom is any of a variety of fleshy, umbrella-shaped *fungi.* Mushrooms most commonly grow in woods and grassy areas. There are about 3,300 species of mushrooms throughout the world. About 3,000 of these species grow in the United States and Canada.

In the past, scientists considered mushrooms and other fungi as nongreen plants. Today, the fungi are most commonly regarded as a separate kingdom of living things. Like other fungi, mushrooms differ from green plants in that they lack *chlorophyll,* the green substance such plants use to make food. Instead, mushrooms survive mainly by absorbing food material from living or decaying plants in their surroundings.

A mushroom consists of two main parts: (1) the mycelium and (2) the fruiting body. The mycelium grows just beneath the surface of the soil and absorbs food materials. This part may live and grow many years. The umbrella-shaped fruiting body grows from the mycelium and lives only a few days. During that time, it produces tiny reproductive cells called *spores* from which new mushrooms grow. The fruiting body of the fungus is the part most people consider the mushroom.

Mushrooms vary greatly in size and color. They measure from about $\frac{3}{4}$ inch (1.9 centimeters) to about 15 inches (38 centimeters) in height. The diameter of the top of a mushroom ranges from less than $\frac{1}{4}$ inch (0.6 centimeters) to about 18 inches (46 centimeters). Most mushrooms have a white, yellow, orange, red, or brown color. Some are blue, violet, green, or black.

Many species of mushrooms are tasty and safe to eat. But others have a bad taste, and some are poisonous. A few of the poisonous species can be fatal if eaten. Mushrooms that are either poisonous or have a bad taste are often referred to as *toadstools.*

How a mushroom obtains food. Mushrooms need carbohydrates, proteins, certain vitamins, and other nutrients. To obtain this food, the mycelium releases proteins called *enzymes* from its hyphae. The enzymes convert the materials on which the hyphae grow into simpler compounds that are absorbed by the mycelium.

Many species of mushrooms are *saprophytes*—that is, they live on dead or decaying materials. Some of these species obtain their food from dead grass or decaying plant matter, or from *humus* (soil formed from decaying plant and animal matter). Other species attack decaying wood, such as fallen trees, old stumps, and even the timber of houses. A few species live on the *dung* (solid body wastes) of animals that graze on grass.

Some mushrooms grow on living plants, especially trees. Such mushrooms are called *parasites.* A few of these mushrooms cause disease and may eventually kill the plants on which they feed.

Other mushrooms grow in or on roots of living green plants without causing harm. This type of association, called a *mycorrhiza,* benefits both the mushroom and the green plant. The mushroom's mycelium absorbs water and certain materials from the soil and passes these on to the plant. In turn, the plant feeds the mushroom. Mushrooms form mycorrhizas with a number of trees—including Douglas-fir, hemlocks, larches, oaks, pines, and poplars—and certain other plants.

See Some mushrooms of North America on the following page.

See **Mushroom** in *World Book* for more information on the following topics:

- Parts of a mushroom
- The life of a mushroom
- Kinds of mushrooms
- The importance of mushrooms

Parts of a mushroom The drawing at the left, *below,* shows the chief parts of a mushroom. The other drawings show the details of the underside of the cap, which consists of either gills, *center,* or tubes, *right.* Tiny basidia on the gills or tubes produce the spores from which new mushrooms grow.

WORLD BOOK illustrations by Patricia J. Wynne

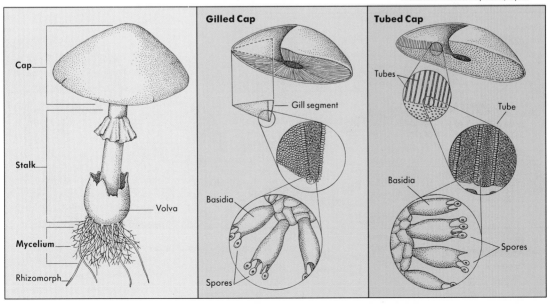

Cap

Stalk

Volva

Mycelium

Rhizomorph

Gilled Cap

Gill segment

Basidia

Spores

Tubed Cap

Tubes

Tube

Basidia

Spores

Some mushrooms of North America

About 3,000 species of mushrooms grow in North America. Twenty-one of them are illustrated below. They are divided into two groups: (1) agarics and (2) boletes. Agarics have gills under their caps, and boletes have tubes. The scientific name of each mushroom appears in italics.

● Poisonous
● Nonpoisonous

WORLD BOOK illustrations by John Eggert

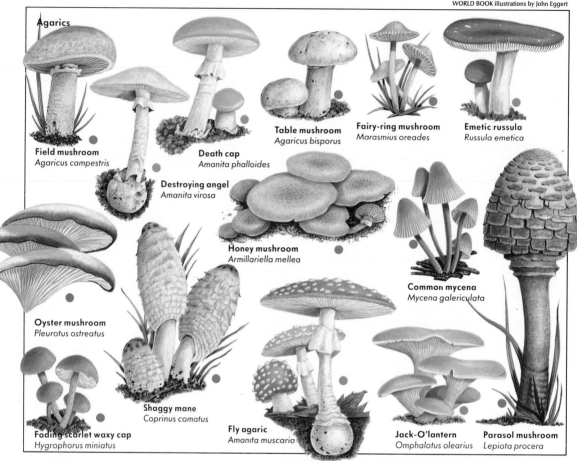

Agarics

Field mushroom
Agaricus campestris

Death cap
Amanita phalloides

Destroying angel
Amanita virosa

Table mushroom
Agaricus bisporus

Fairy-ring mushroom
Marasmius oreades

Emetic russula
Russula emetica

Honey mushroom
Armillariella mellea

Common mycena
Mycena galericulata

Oyster mushroom
Pleurotus ostreatus

Shaggy mane
Coprinus comatus

Fading scarlet waxy cap
Hygrophorus miniatus

Fly agaric
Amanita muscaria

Jack-O'lantern
Omphalotus olearius

Parasol mushroom
Lepiota procera

Boletes

Larch suillus
Suillus grevillei

Slippery Jack
Suillus luteus

Aspen scaber stalk
Leccinum insigne

Frost's bolete
Boletus frostii

Mock oyster
Suillus cavipes

Edible bolete
Boletus edulis

Old man of the woods
Strobilomyces floccopus

Nervous system is an internal communications network that enables an animal to adjust to changes in its environment. Almost all animals, except the simplest kinds, have some type of nervous system.

Animals without a backbone have a nervous system that ranges from a simple net of nerves to a highly organized system of nerve cords and a primitive brain. In human beings and other animals with backbones, the nervous system consists of the brain, the spinal cord, and the nerves. This article deals mainly with the human nervous system.

The human nervous system—especially the highly developed brain—makes people different from all other animals. The human brain functions much like a complicated computer that enables people to speak, solve difficult problems, and produce creative ideas.

The nervous system provides pathways by which information travels from a person's surroundings to the brain. The brain then sends instructions to various muscles via other pathways so that the body can respond to the information. The nervous system also regulates internal functions, such as breathing, digestion, and heartbeat. All of a person's movements, sensations, thoughts, and emotions are products of his or her nervous system.

How the nervous system works

The nervous system is made up of billions of special cells called *neurons* or *nerve cells*. Cordlike bundles of neuron fibers are called *nerves*. The nerves form a network of pathways that conduct information rapidly throughout the body.

A person's reaction to a situation may take only an instant, but it involves many complicated processes within the nervous system. For example, what happens in the nervous system of a person who sees a wild tiger and, an instant later, turns and runs away?

Specialized neurons called *receptors* are located in the ears and eyes and the other sense organs of the body. The receptors translate events in a person's surroundings—such as the sight of a tiger—into nerve messages, which are known as *impulses*. Nerve impulses travel along nerve fibers at speeds of 3 to 300 feet (0.9 to 90 meters) per second.

The receptor cells in the eyes respond to light rays that reflect off the tiger and translate the rays into a pattern of nerve impulses. These impulses then travel through neurons called *sensory neurons* and *association neurons*. The sensory neurons carry information from receptors in the sense organs to association neurons in the brain and the spinal cord.

The neurons in the brain receive the impulses, analyze and interpret the message, and decide what action should be taken. A message consisting of the sight of a wild tiger is, of course, interpreted as danger. The person's brain immediately sends out a message—"Run!" — in the form of nerve impulses.

Next, the impulses travel through *motor neurons*. These nerve cells carry messages from the brain to the muscles and glands, which are called *effectors*. The effectors carry out the brain's instructions. Thus, the leg muscles respond and the person runs away. At the same time, the brain sends messages to various other parts of the body. For example, it sends messages to the heart to beat faster and send more blood to the leg muscles.

Divisions of the nervous system

The nervous system has three main parts, the *central nervous system,* the *peripheral nervous system,* and the *autonomic nervous system.* Each of these parts has special functions.

The central nervous system functions as a "main switchboard" that controls and coordinates the activities of the entire nervous system. The central nervous system consists of the *brain* and the *spinal cord.*

The brain is an extremely complicated organ. It consists of three principal parts, the *cerebrum,* the *cerebellum,* and the *brain stem.* This article provides basic information about the brain. For more detailed information on the brain, see **Brain.**

The cerebrum makes up about 85 per cent of the brain and is the most complex part. It is above the cerebellum and the brain stem and almost surrounds them. Human beings have a highly developed cerebrum that directs their hearing, sight, and touch and their ability to think, use language, and feel emotions. The cerebrum is also the center of learning.

How the nervous system works

The nervous system enables us to adjust to changes in our surroundings. Such *neurons* (nerve cells) as the *receptors* in the eyes translate information from the environment into nerve impulses. *Sensory neurons* carry the impulses to *association neurons* in the brain and spinal cord. *Motor neurons* then carry instructions from the brain to muscles, internal organs, and other body parts.

WORLD BOOK diagrams by Lou Bory Associates

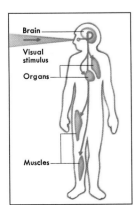

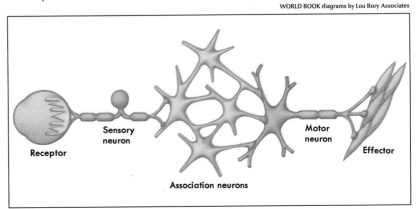

Brain
Visual stimulus
Organs
Muscles

Receptor
Sensory neuron
Association neurons
Motor neuron
Effector

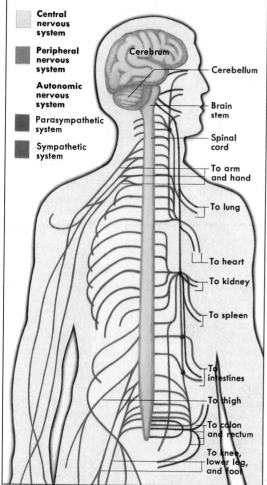

Central
nervous
system

Peripheral
nervous
system

Autonomic
nervous
system

Parasympathetic
system

Sympathetic
system

Cerebrum

Cerebellum

Brain
stem

Spinal
cord

To arm
and hand

To lung

To heart

To kidney

To spleen

To
intestines

To thigh

To colon
and rectum

To knee,
lower leg,
and foot

WORLD BOOK diagram by Lou Bory Associates

The human nervous system has three main parts: (1) the *central nervous system,* (2) the *peripheral nervous system,* and (3) the *autonomic nervous system,* which consists of *sympathetic* and *parasympathetic* divisions. This simplified diagram shows only major nerves. It illustrates peripheral nerves only on the left side of the figure and autonomic nerves only on the right.

The cerebellum, which is about the size of an orange, is slightly above the brain stem. It helps maintain the body's sense of balance and coordinates muscular movements with sensory information.

The brain stem is a stalklike structure that is connected to the spinal cord at the base of the skull. The brain stem contains neurons that relay information from the sense organs. Many neurons that regulate automatic functions, such as balance, blood pressure, breathing, and heartbeat, are also in the brain stem.

The spinal cord is a cable of neurons that extends from the neck about two-thirds of the way down the backbone. The backbone surrounds and protects the spinal cord. The spinal cord contains pathways that carry sensory information to the brain. It also has pathways that relay commands from the brain to the motor neurons.

The peripheral nervous system carries all the messages sent between the central nervous system and the rest of the body. The peripheral nervous system consists of 12 pairs of nerves that originate in the brain, plus 31 pairs of nerves of the spinal cord. These cranial and spinal nerves carry messages to and from every receptor and effector in the body.

The autonomic nervous system is a special part of the peripheral nervous system. The autonomic nervous system regulates such automatic bodily processes as breathing and digestion without conscious control by the brain. This constant regulation enables the body to maintain a stable internal environment.

The autonomic nervous system has two parts, the *sympathetic system* and the *parasympathetic system.* The sympathetic system responds to the body's needs during increased activity and in emergencies. The actions of the sympathetic system include speeding up the heartbeat, sending additional blood to the muscles, and enlarging the pupils of the eyes to use all available light.

The parasympathetic system, in general, opposes the actions of the sympathetic system. The parasympathetic system's functions include slowing down the heartbeat, diverting blood from the muscles to the stomach and intestines, and contracting the pupils of the eyes. The balance of activity between the two systems is controlled by the central nervous system.

The nervous system in other animals

In vertebrates. All vertebrates, including other mammals, as well as amphibians, birds, fish, and reptiles, have nervous systems much like the human nervous system. The neurons that make up the nervous systems of these animals are about the same size and shape as human neurons.

The size of a specific area of the brain may indicate the importance of the function of that area for the animal. For example, dogs have a larger and better developed area for smell than do human beings. In contrast, human beings have a larger and more highly developed *cerebral cortex* than other animals. The cerebral cortex is the outer surface of the cerebrum, where such complicated skills as delicate motor control and the use of language are coordinated.

In invertebrates. Most species of invertebrates that consist of more than one cell have some sort of nervous system. Many of the neurons of these animals are larger than human neurons. In hydras and some other simple invertebrates, the nervous system may be a *nerve net,* in which nerve cells are spread throughout the organism.

Other invertebrates, including worms and insects, have more complicated, centralized nervous systems. These systems consist largely of concentrations of neurons that form a nerve cord. *Ganglia* along the cord serve as centers for organizing and integrating various activities of the animals.

See **Nervous system** in *World Book* for more information on the following topics:

- Parts of a neuron
- How messages are routed
- How neurons carry impulses
- Disorders of the nervous system

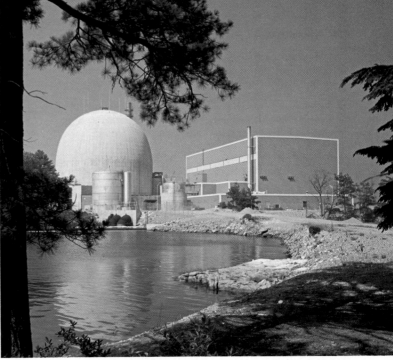

Idaho National Engineering Laboratory

Combustion Engineering, Inc.

The tremendous heat of nuclear energy is created deep within a *nuclear reactor, left,* a device that produces and controls nuclear energy. Water in the reactor keeps the device from melting. A nuclear power plant, *right,* uses the heat from a reactor to produce electricity.

Nuclear energy

Nuclear energy, also called *atomic energy,* is the most powerful kind of energy known. It produces the tremendous heat and light of the sun and the shattering blast of nuclear weapons. Nuclear energy results from changes in the *nucleus* (core) of atoms. Scientists and engineers have found many uses for this energy, especially in producing electricity. But they do not yet have the ability to make full use of nuclear power. If nuclear energy were fully developed, it could supply all the world's electricity for millions of years.

Scientists knew nothing about nuclear energy until the early 1900's. They then began to make important discoveries about matter and energy. They already knew that all matter consists of atoms. But scientists further learned that a nucleus makes up most of the mass of every atom and that this nucleus is held together by an extremely powerful force. A huge amount of energy is concentrated in the nucleus because of this force. The next step was to make nuclei let go of that energy.

Scientists first released nuclear energy on a large scale at the University of Chicago in 1942, three years after World War II began. This achievement led to the development of the atomic bomb. The first atomic bomb was exploded in the desert near Alamogordo, N. Mex., on July 16, 1945. Temperatures at the center of the blast about equaled those at the sun's center. In August, U.S. planes dropped atomic bombs on Hiroshima and Nagasaki, Japan. The bombs largely destroyed both cities and helped end World War II. In 1949, the Soviet Union became the second nation to explode an atomic bomb. Today, at least six nations have nuclear bombs.

Since 1945, peaceful uses of nuclear energy have been developed. The energy released by nuclei creates large amounts of heat. This heat can be used to make steam, and the steam can be used to generate electricity. Engineers have invented devices called *nuclear reactors* to produce and control nuclear energy.

A nuclear reactor operates somewhat like a furnace. But instead of using such fuels as coal or oil, almost all reactors use uranium. And instead of burning in the reactor, the uranium *fissions*—that is, its nuclei split in two. As a nucleus splits, it releases energy largely in the form of heat. The fission of 1 pound (0.45 kilogram) of uranium releases as much energy as the burning of 1,140 short tons (1,030 metric tons) of coal.

Electric power production is by far the most important peaceful use of nuclear energy. Nuclear energy also powers some submarines and other ships. These vessels have a reactor to create heat for making the steam that turns the ship propellers. In addition, the fission that produces nuclear energy is valuable because it releases particles and rays called *nuclear radiation* that have uses in medicine, industry, and science. However, nuclear radiation can be extremely dangerous. Exposure to damaging amounts of radiation can result in a condition called *radiation sickness.*

Nuclear reactions

A nuclear reaction involves changes in the structure of a nucleus. As a result of such changes, the nucleus gains or loses one or more neutrons or protons. It thus changes into the nucleus of a different *isotope* (different form of the same element) or element. If the nucleus changes into the nucleus of a different element, the change is called a *transmutation* (in *World Book,*

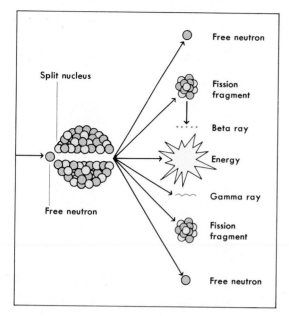

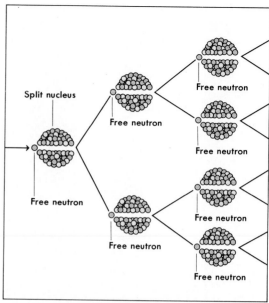

WORLD BOOK diagrams by Arthur Grebetz

Nuclear fission is the chief method of producing nuclear energy. It involves using a free neutron to split a nucleus of a heavy element, such as uranium, into two *fission fragments.* Besides heat energy, fission releases neutrons and such nuclear radiation as gamma rays. The fragments give off beta rays.

A chain reaction results in the continuous fissioning of nuclei and so produces a steady supply of energy. To produce a chain reaction, each fissioned nucleus must give off enough free neutrons to fission at least two more nuclei, *above.* Uranium and plutonium are the materials used to produce a chain reaction.

see **Transmutation of elements**).

Three types of nuclear reactions release useful amounts of energy. These reactions are (1) radioactive decay, (2) nuclear fission, and (3) nuclear fusion. The matter involved in each reaction weighs less after the reaction than it did before. The lost matter has changed into energy.

Radioactive decay, or radioactivity, is the process by which a nucleus *spontaneously* (naturally) changes into the nucleus of another isotope or element. The process releases energy chiefly in the form of particles and rays called nuclear radiation. Uranium, thorium, and several other natural elements decay spontaneously and so add to the natural, or *background,* radiation that is always present on the earth. Nuclear reactors produce radioactive decay artificially. Nuclear radiation accounts for about 10 per cent of the energy produced in a reactor.

Nuclear fission is the splitting of heavy nuclei to release their energy. All nuclear reactors produce energy in this way. To produce fission, a reactor requires a *bombarding particle,* such as a neutron, and a *target material,* such as U-235. Nuclear fission occurs when the bombarding particle splits a nucleus in the target material into two nearly equal parts, called *fission fragments.* Each fragment consists of a nucleus with about half the neutrons and protons of the original nucleus. A fission reaction releases only part of the energy of the nucleus. Most of the energy that is released takes the form of heat. The rest of the released energy takes the form of radiation.

Scientists measure nuclear energy in units called *electron volts.* The burning of one atom of carbon in coal or oil produces about 3 electron volts of energy.

The fissioning of one uranium nucleus produces about 200 million electron volts.

Nuclear fusion occurs when two lightweight nuclei *fuse* (combine) and form a nucleus of a heavier element. The products of the fusion weigh less than the combined weights of the original nuclei. The lost matter has therefore been changed into energy.

Fusion reactions that produce large amounts of energy can be created only by means of extremely intense heat. Such reactions are called *thermonuclear reactions.* Thermonuclear reactions produce the energy of both the sun and the hydrogen bomb.

A thermonuclear reaction can occur only in a special

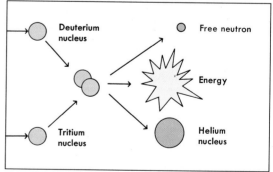

WORLD BOOK diagram by Arthur Grebetz

Nuclear fusion occurs when two lightweight nuclei unite and form a heavier nucleus. In the example above, nuclei of deuterium and tritium unite and form a helium nucleus. This process releases energy and a neutron. Repeated many times, fusion creates the energy of the sun and the hydrogen bomb. But scientists have yet to control fusion for use in energy production.

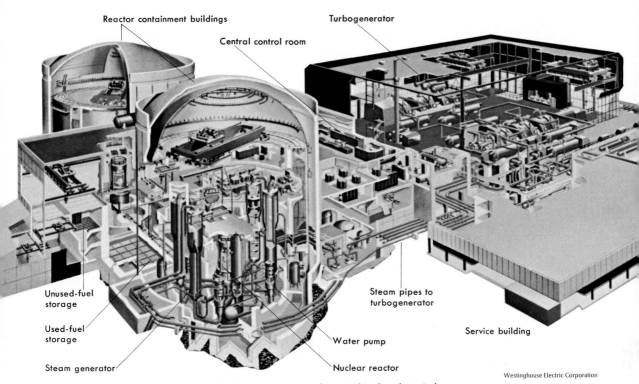

Reactor containment buildings

Central control room

Turbogenerator

Unused-fuel storage

Used-fuel storage

Steam generator

Steam pipes to turbogenerator

Water pump

Nuclear reactor

Service building

Westinghouse Electric Corporation

Nuclear power production requires certain basic equipment, as shown in this plan of a typical nuclear power plant. The equipment makes up two main systems. (1) The *nuclear steam supply system* includes the plant's reactor or reactors, any related steam-generating equipment, and pumps and pipes to move water and steam. Each reactor has its own *containment* building. (2) The *turbogenerator system* consists of a steam turbine and electric generator. Steam from the steam supply system spins the turbine, which drives the electric generator. The electric generator produces electricity. Other equipment includes special safety systems and storage for nuclear fuel.

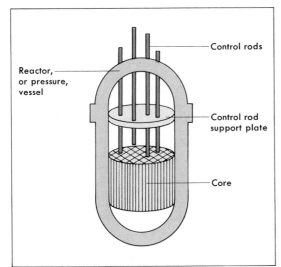

Control rods

Reactor, or pressure, vessel

Control rod support plate

Core

WORLD BOOK diagram by Arthur Grebetz

A typical nuclear reactor consists mainly of a *core; control rods;* and a *reactor,* or *pressure, vessel.* The core holds the uranium that will be fissioned to create heat. The control rods regulate the chain reaction. The reactor vessel holds all other reactor parts and the water that will be heated to produce steam.

form of matter called *plasma.* Plasma is a gas made up of free electrons and free nuclei. Normally, nuclei repel one another. But if a plasma containing lightweight atomic nuclei is heated many millions of degrees, the nuclei begin moving so fast that they break through one another's electrical barriers and fuse.

Problems of controlling fusion. Scientists have not yet succeeded in harnessing the energy of fusion to produce power. In their fusion experiments, scientists generally work with plasmas that are made from one or two isotopes of hydrogen. One such isotope is *tritium,* an artificially made radioactive isotope. Another isotope is *deuterium,* or *heavy hydrogen.* Deuterium is considered an ideal thermonuclear fuel because it can be obtained from ordinary water. A given weight of deuterium can supply about four times as much energy as the same weight of uranium.

See **Nuclear energy** in *World Book* for more information on the following topics:

- The role of nuclear energy in power production
- The science of nuclear energy
- How nuclear energy is produced
- The nuclear energy industry
- The development of nuclear energy

© Harvey Lloyd, The Stock Market
© Alan Gurney, The Stock Market

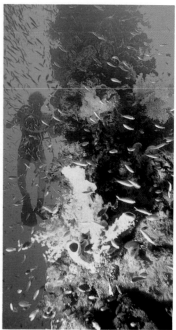

© Barry E. Parker, Bruce Coleman Inc.

The vast ocean covers more than 70 per cent of the earth's surface, from the ice-choked seas of the polar regions, *lower left,* to the warm waters of the tropics, *above.* Its waters move constantly, whether crashing against a rocky coast, *upper left,* or gently rising and falling with the tide.

Ocean

Ocean is the great body of water that covers more than 70 per cent of the earth's surface. People also call it the *sea.* The ocean contains 97 per cent of all the water on the earth.

The ocean provides us with many things. It is far more than a place for swimming, boating, and other recreation. The ocean serves as a source of food, energy, and minerals. Ships use the ocean to carry cargo between continents. But above all else, the sea helps keep the earth's climate healthful by regulating the air temperature and by supplying the moisture for rainfall. If there were no ocean, life could not exist on our planet.

The bottom of the ocean has features as varied as those on land. Huge plains spread out across the ocean floor, and long mountain chains rise toward the surface. Volcanoes erupt from the ocean bottom, and deep valleys gash the floor.

The ocean is a fascinating place that we have only begun to understand. Scientists called *oceanographers* work to discover the secrets of the sea. They study how the ocean moves and how it affects the atmosphere. They investigate how organisms live in the sea and how

various forces shape the sea floor. Such modern tools as satellites and computers have greatly increased scientists' understanding of the ocean.

The world ocean

The waters of the ocean form one great connected body often called the *world ocean* or the *global ocean.* However, the continents divide the world ocean into three major parts. They are, in order of size, the Pacific Ocean, the Atlantic Ocean, and the Indian Ocean. Each ocean includes smaller bodies of water called *seas, gulfs,* or *bays,* which lie along the ocean margins. For example, the Caribbean Sea and the Mediterranean Sea are part of the Atlantic, and the Bering Sea and the South China Sea are part of the Pacific. The word *sea* also means the ocean in general.

The world ocean contains about 97 per cent of all the water on the earth. Most of the remaining water is frozen in glaciers and icecaps. The rest is in lakes and rivers, underground, and in the air.

Area. The world ocean covers about 70 per cent of the earth's surface. Most of the ocean lies in the Southern Hemisphere—that is, south of the equator. The Southern Hemisphere consists of about 80 per cent ocean, and the Northern Hemisphere about 60 per cent.

The Pacific Ocean is the largest ocean by far. It covers about 70 million square miles (181 million square kilometers)—nearly a third of the earth's surface. The Pacific contains about half the water in the world ocean and could hold all the continents. Near the equator, the Pacific stretches about 15,000 miles (24,000 kilometers), almost halfway around the globe. North and South America border the Pacific on the east, and Asia and Australia lie to the west. To the north, the Bering Strait links the Pacific with Arctic waters.

The Atlantic Ocean covers about 36 million square miles (94 million square kilometers), not including the waters of the Arctic. Europe and Africa lie east of the Atlantic, and North and South America lie west.

The Indian Ocean has an area of about 29 million square miles (74 million square kilometers). Africa lies to the west. Australia and Indonesia lie to the east. Asia borders the Indian Ocean on the north.

Depth. The world ocean has an average depth of 12,200 feet (3,730 meters), but parts of the ocean plunge much deeper. The deepest areas occur in *trenches*— long, narrow valleys on the sea floor. The deepest known spot is in the Mariana Trench in the western Pacific Ocean, near the island of Guam. It lies 36,198 feet (11,033 meters) below sea level. If the world's highest mountain, 29,028-foot (8,848-meter) Mount Everest, were placed in that spot, more than 1 mile (1.6 kilometers) of water would cover the mountaintop.

The Pacific is the deepest ocean, with an average depth of 12,900 feet (3,940 meters). The Atlantic is the shallowest ocean, averaging 11,700 feet (3,580 meters) deep. Its deepest known point, 28,374 feet (8,648 meters) below the surface, lies in the Puerto Rico Trench. The Indian Ocean averages 12,600 feet (3,840 meters) deep. Its deepest known spot plunges 25,344 feet (7,725 meters) below sea level in the Java Trench.

Temperature. The surface temperature of the ocean varies from about 28° F. (−2° C) near the North and South poles to about 86° F. (30° C) near the equator. In the polar regions, the surface seawater freezes. The western tropical Pacific has the warmest surface water. Ocean currents affect the surface temperature. As the currents move about in the ocean, they carry warm tropical water toward the poles. Other ocean movements bring colder, deeper water up to the surface and so lower the surface water temperature.

Ocean temperature also varies with depth. In general, the temperature falls as the depth increases. The warm surface waters extend to depths of about 500 feet (150 meters) in the tropics, and about 1,000 feet (300 meters) in the subtropics. Below the surface waters, the temperature drops rapidly, forming a layer called the *thermocline.* The thermocline varies in thickness, from about 1,000 feet (300 meters) to 3,000 feet (910 meters). Below the thermocline, the water cools more slowly. Close to the deep-sea floor, the temperature of the ocean ranges between 34° and 39° F. (1° and 4° C).

Composition. Every natural element can be found in the waters of the ocean. But the ocean is especially known for its salts. Seawater contains, on the average, about 3½ per cent salts. Six elements account for 99 per

Interesting facts about the ocean

WORLD BOOK illustrations by John F. Eggert

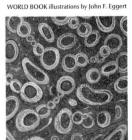

Life began in the ocean according to most scientists. Fossils of one type of sea worm, *right,* show that this organism has remained unchanged for over 500 million years.

There is a bit of "ocean" inside us. The body of an adult male contains about 19 quarts (72 liters) of salt water. The composition of this fluid is similar to seawater.

The ocean floor is in constant motion. The floor of the Atlantic spreads about 1 inch (2.5 centimeters) every year, widening the ocean basin. The Pacific floor spreads even faster, about 5 inches (13 centimeters) every year. But its basin does not widen because the edges of its floor sink under the continents.

Giant kelp, a large brown seaweed, may grow up to 200 feet (161 meters) long, forming great underwater forests in the ocean.

A *tsunami* —a powerful wave caused by an earthquake—can reach a speed of 600 miles (970 kilometers) per hour and travel across an entire ocean.

The world ocean would rise about 200 feet (60 meters) if the Greenland and Antarctic icecaps should suddenly melt. New York City would be submerged, with only the tops of the tallest buildings above water.

cent of the ocean's *salinity* (saltiness). They are, in order of amount, chloride, sodium, sulfur (as sulfate), magnesium, calcium, and potassium. Most of the salty material in the sea consists of the compound sodium chloride, or ordinary table salt.

Many salts in the ocean come chiefly from the wearing away of rocks on land. As rocks break down, rivers carry the salts and other material the rocks consist of to the ocean. Material released by volcanoes and undersea springs also contributes salts to the ocean. Evaporation and precipitation further affect the ocean's salinity. Evaporation removes fresh water from the ocean surface, leaving behind the salts. Evaporation is high in subtropical areas, and so the surface waters are especially salty in those areas. Precipitation returns fresh water to the ocean. Precipitation is greater than evaporation near the equator, making surface waters less salty there. Rivers also bring fresh water to the ocean, which lowers the salinity of seawater near river mouths.

Life in the ocean

An incredible variety of living things reside in the ocean. Marine life ranges from microscopic one-celled organisms to the largest animal that has ever lived—the blue whale, which may measure up to 100 feet (30 meters) long. Ocean plants and plantlike organisms use sunlight and the minerals in the water to grow. Sea animals eat these organisms and one another. Marine plants and plantlike organisms can live only in the sunlit surface waters of the ocean, which is called the *photic zone.* The photic zone extends only about 330 feet (100 meters) below the surface. Beyond that point, the light is insufficient to support plants and plant-like organisms in the sea. Animals, however, live throughout the ocean, from the surface waters to the greatest depths.

All ocean life can be divided into three groups. These groups are (1) the plankton, (2) the nekton, and (3) the benthos.

The plankton consists of plantlike organisms and animals that drift with the ocean currents. They have very little ability to move through the water on their own. Most of them cannot be seen without a microscope. The plantlike organisms of the plankton form the *phytoplankton,* and include such simple organisms as diatoms and other algae. The animals of the plankton form the *zooplankton.* Some minute types of bacteria are included in the plankton.

The phytoplankton consists of several kinds of plantlike organisms. Most have only one cell. The phytoplankton floats in the photic zone, where the organisms obtain sunlight and nutrients. Although the organisms generally drift about, some kinds have long, whiplike parts called *flagella* that enable them to swim. The phytoplankton serves as food for the zooplankton and for some larger marine animals.

The most numerous members of the phytoplankton are diatoms and dinoflagellates. A diatom consists of one cell enclosed in a hard, glasslike shell made of opal. Diatoms live mainly in the colder regions of the ocean. Some even live within sea ice. Most dinoflagellates also are one-celled organisms. They generally live in more tropical regions. A dinoflagellate has two flagella it can use to move in a swirling motion. Some species of dinoflagellates produce powerful poisons. When such species become plentiful, they may discolor the water and create a *red tide* that kills sea animals. Other kinds of phytoplankton include coccolithophores and silicoflagellates.

The zooplankton consists of many kinds of animals, ranging from one-celled organisms to jellyfish up to 6 feet (1.8 meters) wide. The animals live in surface and deep waters of the ocean. Some planktonic animals float about freely throughout their lives. The rest spend only the early part of their lives as plankton. As adults, some

Plankton

Plankton consists of small marine organisms that drift with the ocean currents. The plantlike organisms are called *phytoplankton.* Planktonic animals are known as *zooplankton.*

WORLD BOOK illustrations by Alex Ebel

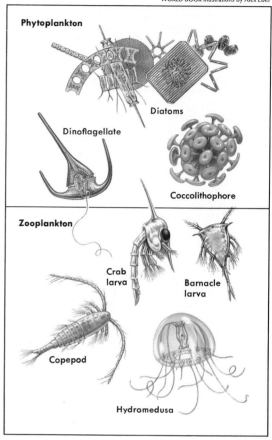

Phytoplankton

Diatoms

Dinoflagellate

Coccolithophore

Zooplankton

Crab larva

Barnacle larva

Copepod

Hydromedusa

become strong swimmers and join the nekton. Others settle to the sea floor or attach themselves to it and become part of the benthos.

Crustaceans make up about 70 per cent of all planktonic animals. A crustacean has jointed legs, and a shell called an *exoskeleton* covers its body. Copepods are the most numerous crustaceans. Krill, which are also crustaceans, serve as food for fish, sea birds, seals, squids, and whales in the waters around Antarctica. Other plankton animals include arrowworms and sea snails.

The nekton consists of animals that can swim freely in the sea. They are strong swimmers and include fish, squids, and marine mammals. Most species of nektonic animals live near the sea surface, where food is plentiful. But many other animals of the nekton live in the deep ocean.

Fish are the most important animals of the nekton. About 13,300 kinds of fish live in the ocean. They differ greatly in size and shape. The smallest fish, the pygmy goby, grows less than $\frac{1}{2}$ inch (13 millimeters) long. The largest fish, the whale shark, measures up to 60 feet (18 meters) long. Such fish as the tuna and the mackerel have streamlined bodies that enable them to move rap-

Animals of the ocean

The creatures shown below represent only a small part of the great variety of animal life found in the ocean.

WORLD BOOK illustrations by Tom Dolan and James Teason

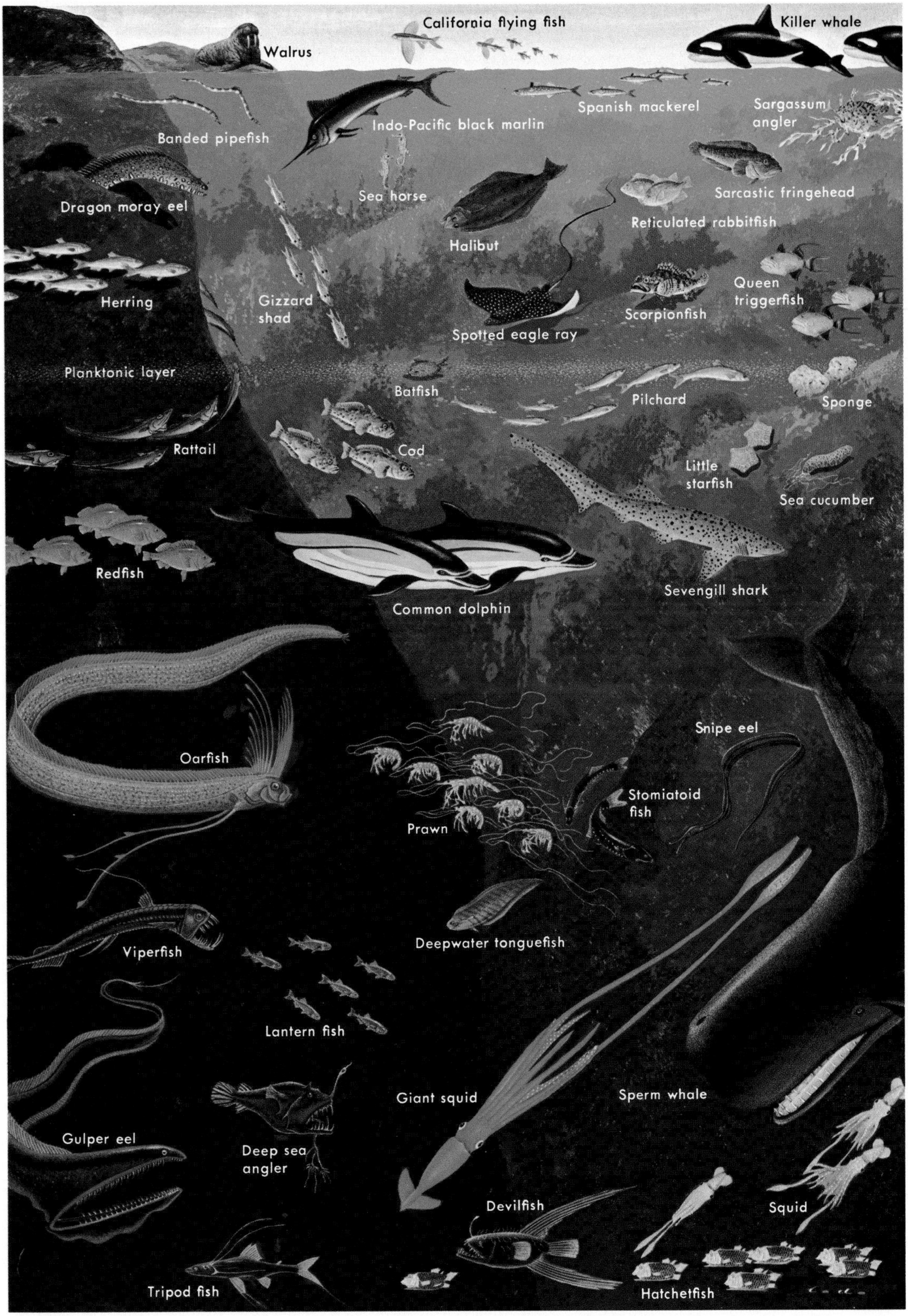
California flying fish
Killer whale
Walrus
Spanish mackerel
Sargassum angler
Banded pipefish
Indo-Pacific black marlin
Sea horse
Sarcastic fringehead
Dragon moray eel
Reticulated rabbitfish
Halibut
Queen triggerfish
Herring
Gizzard shad
Scorpionfish
Spotted eagle ray
Planktonic layer
Batfish
Pilchard
Sponge
Rattail
Cod
Little starfish
Sea cucumber
Redfish
Sevengill shark
Common dolphin
Snipe eel
Oarfish
Stomiatoid fish
Prawn
Viperfish
Deepwater tonguefish
Lantern fish
Giant squid
Sperm whale
Gulper eel
Deep sea angler
Devilfish
Squid
Tripod fish
Hatchetfish

Nekton

Nekton is made up of fish and other animals that have the ability to swim freely in water without the help of currents. Most nektonic creatures live in the upper layer of the ocean.

Benthos

Benthos consists of marine organisms that live on the ocean bottom. Some members of the benthos are attached to the bottom in one position throughout their lives.

WORLD BOOK illustrations by Alex Ebel

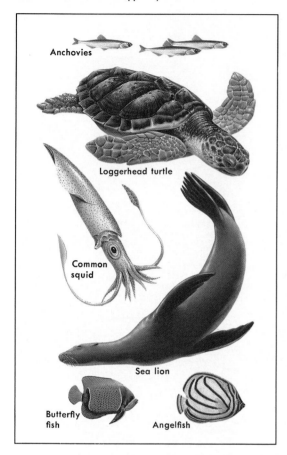

Anchovies

Loggerhead turtle

Common squid

Sea lion

Butterfly fish

Angelfish

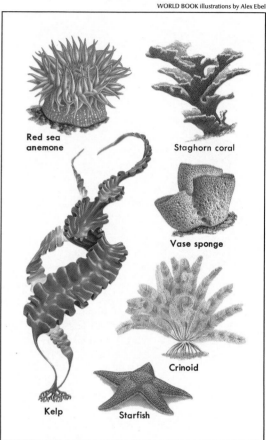

Red sea anemone

Staghorn coral

Vase sponge

Crinoid

Kelp

Starfish

idly through the water in search of food. Other fish, such as cod and flounder, have burrowing whiskers or flat bodies that help them feed along the ocean bottom. Many fish of the deeper parts of the ocean have light-producing organs that may help attract prey. Such fish include deep-sea anglers and lanternfish.

Squids are free-swimming *mollusks* (animals with soft, boneless bodies) that have 10 arms. Related animals include octopuses and cuttlefish. Squids live in surface and deep waters. Squids may measure from less than 1 foot (0.3 meter) to as much as 60 feet (18 meters) long, including the arms. A squid moves backward through the water in a jetlike action by forcing water through a tube that lies beneath its head.

Nektonic mammals include dugongs, manatees, porpoises, and whales, all of which remain in the ocean for their entire lives. Other marine mammals, such as sea lions, sea otters, seals, and walruses, spend time on land.

The benthos is made up of marine organisms that live on or near the sea floor. Animals of the benthos may burrow in the ocean floor, attach themselves to the bottom, or crawl or swim about within the bottom waters.

Where sunlight can reach the sea floor, the benthos includes plants and plantlike organisms, such as kelp and sea grass, which become anchored to the bottom. Among the common animals that live on the sea floor are clams, crabs, lobsters, starfish, and several types of worms. Some fish have features specially suited for life on the ocean floor. For example, halibut and sole, which lie flat on the bottom, have both eyes on the side of the head facing up.

Most bottom-dwelling creatures are part of the plankton and drift with the currents during the early stages of their development. They then sink to the sea floor where, as adults, they become part of the benthos. Such animals include barnacles, clams, corals, oysters, and various snails and worms.

See **Ocean** in *World Book* for more information on the following topics:

- The importance of the ocean
- Life in the ocean
- How the ocean moves
- The benefits of the ocean
- Discovering the secrets of the deep
- Careers in oceanography

Douglas P. Wilson

Many octopuses find their prey on the ocean bottom.

Octopus is a marine animal with a soft body and eight arms, also called *tentacles.* The word *octopus* comes from two Greek words that mean *eight feet.*

Some people call octopuses *devilfish,* probably because of the animal's frightening appearance. An octopus has large eyes and strong, hard jaws that come to a point like a parrot's bill. The octopus uses its arms to catch clams, crabs, lobsters, mussels, and other shellfish, and to break the shells apart. It cuts up food with its horny jaws. Some kinds of octopuses inject a poison that paralyzes their prey. Octopuses rarely if ever attack people.

There are about 50 kinds of octopuses, and most are only about as big as a person's fist. The largest ones measure 28 feet (8.5 meters) from the tip of one arm to the tip of another on the other side of the body.

Octopuses belong to a group of shellfish called *mollusks.* This group also includes clams, oysters, and snails. Like squid and cuttlefish, octopuses are mollusks that have no outside shells. See **Mollusk.**

An octopus has two eyes and sees well. It has the most highly developed brain of all the *invertebrates* (animals without backbones). It has three hearts that pump blood through its body. The animal breathes by means of gills, somewhat as fish do. An octopus swims by drawing water into its body. Then the animal squeezes the water out through its *siphon,* a funnel-shaped open-ing under the head. The force of the expelled water moves the animal backward. The octopus can also squirt a black fluid from the siphon. This fluid forms a dark cloud that hides the animal so it can escape from sharks, whales, human beings, and other enemies.

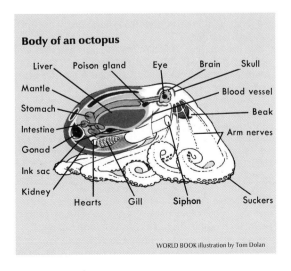

Body of an octopus

Liver, Poison gland, Eye, Brain, Skull, Mantle, Stomach, Intestine, Gonad, Ink sac, Kidney, Blood vessel, Beak, Arm nerves, Hearts, Gill, Siphon, Suckers

WORLD BOOK illustration by Tom Dolan

E. R. Degginger

The ostrich is the world's largest bird. Adults stand nearly 8 feet (2.4 meters) tall and may weigh up to 345 pounds (156 kilograms). The male, *above,* has black and white feathers.

Ostrich is the largest living bird. It may stand nearly 8 feet (2.4 meters) tall and weigh as much as 345 pounds (156 kilograms). Ostriches live on the plains and deserts of Africa. The extinct moas of New Zealand, which were 10 feet (3 meters) tall, were the only birds taller than ostriches. The extinct elephant birds of Madagascar, which weighed about 1,000 pounds (450 kilograms), were the only heavier birds.

The ostrich is the only bird that has only two toes on each foot. The rhea, which is also called the *South American ostrich,* is three-toed, and it is not a true ostrich.

The male ostrich is a handsome bird. It has black feathers on its bulky body, with large white feathers, or plumes, on its small wings and tail. Its long, thin legs and upper neck and its small head have almost no feathers. The bare skin varies in color from pink to blue. Thick black eyelashes surround its eyes, which are almost 2 inches (5 centimeters) in diameter. The female's body, tail, and wings are dull brown.

The male ostrich has a strange voice. It gives a deep roar like that of a lion, but with a strange hissing sound. The ostrich cannot fly, but it is known for its speed. Its long legs can carry it in 15-foot (4.6-meter) steps at speeds up to 40 miles (64 kilometers) per hour. Its speed

and its unusually good eyesight help the ostrich escape from its enemies, mainly lions and people. The belief that the ostrich hides its head in the sand when frightened is not true. If the ostrich is exhausted and cannot run any farther, or if it must defend its nest, it kicks with its powerful legs. Its long toes, the largest of which is 7 inches (18 centimeters) long, have thick nails that become weapons when the bird is cornered.

How the ostrich lives. The ostrich usually eats plants, but it will eat lizards and turtles if it can find them. It also eats much sand and gravel to aid in grinding food for digestion. Ostriches drink water when they find it. But they can live for long periods without drinking if the plants they eat are green and moist.

Ostriches are *polygamous* (the male has more than one mate). Each *cock* (male) digs a shallow nest in sand, and from three to five *hens* (females) lay their eggs in the nest. Each hen lays as many as 10 eggs. Each egg is almost round, nearly 6 inches (15 centimeters) in diameter, and weighs about 3 pounds (1.4 kilograms). The eggs are a dull yellow, and have large pores and a thick shell.

The male sits on the eggs at night. But during the day the hens share the task of keeping them warm. The eggs hatch in five or six weeks. When an ostrich is a month old, it can run as fast as an adult. Ostriches live up to 70 years. Few other birds live so long.

© Giuseppe Mazza

A female ostrich stands guard over a nest of eggs. Three to five females lay their eggs in the same nest.

Crude oil from Saudi Arabia

Crude oil from Venezuela

Crude oil from Australia

Tar sands from Canada

Oil shale from the United States

Top three photos, Standard Oil Company of California; bottom two, WORLD BOOK photos

Most petroleum comes from the earth as a liquid called *crude oil.* Different types of crude oil vary in color and thickness, ranging from a clear, thin fluid to a dark, tarlike substance. In some parts of the world, petroleum also occurs as a solid in certain sands and rocks.

Petroleum

Petroleum is one of the most valuable natural resources in the world. Some people call petroleum *black gold,* but it may be better described as the lifeblood of industrialized countries. Fuels made from petroleum provide power for automobiles, airplanes, factories, farm equipment, trucks, trains, and ships. Petroleum fuels also generate heat and electricity for many houses and business places. Altogether, petroleum provides nearly half the energy used in the world.

In addition to fuels, thousands of other products are made from petroleum. These products range from paving materials to drip-dry fabrics and from engine grease to cosmetics. Petroleum is used to make such items in the home as aspirins, carpets, curtains, detergents, phonograph records, plastic toys, and toothpaste.

Although we use a huge variety of products made from petroleum, few people ever see the substance itself. Most of it comes from deep within the earth as a liquid called *crude oil.* Different types of crude oil vary in thickness and color, ranging from a thin, clear oil to a thick, tarlike substance. Petroleum is also found in solid form in certain rocks and sands.

The word petroleum comes from two Latin words meaning *rock* and *oil.* People gave it this name because they first found it seeping up from the earth through cracks in surface rocks. Today, people often refer to petroleum simply as *oil,* and most petroleum is found in rocks located deep beneath the earth's surface.

People have used petroleum for thousands of years. But few people recognized its full value until the 1800's, when the kerosene lamp and the automobile were invented. These inventions created an enormous demand for two petroleum fuels, kerosene and gasoline. Since about 1900, scientists have steadily increased the variety and improved the quality of petroleum products.

Petroleum, like other minerals, cannot be replaced after it has been used. People are using more and more petroleum each year, and the world's supply is rapidly running out. If present rates of consumption continue, petroleum may become scarce sometime in the mid-2000's.

Most industrialized nations depend heavily on imported petroleum to meet their energy needs. As a result of this dependence, oil-exporting countries have been able to use petroleum as a political and economic weapon by restricting exports to some of these nations. Oil exporters have also strained the economies of a large number of countries, particularly the poorer ones, by drastically increasing the price of petroleum.

To prevent a full-scale energy shortage, scientists are experimenting with artificial forms of oil and with other sources of fuel. But even if new energy sources appear quickly, people will have to rely on petroleum for many years. Conservation of oil has thus become urgent for every country. People now need to be just as inventive in finding ways to conserve petroleum as they have been in finding ways to use it.

Arabian American Oil Company

The Middle East has more than half the world's oil. About a fifth of the total reserves lie in Saudi Arabia alone. Many nations depend on Middle Eastern oil to meet their energy needs.

Gamma from Liaison

Offshore wells provide over 20 per cent of the oil produced in the world. The North Sea, which has some of the richest offshore deposits, is a major source of oil for Western Europe.

© Alan Orling, Black Star

Bituminous sands, or *tar sands,* can be processed into petroleum. The world's largest deposits of these sands lie along the Athabasca River in the Canadian province of Alberta.

Steve Northup, Camera 5

Oil shale contains a substance that yields oil when heated. Huge deposits of oil shale in Colorado, Wyoming, and Utah may someday provide more oil than the oil fields of the Middle East.

How petroleum was formed. Most geologists believe petroleum was formed from remains of organisms that died millions of years ago. This *organic theory* of petroleum formation is based on the presence of certain carbon-containing substances in oil. Such substances could have come only from once living organisms. The process that produced petroleum also produced natural gas. Thus, natural gas is often found in association with crude oil or dissolved in it.

According to the organic theory, water covered much more of the earth's surface in the past than it does today. Masses of tiny organisms lived in shallow water or drifted around near the surface in the open ocean. As these organisms died, their remains settled to the bottom of the ocean and became trapped in *sediments* (particles of mud, sand, and other substances). The sediments piled up and became buried below the surface of the ocean floor.

As the sediments became buried deeper and deeper, they were subjected to increasingly high temperatures and pressures and so were compressed to form *sedimentary rock.* These conditions caused the rock to go through chemical processes that resulted in the formation of a waxy substance called *kerogen.* Kerogen sepa-

rates into a liquid (oil) and a gas (natural gas) when heated to temperatures above about 212° F. (100° C). But if the oil becomes buried too deeply and is exposed to temperatures higher than about 400° F. (200° C), the bonds holding the large, complex oil molecules together weaken and the oil decomposes. The temperature range in which oil can form is called the *oil window.* At temperatures below this range, little oil forms. At great depths, where temperatures are high, most oil decomposes.

Over time, the oil and gas moved upwards through natural passageways in the rock. These passageways included cracks and tiny holes known as *pores.* Geologists believe this movement may have been caused by the presence of water in the rock. Water, which is more dense than oil, could have pushed the oil upward. Another possible cause was the weight of the overlying layers of rock, which would tend to squeeze the oil into holes and cracks in the rock.

Oil and gas escaped to a type of rock called *reservoir rock.* Such rock has two characteristics that enable fluids to move through it: (1) porosity and (2) permeability. Porosity is the presence of small openings, or pores. Permeability means that some of the pores are con-

Where petroleum is found   Most crude oil lies in underground formations called *traps*. In a trap, petroleum collects in the pores of certain kinds of rock. Gas and water are also present in most traps. The most common types of traps are *anticlines, faults, stratigraphic traps,* and *salt domes.*

WORLD BOOK illustrations by Robert Keys

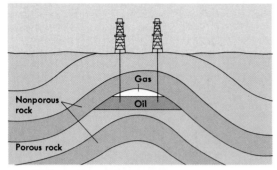

An anticline is an archlike formation.

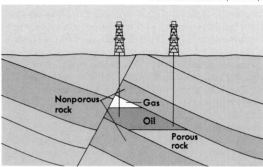

A fault is a fracture in the earth's crust.

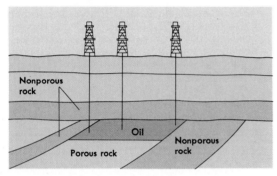

A stratigraphic trap has horizontal layers of rock.

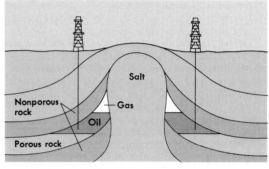

A salt dome is formed by a large mass of salt.

nected by spaces through which fluids can move. Oil and gas moved upward through the connected pore spaces until they reached an impermeable layer of rock. They continued to escape along the underside of the impermeable layer until that layer formed some sort of three-dimensional *trap.* Later, shifts in the earth's crust caused the oceans to draw back. Dry land then appeared over many reservoir rocks and traps.

The most common types of petroleum traps are *anticlines, faults, stratigraphic traps,* and *salt domes.* An anticline is an archlike formation of rock under which petroleum may collect. A fault is a fracture in the earth's crust, which can shift an impermeable layer of rock next to a permeable one that contains oil. Most stratigraphic traps consist of layers of impermeable rock that surround oilbearing rocks. In a salt dome, a cylinder- or cone-shaped formation of salt pushes up through sedimentary rocks, causing the rocks to arch and fracture in its path. Petroleum may accumulate above or along the sides of such a formation.

Most reservoirs and traps lie deep beneath the surface of the earth. However, some reservoirs have formed near the surface, and others have been shifted upward by changes in the earth's crust. Oil from these shallow deposits may reach the surface as *seepages* (trickles) or springs. In some places, such as Venezuela and the island of Trinidad, enough oil has collected at the surface to form a lake.

Today, the organic matter in some sedimentary deposits is being subjected to conditions of pressure, heat, and bacterial action similar to those that formed oil ages ago. But it takes millions of years for useful amounts of oil to develop. People are consuming petroleum much faster than it is being formed.

See **Petroleum** in *World Book* for more information on the following topics:

- Uses of petroleum
- Where petroleum is found
- Exploring for petroleum
- Drilling an oil well
- Recovering petroleum
- Transporting petroleum
- Refining petroleum
- The petroleum industry
- Petroleum conservation
- History of the use of petroleum
- Career opportunities

Planet is any of the nine largest objects that travel around the sun. The earth is a planet that travels around the sun once a year. Going outward from the sun, the planets are Mercury, Venus, Earth, Mars, Jupiter, Saturn, Uranus, Neptune, and Pluto. The sun, the planets and their *satellites* (moons), and smaller objects called asteroids, meteoroids, and comets make up the *solar system.*

The sun and the stars are giant, shining balls of hot gases. The planets are dark, solid bodies, much smaller than the sun and stars. The main difference between the stars and the planets is that the stars produce their own heat and light, but the planets do not. Nearly all light and heat on the planets comes to them from the sun. The planets can be seen only because they reflect the light of the sun. Six of the planets—Mercury, Venus, Mars, Jupiter, Saturn, and Uranus—are bright enough to be seen from the earth without a telescope.

Planets and stars look much alike in the night sky, but there are two ways to tell them apart. First, the planets shine steadily, but the stars seem to twinkle. Second, the planets move in relation to the stars. This movement was first noted by the ancient Greeks, who called the moving objects *planetae,* meaning *wanderers.*

The planets differ greatly in size and in distance from the sun. All of them together weigh less than a hundredth as much as the sun. The diameter of Jupiter, the largest planet, is about a tenth of the sun's. Yet Jupiter is more than 45 times as large as Pluto, the smallest planet. Earth and the three other planets nearest the sun are somewhat similar in size. They are called the *terrestrial* (earthlike) planets. The four largest planets, called *major* planets, are much farther from the sun. Astronomers know little about Pluto, and do not put it in either group.

Suppose the solar system could be shrunk so that the sun were the size of a half dollar. If you placed the sun at home plate on a baseball diamond, all the terrestrial planets would be within 16 feet (5 meters) of home plate. The major planets would begin near the pitcher's mound, and would extend far into the outfield. Pluto, the most distant planet, would be about 420 feet (128 meters) from home plate.

Astronomers do not think there are any planets in the solar system beyond Pluto. But they are almost certain that most of the stars in the universe have planets travel-

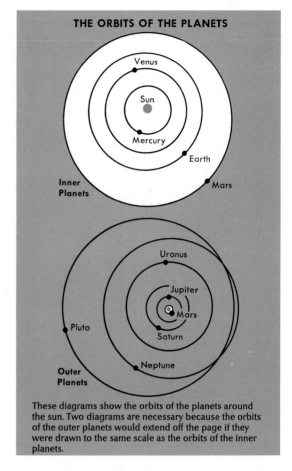

THE ORBITS OF THE PLANETS

Venus
Sun
Mercury
Earth
Mars

Inner Planets

Uranus
Jupiter
Mars
Pluto
Saturn
Neptune

Outer Planets

These diagrams show the orbits of the planets around the sun. Two diagrams are necessary because the orbits of the outer planets would extend off the page if they were drawn to the same scale as the orbits of the inner planets.

ing around them. There are more than 100 billion stars in the *galaxy* (family of stars) that includes the sun, and over 100 billion other galaxies can be seen in the universe. Suppose one star in every galaxy had a planet like the earth, and intelligent life existed on one of every million of these planets. There would be a hundred thousand planets with intelligent life.

Sun   Mercury   Venus   Earth   Mars   Jupiter

The planets vary in size from Jupiter, which has a diameter about 11 times as large as the earth's, to Pluto, with a diameter about a fifth that of the earth.

WORLD BOOK illustrations by Alex Ebel and Herbert F. Herrick

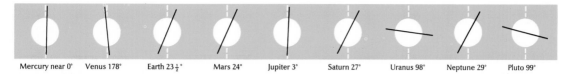

| Mercury near 0° | Venus 178° | Earth 23½° | Mars 24° | Jupiter 3° | Saturn 27° | Uranus 98° | Neptune 29° | Pluto 99° |

The axes of the planets, represented by the solid lines *above,* are imaginary lines around which the planets rotate. A planet's axis is not perpendicular to the path of the planet's orbit around the sun. It tilts at an angle from the perpendicular position indicated by the broken line.

How the planets move

As seen from the earth, the planets and the stars move westward across the sky. A person using a telescope to observe a planet must turn it constantly to keep the planet in view. From night to night, in addition to its motion across the sky, each planet shifts its position slightly eastward in relation to the stars. At certain times, a planet's position may temporarily shift westward, but it always returns to its regular eastward shift.

Orbiting the sun. All the planets move around the sun in the same direction. Three laws of planetary motion describing their orbits were published in the 1600's by the German astronomer Johannes Kepler.

Kepler's first law says that the planets move in *elliptical* (oval-shaped) orbits. As a result, the planets are a little closer to the sun at some points in their orbits than at others. For example, the earth comes within 91,400,000 miles (147,100,000 kilometers) of the sun at its *perihelion* (point of the orbit nearest the sun). It goes 94,500,000 miles (152,100,000 kilometers) from the sun at its *aphelion* (point farthest from the sun).

Kepler's second law is also called the *law of areas.* It says that an imaginary line between the sun and a planet sweeps across equal areas in equal periods of time. When a planet is nearest the sun, the line sweeps across a wide, but short, area, because the planet moves fastest there. When the planet is farthest from the sun, it moves slowest, and the line sweeps across a narrow, long area.

Kepler's third law says that a planet's *orbital period* (the time required to go around the sun) depends on its average distance from the sun. According to this law, the square of the period (the period multiplied once by

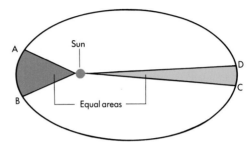

Kepler's second law shows how a planet covers equal areas of its orbit in equal periods of time. The planet travels at a higher speed near the sun, from *A* to *B,* than far from the sun, *C* to *D.*

itself) divided by the cube of the distance (the distance multiplied twice by itself) is the same for all the planets. Thus, a planet four times as far from the sun as another planet takes eight times as long to orbit the sun. This law was once used to find a planet's average distance from the sun after its orbital period had been measured.

Rotation. Each planet rotates as it revolves around the sun. The planets' *rotation periods* (the time required to spin around once) range from less than 10 hours for Jupiter to 243 days for Venus. The earth rotates once every 24 hours, or one day. For information about the earth's rotation and revolution, see **Earth** (How the earth moves; illustration: Three motions of the earth).

Each planet spins around its *rotational axis,* an imaginary line through its center. None of the planets has a rotational axis that is *perpendicular* (at an angle of 90°) to the path of its orbit. The axes tilt at an angle from the perpendicular position. The earth's axis, for example,

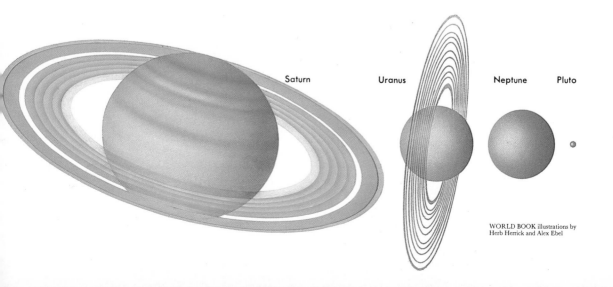

| Saturn | Uranus | Neptune | Pluto |

WORLD BOOK illustrations by
Herb Herrick and Alex Ebel

tilts at about $23\frac{1}{2}°$. Because of the tilt, the equators of the planets do not always face the sun directly. As a result, the planets' northern and southern halves are not heated evenly throughout the year. This uneven heating by the sun produces the changes on the earth that cause the spring, summer, autumn, and winter seasons (see **Season**).

Conditions on the planets

The temperature, atmosphere, surface features, length of days and nights, and other conditions on the planets vary widely. They depend on three things: (1) the planet's distance from the sun, (2) the planet's atmosphere, and (3) the planet's rotation.

Temperature. The planets nearest the sun receive more heat than those far away from it. The temperature on the closest planet, Mercury, rises to about 648° F. (342° C) during the day. On Earth, which is about $2\frac{1}{2}$ times as far from the sun as Mercury, the daytime temperature averages only about 60° F. (16° C). Pluto is over 100 times as far from the sun as Mercury. The tempera-

ture there is probably lower than −300° F. (−184° C).

The temperature on a planet is estimated from measurements of *infrared radiation* (heat waves) and radio waves that the planet sends out. These measurements are difficult to make for objects with low temperatures. For this reason, temperature estimates for cold planets are less reliable than those for warm planets.

Atmosphere is the mixture of gases that surrounds a planet. The atmospheres of the terrestrial planets consist chiefly of carbon dioxide and nitrogen. The atmospheres of the major planets consist mostly of helium, hydrogen, methane, and ammonia. The earth is the only planet with a large amount of oxygen in its atmosphere.

Astronomers determine the kinds of gases in a planet's atmosphere by studying the light, radio waves, and other radiation coming from the planet.

The *atmospheric pressure* (force exerted by the weight of gases) on a planet's surface depends on the amount of gas in the atmosphere. Earth's atmosphere has enough gas to produce a pressure of 14.7 pounds per square inch (1.03 kilograms per square centi-

The planets at a glance*

	Mercury ☿	Venus ♀	Earth ⊕	Mars ♂
Distance from the sun: Mean	35,980,000 mi. (57,900,000 km)	67,230,000 mi. (108,200,000 km)	92,960,000 mi. (149,600,000 km)	141,000,000 mi. (227,900,000 km)
Shortest	28,600,000 mi. (46,000,000 km)	66,800,000 mi. (107,500,000 km)	91,400,000 mi. (147,100,000 km)	128,400,000 mi. (206,600,000 km)
Greatest	43,400,000 mi. (69,800,000 km)	67,700,000 mi. (108,900,000 km)	94,500,000 mi. (152,100,000 km)	154,800,000 mi. (249,200,000 km)
Closest approach to Earth	57,000,000 mi. (91,700,000 km)	25,700,000 mi. (41,400,000 km)	———————— ————————	34,600,000 mi. (55,700,000 km)
Length of year (earth-days) Average orbital speed	87.97 29.76 mi. per sec. (47.89 km per sec.)	224.7 21.77 mi. per sec. (35.03 km per sec.)	365.26 18.51 mi. per sec. (29.79 km per sec.)	686.98 14.99 mi. per sec. (24.13 km per sec.)
Diameter at equator	3,031 mi. (4,878 km)	7,521 mi. (12,104 km)	7,926 mi. (12,756 km)	4,223 mi. (6,796 km)
Rotation period Tilt of axis (degrees)	59 earth-days about 0	243 earth-days 178	23 hrs. 56 min. 23.44	24 hrs. 37 min. 23.98
Temperature	−279 to 801 °F (−173 to 427 °C)	864 °F (462 °C)	−128.6 to 136 °F (−89.6 to 58 °C)	−225.4 ° to 63 °F (−143 ° to 170 °C)
Atmosphere: Pressure	0.00000000003 lb. per sq. in. (0.000000000002 kg per cm²)	1,323 lbs. per sq. in. (93 kg per cm²)	14.7 lbs. per sq. in. (1.03 kg per cm²)	0.1 lb. per sq. in. (0.007 kg per cm²)
Gases	Sodium, helium, hydrogen, oxygen	Carbon dioxide, nitrogen, water vapor, argon, carbon monoxide, neon, sulfur dioxide	Nitrogen, oxygen, carbon dioxide, water vapor	Carbon dioxide, nitrogen, argon, oxygen, carbon monoxide, neon, krypton, xenon, water vapor
Mass (Earth=1) Density (g/cm³) Gravity (Earth=1)	0.056 5.42 0.386	0.815 5.25 0.879	1 5.52 1	0.107 3.94 0.38
Number of known satellites	0	0	1	2

*All figures are approximate.

meter). But the atmosphere of Mars contains so little gas that its surface pressure is only about $\frac{1}{150}$ as great as the earth's. The atmosphere of Venus has so much gas that its surface pressure is as much as 90 times as great as the pressure on the earth.

Astronomers can estimate the amount of gas in a planet's atmosphere by measuring how the temperature varies throughout the atmosphere. A much more accurate, but more difficult, method is to measure changes in radio waves sent through the planet's atmosphere by a passing spacecraft.

Surface features of a planet like the earth include mountains, valleys, lakes, rivers, flat areas, and craters. A planet's surface is shaped partly by conditions on the planet itself, and partly by collisions with meteors.

Studying the planets

Explaining the motion of the planets brought about one of the most interesting disputes in the history of science. The dispute involved two important theories.

One theory of planetary motion was suggested about A.D. 150 by Ptolemy, a Greek astronomer. He believed the earth was the center of the universe. He thought the sun and the planets traveled around the earth once a day. Ptolemy's theory explained what people saw in the sky, and guided their thinking for over a thousand years.

The dispute began in 1543, when the Polish astronomer Nicolaus Copernicus suggested that the earth and the other planets traveled around the sun. This theory made it easier to describe the motions of the planets, and astronomers soon began to use it. But religious leaders called Copernicus a fool for saying that the earth was just another planet. They forbade the use of his writings until 1757.

Discoveries by other astronomers gradually convinced people that the Copernican theory was correct. The Copernican theory gained support after Sir Isaac Newton of England discovered his law of universal gravitation about 1665. This law described the sun's pull on the planets. For more information about how early astronomers solved the puzzle of planetary motions, see **Astronomy** (History) in *World Book*.

Jupiter ♃	Saturn ♄	Uranus ♅	Neptune ♆	Pluto ♇
483,600,000 mi.	888,200,000 mi.	1,786,400,000 mi.	2,798,800,000 mi.	3,666,200,000 mi.
(778,400,000 km)	(1,429,400,000 km)	(2,875,000,000 km)	(4,504,300,000 km)	(5,900,100,000 km)
460,200,000 mi.	838,800,000 mi.	1,702,100,000 mi.	2,774,800,000 mi.	2,749,600,000 mi.
(740,600,000 km)	(1,349,900,000 km)	(2,739,300,000 km)	(4,465,600,000 km)	(4,425,100,000 km)
507,000,000 mi.	937,600,000 mi.	1,870,800,000 mi.	2,824,800,000 mi.	4,582,700,000 mi.
(816,000,000 km)	(1,508,900,000 km)	(3,010,700,000 km)	(4,546,100,000 km)	(7,375,100,000 km)
390,700,000 mi.	762,700,000 mi.	1,607,000,000 mi.	2,680,000,000 mi.	2,670,000,000 mi.
(628,760,000 km)	(1,277,400,000 km)	(2,587,000,000 km)	(4,310,000,000 km)	(4,290,000,000 km)
4,332.7	10,759	30,685	60,190	90,800
8.12 mi. per sec.	5.99 mi. per sec.	4.23 mi. per sec.	3.37 mi. per sec.	2.95 mi. per sec.
(13.06 km per sec.)	(9.64 km per sec.)	(6.81 km per sec.)	(5.43 km per sec.)	(4.74 km per sec.)
88,846 mi.	74,898 mi.	31,763 mi.	30,800 mi.	1,430 mi.
(142,984 km)	(120,536 km)	(51,118 km)	(49,500 km)	(2,300 km)
9 hrs. 55 min.	10 hrs. 39 min.	17 hrs. 8 min.	16 hrs. 7 min.	6 earth-days
3.08	26.73	97.92	28.80	98.8
−234 °F	−288 °F	−357 °F	−353 °F	−387 to −369 °F
(−148 °C)	(−178 °C)	(−216 °C)	(−214 °C)	(−233 to −223 °C)
No surface	No surface	No surface	No surface	?
Hydrogen, helium, methane, ammonia, ethane, acetylene, phosphine, water vapor, carbon monoxide	Hydrogen, helium, methane, ammonia, ethane, phosphine (?)	Hydrogen, helium, methane	Hydrogen, helium, methane, acetylene	Methane, nitrogen (?)
317.892	95.184	14.54	17.15	0.002 (?)
1.33	0.69	1.27	1.64	2.03 (?)
2.53	1.07	0.91	1.14	0.07 (?)
16	18	15	8	1

© Breck Kent, Earth Scenes

A towering sequoia

© Frank Oberle, Bruce Coleman Inc.

Kernels harvested from corn plants

© L. West, Bruce Coleman Inc.

Moss plants growing on a rock

Plants vary greatly in size and form, ranging from tall, majestic trees to tiny, simple mosses. More than 350,000 species of plants grow in all parts of the world. Plants supply people with food and many other useful products. They also add beauty and pleasure to people's lives.

Plant

Plant. Plants grow in almost every part of the world. We see such plants as flowers, grass, and trees nearly every day. Plants also grow on mountaintops, in the oceans, and in many desert and polar regions.

Without plants, there could be no life on the earth. People could not live without air or food, and thus could not live without plants. The oxygen in the air we breathe comes from plants. The food that we eat comes from plants or from animals that eat plants. We build houses and make many useful products from lumber. Much of our clothing is made from the fibers of the cotton plant.

Scientists believe there are more than 350,000 *species* (kinds) of plants, but no one knows for sure. Some tiny plants that grow on the forest floor can barely be seen.

Others tower over people and animals. The largest living things on earth are the giant sequoia trees of California. Some stand more than 290 feet (88 meters) high and measure over 30 feet (9 meters) wide. Plants also are the oldest living things. One bristlecone pine tree in California started growing 4,000 to 5,000 years ago.

Many scientists divide all living things into five main groups called *kingdoms*. These kingdoms are (1) plants, (2) animals, (3) fungi, (4) protists, and (5) monerans. Scientists group organisms in a particular kingdom because the organisms share certain basic characteristics. These characteristics include physical structure, means of obtaining food, and means of reproduction.

Plants have a number of characteristics that set them apart from other living things. For example, both plants and animals are complex organisms that are made up of many types of cells. However, plant cells have thick walls that consist of a material called *cellulose.* Animal cells do not have this material. The cells of monerans and some protists, like those of plants, have cellulose walls. But monerans and protists are simple organisms made up of one cell or only a few types of cells. Bacteria, including blue-green algae, are monerans. Protists include other algae as well as diatoms and protozoans.

All plants develop from a tiny form of the plant called an *embryo.* Monerans, protists, and fungi—such as molds and mushrooms—do not develop from embryos.

Plants also obtain food in ways different from those of most other organisms. Almost all kinds of plants stay in one place for their entire lives. Most plants make their own food from air, sunlight, and water by a process called *photosynthesis.* Fungi cannot make their own food. They obtain the nutrients they need from the animals, plants, and decaying matter on which they live. Animals also cannot make their own food, but most animals can move about to find it.

The importance of plants

Plants supply people with food, clothing, and shelter. Many of our most useful medicines are also made from plants. In addition, plants add beauty and pleasure to our lives. Most people enjoy the smell of flowers, the sight of a field of waving grain, and the quiet within a forest.

Not all plants are helpful to people. Some species grow in fields and gardens as weeds that choke off useful plants. Tiny bits of pollen from certain plants cause such health problems as asthma and hay fever. Some plants are poisonous if eaten. Others, such as poison ivy and poison oak, irritate the skin.

Food. Plants are probably most important to people as food. Sometimes we eat plants themselves, as when we eat apples, peas, or potatoes. But even when we eat meat or drink milk, we are using foods that come from an animal that eats plants.

People get food from many kinds of plants—or parts of plants. The seeds of such plants as corn, rice, and wheat are the chief source of food in most parts of the world. We eat bread and many other products made from these grains, and almost all our meat comes from animals that eat them. When we eat beets, carrots, or sweet potatoes, we are eating the roots of plants. We eat the leaves of cabbage, lettuce, and spinach plants; the stems of asparagus and celery plants; and the flower buds of broccoli and cauliflower plants. The fruits of many plants also provide us with food. They include apples, bananas, berries, and oranges, as well as some nuts and vegetables. Coffee, tea, and many soft drinks get their flavor from plants.

Raw materials. Plants supply people with many important raw materials. Trees give us lumber for building homes and making furniture and other goods. Wood chips are used in manufacturing paper and paper products. Other products made from trees include cork, natural rubber, maple syrup, and turpentine. Most of the world's people wear clothing made from cotton. Threads of cotton are also woven into carpets and other goods. Rope and twine are made from hemp, jute, and sisal plants.

Plants also provide an important source of fuel. In many parts of the world, people burn wood to heat their homes or to cook their food. Other important sources of fuel—coal, oil, and natural gas—also come from plants. Coal began to form millions of years ago, when great forests and swamps covered much of the earth. As the trees in these forests died, they fell into the swamps, which were then covered by mud and sand. The increasing pressure of this mass of materials helped cause the

dead plants to turn into coal. Petroleum and natural gas were formed in ancient oceans by the pressure of mud, sand, and water on decaying masses of plants and animals.

Medicines. Many useful drugs come from plants. Some of these plants have been used as medicines for hundreds of years. More than 400 years ago, for example, some Indian tribes of South America used the bark of the cinchona tree to reduce fever. The bark is still used to make *quinine,* a drug used to treat malaria and other diseases. Another drug, called *digitalis,* is used in treating heart disease. It is made from the dried leaves of the purple foxglove plant. The roots of the Mexican

Plants and the cycle of nature

Plants play an important part in the cycle of nature. They grow by taking energy from the sun, carbon dioxide from the air, and water and minerals from the ground. During the cycle, plants supply us with food and give off the oxygen that we breathe.

WORLD BOOK diagram by David Cunningham

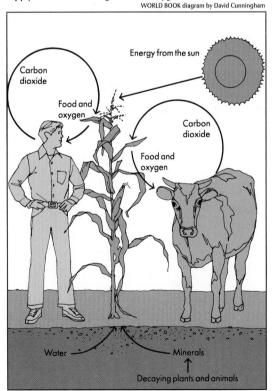

Energy from the sun

Carbon dioxide

Food and oxygen

Carbon dioxide

Food and oxygen

Water

Minerals

Decaying plants and animals

yam are used in producing *cortisone,* a drug useful in treating arthritis and a number of other diseases.

Plants and the cycle of nature. All living things—plants, animals, fungi, protists, and monerans—are linked by the *cycle of nature.* This natural process gives people oxygen to breathe, food to eat, and heat to keep them warm. The sun supplies the energy that runs the cycle.

Plants have a complex relationship with people and animals in the cycle of nature. Plants use sunlight to make their own food, and they give off oxygen during the process. People and animals eat the plants and breathe in the oxygen. In turn, people and animals breathe out carbon dioxide. Plants combine the carbon

dioxide with energy from sunlight and water and minerals from the soil to make more food. After plants and animals die, they begin to decay. The rotting process returns minerals to the soil, where plants can again use them.

Plants also play an important part in *conservation,* the protection of soil, water, wildlife, and other natural resources. Plants help keep the soil from being blown away by the wind or washed away by the water. They slow down the flow of water by storing it in their roots, stems, and leaves. Plants also give wild animals food to eat and a safe place to live. For more information on the importance of plants in nature, see the *World Book* articles on **Balance of nature, Conservation,** and **Ecology.**

Where plants live

Most species of plants live in places that have warm temperatures at least part of the year, plentiful rainfall, and rich soil. But plants can live under extreme conditions. Mosses have been found in Antarctic areas where the temperature seldom rises above 32° F. (0° C). Many desert plants grow in areas where the temperature may rise well above 100° F. (38° C).

Not all kinds of plants grow in all parts of the world. For example, cattails live only in such damp places as swamps and marshes. Cactuses, on the other hand, are found chiefly in deserts. Through long periods of time, many small changes have taken place in various kinds of plants. These changes have enabled the plants to survive in a particular environment.

Many elements make up a plant's environment. One of the most important is the weather—sunlight, temperature, and *precipitation* (rain, melted snow, and other

moisture). The environment of a plant also includes the soil and the other plants and the animals that live in the same area. All these elements form what scientists call a *natural community.*

No two natural communities are exactly alike, but many resemble one another more than they differ. Botanists divide the world into *biomes*—natural communities of plants, animals, and other organisms. Important land biomes include (1) the tundra, (2) forests, (3) chaparrals, (4) grasslands, (5) savannas, and (6) deserts. Forests are often subdivided into smaller biomes, such as temperate deciduous forests and tropical rain forests. In addition, many plants live in *aquatic* (water) regions that are not grouped as a specific biome.

Human beings have greatly affected the natural communities. In North America, for example, great forests once extended from the Atlantic Ocean to the Missis-

Major plant regions of the world

Plants live everywhere except in regions that have permanent ice. But not all plants grow in all regions of the world. This map shows the five major regions in which certain kinds of plants grow best. For example, cacti grow chiefly in deserts, and cattails in *aquatic* (watery) regions.

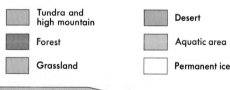

Tundra and high mountain

Forest

Grassland

Desert

Aquatic area

Permanent ice

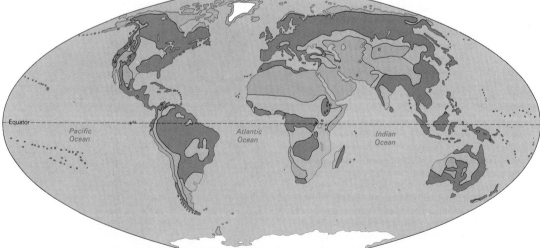

Pacific Ocean

Atlantic Ocean

Indian Ocean

Equator

Adapted from *Physical Elements of Geography,* Fifth Edition by Trewartha, Robinson & Hammond. Copyright © 1967 by McGraw-Hill, Inc. Used by permission of McGraw-Hill Book Company.

WORLD BOOK illustration by Alex Ebel

Plants of the high mountain tundra

Many kinds of mosses, shrubs, and wild flowers survive the long, cold winters of the high mountain tundra. Farther down the mountains, conifers begin to appear.

1. Alpine fir	4. Moss campion	7. Sheep laurel	10. Saxifrage
2. Bristlecone pine	5. Sedum	8. White phlox	11. Mountain avens
3. Englemann spruce	6. Alpine forget-me-not	9. Squawfeather	

WORLD BOOK illustration by John F. Eggert

Plants of the coniferous forest

Towering trees, such as hemlocks, cedars, and Douglas-firs, dominate the temperate coniferous forest on the Olympic Peninsula of Washington. Many small plants grow on the forest floor.

1. Western redcedar	4. Horsetail	7. Piper bellflower
2. Western sword fern	5. Douglas-fir	8. Western hemlock
3. Sitka spruce	6. Wood sorrel	

WORLD BOOK illustration by Lowell Hess

Plants of the tropical rain forest

Trees grow close together in this African rain forest, and vines climb high on the trees. Most of these plants are listed by their scientific names, though all have local common names.

1. *Lophira procera*	6. *Picralima umbellata*
2. *Scottellia kamerunensis*	7. *Diospyros insculpta*
3. *Casearia bridelioides*	8. Lianas
4. *Pausinystalia*	9. Strangler fig
5. *Strombosia pustulata*	10. *Ako ombe*

sippi River. Most of the trees were cleared by advancing settlers, and the forests have been replaced by cities and farms. In other parts of the world, irrigation and the use of fertilizers have enabled plants to be grown on once-barren land.

This section describes the natural plant life in the important land biomes and in aquatic regions. For information on where animals live, see the **Animal** article. For a discussion of the relationship between living things and their environment, see **Ecology**.

The tundra is a cold, treeless area that surrounds the Arctic Ocean, near the North Pole. It extends across the uppermost parts of North America, Europe, and Asia. The land in these regions is frozen most of the year, and the annual precipitation measures only from 6 to 10 inches (15 to 25 centimeters). The upper slopes of the world's highest mountains—the Alps, the Andes, the Himalaya, and the Rockies—have conditions similar to those in the tundra.

Summers in the tundra last only about 60 days, and summer temperatures average only about 45° F. (7° C). The top 1 foot (30 centimeters) or so of the land thaws during the summer, leaving many marshes, ponds, and swamps. Such plants as mosses, shrubs, and wild flowers grow in the tundra. These plants grow in low clumps and so are protected from the wind and cold. A thick growth of *lichens* (organisms made up of algae and fungi) covers much of the land. In *World Book,* see **Tundra.**

Forests cover almost a third of the earth's land area. They consist chiefly of trees, but many other kinds of plants also grow in forests. Some botanists divide the many types of forests into three major groups: (1) coniferous forests, (2) temperate deciduous forests, and (3) tropical rain forests.

Coniferous forests are made up mainly of trees that are *coniferous* (cone-bearing) and evergreen. Most ecologists distinguish between *boreal forests,* also called *taiga,* and *temperate coniferous forests.*

Boreal forests grow in regions that have a short summer and a long, cold winter. The growing season in these regions may last less than three months. Boreal forests are found in the northernmost parts of North America, Europe, and Asia. They also grow in the high mountains of these continents. Trees found in boreal forests include such evergreen conifers as balsam firs, black spruces, jack pines, and white spruces. The pointy, triangular shape of the these trees helps them shed heavy snow.

Few plants grow on the floor of boreal forests. Thick layers of old needles build up beneath the trees. These needles contain acids that are slowly released as the needles decay. Water carries the acids into the soil. The acidic water dissolves many minerals and carries them into the deeper layers of the soil. As a result, the topsoil found in boreal forests is often very sandy and unable to support many types of small plants.

Temperate coniferous forests grow in western North America in areas that have mild, wet winters and dry summers. The redwood forests of northern California and the temperate rain forests found on the Olympic Peninsula of Washington are both examples of temperate coniferous forests. Major trees of the temperate coniferous forest include redwoods and giant sequoias in

WORLD BOOK illustration by Lowell Hess

Plants of the temperate deciduous forest

Trees are the chief plants in a temperate deciduous forest. Most of them lose their leaves every winter. In spring, before the new leaves are fully grown, wild flowers bloom on the forest floor.

1. American elm
2. White oak
3. Mockernut hickory
4. Dogwood
5. Black oak
6. Shagbark hickory
7. Tulip tree
8. May apple
9. Bloodroot
10. Solomon's-seal
11. Jack-in-the-pulpit
12. Bellwort
13. Wild hyacinth
14. Dutchman's-breeches
15. Wild geranium
16. Painted trillium

WORLD BOOK illustration by John F. Eggert

Plants of the chaparral

Thick growths of shrubs and small trees flourish in the hot, dry summers and cool, wet winters of the chaparral. Fires frequently occur during the summer and help stimulate new plant growth.

1. Sugarbush
2. California buckwheat
3. White sage
4. Chamise
5. Black sage
6. Coyote brush
7. California scrub oak
8. Deerweed

WORLD BOOK illustration by Alex Ebel

Plants of the grasslands

Wild grasses, such as big bluestem and prairie cordgrass, once covered the Great Plains of the United States and Canada. Most of these grasslands are now used for crops or for grazing.

1. Indian grass   3. Prairie cordgrass   5. Big bluestem
2. Switchgrass   4. Canada wild rye

the south and Douglas-firs, hemlocks, cedars, and pines in more northern areas.

Temperate deciduous forests cover large areas of North America, central Europe, east Asia, and Australia. In the United States, temperate deciduous forests grow mostly east of the Mississippi River and extend northward into the Northern States and southern Canada, where they become mixed with coniferous forests. Most of these areas have cold winters and warm, wet summers.

Most of the trees in temperate deciduous forests are called *broadleaf trees* because they have broad, flat leaves. They also are *deciduous*—that is, they lose their leaves every fall and grow new ones in the spring. Trees that grow in temperate deciduous forests include basswoods, beeches, birches, hickories, maples, oaks, poplars, tulips, and walnuts. A thick growth of wild flowers, seedlings, and shrubs covers the floor of most of these forests.

Tropical rain forests grow in regions that have warm, wet weather the year around. These regions include Central America and the northern parts of South America, central and western Africa, Southeast Asia, and the Pacific Islands.

Most trees in tropical rain forests are broadleaf trees. Because of the warm, wet weather, they never completely lose their leaves. These trees lose a few leaves at a time throughout the year. Many kinds of trees grow in tropical rain forests, including mahoganies and teaks. The trees grow so close together that little sunlight can reach the ground. As a result, only ferns and other plants that require little sunlight can grow on the forest floor. Many plants, including lichens, orchids, and vines, grow high on the trees.

The heavy rainfall that occurs in tropical rain forests

dissolves much of the nutrients and organic materials out of the soil. As a result, the soils found in tropical rain forests contain a very small amount of nutrients and organic matter. However, the soil is able to support the lush growth found in these forests because fresh nutrients from the decay of fallen leaves are continually being released into the soil.

Chaparrals consist of thick growths of shrubs and small trees. Cork and scrub oaks, manzanitas, and many unusual herbs are often found on chaparrals. Chaparrals occur in areas that have hot, dry summers and cool, wet winters. Such areas are found in the western part of North America, the southern regions of Europe near the Mediterranean Sea, the Middle East, northern Africa, and the southern parts of South America, Africa, and Australia.

During the dry summer season, fires are common on chaparrals. But these fires actually help to maintain the plant life. Many of the plants that grow on chaparrals are either resistant to fire or are able to grow back quickly after they burn. The fires clear the dense vegetation away and expose bare ground to allow for new growth. The heat of the fires also stimulates development in the seeds of some plants. In addition, many types of short-lived, small flowers appear only after a fire has taken place. In *World Book,* see **Chaparral.**

Grasslands are open areas where grasses are the most plentiful plants. In the United States and Canada, most of the natural grasslands are used to grow crops. There, farmers and ranchers grow such grains as barley, oats, and wheat where bluestem, buffalo, and grama grasses once covered the land.

Botanists divide grasslands into *steppes* and *prairies.* Only short grasses grow on steppes. These dry areas include the Great Plains of the United States and Canada,

WORLD BOOK illustration by Lowell Hess

Plants of the desert

Many kinds of cactus plants grow in the desert areas of the American Southwest. Like all desert plants, these cactuses can survive long dry periods and very hot temperatures.

1. Jumping cholla
2. Mesquite
3. Jumping cholla
4. Barrel cactus
5. Saguaro
6. Bur sage
7. Organ-pipe cactus
8. Ocotillo
9. Paloverde
10. Prickly pear
11. Desert marigold
12. Brittlebush
13. Strawberry hedgehog

the *veld* of South Africa, and the plains of the Soviet Union. Taller grasses grow on the prairies of the American Midwest, eastern Argentina, and parts of Europe and Asia. Rolling hills, clumps of trees, and rivers and streams break up these areas. Most of the soil is rich and rainfall is plentiful. As a result, prairie land is used almost entirely to raise food crops and livestock. In *World Book,* see **Grassland.**

Savannas are grasslands with widely spaced trees. Some savannas are found in regions that receive little rain. Others are found in tropical regions, such as the Llamos of Venezuela, the Campos of southern Brazil, and the Sudan of Africa. Most of these areas have dry winters and wet summers. Grasses grow tall and stiff under such conditions. Acacia, baobab, and palm trees grow on many savannas. A wide variety of animals, such as antelope, giraffes, lions, and zebras, roam the savannas of Africa. In *World Book,* see **Savanna.**

Deserts cover about a fifth of the earth's land. A huge desert region extends across northern Africa and into central Asia. This region includes three of the world's great deserts—the Arabian, the Gobi, and the Sahara. Other major desert regions of the world include the Atacama Desert along the western coast of South America, the Kalahari Desert in southern Africa, the Western Plateau of Australia, and the southwest corner of North America.

Some deserts have almost no plant life at all. Parts of the Gobi and the Sahara, for example, consist chiefly of shifting sand dunes. All deserts receive little rain and have either rocky or sandy soil. The temperature in most deserts rises above 100° F. (38° C) for at least part of the year. Some deserts also have cold periods. But in spite of these harsh conditions, many plants live in desert regions. These plants—sometimes called *xerophytes*—include cactuses, creosote bushes, Joshua trees, palm trees, sagebrush, and yuccas. Wild flowers are also found in the desert.

Desert plants do not grow close together. By being spread out, each plant can get water and minerals from a large area. The roots of most desert plants extend over large areas of land, and they capture as much rain water as possible. Cactuses and other *succulent* (juicy) plants store water in their thick leaves and stems. See **Desert.**

Aquatic regions are bodies of fresh or salt water. Freshwater areas include lakes, rivers, swamps, and marshes. Coastal marshes and oceans are saltwater regions. Most aquatic plants, which are also called *hydrophytes,* live in places that receive sunlight. These plants grow near the water surface, in shallow water, or along the shore.

Some kinds of aquatic plants, including eelgrass, live completely under the surface of the water. Other species of aquatic plants, such as duckweed, the smallest known flowering plant, float freely on the surface. Still others, such as the water marigold, grow only partly un-

WORLD BOOK illustration by Alex Ebel

Plants of a freshwater pond

Many species of plants grow in and around ponds and other bodies of fresh water. Some of these plants live completely underwater, but others grow partly in and partly out of the water.

1. Reed grass	5. Blue flag	9. Cattail	13. Water milfoil
2. Black willow	6. Swamp-loosestrife	10. Pickerelweed	14. Bladderwort
3. Silver maple	7. Sphagnum moss	11. White water lily	15. Wild celery
4. Purple loosestrife	8. Sedge	12. Yellow water lily	

Special features of freshwater plants

Plants that live in ponds have special features that enable them to survive. The features of two kinds of these plants, the white water lily and a water milfoil, are shown below.

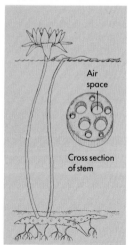

WORLD BOOK illustrations by Margaret Ann Moran

The air spaces in the stem of the white water lily serve two purposes. They help hold the plant upright in the water, and they carry air down through the stem to the roots.

The long, underwater leaves of the water milfoil are especially suited to absorb carbon dioxide from the water. The leaves that grow above water resemble those of land plants.

derwater. Many aquatic plants have air spaces in their stems and leaves. The air spaces help them stand erect or stay afloat.

Aquatic regions have unique conditions that make it difficult for many types of plants to grow there. For example, swamps and marshes, as well as flood plains along many streams and rivers, become flooded leaving the plants that live in these areas completely covered by water. As a result, only a few species of plants are able to survive in aquatic regions. Common freshwater plants include duckweeds, pondweeds, water lilies, sedges, and cattails. Such trees as baldcypresses, blackgums, and willows also grow in fresh water. Saltwater plants include eelgrass, cordgrass, and many types of sedges.

See **Plant** in *World Book* for more information on the following topics:

- Kinds of plants
- Parts of plants
- How plants reproduce
- How plants grow
- How plants change
- Plant enemies
- Classification of plants

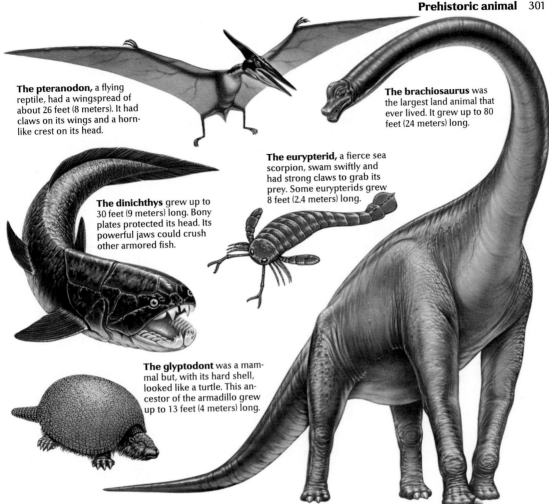

The **pteranodon,** a flying reptile, had a wingspread of about 26 feet (8 meters). It had claws on its wings and a horn-like crest on its head.

The **brachiosaurus** was the largest land animal that ever lived. It grew up to 80 feet (24 meters) long.

The **eurypterid,** a fierce sea scorpion, swam swiftly and had strong claws to grab its prey. Some eurypterids grew 8 feet (2.4 meters) long.

The **dinichthys** grew up to 30 feet (9 meters) long. Bony plates protected its head. Its powerful jaws could crush other armored fish.

The **glyptodont** was a mammal but, with its hard shell, looked like a turtle. This ancestor of the armadillo grew up to 13 feet (4 meters) long.

WORLD BOOK illustrations by Alex Ebel

Prehistoric animal

Prehistoric animal is any animal that lived more than 5,500 years ago—that is, before people invented writing and began to record history. Some prehistoric animals resembled animals alive today. But others were unlike any living animals. They included huge dinosaurs that measured 80 feet (24 meters) long and flying reptiles with a 36-foot (11-meter) wingspread. Other fantastic animals were toothed birds with claws on their wings; fish covered with bony armor; and pig-sized, trunkless ancestors of the elephant. Not all the different prehistoric animals lived at the same time.

The story of prehistoric animals is told by *fossils*. Fossils are shells, bones, animal tracks, outlines of leaves, and any other preserved traces of prehistoric life. Fossils help scientists tell what prehistoric animals looked like and when, where, and how these animals lived.

The oldest known animal fossils are about 700 million years old. However, most scientists who study prehistoric animals believe that the first simple animals lived millions of years earlier. They think that from these sim-

ple creatures more complicated animals gradually developed over millions of years.

The world of prehistoric animals

Prehistoric animals lived mainly during three major periods in the earth's history called *eras*. The *Paleozoic Era* lasted from about 570 million to 240 million years ago. The *Mesozoic Era* lasted from about 240 million to 63 million years ago. The *Cenozoic Era*, the present era, began about 63 million years ago. Throughout each era, great changes occurred in the kinds of animals and plants living on the earth.

The three eras are further divided into shorter periods. Different layers of rock formed in the earth's crust during each period. These rocks tell scientists about changes in the surface features and climate of the earth. From the rocks and the fossils found in them, scientists determine which animals lived during each period.

When animal life began on the earth, the earth looked very different from the way it does today. No plants grew on the bare, rocky land, and most mountains and valleys had not yet formed. Shallow seas covered much of the earth. In these seas, animal and plant life arose.

Early forms of animal life

The first animals were one-celled organisms that lived in the sea. These microscopic animals swam about by means of a whiplike tail. In time, animals made up of many identical cells *evolved* (developed gradually). The separate cells eventually began to serve different functions. These cells became organized into structures for feeding, reproducing, moving about, and sensing changes in the environment.

Animals with backbones are called *vertebrates*. They were the last major group of prehistoric animals to evolve. A vertebrate has several advantages over an invertebrate because it has a skeleton made of bones inside its body. Such a skeleton weighs less than an outer skeleton. It also enables the animal to move more freely. In addition, vertebrates could grow larger than invertebrates because a bony skeleton grows with an animal.

The move onto land was a huge advance in the development of prehistoric animals. Plants appeared on land first, about 430 million years ago. They thus provided food for the animals that came later. The first land animals included insects and spiders. For vertebrates, life on land required major adjustments. They had to breathe with lungs rather than gills. They also had to support their bodies against the pull of gravity. But life on land also had advantages. Oxygen is far more concentrated in air than in water. In addition, there were no enemies to prey on the first land animals.

The Age of Reptiles

The first reptiles were lizardlike creatures that developed about 330 million years ago, near the end of the Mississippian Period. Reptiles evolved from amphibians and resembled them. But reptiles had an important advantage—they could lay their eggs on land. A tough shell prevented reptile eggs from drying out, and special membranes enabled the young to develop inside the eggs. Reptiles thus depended less on water than am-

Animals of the Paleozoic Era Many early forms of animal life developed during the Paleozoic Era, which lasted from about 570 million to 240 million years ago. The era is divided into seven periods. During the first three, all animals lived in the sea. Later, insects, amphibians, and reptiles appeared on land.

WORLD BOOK illustrations by Alex Ebel

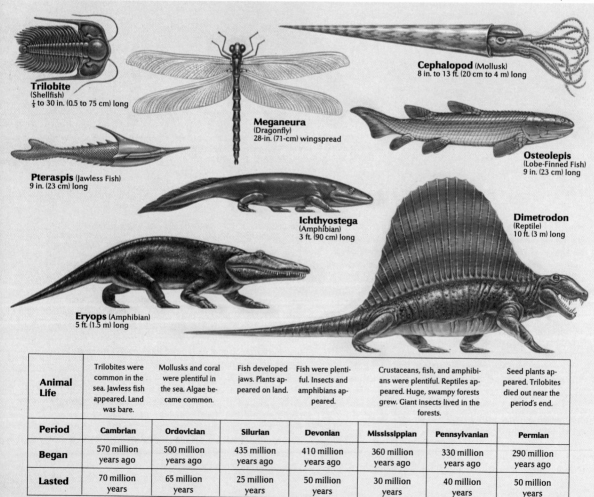

Trilobite (Shellfish) ½ to 30 in. (0.5 to 75 cm) long

Meganeura (Dragonfly) 28-in. (71-cm) wingspread

Cephalopod (Mollusk) 8 in. to 13 ft. (20 cm to 4 m) long

Pteraspis (Jawless Fish) 9 in. (23 cm) long

Osteolepis (Lobe-Finned Fish) 9 in. (23 cm) long

Ichthyostega (Amphibian) 3 ft. (90 cm) long

Dimetrodon (Reptile) 10 ft. (3 m) long

Eryops (Amphibian) 5 ft. (1.5 m) long

Animal Life	Trilobites were common in the sea. Jawless fish appeared. Land was bare.	Mollusks and coral were plentiful in the sea. Algae became common.	Fish developed jaws. Plants appeared on land.	Fish were plentiful. Insects and amphibians appeared.	Crustaceans, fish, and amphibians were plentiful. Reptiles appeared. Huge, swampy forests grew. Giant insects lived in the forests.		Seed plants appeared. Trilobites died out near the period's end.
Period	Cambrian	Ordovician	Silurian	Devonian	Mississippian	Pennsylvanian	Permian
Began	570 million years ago	500 million years ago	435 million years ago	410 million years ago	360 million years ago	330 million years ago	290 million years ago
Lasted	70 million years	65 million years	25 million years	50 million years	30 million years	40 million years	50 million years

phibians did and could lead more active lives on land.

Dinosaurs were the most spectacular Mesozoic reptiles. There were many kinds of dinosaurs, and they varied greatly in size. Some dinosaurs were the largest animals ever to live on land. The smallest kinds were about the size of chickens. Scientists once thought that dinosaurs were slow, clumsy animals. But they now believe that at least some kinds could run fairly fast.

The largest known dinosaurs were the *brachiosaurs*, which measured about 80 feet (24 meters) long. They ate only plants. The worst enemies of plant-eating dinosaurs were meat-eating dinosaurs, such as *tyrannosaurus rex*. By about 63 million years ago, all dinosaurs had died out. Scientists do not know why. But some believe an asteroid hit the earth. Dust from the asteroid could have kept sunlight from reaching the earth, thereby killing the plants that dinosaurs ate. For more information about dinosaurs, see **Dinosaur.**

Other reptiles. While dinosaurs ruled the land, giant reptiles also ruled the seas and the air. Like dinosaurs, they died out at the end of the Mesozoic Era. But smaller reptiles, including crocodiles, lizards, snakes, and turtles, continued into modern times.

Several kinds of marine reptiles lived in the Mesozoic seas. *Ichthyosaurs* resembled porpoises. *Plesiosaurs* were like enormous whales. *Mosasaurs* were gigantic lizards that grew up to 30 feet (9 meters) long.

Flying reptiles called *pterosaurs* were the first vertebrates to conquer the air. Some pterosaurs were no larger than sparrows. Others were huge creatures with a wingspread of 28 feet (8 meters). Pterosaurs had no feathers, but they may have had hair on the membranes of skin that formed their wings.

Invertebrates continued to multiply and evolve during Mesozoic times. Many kinds of mollusks flourished in the seas. They included the spiral-shelled ammonite and ancestors of snails, clams, and squids. Such crustaceans as lobsters, crabs, and shrimp also thrived in Mesozoic seas. Most present-day groups of insects had appeared by the end of the era.

Fish were plentiful during the Age of Reptiles. The first modern bony fish appeared during the Triassic Pe-

Animals of the Mesozoic Era Reptiles dominated the land, sea, and sky during the Mesozoic Era, which is also known as the *Age of Reptiles.* The era lasted from 240 million to 63 million years ago. It is divided into three periods. Many of the reptiles, including the dinosaurs, died out at the end of the era.

WORLD BOOK illustrations by Alex Ebel

Tylosaur (Sea Lizard)
26 ft. (8 m) long

Archaeopteryx
(First Bird) 1 1/2 ft. (46 cm) long

Rhamphorhynchus
(Flying Reptile)
2-ft. (61-cm)
wingspread

Ammonite
(Mollusk)
2 to 72 in. (5 to 183 cm) across

Tyrannosaurus rex
(Dinosaur)
40 ft. (12 m) long

Styracosaurus
(Horned Dinosaur)
20 ft. (6 m) long

	Triassic	Jurassic	Cretaceous
Animal Life	The first turtles, crocodiles, dinosaurs, sea reptiles, flying reptiles, and mammals appeared. The huge supercontinent began to break up into separate continents.	The first birds appeared. Dinosaurs reached their greatest size. Insects were plentiful. Ammonites flourished in the sea. A few small mammals lived on land.	Horned and armored dinosaurs became common. Flowering plants developed. Dinosaurs, flying reptiles, and giant sea reptiles died out at the end of the period.
Period	Triassic	Jurassic	Cretaceous
Began	240 million years ago	205 million years ago	138 million years ago
Lasted	35 million years	67 million years	75 million years

riod, which began about 240 million years ago. Such fish have skeletons made completely of bone. Earlier fish had skeletons made of cartilage or cartilage and bone.

Amphibians. By the end of the Triassic Period, about 205 million years ago, the larger amphibians had died out. But smaller amphibians lived on and became the ancestors of modern frogs, toads, and salamanders.

Birds evolved from dinosaurs during the Mesozoic Era. The oldest known bird was *Archaeopteryx*. It lived about 140 million years ago, during the late Jurassic Period. This bird was about the size of a crow and resembled a reptile in many ways. It had teeth, a reptilelike tail, and claws on each wing. But it was covered with feathers. Prehistoric birds left few fossils because their fragile skeletons were easily crushed.

Mammals, like birds, evolved from reptiles during the Mesozoic Era. They arose from a group of reptiles that gradually developed mammallike skulls, teeth, and bones. The early mammals were small animals, about the size of rats, with furry bodies and pointed snouts.

The Age of Mammals

Mammals began to rule the earth after the dinosaurs and other giant reptiles died out at the end of the Mesozoic Era. The Cenozoic Era, which followed the Mesozoic Era, is also known as the *Age of Mammals*. It began 63 million years ago and continues today.

During early Cenozoic times, conditions on the earth were excellent for the rapid development of many kinds of mammals. New types of living places were created for them as mountains rose and lowland swamps dried up. Being warm blooded and covered with hair, they could adapt more easily than other animals to the cool, dry climate of the early Cenozoic Era.

> See **Prehistoric animal** in *World Book* for more information on Early forms of animal life, The Age of Mammals, and The study of prehistoric animals.

Animals of the Cenozoic Era Mammals became the dominant animals during the Cenozoic Era, which is also known as the *Age of Mammals.* The era began 63 million years ago and continues today. It is divided into two periods and seven epochs. Human beings have lived during only about the last 2 million years.

WORLD BOOK illustrations by Alex Ebel

Procoptodon (Marsupial) 10 ft. (3 m) tall

Smilodon (Saber-Toothed Cat) 6 ft. (1.8 m) long

Megathere (Ground Sloth) 20 ft. (6 m) long

Diatryma (Flightless Bird) 7 ft. (2.1m) tall

Eohippus (First Horse) 1 ft. (30 cm) high at shoulder

Woolly mammoth (Ice Age Mammal) 14 ft. (4.3 m) high at shoulder

Animal Life	The kinds of mammals expanded rapidly.	First camels, horses, and other mammals appeared.	Grassland spread. Primitive apes appeared.	Mammals reached their greatest variety.	Humanlike creatures and many other modern mammals appeared.	Modern human beings developed. The Ice Age began.	Human beings hunted and tamed many animals.
Period	Tertiary					Quaternary	
Epoch	Paleocene	Eocene	Oligocene	Miocene	Pliocene	Pleistocene	Holocene
Began	63 million years ago	55 million years ago	38 million years ago	24 million years ago	5 million years ago	2 million years ago	10,000 years ago
Lasted	8 million years	17 million years	14 million years	19 million years	3 million years	2 million years	10,000 years

Rabbit is a furry animal with long ears and a short, fluffy tail. Rabbits do not walk or run, as most other four-legged animals do. A rabbit moves about by hopping on its hind legs, which are much longer and stronger than its front legs. The animal also uses its front legs when it moves. Rabbits balance on their front legs much as people balance on their hands when they play leapfrog. When chased by an enemy, a rabbit can hop as fast as 18 miles (29 kilometers) an hour. Pet stores sell tame rabbits that have been raised to be pets.

Rabbits live in Africa, Europe, North America, and other parts of the world. They make their homes in fields and prairies where they can hide their young under bushes or among tall grasses. A female rabbit usually has four or five young at a time, and may give birth several times every year. Rabbits in the southern United States, where the weather is warm most of the year, may have babies more than five times a year. In the northern part of the country, rabbits may give birth two to four times between April and September.

Rabbits and hares look much alike, and are often mistaken for each other. Some are even misnamed. For example, the Belgian hare is a rabbit, and the jack rabbit is a hare. Most rabbits are smaller than hares and have shorter ears. The animals can be told apart most easily at birth. A newborn rabbit is blind, it has no fur, and it cannot move about. A newborn hare can see, it has a coat of fine fur, and it can hop a few hours after birth. In addition, the bones in a rabbit's skull have a different size and shape from those in a hare's skull.

The body of a rabbit

Wild rabbits have soft, thick brownish or grayish fur. The fur of pet rabbits may be black, brown, gray, white, or combinations of these colors. An adult wild rabbit grows 8 to 14 inches (20 to 36 centimeters) long and weighs 2 to 5 pounds (0.9 to 2.3 kilograms). Pet rabbits may grow about 8 inches (20 centimeters) longer and weigh 5 pounds (2.3 kilograms) more. Most females are larger than males. Few rabbits live more than a year in the wild because they have little protection against ene-

Robert J. Ellison, NAS

A young cottontail sits motionless to escape hunters, but hops away quickly if they come near.

mies. Many pet rabbits live as long as five years.

A rabbit's eyes are on the sides of its head. As a result, the animal can see things behind or to the side better than in front. Rabbits can move their long ears together or one at a time to catch even faint sounds from any direction. Rabbits also depend on their keen sense of smell to alert them to danger. A rabbit seems to twitch its nose almost all the time.

Rabbits were once classified as *rodents* (gnawing animals). Like beavers, mice, and other rodents, rabbits have chisellike front teeth for gnawing. But unlike rodents, rabbits have a pair of small teeth behind the upper front teeth.

A rabbit's tail is about 2 inches (5 centimeters) long, and is covered with soft, fluffy fur that makes it look round. The fur on the underside of the tail of most kinds of rabbits has a lighter color than that on top. American cottontail rabbits are named for the fur on the underside of their tails. When a cottontail hops, its tail looks somewhat like a bouncing ball of white cotton.

> See **Rabbit** in *World Book* for more information on The life of a rabbit, Kinds of rabbits, and Pet rabbits.

Facts in brief

Names: *Male,* buck; *female,* doe; *young,* kit or kitten.
Gestation period: Cottontails, 26 to 30 days; European rabbits, 28 to 33 days.
Number of young: 2 to 9, usually 4 or 5.
Where found: Africa; Asia; Australia; Europe; New Zealand; North, Central, and South America.
Scientific classification: Rabbits belong to the order *Lagomorpha,* and to the rabbit and hare family, Leporidae. Cottontails belong to the genus of New World rabbits, *Sylvilagus.* European rabbits belong to the genus of Old World rabbits, *Oryctolagus.*

The skeleton of a rabbit

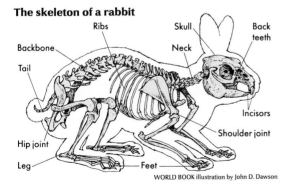

Ribs — Skull — Back teeth
Backbone — Neck
Tail — Incisors
Hip joint — Shoulder joint
Leg — Feet

WORLD BOOK illustration by John D. Dawson

Rabbit tracks in snow

WORLD BOOK illustration by Tom Dolan

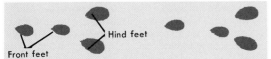

Hind feet
Front feet

© David R. Frazier Photolibrary

Dennis Hallinan, FPG

© Tom Campbell, FPG

Radio broadcasting originates in a studio and can be heard almost anywhere. A disc jockey at a radio station, *above left,* announces and plays recorded music. Many people use small, light-weight portable radios, *above, above right,* to receive broadcasts.

Radio

Radio is one of our most important means of communication. It enables people to send words, music, codes, and other signals to any part of the world. People also use radio to communicate far into space.

The most widespread and familiar use of radio is broadcasting. Radio broadcasts feature music, news, discussions, interviews, descriptions of sports events, and advertising. People wake up to clock radios and ride to their jobs listening to automobile radios. They also spend leisure hours hearing their favorite programs on radio.

Radio works by changing sounds or other signals into *electromagnetic waves,* also called *radio waves.* These waves travel through the air and through space. They also go through some solid objects, such as the walls of buildings. Radio waves travel at the speed of light—186,282 miles (299,792 kilometers) per second. When they reach a radio receiver, the receiver changes them back into the original sounds.

Many people contributed to the development of radio and no one individual can be called radio's inventor. Guglielmo Marconi of Italy sent the first radio communication signals in 1895. Today, radio waves that are broadcast from thousands of stations, along with waves from other sources, fill the air around us continuously.

How radio works

To understand how radio broadcasting works, it is necessary to know what sound is. All sounds consist of vibrations. For example, the sound of a person's voice consists of vibrations of the air that are caused by the person's vibrating vocal cords. Sound travels through the air in the form of waves called *sound waves.* When the waves reach a person's ear, the person hears the original sounds.

During a radio broadcast, a microphone picks up speech and other live sounds that make up the program. An electric current runs through the microphone. When sound waves enter the microphone, they disturb the current in the microphone, creating vibrations in it that match the sound waves. These electric waves are used to produce the radio waves that make up the broadcast. In a similar way, equipment in the radio station changes the prerecorded sounds of a program into electric waves.

From electric waves to radio waves. The electric waves representing the sounds of a program travel over wires to the control board. The control board has many switches and dials. A technician controls the sounds being sent to the board. The technician varies the *volume* (loudness) of each sound and may even blend sounds together. From the control board, the electric waves go to the transmitter.

Transmitting radio waves. In some stations, the transmitter is in the same room as the control board, and the electric waves that make up the program travel between the two instruments over wires. Other stations have their transmitter far from the radio station, at the site of the *transmitting antenna* (the device that sends radio waves through the air). In such cases, the electric waves are passed to the transmitters either by wire or by a special beam of radio waves.

The transmitter strengthens the incoming electric waves representing the broadcast. The transmitter also produces another kind of electric waves called *carrier waves*. It combines the carrier waves with the electric waves from the radio studio. This combination of waves becomes the radio signal that brings the program to radios.

The transmitter sends the radio signal to the antenna. The antenna, in turn, sends the signal out into the air as radio waves. Many stations locate their antennas on towers and in high or open areas, above and away from tall buildings and other structures that might interfere with the radio waves. Some stations, especially small ones, have their antenna on top of the station building or a nearby building.

Kinds of broadcast waves. A radio program is transmitted in one of two ways, depending on the way the carrier wave and program signal are combined. These two kinds of radio transmission are *amplitude modulation* (AM) and *frequency modulation* (FM). In AM transmission, the *amplitude* (strength) of the carrier waves varies to match changes in the electric waves coming from the radio studio. In FM transmission, the amplitude of the carrier waves remains constant. But the *frequency* of the waves (the number of times they vibrate each second) changes to match the electric waves sent from the studio.

An antenna sends out two kinds of AM radio waves—*ground waves* and *sky waves*. Ground waves spread out horizontally from the transmitting antenna. They travel through the air along the earth's surface and follow the curve of the earth for a short distance. Sky waves spread up into the sky. When they reach a layer of the atmosphere called the *ionosphere,* or the *Kennelly-Heaviside layer,* they are reflected back down to earth. This reflection enables AM broadcasts to be received by radios that are great distances from the antenna.

An FM radio antenna sends out waves that travel in the same directions as AM waves, but FM waves that go skyward are not reflected. Instead, they pass through the atmosphere and go into space. The FM waves that spread horizontally travel in what is called *line-of-sight.* This means that FM waves cannot be received farther than the horizon as seen from the antenna. AM broadcasts can be received at much greater distances than FM broadcasts because AM signals bounce off the atmosphere and reach beyond the curve of the earth. Although their range is limited, FM broadcasts have an important advantage over AM broadcasts. FM programs are not affected by static as much as AM programs are. FM transmission also produces a much truer reproduction of sound than does AM.

Broadcasting power and frequency. Another factor that influences the distance a radio program can be broadcast is the power of the transmitter. The strongest AM stations have a power of 50,000 watts. They can be heard far away, especially at night when sky waves are especially effective. For example, 50,000-watt stations in Chicago can be heard at night by listeners in Florida, about 1,000 miles (1,600 kilometers) away. The weakest AM stations operate at 250 watts and usually serve only one or two towns. The power of FM stations ranges from 100 watts, which can broadcast about 15 miles (24 kilometers), to 100,000 watts, which can broadcast about 65 miles (105 kilometers).

Radio terms

Adlib means to speak without a script.

AM stands for *amplitude modulation,* a broadcasting method in which the strength of the carrier waves is changed to match changes in the audio-frequency waves.

Audio-frequency waves are electric waves that represent the sounds of a radio broadcast.

Broadcast band is a group of radio frequencies. One band is for AM broadcasting and one is for FM broadcasting.

Call letters are the initials that identify a radio station, such as station KRKO in Everett, Wash.

Carrier waves "carry" the sounds of a program by being combined with audio-frequency waves.

Channel is the radio frequency assigned to a station.

FM stands for *frequency modulation,* a broadcasting method in which the frequency of the carrier waves is changed to match changes in the audio-frequency waves.

Frequency is the number of times an electric wave vibrates each second.

Ground waves consist of the radio waves that spread along the ground away from a broadcasting antenna.

Ham is a name for the operator of an amateur radio station.

Hertz is a unit used to measure frequency. One hertz equals one vibration per second.

Kilohertz means 1,000 hertz.

Line-of-sight refers to the direct line in which FM waves travel, without "bending" over mountains or the curve of the earth.

Live broadcast consists of sounds made at the moment of the broadcast, without having been prerecorded.

Megahertz means 1 million hertz.

Multiplexing means broadcasting two channels of sound that can be received by stereophonic radios.

Network is an organization that provides radio programming for a group of stations that belong to it.

Prerecorded means recorded on phonograph discs or tape for broadcast at a later time.

Script is a written copy of the words to be spoken during a radio program. It also specifies sound effects, music, and any other sounds to be made during a program.

Sky waves consist of the radio waves that come from a transmitting antenna and go into the sky.

Stereophonic sound comes from at least two radio speakers to match as closely as possible the sounds people would hear with their two ears.

Transistor is a small electronic device that controls the flow of electricity in radio equipment.

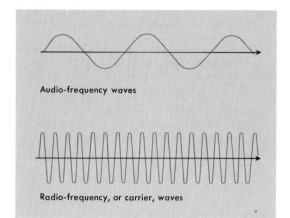

Audio-frequency waves

Radio-frequency, or carrier, waves

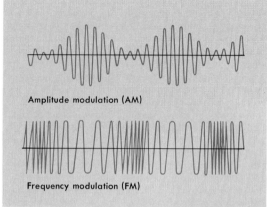

Amplitude modulation (AM)

Frequency modulation (FM)

Radio waves are a combination of two kinds of electric vibrations, *above.* Audio-frequency waves represent voice and other sounds. Radio-frequency waves "carry" audio waves after being combined with them in one of the ways shown at the right.

AM and FM waves. In AM, the height of the combined audio- and radio-frequency waves varies to match the shape of the audio waves. In FM, the frequency of the combined waves changes to match the audio waves.

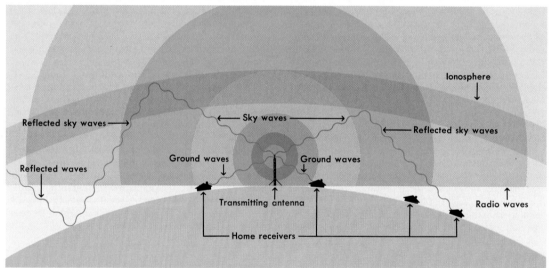

Ionosphere ↓

Reflected sky waves →

← Sky waves →

← Reflected sky waves

Reflected waves

Ground waves ↓

Ground waves ↓

Radio waves ↑

Transmitting antenna

Home receivers

WORLD BOOK diagrams

How broadcast waves travel. An antenna radiates waves in all directions. *Ground waves* reach nearby receivers but cannot go far beyond the horizon. *Sky waves* reflect from the ionosphere and reach distant receivers. They also may reflect from the earth and repeat the process.

Each station broadcasts on a different *channel,* or *assigned frequency.* The use of different frequencies keeps stations from interfering with one another's broadcasts. Frequency is measured in units called *kilohertz* and *megahertz.* One kilohertz equals 1,000 *hertz* (vibrations per second), and one megahertz equals 1,000,000 hertz. AM stations broadcast on frequencies between 535 and 1,605 kilohertz. The AM broadcast band was scheduled to be expanded to 1,705 kilohertz in 1990. The FM band extends from 88 to 108 megahertz.

A program carried by radio waves travels at the speed of light. This speed is 186,282 miles (299,792 kilometers) per second. By contrast, sound waves themselves move through the air at a speed of only about $\frac{1}{5}$ mile (0.3 kilometer) per second. As a result of the great

difference in speed between radio waves and sound waves, a surprising effect occurs. Imagine a live radio broadcast of a concert taking place in New York City. The music would reach radio listeners in California a fraction of a second before it reached the audience in the back of the concert hall.

See **Radio** in *World Book* for more information on the following topics:

•Uses
•How radio works
•The radio industry

•Government regulation of radio
•History

Rain is a form of precipitation that consists of drops of water. Raindrops form when water droplets in clouds combine or when precipitation in the form of ice, such as snow, hail, or sleet, melts.

Formation of rain. Rain develops from water vapor in the atmosphere. This vapor forms when the heat of the sun causes evaporation from the oceans and other bodies of water on the earth. The warm, moist air cools as it rises, and the amount of vapor it can hold decreases. The temperature at which air holds as much vapor as it can is called the *dew point.* When the temperature drops below the dew point, some of the vapor condenses into water droplets, forming clouds.

Water droplets form on tiny particles of matter known as *condensation nuclei.* Such nuclei consist of dust, salt from ocean spray, and chemicals given off chiefly by industrial plants and motor vehicles. As the water droplets form, heat is released, making the clouds warmer. The warmth helps the clouds rise, and they then become cooler. The formation of raindrops in such clouds is explained by the *coalescence theory* and the *ice-crystal theory.*

The coalescence theory applies to much of the rain that forms over the oceans and in the tropics. According to this theory, different sizes of droplets form in clouds. The larger droplets fall faster through a cloud than the smaller droplets do. As a larger droplet falls, it collides and combines with smaller droplets. This process is called *coalescence.* If a large droplet falls about 1 mile (1.6 kilometers) through a cloud, it may combine with a million smaller droplets. In this way, the droplets become too heavy for the air to support them. Some fall to the earth as raindrops. Others having a diameter of more than 0.25 inch tend to split into smaller drops. These drops will move upward if the cloud is rising rapidly. As they begin to grow, they again fall and repeat the coalescence process.

The ice-crystal theory accounts for much of the rainfall in the temperate zone. The process of rain formation based on this theory probably occurs more frequently than coalescence. The ice-crystal process occurs in clouds in which air temperature is lower than 32° F. (0° C), the freezing point of water. In most cases, such clouds consist of droplets of *supercooled water.* Supercooled water is water that remains in a liquid state at temperatures below 32° F. In clouds of this type, ice crystals form on microscopic particles called *ice nuclei.* Most ice nuclei consist of extremely fine particles of soil or volcanic dust.

Ice crystals that form near droplets of supercooled water increase in size when water vapor from cloud droplets is deposited on the crystals. As the crystals fall through a cloud, they may collide and combine with other crystals or with supercooled droplets. Crystals that become too heavy for the air to support fall out of the cloud. Such ice crystals become raindrops if they fall through enough air that is warmer than 32° F.

See **Rain** in *World Book* for more information on Measuring rainfall, Rainfall distribution, and What causes rain.

How rain forms   Weather experts have developed two theories of rain formation—the coalescence theory and the ice-crystal theory. The diagrams below illustrate the processes described by each of these theories.

WORLD BOOK diagrams by Leonard E. Morgan

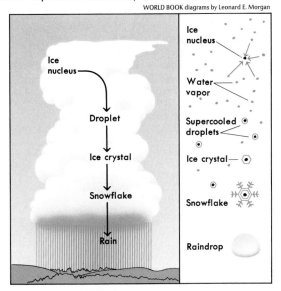

The coalescence theory explains how different sizes of water droplets form in clouds. A droplet forms when water vapor condenses on a particle called a *condensation nucleus.* As a droplet falls through a cloud, it combines with smaller ones. When it becomes too heavy for the air to support, it falls as a raindrop.

The ice-crystal theory applies to clouds of supercooled water droplets. Such a droplet, formed by condensing water vapor, freezes on a particle called an *ice nucleus.* The resulting ice crystal combines with others to form a snowflake. The snowflake becomes rain when it falls through air warmer than 32° F. (0° C).

Rainbow is an arch of brilliant colors that appears in the sky when the sun shines after a shower of rain. It forms in that part of the sky opposite the sun. If the rain has been heavy, the bow may spread all the way across the sky, and its two ends seem to rest on the earth.

The reflection, refraction, and diffraction of the sun's rays as they fall on drops of rain cause this interesting natural phenomenon. These processes produce all the colors of the color spectrum—violet, indigo blue, green, yellow, orange, and red. However, the colors of a rainbow blend into each other so that an observer rarely sees more than four or five clearly. The width of each color band varies, and depends chiefly on the size of the raindrops in which a rainbow forms. Narrow bands are caused by larger drops.

Sunlight is a combination of all colors. Different wavelengths of light exhibit different colors. You see the rainbow when the sun is behind you and the rain is in front of you. As a ray passes into a drop of rain, the water acts like a prism.

The ray is *refracted* (bent) as it enters the drop, and is *diffracted* (dispersed or separated) into different colors. As it strikes the inner surface of the drop, it is *reflected* (turned back). On leaving the drop, it is further refracted and dispersed. Many drops produce a rainbow. Each color is formed by rays that reach the eye at a certain angle, and the angle for a particular color never changes.

A complete bow generally shows two bands of colors. The inner and brighter one is called the *primary* bow. The primary bow exhibits red along the outer edge of the bow, and violet or blue on the inside. A less distinct *secondary* bow is sometimes visible outside the primary bow. The secondary bow is produced by sunlight passing into drops and undergoing a double reflection. As a result, the color order is reversed from that of the primary bow—that is, red appears on the inside and violet or blue on the outside of the secondary bow.

A third bow, called a *tertiary* bow, is sometimes seen outside the secondary bow. It is produced from three internal reflections, and its color order is the same as that of the primary bow. The colors of secondary and tertiary bows are increasingly less intense than those of the primary bow. In fact, they often appear as only bright bows of white light.

How rainbows are formed

Raindrops act as tiny prisms and mirrors to break up sunlight into colors of the spectrum and send colored light back to our eyes. Each drop forms many colors. But the color that reaches our eyes from a particular drop depends on the angle between it and the line formed by the sun's rays. Many raindrops, each sending colored light at certain angles, form a rainbow.

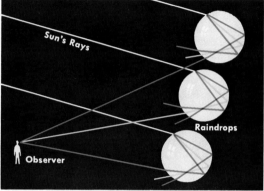

WORLD BOOK diagram by Arnold Ryan Chalfant & Associates

The higher the sun is, the lower the rainbow will be. If the sun is higher than 40 degrees, no bow will be seen. When the sun is near the horizon, an observer on a high mountain might see the entire circle of the rainbow.

Rainbows are often observed in the spray that flies from a garden hose or a sprinkler. Beautiful rainbows often may be seen on sunny days at Niagara Falls.

Why a rainbow is an arc

You see a rainbow as an arc when the sun is behind you and the sky in front of you is filled with moisture. Each band of color occurs at a certain angle. The raindrops in each band lie in an arc. In the red band, for example, all the points of the arc measure about 42° from the line formed by the sun's rays. The other colored bands occur at angles less than 42° from the sun's rays.

WORLD BOOK diagram by Arnold Ryan Chalfant & Associates

Sun's Rays

Sun's Rays

42°

Observer

Rat is a furry mammal that looks like a mouse but is larger. The smallest kinds of rats grow longer and weigh more than the largest mice. Rats, like mice, beavers, and squirrels, are *rodents.* All such animals have chisellike front teeth especially suited for gnawing.

There are about 120 kinds of rats, of which the best known are the *black rat* and the *brown rat.* Both these species live in all parts of the world. Most other kinds of rats live in areas not inhabited by people.

Black rats and brown rats rank among the most serious animal threats to people. They carry the germs of several diseases, including bubonic plague, food poisoning, and typhus. Rats also damage or destroy crops and other food products, and they kill poultry, lambs, and baby pigs. On the other hand, scientists use rats in research projects that have benefited people.

The word *rat* is often used for any long-tailed rodent that is larger than a mouse. But most of these animals are not true rats. They include the *cotton rat,* the *rice rat,* the *kangaroo rat,* and the *woodrat.*

The body of a rat. All species of rats have a slender, scaly tail and long, sharp claws. But black rats and brown rats differ in several ways besides color.

Black rats grow 7 or 8 inches (18 or 20 centimeters) long, not including their tail, and weigh about 10 ounces (280 grams). The tail is longer than the rest of the body. These rats have large ears, a pointed snout, and soft fur. The fur of a black rat may be black, grayish-brown, or smoky-gray. Gray, white, or yellow fur covers the animal's underside. Black rats are also called *roof rats* or *ship rats.*

Brown rats measure from 8 to 10 inches (20 to 25 centimeters) long, not including their tail, and weigh up to 16 ounces (485 grams). The tail is shorter than the rest of the body. Brown rats have small ears, a blunt snout, and coarse fur. They vary in color from brownish-gray to reddish-gray. Other names for the brown rat include *barn rat, gray rat, house rat, Norway rat,* and *sewer rat.*

The life of a rat. Black rats and brown rats originally lived in Asia. They reached Europe by ship or overland. From Europe, they spread to North and South America on ships. More brown rats than black rats live in North America. Some black rats live near coastal seaports in the Northern United States, but most dwell in the Gulf states, such as Louisiana and Texas. Brown rats live throughout the United States.

Both black and brown rats live in large groups, with certain rats *dominating* (having control over) others. Most members of both species build a nest in or near buildings. Black rats live in the upper stories of buildings or in trees. Brown rats are found under floors, within walls, in piles of garbage, or in the ground. If the two species live in the same building, black rats usually occupy the upper levels, and brown rats dwell on the ground level. Rats are cautious creatures and generally avoid anything unfamiliar in their environment. They have a keen sense of smell and can quickly detect approaching danger.

Both black and brown rats eat almost any kind of plant or animal—even other rats of the same or a different species. The brown rat is fierce and aggressive, compared with the milder black rat. Rats feed mostly at night, and sometimes they band together and attack

The skeleton of a rat

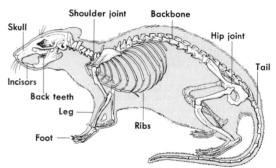

Rat tracks

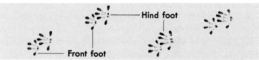

WORLD BOOK illustration by Marion Pahl

such animals as chickens and pigs. Most rats live within an area that may be no more than 150 feet (46 meters) in diameter. But if a food shortage occurs, rats may travel long distances in search of food.

Most black and brown rats mate the year around, and the females give birth to three to six litters annually. A female rat carries her young in her body for about three weeks before they are born. Most black rat litters consist of six or seven babies. Most brown rat litters have eight or nine babies. Newborn rats are blind and deaf. They remain in the nest for about three weeks.

Few rats live more than a year in their natural surroundings because they have so many enemies. Animals that prey on rats include cats, dogs, hawks, owls, snakes, and weasels. In captivity, some rats live more than three years.

See **Rat** in *World Book* for more information on Rats and people.

Alan Blank, Bruce Coleman Inc.

Newborn rats, such as these brown rats, cannot see or hear. They remain in the nest with their mother for about three weeks. Brown rats are common in the United States and Canada.

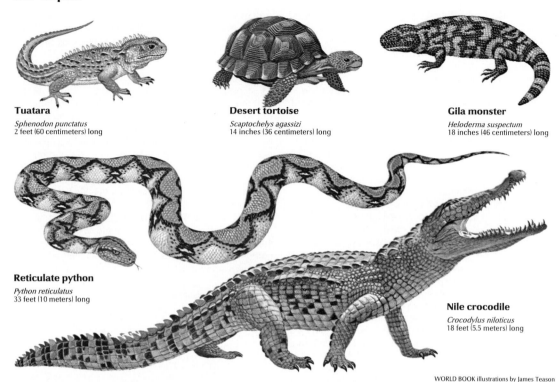

Tuatara
Sphenodon punctatus
2 feet (60 centimeters) long

Desert tortoise
Scaptochelys agassizi
14 inches (36 centimeters) long

Gila monster
Heloderma suspectum
18 inches (46 centimeters) long

Reticulate python
Python reticulatus
33 feet (10 meters) long

Nile crocodile
Crocodylus niloticus
18 feet (5.5 meters) long

WORLD BOOK illustrations by James Teason

Reptiles vary greatly in size, shape, and color. However, they all have skin that consists of dry, tough scales. There are about 6,000 species of reptiles. Most of these animals live on land, but some make their home in the ocean and others dwell in fresh water.

Reptile is an animal that has dry, scaly skin and breathes by means of lungs. There are about 6,000 *species* (kinds) of reptiles, and they make up one of the classes of *vertebrates* (animals that have a backbone). Reptiles include alligators, crocodiles, lizards, snakes, turtles, and the tuatara.

Reptiles are cold-blooded—that is, their body temperature stays about the same as the temperature of their surroundings. To stay alive, these animals must avoid extremely high or low temperatures. Most reptiles that are active during the day keep moving from sunny places to shady spots. Many species of reptiles that live in hot climates are active mainly at night. Reptiles in regions that have harsh winters hibernate during the winter.

The various species of reptiles vary greatly in size. For example, pythons grow more than 30 feet (9 meters) long, and leatherback turtles may weigh more than 1 short ton (0.9 metric ton). On the other hand, some species of lizards measure no more than 2 inches (5 centimeters) long.

Many reptiles live a long time, and some turtles have lived in captivity for more than 100 years. For the length of life of various other reptiles in captivity, see **Animal** (table: Length of life of animals) in *World Book.*

Reptiles live on every continent except Antarctica and in all the oceans except those of the polar regions. They are most abundant in the tropics. Many kinds of lizards and snakes thrive in deserts. Other reptiles, such as rat snakes and box turtles live in forests. Still others, including marine iguanas and sea turtles, spend much of their life in the ocean. Some sea snakes spend their entire life in the water.

Kinds of reptiles

Zoologists divide reptiles into four main groups: (1) lizards and snakes, (2) turtles, (3) crocodilians, and (4) the tuatara.

Lizards and snakes make up the largest group of reptiles. There are nearly 3,000 species of each. Most lizards have four legs, long tails, movable eyelids, and external ear openings. A few species, such as glass snakes and slow worms, have no legs. Lizards thrive in regions that have a hot or warm climate. These animals are also common in deserts.

Snakes have tails that vary in length, depending on the species. But snakes have no legs, eyelids, or ear openings. An unmovable covering of transparent scales protects their eyes. Snakes live mostly in the tropics and in warm regions. However, the European viper lives north of the Arctic Circle, in Finland and Sweden.

Turtles are the only reptiles with a shell. They pull their head, legs, and tail into the shell for protection. There are about 250 species of turtles. They live on land, in fresh water, and in the ocean.

Crocodilians include alligators, caymans, crocodiles, and gavials. There are about 20 species of crocodilians, all of which live in or near water. These reptiles have a long snout, strong jaws, and webbed hind feet. They use their long, powerful tail to swim. All except a few crocodilians dwell in the fresh waters and lowlands of the tropics. Alligators live in the Southeastern United States and in Southern China.

The tuatara inhabits several islands off the coast of New Zealand. It looks like a lizard but is more closely related to the extinct dinosaurs.

The body of a reptile

Reptiles vary greatly in size, shape, and color, but all of them share certain physical characteristics. These characteristics, in addition to the animals' being cold-blooded, include various features of the skin, skeleton, internal organs, and sense organs.

Skin of a reptile consists of scales. Lizards and snakes have a single sheet of overlapping scales. The scales of turtles, crocodilians, and the tuatara grow in the form of individual areas called *plates.* Crocodilians and some lizards have pieces of bone called *osteoderms* within their scales. The skin of such reptiles serves as protective armor.

Many species of reptiles shed their skin several times a year. New scales form under the layer of scales and loosen it. Among snakes, the skin on the snout loosens first. The snake pushes this skin backwards against a rock or the stem of a plant. The animal then crawls out of the old skin and sheds it in one piece. Most lizards shed their skin in large strips, and the skin of crocodilians wears away gradually.

Skeleton of reptiles provides a framework for the head, trunk, and tail. Most reptiles have hip and shoulder bones called *girdles* that support the legs. The majority of snakes do not have girdles. The hip and shoulder girdles of turtles, unlike those of any other animal, are inside the ribcage. The ribs and vertebrae make up the inner layer of the turtle's shell.

Internal organs. Reptiles breathe by means of lungs. Most species have two lungs, but some snakes have only one. The digestive system of reptiles varies among the species, according to the kind of food the animal eats. Reptiles that feed mainly on animals or on such animal products as eggs have a fairly simple stomach and a long intestine. Such reptiles include boa constrictors and Gila monsters. Species that eat plants, including iguanas and most tortoises, have a more complicated stomach. Crocodilians have extremely large stomach muscles that grind flesh into tiny pieces.

Venomous reptiles produce their venom by means of a gland in the mouth. The venom affects the victim's circulatory system or nervous system.

Sense organs. Most reptiles have good vision. Species active during the day have eyes with round pupils. Most species active at night have slitlike eye pupils, which can be closed almost completely in bright light.

The hearing of reptiles varies among the species, but most can hear at least low-pitched sounds. The majority of reptiles have an eardrum, a middle ear, and an inner ear. However, snakes lack a middle ear and cannot hear sounds carried through the air. They "hear" by sensing vibrations from the ground.

See **Reptile** in *World Book* for more information on The body of a reptile, Ways of life, and The evolution of reptiles.

Interesting facts about reptiles

Cold-blooded animals. Reptiles are cold-blooded—that is, their body temperature rarely differs much from the temperature of their surroundings. Reptiles that are active on hot, sunny days cool off by moving to shady spots.

Overlapping scales

Plates

The skin of reptiles. Lizards and snakes have a single sheet of overlapping scales, *left.* Other reptiles grow *plates* (separate areas of scales), *right.* The main function of the skin is to keep water in the animal's body. Reptiles can go without water for long periods, and many species thrive in deserts.

Molting. Many kinds of reptiles *molt* (shed their skin) several times a year. The skin loosens after new scales form under it. The skin of lizards comes off in large strips, as shown at the right.

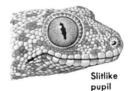

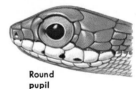

Slitlike pupil

Round pupil

The shape of a reptile's pupil indicates whether the animal is active at night or during the day. Most reptiles active at night have slitlike pupils that can be closed almost completely in bright light. Reptiles active in daytime have round pupils. Most reptiles have good vision, and some can tell the difference among colors.

Egg-laying reptiles include alligators, crocodiles, turtles, a number of snakes and lizards, and the tuatara. The eggs are laid in decayed wood, a nest of leaves and mud, or elsewhere on land. Heat from the sun causes the eggs to hatch.

WORLD BOOK illustrations by James Teason

WORLD BOOK illustration by John F. Eggert

Dinosaurs, the most spectacular reptiles, dominated land animals for millions of years. These creatures died out about 65 million years ago. The diplodocus, *above,* a plant-eating dinosaur that measured about 90 feet (27 meters) long, was one of the largest animals that ever lived.

Respiration is the process by which human beings and other living things obtain and use oxygen. Except for certain microorganisms, all living things require oxygen to live. Respiration also involves the elimination of carbon dioxide, a gas produced when cells use oxygen.

Respiration may be divided into three phases: (1) external respiration, (2) internal respiration, and (3) cellular respiration. In external respiration, or breathing, a plant or animal takes in oxygen from its environment and releases carbon dioxide. In internal respiration, oxygen is carried to the cells of the organism and carbon dioxide is carried away from them. In cellular respiration, oxygen is used in chemical reactions within the cells. These reactions release energy and produce carbon dioxide and water as waste products.

External respiration

Organs of breathing. The lungs are the chief organs of breathing. They are elastic structures in the chest cavity. Each lung contains millions of small air chambers, or sacs, called *alveoli.* A network of tiny blood vessels called *capillaries* lies within the walls of each alveolus. See **Lung.**

Other structures important in breathing are the *chest wall* and the *diaphragm.* The chest wall includes the ribs—which form a protective cage around the chest cavity—and the muscles between the ribs. The diaphragm is a dome-shaped sheet of muscle that separates the chest cavity from the abdomen.

Air enters and leaves the body through the nose and the mouth. The *pharynx* (back of the nose and mouth), the *larynx* (voice box), and the *trachea* (windpipe) are the air passages that connect the nose and mouth with the lungs.

The process of breathing. Breathing consists of two acts, *inspiration* (breathing in) and *expiration* (breathing out). During inspiration, also called *inhalation,* air from the atmosphere is drawn into the lungs. During expiration, or *exhalation,* air is expelled from the lungs.

Inspiration occurs when the diaphragm and the muscles of the chest wall contract. This action makes the chest cavity longer and wider, causing the lungs to expand. The expansion of the lungs creates a slight vacuum in the alveoli, drawing fresh air into the lungs. Oxygen makes up about 20 per cent of the volume of this fresh air. Almost all the rest of it is nitrogen. Only about 0.03 per cent is carbon dioxide.

Expiration results when the diaphragm and other muscles relax, allowing the lungs to retract. This action causes the pressure of the gas in the alveoli to become greater than the atmospheric pressure. As a result, gas flows out of the lungs. Carbon dioxide makes up about 5 per cent and oxygen about 17 per cent of this gas.

Oxygen and carbon dioxide are exchanged between the lungs and the blood through the thin walls of capillaries in the alveoli. Blood entering these capillaries is low in oxygen and high in carbon dioxide. Oxygen that has been inhaled passes into the blood, while carbon dioxide moves from the blood into the alveoli.

See **Respiration** in *World Book* for more information on the following topics:

- External respiration
- Internal respiration
- Cellular respiration
- External respiration in animals without lungs
- Respiration in plants

External respiration   External respiration, or breathing, is the process by which the body takes in oxygen from the atmosphere and releases carbon dioxide into the atmosphere. This exchange of gases takes place in the lungs. Breathing is controlled by an area of the brain called the *respiratory center.*

WORLD BOOK diagrams by Leonard E. Morgan

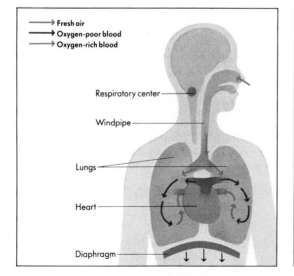

Inspiration—the act of drawing air into the lungs—occurs when the inspiratory muscles contract. Contraction of the *diaphragm,* the chief inspiratory muscle, makes the chest volume larger and thus expands the lungs. This expansion creates a slight vacuum in the lungs, and air flows in from the atmosphere.

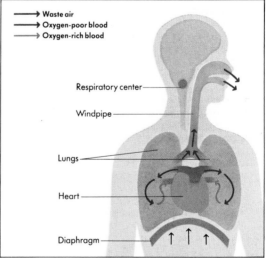

Expiration—the act of letting gas out of the lungs—takes place when the inspiratory muscles relax. The relaxation of these muscles removes the force expanding the lungs, which become smaller. Because of the smaller lung volume, gas pressure inside the lungs increases, and gas flows out into the atmosphere.

Clem Haagner, Bruce Coleman Inc.

E. R. Degginger

African rhinoceroses. The white rhinoceros, *left,* is the largest kind of rhinoceros. All rhinoceroses like to rest in the water after drinking. A charging black rhinoceros, *right,* is a frightening sight. Rhinoceroses have poor vision and often attack things that they do not recognize.

Rhinoceros is a huge animal that ranks as one of the largest land creatures. The rhinoceros has an immense, solid body, and short, clumsy legs. Its thick skin hangs loosely, and most species have little hair. Depending on the kind, the rhinoceros has one or two slightly curving horns that project from its long nose. The horns continue to grow throughout the life of the rhinoceros. The name *rhinoceros* comes from two Greek words and means *nose-horned.*

The animal has three toes on each foot. Each toe ends in a separate hoof. On each front foot is a fourth toe that is *rudimentary,* or no longer used. The rhinoceros differs from the hippopotamus, which has four developed toes. The hippopotamus is a relative of the hog, camel, and cow, and the rhinoceros is more nearly related to the horse.

The rhinoceros eats grass, leafy twigs, and shrubs. In captivity, it is fed hay and diet supplements of proteins, vitamins, and minerals. Wild rhinoceroses live in Africa, in southeastern Asia, and on a few large islands near the Asiatic coast. In prehistoric times, they also roamed over Europe, North America, and northern Asia.

There are five distinct kinds of rhinoceroses—three Asian species and two African. Many Asians believe rhinoceros horns have magical qualities. All species, especially the Asian species, are now nearly extinct and are protected by law and by international trade treaties.

See **Rhinoceros** in *World Book* for more information on Kinds of rhinoceroses.

Ylla, Rapho Guillumette

The great Indian rhinoceros has skin that resembles a suit of armor. Its hide includes large folds of skin and bumps that look like rivets. This rare animal lives in eastern India.

J. C. Stevenson, Animals Animals

A baby rhinoceros begins to grow horns soon after birth. This 3-month-old white rhinoceros has a small horn. Rhinoceroses have three toes on each foot. Each toe has a hoof.

Rock is the hard, solid part of the earth. In many areas, the rock is covered by a layer of soil in which plants or trees may grow. Soil itself is made up of tiny bits of rocks usually mixed with organic materials from plants and animals. Rock also lies beneath the oceans and under the polar icecaps.

Most rocks are *aggregates,* or combinations, of one or more minerals. Basalt, for example, contains crystals of the minerals plagioclase and pyroxene. In some cases, rocks appear to be dense and massive, with no mineral grains. But if you examine a very thin slice of such rock under a microscope, you can see grains of minerals.

Rocks and minerals are useful to us in a number of ways. Builders use granite, marble, and other rocks in construction work. Cement made from limestone and other rocks binds crushed stone into strong, long-lasting concrete for buildings, dams, and highways.

Metals such as aluminum, iron, lead, and tin come from rocks called *ores.* Ores also supply such radioactive elements as radium and uranium. Ore deposits may lie close to the earth's surface, or deep underground. In some regions, deposits of iron or copper ores make up entire mountains.

Some rocks contain valuable nonmetallic minerals such as borax and graphite. All gems, except for amber, coral, and pearl, come from rocks. Diamonds mined in Africa and Arkansas come from a rock called *peridotite.*

Emeralds are found in black limestone in Colombia.

Geologists trace the history of the earth by studying rocks (in *World Book,* see **Geology**). They find oil deposits by studying the structure, age, and composition of rock layers. Other scientists study *fossils* (remains of plants and animals found in rock) to learn about the kind of life that existed millions of years ago (see **Fossil**).

The three main kinds of rocks are: (1) igneous rocks, (2) sedimentary rocks, and (3) metamorphic rocks.

Igneous rock

Deep within the earth there exists *molten* (melted), rock material called *magma.* Magma is under great pressure and is extremely hot (1380° to 2280° F., or 750° to 1250° C). This hot material sometimes rises to the earth's surface through *fissures,* or cracks, caused by earthquakes and other deep movements of the earth's crust. Or, the intense heat and pressure of the magma weakens the rocks above it until they give way. *Igneous rocks* form when magma cools and solidifies. Scientists divide igneous rocks into two groups: extrusive rocks and intrusive rocks.

Extrusive rocks form when magma is *extruded,* or forced out, onto the earth's surface. The magma may emerge as streams of molten rock, partially solid masses of hot lava, or fine cinders and ash. When lava piles up and hardens around a fissure, it forms a volcano.

Exposure to the cooler surface temperatures causes

Common rocks

Rocks are classified into three major groups. *Igneous rock* forms from hardened magma. Hardening of various plant, animal, and mineral materials results in *sedimentary rock. Metamorphic rock* forms when any kind of rock undergoes changes as a result of intense heat and pressure.

Igneous

A. W. Ambler, NAS/Photo Researchers
Basalt

Lee Boltin
Gabbro

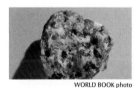
WORLD BOOK photo
Granite

Lee Boltin
Obsidian

Sedimentary

L. S. Stepanowicz, Panographics
Bituminous coal

Lee Boltin
Breccia

L. S. Stepanowicz, Panographics
Flint

WORLD BOOK photo
Limestone

Metamorphic

L. S. Stepanowicz, Panographics
Amphibolite

Charles R. Belinky, Photo Researchers
Gneiss

L. S. Stepanowicz, Panographics
Pink marble

A. W. Ambler, NAS/Photo Researchers
Quartzite

lava to harden in a few hours. The minerals it contains do not have time to form large crystals. It may harden so quickly that it forms *obsidian,* a smooth, shiny *volcanic glass; pumice,* a finely porous rock with air bubbles; or *scoria,* a rough rock that looks like furnace slag. Lava that hardens more slowly forms rocks with tiny mineral crystals. These *finely crystalline* rocks include dark-colored *basalts* and light-colored *felsites.*

Intrusive rocks form from magma that does not rise all the way to the surface of the earth. It may push up the surface rock in the shape of a huge blister. Sometimes it spreads out in sheets between layers of older rocks. The magma may also melt surrounding rocks to create an opening for itself. Beneath the surface, the molten rock cools and hardens slowly. Rocks formed in this way have coarse mineral grains that can be seen with the un-aided eye. These *coarsely crystalline* rocks include the *granites, syenites,* and *gabbros.*

Sedimentary rock

Sedimentary rock consists of materials that once were part of older rocks or of plants and animals. These materials accumulate as *strata* (layers) of loose material. Most of the deposits occur on ocean floors, but some form on land and in fresh water. As time passes, the loose materials harden into solid rocks. Geologists divide these rocks into three groups—clastic sediments, chemical sediments, and organic sediments—based on the materials from which they were formed.

Metamorphic rock

Metamorphic rock is rock that has changed its appearance, and in many cases, its mineral composition. These changes may be caused by hot magma or by pressure and heat due to deep burial or mountain-building movements in the earth's crust. All kinds of rock, including igneous and sedimentary, may go through such *metamorphism* to produce metamorphic rocks. Granite, for example, is an igneous rock that contains quartz, feldspar, and mica in a random arrangement. Metamorphism of granite causes feldspar and quartz crystals to form layers between which mica crystals often lie in wavy bands. The new rock is called *gneiss.* Metamorphism recrystallizes the calcite in limestone to form *marble.* The quartz grains in sandstone grow larger and form connecting crystals to create *quartzite.* Soft shales and clays harden to form *slate,* a rock that easily splits into smooth slabs. Felsites and impure sandstones, limestones, and shales change into *schists* that glisten with mica and other minerals such as hornblende and chlorite. Some minerals, including chlorite and garnet, occur only in metamorphic rocks.

See **Rock** in *World Book* for more information on Igneous rock, Sedimentary rock, and Rocks as a hobby.

Igneous rocks

Rock	Color	Structure
Basalt	Dark, greenish-gray to black.	Dense, microscopic crystals, often form columns.
Gabbro	Greenish-gray to black.	Coarse crystals.
Granite	White to gray, pink to red.	Tightly arranged medium-to-coarse crystals.
Obsidian	Black, sometimes with brown streaks.	Glassy, no crystals, breaks with a shell-like fracture.
Peridotite	Greenish-gray.	Coarse crystals.
Pumice	Grayish-white.	Light, glassy, frothy, fine pores, floats on water.

Lee Boltin
Peridotite

L. S. Stepanowicz, Panographics
Pumice

Sedimentary rocks

Rock	Color	Structure
Breccia	Gray to black, tan to red.	Angular pieces of rock, held together by natural cement.
Coal	Shiny to dull black.	Brittle, in seams or layers.
Flint	Dark gray, black, brown.	Hard, glassy, breaks with a sharp edge.
Limestone	White, gray, and buff to black and red.	Dense, forms thick beds and cliffs. May contain fossils.
Sandstone	White, gray, yellow, red.	Fine or coarse grains cemented together in beds.
Shale	Yellow, red, gray, green, black.	Dense, fine particles, soft, splits easily, smells like clay.

A. W. Ambler, NAS/Photo Researchers
Sandstone

A. W. Ambler, NAS/Photo Researchers
Shale

Metamorphic rocks

Rock	Color	Structure
Amphibolite	Light green to black.	Fine-to-coarse grains, hard, often sparkles.
Gneiss	Gray and pink to black and red.	Medium to coarse crystals arranged in bands.
Marble	Many colors, often mixed.	Medium to coarse crystals, may be banded.
Quartzite	White, gray, pink, buff.	Massive, hard, often glassy.
Schist	White, gray, red, green, black.	Flaky particles, finely banded, feels slippery, often sparkles with mica.
Slate	Black, red, green, purple.	Fine grains, dense, splits into thin, smooth slabs.

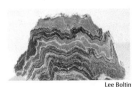
Lee Boltin
Schist

George Whitely, Photo Researchers
Slate

Rocket

NASA

The giant Saturn 5 rocket that carried the first astronauts to the moon rises from its launch tower. Rockets are the only vehicles used for launching people and machines into space.

Rocket is a type of engine that can produce more power for its size than any other kind of engine. A rocket can produce about 3,000 times more power than an automobile engine of the same size. The word *rocket* is also used to describe the vehicle driven by a rocket engine.

Rockets are made in a variety of sizes. Some of the rockets used to shoot fireworks into the sky are only 2 feet (61 centimeters) long. Rockets 50 to 100 feet (15 to 30 meters) long carry giant missiles that may be used to bomb distant enemy targets during wartime. Larger and more powerful rockets lift artificial satellites into orbit around the earth. For example, the Saturn 5 rocket that carried astronauts to the moon stood more than 360 feet (110 meters) high.

A rocket can produce great power, but it burns fuel rapidly. For this reason, a rocket must have a large amount of fuel to work for even a short period of time. The Saturn 5 rocket burned more than 560,000 gallons (2,120,000 liters) of fuel during the first $2\frac{3}{4}$ minutes of flight. Rockets become very hot as they burn fuel. The temperature in some rocket engines reaches 6000° F. (3300° C), about twice the temperature at which steel melts.

People use rockets chiefly for scientific research, space travel, and war. Rockets have been used in war for hundreds of years. In the 1200's, Chinese soldiers fired them against attacking armies. British troops used rockets to attack Fort McHenry in Maryland during the War of 1812 (1812-1814). After watching the battle, Francis Scott Key described "the rockets' red glare" in "The Star-Spangled Banner." During World War I (1914-1918), the French used rockets to shoot down enemy airplanes. Germany attacked London with rockets during World War II (1939-1945). Today's rockets can destroy satellites in orbit around the earth as well as jet airplanes and missiles that fly faster than the speed of sound.

Scientists use rockets for exploration and research in the atmosphere and in space. Rockets carry scientific instruments high in the sky to gather information about the air that surrounds the earth. Since 1957, rockets have shot hundreds of satellites into orbit around the earth. These satellites take pictures of the earth's weather and gather other information for scientific study. Rockets also carry instruments far into space to explore the moon, the planets, and even the space among the planets.

Rockets provide power for human space flights, which began in 1961. In 1969, rockets carried astronauts to the first landing on the moon. In 1981, rocket power launched the first space shuttle into orbit around the earth. In the future, rockets may carry people to Mars and the other planets.

A basic law of motion—discovered in the 1600's by the English scientist Sir Isaac Newton—describes how rockets work. This law states that for every action, there is an equal and opposite reaction (in *World Book,* see **Motion** [Newton's laws of motion]). Newton's law explains why the flow of air from a toy balloon *propels* (drives forward) the balloon in flight. A powerful rocket works similarly.

A rocket burns special fuel in a *combustion* (burning) chamber and creates rapidly expanding gas. This gas presses out equally in all directions inside the rocket. The pressure of the gas against one side of the rocket balances the pressure of the gas against the opposite side. The gas flowing to the rear of the rocket escapes through a nozzle. This exhaust gas does not balance the pressure of gas against the front of the rocket. The uneven pressure drives the rocket forward.

The flow of gas through the nozzle of a rocket is the *action* described in Newton's law. The *reaction* is the continuous *thrust* (pushing force) of the rocket away from the flow of exhaust gas.

Rocket propellant. Rockets burn a combination of chemicals called *propellant.* Rocket propellant consists of (1) a fuel, such as gasoline, kerosene, or liquid hydrogen; and (2) *an oxidizer* (a substance that supplies oxygen), such as nitrogen tetroxide or liquid oxygen. The oxidizer supplies the oxygen that the fuel needs to burn. This supply of oxygen enables the rocket to work in space, which has no air.

Jet engines also work by means of an action-reaction process. But jet fuel does not contain an oxidizer. Jet engines draw oxygen from the air and, for this reason, cannot function outside of the earth's atmosphere. See **Jet propulsion.**

A rocket burns propellant rapidly, and most rockets carry a supply that lasts only a few minutes. But a rocket produces such great thrust that it can hurl heavy vehicles far into space. A rocket burns the most propellant during the first few minutes of flight. During that time, the rocket's speed is held down by air friction, gravity, and the weight of the propellant. Air friction drags on the rocket as long as the rocket travels through the atmosphere. As the rocket climbs higher, the air becomes thinner and the friction decreases. In space, no air friction acts on the rocket. Gravity pulls a rocket toward the earth, but the pull decreases as the rocket travels farther from the earth. As a rocket burns its propellant, the weight it must carry becomes less.

Multistage rockets consist of two or more sections called *stages.* Each stage has a rocket engine and propellant. Engineers developed multistage rockets for long flights through the atmosphere and for flights into space. They needed rockets that could reach greater speeds than were possible with single-stage rockets. A multistage rocket can reach higher speeds because it lightens its weight by dropping stages as it uses up propellant. A three-stage rocket can reach about three times the speed of a single-stage rocket carrying the same amount of fuel.

The first stage, called the *booster,* launches the rocket. After the first stage has burned its propellant, the vehicle drops that section and uses the second stage. The rocket continues using one stage after another. Most space rockets have two or three stages.

Launching a rocket. Space rockets require specially equipped launch sites. All launching activity at a site centers around the launch pad, from which the rocket is fired. A launch site also has (1) assembly buildings, where engineers complete the final steps of rocket construction; (2) service structures, where workers check the rocket before launching; and (3) a control center, where scientists direct the launch and flight of the rocket. Tracking stations, located around the world, record the path of the rocket's flight.

Engineers prepare a rocket for launching in a step-by-step process called the *countdown.* They schedule each step for a specific time during the countdown and launch the rocket when the countdown reaches "zero." Undesirable weather or some other difficulty may cause a *hold,* which temporarily stops the countdown.

How a multistage rocket works

A two-stage rocket carries a propellant and one or more rocket engines in each stage. The first stage launches the rocket. After burning its supply of propellant, the first stage falls away from the rest of the rocket. The second stage then ignites and carries the payload into earth orbit or even farther into space.

WORLD BOOK diagram

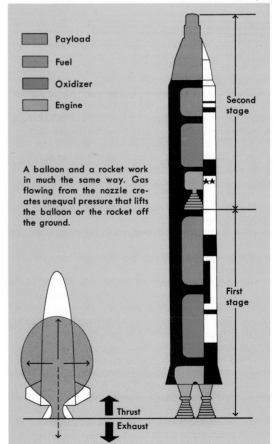

Payload

Fuel

Oxidizer

Engine

Second stage

A balloon and a rocket work in much the same way. Gas flowing from the nozzle creates unequal pressure that lifts the balloon or the rocket off the ground.

First stage

Thrust

Exhaust

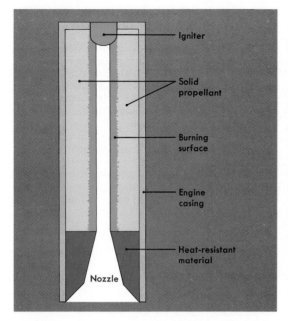

A **solid-propellant rocket** burns a solid material called the *grain*. Engineers design most grains with a hollow core. The propellant burns from the core outward. Unburned propellant shields the engine casing from the heat of combustion.

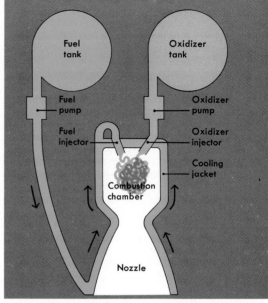

A **liquid-propellant rocket** carries fuel and an oxidizer in separate tanks. The fuel circulates through the engine's cooling jacket before entering the combustion chamber. This circulation preheats the fuel for combustion and helps cool the rocket.

There are four basic kinds of rockets: (1) solid-propellant rockets, (2) liquid-propellant rockets, (3) electric rockets, and (4) nuclear rockets.

Solid-propellant rockets burn a rubbery or plastic-like material called the *grain.* The grain consists of a fuel and an oxidizer in solid form. Unlike some liquid propellants, the fuel and oxidizer of a solid propellant do not burn upon contact with each other. The propellant must be ignited in one of two ways. It may be ignited by the burning of a small charge of *black powder* (a mixture of saltpeter, charcoal, and sulfur) or other chemicals. The propellant also may be ignited by the chemical reaction of a liquid chlorine compound sprayed onto the grain.

The temperature in the combustion chamber of a solid-propellant rocket ranges from 3000° to 6000° F. (1600° to 3300° C). In most of these rockets, engineers use high-strength steel or titanium to build chamber walls that can stand the pressure created at such high temperatures. They also may use fiber glass or special plastic materials.

Solid propellants burn faster than do liquid propellants. But they usually produce less thrust than an equal amount of liquid propellant burned in the same amount of time. Solid propellants remain effective for long periods of storage and present little danger of exploding until ignited. They do not require the pumping and blending equipment needed for liquid propellants. But it is difficult to stop and start the burning of a solid propellant. Astronauts on space flights must stop and start the burning of propellant to control their spacecraft's flight. One method used to stop the burning of solid propellant involves blasting the entire nozzle section from the rocket. But this method prevents restarting.

Solid-propellant rockets are preferred to liquid-propellant rockets by the armed forces. Military rockets must be ready to fire instantly, and solid propellants can be stored better than other kinds of propellants. Solid-propellant rockets provide the power for ICBM's, including the Minuteman 2 and MX, and for such smaller missiles as the Hawk, Talos, and Terrier. Solid-propellant rockets are used as boosters for carrier rockets, as JATO rockets, and as sounding rockets. They are also used in fireworks displays.

Liquid-propellant rockets burn a mixture of fuel and oxidizer in liquid form. These rockets carry the fuel and the oxidizer in separate tanks. A system of pipes and valves feeds the two propellant elements into the combustion chamber. Either the fuel or the oxidizer flows around the outside of the chamber before blending with the other element. This flow cools the combustion chamber and preheats the propellant element for combustion.

Methods of feeding the fuel and oxidizer into the combustion chamber include using (1) pumps or (2) high-pressure gas. The most common method uses pumps. Gas produced by burning a small portion of the propellant drives the pumps, which force the fuel and oxidizer into the combustion chamber. In the other method, high-pressure gas forces the fuel and oxidizer into the chamber. The supply of high-pressure gas may come either from nitrogen or some other gas stored under high pressure, or from the burning of a small amount of the propellant.

Some liquid propellants, called *hypergols,* ignite when the fuel and the oxidizer contact each other. But most liquid propellants require an ignition system. An electric spark may ignite the propellant, or the burning of a small amount of solid propellant in the combustion

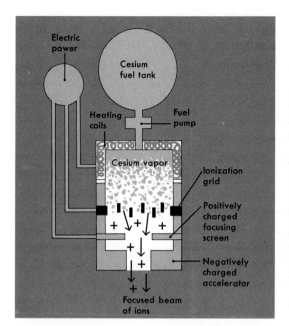

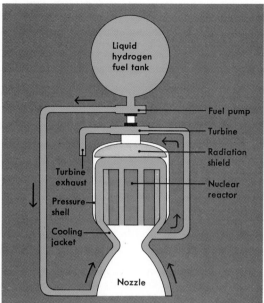

WORLD BOOK diagrams

An ion rocket is a kind of electric rocket. Heating coils in the rocket change a fuel, such as cesium, into a vapor. A hot platinum or tungsten *ionization grid* changes the flowing vapor into a stream of electrically charged particles called *ions.*

A nuclear rocket uses the heat from a nuclear reactor to change a liquid fuel into a gas. Most of the fuel flows through the reactor. Some of the fuel, heated by the nozzle of the rocket, flows through the turbine. The turbine drives the fuel pump.

chamber may do so. Liquid propellants continue to burn as long as the mixture of fuel and oxidizer flows into the combustion chamber.

Thin, high-strength steel or aluminum is used to construct most tanks that hold liquid propellant. Most combustion chambers in these rockets are steel or nickel.

Liquid propellants usually produce greater thrust than do equal amounts of solid propellants burned in the same amount of time. It also is easier to start and stop the burning of liquid propellants than that of solid propellants. The burning can be controlled merely by closing or opening valves. But liquid propellants are difficult to handle. If the propellant elements blend without igniting, the resulting mixture often will explode easily. Liquid propellants also require more complicated rocket construction than do solid propellants.

Scientists use liquid-propellant rockets for most space launch vehicles. For example, liquid-propellant rockets provided the power for the three stages of the Saturn 5 launch vehicle.

Electric rockets use electric power to produce thrust. These rockets include (1) arc jet rockets, (2) plasma jet rockets, and (3) ion rockets. Electric rockets can operate much longer than can other rockets, but they produce less thrust. An electric rocket could not lift a spacecraft out of the earth's atmosphere, but it could propel a vehicle through space. Scientists are working to develop electric rockets for long space flights.

Arc jet rockets heat a propellant gas with an electric spark called an *electric arc.* The spark can heat the gas to a temperature three or four times as great as that produced by a solid- or liquid-propellant rocket.

Plasma jet rockets are a type of arc jet rocket. The flow of propellant gas created by an electric arc con-

tains some electrically charged particles. The mixture of the gas and these particles is called a *plasma.* Plasma jet rockets use an electric current and a magnetic field to increase the speed at which the plasma flows from the rocket.

Ion rockets produce thrust with a flow of electrically charged particles called *ions.* A part of the rocket called the *ionization grid* produces ions as a special gas flows over the surface of the grid. An electric field speeds the flow of the ions from the rocket.

Nuclear rockets heat fuel with a *nuclear reactor,* a machine that produces energy by splitting atoms. Such rockets can produce two or three times more power than do rockets that burn solid or liquid propellant. Scientists are working on the development of nuclear rockets for space travel.

In nuclear rockets, liquid hydrogen is pumped to the reactor through a jacket surrounding the rocket engine. This pumping process helps cool the rocket, and it also preheats the liquid hydrogen. Hundreds of narrow channels pass through the nuclear reactor. As the liquid hydrogen flows through these channels, heat from the reactor changes the fuel into rapidly expanding gas. The gas flows through the exhaust nozzle at speeds up to 22,000 miles (35,400 kilometers) per hour.

See **Rocket** in *World Book* for more information on How rockets are used and History.

Root is one of the three main organs of a plant. The others are the stem and the leaf. Most roots are long and round and grow underground. They anchor the plant in the soil. They also absorb water and minerals that the plant needs to grow. In addition, many roots store food for later use by the plant.

Plants with roots include all seed-producing plants and most spore-producing plants, such as ferns and horsetails. Liverworts, hornworts, and mosses do not have true roots.

Kinds of roots. The first root to develop from a seed is called the *primary* root. It produces many branches called *secondary* roots. The secondary roots, in turn, produce branches of their own.

A plant may develop one of two main kinds of root systems, *taproot* or *fibrous.* In a taproot system, the primary root grows straight down and is called the *taproot.* The taproot remains larger than any of the secondary roots throughout the life of the plant. In some plants, including beets and carrots, the taproot becomes *fleshy* (swollen).

Grass is an example of a plant with a fibrous root system. In such a system, the primary root does not remain larger than the others. Many slender secondary roots grow out in all directions. A fibrous root system may become very extensive. For example, the roots of a rye plant may have a combined length of about 380 miles (612 kilometers).

Some plants have modified roots that perform special functions. Roots that grow from the stem above the ground are called *adventitious roots.* They include the *prop roots* of corn and certain other plants. Prop roots grow down into the soil from the lower part of the stem

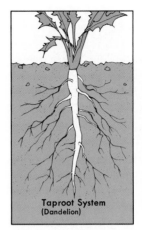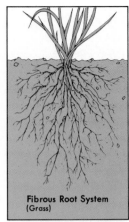

Taproot System
(Dandelion)

Fibrous Root System
(Grass)

WORLD BOOK diagrams by Robert Keys

The two chief kinds of root systems. In a *taproot system,* the primary root grows straight down and remains larger than secondary roots. In a *fibrous root system,* secondary roots grow in all directions and may be as long as the primary root.

and help brace the plant against the wind. Some species of orchids and other plants that live on tree branches send out *aerial roots,* which cling to the branches. Aerial roots absorb water and minerals from the surface of the tree and from the air. Mistletoe is one of the few plants with roots that penetrate the limbs of a tree. These roots, called *sinkers,* absorb food, water, and minerals directly from the tree.

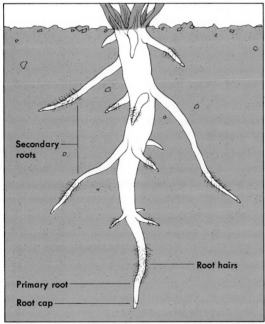

Secondary roots

Root hairs

Primary root

Root cap

WORLD BOOK diagram by Robert Keys

The main parts of a root system are shown above. The *primary root* develops first and produces branches called *secondary roots. Root hairs* grow just above the tip of each root.

See **Root** in *World Book* for more information on Parts of a root and The importance of roots.

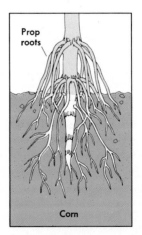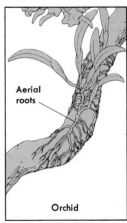

Prop roots

Aerial roots

Corn

Orchid

WORLD BOOK diagrams by Robert Keys

Specialized roots. *Prop roots* grow from a stem and help brace a plant against the wind. *Aerial roots* cling to tree branches and absorb water and minerals from the tree and the air.

NASA

Saturn is encircled by seven major rings. In the photograph at the left, a section of the rings is hidden by the shadow of the planet.

Saturn is the second largest planet. Only Jupiter is larger. Saturn has seven thin, flat rings around it. The rings consist of numerous narrow ringlets, which are made up of ice particles that travel around the planet. The gleaming rings make Saturn one of the most beautiful objects in the solar system. Jupiter and Uranus are the only other planets known to have rings. Their rings are much fainter than those around Saturn.

Saturn's diameter at its equator is about 74,900 miles (120,540 kilometers), almost 10 times that of the earth. The planet can be seen from the earth with the unaided eye, but its rings cannot. Saturn was the farthest planet from the earth that the ancient astronomers knew about. They named it for the Roman god of agriculture.

Orbit. Saturn is the sixth closest planet to the sun. Its mean distance from the sun is about 888,200,000 miles (1,429,400,000 kilometers), compared with about 93,000,000 miles (150,000,000 kilometers) for the earth. At its closest approach to the earth, Saturn is about 762,700,000 miles (1,277,400,000 kilometers) away.

Saturn travels around the sun in an *elliptical* (oval-shaped) orbit. Its distance from the sun is about 937,600,000 miles (1,508,900,000 kilometers) at its farthest point to about 838,800,000 miles (1,349,900,000 kilometers) at its closest point. The planet takes about 10,759 earth-days, or about 29½ earth-years, to go around the sun, compared with 365 days, or one year, for the earth.

Rotation. As Saturn travels around the sun, it spins on its *axis,* an imaginary line drawn through its center. Saturn's axis is not *perpendicular* (at an angle of 90°) to the planet's path around the sun. The axis tilts at an angle of about 27° from the perpendicular position.

Saturn rotates faster than any other planet except Jupiter. Saturn spins around once in only 10 hours 39 minutes, compared to about 24 hours, or one day, for the earth. The rapid rotation of Saturn causes the planet to bulge at its equator and flatten at its poles. The planet's

---

Saturn at a glance

Saturn, shown in blue in the diagram, is the sixth closest planet to the sun. Astronomers still use the ancient symbol for Saturn, *right.*

Pluto
Neptune
Uranus
Saturn
Jupiter
Mars
Earth
Venus
Mercury
Sun

Distance from the sun: *Shortest*—838,800,000 mi. (1,349,900,000 km); *Greatest*—937,600,000 mi. (1,508,900,000 km); *Mean*—888,200,000 mi. (1,429,400,000 km).
Distance from the earth: *Shortest*—762,700,000 mi. (1,277,400,000 km); *Greatest*—1,030,000,000 mi. (1,658,000,000 km).
Diameter: About 74,898 mi. (120,536 km).
Length of year: About 29½ earth-years.
Rotation period: 10 hours 39 minutes.
Temperature: −288° F. (−178° C)
Atmosphere: Hydrogen, helium, methane, ammonia, ethane, and phosphine (?).
Number of satellites: 18.

Jet Propulsion Laboratory

The dark side of Saturn's rings was photographed by *Voyager 1* as it flew by the side opposite the sun. The dense B-ring—the reddish-brown band—appears dark because it blocks much of the sunlight. It is the brightest ring when viewed from earth.

diameter is 8,000 miles (13,000 kilometers) larger at the equator than between the poles.

Surface and atmosphere. Most scientists believe Saturn is a giant ball of gas that has no solid surface. However, the planet seems to have a hot solid inner core of iron and rocky material. Around this dense central part is an outer core that probably consists of ammonia, methane, and water. A layer of highly compressed, liquid metallic hydrogen surrounds the outer core. Above this layer lies a region composed of hydrogen and helium in a *viscous* (syruplike) form. The hydrogen and helium become gaseous near the planet's surface and merge with its atmosphere, which consists chiefly of the same two elements.

A dense layer of clouds covers Saturn. Photographs of the planet show a series of belts and zones of varied colors on the cloud tops. This banded appearance seems to be caused by differences in the temperature and altitude of atmospheric gas masses.

The plants and animals that live on the earth could not live on Saturn. Scientists doubt that any form of life exists on the planet.

Temperature. The tilt of Saturn's axis causes the sun to heat the planet's northern and southern halves unequally, resulting in seasons and temperature changes. Each season lasts about $7\frac{1}{2}$ earth-years, because Saturn takes about 29 times as long to go around the sun as the earth does. Saturn's temperature is always much colder than the earth's, because Saturn is so far from the sun. The temperature at the top of Saturn's clouds averages $-288\ °F\ (-178\ °C)$.

The temperatures below Saturn's clouds are much higher than those at the top of the clouds. The planet gives off about $2\frac{1}{2}$ times as much heat as it receives from the sun. Many astronomers believe that much of Saturn's internal heat comes from energy generated by the sinking of helium slowly through the liquid hydrogen in the planet's interior.

Density and mass. Saturn has a lower *density* than any other planet (in *World Book,* see **Density**). It is only about one-tenth as dense as the earth, and about two-thirds as dense as water. That is, a portion of Saturn would weigh much less than an equal portion of the earth, and would float in water.

Although Saturn has a low density, it has a greater *mass* than any other planet except Jupiter (in *World Book,* see **Mass**). Saturn is 95 times as massive as the earth. The force of gravity is a little higher on Saturn than on earth. A 100-pound (45-kilogram) object on earth would weigh about 107 pounds (49 kilograms) on Saturn.

Rings. The rings of Saturn surround the planet at its equator. They do not touch Saturn. As Saturn orbits the sun, the rings always tilt at the same angle as the equator. Saturn's seven rings consist of thousands of narrow ringlets. The ringlets are made up of billions of pieces of ice. These pieces range from ice particles that are the size of dust to chunks of ice that measure more than 10 feet (3 meters) in diameter.

Saturn's major rings are extremely wide. The outermost ring, for example, may measure as much as 180,000 miles (300,000 kilometers) across. However, the rings of Saturn are so thin that they cannot be seen when they are in direct line with the earth. They vary in thickness from about 660 to 9,800 feet (200 to 3,000 meters). A space separates the rings from one another. Each of these gaps is about 2,000 miles (3,200 kilometers) or more in width. However, some of the gaps between the major rings contain ringlets.

Saturn's rings were discovered in the early 1600's by the Italian astronomer Galileo. Galileo could not see the rings clearly with his small telescope, and thought they were large satellites. In 1656, after using a more powerful telescope, Christiaan Huygens, a Dutch astronomer, described a "thin, flat" ring around Saturn. Huygens thought the ring was a solid sheet of some material. In 1675, Jean Domenique Cassini, a French astronomer, announced the discovery of two separate rings made up of swarms of satellites. Later observations of Saturn resulted in the discovery of more rings. The ringlets were discovered in 1980.

Satellites. In addition to its rings, Saturn has at least 18 satellites. The largest, Titan, has a diameter of about 3,190 miles (5,140 kilometers)—larger than the planets Mercury and Pluto. Titan is one of the few satellites in the solar system known to have an atmosphere. Its atmosphere consists largely of nitrogen.

Many of Saturn's satellites have large craters. For example, Mimas has a crater that covers about one-third the diameter of the satellite. Another satellite, Iapetus, has a bright side and a dark side. The bright side of this satellite reflects about 10 times as much sunlight as the dark side. The satellite Hyperion is shaped somewhat like a squat cylinder rather than like a sphere. Unlike Saturn's other satellites, Hyperion's axis does not point toward the planet.

See **Saturn** in *World Book* for more information on Flights to Saturn.

Steve McCutcheon

Many northern fur seals spend the summer on Alaskan islands and travel south for the winter.

Seal is a sleek sea animal with a body shaped like a torpedo. Seals are excellent swimmers and spend much of their time in the water. But they give birth to their young on land. Most kinds of seals live in the oceans or in inland seas, but a few live in fresh water. The Baikal seal, for example, lives in Lake Baikal in the southern Soviet Union.

Some kinds of seals, including harbor seals and ringed seals, spend much of their time on land or on floating chunks of ice. But northern fur seals stay at sea for eight months. They *migrate* (travel) about 5,000 miles (8,000 kilometers) a year—farther than any other mammal. They swim south from the Bering Sea almost to northern Mexico, and then return north. During the entire trip, the seals swim at a distance of 10 to 100 miles (16 to 160 kilometers) from the coast and never go ashore. No one knows why the seals make their yearly trip.

The largest seal is the southern elephant seal, which lives in the sub-Antarctic waters off South America. The male may grow to be 21 feet (6.4 meters) long and may weigh up to 8,000 pounds (3,600 kilograms). This seal ranks second in size only to whales among all sea mammals. The smallest seal is the ringed seal of the Arctic. It is about 4½ feet (1.4 meters) long and weighs up to 200 pounds (91 kilograms).

Seals make up a group of mammals called *Pinnipedia.* This name comes from Latin words meaning *fin-footed.* A seal's flippers look somewhat like fins.

There are three main groups of pinnipeds: (1) eared seals, which include fur seals and sea lions; (2) earless seals, including harbor seals and elephant seals; and (3) walruses. An earless seal has small ear openings, but no ears on the outside of its body. Walruses also have small ear openings but no outside ears. They are the only pinnipeds with tusks.

The body of a seal

Most kinds of seals have hair on their bodies, but some adult male walruses are almost hairless. Fur seals have thick coats of fine hair. Like all other mammals with fur, seals shed their coats every year and grow new ones. Most species of seals shed a few hairs at a time, much as cats and dogs do. But elephant seals lose large pieces of skin and hair and look ragged.

All seals have a layer of blubber 1 to 6 inches (2.5 to 15 centimeters) thick. It helps keep the animals warm, and gives them energy when they can get no food.

Head. Some kinds of seals have small heads with short noses that give their faces a "pushed in" appearance. An elephant seal has a long, curved nose. The male hooded seal's nose forms a pouch that extends over the top of its head. When the animal is annoyed, it blows air into the pouch. The outer skin of the pouch expands like a balloon, and forms a bright red hood on the

Facts in brief

Names: *male,* bull; *female,* cow; *young,* calf, pup, or whelp; *group,* herd or pod.
Gestation period: About 8 to 12 months, depending on the species.
Number of newborn: Usually 1, rarely 2.
Length of life: 40 years or more.
Where found: Along the coasts of continents in most parts of the world; a few kinds in freshwater lakes and inland seas.
Scientific classification: Seals make up a group of animals called the *pinnipeds.* Traditionally, they have been classified as a suborder of the order Carnivora, which includes such land mammals as bears, cats, and dogs. Some zoologists consider the seals a separate order, Pinnipedia. Fur seals and sea lions belong to the eared seal family, Otariidae. Walruses belong to the walrus family, Odobenida. Elephant seals and harbor seals belong to the earless seal family, Phocidae.

animal's head. The seal uses its hood to frighten enemies. All seals have slitlike nostrils, which they close when they swim under water.

The eyes of most species of seals are large and shiny, but walruses have small eyes. Most seals can see and hear well, but they have a poor sense of smell. All seals have whiskers on the upper lip. The whiskers are sensitive to touch and probably help seals find food.

Flippers. Seals have four legs, but the leg bones above the ankles are buried inside the body. The parts that extend outside, including the feet, form the animal's large, paddlelike flippers. The front flippers of fur seals and sea lions are longer and flatter than those of other species. A fur seal's front flippers may be more than 1½ feet (46 centimeters) long and 6 inches (15 centimeters) wide, and help make this animal a powerful swimmer. The front flippers of earless seals are smaller and narrower than those of fur seals. Earless seals swim by moving their bodies and rear flippers much as fish move their bodies and tails. A frightened fur seal can swim as fast as 10 miles (16 kilometers) per hour for about five minutes.

Fur seals, sea lions, and walruses turn their rear flippers forward and downward to help support their bodies on land. They walk on all four flippers. The rear flippers of earless seals extend straight back, palm to palm. These seals cannot turn their flippers forward. They move themselves across land or ice by rhythmic contractions of their strong belly muscles.

The life of a seal

Most kinds of seals live in groups and may stay together on long ocean journeys. A few species, including the Ross seals of the Antarctic, live alone or with only two or three other seals. Some species, including gray seals and ringed seals, have lived 40 years or more.

Seal rookeries. Every spring, seals go to their breeding grounds, called *rookeries,* to have young and to find mates. Most rookeries are on islands. Rookeries of northern fur seals are large beach areas, and more than 150,000 seals may gather at one rookery.

The northern fur seal *bulls* (males) are the first to arrive at the rookeries. Late in May their bellows and roars can be heard over 1 mile (1.6 kilometers) away as they fight for their choice of places, called *territories,* along the beach. The *cows* (females) come ashore in early July and join the *harem* (group of females) of one of the bulls. A bull's harem consists of 3 to more than 40 cows,

and a few bulls may have over 100 cows. Shortly after a cow arrives on shore, she gives birth to the baby she has carried inside her body for about 12 months. The cow mates again a few days after giving birth.

Bull seals fight to get their territories. They defend their territories and the cows within them. Bulls are not strong enough to hold a territory until they are about 10 years old. The young bachelors, and older bulls without harems, live apart from the others. Most cow seals bear their first young when they are about 5 years old, and usually give birth each year. Some cow seals may bear young until they are 25.

Young. A female seal almost always has one *pup* (baby seal) at a time. Twins are rare. A newborn pup has teeth that are *erupting* (breaking out of the gums), and fine, soft fur covers its body. Sea lion pups have brown fur, and newborn fur seals, elephant seals, and monk seals have black coats. The pups of harp seals, leopard seals, walruses, and other seals that live on floating islands of ice may be white, grayish, or brown.

Northern fur seal pups can swim and can travel on land as soon as they are born. The mothers divide their time between eating at sea and nursing their pups on land. A mother may stay at sea from seven to nine days. After she returns, she hunts for her pup among the hundreds of others on the land. Each mother feeds only her own pup, which she recognizes by its cry and its odor. The pup gets enough milk from its mother to stay alive until its next feeding. Seal milk is rich, and the pups grow quickly. A fur seal weighs about 10 pounds (4.5 kilograms) at birth and from 30 to 35 pounds (14 to 16 kilograms) when its mother leaves it, 3 or 4 months later.

Food. Seals feed on various marine animals. Fur seals and sea lions eat primarily fish and squid, and harbor seals eat mostly fish and octopus. Crabeater seals and ringed seals feed mainly on small shrimp. Elephant seals prefer small sharks and rays, which they capture in deep water, and leopard seals feed on fish and sometimes on penguins. Walruses eat clams.

A seal has sharp, pointed teeth. It cannot chew food because its teeth have no flat surfaces. Seals grasp and tear most of their prey, but they gulp small fish whole.

Enemies. The seal's greatest enemy is the hunter. For hundreds of years, hunters have killed seals for blubber, bones, fur, and meat. During the 1800's, so many seals were killed that only a few survived. Several nations, including the United States, quarreled about how northern fur seals should be hunted. In 1911, Canada, Japan, Russia, and the United States signed an agreement to protect northern fur seals. That year, there were only about 150,000 northern fur seals on the Pribilof Islands. Today, there are about 1 million. The yearly harvest of skins ranged from 20,000 to 24,000. Under the agreement, seals were hunted commercially only on land. Canada and Japan did not hunt northern fur seals because none of the rookeries were in their territory. The Soviet Union and the United States each gave 15 per cent of their catch to Canada and 15 per cent to Japan. In this way, the catch was shared by all the nations in whose territory the seals live. Since 1984, animal protection laws in both the United States and the Soviet Union have ended all commercial harvesting of seals on the Pribilof Islands.

The skeleton of a seal

WORLD BOOK illustration by John D. Dawson

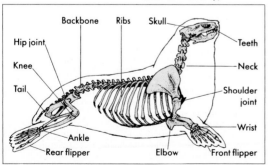

Backbone Ribs Skull
Hip joint
Knee
Tail
Teeth
Neck
Shoulder joint
Wrist
Ankle Elbow Front flipper
Rear flipper

Season is one of the four periods of the year. Each season—spring, summer, autumn, and winter—lasts about three months and brings changes in temperature, weather, and the length of daylight.

During the spring, the days are warm in middle parts of the Northern Hemisphere, the northern half of the earth. Summer follows with hot days and warm nights. In autumn, the days become cooler, leading to the cold of winter. The four periods are called *climatic seasons* when based on these temperature and weather changes.

In the Southern Hemisphere, the climatic seasons differ by about six months. This hemisphere has summer when the Northern Hemisphere has winter.

Some regions do not have all four climatic seasons. In parts of the tropics, for example, temperatures change little. But the amount of rainfall varies greatly, so that these regions have a wet season and a dry season. The polar regions, on the other hand, have a light season and a dark season. In these parts of the world, the sun shines almost all the time in summer and almost never during the winter.

The changing seasons are caused by the changing position of the earth in relation to the sun. Astronomers can tell exactly from the earth's motion around the sun when one season ends and the next one begins. The dates used for the first day of each season mark the beginning of the *astronomical seasons.* The beginning and end of the climatic seasons vary from these dates from place to place and from year to year. The temperature and weather do not change instantly in response to the changing position of the earth in relation to the sun. The warmest and coldest weather generally occurs several weeks after the beginning of the summer and winter astronomical seasons. Heat that has been retained by the oceans plays an important role in producing this delayed response.

The seasons keep changing because the tilt of the earth's axis never changes while the earth circles the sun. One way to understand this is to picture which way the tilt of the axis causes the North Pole to slant at different times of the year. When the North Pole slants toward the sun, the Northern Hemisphere receives the most sunlight and it is summer there. When the pole slants away from the sun, the Northern Hemisphere receives the least sunlight and it is winter. Spring begins when the pole starts to slant toward the sun, and autumn begins when the pole starts to slant away again.

Summer begins in the Northern Hemisphere when the *summer solstice* occurs, on June 20 or 21. The sun is high in the sky and there are more hours of daylight than on any other day. The *winter solstice* marks the beginning of winter in the Northern Hemisphere. It occurs on December 21 or 22. The sun is low in the sky and there are fewer daylight hours on that day than on any other day.

The *vernal equinox* marks the beginning of spring, on March 20 or 21. Autumn begins on September 22 or 23, the *autumnal equinox.* At both points, the sun appears directly above the equator. During each equinox, places on the earth have approximately 12 hours of daylight and 12 hours of darkness.

The change of seasons

The seasons change because places on the earth receive different amounts of sunlight during the year. The tilt of the earth's axis produces the differing amounts. When the North Pole is tilted toward the sun, the Northern Hemisphere has summer. The sun's rays strike the earth from a high angle and each place receives maximum sunlight. When the North Pole is tilted away from the sun, the Northern Hemisphere has winter. The sun's rays come from a lower angle and each place receives minimum sunlight. As the earth moves between these positions, autumn and spring occur.

WORLD BOOK diagram

March 20 or 21 is the first day of spring in the Northern Hemisphere.

June 20 or 21 is the first day of summer in the Northern Hemisphere and of winter in the Southern Hemisphere.

December 21 or 22 is the first day of winter in the Northern Hemisphere and of summer in the Southern Hemisphere.

Northern Hemisphere

Equator

Southern Hemisphere

Summer

Winter

Sun's rays

Sun

Winter

Sun's rays

Summer

Northern Hemisphere

Equator

Southern Hemisphere

September 22 or 23 is the first day of autumn in the Northern Hemisphere.

Earth's orbit around sun

Seed is the specialized part of a plant that produces a new plant. It contains an *embryo* (partly developed plant) that consists of an immature root and stem. A seed also has a supply of stored food and a protective covering.

Seeds are produced by approximately 250,000 kinds of plants. The flowering plants make up the largest group of seed-producing plants. These plants, which botanists call *angiosperms,* include the vast majority of trees, shrubs, and soft-stemmed plants. Seeds are also produced by about 800 kinds of trees and shrubs called *gymnosperms.* Most types of gymnosperms develop cones.

The seeds of different kinds of plants vary greatly in size. The double coconut tree produces the largest seed, which weighs up to 50 pounds (23 kilograms). On the other hand, orchid seeds are so tiny that 800,000 of them weigh no more than an ounce (28 grams). The size of a seed has no relationship to the size of the plant that develops from it. For example, the giant redwood tree grows from a seed that is only $\frac{1}{16}$ inch (1.6 millimeters) long.

The number of seeds produced by an individual plant varies according to the size of the seeds. A coconut tree has only a few large seeds, but an orchid or pigweed plant produces millions of tiny ones.

Kinds of seeds. Seeds develop from structures called *ovules,* which are in the flowers or on the cones of a plant. Botanists divide seeds into two main groups, *enclosed seeds* and *naked seeds.*

Enclosed seeds are produced by angiosperms. Their ovules are enclosed by an *ovary,* a structure within the flower. As the seed ripens, the ovary enlarges and forms a fruit, which provides some protection for the developing seed. In some plants, the ovaries develop into fleshy fruits, such as apples and peaches. Other plants, such as peas and poppies, have dry fruits that form pods or capsules. In grain plants, such as corn and wheat, the ovary and ovule join together, forming a hard kernel.

Naked seeds are produced by gymnosperms. These trees and shrubs produce ovules on the upper surface of the scales that form their cones. Gymnosperms have no ovaries, and so their seeds are not enclosed during development. However, the scales of the cones close up together when the seeds are ripening and provide some protection for the seeds.

The parts of a seed. Seeds consist of three parts: (1) the embryo, (2) the food storage tissue, and (3) the seed coat.

The embryo is the part of the seed from which the mature plant develops. It contains the parts that develop into the *primary root,* the first root to grow; the stem; and the first leaves of the new plant. The embryo also has one or more specialized leaflike structures called *cotyledons.* Angiosperms have either one or two cotyledons. Those with one cotyledon are called *monocotyledons* or *monocots.* Angiosperms with two cotyledons are called *dicotyledons* or *dicots.* Gymnosperms have from two to eight cotyledons.

The cotyledons absorb and digest food from the food storage tissue of the seed. In angiosperm seeds, this tissue is called the *endosperm.* The cotyledons of some dicotyledon seeds quickly absorb all the food in the endosperm. The cotyledons then store the food that the embryo needs for growth. In gymnosperm seeds, food is stored in tissue called the *megagametophyte.*

The seed coat covers the embryo and food storage tissue and protects them from injury, insects, and loss of water. Seed coats range from thin, delicate layers of tissue to thick, tough coverings.

See **Seed** in *World Book* for more information on the following topics:

•How seeds develop   •How seeds sprout
•How seeds are spread •How people use seeds

The parts of a seed

A seed consists of an embryo, food storage tissue, and a seed coat. The embryo contains the parts that form a new plant. It also has one or more *cotyledons,* which absorb and digest food from the food storage tissue. The seed coat protects the seed from injury, insects, and loss of water.

WORLD BOOK diagrams by James Teason

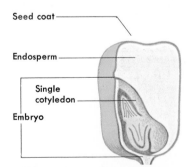

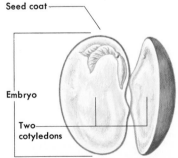

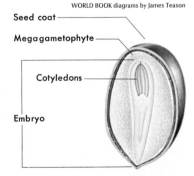

A monocotyledon seed, such as this corn seed, has one cotyledon. Its food storage tissue is called the *endosperm.*

A dicotyledon seed has two cotyledons. In the bean seed shown above, the cotyledons serve as the food storage tissue.

A gymnosperm seed, such as this pine seed, stores food in the *megagametophyte* and has two or more cotyledons.

The oceanic whitetip shark, *left*, has a graceful, torpedolike body. The fish's streamlined shape enables it to move swiftly through the water with little effort. This shark is named for the white markings on the tips of its fins. It is one of the most common species of large shark.

Peter Lake from Peter Schub

Shark is a meat-eating fish and one of the most feared sea animals. Scientists classify about 350 species of fish as sharks. These fish live in oceans throughout the world but are most common in warm seas.

Sharks vary greatly in size and habits. Whale sharks, the largest kind of shark—and the largest of all fish—may grow up to 40 feet (12 meters) long. They may weigh over 15 short tons (14 metric tons), more than twice as much as an African elephant. The smallest sharks may measure only 5 inches (13 centimeters) long and weigh about 1 ounce (28 grams).

Some kinds of sharks live in the depths of the ocean. Other kinds are found near the surface. Some species live in coastal waters, but others dwell far out at sea. A few species enter rivers and lakes that have outlets to the sea.

All sharks are *carnivores* (meat-eaters). Most of them eat live fish, including other sharks. In fact, a shark's most common natural enemy is a larger shark. Most sharks eat their prey whole, or they tear off large chunks of flesh. Some sharks crush their prey. Others scoop out small pieces of flesh from large fish. Sharks also feed on dead or dying animals.

Sharks have the reputation of attacking human be-

ings. But fewer than 100 shark attacks a year are reported throughout the world.

The body of a shark

Sharks differ from most other kinds of fish in a number of ways. For example, sharks have a boneless skeleton made of a tough, elastic substance called *cartilage.* Most species of sharks have a rounded body, shaped somewhat like a torpedo. This streamlined shape aids in swimming. Angel sharks, which live near the ocean bottom, have a flat body similar to that of skates and rays.

Sharks have fewer young at a time than most fish do. Some species give birth to 60 or more *pups* in a litter, but most have far fewer. The parents do not take care of the young—and may even eat them.

Shark eggs, unlike those of most fish, are fertilized inside the female's body. The male shark has two organs called *claspers,* which release sperm into the female, where it fertilizes the eggs. Among most species of sharks, the eggs hatch inside the female, and the pups are born alive. At least 40 species lay their eggs outside their bodies.

Tail and fins. Sharks can travel with great bursts of speed when excited. Scientists recorded a blue shark

The body of a shark

WORLD BOOK diagram by Marion Pahl

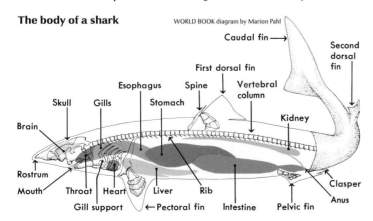

Brain
Skull
Gills
Esophagus
Stomach
Spine
First dorsal fin
Vertebral column
Caudal fin →
Second dorsal fin
Kidney
Rostrum
Mouth
Throat
Heart
Liver
Rib
Intestine
Pelvic fin
Clasper
Anus
Gill support
← Pectoral fin

Kent Cambridge Scientific, Inc.

A shark's skin is covered with tiny toothlike scales. The scales pictured above were photographed with an electron microscope.

Marine Studios, Marineland of Florida

The mouth of a white shark has two rows of razor-sharp teeth. New teeth regularly replace the old teeth. The replacement teeth lie out of sight along the inside of the jaws.

traveling at bursts of 43 miles (69 kilometers) per hour. The fastest-swimming sharks have a crescent-shaped tail that provides power for swimming. The upper part of the tail usually is longer than the lower part. Stiff *pectoral* (side) fins help lift and balance the front of the body.

Most fish have a *swim bladder,* a gas-filled organ that helps them remain at a certain depth without sinking. Sharks lack this organ. Instead, they have a large liver filled with oil. This oil is lighter than water, and it helps the shark keep from sinking. Even so, sharks must swim constantly or they will sink.

Teeth and scales. A shark's mouth is on the underside of the head among all species except the angel, megamouth, whale, and wobbegong sharks. The mouth of these sharks is at the front of the head. A shark has several rows of teeth. New teeth replace the rows of old teeth regularly—as often as every one to two weeks. Some sharks have molarlike grinding teeth. Others have razorlike cutting teeth, and still others have pointed teeth. Some people believe that sharks must turn over on their back to bite, but this is not true.

Small, toothlike scales cover a shark's body. These *placoid* scales make the skin of a shark very rough. Dried sharkskin, called *shagreen,* was once used as sandpaper.

Gills. Sharks get oxygen from the water through gills, as do other fish. But sharks have no *gill cover,* a bony plate that shields the gills of most fish. Instead, sharks have from five to seven slits in the skin on each side of

the head. Water passes out of these slits after the shark's gills remove the oxygen.

Most sharks cannot pump water over their gills, as do the majority of fish. Sharks rely on their constant swimming to force water through their mouth and over their gills. This process of forcing water is known as *ram-jet ventilation.*

Senses. Sharks have keen senses that enable them to compete successfully for prey. They have excellent hearing, though it is limited to low-pitched sounds. Sharks can home in on prey by its sounds. Some scientists believe that the shark's *lateral line* detects the lowest-pitched sounds. The lateral line is a sensory system of fluid-filled canals that runs down both sides of the shark's body, from its head to its tail. The lateral line also detects water movement.

Sharks have highly sensitive eyes that can see extremely well in dim light. Sharks even possess a crude form of color vision. However, they may not be able to see details clearly. Sharks have been called "swimming noses." It was once widely believed that sharks relied mainly on their sense of smell to hunt prey. However, little evidence exists of a special sensitivity for smells in sharks.

Sharks can detect incredibly small electrical fields. The head of a shark has a large number of small pores that lead to an elaborate system of sensory tubes. These tubes, called *ampullae of Lorenzini,* are sensitive to electrical fields. Sharks can locate and capture a fish by sensing the small electrical field produced by its gills. Sharks also seem to use their electrical sense for navigation and migration.

See **Shark** in *World Book* for more information on Kinds of sharks and Sharks and people.

Some kinds of sharks

WORLD BOOK illustration by Marion Pahl

White shark
Carcharodon carcharias
Up to 21 feet
(6.4 meters) long

Nurse shark
Ginglymostoma cirratum
Up to 14 feet
(4.3 meters) long

Shortfin mako
Isurus oxyrinchus
Up to 12 feet
(3.7 meters) long

Scalloped shark
Sphyrna lewini
Up to 14 feet
(4.3 meters) long

Whale shark
Rhincodon typus
Up to 40 feet
(12 meters) long

Thresher shark
Alopias vulpinus
Up to 20 feet
(6.1 meters) long

Skeleton is the flexible, bony framework of any vertebrate animal. It gives the body shape, protects vital organs, and provides a system of levers, operated by muscles, that enables the body to move. The skeleton houses *bone marrow,* the blood-forming tissues. It stores such elements as calcium and phosphorus and releases them to the blood. It also contains smaller amounts of magnesium, potassium, and sodium.

The human skeleton has about 206 separate bones. That is, a human being generally forms that many bones out of cartilage while developing to maturity. Sixty bones are in the hands and arms alone.

Bones are joined to neighboring bones by joints. Joints are either immovable, as in the skull, or movable, as in the arms and legs. The bones fit together and are held in place by strong bands of flexible tissue called *ligaments.* The human skeleton is divided into two main parts, the *axial skeleton,* and the *appendicular skeleton.*

The axial skeleton is made up of the bones of the head, neck, and trunk. The spine (*spinal column* or *backbone*) forms an axis that supports the other parts of the body. The skull is at the top of the spine. The spine consists of separate bones, called *vertebrae,* with fibrous discs between them. Seven bones make up the *cervical*

vertebrae (neck bones). The 12 *thoracic* vertebrae are at the back of the chest.

The ribs are attached to the thoracic vertebrae. There are usually 12 ribs on each side of the body. The upper ribs fasten in front to the *sternum* (breastbone).

The five *lumbar* vertebrae lie in the lower part of the back. Below the last lumbar vertebra is the *sacrum.* In babies, five separate bones make up the sacrum. In adults, these bones have grown together into one solid structure. The pelvis is attached to the sacral segment of the spine by *sacroiliac joints.* The coccyx is at the bottom of the spine.

The appendicular skeleton is made up of the bones of the arms and legs and their supports. The *shoulder girdle* consists of the *scapula,* (shoulder blade) and the *clavicle* (collarbone). The skeleton of the arm is divided into the *humerus* (upper arm); *radius* and *ulna* (forearm); *carpus* (wrist bones); *metacarpus* (palm); and *phalanges* (fingers). The bones of the leg consist of the *femur* (thigh); *tibia* and *fibula* (leg); *tarsus* (back of the foot); *metatarsus* (forefoot); and *phalanges* (toes). The leg is attached to the trunk by a *pelvic girdle* made up of two hip bones. Each consists of three bones, the *ilium,* the *ischium,* and the *pubis.* These bones are fused in adults.

The human skeleton

The skeleton is a strong, flexible framework that supports the body and protects the internal organs. It also provides a system of levers, operated by the muscles, that enables the body to move. The human skeleton consists of about 206 bones, some of which are *fused* (joined) in adults.

WORLD BOOK illustrations by Zorica Dabich

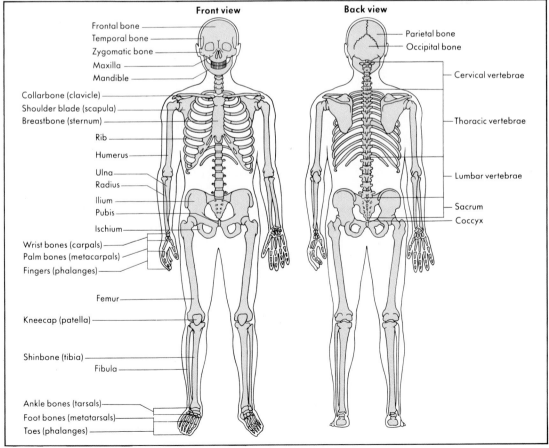

Front view

Back view

Frontal bone
Temporal bone
Zygomatic bone
Maxilla
Mandible

Parietal bone
Occipital bone
Cervical vertebrae

Collarbone (clavicle)
Shoulder blade (scapula)
Breastbone (sternum)

Thoracic vertebrae

Rib
Humerus
Ulna
Radius
Ilium
Pubis
Ischium

Lumbar vertebrae

Sacrum
Coccyx

Wrist bones (carpals)
Palm bones (metacarpals)
Fingers (phalanges)

Femur

Kneecap (patella)

Shinbone (tibia)
Fibula

Ankle bones (tarsals)
Foot bones (metatarsals)
Toes (phalanges)

Skin is the organ that covers the bodies of human beings and many other animals. In human beings, the skin protects the body in a wide variety of ways. For example, the skin is almost completely waterproof and so prevents the escape of the fluids that bathe body tissues. It also prevents bacteria and chemicals from entering most parts of the body. The skin protects underlying tissues from harmful rays of the sun.

In addition, the skin helps keep the internal temperature of the body within normal levels. Glands in the skin release sweat when a person becomes overheated. The sweat evaporates and so cools the body. When a person becomes too cool, the body retains heat by narrowing the blood vessels in the skin. As a result, the flow of blood near the surface of the body decreases, and the body gives off less heat. The skin has many nerve endings that are sensitive to cold and heat, as well as pain, pressure, and touch.

The skin is the largest organ of the human body. If the skin of a 150-pound (68-kilogram) adult male were spread out flat, it would cover about 20 square feet (1.8 square meters).

Structure of the skin

The skin has three layers of tissue: (1) epidermis, (2) dermis, and (3) subcutaneous tissue. The epidermis, the outermost layer, is about as thick as a sheet of paper over most parts of the body. The dermis, the middle layer, is between 15 and 40 times as thick as the epidermis. The subcutaneous tissue, the innermost layer, varies greatly in thickness among individuals. In all people, however, the subcutaneous tissue is much thicker than the epidermis and dermis. In addition to these tissues, the skin includes the hair, nails, and certain kinds of glands.

Epidermis has four layers of cells. From the outermost to the innermost, they are the *horny, granular, spinous,* and *basal layers.* The horny layer consists of between about 15 and 40 rows of dying cells. These cells are filled with a tough, waterproof protein called *keratin.* The granular layer consists of one or two rows of dying cells that contain small grains of a substance called *keratohyaline.* The spinous layer is composed of between about 4 and 10 rows of living cells that have spinelike projections where the cells touch one another. The basal layer is also made up of living cells. It consists mainly of a single row of tall, narrow *basal cells.* The basal layer also includes cells called *melanocytes.* These cells produce a brown pigment called *melanin.*

The basal cells divide continually and form *daughter cells.* Some daughter cells remain in the basal layer. Others move toward the outer surface of the skin and eventually form the upper layers of the epidermis. These cells are called *keratinocytes,* and they produce keratin. Keratin is found only in the epidermis, hair, and nails. Keratin makes the skin tough. It also prevents fluids and certain substances from passing through the skin. As the keratinocytes move upward through the epidermis, they become filled with more and more keratin. By the time they reach the surface of the skin, they have died and become flat and dry. Eventually, they are shed as thin flakes.

Dermis is made up chiefly of blood vessels, nerve endings, and connective tissue. The blood vessels nourish both the dermis and the epidermis. The surface of the dermis has many tiny elevations called *papillae* that fit into pits on the undersurface of the epidermis. They help connect the dermis to the epidermis. The papillae contain nerve endings that are sensitive to touch. The nerve endings are especially numerous on the palms and fingertips.

Subcutaneous tissue consists mainly of connective tissue, blood vessels, and cells that store fat. The subcutaneous tissue helps protect the body from blows and other kinds of injuries. It also helps retain body heat. The amount of fat in the subcutaneous tissue may increase after a person overeats. If the body needs extra food energy, it breaks down this stored fat.

Hair, nails, and glands. Hair, nails, and the glands in the skin are called *epidermal appendages.* They are

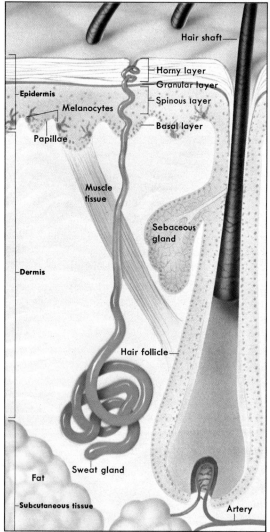

Hair shaft

Horny layer
Granular layer
Spinous layer

Epidermis

Melanocytes

Basal layer

Papillae

Muscle tissue

Sebaceous gland

Dermis

Hair follicle

Sweat gland

Fat

Subcutaneous tissue

Artery

WORLD BOOK illustration by Charles Wellek

Human skin has three layers of tissue—the *epidermis,* the *dermis,* and *subcutaneous tissue.* The epidermis consists of four layers of cells—*horny, granular, spinous,* and *basal.* The skin also has hair and two kinds of glands, *sebaceous* and *sweat.*

formed from the basal cells of the epidermis.

Hair. Most of the skin is covered by tiny hairs. The scalp and some other parts of the body have large hairs. The palms of the hands and the soles of the feet have no hair at all. Part of each hair extends below the surface of the skin. This part lies in a baglike structure called the *follicle.* The end of the hair, called the *bulb,* is the only living part of a hair. It lies in the dermis or subcutaneous tissue. The cells of the bulb divide rapidly and account for the growth of a hair. The hair cells above the bulb contain a form of keratin called *hard keratin.*

Nails. A nail has three parts, the *matrix, plate,* and *bed.* The matrix lies under the surface of the skin at the base of the nail. Most of the matrix is covered by skin. But part of the matrix forms a whitish half moon that can be seen at the base of the nail. The plate is the hard outer part of the nail. It consists of many layers of flat, dead cells that contain keratin. The bed lies under the plate. The cells of the bed and plate are formed in the matrix. Newly formed cells push the older ones toward the tip of the nail. This pushing process results in the growth of the nail.

Glands. The skin has two kinds of glands, *sebaceous* and *sweat.* Sebaceous glands empty into hair follicles. These glands secrete an oil called *sebum,* which lubricates the hair and the surface of the skin.

There are two types of sweat glands, *eccrine* and *apocrine.* Eccrine glands produce the sweat that cools the body. They are located throughout the surface of the skin but are particularly numerous on the forehead, palms, and soles. Some eccrine glands produce secretions continually. Others become active only when a person is under physical or emotional stress. Eccrine

Skin color

Skin color depends mainly on the amount of brown pigment, called *melanin,* in the skin. In light skin, *below left,* cells known as *melanocytes* produce a small amount of melanin. In dark skin, *below right,* these cells produce more melanin.

WORLD BOOK illustrations by Charles Wellek

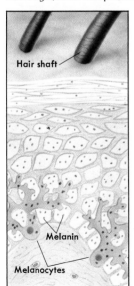

Light skin

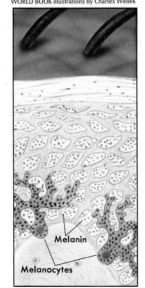

Dark skin

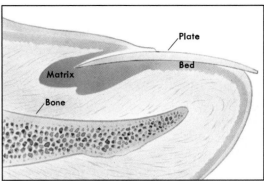

WORLD BOOK illustration by Charles Wellek

The nails of the fingers and toes are formed from certain cells of the skin. A nail has three parts—the *matrix, bed,* and *plate.* The matrix produces the cells of the bed and plate.

glands release their secretions onto the surface of the skin. Apocrine glands produce sweat that has no important function. Most of these glands are in the armpits and around the *genitals* (external sex organs). They release their secretions into hair follicles.

Sweat is odorless until after it has been broken down by bacteria on the surface of the skin. After this process occurs, sweat has what many people consider an unpleasant odor. Apocrine sweat smells stronger than eccrine sweat, and so the armpits and genital area are the chief sources of body odor.

Skin color

The color of the skin varies greatly among races and individuals. Skin color depends mainly on the amount of the brown pigment melanin produced in the skin. Melanin is formed by the melanocytes in the epidermis. People of all races have about the same number of melanocytes. However, the melanocytes of dark-skinned people produce more melanin than do those of light-skinned people. The amount of melanin produced in each person's skin is determined mainly by heredity. However, exposure to sunlight increases the production of melanin, causing light skin to tan. In some cases, melanin builds up in small spots, forming freckles. Most freckles appear on the face and hands. Exposure to sunlight may increase freckling.

As a person grows older, the melanocytes produce melanin at uneven rates, which causes some areas of the skin to remain light and others to darken. These dark spots are sometimes called *age spots* or *liver spots.* As a person ages, the skin also becomes thinner and drier and so starts to wrinkle and turn scaly. In addition, the skin of an old person bruises and chaps more easily and heals more slowly.

See **Skin** in *World Book* for more information on Skin disorders and Animal skin.

The North American hognose snake sometimes plays dead when threatened by an enemy. The illustration at the left above shows the hognose in a natural position. When playing dead, the snake rolls over on its back and hangs out its tongue, *right.*

WORLD BOOK illustrations by Alex Ebel

One of the largest snakes is the anaconda of South America. It has a stout body and may grow up to 30 feet (9 meters) long. Only the reticulate python of Asia rivals it in size.

Snake

Snake is an animal with a long, legless body covered by dry scales. To move about on land, a snake usually slides on its belly. Many snakes have such a flexible body that they can coil into a ball. The eyes of a snake are covered by clear scales instead of movable eyelids. As a result, its eyes are always open. Snakes have a narrow, forked tongue, which they repeatedly flick out. They use the tongue to bring odors to a special sense organ in the mouth.

Snakes belong to an *order* (group) of animals called *reptiles.* Reptiles also include crocodiles, lizards, and turtles. Like other reptiles, snakes can maintain a fairly steady body temperature by behavioral means. For example, they raise their body temperature by lying in the sun or lower it by crawling into the shade. In contrast, mammals and birds have internal mechanisms that regulate their body temperature.

Scientists have evidence that snakes developed from lizards about 100 million years ago. Snakes resemble lizards more than they do other reptiles. But unlike most lizards, snakes lack legs, movable eyelids, and external ear openings. Their scales and skulls also differ from those of lizards. Because of their special eye structure, snakes are thought to have developed from lizards that burrowed underground. Their loss of legs is also thought to have occurred as a result of this burrowing phase.

Snakes live almost everywhere on the earth. They live in deserts, forests, oceans, streams, and lakes. Many snakes are ground dwellers, and some live underground. Others dwell in trees, and still others spend most of their time in water. Only a few areas in the world have no snakes. Snakes cannot survive where the ground stays frozen the year around. Thus, no snakes live in the polar regions or at high elevations in mountains. In addition, snakes are often absent from islands, including Ireland and New Zealand.

Interesting facts about snakes

One of the smallest snakes is the Braminy blind snake, which lives in the tropics and grows only 6 inches (15 centimeters) long. It has tiny eyes that are covered by head scales.

An African Gaboon viper in a zoo once fasted for $2\frac{1}{2}$ years. Snakes in zoos sometimes do not eat for 6 months to 3 years.

Gaboon viper

The fastest snake is probably the black mamba of Africa. It was timed moving at the speed of 7 miles (11 kilometers) per hour over a short distance.

Black mamba

The African ball python protects itself from enemies by coiling into a ball with its head in the middle. Many other snakes also use this method of defense.

Ball python

Green tree pythons may be yellow or brown when hatched. Snakes of both colors may hatch from the same batch of eggs. They turn green as they grow older. Green tree pythons live in New Guinea.

Green tree pythons

The ringhals, or spitting cobra, of Africa can squirt venom 6 to 8 feet (1.8 to 2.4 meters). The snake aims for the eyes of its enemy. The venom causes a painful, burning sensation and can produce blindness.

Ringhals

WORLD BOOK illustrations by Alex Ebel

© Gordon Wiltsie, Bruce Coleman Inc.

Male rattlesnakes battle for the right to mate with a female. The snakes rear up and lunge at each other repeatedly. The combat continues until one snake is forced down and retreats.

There are about 2,700 kinds of snakes. The greatest variety dwell in the tropics. The largest snakes are the anaconda of South America and the reticulate python of Asia. Both may grow up to 30 feet (9 meters) long. One of the smallest snakes is the Braminy blind snake, which lives in the tropics and grows only 6 inches (15 centimeters) long. Like other blind snakes, the Braminy blind snake has eyes, but they are covered by head scales. Blind snakes probably can distinguish only light and dark.

Some snakes are poisonous. They have two hollow or grooved fangs in the upper jaw. The snakes inject *venom* (poison) through their fangs when they bite. About 270 kinds of snakes have venom that is harmful or fatal to human beings. About 25 kinds cause most of the deaths from snakebites. These snakes include the Indian cobra of southern Asia, the black mamba and the saw-scaled viper of Africa, and the tiger snake of Australia.

Some people fear and dislike snakes, partly because some kinds are poisonous and partly because their appearance and ways of life seem strange. Throughout history, snakes have been the subjects of many myths and superstitions. The fear of snakes results from a lack of knowledge about the animals. Most snakes are harmless to people. In addition, snakes are helpful in controlling rats and other rodents.

The bodies of snakes

Body shape. Snakes vary greatly in body shape. For example, some snakes, such as the Gaboon viper of Africa, have a stout body. Certain tree snakes, on the other hand, have an extremely thin, long body that resembles a vine. The bodies of sea snakes are flattened from side to side.

The males and females of most species of snakes do not differ greatly in body shape and appearance. However, among some species, the females are larger than the males. In some other species, the males are larger. One species in which the males and females differ greatly in appearance is the langaha of Madagascar.

Male langahas have a conelike stub on the snout. The females have a long snout shaped somewhat like a maple leaf.

Scales and color. The body of a snake is covered with dry scales, which may be smooth or have ridges. The majority of snakes have overlapping scales that stretch apart. Among most species, the belly scales, which are called *scutes,* consist of one row of large scales extending from the neck to the tail. The side and back scales vary in size and shape among species.

The scaly skin of a snake has two layers. The inner layer of skin consists of cells that grow and divide. The cells die as they are pushed upward by new cells. The dead cells form the outer layer of skin. From time to time, a snake sheds the outer layer of skin because it becomes worn.

The skin-shedding process is called *molting.* For a short time before molting, a snake is less active than usual. The animal's eyes become clouded and then clear again just before it molts. The snake loosens the skin around the mouth and head by rubbing its nose on a rough surface. The snake then crawls out of the old skin, turning it inside out in the process.

How often a snake molts depends chiefly on its age and how active it is. Young snakes shed more often than old ones. Snakes that live in warm climates are active for longer periods than those that live in cooler climates. As a result, they molt more frequently. Some pythons of the tropics shed six or more times a year. In contrast, some North American rattlesnakes average two or three molts a year. A new segment may be added to the rattle on the tail each time they molt.

E. R. Degginger

A snake sheds its skin by rubbing its nose on a rough surface, which loosens the skin about the head. It then crawls out of the skin. This snake is a North American rainbow water snake.

A snake's color comes chiefly from special *pigment cells* in deep layers of the skin. But some color may be due to the way light is reflected from the surface of the scales.

See **Snake** in *World Book* for more information on the following topics:

- The bodies of snakes
- Ways of life among snakes
- Classification of snakes
- The importance of snakes

The anatomy of a snake

This drawing of a male water moccasin shows the skeleton and internal organs. A snake's skeleton consists of a skull and many vertebrae and ribs. Most of the animal's internal organs are long and thin. Only poisonous snakes have fangs and venom glands.

WORLD BOOK diagram by James Teason

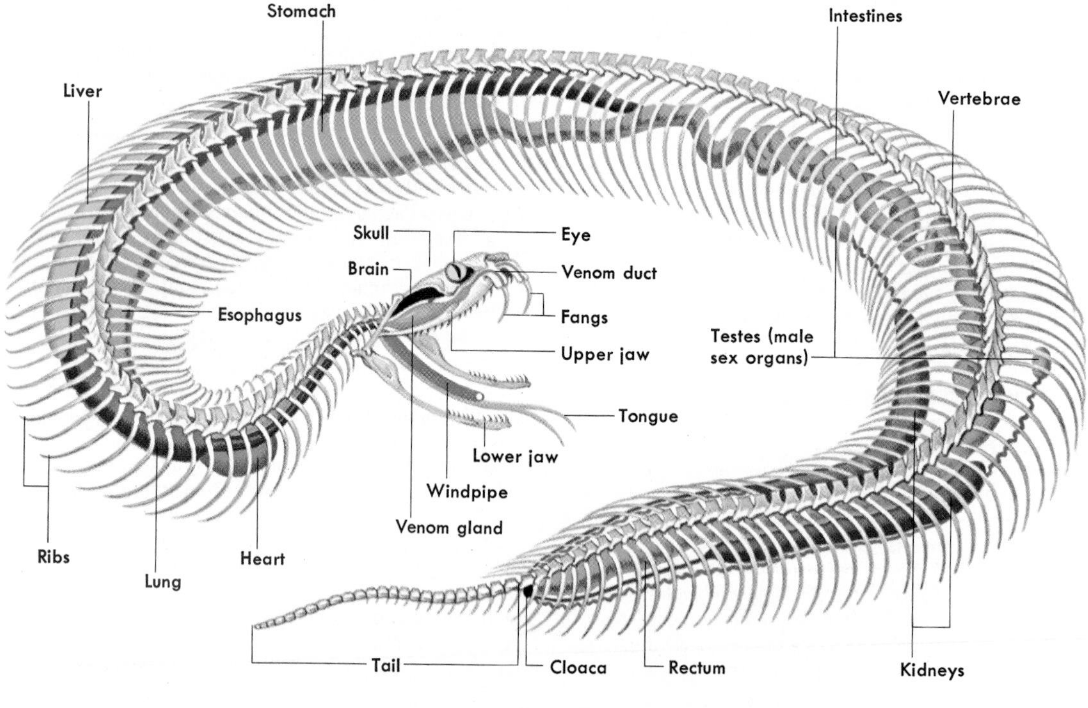

Stomach

Intestines

Liver

Vertebrae

Skull

Eye

Brain

Venom duct

Esophagus

Fangs

Upper jaw

Testes (male sex organs)

Tongue

Lower jaw

Windpipe

Venom gland

Ribs

Heart

Lung

Tail

Cloaca

Rectum

Kidneys

Solar energy is energy given off by the sun. It consists of light, heat, and other forms of electromagnetic radiation. Solar energy is produced by nuclear reactions that take place inside the sun.

Every 40 minutes, the sun delivers as much energy to the earth's surface as all the people on the earth use in a year. People directly use only a fraction of the solar energy that reaches the earth. Scientists are developing new ways to capture solar energy and to put it to use where—and when—it is needed.

How solar energy affects the earth

The sun is the chief source of energy for all life on the earth. Life depends on the sun for heat and light. It also depends on the sun for food. Plants use solar energy to produce food during *photosynthesis.* Some of the plants are eaten by animals, which, in turn, are eaten by other animals.

Energy from the sun also sets the earth's weather in motion. For example, precipitation occurs when water evaporated by the sun condenses and falls back to the earth. Wind occurs because the sun's rays are more direct—and thus stronger—at the equator than they are at the poles. The strong rays in tropical regions warm the air there, causing it to rise. Cooler air from the polar regions then flows under the warm tropical air. These movements create air currents that circulate around the earth. The currents are influenced by the earth's rotation, the surface features of the continents, and variations in the amount of moisture in the atmosphere. Simi-larly, ocean currents are formed by wind and by the sun's warming of tropical waters, under which cold polar waters flow.

Stored solar energy

Precipitation, wind, and ocean currents all can be viewed as stored solar energy. Much of the precipitation that falls on land flows into rivers. Hydroelectric power stations built along the rivers collect the energy of the moving water. People use wind to power sailboats and windmills. Large groups of windmills called *wind farms* have been set up to generate electricity in areas where the wind is steady and strong. Scientists and engineers are developing methods of using the energy of ocean waves. They also are exploring ways to harness the heat energy in ocean water.

Solar energy also is stored in plants and animals. This energy can be used in a variety of ways. For example, trees can be burned as firewood. Such crops as corn, sugar cane, and sugar beets can be fermented to produce alcohol, a fuel similar to gasoline. Petroleum, coal, and natural gas developed from the remains of plants that lived millions of years ago. Thus, these fuels contain solar energy that has been stored in the earth for ages. As supplies of these fuels diminish, people are working to increase the direct use of the sun's energy.

Capturing direct solar energy

People have devised a number of ways to make direct use of the sun's energy. These uses include heating

How solar energy affects the earth

The sun is our chief source of energy. Plants need sunlight to grow, and animals depend on plants for food and on the sun for warmth. Solar energy heats homes and greenhouses; produces wind power; and generates water power through evaporation and rainfall. Coal and petroleum are stored solar energy from very long ago and cannot be renewed once they are used.

WORLD BOOK illustration by Oxford Illustrators Limited

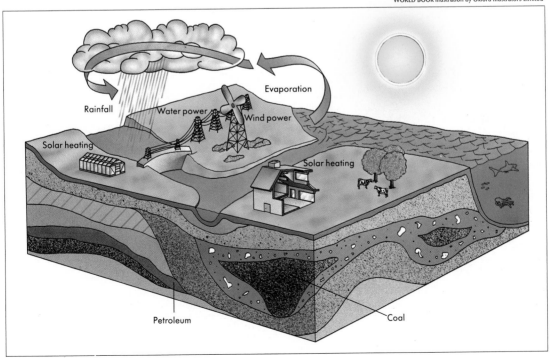

water, heating and cooling buildings, generating electricity, and cooking food.

Solar heating. Many people in warm climates heat water with simple, inexpensive *batch heaters.* A batch heater consists mainly of an insulated tank with several layers of clear glass covering the side of the tank that faces south. The outside of the tank is blackened because black absorbs more sunlight than any other color. The black surfaces convert the sunlight to heat and thus warm the water. The glass prevents most of the heat from escaping from the tank. The hot water rises to the top of the tank and flows directly to a faucet.

Devices called *flat-plate collectors* are used to heat water and the air inside buildings. A flat-plate collector consists chiefly of an insulated box covered by one or more layers of clear glass or plastic. Inside the box is a plate of black metal or black plastic. The plate absorbs sunlight and converts it to heat, which becomes trapped under the glass. Air, water, or some other fluid circulates through tubes welded to the plate and absorbs heat from the plate. The heated fluid then flows to a heat exchanger, where it transfers its heat to water. The heated water is stored in a tank and is pumped from the tank to faucets in the house.

Many buildings use *passive solar energy systems* for heating air. In most cases, these buildings have large south-facing windows to trap heat. During the day, sunlight passes through the windows and heats walls and floors made of stone or brick. At night, the walls and floors release the heat. Additional heat may be stored by placing water or special *phase-change materials* inside the walls. These phase-change materials melt at about room temperature. As they melt, the materials store large amounts of heat. The materials later release the heat as they become solid again. In buildings with passive solar energy systems, special insulating shades or shutters help keep heat from escaping through the windows at night.

See **Solar energy** in *World Book* for more information on Capturing direct solar energy and History of solar energy.

How solar energy heats a house

WORLD BOOK illustrations by Oxford Illustrators Limited

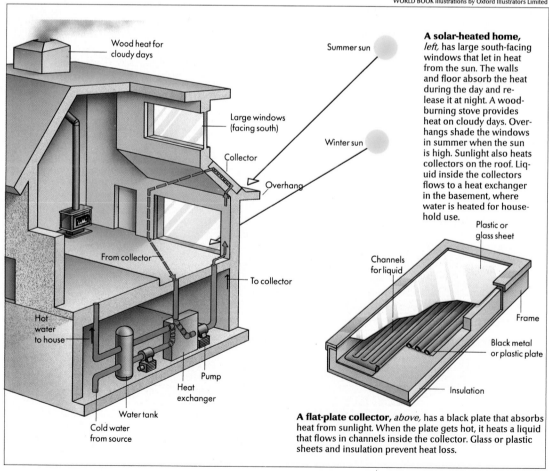

Wood heat for cloudy days

Summer sun

Large windows (facing south)

Collector

Winter sun

Overhang

From collector

To collector

Hot water to house

Channels for liquid

Plastic or glass sheet

Frame

Black metal or plastic plate

Insulation

Pump

Heat exchanger

Water tank

Cold water from source

A solar-heated home, *left,* has large south-facing windows that let in heat from the sun. The walls and floor absorb the heat during the day and release it at night. A wood-burning stove provides heat on cloudy days. Overhangs shade the windows in summer when the sun is high. Sunlight also heats collectors on the roof. Liquid inside the collectors flows to a heat exchanger in the basement, where water is heated for household use.

A flat-plate collector, *above,* has a black plate that absorbs heat from sunlight. When the plate gets hot, it heats a liquid that flows in channels inside the collector. Glass or plastic sheets and insulation prevent heat loss.

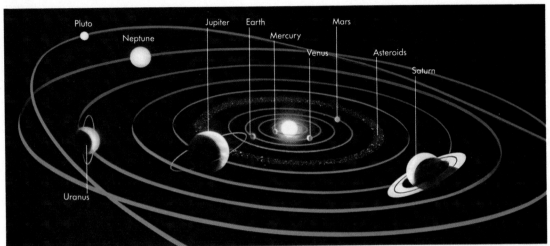

WORLD BOOK illustration by Rob Wood

The solar system includes many different objects that travel around the sun. These objects vary from planets much larger than the earth to tiny meteoroids and dust particles.

Solar system

Solar system consists of a star called the *sun* and all the objects that travel around it. The solar system includes (1) the earth and eight other *planets,* along with the *satellites* (moons) that travel around most of them; (2) planetlike objects called *asteroids;* (3) chunks of iron and stone called *meteoroids;* (4) bodies of dust and frozen gases called *comets;* and (5) drifting particles called *interplanetary dust* and electrically charged gas called *plasma* that together make up the *interplanetary medium.*

The solar system is shaped like a disk. It is only a tiny part of a *galaxy* (family of stars) called the *Milky Way.* The Milky Way consists of hundreds of billions of stars, including the sun. Some of the other stars may also have planets orbiting them. The Milky Way, which also has a disklike shape, is about 100,000 light-years across, and about 10,000 light-years thick at its center. A *light-year* is the distance light travels in one year at a speed of 186,282 miles (299,792 kilometers) per second. The solar system is less than one *light-day* (the distance light travels in one day) across.

Distances within the solar system are measured in *astronomical units* (AU). One astronomical unit equals the average distance between the earth and the sun—about 93 million miles (150 million kilometers). The distance between the sun and Pluto, the outermost planet, averages about 39 AU.

Parts of the solar system

The sun is the center of the solar system. Its *mass* is about 740 times as great as that of all the planets combined (in *World Book,* see **Mass**). The huge mass of the sun creates the gravitation that keeps the other objects traveling around the sun in an orderly manner.

The sun continuously gives off energy in several forms—visible light; invisible *infrared, ultraviolet, X,* and *gamma rays;* radio waves; and *plasma.* The flow of

plasma, which becomes part of the interplanetary medium and drifts throughout the solar system, is called the *solar wind.* The surface of the sun changes continuously. Bright spots called *plages* and dark spots called *sunspots* frequently form and disappear. Gases often shoot up violently from the surface. For more information on the sun, see the article **Sun.**

Planets are the largest objects in the solar system except for the sun. Unlike the sun, the planets do not produce their own energy. Instead, the planets reflect the heat and visible light produced by the sun. The two largest planets, Jupiter and Saturn, send out radio radiation. Jupiter's radio waves are so strong they can be picked up on the earth by radio telescopes. The four planets nearest the sun—Mercury, Venus, Earth, and Mars—are called *terrestrial* (earthlike) planets. They appear to consist chiefly of iron and rock. The terrestrial planets and Pluto are the smallest planets. The earth has one satellite, Mars has two, and Pluto has one. Mercury and Venus have no satellites.

The four largest planets—Jupiter, Saturn, Uranus, and Neptune—are called the *giant* planets. They are made up chiefly of hydrogen, helium, ammonia, and methane. Compared to the terrestrial planets, they contain little iron and rock. Each of the giant planets has several satellites. Jupiter, Saturn, and Uranus also have rings around them. But only Saturn's large, bright rings can be easily seen through a small telescope.

All the planets are surrounded by varying kinds and amounts of gases. The gases surrounding a planet are called its *atmosphere.* The earth is the only planet that has enough oxygen surrounding it and enough water on its surface to support life as we know it. For a more complete description of the planets, see **Planet** and the separate articles on **Earth, Jupiter, Mars, Mercury, Saturn,** and **Venus.** In *World Book,* see **Neptune, Pluto,** and **Uranus.**

WORLD BOOK illustration by Rob Wood

The Milky Way is made up of hundreds of billions of stars. Many stars have their own solar systems. This side view of the Milky Way shows the sun's position in the galaxy.

Asteroids, also called *planetoids,* are small, irregularly shaped objects made of rock or metal or a mixture of the two substances. Most asteroids are between the orbits of Mars and Jupiter. Astronomers have figured out the orbits of about 4,000 asteroids. About 30 asteroids have diameters greater than 120 miles (190 kilometers). Many others are less than a mile (1.6 kilometers) across. The asteroid belt between Mars and Jupiter also includes dust particles. Astronomers believe these particles were formed by continuing collisions between asteroids.

Meteoroids are small chunks of iron and rock thought to result from collisions between asteroids. They also may be formed when comets disintegrate into fragments. Many meteoroids fall into the earth's atmosphere, but most are burned up by friction before they reach the earth. Meteoroids are called *meteors* while falling through the atmosphere, and *meteorites* if they are found on the earth's surface. See **Meteor.**

Comets are small bodies that move around the sun. Most comets have three parts: (1) a solid *nucleus,* or center, made of frozen gases and dust; (2) a round *coma,* or head, that surrounds the nucleus and consists of dust particles mixed with gases; and (3) a long *tail* of dust and gases that escape from the head. Most comets stay near the outer edge of the solar system. Some come near the sun, where their bright heads and long, shining tails provide a spectacular sight. See **Comet.**

Formation of the solar system

Astronomers do not have enough information to describe the formation of the solar system completely. Many ideas have been suggested, but parts of all of them have been proved wrong.

Until the mid-1900's, theories of how the solar system was formed could be based on only five observations. (1) The sun and most other parts of the solar system spin in the same direction on their *axes* (imaginary lines drawn through their centers). (2) Most parts of the solar system travel around the sun in the same direction that the sun spins. (3) Most satellites travel around their planets in the same direction that the planets travel around the sun. (4) Going outward from the sun, the distance between the orbits of the planets increases. (5) The solar system has a circular shape.

The theories that have been suggested to explain the above observations can be divided into two general groups. These groups are *monistic theories* and *dualistic theories.* Most astronomers believe that some form of monistic theory will someday be proved correct.

Monistic theories are based on the belief that the solar system was formed from a single flat cloud of gas

called the *solar nebula.* According to some monistic theories, all parts of the solar system were formed at the same time. Other monistic theories suggest that the sun was formed first, and the planets and other objects came later from the remaining gas. The first monistic theory was proposed in the early 1600's by the French scientist and philosopher René Descartes. In the late 1700's, Pierre Simon Laplace of France suggested the monistic theory called the *nebular hypothesis.*

Dualistic theories are based on the belief that the solar system was formed when some huge object passed near the sun. According to these theories, the force of gravity of the passing object pulled a long stream of gas out from the sun. The planets and other objects were formed from this gas. The first dualistic theory was proposed in the 1700's by the French scientist Comte de Buffon. Buffon believed the passing object was a large comet, which he incorrectly thought was as large as a star. In the early 1900's, Thomas Chamberlin and Forest Moulton, both of the University of Chicago, offered a dualistic theory called the *planetesimal hypothesis.*

Theories since the mid-1900's are helping scientists come closer to learning how the solar system was formed. For example, astronomers have discovered that the Milky Way is at least twice as old as the solar system. For that reason, the processes of star formation seen in the galaxy today are probably similar to the processes that formed the sun.

The study of meteorites is producing new information about temperatures, pressures, and other conditions that probably existed during the formation of the solar system. Measurements of the radioactivity of meteorites indicate that they were formed at about the same time as the solar system, about 4.6 billion years ago.

The exploration of the moon has provided scientists with a better understanding of how and when the moon was formed. They have learned that the moon was once geologically active, as the earth is today. Rock samples brought back by the Apollo astronauts in the late 1960's revealed that volcanic eruptions occurred on the moon more than 3 billion years ago.

Data collected by space probes indicate that the atmospheres and interiors of most of the planets differ greatly from those of the earth. By studying the planets, scientists hope to discover how various chemical elements are spread throughout the solar system. They also hope to learn why some planets have large amounts of carbon dioxide in their atmospheres, and whether the major planets have gaseous or liquid surfaces.

Studies of the sun may lead to the discovery of how the interior of the sun heats its outer atmosphere. They also may help explain why the formation of sunspots reaches a peak about every 11 years.

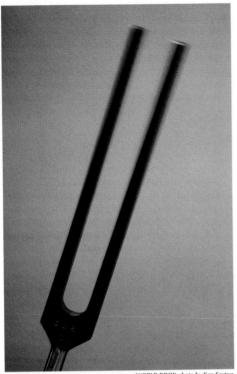

WORLD BOOK photo by Ken Sexton

A tone-producing tuning fork

Jerry Herman, FPG

A male frog sounding a mating call

Dennis Hallinan, FPG

Trombonists in a marching band

All sounds are produced by vibrations. When a tuning fork is struck, the vibration of its prongs generates a tone. A frog croaks by forcing air over its vocal cords, making them vibrate. A trombone produces sound when the player causes the air inside the instrument to vibrate.

Sound

Sound surrounds us all the time. The buzzing of an alarm clock or the chirping of birds may awaken us in the morning. Throughout the day, we hear many kinds of sounds, such as the clatter of pots and pans, the roar of traffic, and the voices of people. As we fall asleep at night, we may listen to the croaking of frogs or the whistle of the wind.

All the sounds we hear have one thing in common. Every sound is produced by vibrations of an object. When an object vibrates, it makes the surrounding air vibrate. The vibrations in the air travel outward in all directions from the object. When the vibrations enter our ears, the brain interprets them as sounds (see **Ear** [The sense of hearing]). Although many of the sounds we hear travel through the air, sound can move through any material. For example, sound travels well through solid earth. You may have read that American Indians used to put their ears to the ground to listen for distant hoofbeats.

Sound has great importance in our lives. First of all, sound makes it possible for us to communicate with one another through speech. Many sounds, such as music and the singing of birds, provide pleasure. The sounds of radio and television broadcasts bring us entertainment and information. We are warned of danger by such sounds as automobile horns and fire alarms.

The nature of sound

If you drop a pebble into a still pond, you will see a series of waves travel outward from the point where the pebble struck the surface. Sound also travels in waves as it moves through the air or some other *medium* (substance). The waves are produced by a vibrating object. As a vibrating object moves outward, it compresses the surrounding medium, producing a region of compression called a *condensation.* As the vibrating object then moves inward, the medium expands into the space formerly occupied by the object. This region of expansion is called a *rarefaction.* As the object continues to move outward and inward, a series of condensations and rarefactions travels away from the object. *Sound waves* consist of these condensations and rarefactions.

Sound waves must travel through a medium. Thus, sound is absent in outer space, which contains no material for a vibrating object to compress and expand.

The nature of a particular sound can be described in terms of (1) frequency and pitch, (2) intensity and loudness, and (3) quality.

Frequency and pitch. The number of condensations or rarefactions produced by a vibrating object each second is called the *frequency* of the sound waves. The more rapidly an object vibrates, the higher will be the frequency. Scientists use a unit called the *hertz* to measure frequency. One hertz equals one *cycle* (vibration) per second. As the frequency of sound waves increases,

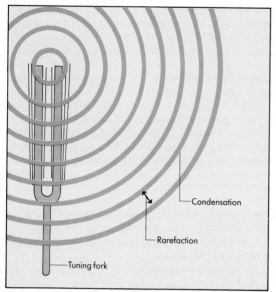

WORLD BOOK diagram by Bill and Judie Anderson

Sound waves form when a vibrating object causes the surrounding *medium* (substance) to vibrate. As the object moves outward, it produces a region of compression called a *condensation*. As the object then moves inward, a region of expansion known as a *rarefaction* forms. Sound waves consist of the series of condensations and rarefactions generated by the object.

the *wavelength* decreases. Wavelength is the distance between any point on one wave and the corresponding point on the next one.

Most people can hear sounds with frequencies from about 20 to 20,000 hertz. Bats, dogs, and many other kinds of animals can hear sounds with frequencies far above 20,000 hertz. Different sounds have different frequencies. For example, the sound of jingling keys ranges from 700 to 15,000 hertz. A person's voice can produce frequencies from 85 to 1,100 hertz. The tones of a piano have frequencies ranging from about 30 to 15,000 hertz.

The frequency of a sound determines its *pitch*—the degree of highness or lowness of the sound as perceived by a listener. High-pitched sounds have higher frequencies than low-pitched sounds. Musical instruments can produce a wide range of pitches. For example, a trumpet has valves that can shorten or lengthen the vibrating column of air inside the instrument. A short column produces a high-frequency, high-pitched sound. A long column results in a note of low frequency and low pitch.

Intensity and loudness. The *intensity* of a sound is related to the amount of energy flowing in the sound waves. Intensity depends on the *amplitude* of the vibrations producing the waves. Amplitude is the distance that a vibrating object moves from its position of rest as it vibrates. The larger the amplitude of vibration is, the more intense will be the sound.

The *loudness* of a sound refers to how strong the sound seems to us when it strikes our ears. At a given frequency, the more intense a sound is, the louder it seems. But equally intense sounds of different frequencies are not equally loud. The ear has low sensitivity to

sounds near the upper and lower limits of the range of frequencies we can hear. Thus, a high-frequency or low-frequency sound does not seem as loud as a sound of the same intensity in the middle of the frequency range.

Water waves in a pond get weaker as they travel away from their source. In the same way, sound waves lose intensity as they spread outward in all directions from their source. Thus, the loudness of a sound decreases as the distance increases between a person and the source of the sound. You can observe this effect in a large field by walking away from a friend who is talking at a constant level. As you move farther and farther away, the voice of your friend gets fainter and fainter.

Sound quality, also called *timbre,* is a characteristic of musical sounds. Quality distinguishes between sounds of the same frequency and intensity produced by different musical instruments.

Almost every musical sound consists of a combination of the actual note sounded and a number of higher tones related to it. The actual note played is the *fundamental.* The higher tones are *overtones* of the fundamental. For example, when a note is produced by a violin string, the string vibrates as a whole and produces the fundamental. But the string also vibrates in separate sections at the same time. It may vibrate in two, three, four, or more parts. Each of these vibrations produces an overtone of higher frequency and pitch than the fundamental. The greater the number of vibrating parts is, the higher will be the frequency of the overtone.

The number and strength of the overtones help determine the characteristic sound quality of a musical instru-

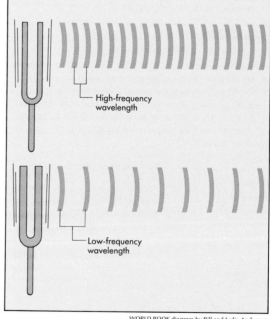

WORLD BOOK diagram by Bill and Judie Anderson

Frequency of sound waves is the number of condensations or rarefactions produced by a vibrating object each second. The more rapidly an object vibrates, the higher will be the frequency. As the frequency increases, the *wavelength* decreases. The frequency of a sound determines its pitch. High-pitched sounds have higher frequencies than low-pitched sounds.

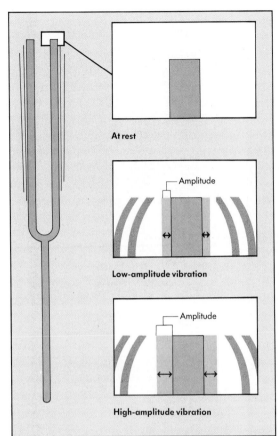

Amplitude is the distance that a vibrating object moves from its position of rest as it vibrates. The larger the amplitude of vibration is, the more intense will be the sound.

At rest

Low-amplitude vibration

Amplitude

High-amplitude vibration

Amplitude

WORLD BOOK diagram by Bill and Judie Anderson

Terms used in the study of sound

Acoustics is the science of sound and of its effects on people.
Beats are periodic variations in the loudness of a sound. Beats are heard when two tones of slightly different frequencies are sounded at the same time.
Condensation is a region of compression in a sound wave.
Decibel is the unit used to measure the intensity level of a sound. A 3,000-hertz tone of zero decibels is the weakest sound that the normal human ear can hear.
Frequency of sound waves refers to the number of condensations or rarefactions produced by a vibrating object each second.
Hertz is the unit used to measure frequency. One hertz equals one *cycle* (vibration) per second.
Infrasound is sound with frequencies below the range of human hearing.
Intensity of a sound is related to the amount of energy flowing in the sound waves.
Phon is a unit often used to measure the loudness level of tones. The loudness level in phons of any tone is the intensity level in decibels of a 1,000-hertz tone that seems equally loud.
Pitch is the degree of highness or lowness of a sound as perceived by a listener.
Rarefaction is a region of expansion in a sound wave.
Resonance frequency is approximately the frequency at which an object would vibrate naturally if disturbed in some way.
Sound quality, also called *timbre,* is a characteristic of musical sounds. Sound quality distinguishes between notes of the same frequency and intensity produced by different musical instruments.
Ultrasound is sound with frequencies above the range of human hearing.

ment. For instance, a note on the flute sounds soft and sweet because it has only a few, weak overtones. The same note played on the trumpet has many, strong overtones and thus seems powerful and bright.

How sound behaves

The speed of sound depends on the medium through which the sound waves travel. The properties of a medium that determine the speed of sound are *density* and *compressibility.* Density is the amount of material in a unit volume of a substance. Compressibility measures how easily a substance can be crushed into a smaller volume. The denser a medium is and the more compressible it is, the slower the speed of sound is.

In general, liquids and solids are denser than air. But they are also far less compressible. Therefore, sound travels faster through liquids and solids than it does through air. Compared with its speed through air, sound travels about 4 times faster through water and about 15 times faster through steel. The speed of sound through air is commonly measured at sea level at 59° F. (15° C). At that temperature, sound travels 1,116 feet (340 meters) per second. But the speed of sound increases as air temperature rises. For instance, sound travels 1,268 feet (386 meters) per second through air at 212° F. (100° C).

The speed of sound is much slower than the speed of light. In a vacuum, light travels 186,282 miles (299,792 kilometers) per second—almost a million times faster than sound. As a result, we see the flash of lightning during a storm before we hear the thunder. If you watch a carpenter hammering on a distant building, you will see the hammer strike before you hear the blow.

You may have noticed that the pitch of a train whistle seems higher as the train approaches and lower after the train passes and moves away. The sound waves produced by the whistle travel through the air at a constant speed, regardless of the speed of the train. But as the train approaches, each successive wave produced by the whistle travels a shorter distance to your ears. The waves arrive more frequently, and the pitch of the whistle appears higher. As the train moves away, each successive wave travels a longer distance to your ears. The waves arrive less frequently, producing a lower apparent pitch. This apparent change in pitch produced by moving objects is called the *Doppler effect.* To a listener on the train, the pitch of the whistle does not change.

Jet airplanes sometimes fly at supersonic speeds. A plane flying faster than the speed of sound creates *shock waves,* strong pressure disturbances that build up around the aircraft. People on the ground hear a loud noise, known as a *sonic boom,* when the shock waves from the plane sweep over them.

See **Sound** in *World Book* for more information on the following topics:

- How some familiar sounds are produced
- How sound behaves
- Working with sound
- The study of sound

The space shuttle blasts off

Jim Tuten, Black Star

NASA

A solar wind experiment on the moon

NASA

A space probe photo of Saturn

The exploration of space provides knowledge about the moon, the planets, and the stars. Explorers have performed experiments on the moon, and space probes have photographed Saturn and other planets. The space shuttle not only can launch satellites but can also retrieve them.

Space travel

Space travel is humanity's greatest adventure—the chance to explore the moon, the planets, and the stars. Giant rockets lift off with a roaring blast of orange flame. They climb into the blue sky, leaving a white trail. Then they speed out of sight into space, where the sky is always black and the stars always shine. Rockets may carry people on their way to conduct scientific experiments, or they may carry an artificial satellite to explore a distant planet.

The space age began on Oct. 4, 1957. On that day, the Union of Soviet Socialist Republics (U.S.S.R.) launched

Sputnik I, the first artificial satellite to circle the earth. The first manned space flight was made on April 12, 1961, when a Soviet cosmonaut, Yuri A. Gagarin, orbited the earth in a spaceship. The next month, U.S. astronaut Alan B. Shepard, Jr., made a 15-minute space flight, but he did not go into orbit. On Feb. 20, 1962, John H. Glenn, Jr., became the first American to orbit the earth.

During the years that followed these first space expeditions, many flights carried people into orbit around the earth. Then, on Dec. 24 and 25, 1968, United States astronauts Frank Borman, William A. Anders, and James A. Lovell, Jr., orbited the moon 10 times in their Apollo 8 spacecraft.

Human beings first set foot on the moon on July 20,

1969. U.S. astronaut Neil A. Armstrong stepped out of the Apollo 11 lunar module, *Eagle,* and at 10:56 p.m. E.D.S.T., put his left foot on a rocky lunar plain. After he had walked around for 18 minutes, astronaut Edwin E. Aldrin, Jr., joined him. For about two hours, the astronauts explored near the module and set up experiments. *Eagle* was on the moon almost 22 hours before Armstrong and Aldrin lifted off to rejoin the command module *Columbia,* piloted by astronaut Michael Collins.

A new era in space exploration dawned on April 12, 1981, when U.S. astronauts John W. Young and Robert L. Crippen took off in the first space shuttle. The space shuttle was the first manned spacecraft designed to be reusable. It permits space flights to be scheduled on a routine basis. On a typical mission, the shuttle rockets into space with its crew, remains in orbit for about a week, and then lands on the earth like an airplane. It can be ready for another flight in about four weeks.

During the years since the space age began, many uses for space travel have been discovered. The space age developed a huge industry called the aerospace industry to design and build space equipment. A new field of medicine called space medicine came into being to study the problems of living and working in space. Weather forecasters receive warning of storms with pictures taken by weather satellites. Telephone calls and television pictures are sent around the world by communications satellites. Signals from navigation satellites enable ship navigators, leaders of scientific expeditions, and search and rescue forces to determine their positions with great accuracy. Scientific satellites and space probes discovered the Van Allen radiation belt around the earth and made many other discoveries.

During the early years of the space age, success in space became a measure of a country's leadership in science, engineering, and national defense. As a result, the United States and the Soviet Union competed with one another in developing their space programs. Each of them, for example, sought to build better rockets and spacecraft than the other in order to reach the moon first. But both nations began to realize that they could benefit from working together on selected scientific projects. In 1975, the U.S. and the Soviet Union cooperated in their first joint space mission. An Apollo spacecraft piloted by three United States astronauts docked with a Soyuz craft manned by two Soviet cosmonauts. The principal area of cooperation between U.S. and Soviet space programs has been in space medicine.

People have always wanted to explore the unknown. Many people believe that we should explore space simply because we have the means to do so. Scientists hope that space travel will answer many questions about the universe—how the sun, the planets, and the stars were formed, and whether life exists elsewhere.

Space travel terms

Ablation is the melting away of a spacecraft's heat shield during reentry.

Aerospace includes the atmosphere and the regions of space beyond it.

Aphelion is the point farthest from the sun in the path of a solar satellite.

Apocynthion is the point farthest from the moon in the orbit of a lunar satellite.

Apogee is the point farthest from earth in the orbit of an earth satellite.

Artificial satellite is a spacecraft that circles the earth or other celestial body. The term is usually shortened to *satellite,* but it then also applies to natural moons.

Astro is a prefix meaning *star.* It also means *space* in such words as *astronautics* (the science of space flight).

Astronaut is a United States space pilot.

Attitude is the position of a spacecraft in relation to some other point, such as the spacecraft's direction of flight, the position of the sun, or the position of the earth.

Biosatellite is an artificial satellite that carries animals or plants.

Booster is the propulsion system that provides most of the energy for a spacecraft to go into orbit.

Burnout is the point in the flight of a rocket when its propellant is used up.

Capsule is a manned spacecraft or a small package of instruments carried by a larger spacecraft.

Cosmonaut is a Soviet space pilot.

Eccentricity is the variation of a satellite's path from a perfect circle.

Escape velocity is the speed a spacecraft must reach to coast away from the pull of gravity.

Exhaust velocity is the speed at which the burning gases leave a rocket.

Gantry is a special crane or movable tower used to service launch vehicles.

Heat shield is a covering on a spacecraft to protect the craft and astronaut from high temperatures of reentry.

Hypergol consists of propellants that ignite when mixed together.

Inclination is the angle between the plane of a spacecraft's orbit and the earth's equator.

LOX or **liquid oxygen** is a common oxidizer. It is made by cooling oxygen to −183° C (−297° F.).

Module is a single section of a spacecraft that can be disconnected and separated from other sections.

Orbit is the path of a satellite in relation to the object around which it revolves.

Oxidizer is a substance that mixes with the fuel in a rocket, furnishing oxygen that permits the fuel to burn.

Pericynthion is the point closest to the moon in the orbit of a lunar satellite.

Perigee is the point closest to earth in the orbit of an earth satellite.

Perihelion is the point closest to the sun in the path of a solar satellite.

Period is the time it takes for a satellite to make one revolution.

Propellant is a substance burned in a rocket to produce thrust. Propellants include fuels and oxidizers.

Reentry is that part of a flight when a returning spacecraft begins to descend through the atmosphere.

Rendezvous is a space maneuver in which two or more spacecraft meet.

Revolution is one complete cycle of a heavenly body or an artificial satellite in its orbit.

Spacecraft is an artificially created object that travels through space.

Stage is one of two or more rockets combined to form a launch vehicle.

Thrust is the push given to a rocket by its engines.

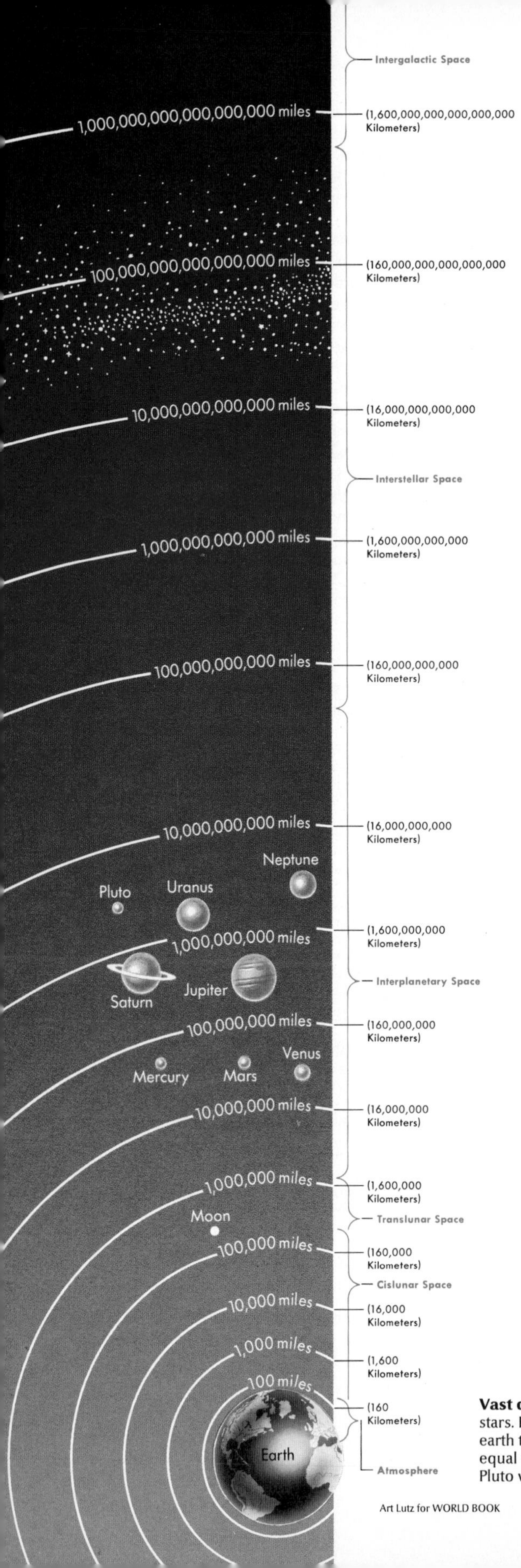

Intergalactic Space

1,000,000,000,000,000,000 miles — (1,600,000,000,000,000,000 Kilometers)

100,000,000,000,000,000 miles — (160,000,000,000,000,000 Kilometers)

10,000,000,000,000 miles — (16,000,000,000,000 Kilometers)

Interstellar Space

1,000,000,000,000 miles — (1,600,000,000,000 Kilometers)

100,000,000,000 miles — (160,000,000,000 Kilometers)

10,000,000,000 miles — (16,000,000,000 Kilometers)

Neptune

Pluto   Uranus

1,000,000,000 miles — (1,600,000,000 Kilometers)

Interplanetary Space

Saturn   Jupiter

100,000,000 miles — (160,000,000 Kilometers)

Venus

Mercury   Mars

10,000,000 miles — (16,000,000 Kilometers)

1,000,000 miles — (1,600,000 Kilometers)

Translunar Space

Moon

100,000 miles — (160,000 Kilometers)

Cislunar Space

10,000 miles — (16,000 Kilometers)

1,000 miles — (1,600 Kilometers)

100 miles — (160 Kilometers)

Earth

Atmosphere

Art Lutz for WORLD BOOK

What is space?

Space continues in all directions, and has no known limits. The moon moves through space around the earth. The earth and the other planets circle in space around the sun. The sun and billions of other stars make up a giant *galaxy* whirling through space. Countless other galaxies are scattered throughout space as far as we can see with the largest telescopes.

The beginning of space. Space begins where the earth's *atmosphere* (air) is too thin to affect objects moving through it. Near the earth's surface, air is plentiful. But higher above the earth, the air becomes thinner and thinner until it fades to almost nothing, and space begins. Space usually is said to begin about 100 miles (160 kilometers) above the earth. At this height, a satellite may continue circling the earth for months. But, even there, enough air is still present to slow a satellite and cause it to fall. Solar storms in the upper atmosphere may also cause satellites to fall sooner than expected.

From the earth to the moon. The atmosphere continues beyond 100 miles (160 kilometers) above the earth. But it is not like the air near the earth. It consists of widely scattered atoms and molecules of gas, and radiation. The radiation consists mostly of electrons, protons, and other subatomic particles. The particles carry electric charges. They are "trapped" in space by the earth's magnetic field. Scientists call the part of the atmosphere that contains these particles the *magnetosphere.*

Space between the earth and moon is called *cislunar* space (*cis* means *on this side,* and *lunar* means *of the moon*). As the moon is approached through cislunar space, the earth's gravity becomes weaker and the moon's gravity becomes stronger. The combined gravities of the earth and the moon are effective to about 1,000,000 miles (1,600,000 kilometers) from the earth. This distance is sometimes called *translunar space.*

Space between the planets is called *interplanetary space.* The sun's gravity controls interplanetary space. But each planet and moon also has its own gravity. Vast distances separate the bodies that move in interplanetary space. The sun is about 93 million miles (150 million kilometers) from the earth. Venus, the closest planet to the earth, approaches only to within about 25 million miles (40 million kilometers) of the earth. Interplanetary space reaches far beyond Pluto, the planet most distant from the earth. It ends where the sun's gravity is no longer effective—perhaps 50 billion miles (80 billion kilometers) from the earth.

To the stars and beyond. We find even greater distances in *interstellar space* (space between the stars). *Proxima Centauri,* the nearest star outside the solar system, is over 25 trillion miles (40 trillion kilometers) away. To cover such great distances, a spacecraft would have to travel almost as fast as light. Even then, a round trip to a star could take a space traveler's whole lifetime. Interstellar space reaches unimaginable distances. Then *intergalactic space* (space between the galaxies) begins.

Vast distances separate the earth from the moon, the planets, and the stars. In the illustration at the left, these bodies appear much closer to the earth than they actually are. If the diagram had been drawn with 1 inch equal to 1,000 miles (or 1 centimeter equal to 630 kilometers), the picture of Pluto would have to be 40 miles (64 kilometers) from that of the earth.

A spacecraft may make several kinds of trips into space. It may be launched into orbit around the earth, rocketed to the moon, or sent past a planet. For each trip, the spacecraft must be launched at a particular *velocity* (speed and direction). The job of the launch vehicle is to give the spacecraft this velocity. If the spacecraft carries a crew, the spacecraft itself must be able to slow down and land safely on the earth.

Overcoming gravity is the biggest problem in getting into space. Gravity pulls everything to the earth and gives objects their weight. A rocket overcomes gravity by producing *thrust* (a pushing force). Thrust, like weight, can be measured in pounds or newtons. To lift a spacecraft, a rocket must have a thrust greater than its own weight and the added weight of the spacecraft. The extra thrust *accelerates* the spacecraft. That is, it makes the spacecraft go faster and faster until it reaches the velocity needed for its journey.

Rocket engines create thrust by burning large amounts of fuel. As the fuel burns, it becomes a hot gas. The heat creates an extremely high pressure in the gas. This pressure does two things: (1) it pushes the flaming gas backward and out through the rocket nozzle; (2) it pushes the rocket forward. This forward push on the rocket is the thrust.

Rocket fuels are called *propellants*. Liquid-propellant rockets work by combining a fuel, such as kerosene or liquid hydrogen, with an *oxidizer,* such as liquid oxygen (LOX). The fuel and oxidizer burn violently when mixed. Solid-fuel rockets use dry chemicals as propellants.

Engineers rate the efficiency of propellants in terms of the thrust that 1 pound (0.45 kilogram) of fuel can produce in one second. This measurement is known as the propellant's *specific impulse.* Liquid propellants have a higher specific impulse than most solid propellants. But some, including LOX and liquid hydrogen, are difficult and dangerous to handle. They must be loaded into the rocket just before launching. Solid propellants are loaded into the rocket at the factory, and are then ready to use.

The primary vehicle for research and exploration in the United States space program is the space shuttle. The space shuttle takes off like a rocket, orbits the earth like a spacecraft, and lands like an airplane. It consists of an *orbiter,* an *external tank,* and two *solid rocket boosters.*

The orbiter resembles an airplane. It carries the crew and the *payload* (cargo). The orbiter has three liquid rocket engines near its tail. Propellants are fed to the engines from the external tank. The external tank holds more than 1½ million pounds (680,000 kilograms) of propellant, which consists of liquid hydrogen and LOX. Each solid rocket weighs about 1.3 million pounds (589,000 kilograms) and produces about 2.6 million pounds (1.2 million kilograms) of thrust.

The orbiter's engines, combined with the solid rocket boosters, provide the thrust to launch the space shuttle. After two minutes of flight, the boosters separate from the orbiter. The orbiter continues into space and releases the external tank just before entering orbit.

Returning to the earth involves problems opposite to those of getting into space. The spacecraft must lose

WORLD BOOK illustration by Zorica Dabich

The space shuttle takes off by using the fuel in its solid rocket boosters and external tank. After the fuel has been used, the boosters return to the earth by parachute and the tank falls into the ocean. In orbit, the spacecraft's payload bay doors are opened for such purposes as releasing or retrieving a satellite.

speed instead of gaining it. The space shuttle orbiter has two smaller engines that are fired to slow down the spacecraft and modify its orbit for the return to earth. These engines are also used for maneuvering during orbit. The orbiter enters the earth's atmosphere at a speed of more than 16,000 miles (25,800 kilometers) per hour. As the spacecraft slows down, friction with the air produces intense heat. The temperature of the wings may reach 2750° F. (1510° C). A *thermal protection system* shields the orbiter from this heat. The thermal protection system consists of more than 25,000 ceramic tiles bonded to the body of the spacecraft. About an hour after the shuttle's engines are fired to bring it out of its orbit, the spacecraft lands on a runway. The shuttle touches down at a speed of about 200 miles (320 kilometers) per hour.

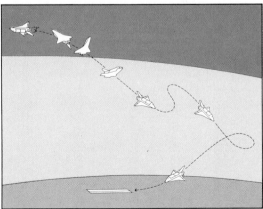

WORLD BOOK illustration by Zorica Dabich

The orbiter returns to the earth by firing two engines that reduce its speed. The spacecraft enters the earth's atmosphere at a speed of more than 16,000 miles (25,800 kilometers) per hour and maneuvers into landing position. It lands on a runway at a speed of about 200 miles (320 kilometers) per hour.

A launch vehicle is a rocket or a combination of rockets used to launch satellites, space probes, and other spacecraft. The United States uses several launch vehicles with a wide range of lifting power. These vehicles can launch many kinds of spacecraft to various distances. A rocket must burn a large amount of fuel to launch a spacecraft, and so a launch vehicle consists mostly of fuel tanks. The more powerful it is, the larger it must be to hold the needed fuel. See **Rocket.**

The building block idea. Engineers use a few basic rockets and rocket engines to build a family of launch vehicles. They call this method the "building block" idea. Here is how it works. The part of a launch vehicle that provides most of the propulsion for a spacecraft is called the *booster* stage. Atlas boosters orbited U.S. astronauts in the Mercury program. An Atlas combined with an Agena second stage launched many *Mariner* space probes to Mars and Venus. The combined vehicle was called an Atlas-Agena. The Atlas-Centaur, a more powerful vehicle, combines the Atlas with a Centaur second stage. The Atlas-Centaur has launched heavy sat-

ellites, such as the *Orbiting Astronomical Observatories* and the *Intelsat* communications satellites.

The Titan family of launch vehicles developed from the Titan missile. The Titan 2 launched U.S. astronauts in the Gemini program. Later vehicles in the Titan series have had two solid-fuel booster rockets attached to their sides. These *piggyback boosters* provide extra thrust to launch heavier payloads. For example, the Titan 2 liquid-fuel vehicle could lift 8,600 pounds (3,900 kilograms) into a low orbit of the earth. But with two solid-fuel boosters strapped to it, the Titan today can lift 39,000 pounds (18,000 kilograms) into earth orbit. The Titan 3 had enough power to launch heavy probes to Mars and other planets. The Titan 34D was used chiefly for lifting large military payloads into orbit. It was replaced in 1989 by the Titan 4, which is the most powerful vehicle in the series.

Engineers have used rocket engines as well as whole rockets for building blocks. For example, the Saturn family of launch vehicles used three basic engines, the H-1, F-1, and J-2. Saturn vehicles carried the first astro-

U.S. launch vehicles

Launch vehicle	Stages	Takeoff thrust		Payload
* Vanguard	3	28,000 lbs.	125,000 N†	50 lbs. (23 kg) in earth orbit
* Jupiter C	4	82,000 lbs.	365,000 N	30 lbs. (14 kg) in earth orbit
Scout	4	107,200 lbs.	476,850 N	410 lbs. (186 kg) in earth orbit, 85 lbs. (39 kg) to moon
* Juno 2	4	150,000 lbs.	667,000 N	100 lbs. (45 kg) in earth orbit
* Mercury-Redstone	1	82,000 lbs.	365,000 N	3,000 lbs. (1,400 kg) suborbital
Delta	3	205,000 lbs.	911,900 N	3,900 lbs. (1,770 kg) in earth orbit; 1,050 lbs. (476 kg) to moon
Delta 2	3	635,000 lbs.	2,825,000 N	8,780 lbs. (3,980 kg) in earth orbit
* Mercury-Atlas	1 $\frac{1}{2}$**	367,000 lbs.	1,632,000 N	3,000 lbs. (1,400 kg) in earth orbit
* Atlas-Agena	2 $\frac{1}{2}$**	400,000 lbs.	1,800,000 N	7,700 lbs. (3,490 kg) in earth orbit; 1,430 lbs. (649 kg) to moon; 1,000 lbs. (450 kg) to Mars or Venus
Atlas-Centaur	2 $\frac{1}{2}$**	400,000 lbs.	1,800,000 N	10,300 lbs. (4,672 kg) in earth orbit; 2,500 lbs. (1,130 kg) to moon; 2,200 lbs. (998 kg) to Mars or Venus
Atlas E	1 $\frac{1}{2}$**	390,000 lbs.	1,735,000 N	2,000 lbs. (910 kg) in earth orbit
Atlas H	1 $\frac{1}{2}$**	439,000 lbs.	1,953,000 N	3,200 lbs. (1,450 kg) in earth orbit
* Titan 2	2	430,000 lbs.	1,913,000 N	8,600 lbs. (3,900 kg) in earth orbit
* Titan 3C	3 or 4	2,400,000 lbs.	10,700,000 N	26,000 lbs. (11,800 kg) in earth orbit; 6,200 lbs. (2,810 kg) to moon
* Titan 34D	3 or 4	2,600,000 lbs.	11,570,000 N	31,000 lbs. (14,100 kg.) in earth orbit
* Titan-Centaur	4	2,400,000 lbs.	10,700,000 N	35,000 lbs. (15,900 kg) in earth orbit; 11,500 lbs. (5,216 kg) interplanetary missions
Titan 4	3 or 4	2,788,000 lbs.	12,402,000 N	39,000 lbs (18,000 kg) in earth orbit
Space shuttle system	3	6,925,000 lbs.	30,802,000 N	65,000 lbs. (29,500 kg) in earth orbit
* Saturn V	3	7,570,000 lbs.	33,670,000 N	285,000 lbs. (129,300 kg) in earth orbit; 107,000 lbs. (48,530 kg) to moon; 70,000 lbs. (32,000 kg) to Mars or Venus

*No longer in use.
**Half stage is droppable booster engine.
†*N* is the abbreviation for *newton,* the unit of force in the metric system.

Jupiter C	Vanguard	Scout	Juno 2	Mercury-Redstone	Mercury-Atlas	Atlas-Agena	Atlas-Centaur	Titan 2
68 $\frac{1}{4}$ ft. (20.8 m)	72 ft. (21.9 m)	72 ft. (21.9 m)	76 ft. (23.2 m)	83 ft. (25.3 m)	95 $\frac{1}{4}$ ft. (29.1 m)	102 ft. (31.1 m)	109 ft. (33.2 m)	109 ft. (33.2 m)

nauts to the moon in the Apollo program. These vehicles also orbited the first U.S. space station, *Skylab*. The Saturn 1B had two stages. The first stage used eight H-1 engines, and the second stage used one J-2 engine. The more powerful Saturn V consisted of three stages. The first stage had five F-1 engines, the second stage five J-2 engines, and the third stage one J-2 engine.

Space shuttle systems began to operate in the early 1980's. A space shuttle does the work of a launch vehicle. However, unlike other launch vehicles, it can make more than one flight.

The shuttle system has three main stages: (1) an orbiter, which has three main engines, (2) an external tank, and (3) two solid rocket boosters. The orbiter lifts off by means of its own engines and the solid rocket boosters. The external tank feeds propellant to the engines. After two minutes, the booster rockets separate from the orbiter and return to the earth by parachutes. The boosters can be used again. The orbiter releases the external tank just before going into orbit. The tank breaks up over the ocean. Two pilot astronauts operate the orbiter. Other astronauts handle cargo, conduct experiments, or perform tasks outside the craft. On some flights, *payload specialists* carry out scientific experiments and other duties connected with the payload. The space shuttle can normally carry up to seven crew members. After the mission's completion, the orbiter enters the earth's atmosphere and lands on a runway.

NASA

Solid rocket boosters of the space shuttle are released at an altitude of about 27 miles (43 kilometers), after two minutes of flight. The boosters return to the earth by parachute and can be used again on another flight.

WORLD BOOK illustrations by Oxford Illustrators Limited

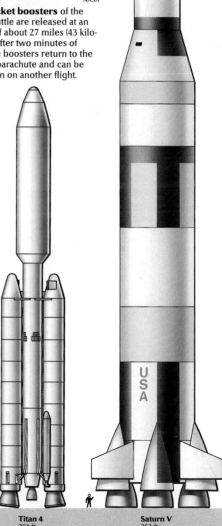

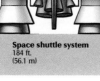

Delta	**Titan-Centaur**	**Space shuttle system**	**Titan 4**	**Saturn V**
116 feet	160 ft.	184 ft.	204 ft.	363 ft.
(35.4 m)	(48.8 m)	(56.1 m)	(62 m)	(110.6 m)

This section describes the Apollo spacecraft that took U.S. astronauts to the moon in 1969 and the early 1970's. The Soyuz spacecraft that carry Soviet cosmonauts to orbiting space stations are similar.

The Apollo spacecraft were lifted into space atop the Saturn launch vehicles. The spacecraft had the general shape of a cone. They were launched with the narrow end pointing up to reduce air resistance during the flight through the atmosphere. They descended through the atmosphere backwards—with the broad end pointing in the direction of flight. In this way, they lost speed quickly, because the broad end offered great resistance to the air. Spacecraft like the Apollo *lunar module* were not streamlined at all. This spacecraft was designed to operate only near the moon, where there is no air.

Life-support systems supplied the astronauts with oxygen, food, and water. Oxygen and water were carried in tanks. Food was freeze-dried and stored in meal-size packages. Solid body wastes were sealed into plastic bags and stored aboard the spacecraft. Liquid wastes were released into space.

Communications and navigation equipment. The astronauts needed a radio to report to scientists and engineers on the ground. They could answer their questions and ask for directions in an emergency. The Apollo spacecraft carried a television camera so that pictures from space or the moon could be sent to the earth during the flight. Navigation equipment included sextants, gyroscopes, and small electronic computers. The astronauts used this equipment to find their position in space

and to check their course. *Telemetry* equipment sent information about all spacecraft systems to ground stations.

Control systems enabled the astronauts to put the spacecraft in any position. They did this by firing tiny rocket motors located at various places on the outside of the craft. By operating these motors, the astronauts could tilt the craft, point it to either side, and roll it right or left. To reenter the atmosphere, the craft had to point a certain way, or else it might have skipped away from earth or descended too fast and burnt up.

Reentry and landing equipment. The engines of the propulsion system were used for maneuvering in space. The engines were fired in the direction opposite to that of orbit to slow the spacecraft down and cause it to fall out of orbit. The *heat shield* protected the astronauts from the intense heat generated when the craft plunged through the atmosphere. When the spacecraft had lost enough speed and altitude, parachutes opened and lowered it gently to the earth.

See **Space travel** in *World Book* for more information on the following topics:

- •Living in space
- •Orbiting the earth
- •Reaching the moon
- •Space stations
- •Reaching the planets and
    the stars

- •Artificial satellites
- •Space probes
- •Steps in the conquest of
    space

Manned spacecraft

Four U.S. and two Soviet spacecraft are shown below. Vostok and Mercury capsules each carried one space pilot. The Gemini spacecraft carried two astronauts. Three astronauts orbited the moon in the Apollo command module. Two of them landed on the moon in the lunar module. The Apollo service module carried a rocket engine used during the flight. The Soviet Soyuz can carry three cosmonauts.

WORLD BOOK illustrations by Oxford Illustrators Limited

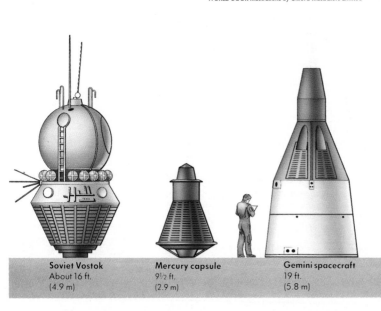

Soviet Vostok
About 16 ft.
(4.9 m)

Mercury capsule
9½ ft.
(2.9 m)

Gemini spacecraft
19 ft.
(5.8 m)

Apollo command and service modules
35⅓ ft.
(10.8 m)

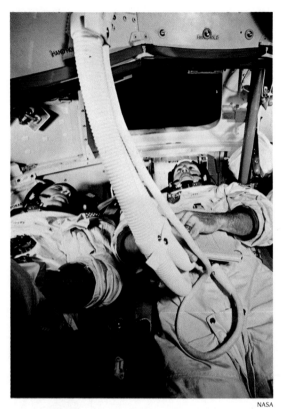

NASA

Inside an Apollo command module simulator, astronauts
William A. Anders, *left,* and James A. Lovell, Jr., *right,* train for a
flight around the moon.

NASA

Inside an Apollo lunar module simulator, astronaut Neil A.
Armstrong practices a moon landing. Through a window to his
left, he sees a simulated moonscape.

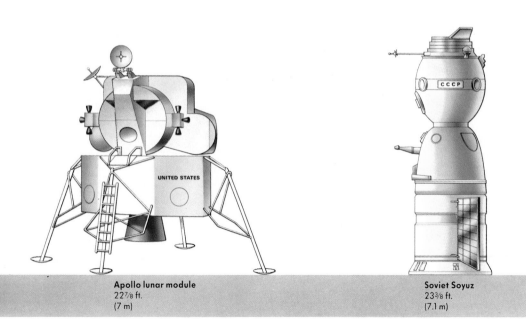

Apollo lunar module
22⁷/₈ ft.
(7 m)

Soviet Soyuz
23³/₈ ft.
(7.1 m)

Spider

Spider is a small, eight-legged animal that spins silk. Spiders are best known for the silk webs they spin. They use their webs to catch insects for food. Even insects that are larger and stronger than spiders cannot escape from the threads of a spider's web.

All spiders spin silk, but some kinds of spiders do not make webs. The bolas spider, for example, spins a single line of silk with a drop of sticky silk at the end. When an insect flies near, this spider swings the line at it and traps the insect on the sticky ball.

All spiders have fangs, and most kinds of spiders have poison glands. Spiders use their fangs and poison glands to capture animals for food. A spider's bite can kill insects and other small animals, but few kinds of spiders are harmful to human beings. In North America, only six kinds of spiders have bites that can harm people. These spiders are the brown recluse spider, the sac spider, the black widow, the brown widow, the red-legged widow, and the varied widow. Of the four widow spiders, only the females are known to bite humans. The bites of these six spiders often cause only mild reactions in people. Usually, a person must severely irritate a spider before it will bite.

Spiders are helpful to people because they eat harmful insects. Spiders eat grasshoppers and locusts, which destroy crops, and flies and mosquitoes, which carry diseases. Although spiders feed mostly on insects, some spiders capture and eat tadpoles, small frogs, small fish, and mice. Spiders even eat each other. Most female

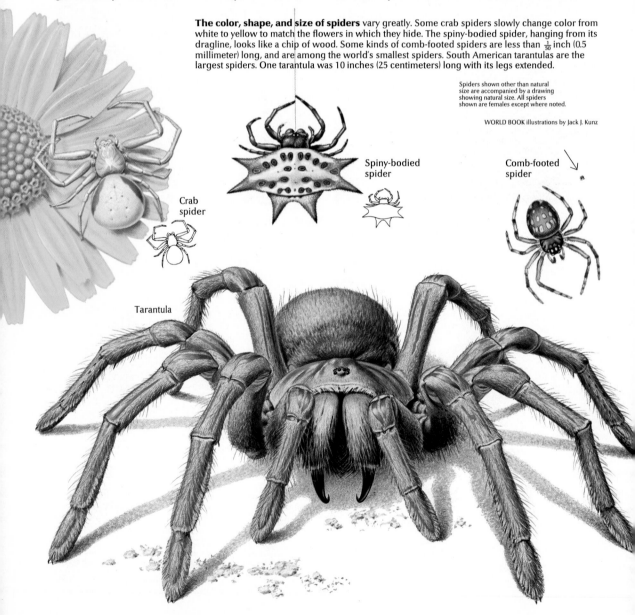

The color, shape, and size of spiders vary greatly. Some crab spiders slowly change color from white to yellow to match the flowers in which they hide. The spiny-bodied spider, hanging from its dragline, looks like a chip of wood. Some kinds of comb-footed spiders are less than $\frac{1}{50}$ inch (0.5 millimeter) long, and are among the world's smallest spiders. South American tarantulas are the largest spiders. One tarantula was 10 inches (25 centimeters) long with its legs extended.

Spiders shown other than natural size are accompanied by a drawing showing natural size. All spiders shown are females except where noted.

WORLD BOOK illustrations by Jack J. Kunz

Crab
spider

Spiny-bodied
spider

Comb-footed
spider

Tarantula

spiders are larger and stronger than male spiders, and occasionally eat the males.

Spiders live anywhere they can find food. They can be seen in fields, woods, swamps, caves, and deserts. One kind of spider spends most of its life under water. Another kind lives near the top of Mount Everest, the world's highest mountain. Some spiders live in houses, barns, or other buildings. Others live on the outside of buildings—on walls, on window screens, or in the corners of doors and windows.

There are more than 30,000 known kinds of spiders, but scientists believe there may be as many as 50,000 to 100,000 kinds. Some kinds are smaller than the head of a pin. Others are as large as a person's hand. One spider, a South American tarantula, measured 10 inches (25 centimeters) long with its legs extended.

Many people think spiders are insects. However, scientists classify spiders as *arachnids,* which differ from insects in a number of ways. Spiders have eight legs. Ants, bees, beetles, and other insects have only six legs. In addition, most insects have wings and *antennae* (feelers), but spiders do not. Other arachnids include daddy longlegs, scorpions, and mites and ticks. Scientists also classify spiders as either *true spiders* or *tarantulas* according to certain differences in their bodies, such as the way the fangs point and move.

The spider's body

Spiders may be short and fat, long and thin, round, oblong, or flat. Their legs are short and stubby, or long and thin. Most spiders are brown, gray, or black. But some are as beautifully colored as lovely butterflies.

The bolas spider does not trap insects in a web. Instead, it spins a line of silk with a drop of sticky silk at the end. The spider swings the line at an insect and traps it on the sticky ball.

WORLD BOOK illustrations by Jack J. Kunz

Bolas spider

The ogre-faced stick spider traps insects in a web of sticky silk. Its front legs stretch the web to several times its normal size and sweep it over the insect like a net.

Ogre-faced stick spider

The purse-web spider extends the silk lining of its burrow up the side of a tree to make a tube-shaped web. The spider bites through the tube to seize insects crawling over its web.

Purse-web spider

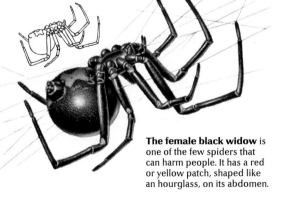

Wolf spider

Jumping spider

Spiderlings travel in interesting ways. Baby wolf spiders ride on their mother's back. A young jumping spider travels by *ballooning.* It raises its abdomen so that the wind can pull silk threads from its spinnerets. The wind catches and lifts the silk, pulling the spiderling into the air.

Black widow

The female black widow is one of the few spiders that can harm people. It has a red or yellow patch, shaped like an hourglass, on its abdomen.

A spider has no bones. Its tough skin serves as a protective outer skeleton. Hairs, humps, and *spines* (bristles of skin) cover the bodies of most spiders.

A spider's body has two main sections: (1) the *cephalothorax,* which consists of the head joined to the *thorax* (chest); and (2) the *abdomen.* Each of these sections has *appendages* (attached parts). A thin waist called the *pedicel* connects the cephalothorax and the abdomen.

Eyes. A spider's eyes are on top and near the front of its head. The size, number, and position of the eyes vary among different species. Most species have eight eyes, arranged in two rows of four each. Other kinds have six, four, or two eyes. Some spiders have better vision than others. For example, hunting spiders have good eyesight at short distances. Their eyesight enables them to form images of their prey and mates. Web-building spiders have poor eyesight. Their eyes are used for detecting changes in light. Some species of spiders that live in caves or other dark places have no eyes at all.

Mouth. A spider's mouth opening is below its eyes. Spiders do not have chewing mouth parts, and they eat only liquids. Various appendages around the mouth

opening form a short "straw" through which the spider sucks the body fluid of its victim.

The spider can eat some of the solid tissue of its prey by *predigesting* it. To do this, the spider sprays digestive juices on the tissue. The powerful juices dissolve the tissue. By predigestion and sucking, a large tarantula can reduce a mouse to a small pile of hair and bones in about 36 hours.

Chelicerae are a pair of appendages that the spider uses to seize and kill its prey. The chelicerae are above the mouth opening and just below the spider's eyes. Each chelicera ends in a hard, hollow, pointed claw, and these claws are the spider's fangs. An opening in the tip of the fang connects with the poison glands. When a spider stabs an insect with its chelicerae, poison flows into the wound and paralyzes or kills the victim.

The fangs of tarantulas point straight down from the head, and the poison glands are in the chelicerae. In true spiders, the fangs point crosswise, and the poison glands extend back into the cephalothorax.

Spiders also use chelicerae to crush prey. Some species use them to dig burrows in the ground as nests.

WORLD BOOK illustration by John F. Eggert

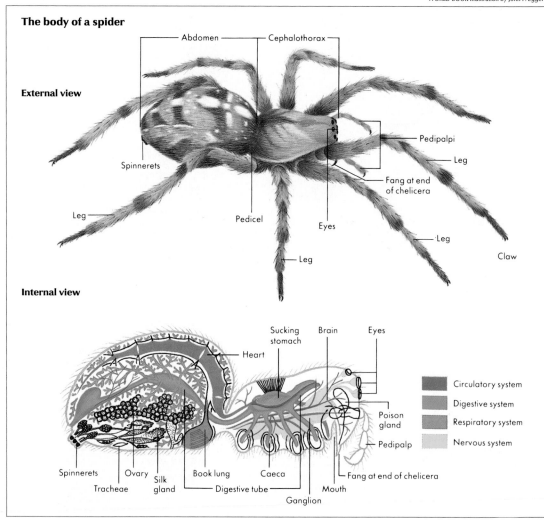

The body of a spider

External view

Abdomen — Cephalothorax

Pedipalpi

Leg

Spinnerets

Fang at end of chelicera

Leg

Pedicel

Eyes

Leg

Leg

Claw

Internal view

Sucking stomach   Brain   Eyes

Heart

Circulatory system

Digestive system

Poison gland

Respiratory system

Pedipalp

Nervous system

Spinnerets   Ovary   Silk gland   Book lung   Caeca

Fang at end of chelicera

Tracheae   Digestive tube   Mouth

Ganglion

Pedipalpi are a pair of appendages that look like small legs. One pedipalp is attached to each side of the spider's mouth, and they form the sides of the mouth. Each pedipalp has six *segments* (parts). In most kinds of spiders, the segment closest to the body bears a sharp plate with jagged edges. The spider uses this plate to cut and crush its food. In adult male spiders, the last segment of each pedipalp bears a reproductive organ.

Legs. A spider has four pairs of legs, which are attached to its cephalothorax. Each leg has seven segments. In most kinds of spiders, the tip of the last segment has two or three claws. A pad of hairs called a *scopula* may surround the claws. The scopula sticks to smooth surfaces and helps the spider walk on ceilings and walls. Each leg also is covered with sensitive bristles that serve as organs of touch and perhaps organs of smell. Some bristles pick up vibrations from the ground or air, or the spider's leg. Others detect chemicals in the environment.

When a spider walks, the first and third leg on one side of its body move with the second and fourth leg on the other side. Muscles in the legs make the legs bend at the joints. But spiders have no muscles to extend their legs. The pressure of the blood in their bodies makes their legs extend. If a spider's body does not contain enough fluids, its blood pressure drops. The legs draw up under the body, and the animal cannot walk.

Spinnerets are short, fingerlike organs with which the spider spins silk. They are attached to the rear of the abdomen. Most kinds of spiders have six spinnerets, but some have four or two. The tip of a spinneret is called the *spinning field.* The surface of each spinning field is covered by as many as a hundred *spinning tubes.* Through these tubes, liquid silk flows from silk glands in the spider's abdomen to the outside of its body. The silk then hardens into a thread.

Respiratory system. Spiders as a group have two kinds of breathing organs—*tracheae* and *book lungs.* Tracheae, found in almost all kinds of true spiders, are small tubes which carry air directly to the body tissues. Air enters the tubes through the *spiracle,* an opening in front of the spinnerets in most kinds of true spiders.

Book lungs are in cavities in the spider's abdomen. Air enters the cavities through a tiny slit on each side and near the front of the abdomen. Each lung consists of 15 or more thin, flat folds of tissue arranged like the pages of a book. The sheets of tissue contain many blood vessels. As air circulates between the sheets, oxygen passes into the blood. Tarantulas have two pairs of book lungs. Most true spiders have one pair.

Circulatory system. The blood of spiders contains many pale blood cells and is slightly bluish in color. The heart, a long, slender tube in the abdomen, pumps the blood to all parts of the body. The blood returns to the heart through open passages instead of closed tubes, such as those of the human body. If the spider's skin is broken, the blood quickly drains from its body.

Digestive system. A digestive tube extends the length of the spider's body. In the cephalothorax, the tube is larger and forms a *sucking stomach.* When the stomach's powerful muscles contract, the size of the stomach increases. This causes a strong sucking action that pulls the food through the stomach into the intestine. Juices in the digestive tube break the liquid food into particles small enough to pass through the walls of the intestine into the blood. The food is then distributed to all parts of the body. Food is also pulled through the stomach into a fingerlike cavity called the *caeca.* The ability to store food in the caeca enables spiders to go for long periods of time without eating.

Nervous system. The central nervous system of a spider is in the cephalothorax. It includes the brain, which is connected to a large group of nerve cells called the *ganglion.* Nerve fibers from the brain and ganglion run throughout a spider's body. The nerve fibers carry information to the brain from sense organs on the head, legs, and other parts of the body. The brain can also send signals through the nerve fibers to control the activities of the body.

WORLD BOOK illustrations by John F. Eggert

Spider faces

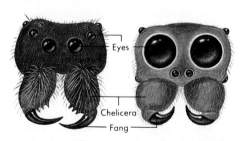

Wolf spider
Lycosa carolinensis

Tarantula
Lasiodora

Eyes

Chelicera

Fang

Jumping spider
Phidippus variegatus

Ogre-faced stick spider
Deinopis spinosus

Eyes

Chelicera

Fang

Spider feet

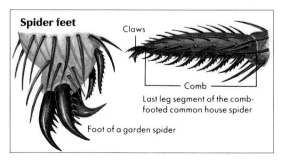

Claws

Comb

Last leg segment of the comb-footed common house spider

Foot of a garden spider

See **Spider** in *World Book* for more information on the following topics:

- The spider's silk
- Hunting spiders
- Web-spinning spiders
- The life of a spider

Ed. Cesar, N.A.S.

Douglas squirrel and young

Alvin E. Staffan, N.A.S.

Eastern gray squirrel

Squirrel is a furry-tailed animal with large, black eyes and rounded ears. Many squirrels are lively animals with long, bushy tails. They scamper about the ground or in trees. These *tree squirrels* are often seen in parks and woodlands. They include gray squirrels, fox squirrels, red squirrels, and flying squirrels. But many kinds of squirrels have short tails and never climb trees. They are called *ground squirrels,* and include chipmunks, marmots, prairie dogs, and woodchucks.

Squirrels live throughout the world except in Australia, Madagascar, and southern South America. One of the smallest squirrels is the African pygmy squirrel, found in western Africa. It weighs about ½ ounce (14 grams) and is 3 inches (8 centimeters) long without the 2-inch (5-centimeter) tail. The marmot is the largest squirrel. It weighs up to 20 pounds (9 kilograms) and grows as long as 30 inches (76 centimeters), including a 10-inch (25-centimeter) tail.

There are over 300 kinds of squirrels. They make up the squirrel family, called Sciuridae. Squirrels are one of the largest families of *rodents* (gnawing animals). Like other rodents, squirrels have chisel-like front teeth.

Many kinds of squirrels, especially tree squirrels and chipmunks, are easy to tame. They may learn to take nuts and other food from a person's hand. But even a tame squirrel may bite or scratch a person and cause a serious wound.

The word *squirrel* comes from two Greek words that mean *shadow tail.* At first, the word may have been used only for tree squirrels, whose large, bushy tails curl over their backs and seem to keep them in the shade.

The rest of this article is about tree squirrels only. To learn more about the various kinds of ground squirrels, see the *World Book* articles on **Chipmunk; Marmot; Prairie dog;** and **Woodchuck.**

Homes. Most kinds of tree squirrels are active, noisy animals. They seem to scold one another continually in a variety of loud chirps, whistles, and noises that sound somewhat like *chirrrr.*

Many squirrels have two homes—a warm, permanent one, and a temporary one that is cool enough for hot days. The permanent home may be a den in a hollow tree trunk, or a sturdy nest built on a branch. A squirrel's den is lined with dry leaves and strips of bark. In winter, several squirrels may share a den. A permanent nest is

Facts in brief

Common name	Scientific name	Gestation period	Number of young	Life span (in captivity)
Flying squirrel	*Glaucomys*	40 days	2-6	7-13 years
Fox squirrel	*Sciurus*	45 days	2-4	9 years
Gray squirrel	*Sciurus*	44 days	2-5	8-15 years
Red squirrel	*Tamiasciurus*	40 days	4	8-9 years

© E. Hanumantha Rao, N. H. P. A.

The black giant squirrel lives in forests in Southeast Asia. It weighs up to 6½ pounds (3 kilograms) and has a very long tail.

made of layers of twigs and leaves packed together to keep out rain, snow, and wind. A temporary nest is only a loose pile of twigs and leaves. It soon falls apart, and a squirrel may have to build several each summer.

Squirrels move about easily in trees or on rooftops or telephone wires. They spread their legs straight out and leap from place to place. Squirrels use their bushy tails to keep their balance when they jump.

Food. Squirrels eat berries, corn, fruits, mushrooms, nuts, and seeds. They spend much time searching for food. A squirrel is especially busy in autumn, when it gathers food for the winter. Squirrels store food in holes in the ground, in trees, or in their dens.

Red squirrels are famous for the many pine cones they cut and store for food. A red squirrel may cut more than a hundred cones from a tree in an hour. Then the animal rushes to the ground, gathers the cones, and hides them. The hiding place may be a hollow tree stump. Or the squirrel may pile the cones around a stone or a log and cover them with leaves. When winter comes, the squirrel may have 3 to 10 bushels of cones.

Young. A female squirrel carries her young in her body for 36 to 45 days before birth. She may give birth twice a year, and usually from two to six young are born at a time. Newborn squirrels have no fur, and their eyes are closed. Red squirrels and flying squirrels may open their eyes 26 to 28 days after birth, but gray squirrels may take as long as 37 days. When squirrels are 5 to 8 weeks old, they have all their fur and begin to search for their own food. They start to have their own families when they are about a year old.

Enemies. Human beings are the greatest enemies of squirrels. People hunt most kinds of squirrels for sport, but they hunt tree squirrels especially for meat and fur. Other enemies include bobcats, cats, coyotes, dogs, and foxes. Tree squirrels race for the nearest tree when an enemy comes near. Squirrels may live for 2 to 6 years in the wild. Some have lived for 15 years in captivity.

See **Squirrel** in *World Book* for more information on Kinds of tree squirrels.

© Pat and Tom Lesson, Photo Researchers

The Kaibab squirrel, or tassel-eared squirrel, has tufts of fur on its ears. It lives in pine forests near the Grand Canyon.

The body of a squirrel

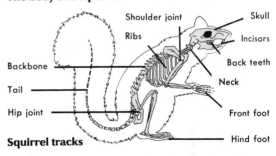

Squirrel tracks

WORLD BOOK illustration by Tom Dolan

Where squirrels live

The yellow areas show where squirrels are found.

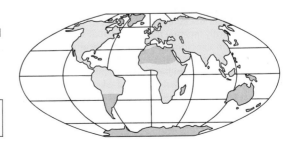

© California Institute of Technology and
Carnegie Institution of Washington, from Hale Observatories

Like gleaming jewels, stars sparkle against the night sky. Some are surrounded by hazy clouds of dust. The telescope and camera that were used to make this picture caused circles and cross-shaped "rays" to appear around some stars. Astronomers call this group of stars *the Pleiades.* The inset on the opposite page shows how these stars look when seen without a telescope.

Star

Star is a huge ball of glowing gas in the sky. The sun is a star. It is the only star close enough to the earth to look like a ball. The other billions of stars are so far away that they appear to be no more than pinpoints of light—even through powerful telescopes.

There are more than 200 billion billion (200,000,000,-000,000,000,000) stars. Suppose that everyone in the world were to count the stars. Each person could count more than 50 billion of them without the same star being counted twice.

In spite of their appearance, stars are enormous objects. The sun is only a medium-sized star, but its diameter is more than 100 times the diameter of the earth. The largest stars would more than fill the space between the earth and the sun. Such stars have a diameter that is about 1,000 times as large as the sun's. The smallest stars are smaller than the earth.

We can hardly imagine the great size of some stars. But even large stars look like tiny dots because they are so far away. The nearest star—other than the sun—is more than 25 million million miles (40 million million kilometers) away. The fastest jet would take a million years to fly that far. But even this great distance is only one-billionth the distance to the farthest stars.

Stars differ greatly in color and brightness, because they differ in temperature and size. Some stars look yel-low, like the sun. Others glow blue or red. The stars we see at night are a mixture of nearby stars that are fairly dim and distant stars that are very bright.

Stars twinkle because starlight comes to us through moving layers of air that surround the earth. The stars shine day and night, but we can see them only when the sky is dark and clear. During the day, sunlight brightens the sky and keeps us from seeing the stars.

At night, the stars seem to move across the sky—as the sun does during the day. This "movement" comes from the spinning of the earth, not from the movement of the stars. The stars themselves do move, but their motion cannot be seen because they are so far from the earth. However, their slow change in position can be determined through precise measurements over many years.

A star is made up mainly of two gases: hydrogen and helium. The great weight of a star makes the temperature at its center high enough for a nuclear reaction between hydrogen atoms to take place. The energy released by the reaction keeps stars shining until much of the hydrogen in the star's center is used up.

Most stars began shining about 10 billion years ago. But new stars are still forming within the clouds of gas and dust of the Milky Way and other galaxies. The sun itself was probably formed in this way, developing from a

Minolta Corporation

The stars of the Pleiades, shown in the above inset, appear in a closely spaced group. The ancient Greeks named these stars for the seven sisters of an ancient story. A stargazer without a telescope can easily see the six brightest stars of the Pleiades.

rotating mass of gas and dust about five billion years ago.

People have studied the stars since ancient times. Early farmers watched the stars to know when to plant their crops. Travelers learned to use the stars to tell directions. Ancient peoples made up stories about people, animals, and other things they saw pictured in certain groups of stars. These groups of stars are called *constellations.* See **Astronomy** (maps: The stars and constellations); in *World Book,* see **Constellation.**

Some starlike objects that we see in the sky are not stars. A few of these objects are planets. Meteors look like falling stars but are really pieces of rock or metal that burn up as they shoot through the air. For more information, see the articles on **Planet** and **Meteor.**

Stars in the universe

Stars are not spread evenly throughout the universe. They are gathered in huge groups of billions of stars called *galaxies.* The sun belongs to a galaxy called the Milky Way. This galaxy has a shape like a pancake with a bulge in the center. The sun and the nine planets—including the earth—lie in the flat portion of the galaxy.

How many stars are there? No one knows exactly how many stars there are. On a clear, dark night, a per-

Star terms

Absolute magnitude is a star's brightness if the star were 32.6 light-years from the earth. It is a measure of the amount of energy the star gives off.

Apparent magnitude is a star's brightness as seen from the earth. Apparent magnitude depends on the star's absolute magnitude and its distance from the earth.

Binary star is a pair of stars revolving around each other.

Black hole is a collapsed star that has become invisible. It has so much gravitation that not even light can escape from it.

Light-year is the distance light travels in one year—5,880,000,000,000 miles (9,460,000,000,000 kilometers).

Neutron star is a small star made almost entirely of atomic particles called *neutrons.*

Nova is a star that suddenly becomes thousands of times brighter, and then becomes dim again.

Proper motion is the change in a star's position among other stars.

Spectral class identifies a star's surface temperature on the basis of the star's spectrum.

Supernova is a star that explodes and then becomes billions of times brighter for a few weeks. Supernovae may leave behind neutron stars or black holes.

Variable star is a star whose brightness changes.

White dwarf is a small, white star with a large amount of material packed into an extremely small space.

Stars at a glance

Number: About 200 billion billion stars in the known universe.

Age: Up to 15 billion years. Most stars are between 1 million and 10 billion years old.

Composition: About 75 per cent hydrogen; 22 per cent helium; and traces of most other elements, including—in order of next highest percentages—oxygen, neon, carbon, and nitrogen.

Mass: From $\frac{1}{20}$ the mass of the sun to 100 times the mass of the sun.

Nearest star excluding the sun: Proxima Centauri, 4.3 light-years away.

Farthest stars: In galaxies billions of light-years away.

Brightest star excluding the sun: Sirius (according to apparent magnitude).

Largest stars: Have a diameter of about 1 billion miles (1.6 billion kilometers)—about 1,000 times that of the sun.

Smallest known stars: Neutron stars that have a diameter of 10 miles (16 kilometers).

Colors: From blue through white, yellow, and orange, to red, depending on the star's surface temperature.

Temperature: *Surface,* from about 50,000° F. (28,000° C) on blue stars to about 5000° F. (2800° C) on red stars; *interior,* more than 2,000,000° F. (1,100,000° C).

Energy source: Nuclear fusion that changes hydrogen into helium and energy.

son can see about 3,000 stars. Through the course of a year, different stars become visible. Altogether, about 6,000 stars can be seen from the earth. But these are just the brightest stars—the ones visible without a telescope.

A telescope brings many dim stars into view. For example, a total of about 600,000 stars can be seen through a telescope with a lens 3 inches (7.6 centimeters) in diameter. The largest telescopes make it possible to detect billions of individual stars and more than 1 billion galaxies. Astronomers believe these galaxies consist of a total of about 200 billion billion stars.

Only a few stars have names. Ancient stargazers named the brightest stars, such as Betelgeuse and Rigel in the constellation Orion. Today, astronomers use a letter of the Greek alphabet with the name of a constellation to identify stars that can be seen with the naked eye.

For example, Betelgeuse is called *Alpha Orionis* and Rigel is *Beta Orionis.* Faint stars are numbered and are listed in various catalogs of stars.

The size of stars varies from neutron stars that have a diameter of 10 miles (16 kilometers) to giant stars far larger than the sun. The sun itself is a medium-sized star with a diameter of 865,000 miles (1,392,000 kilometers)—109 times that of the earth. Astronomers divide stars into five main groups by size: (1) supergiants, (2) giants, (3) medium-sized stars, (4) white dwarfs, and (5) neutron stars. A star may change groups during its lifetime.

Supergiants, the largest known stars, include such stars as Antares and Betelgeuse. Antares has a diameter 330 times that of the sun. Betelgeuse actually expands and shrinks. Its diameter varies from 375 to 595 times that of the sun. The largest supergiants have diameters about a thousand times as large as the sun's.

Giants have diameters about 10 to 100 times as large as the sun's. The diameter of Aldebaran, for example, measures 36 times that of the sun.

Medium-sized stars, commonly called *main-sequence* or *dwarf* stars, are about as large as the sun. Their diameters vary from about a tenth that of the sun to about 10 times the sun's diameter. Well-known stars in this group include Altair, Sirius, and Vega.

White dwarfs are small stars. The smallest white dwarf, van Maanen's Star, has a diameter of 5,200 miles (8,370 kilometers)—less than the distance across Asia.

Neutron stars are the tiniest stars. They have as much mass as the sun, but are so compact that they are only about 12 miles (20 kilometers) in diameter. Some send out short bursts of radio waves at regular intervals. These rapidly spinning neutron stars are called *pulsars.*

The distance of stars. The sun is about 93 million miles (150 million kilometers) from the earth. The star nearest the sun, Proxima Centauri, seems like only a pinpoint of light because it is about 25 million million miles (40 million million kilometers) from the earth.

Astronomers measure the distance between stars in units called *light-years.* For example, Proxima Centauri is 4.3 light-years from the sun. A light-year equals 5.88 million million miles (9.46 million million kilometers). This is the distance light travels in one year at a speed of 186,282 miles (299,792 kilometers) per second. Some stars in the Milky Way are as far as 80,000 light-years from the sun and the earth.

The Milky Way's closest "neighbor" is a galaxy 200,000 light-years away. The most distant stars are in galaxies billions of light-years away from the Milky Way.

The sun lies about 25,000 light-years from the center of the Milky Way. It belongs to a part of the Galaxy where the distance between stars averages 4 to 5 light-years. In some other parts of the Milky Way, the stars are much closer. In globular clusters, for example, less than one-hundredth of a light-year separates the stars.

Why stars shine. A star's energy source lies deep within it. There, hydrogen nuclei change into helium nuclei through a process called *nuclear fusion.* During this process, the mass of helium produced does not wholly equal the mass of hydrogen used up. Some of the material that makes up the original hydrogen changes into energy rather than into helium.

Nuclear fusion creates so much energy that the temperature at the center of the star reaches millions of degrees. The energy eventually escapes from the star in the form of light. Most stars have enough hydrogen to shine steadily for billions of years. When a star has used up a large portion of the hydrogen in its center, it begins to change rapidly. A star such as the sun will swell up to become a red giant, then slowly lose material and shrink to become a white dwarf.

Color, temperature, and brightness. Starlight has a variety of color. Rigel sparkles with blue light and Vega seems white. Capella's gleam looks yellow and Betelgeuse glows red. Others have in-between colors, such as blue-white Sirius and orange-red Arcturus.

A star's color indicates the temperature of its surface. This temperature varies from about 5000° F. (2800° C) for red stars, such as Betelgeuse, to about 50,000° F. (28,000° C) for blue stars, such as Rigel. Stars of other colors have surface temperatures somewhere in between. The sun, a yellowish star, has a temperature of about 10,000° F. (5500° C).

The stars that appear the brightest are not always the largest nor the nearest to the earth. Brightness also depends on the amount of light energy that a star sends out. Rigel is smaller and farther from the earth than is Betelgeuse. But because it is much hotter, Rigel sends out more light energy and looks brighter than Betelgeuse.

Star motions. Every day, the sun and all the other stars seem to move across the sky, rising in the east and setting in the west. The rising and setting comes from the spinning of the earth, not from the motion of the stars. See **Earth** (How the earth moves).

Stars do move, but a star's motion produces only a slight change in its position among other stars. Astronomers measure this change, called *proper motion,* by comparing photographs taken at regular intervals. Barnard's Star has the greatest known proper motion. It

National Optical Astronomy Observatories

A *globular cluster, above,* is a ball-like star cluster that consists of thousands of stars. Irregularly shaped star clusters, called *open clusters,* have from 10 to a few hundred stars.

The Milky Way galaxy

The Milky Way is one of more than a billion groups of stars called *galaxies* that are found throughout the universe. The Milky Way is a *spiral galaxy,* with bright arms curving out from its central disk. The sun and its planets—including the earth—are part of the Milky Way.

WORLD BOOK illustration by Anne Norcia

Sun

takes 180 years for this star to move half a degree—an angle equal to the diameter of the moon as seen from the earth. The closer a star is to the earth, the easier it is for astronomers to measure its proper motion. However, most stars are so far away that their proper motion is too small to be measured.

The sun itself moves at a speed of 12 miles (19 kilometers) per second through the Milky Way. In addition, the sun and all the other stars of the Milky Way orbit the center of the Galaxy. This spinning motion of the Milky Way gives the sun and the stars near it a speed of 156 miles (250 kilometers) per second. It takes about 250 million years for the sun to make one trip around the center of the Galaxy.

Star groups. The Milky Way has more than 100 billion stars. Many of these stars are in smaller groups called star clouds and star clusters. Pairs of stars are called double stars.

Star clouds look like bright, hazy areas when seen without a telescope. The brightness comes from the millions of stars that make up these areas. Such clouds form a background against which astronomers can see dark clouds of *interstellar* (between-the-stars) dust.

Star clusters may be either ball-like or of irregular shapes. Ball-like clusters, called *globular clusters,* contain from 10,000 to a million stars densely packed together by their shared gravitation. About 100 globular clusters lie around the center of the Milky Way. The stars in globular clusters are among the oldest in our galaxy. Irregularly shaped clusters, called *open clusters* or *galactic clusters,* have from 10 to a few hundred stars.

They lie within the main "pancake" of the Milky Way. They include some of the youngest stars in our galaxy.

Double stars, also called *binaries,* consist of a pair of stars that orbit each other and are held together by gravity. Many double stars belong to larger groups that include other double stars and single stars. Such groups are called *multiple stars.* Double stars are especially important because the *masses* of such stars can be determined by measuring their orbits. The mass of a star is the amount of matter it contains.

See **Star** in *World Book* for more information on the following topics:

- How people use the stars
- Kinds of stars
- How stars produce energy
- The birth and death of a star
- Studying the stars

E. R. Degginger   E. R. Degginger   © G. I. Bernard, NHPA

Plant stems can be divided into two kinds, *herbaceous* and *woody.* Herbaceous stems, like those of the orchid, *left,* and the rose, *center,* have soft tissue and produce small plants. A woody stem, like that of the atlas cedar, *right,* has hard, tough tissue. Trees and shrubs have woody stems.

Stem is the part of a plant that produces and supports buds, leaves, flowers, and fruit. Most stems hold the leaves in a position to receive sunlight needed to manufacture food. The stem also carries water and minerals from the roots to the leaves for use in food production. The sugar made in the leaves is conducted by the stem to other parts of the plant.

All plants have stems except liverworts, hornworts, and mosses. But the stems of various kinds of plants differ greatly in size and appearance. For example, lettuce plants have very short stems that are barely visible under the large leaves. California redwood trees have huge stems—their trunks—that may grow 12 feet (3.7 meters) wide and over 350 feet (107 meters) high.

Most stems grow erect above the ground. A few

kinds grow underground or horizontally along the ground. Buds develop on the stem at points called *nodes* and produce branches, leaves, or flowers. The space between each node is called an *internode.*

There are two chief kinds of stems, *herbaceous stems* and *woody stems.* Herbaceous stems have soft tissues, produce small plants, and grow very little in diameter. Most herbaceous stems live only one growing season. Such plants as alfalfa, clover, and garden peas have herbaceous stems.

Woody stems are hard and thick. They have tough, woody tissues and may live for hundreds of years. Each growing season, woody stems develop new tissues that cause them to grow in diameter. Trees and shrubs have woody stems.

The structure of stems The various kinds of stems differ in structure. Herbaceous stems have only *primary tissues,* which develop from cell division at the tip of the stem. Woody stems have both primary and *secondary tissues.* Secondary tissues cause woody stems to develop wood and bark and to grow thicker. The diagrams below show the internal structures of the herbaceous stems and of a woody stem.

WORLD BOOK diagrams by Marion Pahl

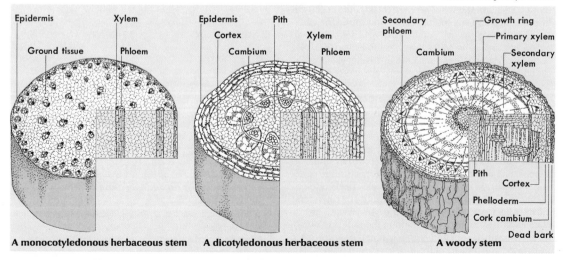

A monocotyledonous herbaceous stem   **A dicotyledonous herbaceous stem**   **A woody stem**

Steve Terrill

The sun is only one of billions of stars in the universe. But it is more important to us than any other object in the sky. All life on earth depends on the energy released by the sun as heat and light. The sun gets its enormous energy from nuclear reactions near its center.

Sun

Sun is a huge, glowing ball of gases at the center of the solar system. The earth and the other eight planets travel around it. The sun is only one of billions of stars in the universe. As a star, there is nothing unusual about it. But the sun is more important to people than any other star. Without the heat and light of the sun, there could be no life on the earth.

The *diameter* (distance through the center) of the sun is about 865,000 miles (1,392,000 kilometers), about 109 times the diameter of the earth. Because the sun is about 93 million miles (150 million kilometers) from the earth, it does not appear larger than the moon. But the sun's diameter is 400 times as large as that of the moon. The sun is also almost 400 times farther from the earth than is the moon.

If the sun were the size of a skyscraper, the earth would be the size of a person. The moon would be the size of a cocker spaniel standing next to the person. Jupiter, the largest planet, would be the size of a small building. The nearest star also would be about the size of a skyscraper. But it would be about 7 million miles (11 million kilometers) away.

The sun is nearer the earth than is any other star. For this reason, scientists study the sun to learn about stars much farther away. The visible surface of the sun consists of hot gases that give off light and heat. Only about one two-billionth of the sun's light and heat reaches the earth. The rest of the light and heat is lost in space.

The temperature of any place on the earth depends on the position of the sun in the sky. The temperature greatly affects the weather of a region. Tropical regions near the equator have a hot climate because the sun shines almost directly overhead at noon. Regions near the North Pole and the South Pole have a cold climate because the sun never rises far above the horizon.

The Egyptians, Greeks, and many other ancient peoples thought the sun was a god. They worshiped the sun, made offerings to it, and built temples to honor it. Many early beliefs about the sun began when people tried to explain the sun's movement across the sky.

Today, we know we must have the sun as a source of heat, light, and other kinds of energy. All life on the earth—people, animals, and plants—depends on this energy from the sun. Plants use sunlight to make their own food and in the process give off oxygen. People and animals eat the plants and breathe in the oxygen. In turn, people and animals breathe out carbon dioxide, which plants combine with energy from sunlight and water from the soil to produce more food.

Scientists estimate that the sun and the rest of the objects in the solar system are about 4,600,000,000 years old. They believe that the sun will continue to be a source of energy for at least another 5 billion years.

The sun at a glance

Distance from the earth: *Shortest*—about 91,400,000 miles (147,100,000 kilometers); *Greatest*—about 94,500,000 miles (152,100,000 kilometers); *Mean*—about 93 million miles (150 million kilometers). Sunlight takes about 8 minutes and 20 seconds to reach the earth, traveling at 186,282 miles (299,792 kilometers) per second.
Diameter: About 865,000 miles (1,392,000 kilometers), approximately 109 times that of the earth.
Volume: About 1,300,000 times that of the earth.
Mass: 99.8 per cent of the mass of the solar system; about 333,000 times that of the earth.
Temperature: *Surface*—about 10,000° F. (5500° C); *Center*—about 27,000,000° F. (15,000,000° C).
Age: About 4,600,000,000 years.
Rotation period: About 1 month.
Revolution period in the Milky Way: About 225 million years.
Chemical makeup: Hydrogen, about 75 per cent; helium, almost 25 per cent; at least 70 other elements make up the remaining 1 to 2 per cent.
Density: *Convection zone*—about $\frac{1}{10}$ that of water; *Radiative zone*—about equal to that of water; *Core*—about 100 times that of water.

    The size of the sun. The sun is closer to the earth than is any other star, and so it looks larger than other stars. Compared with the planets in the solar system, the sun is large. For example, the diameter of the sun is about 865,000 miles (1,392,000 kilometers). This distance is about 109 times the diameter of the earth. The sun's diameter is also nearly 10 times the diameter of Jupiter, the largest planet, and about 400 times the diameter of the moon.
    Compared with other stars, the sun is only medium-sized. In fact, it is one of many stars that astronomers call *yellow dwarfs.* Some stars have a diameter 10 times as small as that of the sun. Other stars have a diameter as large as 1,000 times that of the sun. Astronomers call these huge stars *supergiants.* One supergiant, Betelgeuse, has a diameter that is about 460 times that of the sun. If the sun grew to be the size of Betelgeuse, it would swallow up Mercury, Venus, Earth, and Mars.
    From the earth, the sun looks like a circle. Astronomers often use the term *disk* for the part of the sun that can be seen from the earth. Some astronomers have measured the disk and found that it is slightly flattened in some places. But other astronomers are not certain how correct these measurements are.
    Distance to the sun. The earth's distance from the sun varies from about 91,400,000 to 94,500,000 miles (147,100,000 to 152,100,000 kilometers). This distance varies because the earth travels around the sun in an orbit that has an *elliptical* (oval) shape. The average distance between the earth and the sun is about 93 million miles (150 million kilometers).
    Suppose that the orbit of the earth were the same as the orbit of Venus. The earth would then be so close to the sun that it would be too hot to support life as we know it. Now suppose that the orbit of the earth were the same as the orbit of Mars. The earth would then be so far away from the sun that it would probably be too cold to support anything but the sturdiest and simplest forms of life.
    Light travels at a speed of 186,282 miles (299,792 kilo-

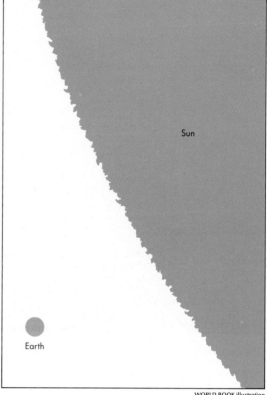

WORLD BOOK illustration
The sun is the largest object in the solar system. Its diameter is about 109 times the diameter of the earth, and its volume is about 1,300,000 times that of the earth.

meters) per second. At this speed, light from the sun takes about 8 minutes and 20 seconds to reach the earth. When a spacecraft is escaping from the pull of the earth's gravity, it must travel at a speed of 25,000 miles (40,200 kilometers) per hour. If the spacecraft could maintain this speed on a journey to the sun—and not burn up—the trip would take 154 days, or slightly longer than five months.
    The sun's brightness. The light and heat of the sun come from its surface. The amount of light and heat stays fairly constant, so that the actual brightness of the sun changes little. The changes in brightness that seem to take place result from weather conditions in the earth's atmosphere. These conditions affect the amount of sunlight that reaches any particular place on the earth. Sometimes a small increase in brightness may result from eruptions of gases on the sun's surface. Most of these eruptions, called *flares,* last from 10 minutes to an hour. But any changes in the total brightness of the sun caused by flares are not visible to the naked eye.
    Sunlight contains all the colors of the rainbow. These colors blend to form white light, and so sunlight is white (see **Color** [The relation between color and light]). But at times, some of the colors become scattered. We see only the remaining colors, and the sunlight appears colored. For example, when the sun appears high in the

sky, some of the blue light rays are scattered in the earth's atmosphere. At such times, the sky looks blue and the sun appears to be yellow. At sunrise or sunset, the sun is near the horizon and the light must follow a longer path through the earth's atmosphere. As a result, more of the blue and green rays are scattered in the atmosphere, and the sun looks red. On rare occasions, the sun may look bright green for a moment when only an edge is visible above the horizon. This *green flash* occurs because the red rays of light are hidden below the horizon and the blue rays are scattered in the atmosphere.

The sun's heat. Of course, astronomers cannot measure the sun's temperature directly. They have determined it from indirect measurements on sunlight and from mathematical equations that are based on known physical laws. Astronomers estimate that the temperature at the center of the sun reaches about 27,000,000° F. (15,000,000° C).

The sun's energy is produced at its center. This energy gradually flows to the surface. Midway between the sun's interior and its surface, the sun's temperature is approximately 4,500,000° F. (2,500,000° C). The temperature decreases to about 10,000° F. (5500° C) at the surface of the sun.

When the energy produced at the sun's center reaches the surface, it is sent out into space as radiant energy in the form of heat and light. People once thought this heat and light came from something that was burning. Today, scientists know that the sun's light and heat come from *thermonuclear reactions* in the center of the sun. Such reactions occur when lightweight atoms join and form heavier atoms. For more information about the thermonuclear reactions of the sun, see the **Sun** article in *World Book.*

The sun's mass makes up 99.8 per cent of the mass of the entire solar system (in *World Book,* see **Mass**). The mass of the sun is about 1,047 times that of Jupiter, the largest planet in the solar system. The sun's mass is about 333,000 times that of the earth.

Because the sun is so massive, the force of gravity at its surface is much greater than the force of gravity at the surface of any of the planets. As a result, objects would weigh more on the sun than they would on any planet. A person who weighs 100 pounds (45 kilograms) on the earth would weigh about 2,800 pounds (1,270 kilograms) on the sun.

Through the force of gravity, the sun controls the orbits of the planets. The force of gravity also pulls the sun's gases toward the center of the sun. If there were nothing to balance the force of gravity on the sun, the sun would collapse. But it does not collapse because its gases are extremely hot. Hot gases have high pressure and try to expand. The pressure of the gases balances the force of gravity. As a result, the sun keeps its size and shape.

What the sun is made of. About three-fourths of the mass of the sun consists of hydrogen, the lightest known element. Almost a fourth of the sun's mass consists of helium. Scientists discovered this gas on the sun before they found it on the earth. The word *helium* comes from a Greek word meaning *sun.*

Of the 109 known elements, 91 occur naturally in or on the earth. The other elements are artificially created. At least 70 of the earth's natural elements have been found on the sun. But all these elements—except hydrogen and helium—make up only between 1 and 2 per cent of the mass of the sun. Scientists were able to identify the elements on the sun by studying the *spectrum* (pattern of colored lines) of light from the sun (in *World Book,* see **Light** [Electromagnetic waves]).

How the sun moves. Like the earth, the sun spins like a top. And, just as the earth revolves around the sun, the sun revolves around the center of the Milky Way galaxy.

The earth takes a day to rotate once on its *axis,* an imaginary line through the North and South poles. But the sun takes about a month to spin around once on the axis through its poles. The regions near the sun's equator rotate once in a few days less than a month. The regions near the sun's poles take a few days more than a month to spin around once. The difference in the rates of rotation is made possible by the sun's being a ball of gases. If the sun were a solid body, it could not rotate at different rates in different parts.

The earth takes a year to revolve around the sun, but the sun takes about 225 million years to make one revolution around the center of the Milky Way. During this period, the sun travels about 10 billion times as far as the distance between it and the earth.

Sun terms

Chromosphere is the middle region of the sun's atmosphere.
Convection zone is the outermost third of the sun's interior. It ends just below the sun's surface.
Core is the center of the sun, the region in which nuclear reactions produce the sun's energy.
Corona is the region of the sun's atmosphere above the chromosphere.
Coronal holes are regions of relatively low temperature and density in the corona. They are the chief source of solar wind.
Disk is the part of the sun that can be seen from the earth.
Faculae, flocculi, or plages are particularly bright patches of gas in the upper photosphere and in the chromosphere. They appear above groups of sunspots.
Flares are bursts of light on the sun's surface. They release huge amounts of the sun's energy.
Granules are small patches of gas that make up the photosphere of the sun.
Photosphere is the visible surface of the sun, the innermost part of the sun's atmosphere.
Prominences are huge, bright arches of gas that rise from the edge of the disk and flow back into the sun.
Radiative zone is the middle third of the sun's interior.
Solar radiation is the sun's energy given off as light and heat and in other forms, including radio waves, ultraviolet rays, and X rays.
Solar wind is the expansion of gases from the sun's corona.
Spicules are streams of gas that shoot up briefly from the chromosphere.
Sunspots are dark patches on the sun's surface that appear and disappear in regular cycles. A complete sunspot cycle consists of two 11-year periods of sunspot activity.
Thermonuclear fusion is a type of nuclear reaction that produces the sun's energy. It occurs when the nuclei of two hydrogen atoms combine to form the nucleus of a helium atom.

Heat and light for life. All life on the earth depends on the sun for heat and light. The steady flow of heat and light from the sun made possible the development of life on the earth. If the sun's heat and light were to vary significantly, life would be endangered. Sometimes the earth would be too hot for life to exist, and sometimes it would be too cold.

The earth's atmosphere helps trap the heat of the sun. The atmosphere lets sunlight through to the surface of the earth. The light warms the earth, but the heat it creates cannot easily pass through the atmosphere into space. As a result, the earth is warmed by the sun. This behavior of the atmosphere is called the *greenhouse effect* because it resembles the action of a greenhouse. A greenhouse lets sunlight in to heat the plants, but the heat passes back through the roof and walls very slowly. (In *World Book,* see **Greenhouse effect.**

Life also depends on the sun for food. All living things—both plants and animals—are part of a process called the *food chain.* The food chain starts with green plants. These plants make their own food through the process of *photosynthesis.* During photosynthesis, plants combine energy from sunlight with carbon dioxide from the air and water from the soil to make food. In the process, the plants give off oxygen. Some plants are eaten by animals, which in turn are eaten by larger animals. People eat both animals and plants. Human beings and animals breathe the oxygen that the plants release during photosynthesis. They exhale the carbon dioxide that, in turn, is used by plants.

Sunlight can also be harmful. Too much strong sunlight can burn the skin. The sun can seriously injure the eyes if a person looks at it directly.

Weather. Sunlight has a great influence on the earth's weather. For example, it evaporates water from rivers, lakes, and oceans, and this water later falls as rain or snow. When the water is suspended in the atmosphere, clouds appear. They reflect sunlight back into space. Sunlight also comes to the earth at various angles during different seasons. Clouds, and the angle at which sunlight reaches the earth, result in uneven heating of the earth's atmosphere. This uneven heating causes differences in air pressure. Air moves from high pressure areas to low pressure areas, causing wind and changes in weather. See **Weather.**

The sun as an energy source. Until human beings learned to develop nuclear energy, sunlight supplied their energy needs. Plants used sunlight for photosynthesis. Animals ate the plants, and people used both plants and animals for food, clothing, and shelter.

People also use the energy in *fossil fuels*—coal, oil, and natural gas. These fuels come from plants and animals that lived millions of years ago. After the plants and animals died, they were buried by soil in swamplands or on the sea floor. By burning coal, and by refining oil and natural gas, energy is released from the sun that was stored in the fossils millions of years ago.

In addition, people use sunlight for power in other ways. For example, the effects of sunlight cause wind, which some people use to power windmills. Sunlight also evaporates water, which falls as rain. The rain forms rivers. Hydroelectric power plants on the rivers use the power of moving water to generate electricity. Solar furnaces use mirrors to focus sunlight to heat water in boilers. Solar energy cells provide power for artificial satellites and spacecraft. See **Solar energy.**

The greenhouse effect

The atmosphere of the earth traps heat from the sun, much as a greenhouse does. The greenhouse lets sunlight in to heat the plants, but it prevents much of the heat from getting out. In a similar way, the atmosphere lets sunlight through to the surface of the earth. The sunlight warms the earth, but the heat that is created cannot easily pass back through the atmosphere into space.

WORLD BOOK diagram by Herb Herrick

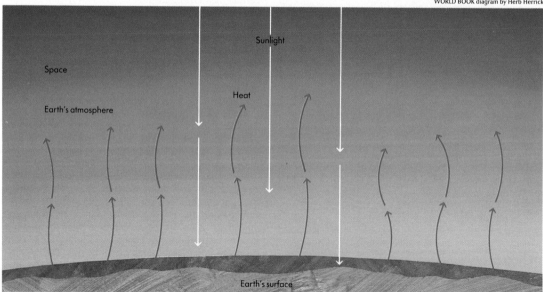

The sun's interior. The inner third of the interior of the sun is called the sun's *core.* The temperature in the core is about 27,000,000° F. (15,000,000° C). The material that makes up the core is more than 100 times as dense as water, but it still consists of gases (in *World Book,* see **Density**). Thermonuclear reactions, which produce the sun's light and heat, occur in the core.

Beyond the core is the *radiative zone,* which extends through about the middle third of the sun's interior. In the radiative zone, the average temperature is about 4,500,000° F. (2,500,000° C), and the gases are about as dense as water. The parts of the radiative zone that are nearer the sun's surface are cooler than those that are closer to the sun's core. Because radiant heat normally flows from a hot place to a cooler one, the energy produced in the sun's core flows through the radiative zone, toward the surface of the sun. This outward flow of heat is called *radiation.*

The *convection zone* begins about two-thirds of the way from the center of the sun and ends about 137 miles (220 kilometers) below the sun's surface. The temperature in this zone is about 2,000,000° F. (1,100,000° C), and the gases are about a tenth as dense as water. The gases are so cloudy that energy from the sun's core cannot travel through the convection zone by radiation. In-stead, the energy causes the gases to undergo violent churning motions called *convection* and *turbulence.* These motions carry most of the sun's energy to the surface.

The sun's surface, or *photosphere,* is about 340 miles (547 kilometers) thick, and its temperature is about 10,000° F. (5500° C). The photosphere is actually the innermost layer of the sun's atmosphere. It is from one-millionth to 1 ten-millionth as dense as water.

The photosphere contains many small patches of gas called *granules.* A typical granule lasts only 5 to 10 minutes, and then it fades away. As old granules fade away, the sun's surface becomes marked with new ones. Scientists believe the granules are produced by the violent churning of the gases in the convection zone.

The photosphere also has dark spots called *sunspots.* See the **Sun** article in *World Book* for more information on sunspots.

The photosphere gives off the sun's energy in the form of heat and light. The sunlight given off by the photosphere is made up of many colors. These colors are not all equally bright. Various elements in the photosphere absorb some of the colors and prevent the sun from giving off those colors. Scientists can see what colors are absorbed by passing sunlight through a glass

Inside the sun

Beneath the sun's *photosphere* (surface) are the violently churning convection zone, the radiative zone, and the core, where the sun's energy is produced. This energy flows from the core to the photosphere and then out into space as radiant heat and light.

WORLD BOOK diagram by Herb Herrick

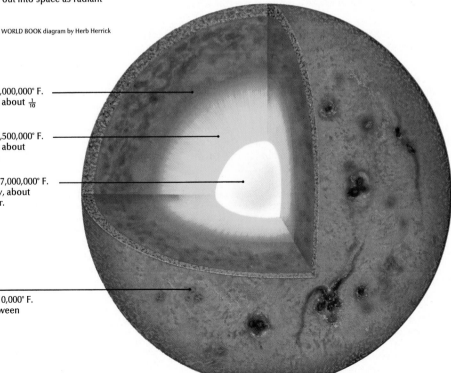

Convection zone
Temperature, about 2,000,000° F. (1,100,000° C). Density, about $\frac{1}{10}$ that of water.

Radiative zone
Temperature, about 4,500,000° F. (2,500,000° C). Density, about equal to that of water.

Core
Temperature, about 27,000,000° F. (15,000,000° C). Density, about 100 times that of water.

Photosphere
Temperature, about 10,000° F. (5500° C). Density, between $\frac{1}{1,000,000}$ and $\frac{1}{10,000,000}$ that of water.

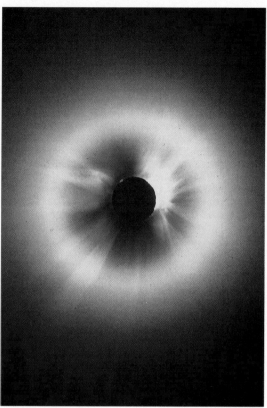

NASA

Los Alamos Scientific Laboratory

The sun's corona, the outer edge of its atmosphere, can be studied during a solar eclipse. The sun showed little activity during the eclipse at the left. However, in the eclipse at the right, it displayed prominences and possible *coronal holes,* regions of lower temperature and density.

prism to form a spectrum. Where light has been absorbed, dark lines appear on the spectrum. These lines are called *Fraunhofer lines,* after Joseph von Fraunhofer, a German physicist who studied them during the early 1800's. Each element has its own characteristic pattern of Fraunhofer lines. Astronomers learned what elements are on the sun by comparing the Fraunhofer lines of the sun's spectrum with the lines that various elements show in laboratory experiments.

In photographs of the sun, the region near the edge of the disk does not appear so bright as the central region. This effect is called *limb darkening.* It occurs because light from the central region follows a more direct path to the earth than does light from the edge of the disk. As a result, less of the central light is absorbed by the sun's gases, and more light from deep within the photosphere can be seen. The deeper gases are hotter than those near the surface, and the hotter gases give off brighter light.

Above the surface. About 100 miles (160 kilometers) above the photosphere, the temperature is about 7200° F. (4000° C). Above this point, the temperature rises again. In the *chromosphere* (the middle region of the sun's atmosphere), the temperature reaches about 50,000° F. (27,800° C).

The chromosphere consists of hot gas in violent motion. Some of the gas forms streams called *spicules* that measure as much as 500 miles (800 kilometers) thick and shoot up as high as 10,000 miles (16,000 kilometers). A spicule lasts up to 15 minutes.

The temperature of the sun's atmosphere climbs rapidly above the chromosphere. A region above the chromosphere called the *corona* has an average temperature of about 4,000,000° F. (2,200,000° C). The atoms of the corona are so far apart that the gases of the corona have little heat. If it were possible for an astronaut to be in the corona and shielded from the direct rays of the sun, the astronaut's space suit would have to be heated.

The temperature drops slowly from the corona outward into space. The corona has no well-defined boundary. Its gases expand constantly away from the sun. This expansion of its gases is called *solar wind.*

See **Sun** in *World Book* for more information on the following topics:

- People and the sun
- The sun as a star
- How the sun produces energy
- The sun's stormy activity
- Studying the sun

Swan is a water bird closely related to ducks and geese. Like ducks and geese, swans have a flattened bill; a long neck; water-repellent feathers; long, pointed wings; a short tail; short legs; and webbed feet. But most swans are larger and have a much longer neck than ducks or geese.

Swans nest on all continents except Africa and Antarctica. They live chiefly in regions with a mild or cold climate. Their webbed feet make swans good swimmers, but they also walk well on land. Swans make several vocal sounds, from whistles to trumpetlike calls. Most swans have white feathers. Male swans are called *cobs*, females are called *pens*, and their offspring are called *cygnets*.

Habits. Most swans nest along the shores of marshes and ponds in the summer. They move to large lakes and bays in the winter. Swans feed mostly on underwater plants. Because of their long necks, they can graze in much deeper water than ducks. Swans also eat grasses along the shore. Occasionally, they eat grain in upland fields.

When they are 2 or 3 years old, swans choose mates during highly vocal courtship displays. In one such display, called the *triumph ceremony,* the male and female face each other, raise their wings, and call loudly. Mated swans usually stay together for life. Some swans in captivity have lived more than 50 years.

Swans use grasses and other plant material to build large nests. The female usually lays four to six whitish eggs. Among most swans, only the female sits on the eggs to keep them warm. But the male black swan shares this duty with the female. The eggs must be warmed 30 to 35 days before they hatch. During this period, swans will attack foxes, dogs, people, and any other possible threats to their eggs. When cygnets hatch, they are covered with grayish-white down. They soon grow their flight feathers and can fly at 7 to 14 weeks of age. Small cygnets may ride on their parents' backs. Swans have strong family ties. The young may remain with their parents until it is time to choose a mate.

See **Swan** in *World Book* for more information on Kinds of swans.

The swan swims and flies gracefully, though it is one of the largest birds. Its beauty has inspired composers, painters, and writers. Four of the seven species of swans are shown below.

Black-necked swan
Cygnus melanocoryphus
Found in South America
Body length: 45 inches
(114 centimeters)

Black swan
Cygnus atratus
Found in Australia
Body length: 40 inches
(100 centimeters)

Mute swan
Cygnus olor
Found in temperate Eurasia
Body length: 60 inches
(150 centimeters)

Tundra swan
Cygnus columbianus
Found in North American and Eurasian tundras
Body length: 52 inches
(132 centimeters)

WORLD BOOK illustrations by Walter Linsenmaier

Teeth

Teeth are hard, bonelike structures in the upper and lower jaws of human beings and many kinds of animals. They are the hardest parts of the body.

People use their teeth chiefly to chew food. Chewing is the first step in the process of *digestion.* Digestion begins as the teeth chop and grind chunks of food into smaller pieces. As the teeth chew the food, it is mixed with *saliva,* a liquid produced in the mouth. The food becomes a moist pulp, which is easy to swallow. The food is further broken down in the stomach and the small intestine, where it is absorbed by the blood. The blood carries the digested food to all parts of the body. Without teeth, people could not eat foods that must be chewed. They could only swallow soft foods and liquids.

Teeth also play an important part in speech. The teeth and tongue are used together to form many sounds that make up words. To produce the *th* sound, for example, the tip of the tongue is placed against the upper front teeth. A person who lacks these teeth may be unable to make the sound.

Teeth also help support the muscles around the mouth and so contribute to a person's appearance. People who have lost their teeth lack this support. Unless they wear artificial teeth, they may have deep, saggy lines around the mouth.

Like human beings, most animals use their teeth to chew food. They also use their teeth to obtain food. Many animals that eat plants tear off the leaves or stalks of the plants with their teeth. Most meat-eating animals use their teeth to seize and kill prey.

Kinds of teeth

Human beings grow two sets of teeth: (1) deciduous teeth and (2) permanent teeth. The individual deciduous teeth appear and fall out gradually early in life. They are replaced, one by one, by the permanent teeth. See the table *Ages at which teeth appear* for the times the various kinds of teeth generally appear.

Deciduous and permanent teeth have the same basic structure. Each tooth has a *crown* and one or more *roots.* The crown is the part of the tooth that can be seen in the mouth. The root or roots are covered by the bone and gums. The roots hold the tooth in a socket in the jawbone.

Deciduous teeth are also called *baby teeth, milk teeth,* or *primary teeth.* They start to form about $7\frac{1}{2}$ months before a baby is born. They begin as oval or round swellings called *buds,* which gradually develop into teeth. When a baby is born, parts of all the deciduous teeth are present deep within the jaws. As the teeth grow, they push through the gums. This process is called *eruption* or *teething.* Babies begin to teethe at about 6 to 9 months of age. Most children have all their deciduous teeth by about 2 years of age.

There are 20 deciduous teeth, 10 in each jaw. They consist of three kinds of teeth: (1) incisors, (2) canines, and (3) molars. Each jaw has 4 incisors, 2 canines, and 4 molars. The incisors and canines are used to bite into food, and the molars to grind food. The positions of these teeth in the mouth are shown in the illustration *Kinds of teeth.*

The deciduous teeth help the permanent teeth erupt in their normal positions. Most of the permanent teeth form near the roots of the deciduous teeth. When a child is about 3 years old, the roots of various deciduous teeth begin to dissolve slowly. By the time a permanent tooth is ready to erupt, the root of the deciduous tooth has completely dissolved. The crown of the tooth then becomes loose and falls out.

Permanent teeth, like deciduous teeth, begin to develop before birth. But most of their growth occurs after birth. The permanent teeth begin to erupt after the deciduous teeth start to fall out.

The first permanent teeth appear when a child is about 6 or 7 years old. Between the ages of 6 and 12, a child has some permanent and some deciduous teeth in the mouth. The last permanent teeth erupt when a person is 17 to 21 years old.

There are 32 permanent teeth, 16 in each jaw. They are larger than the deciduous teeth and consist of four kinds of teeth. The four kinds are (1) incisors, (2) canines, (3) premolars, and (4) molars. Each jaw has 4 incisors, 2 canines, 4 premolars, and 6 molars. The following discussion describes the four kinds of permanent teeth. Their positions in the mouth are shown in the illustration *Kinds of teeth.*

Incisors are the chief biting teeth. They have a sharp, straight cutting edge. In most cases, incisors have one root. The central incisors of the lower jaw are the smallest permanent teeth.

Canines are used with the incisors to bite into food. They are also used to tear off pieces of food. The name for these teeth comes from another word for *dog*—that is, *canine.* The canine teeth resemble a dog's fangs. They have a sharp, pointed edge and one root. Canines are

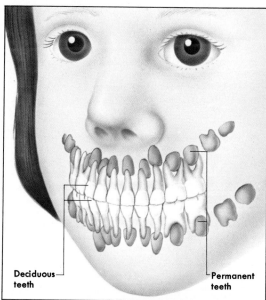

WORLD BOOK diagram by Charles Wellek

The teeth of a child. By the time a child is about 4 years old, most of the permanent teeth have formed within the jaws near the roots of the deciduous teeth. The deciduous teeth, all of which have erupted by about age 2, will gradually fall out and be replaced, one by one, by the permanent teeth.

Kinds of teeth

The illustrations below show the kinds of deciduous and permanent teeth and their positions in the mouth.

WORLD BOOK diagrams by Charles Wellek

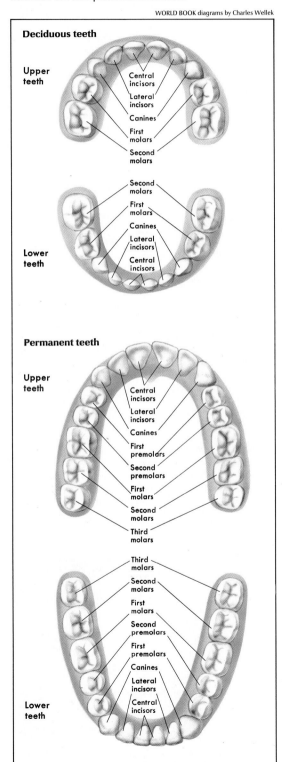

Deciduous teeth

Upper teeth
- Central incisors
- Lateral incisors
- Canines
- First molars
- Second molars

Lower teeth
- Second molars
- First molars
- Canines
- Lateral incisors
- Central incisors

Permanent teeth

Upper teeth
- Central incisors
- Lateral incisors
- Canines
- First premolars
- Second premolars
- First molars
- Second molars
- Third molars

Lower teeth
- Third molars
- Second molars
- First molars
- Second premolars
- First premolars
- Canines
- Lateral incisors
- Central incisors

Ages at which teeth appear*

Deciduous teeth:	Lower teeth	Upper teeth
Central incisors	6 months	7 months
Lateral incisors	7 months	9 months
Canines	16 months	18 months
First molars	12 months	14 months
Second molars	20 months	24 months
Permanent teeth:	**Lower teeth**	**Upper teeth**
Central incisors	6-7 years	7-8 years
Lateral incisors	7-8 years	8-9 years
Canines	9-10 years	11-12 years
First premolars	10-12 years	10-11 years
Second premolars	11-12 years	10-12 years
First molars	6-7 years	6-7 years
Second molars	11-13 years	12-13 years
Third molars	17-21 years	17-21 years

* The ages given are approximate. In many cases, individual teeth may erupt at an earlier or later age.

also called *cuspids* or *dogteeth*. The upper canines are sometimes known as *eyeteeth*.

Premolars are used to crush and grind food. They have a broad, lumpy top instead of a sharp biting edge. The small surface lumps are called *cusps*. The cusps enable the teeth to mash pieces of food.

Premolars are sometimes called *bicuspids* because, in most cases, they have two cusps. The prefix *bi* means *two*. The first upper premolars normally have two roots. The other premolars have one root. The premolars erupt in the place of the deciduous molars.

Molars, like premolars, are used to grind food. They are shaped much like premolars but are larger. The various molars normally have three to five cusps and two or three roots.

The permanent molars do not form beneath any of the deciduous teeth. They develop as the jaws grow, which makes space for them. Some adults lack one or more of the third molars, which are commonly called *wisdom teeth*. In many cases, the jaws do not grow large enough to provide space for the wisdom teeth. As a result, the wisdom teeth may become *impacted*—that is, wedged between the jawbone and another tooth. The wisdom teeth must then be removed.

Parts of a tooth

A tooth consists of four kinds of tissues. They are (1) pulp, (2) dentin, (3) enamel, and (4) cementum. Connective tissue surrounds the root of the tooth. This tissue, called the *periodontal ligament,* holds the root in the socket in the jaw.

Pulp is the innermost layer of a tooth. It consists of connective tissue, blood vessels, and nerves. The blood vessels nourish the tooth. The nerves transmit sensations of pain to the brain.

The pulp has two parts, the *pulp chamber* and the *root canal.* The pulp chamber lies in the crown of the tooth. The root canal lies in the root of the tooth. Blood vessels and nerves enter the root canal through a small hole at the tip of the root. They extend through the root canal and into the pulp chamber.

Dentin is a hard, yellow substance that surrounds the pulp. It makes up most of a tooth. Dentin is harder than bone. It consists mainly of mineral salts and water but also has some living cells.

Parts of a tooth

The *crown,* or visible part of a molar tooth, includes projections called *cusps.* The *root* extends into the bone of the jaw. A tissue called *dentin* makes up most of the tooth. A layer of *enamel* covers the dentin of the crown, and *cementum* overlies the dentin of the root. Within the dentin lies the *pulp,* including the *pulp chamber* and the *root canal,* through which blood vessels and nerves enter the tooth. The *periodontal ligament* surrounds the root and holds the tooth in its socket.

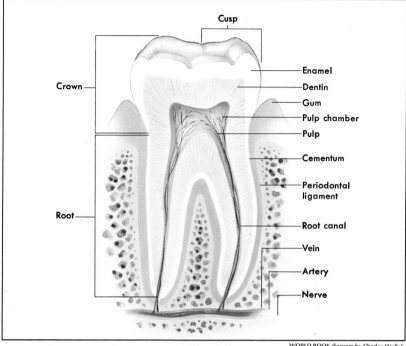

WORLD BOOK diagram by Charles Wellek

Filling a cavity

These illustrations show how a dentist fills a cavity. The dentist usually begins by injecting a drug called an *anesthetic* into the gums near the tooth. The anesthetic prevents the patient from feeling the pain that drilling might produce.

WORLD BOOK diagrams by Charles Wellek

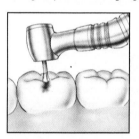

Drilling. The dentist uses a drill to remove decayed and soft parts of the tooth and to form undercuts or ledges that will help hold the filling.

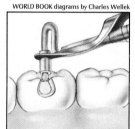

Filling. An instrument is used to place filling material into the hole. Silver amalgam, made from silver, copper, and tin, is a commonly used filling.

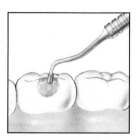

Packing. Using another instrument, the dentist firmly packs the filling into the hole. The filling is then allowed to harden slightly.

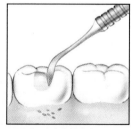

Shaping. The dentist carefully carves the filling to restore the original shape of the tooth. Finally, any rough edges are smoothed down.

Enamel overlies the dentin in the crown of the tooth. It forms the outermost covering of the crown. Enamel is the hardest tissue in the body. It enables a tooth to withstand the pressure placed on it during chewing. Enamel consists of mineral salts and a small amount of water. Enamel is white but transparent. The yellow color of the dentin shows through the enamel, and so most teeth appear slightly yellowish.

As a person grows older, small amounts of enamel begin to wear away. This process, called *attrition,* results from the use of the teeth over a long period. As the enamel wears away, the dentin becomes exposed.

Cementum overlies the dentin in the root of the tooth. In most cases, the cementum and enamel meet where the root ends and the crown begins. As the surface of the tooth wears away, the tooth grows farther

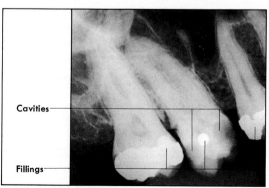

Patrick D. Toto

An X ray of the teeth shows cavities and fillings. Cavities appear as dark spots. Fillings show up as distinct white areas.

out of its socket, exposing the root. These areas may then become more sensitive to hot and cold liquids. Cementum is about as hard as bone. Like dentin and enamel, it consists mainly of mineral salts and water.

Periodontal ligament consists of small fibers. These fibers extend through the cementum and into the bony socket, which is called the *alveolus*. Besides anchoring the tooth in the alveolus, the periodontal ligament serves as a shock absorber during chewing.

Teeth of animals

Many kinds of animals have teeth. However, birds, toads, turtles, and some types of insects and whales do not have teeth.

Cats, dogs, and most other mammals have *heterodont teeth*—that is, they have at least two types of teeth, which have different uses. For example, they may have incisors for biting into food and molars for crushing or grinding food.

The teeth of various kinds of mammals differ in shape and size, depending chiefly on what the animals eat. For example, plant-eating mammals, such as elephants, giraffes, and sheep, have unusually broad, flat molars. They use the molars to chew and mash plants. Meat-eating mammals, such as lions, tigers, and wolves, have long, pointed canines. They use the canines to rip and tear the bodies of their prey.

Some mammals have teeth that grow continuously. The tusks of elephants are actually incisors that have become very long. The tusks have an open pulp, which enables them to keep growing. Beavers, rats, and other rodents also have teeth that grow continuously. But most of the growth is worn down by continual use of the teeth, and so the teeth of these animals do not lengthen greatly.

Unlike most mammals, many fish and most reptiles have *homodont teeth*—that is, all their teeth are about the same size and shape and have only one use. In general, animals that have homodont teeth use their teeth to catch prey. Fish and reptiles lose and replace their teeth continuously.

Snakes have teeth that curve back toward the throat. Snakes swallow their prey whole and use their teeth to pull the prey back into the throat. In poisonous snakes, certain teeth have a canal or a groove, through which poison can be ejected. The poison comes from glands in the roof of the mouth.

See **Teeth** in *World Book* for more information on Care of the teeth and gums and Diseases and defects of the teeth.

Some animal teeth   Animal teeth vary in size and shape. Most mammals have *heterodont teeth,* which consist of two or more types: incisors and canines for biting and tearing food, and molars for crushing it. Most reptiles and many fish have *homodont teeth,* a single type that generally is used to catch prey.

WORLD BOOK diagrams by Patricia J. Wynne

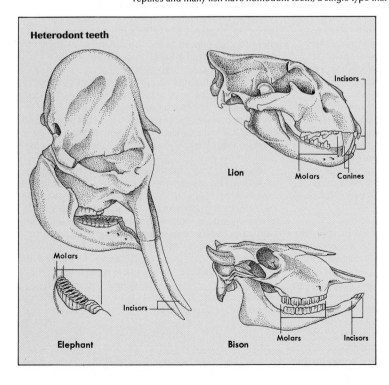

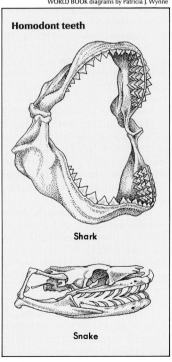

The Olympic Games; Eiji Miyazawa, Black Star

Sports events

"Sesame Street"; Children's Television Workshop

Learning and fun for children

WMAQ-TV (WORLD BOOK photo by Steve Hale)

The latest news

"Wheel of Fortune" (Merv Griffin Enterprises)

Game shows

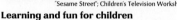

Television is sometimes called "the device that brings the world into the home." TV provides millions of home viewers with a wide variety of entertainment, information, and special events. The pictures on this and the following page show some examples of television's far-reaching coverage.

Television

Television, also called TV, is one of our most important means of communication. It brings pictures and sounds from around the world into millions of homes. People with a television set can sit at home and watch the President make a speech or visit a foreign country. They can see a war being fought, and they can watch government leaders try to bring about peace. Through television, viewers can see and learn about people, places, and things in faraway lands. Television even takes viewers out of this world with coverage of America's astronauts as the astronauts explore outer space.

In addition to all these things, television brings its viewers a steady stream of programs that are designed to entertain. In fact, TV provides many more entertainment programs than any other kind. The programs include action-packed dramas; light comedies; soap operas; sporting events; cartoon, quiz, and variety shows; and motion pictures.

About 89 million homes in the United States—or about 97 per cent of all the country's homes—have at least one TV set. About 60 per cent of American homes have two or more TV's. Altogether, there are about 214 million sets in the United States. On the average, a TV set is in use in each home for about 7 hours each day. As a result, TV has an important influence on how people spend their time and on what they see and learn.

Because of its great popularity, television has become a major way to reach people with advertising messages. Most TV stations carry hundreds of commercials each day. In the mid-1980's, about $24 billion a year was spent on television advertising in the United States. The use of television advertising has greatly changed the process of getting elected to public office in the United States. Before TV, candidates relied chiefly on public appearances to urge people to vote for them. Today, most candidates for high office reach many more people through TV than they reach in person.

The name *television* comes from a Greek word meaning *far* and a Latin word meaning *to see.* Thus, *television* means *to see far.* Most pictures and sounds received by a television set are beamed from a television station on electronic signals called *electromagnetic waves.* The television set changes these waves back into pictures and sounds.

Many scientists contributed to the development of television, and no one person can be called its inventor. Experiments leading to the invention of TV began in the 1800's, but progress was slow. Television as we know it today was not developed until the 1920's, and it had little importance in communication until the late 1940's. But during one 10-year period—the 1950's—it became part of most households in the United States. Since then, television has gained importance in most other countries. In addition, many organizations, including businesses, hospitals, and schools, now use television for their own special purposes.

A person looking directly at a scene sees the entire view all at once. But television cannot send a picture of an entire scene all at once. It can send only one tiny part of the picture after another until it has sent the complete picture. A TV camera divides a picture into several hundred thousand tiny parts by a process called *scanning*. As the camera scans the picture, it creates electronic signals from each part of the picture.

A TV set uses these signals in re-creating the picture on its screen. The scanning process puts the picture back together piece by piece. A person watching TV does not realize this is happening. The process works so quickly that the viewer sees only a complete picture.

Sending television pictures and sounds involves three basic steps. (1) The light and sound waves from the scene being televised must be changed into electronic signals. (2) These signals must be transmitted to the television receiver. (3) The receiver must unscramble the signals and change them back into copies of the light and sound waves that came from the original scene.

Creating television signals

A television signal begins when light from the scene being televised enters a television camera. The camera changes the light into electronic signals. At the same time, a microphone picks up the sounds from the scene and changes them into electronic signals. Television engineers call the signals from a camera *video* and the signals from a microphone *audio*.

The television camera. In producing a compatible color signal, the TV camera must: (1) capture the image of the scene being telecast; (2) create video signals from the image; and (3) encode the color signals for transmission. To perform these tasks, a television camera uses a lens, a system of mirrors and filters, camera tubes, and complex electronic circuits. Some of the electronic circuits used by the camera are located elsewhere in the TV station and connected to the camera by wires.

Capturing the image. The lens gathers the *image* (picture) of the scene in front of the camera. Like the lenses in other cameras and the human eye, the TV lens *focuses* (collects and bends) the light from the scene in order to form a sharp image. This image contains all the colors of the scene. However, in order to produce color signals, the camera must split the full-color image into three separate images—one for each of the *primary colors* (red, blue, and green).

Creating the video signals. A camera tube changes the light image into video signals. A black-and-white camera has only one camera tube. Most high-quality color cameras have three such tubes, which are improved versions of a tube called the *vidicon*.

A vidicon tube has a glass *faceplate* at its front end. In back of the faceplate is a transparent coating called the *signal plate*. A second plate, called the *target*, lies behind the signal plate. The target consists of a layer of *photoconductive material* that conducts electricity when exposed to light. At the rear of the tube is a device called an *electron gun*.

Light from the image reaches the target after passing through the faceplate and the signal plate. The light causes negatively charged particles called *electrons* in the photoconductive material to move toward the signal plate. This movement leaves the back of the target with a positive electric charge. The strength of the positive charge on any area of the target corresponds to the brightness of the light shining on that area. The camera tube thus changes the light image gathered by the lens into an identical electric image of positive charges on the back of the target.

The electron gun shoots a beam of electrons across the back of the target. The beam moves across the target in an orderly pattern called a *scanning pattern*. As the beam moves across the target, it strikes areas with different amounts of positive charge. Areas of the target that have the strongest charge attract the most electrons from the beam. This occurs because particles of unlike electric charge attract each other. Other areas of the target attract fewer electrons. The electrons from the beam move through the target and cause an electric current to flow in the signal plate. The voltage of this current changes from moment to moment, depending on whether the beam is striking a bright or dim part of the image. This changing voltage is the video signal from that camera tube.

The electron gun scans the target much as a person reads—from left to right, top to bottom. But unlike the way a person reads, the electron beam skips every other line on the target. After the beam scans the top line, it quickly snaps back to the left. Then, it scans the third line, fifth line, and so on. When the beam reaches the bottom of the target, it snaps back and then scans line two, line four, line six, and so on.

The scanning pattern of TV cameras in the United States is made up of 525 lines ($262\frac{1}{2}$ odd-numbered and $262\frac{1}{2}$ even-numbered lines). The beam completes the scanning of one *field* each time it scans $262\frac{1}{2}$ lines. Two fields make up a complete television picture, called a *frame*. The electron beam moves with such extreme speed that it produces 30 complete frames in a second. This speed is fast enough so the television picture shows moving objects smoothly.

Transmitting television signals

Most television signals are broadcast through the air. Engineers at a television station use a device called a transmitter to produce a TV signal from separate audio and video signals. The signal is then carried by wire to an antenna and broadcast. The signal is called an *electromagnetic wave*. Such waves can travel through the air at the speed of light, about 186,282 miles (299,792 kilometers) per second. But the signal can be received clearly only up to a distance of about 150 miles (241 kilometers). To send TV signals farther, other means of transmitting must be used. These include coaxial cable and fiber optic cable, microwaves, and satellites.

Broadcasting. Before a television signal is broadcast, the transmitter boosts its *frequency* (rate of vibration). A television signal needs a high frequency to carry the picture information through the air. The transmitter amplifies the signal so it has enough power to reach a large area.

Coaxial cable and fiber optic cable are used to carry television signals for long distances or to areas that have difficulty receiving signals. The television networks often send programs to their affiliated stations throughout the country through coaxial cables. The affiliates then broadcast the programs to their viewers.

How color television is transmitted

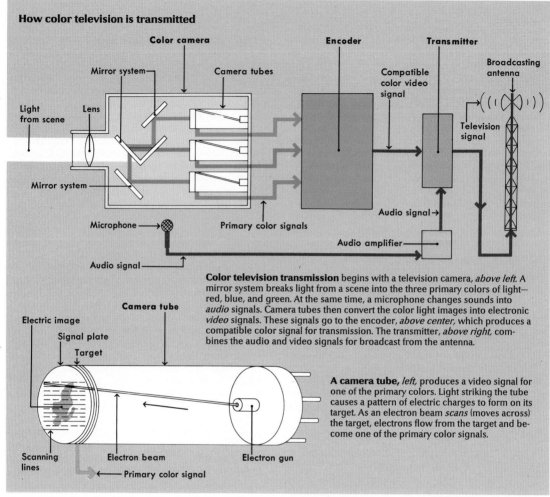

Color television transmission begins with a television camera, *above left.* A mirror system breaks light from a scene into the three primary colors of light—red, blue, and green. At the same time, a microphone changes sounds into *audio* signals. Camera tubes then convert the color light images into electronic *video* signals. These signals go to the encoder, *above center,* which produces a compatible color signal for transmission. The transmitter, *above right,* combines the audio and video signals for broadcast from the antenna.

A camera tube, *left,* produces a video signal for one of the primary colors. Light striking the tube causes a pattern of electric charges to form on its target. As an electron beam *scans* (moves across) the target, electrons flow from the target and become one of the primary color signals.

WORLD BOOK diagram by Mas Nakagawa

Cable television systems use coaxial or fiber optic cables to carry signals to the homes of persons who subscribe to the service.

Microwaves are electromagnetic waves, similar to television signals. Tall relay towers spaced about 30 miles (48 kilometers) apart across the country carry programs from the networks to affiliate stations on these waves. Equipment in a tower automatically receives, amplifies, and then retransmits the microwave signal to the next tower. The affiliate stations change the microwave signals back into TV signals.

Satellites carry television signals between stations where cables or microwave towers cannot be built. For example, satellites relay signals across oceans. Satellites work like relay towers in space. They receive coded TV signals from a special earth station, amplify them, and send them on to another earth station. The two stations may be thousands of miles or kilometers apart.

Receiving television signals

The television signal from a transmitter is fed into a home television set through a *receiving antenna* or *aerial.* The set uses the signal to make copies of the pic-

tures and sounds from the televised scene. In reproducing the television program, a TV set uses a tuner, amplifiers and separators, and a picture tube.

Receiving antenna. A good antenna collects a strong enough television signal for the receiver to produce a picture. A simple indoor antenna, commonly called *rabbit ears*, picks up a strong enough signal within a few miles or kilometers of the transmitter. At greater distances, a more elaborate antenna mounted on the roof may be needed. The best reception results when the antenna is pointed toward the desired station. Some antennas can be rotated by remote control to align them with widely separated stations.

Tuner. Signals from the antenna are fed into the set's tuner. The tuner selects only the signal from the station the viewer wants to receive. It shuts out all others. Most TV sets have two tuning devices. One device selects the VHF channels, 2 through 13, and the other device selects the UHF channels, 14 through 69.

Amplifiers and separators. From the tuner, the television signal goes to a group of complicated electronic circuits in the set. These circuits amplify the signal and separate the audio and video portions of it. The audio

How color television is received

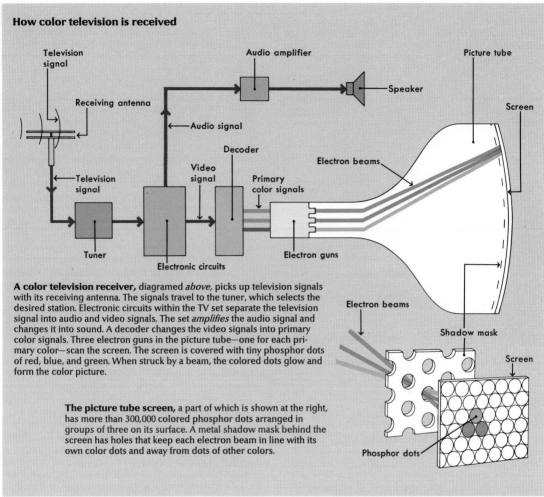

A color television receiver, diagramed *above,* picks up television signals with its receiving antenna. The signals travel to the tuner, which selects the desired station. Electronic circuits within the TV set separate the television signal into audio and video signals. The set *amplifies* the audio signal and changes it into sound. A decoder changes the video signals into primary color signals. Three electron guns in the picture tube—one for each primary color—scan the screen. The screen is covered with tiny phosphor dots of red, blue, and green. When struck by a beam, the colored dots glow and form the color picture.

The picture tube screen, a part of which is shown at the right, has more than 300,000 colored phosphor dots arranged in groups of three on its surface. A metal shadow mask behind the screen has holes that keep each electron beam in line with its own color dots and away from dots of other colors.

WORLD BOOK diagram by Mas Nakagawa

signals are changed into sound waves by the speaker. The video signals go to the *picture tube,* or *kinescope,* where they re-create the picture.

A color set has circuits that use the color burst to separate the video signal into the two chrominance signals and the luminance signal. Another group of circuits, called the *decoder* or *matrix,* transforms these signals into red, blue, and green signals that duplicate the signals from the three camera tubes.

The picture tube transforms the video signals into patterns of light that duplicate the scene in front of the camera. One end of the picture tube is rectangular and nearly flat. This end forms the screen of the television set. Inside the set, the picture tube tapers to a narrow neck. The neck of a color picture tube holds three electron guns—one each for the red, blue, and green signals. A black-and-white tube has only one electron gun.

Each electron gun in a color picture tube shoots a separate beam of electrons at the screen. Each beam scans the screen just as the beam in each camera tube scanned its target. The synchronization signal, which is a part of the video signal, ensures that the picture tube's scanning pattern follows exactly the pattern used by the

camera. The beams must be in step with each other in order to produce a picture.

The screen of most color tubes is coated with more than 300,000 tiny phosphor dots. The dots are grouped in triangular arrangements of three dots each—one red, one blue, and one green. These dots glow with their respective color when struck by an electron beam. A metal plate perforated with thousands of tiny holes lies about $\frac{1}{2}$ inch (13 millimeters) behind the screen of a color tube. This plate is called the *shadow mask.* Its holes keep the beams from hitting any color dots but their own.

See **Television** in *World Book* for more information on the following topics:

- Uses of television
- Producing television programs
- The television industry
- Effects of television
- How television works
- Government regulations
- Television in other lands
- History

Ylla, Rapho Guillumette

The tiger's coloration helps conceal the animal in its natural surroundings. This female tiger could easily go unseen because her stripes blend with the tall grasses.

Tiger is the largest member of the cat family. People admire the tiger for its strength and beauty, but they fear it because it has been known to kill and eat human beings. Yet almost all wild tigers avoid people. Probably only 3 or 4 of every 1,000 tigers ever eat people, and some of these are sick or wounded animals that can no longer hunt large prey.

Wild tigers are found only in Asia. Until the 1800's, many lived throughout most of the southern half of the continent. Tigers still live in some of this area, but only a few are left. People have greatly reduced the number of tigers by hunting them and by clearing the forests in which they lived. Today, wildlife experts consider the tiger an endangered species. In the past, wild tigers were captured for zoos. Today, enough tigers for zoos are born in captivity.

The body of a tiger. Adult male tigers weigh about 420 pounds (191 kilograms) and are 9 feet (2.7 meters) long, including a 3-foot (0.9-meter) tail. Tigresses weigh about 300 pounds (136 kilograms) and are 8 feet (2.4 me-

ters) long. The tiger's coat ranges from brownish-yellow to orange-red and is marked by black stripes. The stripes vary greatly in length, width, and spacing. The fur on the throat, belly, and insides of the legs is whitish. Many tigers have a ruff of hair around the sides of the head, but the hair is not so long as the mane of lions. The tigers of Manchuria, where the winters are bitter cold, have long, shaggy, winter coats.

The tiger looks different from the lion because of its stripes and more colorful coat. But the two animals have similar bodies. In fact, tigers and lions have mated in zoos. The offspring are called *tiglons, tigons,* or *ligers.*

See **Tiger** in *World Book* for more information on How a tiger hunts and The life of a tiger.

Facts in brief

Names: *Male,* tiger; *female,* tigress; *young,* cub.
Gestation period: 98 to 109 days.
Number of newborn: 1 to 6, usually 2 or 3.
Length of life: Up to 20 years.
Where found: Chiefly in Bangladesh, India, Nepal, and Southeast Asia, including Sumatra; also a few in China, Iran, Java, and Korea, and along the Siberian-Manchurian border.
Scientific classification: Tigers belong to the class Mammalia and the order Carnivora. They are in the cat family, Felidae, and the genus *Panthera.* All tigers are of the same species, *P. Tigris.*

The skeleton of a tiger

WORLD BOOK diagram

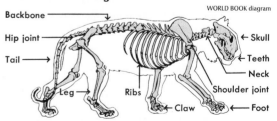

Backbone — Hip joint — Tail — Leg — Ribs — Claw — Skull — Teeth — Neck — Shoulder joint — Foot

Tiger tracks

← Front feet
Hind feet →

Tornado is a powerful, twisting windstorm. The winds of a tornado are the most violent winds that occur on the earth. They whirl around the center of the storm at speeds of more than 200 miles (320 kilometers) per hour. Most tornadoes measure several hundred yards or meters in diameter, and many have caused widespread death and destruction.

A tornado is a rotating funnel cloud that extends downward from a mass of dark clouds. Some funnels do not reach the earth. Others may strike the surface of the earth, withdraw into the dark clouds above, and then dip down and strike the earth again. In the United States, most funnel clouds tend to travel toward the northeast.

The winds of a tornado whirl in a counterclockwise direction in the Northern Hemisphere and clockwise in the Southern Hemisphere. People in some regions call a tornado a *twister* or a *cyclone*. A tornado that occurs over a lake or ocean is called a *waterspout*.

Most tornadoes last less than an hour. These storms travel a distance of about 20 miles (32 kilometers) at a speed of 10 to 25 miles (16 to 40 kilometers) per hour. Some tornadoes last several hours and measure up to 1$\frac{1}{2}$ miles (2.4 kilometers) in diameter. They may travel 200 miles (320 kilometers) or more at a speed of up to 60 miles (97 kilometers) per hour. Such tornadoes are especially destructive.

The greatest killer tornado in history roared through Missouri, Illinois, and Indiana on March 18, 1925, and killed 689 persons. This tornado was one of the largest and fastest tornadoes ever recorded. Its path measured about 220 miles (354 kilometers) long and up to a mile (1.6 kilometers) wide. The storm traveled at a speed of about 60 miles (97 kilometers) per hour.

The story of a tornado. Most tornadoes in the United States strike the Midwest and the states that border the Gulf of Mexico. Scientists do not know exactly why tornadoes develop.

Most tornadoes form along a *front* (boundary) between cool, dry air from the north and warm, humid air from the Gulf of Mexico. A narrow zone of *cumulonimbus* (thunderstorm) clouds develops along such a front.

This zone of clouds, called a *squall line,* produces violent weather.

The violent weather produced by a squall line results when a mass of warm, humid air rises extremely rapidly. As this air rises, more warm air rushes in to replace it. The inrushing air also rises and, in some cases, begins to rotate. The rotating air then forms into a tornado.

Most tornadoes occur in spring on a hot, humid day in the afternoon or in the early evening. Large thunderclouds appear in the sky, and thunder begins to rumble in the distance. A nearby cloud becomes dark and dense. Rounded masses at the bottom of the cloud start to twist. One of the twisting masses then forms a funnel cloud that gradually extends downward. Heavy rain and some hail begin to fall, and flashes of lightning occur. A hissing sound begins as the funnel cloud extends toward the earth. If the funnel touches the ground, it stirs up dirt and debris. The hissing becomes a loud roar.

The violent, rotating winds of a tornado blow down almost everything in its path. In addition to the force of the wind, the explosive force of a tornado can demolish a small building. It does so primarily by causing a difference in air pressure between the inside and outside of the building. When a tornado passes over a house, it sucks up air from around the structure. The air pressure outside the house drops suddenly, but the air pressure inside remains the same. As a result, the pressure inside the house is greater than that outside. Because the pressure difference cannot equalize quickly enough, the building explodes outward.

The tremendous lifting force of a tornado results from a powerful updraft of air inside the funnel. Tornadoes have uprooted large trees, overturned railroad cars, and carried such heavy objects as automobiles hundreds of feet or meters.

See **Tornado** in *World Book* for more information on Protection against tornadoes.

Where tornadoes occur

Tornadoes frequently hit the Midwestern and Southern States. The Western States have few tornadoes. The map shows the number of tornadoes that occurred in each region during a 12-year period.

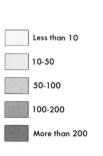

Less than 10

10-50

50-100

100-200

More than 200

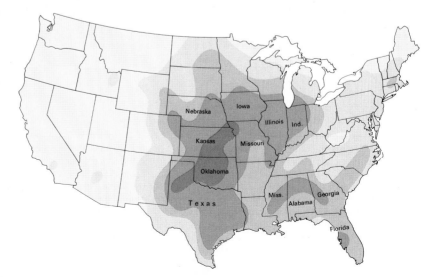

WORLD BOOK map

David Muench

The magnificent giant sequoias of California rank among the world's oldest and largest living things. Some of these trees are thousands of years old and over 200 feet (61 meters) tall.

Tree

Tree is the largest of all plants. The tallest trees grow higher than 30-story buildings. Many trees also live longer than other plants. Some trees live for thousands of years. They are the oldest known living things.

People do not think of trees the way they think of other plants, most of which grow only a short time and then die. People think of trees as permanent parts of the landscape. Year after year, large, old trees shade houses and streets from the sun. Their buds and flowers are a sign of spring each year, and their colorful leaves brighten in autumn in many areas.

Trees continue to grow as long as they live. A tree's leaves make food that keeps the tree alive and helps it grow. Where winters are cold, many trees lose their leaves in autumn. Other trees keep their leaves during the winter and so stay green all year long. Trees that shed their leaves in autumn rest during the winter. In spring, they grow new leaves and flowers. The flowers grow into fruits, which contain seeds for making new trees. Some tree fruits, such as apples and oranges, taste good. Fruit growers raise large amounts of these fruits for sale. Trees also make new wood each year

Theodore F. Welch, Van Cleve Photography

Dwarf trees never reach full size. Some, such as this miniature cypress tree, are deliberately kept small by a special pruning process. But many dwarf trees grow naturally in arctic regions.

WORLD BOOK illustration by James Teason

Coconut

Coconut palm

The coconut palm provides wood and other building materials. The tree's nuts provide sweet-tasting milk and meat. Oil from dried coconut meat is used in making such products as margarine and soap.

Interesting facts about trees

The world's largest living thing is the General Sherman Tree, a giant sequoia in Sequoia National Park in California. It towers more than 275 feet (83.8 meters) and has a trunk about 37 feet (11 meters) wide. It probably dates from before 200 B.C.

The traveler's-tree, which grows in Madagascar, stores up to 1 pint (0.5 liter) of water inside the base of each of its long leaf stalks. The tree received its name because it provides thirsty travelers with fresh drinking water.

Traveler's-tree

The tallest trees are California's redwoods, which may tower more than 360 feet (110 meters). Australia's eucalyptuses may grow more than 300 feet (91 meters) tall.

The thickest tree trunk is that of a Montezuma baldcypress near Oaxaca, Mexico. Its diameter exceeds 40 feet (12 meters).

The baobab tree of Africa is one of the most useful trees. It has a huge trunk, which people hollow out to store water in or to live in. They eat the tree's leaves, fruit, seeds, and roots and use its parts in many other ways.

Baobab

The oldest trees are California's bristlecone pines and giant sequoias. Some bristlecone pines have lived between 4,000 and 5,000 years. The oldest sequoias are about 3,500 years old.

The banyan tree of India spreads by growing trunklike roots from its branches. In time, a banyan may cover acres of ground.

The ombu tree of Argentina is one of the hardiest trees. It can live with little water and can survive insect attacks, violent storms, and intense heat. The tree's wood is so moist it will not burn and so spongy it cannot be cut down.

Ombu

The largest seeds are the nuts of the coco-de-mer, or double coconut palm, of the Seychelles, an island group in the Indian Ocean. A nut may weigh up to 50 pounds (23 kilograms).

when the weather turns warmer. Wood is one of the most valuable parts of a tree. Mills and factories use wood to manufacture lumber, paper, and many other products.

A tree differs from other plants in four main ways. (1) Most trees grow at least 15 to 20 feet (4.6 to 6.1 meters) tall. (2) They have one woody stem, which is called a *trunk.* (3) The stem grows at least 3 to 4 inches (8 to 10 centimeters) thick. (4) A tree's stem can stand by itself. All other plants differ from trees in at least one of these ways. For example, no plant with a soft, juicy stem is a tree. Most of these plants, called *herbs,* are much shorter than most trees. *Shrubs,* like trees, have woody stems. But most shrubs have more than one stem, and

none of the stems grows so thick or so tall as a tree trunk. Some jungle *vines* grow more than 200 feet (61 meters) long and have a woody stem. But the stems of most vines cannot support themselves.

There are thousands of kinds of trees. But most trees belong to one of two main groups—the broadleaf trees and the needleleaf trees. These two types of trees grow in Europe, North America, and many other parts of the world. Most other types of trees, such as palms and tree ferns, grow mainly in warm regions.

Kinds of trees

There are about 20,000 kinds of trees. More than 1,000 kinds grow in the United States. They range from mighty forest trees to fragile ornamentals. The greatest variety of trees grow in wet tropical regions.

Scientists who study plants divide plants with similar characteristics into various groups. These scientists, called *botanists,* do not put trees in a separate group of plants. Instead, each kind of tree is grouped with other plants that have certain features in common with it. Therefore, a group of plants may include certain trees, certain shrubs or vines, and certain herbs. For example, locust trees, broom plants, and clover all belong to the same *family.* These plants are grouped together because they reproduce in the same way and have similar flowers. On the other hand, some trees that look much alike, such as tree ferns and palms, belong to different groups of plants.

Trees also can be divided into six groups according to various features they have in common. These six groups are: (1) broadleaf trees; (2) needleleaf trees; (3) palm, pandanus, and lily trees; (4) cycad trees; (5) tree ferns; and (6) ginkgo trees.

The six main groups of trees

Trees can be divided into the six main groups illustrated below. All the trees in each group are similar in appearance and have other features in common.

Silver maple
Fruit   Leaf

Broadleaf trees are known for their autumn colors, bare winter branches, and spring flowers, which develop into fruits.

Red, or Norway, pine
Needles and cone

Needleleaf trees have needlelike or scalelike leaves and bear their seeds in cones. Most are evergreen.

Royal palm
Fruit

Palms and pandanus and lily trees form a group of mainly tropical trees. Most palms have huge leaves and no branches.

South African cycad
Leaves and cones

Cycad trees live only in warm, moist regions. They bear heavy cones that may grow 3 feet (91 centimeters) long.

West Indies tree fern
Leaflet and spore cases

Tree ferns are the only trees that have no flowers, fruits, or seeds. They reproduce by means of *spores.*

Seeds   Ginkgo   Leaf

WORLD BOOK illustrations by James Teason

Ginkgo trees are a single species. They bear seeds but not fruits or cones. The seeds have an unpleasant odor.

A tree has three main parts: (1) the trunk and branches; (2) the leaves; and (3) the roots. The branches and leaves together are called the *crown*. The trunk supports the crown and holds it up to the sunlight. Tree ferns, cycads, and most palms have no branches. Their crowns consist only of leaves. The roots of most trees are hidden in the ground, but they may take up as much space as the trunk and crown do above the ground. Other important parts of a tree include the seeds and the seed-forming structures.

Trunk and branches give a tree its shape. The trunks of most needleleaf trees grow straight up to the top of the tree. The branches grow out from the trunk. On most needleleaf trees, the branches near the top are shorter than those farther down, which gives the crown a spirelike shape. The trunks of most broadleaf trees do not reach to the top of the tree. Instead, the trunk divides into spreading branches near the base of the crown, giving the crown a rounded shape. The trunks of

a few broadleaf trees, such as black willows and white poplars, sometimes divide so close to the ground that the trees seem to have more than one trunk.

The trunks, branches, and roots of broadleaf and needleleaf trees consist of four layers of plant tissue wrapped around one another. These layers, from innermost to outermost, are: (1) the *xylem,* (2) the *cambium,* (3) the *phloem,* and (4) the *cork.*

The xylem is the woody, central part of the trunk. It has tiny pipelines that carry water with a small amount of dissolved minerals from the roots to the leaves. This water is called *sap.* The cambium, which surrounds the xylem, is a thin layer of growing tissue. Its job is to make the trunk, branches, and roots grow thicker. The phloem, also called the *inner bark,* is a layer of soft tissue surrounding the cambium. Like the xylem, the phloem has tiny pipelines. The food made by the leaves moves through the phloem to the other parts of a tree. In palms and tree ferns, the xylem and phloem are not

Parts of a tree

These diagrams show the three main parts of a tree: (1) the leaves, (2) the trunk and branches, and (3) the roots. The branches and leaves together make up a tree's *crown.* The diagrams also show the main types of tissue that compose most trees.

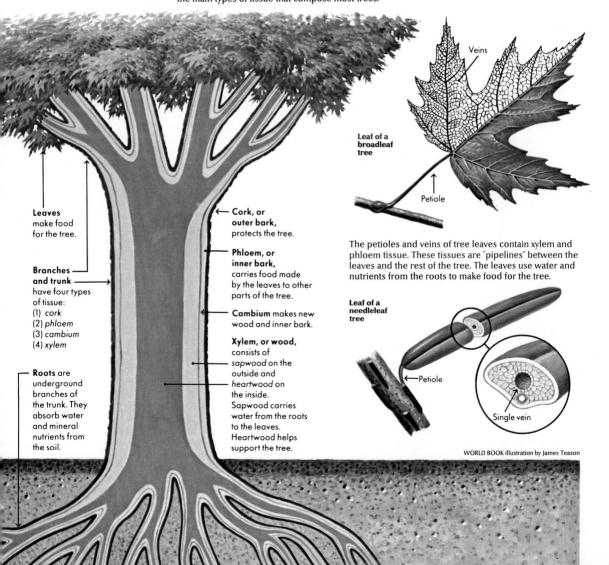

Veins

Leaf of a broadleaf tree

Petiole

Leaves make food for the tree.

Branches and trunk have four types of tissue:
(1) *cork*
(2) *phloem*
(3) *cambium*
(4) *xylem*

Roots are underground branches of the trunk. They absorb water and mineral nutrients from the soil.

← **Cork, or outer bark,** protects the tree.

Phloem, or inner bark, carries food made by the leaves to other parts of the tree.

Cambium makes new wood and inner bark.

Xylem, or wood, consists of *sapwood* on the outside and *heartwood* on the inside. Sapwood carries water from the roots to the leaves. Heartwood helps support the tree.

The petioles and veins of tree leaves contain xylem and phloem tissue. These tissues are "pipelines" between the leaves and the rest of the tree. The leaves use water and nutrients from the roots to make food for the tree.

Leaf of a needleleaf tree

Petiole

Single vein

WORLD BOOK illustration by James Teason

Seeds of broadleaf and needleleaf trees

Cherry   Elm   Walnut

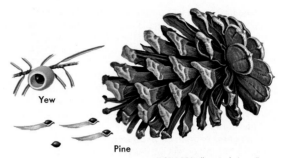

Yew   Pine

WORLD BOOK illustration by James Teason

Seeds of broadleaf trees, or *angiosperm seeds,* have protective coverings. The seed and covering together are called a fruit. Cherry and walnut seeds are enclosed in a pit or shell with a fleshy outer covering. Elm seeds have thin, winged coverings.

Seeds of needleleaf trees, or *gymnosperm seeds,* do not have protective coverings. The seeds of most needleleaf trees lie in cones and are released after the cones ripen. The yew and a few other coneless needleleaf trees have berrylike seeds.

separate layers. Instead, bits of xylem and phloem are connected and form small double pipelines scattered throughout the trunk.

The cork layer is the *outer bark* of a tree. It forms a "skin" of hard, dead tissue that protects the living inner parts from injury. The bark stretches to let the trunk and branches grow thicker. The bark of some trees, such as beeches and birches, is smooth because it stretches easily. But the bark of most other trees does not stretch so well. As the trunk and branches grow thicker, they push against the bark. It finally cracks and dries and so becomes grooved and rough. Most trees replace old bark from time to time with a new layer.

Leaves of various species of trees differ greatly in size and shape. Palms have leaves over 20 feet (6 meters) long. The leaves of some needleleaf trees are less than $\frac{1}{2}$ inch (13 millimeters) long. Some broadleaf trees have *compound leaves* made up of small leaflets.

The main job of the leaves is to make food for the tree. Every leaf has one or more *veins,* which consist of xylem and phloem tissue. The tissue that surrounds the veins contains tiny green bodies called *chloroplasts.* Water from the roots passes through the xylem of the trunk, branches, and leaves to the chloroplasts, which use the water to make food sugar. Only a small amount of the water carried to the leaves is used to make sugar. The leaves lose most of the water to the atmosphere through *transpiration* (evaporation). Like the water and dissolved minerals carried from the roots, the food made by the leaves is also called *sap.* It travels through the phloem of the leaves, branches, and trunk to parts of the tree where it is needed.

Almost all leaves are green in the spring and summer. Their color comes from chlorophyll, a green substance in the chloroplasts. Most trees also have reds and yellows in their leaves. But the green conceals these colors. In late summer and early autumn, the chlorophyll in the leaves of many broadleaf trees breaks down. The leaves then die. But before the leaves fall, they reveal their hidden reds and yellows. After the chlorophyll breaks down, the leaves of many trees also develop scarlets and purples.

Roots are long, underground branches of the trunk. They have the same layers of tissue as the trunk. The roots anchor a tree in the ground and absorb water with dissolved minerals from the soil. The main roots branch out into small roots, which, in turn, branch out into still

smaller roots. The main roots of most trees begin to branch out 1 or 2 feet (30 or 61 centimeters) under the ground. Some trees have one main root larger than the others. This root, called a *taproot,* extends straight down 15 feet (5 meters) or more.

A tree develops millions of small roots. Each root grows longer at its tip, which is as small as a thread. As a root tip grows, it pushes through particles of soil. Thousands of fine, white *root hairs* grow just back of the root tip. When the tip comes in contact with drops of water in the soil, the hairs soak up the water and dissolved minerals. The xylem layer of the roots, trunk, and branches carries this sap to the leaves.

Seeds are the means by which all trees except tree ferns reproduce. Tree ferns reproduce by spores.

Angiosperms—broadleaf trees and palm, pandanus, and lily trees—produce seeds by means of flowers. Some broadleaf trees, such as horsechestnuts and magnolias, produce large, showy flowers. Many others have small, plain-looking flowers. Most palm, pandanus, and lily trees have small flowers that grow in bunches. Sometimes these are brightly colored and fragrant.

The seeds of angiosperms are enclosed to form a fruit. The fruits of some broadleaf trees, such as apples and cherries, have a fleshy outer covering. The fruits of other broadleaf trees, including acorns and beechnuts, are hard nuts. Ashes, elms, and maples have thin, winged fruits. Palm, pandanus, and lily trees have a variety of fruits, ranging from nuts to berries.

Gymnosperms—needleleaf trees, cycads, and ginkgoes—do not have flowers or fruits. Their seeds are produced in cones or similar structures. The seeds of needleleaf trees and cycads have no protective coverings. Ginkgo seeds have a fleshy outer covering, but the covering is not a true fruit.

See **Tree** in *World Book* for more information on the following topics:

- The importance of trees
- Kinds of trees
- The parts of a tree
- How a tree grows
- Familiar broadleaf and needleleaf trees of North America
- Trees around the world
- Planting and caring for trees
- Scientific classification of trees

E. R. Degginger

William M. Stephens, Tom Stack & Associates

Clem Haagner, Bruce Coleman Inc.

Turtles live in a variety of habitats. The painted turtle, *upper left,* makes its home in fresh water. It uses its webbed feet for both swimming and walking. The green turtle, *lower left,* dwells in the sea. It has long, paddlelike flippers. The leopard tortoise, *above,* lives on land. Its stumpy legs and feet are well suited for walking on dry, rough ground.

Turtle is the only reptile with a shell. Most kinds of turtles can pull their head, legs, and tail into their shell, which serves as a suit of armor. Few other backboned animals have such excellent natural protection.

Turtles, like all reptiles, are cold-blooded—that is, their body temperature stays about the same as the temperature of the surrounding air or water. Turtles cannot be warm and active in cold weather, and so they cannot live in regions that are cold throughout the year. They live almost everywhere else—in deserts, forests, grasslands, lakes, marshes, ponds, rivers, and the sea.

There are about 250 species of turtles, about 50 of which live in North America north of Mexico. Some turtles live only on land, but others spend almost their entire life in the sea. Most other species dwell mainly in fresh water or live about equally on land and in fresh water. Many turtles live their entire life within a few miles or kilometers of where they were hatched. But large numbers of sea turtles migrate thousands of miles or kilometers from their birthplace.

Turtles vary greatly in size. The largest turtle species, the leatherback turtle, grows from 4 to 8 feet (1.2 to 2.4 meters) long. But the common bog turtle measures only about 4 inches (10 centimeters) in length.

Sea turtles, all of which swim rapidly, rank as the fastest turtles. One of these species, the green turtle, can swim for brief periods at a speed of nearly 20 miles (32

kilometers) per hour. On land, many kinds of turtles are slow, lumbering creatures. But some kinds of land turtles can move with surprising speed. For example, the smooth softshell turtle, a fresh-water species of North America, often can outrun a man on level ground.

The first turtles lived more than 185 million years ago. The *Archelon,* a sea turtle of about 25 million years ago, grew about 12 feet (3.7 meters) long. This creature died out, as did many other species. Today, many species of turtles face extinction because people hunt them for food and for their shells and gather their eggs. People also destroy their natural homes to make way for cities and farms.

At one time, pet shops throughout the United States sold thousands of painted turtles and red-eared turtles yearly. But medical researchers discovered that many of these turtles carried bacteria that cause *salmonella poisoning,* a serious illness in human beings. In 1975, the U.S. Food and Drug Administration banned the sale of most pet turtles.

The body of a turtle

Shell. Most species of turtles can pull their head, legs, and tail into their shell for protection. A few kinds of turtles, particularly sea turtles, cannot withdraw into their shell.

A turtle's shell consists of two layers. The inner layer

is made up of bony plates and is actually part of the skeleton. Among most species, the outer layer consists of hard, horny structures called *scutes,* which are formed from skin tissue. Soft-shelled turtles and the leatherback turtle have an outer layer of tough skin rather than scutes. The part of the shell that covers the turtle's back is called the *carapace,* and the part that covers the belly is called the *plastron.* The carapace and the plastron are joined along each side of the body by a bony structure called the *bridge.*

Most turtles that live on land have a high, domed shell. Those that live in water have a flatter, more streamlined shell. Some species of turtles, including Blanding's turtle, box turtles, and mud turtles, have a hinged plastron. They can close the plastron tightly against the carapace after withdrawing into their shell.

The shells of some kinds of turtles are plain black, brown, or dark green. But others have bright green, orange, red, or yellow markings.

Head. The head of most species of turtles is covered by hard scales. Turtles have no teeth, but they have a beak with a hard, sharp edge that they use to cut food. Many turtles have powerful jaws, with which they tear food and capture prey.

Legs and feet. A turtle's legs and feet vary according to the habitat of the species. Land turtles, particularly tortoises, have heavy, short, clublike legs and feet. Most fresh-water turtles have longer legs and webbed feet. Sea turtles have legs shaped like long paddles, with flippers instead of feet.

The hip bones and shoulder bones of the turtles, unlike those of any other animal, are inside the ribcage. This unusual feature enables most kinds of turtles to pull their legs inside their shell. Some species cannot withdraw their legs because the shell is too small.

William M. Partington, NAS   Hladik, Jacana

Turtles have a hard beak. Among most species, such as the mud turtle, *left,* the beak is not covered. But a soft-shelled turtle, *right,* has fleshy lips that cover its beak.

Senses. Turtles have a well-developed sense of sight and of touch. Scientific experiments indicate that they also have a good sense of smell, at least for nearby objects. Turtles have a middle ear and inner ear, and a *tympanic membrane* (eardrum) forms their outer ear. A turtle can hear low-pitched sounds about as well as a human being can.

The life of a turtle

Young. Turtles hatch from eggs, which are fertilized within the female's body. One mating can result in the fertilization of all the eggs of a female for several years. Most kinds of turtles lay their eggs between late spring and late autumn, and some lay eggs more than once during this period. For example, a green turtle may lay as many as seven *clutches* (groups) of eggs during one breeding season.

All turtles, including sea and fresh-water species, lay

The skeleton of a land turtle
Bottom view

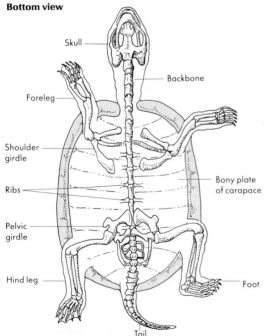

Skull

Backbone

Foreleg

Shoulder girdle

Ribs

Pelvic girdle

Bony plate of carapace

Hind leg

Foot

Tail

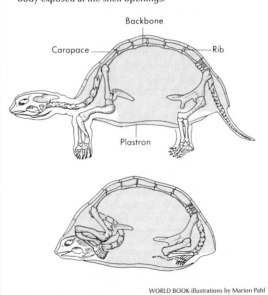

A turtle's shell provides excellent protection. Most turtles retract their head by pulling their long, flexible neck straight back in a U-curve. Scales protect the parts of the body exposed at the shell openings.

Backbone

Carapace

Rib

Plastron

WORLD BOOK illustrations by Marion Pahl

R. R. Pawlowski, Bruce Coleman Inc.

All turtles lay their eggs on land. Among most species, the female digs a hole in the ground, lays her eggs and covers them, and then leaves them. The sun's heat hatches the eggs. The female shown above is one of the side-necked species.

their eggs on land. Among most species, the female digs a hole in the ground with her back feet when ready to lay her eggs. She lays the eggs in the hole and covers them with soil, sand, or rotting plant matter. The number of eggs laid varies. An African pancake tortoise lays only one egg per clutch, but a sea turtle may lay 200 eggs at a time.

The female turtle walks away after covering her eggs and does not return. The warmth of the sun hatches the eggs. The temperature at which the eggs are incubated also determines the sex of the hatchlings. Newly hatched turtles must dig their way to the surface of the ground, obtain food, and protect themselves—all on their own.

Many animals prey on turtle eggs and newborn turtles. Various birds and mammals flock to beaches and eat baby sea turtles as they crawl toward the water. Fish attack many others as they enter the sea. Skunks, raccoons, and snakes dig up the nests of fresh-water turtles and devour the eggs.

Alan Blank, Bruce Coleman Inc.

A baby desert tortoise hatches from its egg after about 100 days. Young turtles have a horny growth on the tip of their beak. This growth, called a *caruncle,* helps break open the shell.

Scientists believe turtles live longer than any other backboned animal. Some box turtles and tortoises have lived more than 100 years. Most of a turtle's growth occurs during the animal's first 5 to 10 years. The turtle continues to grow after reaching this age, but at a much slower rate.

Food. Most kinds of turtles eat both animals and plants. The organisms eaten by a turtle vary among the species. A few kinds of turtles, including green turtles and tortoises, feed almost entirely on plants. Certain fresh-water species, such as map turtles and soft-shelled turtles, eat chiefly animals.

Hibernation. Turtles, like other cold-blooded animals, cannot remain active in cold weather. Species that live in regions with harsh winters must hibernate. Most fresh-water turtles hibernate by burrowing into the warm, muddy bottom of a pond, stream, or other body of water. Land turtles bury themselves in soil or under rotting vegetation.

See **Turtle** in *World Book* for more information on Kinds of Turtles and Turtles and human beings.

Jim Teason

The common snapping turtle has a small shell in relation to the rest of its body. The snapper cannot retreat into its shell for protection, and so it depends on its strong jaws for defense.

E. R. Degginger

A soft-shelled turtle has a round, flat shell covered by leathery skin. Most softshells also have paddlelike legs and a long, flexible nose that serves as an underwater breathing tube.

Venus is known as the earth's "twin" because the two planets are so similar in size. The diameter of Venus is about 7,520 miles (12,100 kilometers), about 400 miles (644 kilometers) smaller than that of the earth. No other planet comes closer to the earth than Venus. At its closest approach, it is about 25.7 million miles (41.4 million kilometers) away.

As seen from the earth, Venus is brighter than any other planet or even any star. At certain times of the year, Venus is the first planet or star that can be seen in the western sky in the evening. At other times, it is the last planet or star that can be seen in the eastern sky in the morning.

When Venus is near its brightest point, it can be seen in daylight. Ancient astronomers called the object that appeared in the morning Phosphorus, and the object that appeared in the evening Hesperus. Later, they realized these objects were the same planet. They then named it Venus in honor of the Roman goddess of love and beauty.

Orbit. Venus is closer to the sun than any other planet except Mercury. Its mean distance from the sun is about 67.2 million miles (108.2 million kilometers), compared with about 93 million miles (150 million kilometers) for the earth and 36 million miles (57.9 million kilometers) for Mercury.

Venus travels around the sun in a nearly circular orbit. The planet's distance from the sun varies from about 67.7 million miles (108.9 million kilometers) at its farthest point to about 66.8 million miles (107.5 million kilometers) at its closest point. The orbits of all the other planets are more *elliptical* (oval-shaped).

Venus takes about 225 earth-days, or about $7\frac{1}{2}$ months, to go around the sun once, compared with 365 days, or one year, for the earth.

Phases. When viewed through a telescope, Venus can be seen going through "changes" in shape and size. These apparent changes are called *phases,* and they resemble those of the moon. They result from different parts of Venus' sunlit areas being visible from the earth at different times.

As Venus and the earth travel around the sun, Venus can be seen near the opposite side of the sun about every 584 days. At this point, almost all its sunlit area is visible. As Venus moves around the sun toward the earth, its sunlit area appears to decrease and its size seems to increase. After about 221 days, only half the planet is visible. After another 71 days, Venus nears the same side of the sun as the earth, and only a thin sunlit area can be seen.

When Venus is moving toward the earth, the planet can be seen in the early evening sky. When moving away from the earth, Venus is visible in the early morning sky.

Rotation. As Venus travels around the sun, it rotates very slowly on its axis, an imaginary line drawn through its center. Venus' axis is not *perpendicular* (at an angle of 90°) to the planet's path around the sun. The axis tilts at an angle of approximately 178° from the perpendicular position. Venus is the only planet that does not rotate in the same direction in which it travels around the sun. The planet rotates in the *retrograde* (opposite) direction. Venus spins around once every 243 earth-days.

NASA

Venus is the closest planet to the earth. Thick clouds of sulfuric acid and sulfur cover the planet's surface. This picture of Venus was transmitted back to the earth by the U.S. *Pioneer Venus 1* space probe in December 1978.

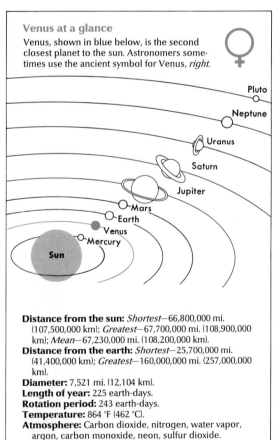

Venus at a glance

Venus, shown in blue below, is the second closest planet to the sun. Astronomers sometimes use the ancient symbol for Venus, *right.*

Pluto
Neptune
Uranus
Saturn
Jupiter
Mars
Earth
Venus
Mercury
Sun

Distance from the sun: *Shortest*—66,800,000 mi. (107,500,000 km); *Greatest*—67,700,000 mi. (108,900,000 km); *Mean*—67,230,000 mi. (108,200,000 km).
Distance from the earth: *Shortest*—25,700,000 mi. (41,400,000 km); *Greatest*—160,000,000 mi. (257,000,000 km).
Diameter: 7,521 mi. (12,104 km).
Length of year: 225 earth-days.
Rotation period: 243 earth-days.
Temperature: 864 °F (462 °C).
Atmosphere: Carbon dioxide, nitrogen, water vapor, argon, carbon monoxide, neon, sulfur dioxide.
Number of satellites: None.

Surface and atmosphere. Although Venus is called the earth's "twin," its surface conditions appear to be very different from those of the earth. Astronomers have had difficulty learning about the surface of Venus because the planet is always surrounded by thick clouds of sulfuric acid and sulfur. They have used radar, radio astronomy equipment, and space probes to "explore" Venus and to form some idea of the conditions on the planet.

The surface of Venus is extremely hot and dry. Photographs from surface lander equipment and radar measurements indicate that the planet has surface features as varied as those of the earth. These features include mountains, canyons and valleys, and flat plains. There are two mountain regions on Venus that are the size of entire continents on the earth. Some parts of Venus' surface are covered with fine dust and others with large sharp-edged rocks. There is no water on the planet's surface because the high surface temperature would make the water boil away. There may be some active volcanoes on Venus, which could help account for the sulfuric acid in the clouds above the planet.

The atmosphere of Venus is heavier than that of any other planet. It consists primarily of carbon dioxide, with small amounts of nitrogen and water vapor. The planet's atmosphere also contains minute traces of argon, carbon monoxide, neon, and sulfur dioxide. The *atmospheric pressure* (force exerted by the weight of the gases) on Venus is estimated at 1,323 pounds per square inch (93 kilograms per square centimeter), compared with about 14.7 pounds per square inch (1.03 kilograms per square centimeter) on the earth.

The plants and animals that live on the earth could not live on Venus, because of the high temperature and the lack of sufficient oxygen. Astronomers do not know whether any form of life exists on Venus, but they doubt that it does.

Temperature. The temperature of the uppermost layer of Venus' clouds averages about 55° F. (13° C). However, the temperature of the planet's surface is about 864° F. (462° C)—higher than that of any other planet and hotter than most ovens.

Most astronomers believe that Venus' high surface temperature can be explained by the "greenhouse" heat theory. A greenhouse lets in radiant energy from the sun, but it prevents much of the heat from escaping. The thick clouds and dense atmosphere of Venus work in much the same way. The sun's radiant energy readily filters into the planet's atmosphere. But the large particles of sulfur in Venus' clouds—and the water vapor and great quantity of carbon dioxide in the atmosphere—seem to trap much of the solar energy at the planet's surface.

Mass and density. The *mass* of Venus is about four-fifths that of the earth (in *World Book,* see **Mass**). The force of gravity on Venus is slightly less than on the earth. For this reason, an object weighing 100 pounds on the earth would weigh about 88 pounds on Venus. Venus is also slightly less *dense* than the earth (in *World Book,* see **Density**). A portion of Venus would weigh a little less than an equal-sized portion of the earth.

Flights to Venus. Venus was the first planet to be observed by a passing spacecraft. The unmanned U.S. spacecraft *Mariner 2* passed within 21,600 miles (34,760

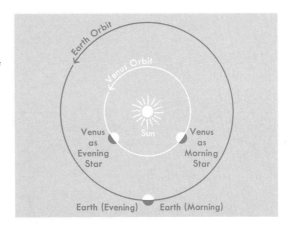

Venus appears in the evening sky when moving toward the earth. It is in the morning sky after it has passed between the sun and the earth and begins moving away from the earth.

kilometers) of Venus on Dec. 14, 1962, after traveling through space for more than $3\frac{1}{2}$ months. It made various measurements of conditions on and near Venus. For example, instruments carried by the spacecraft measured the high surface temperatures of the planet.

Two unmanned Soviet spacecraft "explored" Venus in 1966. *Venera 2* passed within 25,000 miles (40,200 kilometers) of the planet on February 27, and *Venera 3* crashed into Venus on March 1.

In October 1967, spacecraft from both the United States and the Soviet Union reached Venus. On October 18, the Soviet spacecraft *Venera 4* dropped a capsule of instruments into Venus' atmosphere by parachute. On October 19, the U.S. spacecraft *Mariner 5* passed within 2,480 miles (3,991 kilometers) of Venus. Both probes reported large amounts of carbon dioxide in the planet's atmosphere. On Dec. 15, 1970, the Soviet spacecraft *Venera 7* landed on Venus. The U.S. planetary probe *Mariner 10* flew near Venus on Feb. 5, 1974. The probe reported that the planet has no magnetic field.

On October 22, 1975, the unmanned Soviet spacecraft *Venera 9* landed on Venus and provided the first close-up photograph on the planet's surface. Three days later, another Soviet space vehicle, *Venera 10,* reached Venus. It photographed Venus' surface and measured its atmospheric pressure.

Four unmanned spacecraft reached Venus in December 1978. The U.S. *Pioneer Venus 1* began orbiting the planet on December 4. It transmitted radar photographs of Venus and measured temperatures at the top of the planet's clouds. On December 9, the U.S. *Pioneer Venus 2* entered the planet's atmosphere and measured its density and chemical composition. On December 21, the Soviet craft *Venera 12* landed on Venus. A second Soviet lander, *Venera 11,* reached the planet's surface four days later. Both probes sent back data on the lower atmosphere of Venus. Two more Soviet spacecraft landed on Venus in 1982—*Venera 13* on March 1 and *Venera 14* on March 5. Both probes transmitted photographs of Venus and analyzed soil samples. The U.S. spacecraft *Magellan,* launched in May 1989, was scheduled to reach Venus in August 1990 on a mission to map the planet with radar.

Dr. Harold Simon, Tom Stack & Associates

Robert Goodman, Black Star

The eruption of a volcano can produce spectacular sights. At the left, great clouds of dense gas and dust pour from Surtsey, a volcanic island off the south coast of Iceland. At the right, enormous fountains of glowing lava shoot out of the volcano Kilauea in Hawaii.

Volcano

Volcano is an opening in the earth's surface through which lava, hot gases, and rock fragments *erupt* (burst forth). Such an opening forms when melted rock from deep within the earth blasts through the surface. Most volcanoes are mountains, particularly cone-shaped ones, which were built up around the opening by lava and other materials thrown out during eruptions.

Eruptions of volcanic mountains are spectacular sights. In some eruptions, huge fiery clouds rise over the mountain, and glowing rivers of lava flow down its sides. In other eruptions, red-hot ash and cinders shoot out the mountaintop, and large chunks of hot rock are blasted high into the air. A few eruptions are so violent they blow the mountain apart.

Some eruptions occur on volcanic islands. Such islands are the tops of volcanic mountains that have been built up from the ocean floor by repeated eruptions. Other eruptions occur along narrow cracks in the ocean floor. In such eruptions, lava flows away from the cracks, building up the sea bottom.

How a volcano is formed

Powerful forces within the earth cause volcanoes. Scientists do not fully understand these forces. But they have developed theories on how the forces create volcanoes. This section describes how most scientists explain the beginning and eruption of a volcano.

The beginning of a volcano. A volcano begins as *magma,* melted rock inside the earth. Magma results from the extreme heat of the earth's interior. At certain depths, the heat is so great it partly melts the rock inside the earth. When the rock melts, it produces much gas, which becomes mixed with the magma. Most magma forms 50 to 100 miles (80 to 160 kilometers) beneath the surface. Some develops at depths of 15 to 30 miles (24 to 48 kilometers).

The gas-filled magma gradually rises toward the earth's surface because it is lighter than the solid rock around it. As the magma rises, it melts gaps in the surrounding rock. As more magma rises, it forms a large chamber as close as 2 miles (3 kilometers) to the surface. This *magma chamber* is the reservoir from which volcanic materials erupt.

The eruption of a volcano. The gas-filled magma in the reservoir is under great pressure from the weight of the solid rock around it. This pressure causes the magma to blast or melt a *conduit* (channel) in a fractured or weakened part of the rock. The magma moves up through the conduit to the surface. When the magma nears the surface, the gas in the magma is released. The gas and magma blast out an opening called the *central vent.* Most magma and other volcanic materials then erupt through this vent. The materials gradually pile up around the vent, forming a volcanic mountain, or volcano. After the eruption stops, a bowllike crater generally forms at the top of the volcano. The vent lies at the bottom of the crater.

Once a volcano has formed, not all the magma from

later eruptions reaches the surface through the central vent. As the magma rises, some of it may break through the conduit wall and branch out into smaller channels. The magma in these channels may escape through a vent formed in the side of the volcano. Or it may remain below the surface.

Kinds of volcanic materials

Three basic kinds of materials may erupt from a volcano. They are (1) lava, (2) rock fragments, and (3) gas. The material that erupts depends chiefly on how sticky or fluid a volcano's magma is.

Lava is the name for magma that has escaped onto the earth's surface. When lava comes to the surface, it is red hot and may have a temperature of more than 2012° F. (1100° C). Highly fluid lava flows rapidly down a volcano's slopes. Sticky lava flows more slowly. As the lava cools, it hardens into many different formations. Highly fluid lava hardens into smooth, folded sheets of rock called *pahoehoe* (pronounced *pah HOH ee HOH ee*). Stickier lava cools into rough, jagged sheets of rock called *aa* (*AH ah*). Pahoehoe and aa cover large areas of Hawaii, where the terms originated. The stickiest lava forms flows of boulders and rubble called *block flows*. It may also form mounds of lava called *domes*.

Other lava formations include *spatter cones* and *lava tubes*. Spatter cones are steep hills up to 100 feet (30 meters) high. They build up from the spatter of fountain-like eruptions of thick lava. Lava tubes are tunnels formed from fluid lava. As the lava flows, its outer surface cools and hardens. But the lava underneath continues to flow. After it drains away, it leaves a tunnel.

Rock fragments, generally called *tephra* (*TEHF ruh*), are formed from sticky magma. Such magma is so sticky that its gas cannot easily escape when the magma approaches the surface or central vent. Finally, the trapped gas builds up so much pressure that it blasts the magma into fragments. Tephra includes, from smallest to largest, *volcanic dust, volcanic ash,* and *volcanic bombs.*

Volcanic dust consists of particles less than $\frac{1}{100}$ inch (0.25 millimeter) in diameter. Volcanic dust can be carried great distances. In 1883, the eruption of Krakatoa in Indonesia shot dust 17 miles (27 kilometers) into the air. The dust was carried around the earth several times and produced brilliant red sunsets in many parts of the world. Some scientists believe that large quantities of volcanic dust can affect the climate by reducing the amount of sunlight that reaches the earth.

Volcanic ash is made up of fragments less than $\frac{1}{5}$ inch (0.5 centimeter) in diameter. Most volcanic ash falls to the surface and becomes welded together as rock called *volcanic tuff*. Sometimes, volcanic ash combines with water in a stream and forms a boiling *mudflow*. Mudflows may reach speeds of 60 miles (97 kilometers) per hour and can be highly destructive.

Volcanic bombs are large fragments. Most of them range from the size of a baseball to that of a basketball. The largest bombs may measure more than 4 feet (1.2 meters) across and weigh up to 100 short tons (91 metric tons). Small volcanic bombs are generally called *cinders.*

Gas pours out of volcanoes in large quantities during most eruptions. The gas is made up chiefly of steam. But it includes carbon dioxide, nitrogen, sulphur dioxide, and other gases. Most of the steam comes from a volcano's magma. But some may also be produced when rising magma heats water in the ground. Volcanic gas carries a large amount of volcanic dust. This combination of gas and dust looks like black smoke.

Kinds of volcanoes

Scientists divide volcanoes into three main groups: (1) shield volcanoes, (2) cinder cones, and (3) composite

How a volcanic mountain erupts

An eruption begins when *magma* (melted rock inside the earth) rises toward the surface, *left,* and collects in a *magma chamber* under the volcano. Pressure on the chamber forces the magma up through the *conduit, right*. In the *composite volcano* shown here, the magma erupts through the central and side vents as gas and mostly lava or mostly *tephra* (dust and other fragments).

WORLD BOOK illustrations by David Cunningham

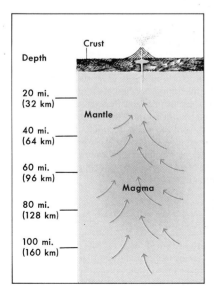

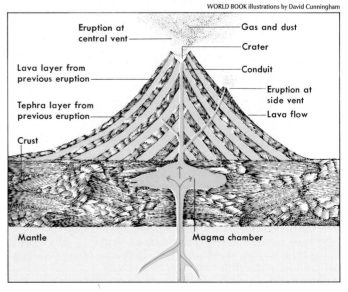

The three main kinds of volcanoes

Gordon A. Macdonald, Hawaii Institute of Geophysics

Cinder cones, such as Mexico's Paricutín, *above,* form when mainly tephra erupts from the central vent and piles up around it.

Gordon A. Macdonald, Hawaii Institute of Geophysics

Composite volcanoes are created by repeated eruptions of lava and tephra. The materials pile up in alternate layers, forming a cone-shaped mountain. Mayon Volcano in the Philippines, *above,* is one of the most perfectly shaped volcanoes.

Tom Nebbia, Click/Chicago

A shield volcano forms when lava erupts from several vents, spreads out widely, and builds up a low, broad mountain. Most shield volcanoes have many craters on their summits. The larger craters are called *calderas.* Hawaii's Mauna Loa, *above,* was formed by thousands of layers of overlapping lava.

shaped mountain. The famous Mauna Loa in Hawaii is a shield volcano. Thousands of separate, overlapping lava flows, each less than 50 feet (15 meters) thick, formed Mauna Loa.

Cinder cones build up when mostly tephra erupts from a vent and falls back to earth around the vent. The accumulated tephra, which is generally cinders, forms a cone-shaped mountain. Paricutín in western Mexico is a well-known cinder cone. It began in 1943, when a crack opened in the ground of a cornfield. When the eruptions ended in 1952, the top of the cone was 1,345 feet (410 meters) above its base.

Composite volcanoes are formed when both lava and tephra erupt from a central vent. The materials pile up in alternate layers around the vent and form a towering, cone-shaped mountain. Composite volcanoes include Japan's beautiful Mount Fuji; Mayon Volcano in the Philippines; and Italy's Vesuvius. In A.D. 79, Vesuvius erupted, burying the nearby towns of Pompeii, Herculaneum, and Stabiae under a mass of ashes, dust, and cinders. Mount St. Helens, which has erupted several times since 1980, is one of the most active composite volcanoes in the United States.

Occasionally, the magma chamber of a shield volcano, cinder cone, or composite volcano may become nearly empty. This happens when most of a volcano's magma erupts onto the surface. Because the chamber is empty, it can no longer support the volcano above. As a result, a large part of the volcano collapses, forming a huge crater called a *caldera.* Scenic Crater Lake in Oregon is a caldera that has filled with water. It is about 6 miles (10 kilometers) across at its widest point and 1,932 feet (589 meters) deep.

volcanoes. These groups are based on the shape of the volcanoes and the type of material they are built of.

Shield volcanoes are formed when a large amount of free-flowing lava spills from a vent and spreads widely. The lava gradually builds up a low, broad, dome-

See **Volcano** in *World Book* for more information on Why volcanoes occur in certain places, The study of volcanoes, and Benefits of volcanoes.

Where volcanoes occur

This map shows the location of many volcanoes. It also shows the earth's large, rigid plates. Volcanoes usually occur along the edges of the plates.

∴·∵ Volcanoes

Plate boundary

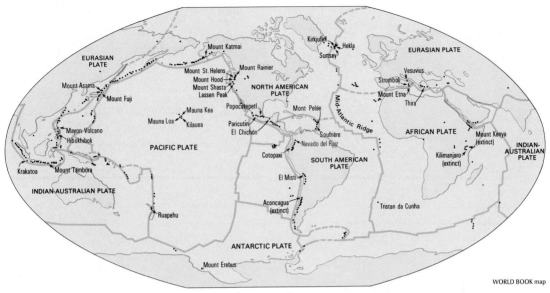

WORLD BOOK map

Some famous volcanoes

Name	Location	Height above sea level		Interesting facts
		In feet	In meters	
*Aconcagua	Argentina	22,831	6,959	Highest mountain in Western Hemisphere; volcano extinct.
*Cotopaxi	Ecuador	19,347	5,897	Eruption in 1877 produced mudflow that traveled about 150 miles (241 kilometers) and killed about 1,000 people.
El Chichón	Mexico	3,478	1,060	Eruption in 1982 killed 187 people and released a cloud of dust and sulfur dioxide gas high into the atmosphere.
Hibokhibok	Philippines	4,363	1,330	In 1951, red-hot cloud of gas and dust killed about 500 people.
*Krakatoa	Indonesia	2,667	813	Great eruption in 1883 heard about 3,000 miles (4,800 kilometers) away; produced sea waves almost 130 feet (40 meters) high that drowned about 36,000 people on nearby islands.
*Lassen Peak	California	10,457	3,187	One of several volcanoes in the Cascade Range; last erupted in 1921.
*Mauna Loa	Hawaii	13,677	4,169	World's largest volcano; rises almost 30,000 feet (9,100 meters) from ocean floor and is about 60 miles (97 kilometers) wide at its base.
*Mont Pelée	Martinique	4,583	1,397	Glowing cloud from 1902 eruption destroyed town of St. Pierre, killing about 38,000 people in minutes.
*Mount Etna	Sicily	11,122	3,390	About 20,000 people killed in 1669 eruption.
Mount Katmai	Alaska	6,715	2,047	Eruption in 1912 produced glowing flood of hot ash that traveled about 15 miles (24 kilometers) and formed Valley of Ten Thousand Smokes.
*Mount St. Helens	Washington	8,364	2,549	In 1980, violent eruptions released large amounts of molten rock and hot ash; killed 57 people.
Mount Tambora	Indonesia	9,350	2,850	In 1815, eruption released 6 million times more energy than that of an atomic bomb; killed about 92,000 people.
Nevado del Ruiz	Colombia	17,717	5,400	Eruption in 1985 triggered mud slides and floods; destroyed city of Armero and killed about 25,000 people.
*Paricutín	Mexico	9,213	2,808	Began in farmer's field in 1943; built cinder cone over 500 feet (150 meters) high in six days.
*Stromboli	Mediterranean Sea	3,031	924	Active since ancient times; erupts constantly for months or even years.
Surtsey	North Atlantic Ocean	568	173	In 1963, underwater eruption began forming island of Surtsey; after last eruption of lava in 1967, island covered more than 1 square mile (2.6 square kilometers).
Thira (formerly Santorin)	Mediterranean Sea	1,850	564	Eruption in about 1500 B.C. may have destroyed Minoan civilization on Crete; legend of lost continent of Atlantis may be based on this eruption.
*Vesuvius	Italy	4,190	1,277	In A.D. 79, produced history's most famous eruption, which destroyed towns of Herculaneum, Pompeii, and Stabiae.

*Has a separate article in *World Book.*

Waterfalls flow over rocky cliffs.

Cameramann International, Ltd. from Marilyn Gartman

Frederick Figall from Artstreet

A flood can cause enormous destruction of property.

© Robert Frerck, Woodfin Camp, Inc.

Waterways are used to transport bulky goods.

Water

Water is the most common substance on earth. It covers more than 70 per cent of the earth's surface. It fills the oceans, rivers, and lakes, and is in the ground and in the air we breathe. Water is everywhere.

Without water, there can be no life. Every living thing—plants, animals, and people—must have water to live. In fact, every living thing consists mostly of water. Your body is about two-thirds water. A chicken is about three-fourths water, and a pineapple is about four-fifths water. Most scientists believe that life itself began in water—in the salty water of the sea.

Ever since the world began, water has been shaping the earth. Rain hammers at the land and washes soil into rivers. The oceans pound against the shores, chiseling cliffs and carrying away land. Rivers knife through rock, carve canyons, and build up land where they empty into the sea. Glaciers plow valleys and cut down mountains.

Water helps keep the earth's climate from getting too hot or too cold. Land absorbs and releases heat from the sun quickly. But the oceans absorb and release the sun's heat slowly. So breezes from the oceans bring warmth to the land in winter and coolness in summer.

Throughout history, water has been people's slave—and their master. Great civilizations have risen where water supplies were plentiful. They have fallen when these supplies failed. People have killed one another for a muddy water hole. They have worshiped rain gods

and prayed for rain. Often, when rains have failed to come, crops have withered and starvation has spread across a land. Sometimes the rains have fallen too heavily and too suddenly. Then rivers have overflowed their banks, drowning everything and everyone in their paths.

Today, more than ever, water is both slave and master to people. We use water in our homes for cleaning, cooking, bathing, and carrying away wastes. We use water to irrigate dry farmlands so we can grow more food. Our factories use more water than any other material. We use the water in rushing rivers and thundering waterfalls to produce electricity.

Our demand for water is constantly increasing. Every year, there are more people in the world. Factories turn out more and more products, and need more and more water. We live in a world of water. But almost all of it—about 97 per cent—is in the oceans. This water is too salty to be used for drinking, farming, and manufacturing. Only about 3 per cent of the world's water is *fresh* (unsalty). Most of this water is not easily available to people because it is locked in glaciers and icecaps. By the year 2000, the world demand for fresh water may be double what it was in the 1980's. But there will still be enough to meet people's needs.

There is as much water on earth today as there ever was—or ever will be. Almost every drop of water we use finds its way to the oceans. There, it is evaporated by the

Ice is the solid form of water.

© E. Schulthess, Black Star

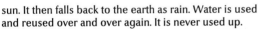

© Alexander Lowrey, Photo Researchers

Many people enjoy the recreational uses of water.

Bureau of Reclamation

Falling water from a dam produces energy.

sun. It then falls back to the earth as rain. Water is used and reused over and over again. It is never used up.

Although the world as a whole has plenty of fresh water, some regions have a water shortage. Rain does not fall evenly over the earth. Some regions are always too dry, and others too wet. A region that usually gets enough rain may suddenly have a serious dry spell, and another region may be flooded with too much rain.

Some regions have a water shortage because the people have managed their supply poorly. People settle where water is plentiful—near lakes and rivers. Cities grow, and factories spring up. The cities and factories dump their wastes into the lakes and rivers, polluting them. Then the people look for new sources of water. Shortages also occur because some cities do not make full use of their supply. They have plenty of water, but they do not have enough storage tanks and distribution pipes to meet the people's needs.

As our demand for water grows and grows, we will have to make better and better use of our supply. The more we learn about water, the better we will be able to meet this challenge.

Interesting facts about water

How much water is on the earth? There are about 326 million cubic miles (1.4 billion cubic kilometers) of water. There are over a million million (1,000,000,000,000) gallons of water per cubic mile (0.9 million million liters per cubic kilometer).

How much of the earth's water is fresh? Only about 3 per cent of the earth's water is fresh. About three-fourths of the fresh water is frozen in glaciers and icecaps. Glaciers and icecaps contain as much water as flows in all the earth's rivers in about 1,000 years.

How much water do living things contain? All living things consist mostly of water. For example, the body of a human being is about 65 per cent water. An elephant is about 70 per cent water. A potato is about 80 per cent water. A tomato is about 95 per cent water.

How much water does a person take in over a lifetime? On the average, a person takes in about 16,000 gallons (60,600 liters) of water during his or her life.

What are the different forms of water? Water is the only substance on earth that is naturally present in three different forms—as a liquid, a solid (ice), and a gas (water vapor).

How much water does a person use every day? On the average, each person in the United States uses about 70 gallons (260 liters) of water a day in the home.

What is the largest single use of water? The largest single use of water is by industry. It takes about 150 gallons (568 liters) of water to make the paper for one Sunday newspaper, and about 160 gallons of water per pound (1,340 liters per kilogram) of aluminum.

Can water ever be used up? Water is used and reused over and over again—it is never used up. Every glass of water you drink contains molecules of water that have been used countless times before.

Nature's water cycle

The waters of the earth move continuously from the oceans, to the air, to the land, and back to the oceans again. The sun's heat evaporates water from the oceans. The water rises as invisible vapor, and falls back to the earth as rain, snow, or some other form of moisture. This moisture is called *precipitation*. Most precipitation drops back directly into the oceans. The remainder falls on the rest of the earth. In time, this water also returns to the sea, and the cycle starts again. This unending circulation of the earth's waters is called the *water cycle* or *hydrologic cycle*.

Because of nature's water cycle, there is as much water on earth today as there ever was—or ever will be. Water changes only from one form to another, and moves from one place to another. The water you bathed in last night might have flowed in the Soviet Union's Volga River last month. Or perhaps Alexander the Great drank it more than 2,000 years ago.

The waters of the earth. The earth has a tremendous amount of water, but almost all of it is in the oceans. The oceans cover about 70 per cent of the earth's surface. They contain about 97 per cent of all the water on earth, and are the source of most precipitation that falls to earth. Ocean water is too salty to be used for drinking, agriculture, or industry. But the salt is left behind during evaporation, and the precipitation that falls to earth is fresh water.

Only about 3 per cent of the water on earth is fresh water—and most of it is not easily available to people. It includes water locked in glaciers and icecaps, more than 2 per cent of the earth's water. About half of 1 per cent of the earth's water is beneath the earth's surface. Rivers and lakes contain only about one-fiftieth of 1 per cent of the earth's water.

Water in the air. At one time or another, all the water on earth enters the air, or atmosphere, as water vapor. This vapor becomes the life-giving rain that falls to the earth. Yet, the atmosphere contains only one-thousandth of 1 per cent of the earth's water.

Moisture in the air comes mostly from evaporation. The sun's heat evaporates water from land, lakes, rivers, and, especially, the oceans. About 85 per cent of the vapor in the air comes from the oceans. Plants also add moisture. After plants have drawn water from the ground through their roots, they pass it out through their leaves as vapor in a process that is called *transpiration*. For example, a birch tree gives off about 70 gallons (260 liters) of water a day. A corn field gives off about 4,000 gallons of water per acre (37,000 liters per hectare) daily.

Precipitation. Vapor is carried by the air moving over the earth. The moisture-filled air cools wherever it is forced up by colder air or by mountains or hills. As the air cools, the vapor *condenses* into droplets of liq-

The water cycle

This diagram traces the never-ending circulation of the earth's water as it makes its long journey from the oceans, to the air, to the land, and back to the oceans again.

WORLD BOOK diagram by George Suyeoka

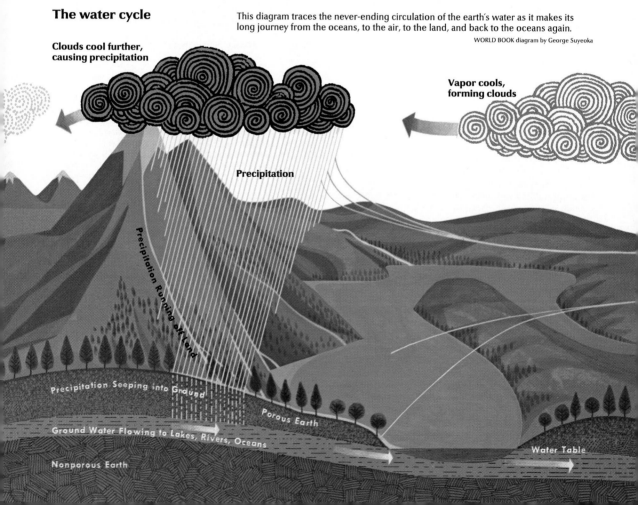

Clouds cool further, causing precipitation

Vapor cools, forming clouds

Precipitation

Precipitation Running off Land

Precipitation Seeping into Ground

Porous Earth

Ground Water Flowing to Lakes, Rivers, Oceans

Water Table

Nonporous Earth

uid water, forming clouds. The droplets fall to the earth as rain. If the vapor is chilled enough, it condenses into ice crystals, and falls as snow.

About 75 per cent of the precipitation falls back directly on the oceans. Some of the rest evaporates immediately—from the surface of the ground, from rooftops, from puddles in the streets. Some of it runs off the land to rivers. From the rivers, it flows back to the sea. The rest of the precipitation soaks into the earth and becomes part of the *ground water* supply. Ground water moves slowly through the ground to the rivers and returns to the sea. This movement of ground water to rivers keeps the rivers flowing during periods when there is no rain.

How water shapes the earth. Water changes the face of the earth as it moves through the great water cycle. Water wears down mountains, carves valleys, and cuts deep canyons. It also builds deltas and straightens coastlines.

During precipitation, some water falls on highlands and mountains. The force of gravity pulls the water downhill. As the water flows to lower levels, it *erodes* (wears away) the soil and rocks. In this way, after many thousands of years, mountains are worn down. The water that runs off the land during precipitation cuts small channels. The small channels drain into larger channels. The larger channels drain into still larger

ones, until finally the water empties into the main stream that runs to the sea. The water carries to the sea the materials it has eroded from the land.

Some of the precipitation that falls is captured in mountain glaciers. As the glaciers slide down mountainsides, they cut the mountains into sharp and jagged peaks.

The ocean also changes the face of the land. As waves pound against the shore, they cut away land and leave steep cliffs. Much of the material the waves wear away from the land is carried far out to sea. Some piles up near shore in sand bars. For more information on how water shapes the earth, see the *World Book* articles **Earth** (How the earth changes); **Erosion; Ocean** (The changing shoreline).

How water began. The question of how water began on earth is part of the question of how the earth itself began. Many scientists believe the earth was formed from materials that came from the hot sun. These materials included the elements that make up water. As the earth cooled and grew solid, water was trapped in rocks in the earth's crust. The water was gradually released, and the ocean basins filled with water. Other scientists have other ideas about how the earth and water began. For a discussion of these ideas, see the *World Book* articles **Earth** (How the earth began) and **Ocean** (How the oceans began).

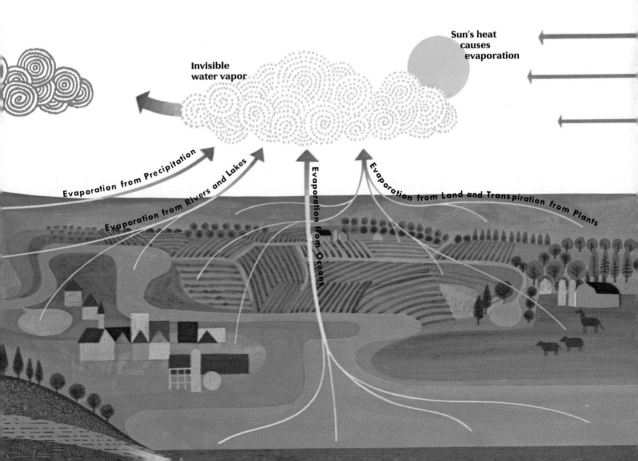

Sun's heat causes evaporation

Invisible water vapor

Evaporation from Precipitation

Evaporation from Rivers and Lakes

Evaporation from Oceans

Evaporation from Land and Transpiration from Plants

Shortages of fresh water have troubled people throughout history. Today, they trouble people more than ever because the demand for water is growing rapidly. Many people fear that the world does not have enough water to meet all our needs. Yet the world has—and always will have—the same amount of water it has always had. All the water we use passes through the great water cycle and can be used again and again.

The total amount of water on earth is enough for all our needs. However, the earth's water is distributed unevenly. Some regions suffer a constant *drought* (lack of rain). Other regions generally have plenty of water, but they may be struck by drought at times. In addition, people have created many water problems by mismanaging the supply.

World distribution of water. The earth has an enormous amount of water—about 326 million cubic miles (1.4 billion cubic kilometers) of it. In a cubic mile, there are more than a million million—1,000,000,000,000— gallons, or 3.8 million million liters. But 97 per cent of this water is in the salty oceans, and more than 2 per cent is in glaciers and icecaps. The rest totals less than 1 per cent. Most of this water is underground, and the remainder includes the water in lakes, rivers, springs, pools, and ponds. It also includes rain and snow, and the vapor in the air.

A country's water supply is determined by its precipitation. In regions with plenty of precipitation year after year, there is plenty of water in lakes, rivers, and underground reservoirs.

The earth as a whole receives plentiful rain. If this rain fell evenly, all the land would receive about 26 inches (66 centimeters) a year. But the rain is distributed unevenly. For example, over 400 inches (1,000 centimeters) drenches northeastern India every year. But northern Chile may not get rain for years.

Generally, the world's most heavily populated areas receive enough rain for their needs. These areas include most of Europe, Southeast Asia, the Eastern United States, India, much of China, and the northwestern region of the Soviet Union. But about half the earth's land does not get enough rain. These dry areas include most of Asia, central Australia, most of northern Africa, and the Middle East.

The United States has plenty of water. It averages about 30 inches (76 centimeters) of rain annually. This total is large, but it is distributed unevenly. Over 135 inches (343 centimeters) soaks parts of western Washington each year, but Nevada averages only about 7 inches (18 centimeters). Most states east of the Mississippi get 30 to 50 inches (76 to 130 centimeters) of precipitation a year—more than enough to grow crops. But large regions in the West get less than 10 inches (25 centimeters). There, only a little grass and shrubs can grow without irrigation.

Canada's annual precipitation is also distributed unevenly. In the southeast, it ranges from 30 inches (76 centimeters) in central Ontario to 55 inches (140 centimeters) in eastern Nova Scotia. From 14 to 20 inches (36 to 51 centimeters) of precipitation falls in most of the Prairie Provinces. Parts of the west coast get over 100 inches (250 centimeters).

Water shortages. Many regions of the world have a constant water shortage because they never get enough rain. But even a region that normally has enough rain may suddenly have a dry year or several dry years. The climates in regions that receive only light rainfall are especially changeable. Such regions can have a series of destructive dry years.

In the 1930's, one of the worst droughts in United States history struck the Southwest, an already dry region. Winds whipped the dry soil into gigantic dust storms, and most of the region became known as the *Dust Bowl*. Hundreds of farm families had to leave their homes.

Periods of low rainfall alternate with periods of high rainfall from year to year and from place to place. During the 1960's, for example, drought struck the Northeastern United States, and parts of China, Brazil, Nicaragua, Portugal, and other countries. Meanwhile, floodwaters spilled over the land in the Midwestern and Western United States, and in parts of Italy, Mexico, Honduras, and other countries.

Many regions have water shortages because the people have not prepared for a period of less than normal rainfall. These water shortages could have been prevented if the people had built artificial lakes, storage tanks, and other facilities to carry them through a drought.

The United States is especially rich in water. But every year, a number of U.S. communities must ration their water. As a result, many people fear that the country is running out of water. The United States as a whole has as much water today as the land had when Christopher Columbus sailed to the New World. But rainfall patterns change. In addition, the demand for water is increasing faster in the United States than in any other country. More and more Americans want air conditioners, garbage disposers, automatic washers, and an extra bathroom. Industry also demands more water as production rises. When drought strikes a water-hungry U.S. community, the effects can be severe—especially if the people are not prepared.

During the 1960's, rainfall in the Northeastern United States fell below normal for several years. Many cities had to restrict the use of water. New York City suffered especially, because it is so heavily populated. To save water, people turned off their air conditioners and let their lawns wither. Restaurants tried not to serve water to customers. The city was declared a disaster area. New York City's troubles came about because the city did not have enough storage tanks, distribution lines, and other facilities to supply the city with water during a long period of light rainfall.

Water management and conservation. Throughout history, people have attempted to increase their water supply by trying to "make rain." They have prayed to rain gods and performed rain dances. They have sprayed the clouds with chemicals to make them release their moisture. People also have always looked to the sea as a source of water. But often, people do not need more water. They only need to manage the supply better.

Many water problems in the United States have arisen because the country has had a plentiful and easily available water supply. Water has been cheap, and people have been careless and wasteful. They have dumped untreated sewage and other wastes into rivers and lakes, spoiling the water. In most U.S. cities, people pay about 45 cents per 1,000 gallons (3,800 liters) of water. In contrast, New York City, which has had severe water shortages, supplies free water to many people. Many landlords pay a fixed fee, and the tenants can let the water run as long as they like, wasting much of it. Neither the tenant nor the landlord pays a penny extra.

The supply of cheap, easily available water is shrinking in the United States. The development of new supplies will become more and more costly. It will then be cheaper to reuse water from old supplies. For example,

steel companies use great quantities of water for cooling. As costs rise, the companies may reuse a small amount of water in a circulating cooling system.

See **Water** in *World Book* for more information on the following topics:

- Water in our daily lives
- City water systems
- Fresh water from the sea
- What water is and how it behaves
- Water and the course of history

The unequal distribution of precipitation

- Always Enough Rain
- Usually Enough Rain
- Usually Not Enough Rain
- Never Enough Rain

WORLD BOOK map

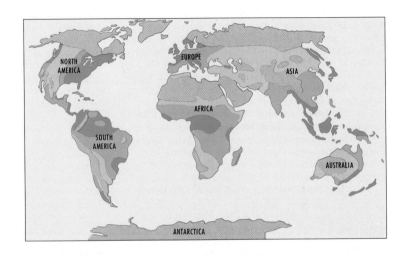

Artstreet

A tropical rain forest receives plentiful rainfall and remains green throughout the year.

Photri from Marilyn Gartman

A desert receives little rainfall, resulting in a dry landscape that can support little vegetation or animal life.

Artstreet

A drought occurs when a region receives less than normal rainfall over a long time, often leaving soil parched and cracked.

AP/Wide World

A mudslide can occur when a sudden downpour drenches an area that seldom receives large amounts of rain.

Water pollution is one of our most serious environmental problems. It occurs when water is contaminated by such substances as human and other animal wastes, toxic chemicals, metals, and oils. Pollution can affect rain, rivers, lakes, oceans, and the water beneath the surface of the earth, called *ground water.*

Sources

There are three chief sources of water pollution: (1) industrial wastes, (2) sewage, and (3) agricultural chemicals and wastes.

Industrial wastes. U.S. industries discharge three to four times as many pollutants into wastewater as do all the country's sewerage systems. These wastewaters contain many toxic chemicals. Much of this chemical waste is discharged directly into water systems. Also, the burning of coal, oil, and other fuels by power plants, factories, and automobiles produces sulfur and nitrogen oxides. These pollutants cause *acid rain,* which falls to the earth and enters streams and lakes.

Some industries use large amounts of water to cool equipment. Heat from the equipment makes the water hot. When discharged into a river or lake, it may cause *thermal pollution* that can harm plant and animal life.

Sewage consists of human wastes, garbage, and water that has been used for laundering or bathing. By the year 2020, the United States will probably produce three times as much sewage as it did in 1970. Most of the sewage in the United States goes through treatment plants that remove solids and such dissolved substances as nitrogen and phosphorus. About 10 per cent passes through *septic tanks* before filtering through *leaching fields* into the land. The remaining 10 per cent of the sewage in the United States goes untreated directly into waterways or the ocean.

Agricultural chemicals and wastes. Water from rain or melted snow flows from farmland into streams and carries chemical fertilizers and pesticides that farmers have used on the land. Animal wastes also may cause water pollution, particularly from feed lots with large numbers of animals. Cattle, hogs, sheep, and poultry that are raised on feed lots do not distribute their wastes over widespread pastureland. Instead, much of their wastes runs off into nearby streams. Water used for irrigation also may be polluted by salt, agricultural pesticides, and toxic chemicals on the soil surface before it flows back into the ground.

See **Water pollution** in *World Book* for more information on Effects and Control.

How eutrophication affects a lake

Eutrophication, the process by which wastes add nutrients to water, changes the balance of life there. The diagram at the left shows a lake with few waste nutrients added. Algae grow, using nutrients already in the lake, and provide food for fish. As the fish and algae die, their remains become organic wastes. Bacteria, using oxygen from the water, convert these wastes into nutrients and the cycle repeats. Nutrients and organic wastes added by people unbalance the cycle, as shown at the right. Nutrients increase the growth of algae. As the algae die, they add to the wastes. Bacteria use so much oxygen converting wastes into nutrients that few fish survive.

Balanced cycle

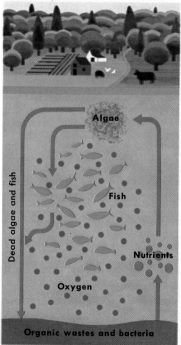

Unbalanced cycle

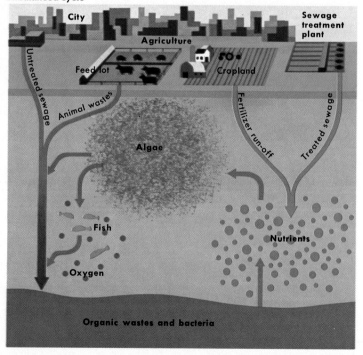

WORLD BOOK illustration by George Suyeoka

Milt and Joan Mann

A television weather report gives the day's weather conditions locally and across the nation. It also predicts the local weather for the next several days. Millions of people rely on TV forecasts to find out what kind of weather they can expect in the coming days.

Weather

Weather is the condition of the air that surrounds the earth. The weather may be hot or cold, cloudy or clear, windy or calm. It may bring rain, snow, sleet, or hail.

The weather affects our lives in numerous ways. For example, the type of clothing we wear depends largely on the weather. We put on heavy clothes when it is cold and dress lightly when it is hot. We also heat our homes in cold weather and cool them in hot weather. In many cases, we decide whether to spend our leisure time outdoors or inside according to the weather. The weather even affects our moods. People often feel more cheerful on a sunny day than on a gloomy one.

The weather has an enormous impact on agriculture. Farmers need clear weather to plant and harvest their crops. The plants require the right amount of sunlight and rain to grow and ripen. A storm or a sudden frost can damage or kill much of a crop. In such cases, the food produced from the plants that survive costs more.

Industry, transportation, and communication also suffer during bad weather. The construction of buildings, bridges, and roads may be delayed by rain, snow, or extreme cold. Snow may make trains late. Fog often prevents airplanes from taking off. Icy highways slow traffic.

Storms may break power lines and telephone wires. Thunderstorms may disrupt radio and television broadcasts. Even more serious is the loss of lives that sometimes results from severe storms.

Weather is not the same as climate. Weather is the condition of the air during a brief period. Climate is the average weather of an area over a long time. Scientists often describe climate in terms of the average temperature of a region and the amount of rain and snow the area receives. A region's weather may change greatly from day to day. But the average temperature and the amount of rain and snow remain about the same from year to year. See **Climate**.

People have tried to predict the weather for thousands of years. Today, scientists use complex instruments, such as radar, satellites, and computers, to forecast the weather. The forecasts are broadcast on radio and television stations and published in newspapers. Modern scientific instruments have made weather forecasting today more accurate than ever before. But predicting the weather remains a difficult, inexact science.

All weather develops in the *atmosphere,* the air that surrounds the earth. The atmosphere consists chiefly of the gases nitrogen and oxygen. It also has small amounts of other gases. Water vapor and particles of dust are mixed in the atmosphere. The atmosphere extends far above the earth's surface. Above a height of about 100 miles (160 kilometers), there is almost no air. This region is called *space.*

Nearly all weather occurs in the lowest layer of the atmosphere. This layer, called the *troposphere,* begins at the surface of the earth and extends from 6 to 10 miles (10 to 16 kilometers) away from the surface. Weather conditions in the troposphere—and on the earth—depend on four elements: (1) temperature, (2) air pressure, (3) wind, and (4) moisture.

Temperature is the degree of heat in the atmosphere. This heat comes from the sun. But only about one two-billionth of the heat given off by the sun enters the atmosphere. The rest is lost in space. About 34 per cent of the sunlight that enters the atmosphere is reflected back into space, chiefly by clouds. About 19 per cent is absorbed by the atmosphere and warms the air. However, the atmosphere gets most of its heat in another way. About 47 per cent of the sunlight that enters the atmosphere reaches the earth's surface and warms the ground and the seas. Heat from the ground and the seas then warms the atmosphere. The atmosphere absorbs the heat and prevents it from easily passing back into space. This result is called the *greenhouse effect* because the process resembles the way a greenhouse works. A greenhouse is a glass or clear plastic building in which plants can be grown throughout the year. A greenhouse lets sunlight in to heat the plants, but it prevents much of the heat from escaping.

Air pressure is the force of the atmosphere pushing on the earth. Temperature has a great effect on air pressure. Warm air weighs less than cool air. As a result, warm air puts less pressure on the earth than does cool air. The warm air forms a *low-pressure area,* also called a *low.* Cool air forms a *high-pressure area,* or a *high.* The force of air pressure tends to push air from high-pressure areas to low-pressure areas.

Wind is the movement of air from a high-pressure area to a low-pressure area. The greater the difference

Weather terms

Air mass is an enormous body of air that forms over a region in which the temperature is fairly constant. The air mass takes on the temperature of the region and has a great influence on the weather.

Front is a zone that develops when the edge of a cold air mass and the edge of a warm air mass meet. Most changes in the weather occur along fronts.

High-pressure area is an area in which the force of the atmosphere on the earth is relatively high. High-pressure areas usually have clear skies.

Humidity is the measure of the amount of water vapor in the air.

Low-pressure area is an area in which the force of the atmosphere on the earth is relatively low. Low-pressure areas usually have cloudy skies.

Precipitation is moisture that falls from clouds in the form of rain, snow, sleet, or hail.

Temperature is the degree of heat in the atmosphere.

Wind is the movement of air. Air tends to move from a high-pressure area to a low-pressure area. Winds are named for the direction from which they blow. For example, a north wind blows from the north.

Wind chill is an estimate of how cold the wind makes a person feel. For example, when the temperature is 20° F. (−6.7° C) and the wind is blowing at 10 miles (16 kilometers) per hour, the wind chill temperature is 3° F. (−16.1° C). Thus, a person feels as cold as when the temperature is 3° F. (−16.1° C) and the wind is calm.

in pressure between the two areas, the stronger the wind will be. Winds are named for the direction from which they blow. For example, a north wind blows from the north.

As air moves into a low-pressure area, it forces some of the air that was already there to move upward. The rising air expands and cools. Cool air cannot hold as much water vapor as warm air can. As a result, the water vapor in the air *condenses*—that is, it changes into tiny drops of water. The drops are held aloft by the rising air. When billions of these drops of water cluster together, they form a cloud. Thus, low-pressure areas are usually cloudy.

As air near the ground flows out of a high-pressure area, the air above sinks and replaces it. The sinking air is compressed and becomes warmer. Because the warmer air can hold more water vapor, it can evaporate

Weather extremes around the world

Highest temperature recorded was 136° F. (58.0° C) at Al Aziziyah, Libya, on Sept. 13, 1922. The highest temperature recorded in North America was 134° F. (57° C) in Death Valley, Calif., on July 10, 1913.

Lowest temperature observed on the earth's surface was −128.6° F. (−89.2° C) at Vostok Station in Antarctica, on July 21, 1983. The record low in the United States was −80° F. (−62° C) at Prospect Creek, Alaska, on Jan. 23, 1971.

Highest air pressure at sea level was recorded at Agata, in the Soviet Union, on Dec. 31, 1968, when the barometric pressure reached 32.01 inches (81.31 centimeters or 108.4 kilopascals).

Lowest air pressure at sea level was estimated at 25.69 inches (65.25 centimeters or 87.00 kilopascals), during a typhoon in the Philippine Sea on Oct. 12, 1979.

Strongest winds measured on the earth's surface were recorded at Mount Washington, N.H., on April 12, 1934. For five minutes the wind blew at 188 mph (303 kph). One gust reached 231 mph (372 kph).

Driest place on earth is Arica, Chile. In one 59-year period, the

average annual rainfall was $\frac{3}{100}$ inch (0.76 millimeter). No rain fell in Arica for a 14-year period.

Heaviest rainfall recorded in 24 hours was 73.62 inches (186.99 centimeters) on March 15-16, 1952, at Cilaos, on the island of Reunion in the Indian Ocean. The most rain in one year was at Cherrapunji, India. From August 1860 to July 1861, 1,041.78 inches (2,646.12 centimeters) fell. The wettest place is Mount Waialeale, on the island of Kauai in Hawaii, with an average annual rainfall of 460 inches (1,168 centimeters).

Heaviest snowfall recorded in North America in 24 hours—76 inches (193 centimeters)—fell at Silver Lake, Colo., on April 14-15, 1921. The most snow recorded in North America in one winter—1,122 inches (2,850 centimeters)—fell at Rainier Paradise Ranger Station in Washington in 1971-1972.

Largest hailstone in the United States fell in Coffeyville, Kans., on Sept. 3, 1970. The hailstone measured $17\frac{1}{2}$ inches (44.5 centimeters) in circumference, and it weighed $1\frac{2}{3}$ pounds (0.76 kilogram).

Source: National Oceanic and Atmospheric Administration.

Elements of weather   All weather develops in the atmosphere. Weather conditions in the atmosphere—and on the earth—depend on four elements: (1) temperature, (2) air pressure, (3) wind, and (4) moisture.

WORLD BOOK diagrams by Zorica Dabich

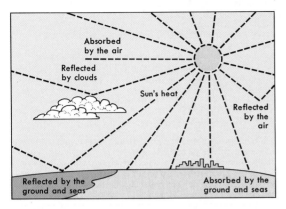

Temperature is the degree of heat in the atmosphere. The ground, seas, and air absorb about two-thirds of the sun's heat that enters the atmosphere. The rest is reflected into space.

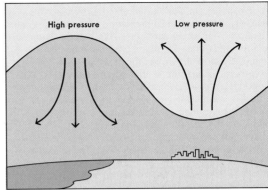

Air pressure is the force of the atmosphere on the earth. Warm air weighs less than cool air. Warm air thus forms an area of low pressure and cool air forms an area of high pressure.

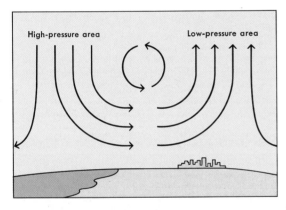

Wind is the movement of air. Air moves from a high-pressure area to a low-pressure area. As air moves into a low-pressure area, it forces the air that was already there to move upward.

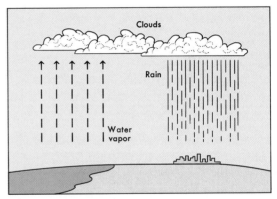

Moisture enters the air as water vapor, which comes from the oceans. As the vapor rises, it may change into drops of water and form clouds. If the drops get big enough, they fall to earth.

any clouds in the area. As a result, high-pressure areas are usually clear.

Moisture enters the atmosphere in the form of water vapor. Nearly all the vapor comes from water that evaporates from the oceans. The amount of water vapor in the air is called *humidity.* The more moisture there is in the air, the higher the humidity. Air that holds as much moisture as it can is *saturated.* The temperature at which the air becomes saturated is called the *dew point.* If the temperature falls below the dew point, the moisture in the air condenses.

On calm, clear nights, the air just above the ground cools rapidly. If the temperature of this air falls below the dew point, drops of water settle on grass, leaves, and windows and other surfaces. These drops of water are called *dew.* If the dew point is at or below freezing, *frost* forms. Sometimes, warm, moist air near the ground is cooled to its dew point. In such cases, low clouds called *fog* may develop. Fog can form at night or during the day.

A cooling of the air may also cause moisture to fall to the earth as *precipitation.* Precipitation may occur in the

form of *rain, snow, sleet,* or *hail.* Rain falls when the drops of water that form clouds combine and become so heavy that the air can no longer hold them up. If the temperature of the clouds is below freezing, ice crystals form. The ice crystals can turn to snow if the temperature of the air near the ground is as high as about 37° F. (2.78° C). If the temperature is between about 37° and 39° F. (2.78° and 3.89° C), the crystals change to sleet. At higher temperatures, the ice crystals melt as they fall and reach the earth as rain. Hail forms when strong air currents carry ice crystals up and down between the top and bottom layers of a thundercloud. The crystals become larger and larger until they fall to the earth as hailstones.

See **Weather** in *World Book* for more information on How weather develops and changes, Weather forecasting, and Development of weather forecasting.

Weights and measures are the standards used to find the size of things. People in the United States and a few other countries use standards that belong to the *customary,* or *English, system of measurement.* This system was developed in England from older measurement standards, beginning about the 1200's. People in nearly all other countries—including England—now use a system of measurement called the *metric system.* The metric system was created in France in the 1790's. In 1975, the United States Congress passed the Metric Conversion Act, which called for a voluntary changeover to the metric system. For more information on metric measurement, see the article on the **Metric system.**

Weights and measures form one of the most important parts of our life today. Many weights and measures

Metric conversion table

This table can help you change measurements into or out of metric units. To use it, look up the unit you know in the left-hand column and multiply it by the number given. Your answer will be approximately the number of units in the right-hand column.

When you know:	Multiply by:	To find:
Length and distance		
inches (in.)	25	millimeters
feet (ft.)	30	centimeters
yards (yd.)	0.9	meters
miles (mi.)	1.6	kilometers
millimeters (mm)	0.04	inches
centimeters (cm)	0.4	inches
meters (m)	1.1	yards
kilometers (km)	0.6	miles
Surface or area		
square inches (sq. in.)	6.5	square centimeters
square feet (sq. ft.)	0.09	square meters
square yards (sq. yd.)	0.8	square meters
square miles (sq. mi.)	2.6	square kilometers
acres	0.4	hectares
square centimeters (cm²)	0.16	square inches
square meters (m²)	1.2	square yards
square kilometers (km²)	0.4	square miles
hectares (ha)	2.5	acres
Volume and capacity (liquid)		
fluid ounces (fl. oz.)	30	milliliters
pints (pt.), U.S.	0.47	liters
pints (pt.), imperial	0.568	liters
quarts (qt.), U.S.	0.95	liters
quarts (qt.), imperial	1.137	liters
gallons (gal.), U.S.	3.8	liters
gallons (gal.), imperial	4.546	liters
milliliters (ml)	0.034	fluid ounces
liters (l)	2.1	pints, U.S.
liters (l)	1.76	pints, imperial
liters (l)	1.06	quarts, U.S.
liters (l)	0.88	quarts, imperial
liters (l)	0.26	gallons, U.S.
liters (l)	0.22	gallons, imperial
Weight and mass		
ounces (oz.)	28	grams
pounds (lb.)	0.45	kilograms
short tons	0.9	metric tons
grams (g)	0.035	ounces
kilograms (kg)	2.2	pounds
metric tons (t)	1.1	short tons
Temperature		
degrees Fahrenheit (° F.)	$\frac{5}{9}$ (after subtracting 32)	degrees Celsius
degrees Celsius (° C)	$\frac{9}{5}$ (then add 32)	degrees Fahrenheit

Miscellaneous weights and measures

Angstrom is a unit once used with the metric system to measure small distances. It equals 0.0000001 of a millimeter (0.0000000039 inch).

Assay ton, used for testing ore, equals 29.167 grams (1.029 ounces).

Bolt, used in measuring cloth, equals 120 feet (36.6 meters).

Butt, formerly used for liquids, equals 126 gallons (477 liters).

Carat, used to weigh precious stones and pearls, equals 200 milligrams (0.007 ounce).

Catty, used to measure tea and other materials, weighs about $1\frac{1}{3}$ pounds (0.6 kilogram).

Chaldron, a capacity measure, equals 36 imperial bushels (1.31 cubic meters).

Cubit, in the customary system, is 18 inches (46 centimeters). It is based on the length of the forearm.

Ell, used in measuring cloth, equals 45 inches (114 centimeters).

Firkin, used to measure lard or butter, equals either about 9 imperial gallons (40.9 liters) or about 56 pounds (25 kilograms).

Fortnight is a period of 14 days.

Hand, used to measure the height of horses, from the ground to the withers, equals 4 inches (10 centimeters).

Hogshead, used to measure liquids, equals 63 gallons (238 liters).

Kilderkin, used to measure liquids, equals 18 imperial gallons (82 liters).

Knot is a speed of 1 nautical mile (1.1508 statute miles or 1.852 kilometers) per hour.

Light-year, the distance light travels in a year. It is about 5.88 trillion miles (9.46 trillion kilometers).

Line, used to measure buttons, is $\frac{1}{40}$ inch (0.6 millimeter).

Load, of earth or gravel, equals 1 cubic yard (0.76 cubic meter).

Mole is a metric base unit for the amount of a substance. It equals 602,257,000,000,000,000,000,000 atoms, molecules, or whatever other elemental particles are being measured.

Nail, used in measuring cloth, equals 2.25 inches (5.72 centimeters).

Palm equals 3 or 4 inches (8 or 10 centimeters).

Perch, used for masonry, equals 24.75 cubic feet (0.7 cubic meter).

Perch, a measure of length in the customary system, equals 1 rod (5.03 meters).

Pin, used to measure liquids, equals $4\frac{1}{2}$ gallons (17 liters).

Pipe, used to measure liquids, equals 126 gallons (477 liters).

Pole, a measure of length in the customary system, equals 1 rod (5.03 meters).

Puncheon, used to measure liquids, equals 84 gallons (318 liters).

Quarter, used to measure grain, equals 25 pounds (11 kilograms).

Rood, used to measure land, equals $\frac{1}{4}$ acre (0.1 hectare).

Score is a group of 20.

Skein, used to measure yarn, equals 360 feet (110 meters).

Square, used to measure floor or roofing material, is an area of 100 square feet (9.3 square meters).

Tierce, used to measure liquids, equals 42 gallons (159 liters).

Tun, used to measure liquids, equals 252 gallons (954 liters).

Vara, used to measure land, equals $33\frac{1}{3}$ inches (84.6 centimeters) in Texas; 33 inches (84 centimeters) in California; and from 32 to 43 inches (81 to 109 centimeters) in Spain, Portugal, and Latin-American countries.

have had a fascinating history. For a complete discussion of the history of measurement, see **Measurement** in *World Book*.

The tables in this article show how to convert from customary to metric units and from metric to customary units. Suppose you want to change customary units to metric units. Multiply the number of customary units—inches, feet, pounds, and so on—by the number of metric units in *one* of the customary unit. For example, if you want to change 22 miles to kilometers, multiply 22, the number of miles, by 1.6093, the number of kilometers that make up 1 mile: $22 \times 1.6093 = 35.4046$. Therefore, 22 customary-unit miles equal 35.4046 metric-unit kilometers.

Length and distance

Lengths and distances are measured from one point to another, usually along a straight line. Length usually refers to the measurement of an object. Distance usually refers to the measurement of the space between two places. The customary and metric units for length and distance are listed in the tables below. The tables also show the nautical units used to measure distances at sea, and the chain units used to survey land.

Customary			Metric		Metric			Customary	
1 inch (in.)		=	2.54	cm	1 nano-				
1 foot (ft.)	= 12 in.	=	30.48	cm	meter (nm)		=	0.00000003937	in.
1 yard (yd.)	= 3 ft.	=	0.9144	m	1 micron (μ)	= 1,000 nm	=	0.00003937	in.
1 rod (rd.)	= 5½ yd.	=	5.0292	m	1 milli-				
1 furlong (fur.)	= 40 rd., or ⅛ mi.	=	201.168	m	meter (mm)	= 1,000 μ	=	0.03937	in.
1 statute, or land,					1 centi-				
					meter (cm)	= 10 mm	=	0.3937	in.
mile (mi.)	= 5,280 ft.,	=	1.6093	km	1 deci-				
	or 0.86897624				meter (dm)	= 10 cm	=	3.937	in.
	nautical mi.				1 meter (m)	= 10 dm	=	39.37	in.
1 statute					1 deka-				
league	= 15,840 ft.,	=	4.8280	km	meter (dam)	= 10 m	= 393.7		in.
	or 3 statute mi.,				1 hecto-				
	or 2.6069287				meter (hm)	= 10 dam	= 328.0833		ft.
	nautical mi.				1 kilometer (km)	= 10 hm	=	0.62137	mi.

Nautical

				Customary		Metric	
1 span		=		9	in.	= 22.8	cm
1 fathom (fm.)	= 8 spans	=		6	ft.	= 1.83	m
1 cable's length	= 120 fathoms	=		720	ft.	= 219.46	m
1 nautical mile, or 1 International Nautical Mile (INM)		=		6,076.11549	ft., or 1.150779 statute mi.	= 1.852	km
1 nautical league	= 3 nautical mi.	=		18,228.346	ft., or 3.452338 statute mi.	= 5.556	km

Surveyor's, or Gunter's, Chain

			Customary		Metric	
1 link (li.)		=	7.92	in.	= 20.12	cm
1 chain (ch.)	= 100 li.	=	66	ft.	= 20.12	m
1 furlong (fur.)	= 10 ch.	=	660	ft.	= 201.168	m
1 statute mile (mi.)	= 8 fur.	=	5,280	ft.	= 1.6093	km

Engineer's Chain

			Customary		Metric	
1 link (li.)		=	1	ft.	= 30.48	cm
1 chain (ch.)	= 100 li.	=	100	ft.	= 30.48	m
1 mile (mi.)	= 52.8 ch.	=	5,280	ft.	= 1.6093	km

Surface or area

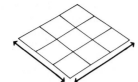

An area of land or the surface of an object is measured in square units. These units result from multiplying the length of the area or object by its width. The square units of both the customary and metric systems are based on units of length and distance. A small 2, placed to the right and above the symbol for a metric unit, indicates a square unit.

Customary			Metric	Metric			Customary	
1 square inch (sq. in.)		=	6.4516 cm²	1 square millimeter (mm²)		=	0.002	sq. in.
1 square foot (sq. ft.)	= 144	sq. in. =	0.0929 m²	1 square centimeter (cm²)	= 100 mm² =		0.155	sq. in.
1 square yard (sq. yd.)	= 9	sq. ft. =	0.8361 m²	1 square decimeter (dm²)	= 100 cm² =		15.5	sq. in.
1 square rod (sq. rd.)	= 30¼	sq. yd.=	25.293 m²	1 square meter (m²)	= 100 dm² =	1,550		sq. in.
1 acre	= 160	sq. rd. =	0.4047 ha	1 square dekameter (dam²)	= 100 m² =	119.6		sq. yd.
1 square mile (sq. mi.)	= 640	acres =	258.9988 ha,	1 square hectometer (hm²)	= 100 dam² =		2.4711	acres
		or	2.590 km²	1 square kilometer (km²)	= 100 hm² =		247.105	acres,
						or	0.3861	sq. mi.

Metric Land Measurement

Metric				Customary	
1 centiare (ca)			=	1,550	sq. in.
1 are (a)	=	100 ca	=	119.6	sq. yd.
1 hectare (ha)	=	100 a	=	2.4711	acres
1 square kilometer (km²)	=	100 ha	=	247.105	acres,
			or	0.3861	sq. mi.

Surveyor's Land Measurement

			Customary			Metric
1 square link (sq. li.)		=	62.73 sq. in.	=	404.686 cm²
1 square pole (sq. p.)	= 625 sq. li.	=	30.25 sq. yd.	=	25.293 m²
1 square chain (sq. ch.)	= 16 sq. p.	=	484 sq. yd.	=	404.686 m²
1 acre	= 10 sq. ch.	=	4,840 sq. yd.	=	4,046.856 m²
1 section (sec.)	= 640 acres	=	1 sq. mi.	=	2.590 km²
1 township (tp.)	= 36 sec.	=	36 sq. mi.	=	93.240 km²

Volume and capacity

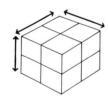

Volume refers to the amount of space occupied by an object. Capacity is the amount of a substance that a container can hold. Volume and capacity are both measured in cubic units. Cubic units combine length, width, and depth. But the names of many common cubic units, such as liter and quart, do not include the word *cubic*. A small 3, placed to the right and above the symbol for a metric unit, indicates a cubed unit.

Volume Measurement

Customary			Metric
1 cubic inch (cu. in.)		=	16.387 cm³
1 cubic foot (cu. ft.)	= 1,728 cu. in.	=	0.0283 m³
1 cubic yard (cu. yd.)	= 27 cu. ft.	=	0.7646 m³

Metric			Customary	
1 cubic milli-meter (mm³)		= 0.00006	cu. in.	
1 cubic centi-meter (cm³)	= 1,000 mm³	= 0.0610	cu. in.	
1 cubic deci-meter (dm³)	= 1,000 cm³	= 0.0353	cu. ft.	
1 cubic meter (m³)	= 1,000 dm³	= 1.308	cu. yd.	
1 cubic deka-meter (dam³)	= 1,000 m³	= 1,308	cu. yd.	
1 cubic hecto-meter (hm³)	= 1,000 dam³	= 1,308,000 cu. yd.		

Metric Capacity Measure

Metric			Customary	
1 milliliter (ml)		=	0.0610	cu. in.
1 centiliter (cl)	= 10 ml	=	0.6103	cu. in.
1 deciliter (dl)	= 10 cl	=	6.1025	cu. in.
1 liter (l)	= 10 dl	=	61.025	cu. in.,
		or	1.057	liquid qt.,
		or	0.908	dry qt.
1 dekaliter (dal)	= 10 l	=	610.25	cu. in.
1 hectoliter (hl)	= 10 dal	=	6,102.55	cu. in.
1 kiloliter (kl)	= 10 hl	=	35.316	cu. ft.,
		or	264.179	gal.,
		or	28.38	bu.

Household Capacity Measurement

Customary				Metric	
1 teaspoon		=	⅙ fl. oz. =	4.9	ml
1 table-spoon	= 3 teaspoons	=	½ fl. oz. =	14.8	ml
1 cup	= 16 tablespoons	=	8 fl. oz. =	236.6	ml
1 pint	= 2 cups	=	16 fl. oz. =	473.2	ml
1 quart	= 2 pints	=	32 fl. oz. =	946.3	ml
1 gallon	= 4 quarts	=	128 fl. oz. =	3.785	l

Customary Liquid Capacity Measurement

	Customary		Metric
1 gill (gi.)		= 7.219 cu. in.	= 0.1183 l
1 pint (pt.)	= 4 gi.	= 28.875 cu. in.	= 0.4732 l
1 quart (qt.)	= 2 pt.	= 57.75 cu. in.	= 0.9463 l
1 gallon (gal.)	= 4 qt.	= 231 cu. in.	= 3.7854 l
1 barrel (bbl.), liquids	= 31.5 gal.	= 4.21 cu. ft.	= 119.24 l
1 barrel (bbl.), petroleum	= 42 gal.	= 5.61 cu. ft.	= 158.98 l

Imperial	Customary		Metric
1 imperial pint	= 1.201 U.S. pt.	= 34.6775 cu. in.	= 0.568 l
1 imperial quart	= 1.201 U.S. qt.	= 69.354 cu. in.	= 1.13652 l
1 imperial gallon	= 1.201 U.S. gal.	= 277.42 cu. in.	= 4.54609 l

Customary Dry Capacity Measurement

	Customary		Metric
1 pint (pt.)		= 33.600 cu. in.	= 550.61 cm^3
1 quart (qt.)	= 2 pt.	= 67.20 cu. in.	= 1,101.22 cm^3
1 peck (pk.)	= 8 qt.	= 537.61 cu. in.	= 8,809.77 cm^3
1 bushel (bu.)	= 4 pk.	= 2,150.42 cu. in.	= 0.035239 m^3
1 barrel (bbl.)		= 4.08 cu. ft.	= 0.115627 m^3

Imperial	Customary		Metric
1 imperial pint	= 1.032 U.S. pt.	= 34.6775 cu. in.	= 568.26092 cm^3
1 imperial quart	= 1.032 U.S. qt.	= 69.354 cu. in.	= 1,136.52 cm^3
1 imperial bushel	= 1.032 U.S. bu.	= 2,219.36 cu. in.	= 0.03637 m^3

Apothecaries' Fluid Measurement

		Customary	Metric
1 minim or drop (min. or ♏)		= 0.002083 fl. oz.	= 0.0616 ml
1 fluid dram (fl. dr. or fʒ)	= 60 min.	= 0.125 fl. oz.	= 3.6966 ml
1 fluid ounce (fl. oz. or f℥)	= 8 fl. dr.	= 1 fl. oz.	= 0.0296 l
1 pint (O.)	= 16 fl. oz.	= 16 fl. oz.	= 0.4732 l
1 gallon (C.)	= 8 O.	= 128 fl. oz.	= 3.7853 l

Shipping Capacity Measurement

		Customary	Metric
1 barrel bulk		= 5 cu. ft.	= 0.1416 m^3
1 shipping ton, or 1 measurement ton, or 1 freight ton,	= 8 barrels bulk	= 40 cu. ft.	= 1.1327 m^3
1 displacement ton		= 35 cu. ft.	= 0.9911 m^3
1 register ton		= 100 cu. ft.	= 2.8317 m^3

Weight and mass

The customary system measures the weight of various materials. Avoirdupois weight measures ordinary materials. Apothecaries' weight once measured drugs and medicines. Troy weight measures precious metals and gems. The metric system measures *mass* (amount of material something contains). An object's mass does not change, but its weight decreases with altitude. Mass and weight are equal at sea level, and the comparisons in this table are based on that location.

Avoirdupois Weight

		Metric
1 grain (gr.)	=	0.0648 g
1 dram (dr.)	= 27.34375 gr.	= 1.7718 g
1 ounce (oz.)	= 16 dr.	= 28.3495 g
1 pound (lb.)	= 16 oz.	= 453.5924 g, or 0.4536 kg
1 hundred-weight (cwt.)	= 100 lb.	= 45.3592 kg
1 short ton	= 2,000 lb.	= 907.18 kg, or 0.9072 t

Special British Units	Customary	Metric
1 stone (st.)	= 14 lb.	= 6.35 kg
1 hundred-weight (cwt.)	= 112 lb.	= 50.80 kg
1 long ton	= 2,240 lb.	= 1,016.05 kg, or 1.0160 t

Metric Weight

		Avoirdupois
1 milligram (mg)		= 0.0154 gr.
1 centigram (cg)	= 10 mg	= 0.1543 gr.
1 decigram (dg)	= 10 cg	= 1.5432 gr.
1 gram (g)	= 10 dg	= 15.4324 gr.
1 dekagram (dag)	= 10 g	= 0.3527 oz.
1 hectogram (hg)	= 10 dag	= 3.5274 oz.
1 kilogram (kg)	= 10 hg	= 2.2046 lb.
1 metric ton (t)	= 1,000 kg	= 2,204.62 lb.

Apothecaries' Weight

				Avoirdupois		Metric
1 grain (gr.)			=	0.002286 oz.	=	0.0648 g
1 scruple (s. ap. or ℈)	= 20 gr.		=	0.04571 oz.	=	1.296 g
1 dram (dr. ap. or ʒ)	= 3 s. ap.		=	0.1371 oz.	=	3.888 g
1 ounce (oz. ap. or ℥)	= 8 dr. ap.		=	1.0971 oz.	=	31.1035 g
1 pound (lb. ap. or ℔)	= 12 oz. ap.		=	13.1657 oz.	=	373.24 g, or 0.3732 kg

Troy Weight

				Avoirdupois		Metric
1 grain (gr.)			=	0.002286 oz.	=	0.0648 g
1 pennyweight (dwt.)	= 24	gr.	=	0.054857 oz.	=	1.56 g
1 ounce (oz. t.)	= 20	dwt.	=	1.0971 oz.	=	31.1035 g
1 pound (lb. t.)	= 12	oz. t.	=	13.1657 oz.	=	373.24 g, or 0.3732 kg

Time

Both the customary and metric systems use the same units to measure time. The shortest unit of time in the customary system is the second. But the metric system has four units of time shorter than the second.

1 picosecond (ps)			=	0.000000000001 s
1 nanosecond (ns)			=	0.000000001 s
1 microsecond (µs)	=	1,000 ns	=	0.000001 s
1 millisecond (ms)	=	1,000 µs	=	0.001 s
1 second (s)	=	1,000 ms	=	$\frac{1}{3,600}$ h.
1 minute (min.)	=	60 s	=	$\frac{1}{60}$ h.
1 hour (h.)	=	60 min.		
1 day (d.)	=	24 h.		
1 week (wk.)	=	7 d.		
1 common lunar year (yr.)	=	354 d.		
1 common solar year	=	365 d.		
1 leap year	=	366 d.		
1 decade	=	10 yr.		
1 century	=	100 yr.		
1 millennium	=	1,000 yr.		

Temperature

The customary system measures temperature in Fahrenheit degrees. The metric system measures temperatures in Celsius degrees. The two temperature scales are shown below, with the freezing and boiling points of water indicated on both.

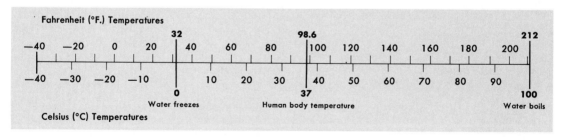

James Hudnall

A mother whale and her calf remain close together for at least a year. This baby humpback whale is resting on its mother's back as she swims along just beneath the surface of the water.

Whale

Whale is a huge sea animal that looks much like a fish. But whales are not fish. They belong instead to the group of animals called *mammals.* Other mammals include chimpanzees, dogs, and human beings. Like these mammals, whales have a highly developed brain and so are among the most intelligent of all animals.

Most whales are enormous creatures. One kind, the blue whale, is the largest animal that has ever lived. Blue whales may grow up to 100 feet (30 meters) long and can weigh more than 220 short tons (200 metric tons). However, some kinds of whales are much smaller. Belugas and narwhals, for example, grow only 10 to 15 feet (3 to 5 meters) long.

Whales have the same basic shape as fish, but they differ from fish in many ways. The most visible difference is the tail. Fish have *vertical* (up and down) tail fins, but whales have sideways tail fins. Fish breathe by means of gills, which absorb dissolved oxygen from water. Whales, on the other hand, have lungs and must come to the surface to breathe. But they can hold their breath for long periods. One kind of whale, the sperm

whale, can hold its breath up to 75 minutes.

Like other mammals, whales give birth to live young and feed them with milk produced by the mother's body. Most fish, however, lay eggs and do not feed their offspring. Whales are also *warm-blooded*—that is, their body temperature remains about the same regardless of the temperature of their surroundings. Almost all fish are *cold-blooded.* Their body temperature changes with changes in the temperature of the water.

Down through the ages, whales have gradually lost some of the characteristics of mammals. For example, hair covers the bodies of most mammals. But whales have only a few stiff hairs on the head. Most mammals also have four legs. A whale has no hind legs. The only traces of them that remain are two tiny hipbones. In addition, the front legs have developed into flippers, which help a whale steer and keep its balance.

People have hunted whales since prehistoric times. In early days, people killed whales for their meat and for whale oil, which they used as a fuel for lamps and for cooking. Today, people in Japan, as well as native peo-

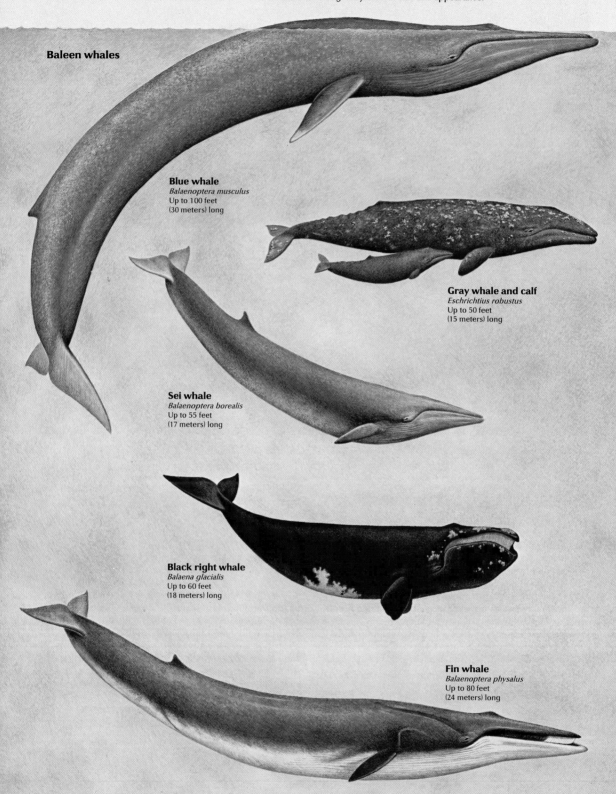

Some kinds of whales

The illustrations on this page and the following page show some of the major kinds of baleen and toothed whales. Baleen whales include nearly all the extremely large types of whales. Among toothed whales, only the sperm whale can compare in size with baleen whales. Unlike baleen whales, the various kinds of toothed whales differ greatly in both size and appearance.

Baleen whales

Blue whale
Balaenoptera musculus
Up to 100 feet
(30 meters) long

Gray whale and calf
Eschrichtius robustus
Up to 50 feet
(15 meters) long

Sei whale
Balaenoptera borealis
Up to 55 feet
(17 meters) long

Black right whale
Balaena glacialis
Up to 60 feet
(18 meters) long

Fin whale
Balaenoptera physalus
Up to 80 feet
(24 meters) long

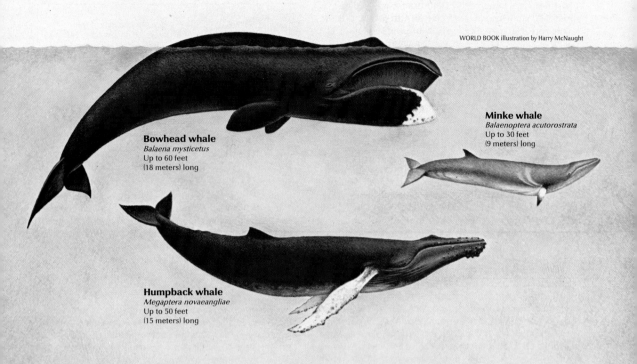

WORLD BOOK illustration by Harry McNaught

Bowhead whale
Balaena mysticetus
Up to 60 feet
(18 meters) long

Minke whale
Balaenoptera acutorostrata
Up to 30 feet
(9 meters) long

Humpback whale
Megaptera novaeangliae
Up to 50 feet
(15 meters) long

Toothed whales

Sperm whale
Physeter macrocephalus
Up to 60 feet
(18 meters) long

Killer whale
Orcinus orca
Up to 30 feet
(9 meters) long

Baird's beaked whale
Berardius bairdii
Up to 40 feet
(12 meters) long

Pilot whale
Globicephala melaena
Up to 28 feet
(8.5 meters) long

Narwhal
Monodon monoceros
Up to 15 feet
(5 meters) long

Beluga
Delphinapterus leucas
Up to 15 feet
(5 meters) long

ples on several other Pacific islands and in Arctic regions, still eat whale meat. Whale oil and other parts of whales are used to make a variety of products, such as cosmetics, fertilizer, glue, medicines, and soap.

During the 1900's, whaling fleets have killed huge numbers of whales and so have seriously endangered the survival of some kinds of whales. For this reason, the International Whaling Commission limits the number of whales that may be killed each year. The International Whaling Commission also completely prohibits the killing of certain kinds of whales. The United States government forbids the import of whale products.

Whales belong to a group of mammals called *cetaceans* (pronounced *see TAY shuhnz*). This name comes from a Latin word meaning *large sea animal.* Scientists have identified at least 75 kinds of cetaceans. They divide the various kinds into two major groups—*baleen whales,* which do not have teeth, and *toothed whales,* which have teeth.

Kinds of baleen whales

Baleen whales have no teeth. Instead, they have hundreds of thin plates in the mouth. A whale uses these plates to strain out food from the water. The plates are called *baleen* or *whalebone* and consist of the same material as human fingernails. The baleen hangs from the whale's upper jaw. The inside edges of the plates have brushlike fibers that filter out the food. Baleen whales feed mainly on *plankton*—drifting masses of tiny plants and animals.

There are 10 kinds of baleen whales. Scientists divide them into three groups: (1) *right whales,* including bowhead whales, black right whales, and pygmy whales; (2) *gray whales;* and (3) *rorquals,* including blue whales, Bryde's whales, fin whales; humpback whales; minke whales, and sei whales.

Kinds of toothed whales

Unlike baleen whales, toothed whales have teeth. There are about 65 kinds of toothed whales. They differ greatly in size, in shape, and in the number of teeth they have. Some toothed whales eat fish, and others eat such animals as cuttlefish and squid.

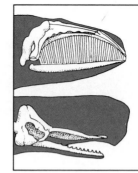

Baleen consists of thin plates that hang from the upper jaw of baleen whales. Baleen is made of the same type of material as human fingernails.

Peglike teeth grow from the lower jaw of nearly all species of toothed whales. Some species have teeth in the upper jaw as well.

WORLD BOOK illustration by Marion Pahl

Scientists divide the various kinds of toothed whales into five groups: (1) sperm whales; (2) beaked whales; (3) belugas and narwhals; (4) dolphins and porpoises; and (5) river dolphins. Most people do not consider dolphins and porpoises to be whales. But scientists classify them as toothed whales because they have the same basic body features as other toothed whales.

The bodies of whales

Several features of the whale body suggest that whales are closely related to hoofed mammals, particularly split-hoofed mammals, such as cattle and deer. Some scientists believe that whales developed from primitive meat-eating mammals. The oldest whale fossil yet discovered dates from about 45 million years ago. However, scientists think that whales probably began to develop as early as 70 million years ago.

Whales basically have the same body features as other mammals. But whales have many special characteristics suited to living in water. Also, living in water enables them to reach enormous sizes. A land animal can grow only so big before its bones and muscles can no longer support its body weight. But the *buoyancy* (lift) of water helps support a whale's body and makes it possible for whales to grow far larger than any land animal.

Body shape. Whales have a highly streamlined shape, which enables them to swim with a minimum of resistance. Their shape resembles that of fish. But a

William A. Watkins, Woods Hole Oceanographic Institution

A baleen whale has no teeth. Instead, it has hundreds of thin plates called *baleen.* It uses these plates to filter out food from the water. Baleen whales form one of the two major groups of whales. Toothed whales make up the other group.

Bruce Coleman Inc.

Toothed whales use their teeth only to capture prey, not to chew it. All toothed whales swallow their food whole.

The body of a female fin whale

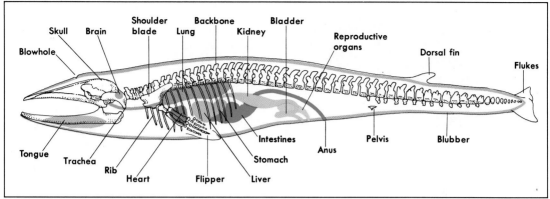

WORLD BOOK illustration by Marion Pahl

whale's powerful tail fins, called *flukes,* are horizontal instead of vertical like the tail fins of a fish. A whale propels itself by moving its flukes up and down. Most fish swim by swinging their tail fins from side to side.

The ancestors of whales lived on land and had four legs. But after these animals moved into the sea, their body features gradually changed. Over millions of years, the front legs developed into flippers and the hind legs disappeared. A whale uses its flippers to help in steering and in keeping its balance.

Skeleton. A whale's backbone, ribcage, and shoulder blades resemble those of other mammals. The absence of hind legs, however, distinguishes the whale from most other mammals. Two small bones buried in the hip muscles are all that remain of the whale's hind legs.

Almost all mammals have seven neck vertebrae. But in whales, these vertebrae are greatly compressed into a short length or joined together into one bone. This feature keeps the head from moving about as a whale swims. It also contributes to the whale's streamlined shape by joining the head directly to the body.

Skin and blubber. Whales have smooth, rubbery skin that slips easily through the water. Most mammals are covered with hair, which holds warm air next to the body. Whales, however, do not have a coat of hair to provide them with insulation. A few bristles on the head are all the hair that whales have.

Beneath the skin, whales have a layer of fat called *blubber,* which keeps them warm. Actually, rorquals have more difficulty getting rid of excess heat than keeping warm. Their blubber, therefore, never grows more

than about 6 inches (15 centimeters) thick. In contrast, right whales may have a layer of blubber up to 20 inches (50 centimeters) thick. If food is scarce, whales can live off their blubber for a long time. Blubber is lighter than water, and so it also increases the buoyancy of whales.

Respiratory system. Like all other mammals, whales have lungs. They must therefore come to the surface regularly to breathe. Baleen whales usually breathe every 5 to 15 minutes, but they can go as long as 40 minutes without breathing. A sperm whale can hold its breath up to 75 minutes.

Whales can go for long periods without breathing for several reasons. Their muscles store much more oxygen than do the muscles of other mammals. Human beings, for example, store only about 13 per cent of their oxygen supply in the muscles, compared with about 41 per cent for whales. During a dive, a whale's body greatly reduces the blood flow to the muscles but keeps a normal flow to the heart and brain. The heartbeat also slows, which helps save oxygen. After a dive, a whale must take several breaths to recharge its tissues with oxygen before diving again.

When a whale comes up to breathe, it rolls forward as it breaks the surface. This movement gives the whale only about two seconds to blow out and breathe in up to 2,100 quarts (2,000 liters) of air. Whales breathe through nostrils, called *blowholes,* at the top of the head. Toothed whales have one blowhole, but baleen whales have two. Powerful muscles and valves open the blowholes wide for whales to breathe, and then the openings snap tightly shut.

WORLD BOOK illustration by Marion Pahl

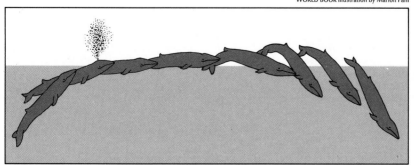

A rapid forward roll enables a whale to surface, breathe, and begin a new dive in one continuous motion. This movement gives the whale only about two seconds to exhale and inhale. Many kinds of whales throw their *flukes* (tail fins) clear of the water when beginning a deep dive.

Jen and Des Bartlett, Bruce Coleman Inc.

Impressive leaps from the water are performed by some species of whales. Scientists call this behavior *breaching*. The right whale shown above is breaching off the coast of Argentina.

When a whale exhales, it produces a cloud called a *blow* or *spout*. The blow consists chiefly of water vapor. It may also include mucus and oil droplets. Experts can identify the species of a whale by the height and shape of its blow. Blows range in height from about 6 feet (1.8 meters) in humpback whales to 25 feet (8 meters) in sperm whales. Right whales have a double V-shaped blow, and rorquals have a pear-shaped one. Sperm whales blow forward and to the left.

Senses. Whales have no sense of smell, and most species have poor eyesight. Studies indicate that some kinds of toothed whales may have a limited sense of taste, but most whales cannot taste. However, all whales have well-developed senses of touch and hearing. Their keen hearing provides them with most of their information about their surroundings. They can hear an extremely wide range of sounds, including low- and high-pitched sounds far beyond the range of human hearing. Unlike people, whales can also tell from what direction a sound is coming underwater.

Toothed whales produce sounds within the *nasal sac system,* a series of air-filled pouches around the blowhole. The whales locate underwater objects by listening for the echoes produced when objects reflect the sounds. From the echoes, they determine the distance to an object and the direction in which it lies. This method of navigation is called *echolocation*. Biologists do not know for sure whether baleen whales echolocate, but some experts believe that they do.

The future of whales

Many of the larger kinds of whales face an uncertain future. Whalers have killed so many blue, bowhead, humpback, and right whales that those species have been threatened with extinction. Overhunting has also greatly reduced the number of fin and sei whales.

In 1946, the major whaling countries formed the International Whaling Commission (IWC) to protect whales from overhunting and to regulate the whaling industry. For many years, the IWC established unrealistically high *quotas* (limits) on the number of whales that could be killed. During the 1960's, the commission began to set reduced quotas and banned the hunting of several whale species. IWC quotas declined further during the 1970's, and in 1979 the commission limited the use of factory ships.

In 1982, the IWC voted for a *moratorium* (temporary halt) on commercial whaling, beginning with the 1985 and the 1986 hunting seasons. By 1988, all nations had halted commercial whaling. Several nations, however, have continued to kill whales for purposes of scientific research, a practice that has stirred controversy. The IWC planned to determine by 1990 whether whale numbers had grown enough to support renewed hunting.

The United States has strongly opposed commercial whaling. In 1971, the U.S. government ordered an end to commercial U.S. whaling and outlawed the importation of whale products. Federal law also calls for *sanctions* (penalties) against any nation that disregards IWC rules.

Public opinion in the United States, Canada, and some European countries has been strongly opposed to commercial whaling. For example, in 1973, antiwhaling groups agreed to *boycott* (refuse to buy) products from Japan and the Soviet Union until those countries stopped commercial whaling. Public opinion also played a major role in the passage of the IWC moratorium on commercial whaling.

The IWC permits native peoples who have traditionally depended on whales for food to continue hunting whales. These peoples include Eskimos of Alaska, Greenland, and the Soviet Union. They eat whale blubber, meat, and skin. The IWC regulates which whales these people may hunt and the hunting methods used.

Most biologists believe that all species of whales have been saved for the present. However, complete protection of endangered species must continue for a long time to allow them to recover from years of extreme overhunting. Even with protection, some species may not be able to recover. For example, the right whale has been fully protected since 1935, but it has not yet made a significant comeback.

Every year, the number of people in the world increases about $1\frac{1}{2}$ per cent, and so the demand for food rises constantly. This fact may threaten the survival of whales. If the population does not level off, people may have to compete with whales for food in the sea. Some nations have already begun experimental fishing for krill, the main food of whales in Antarctic waters.

See **Whale** in *World Book* for more information on the following topics:

- Kinds of baleen whales
- Kinds of toothed whales
- The life of whales
- The early days of whaling
- Modern whaling

Woodpecker is a bird that uses its long, chisellike bill for drilling into trees. Woodpeckers bore holes in bark and wood to find food and build nests. These small- to medium-sized birds live in almost all parts of the world.

Body. Woodpeckers have several features that are especially useful to their way of life. Strong feet and sharp claws enable the birds to climb up and down tree trunks and to cling to bark. Most woodpeckers have two front toes and two hind toes, an arrangement that helps them to climb without falling backwards. Stiff tail feathers brace the birds against the tree trunk. Strong neck muscles propel the bird's head rapidly back and forth while it drills. Muscles on the head act as shock absorbers, protecting the skull from the impact of the drilling.

Many woodpeckers have black and white or brown and white feathers, and many are banded or spotted. Most of the males have some red feathers on their head. Some woodpeckers also have yellow or green feathers.

Habits. Woodpeckers use their bill to probe bark and wood for the adult insects and insect larvae they eat. They draw the food out with an extremely long, sticky tongue that has a barbed tip. Some woodpeckers also catch insects on the ground or in the air. In addition, many woodpeckers eat fruit and nuts. The wood-boring insects that woodpeckers eat are available the year around. For this reason, few woodpeckers migrate.

For their nests, woodpeckers dig holes in the trunks of trees. The nest may extend 6 to 18 inches (15 to 45 centimeters) below the entrance hole. It has no lining except for some wood chips. A female woodpecker lays from two to eight pure-white eggs.

A woodpecker's call consists of a series of harsh notes. The birds also drum with their bills on dead branches or on anything hollow. They use this sound to advertise their presence and defend their territory. Except for nesting pairs, most woodpeckers live alone.

Kinds. There are about 200 species of woodpeckers, but only about 23 species live in North America. Their habitat ranges from evergreen forests to arid deserts.

The large *ivory-billed woodpecker* once lived in the swampy forests of the southeastern United States. Logging has destroyed most of its habitat, and for many years it was feared to be extinct. In 1986, at least two ivory-billed woodpeckers were sighted in Cuba.

M. Vinciguerra, N.A.S.

The male pileated woodpecker, *left,* is often mistaken for the ivory-billed woodpecker. It is found in eastern North America and in parts of the Northwest. Both sexes have a high crest on the head.

Ivory-billed woodpecker
Campephilus principalis
Once found in southeastern United States, now known only in Cuba
Body length: 20 inches (51 centimeters)

Green woodpecker
Picus canus
Found in Eurasian forests
Body length: 12 inches
(30 centimeters)

WORLD BOOK illustration by Marion Pahl

Hairy woodpecker
Dendrocopos villosus
Found in North America
Body length: 10 inches
(25 centimeters)

WORLD BOOK illustrations
by Guy Coheleach

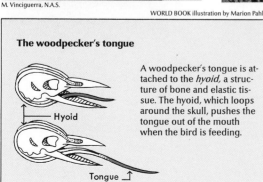

The woodpecker's tongue

A woodpecker's tongue is attached to the *hyoid,* a structure of bone and elastic tissue. The hyoid, which loops around the skull, pushes the tongue out of the mouth when the bird is feeding.

Hyoid

Tongue